THE LAW OF THE SEA AND CLIMATE CHANGE

Our oceans are suffering under the impacts of climate change. Despite the critical role that oceans play in climate regulation, international climate law and the law of the sea are developed as two different, largely separate, legal regimes. The main objective of this book is to assess how the law of the sea can be interpreted, developed and applied to support the objectives of the United Nations Climate Regime. By identifying the potential and constraints of the law of the sea regime in supporting and complementing the climate regime in the mitigation of and adaptation to climate change, this book offers a new perspective on the law of the sea and its capacity to evolve to respond to systemic challenges, and its potential to adapt and ensure a resilient and sustainable future.

Elise Johansen is an Associate Professor at the Norwegian Centre for the Law of the Sea at UiT the Arctic University of Norway, Tromsø. She has published extensively on international law of the sea, environmental and climate law. She teaches courses in the law of the sea in Norway and the US. Johansen is currently leading one of NCLOS's five main research programmes.

Signe Veierud Busch is an Associate Professor at the Norwegian Centre for the Law of the Sea at UiT the Arctic University of Norway, Tromsø. Her primary research interests are dispute settlement, maritime limits and climate change. Drawing on her research experience and results, she is currently leading a research programme with the purpose of rethinking the spatial architecture of the law of the sea and ocean governance.

Ingvild Ulrikke Jakobsen is Professor at the Norwegian Centre for the Law of the Sea at UiT the Arctic University of Norway, Tromsø. Jakobsen has published extensively within international and national environmental law, the law of the sea and ocean governance. She has broad experience in leading and collaborating in interdisiplinary research projects and has acted as Vice Dean of Research at the Faculty of Law, UiT for several years.

The Law of the Sea and Climate Change

SOLUTIONS AND CONSTRAINTS

Edited by

ELISE JOHANSEN

UiT The Arctic University of Norway

SIGNE VEIERUD BUSCH

UiT The Arctic University of Norway

INGVILD ULRIKKE JAKOBSEN

UiT The Arctic University of Norway

CAMBRIDGE
UNIVERSITY PRESS

CAMBRIDGE
UNIVERSITY PRESS

Shaftesbury Road, Cambridge CB2 8EA, United Kingdom

One Liberty Plaza, 20th Floor, New York, NY 10006, USA

477 Williamstown Road, Port Melbourne, VIC 3207, Australia

314–321, 3rd Floor, Plot 3, Splendor Forum, Jasola District Centre, New Delhi – 110025, India

103 Penang Road, #05–06/07, Visioncrest Commercial, Singapore 238467

Cambridge University Press is part of Cambridge University Press & Assessment, a department of the University of Cambridge.

We share the University's mission to contribute to society through the pursuit of education, learning and research at the highest international levels of excellence.

www.cambridge.org
Information on this title: www.cambridge.org/9781108827430

DOI: 10.1017/9781108907118

First published 2021
First paperback edition 2026

A catalogue record for this publication is available from the British Library

Library of Congress Cataloging-in-Publication data
NAMES: Johansen, Elise, Dr., editor. | Busch, Signe Veierud, editor. | Jakobsen, Ingvild Ulrikke, 1974– editor.
TITLE: The law of the sea and climate change : solutions and constraints / edited by Elise Johansen, The Arctic University of Norway; Signe Busch, The Arctic University of Norway; Ingvild Ulrikke Jakobsen, The Arctic University of Norway.
DESCRIPTION: Cambridge, United Kingdom ; New York, NY : Cambridge University Press, 2020. | Includes bibliographical references and index.
IDENTIFIERS: LCCN 2020047287 (print) | LCCN 2020047288 (ebook) | ISBN 9781108842266 (hardback) | ISBN 9781108907118 (ebook)
SUBJECTS: LCSH: Climatic changes – Law and legislation. | Law of the sea.
CLASSIFICATION:LCC K3585.5 .L393 2020 (print) | LCC K3585.5 (ebook) | DDC 344.04/6342–dc23
LC record available at https://lccn.loc.gov/2020047287
LC ebook record available at https://lccn.loc.gov/2020047288

ISBN 978-1-108-84226-6 Hardback
ISBN 978-1-108-82743-0 Paperback

Contents

List of Contributors — *page* viii

Preface — xv

Acknowledgements — xvii

International Instruments — xviii

Table of Cases — xxi

List of Abbreviations — xxiv

1 **The Role of the Oceans in Regulating the Earth's Climate: Legal Perspectives**
Elise Johansen — 1

2 **Climate Change and the Anthropocene: Implications for the Development of the Law of the Sea**
Davor Vidas, Jan Zalasiewicz, Mark Williams and Colin Summerhayes — 22

3 **Mitigation and Adaptation**
Robin Kundis Craig — 49

4 **Protecting the Marine Environment from Climate Change: The LOSC Part XII Regime**
Alan Boyle — 81

5 **Ocean Acidification**
Karen N. Scott — 104

6 Regulating Greenhouse Gases from Ships: Some Light at the End of the Funnel?
Henrik Ringbom 129

7 Carbon Capture and Storage and the Law of the Sea
Nigel Bankes 160

8 Ocean Fertilization
Elise Johansen 184

9 Offshore Renewable Energy and the Law of the Sea
Maria Madalena das Neves 206

10 Marine Protected Areas and Climate Change
Ingvild Ulrikke Jakobsen 234

11 Integrating Climate Change in International Fisheries Law
Erik J. Molenaar 263

12 Adaptation of Aquaculture to Climate Change: The Relevance of Temporal International Framework from a Norwegian Perspective
Irene Dahl 289

13 Law of the Sea Responses to Sea-Level Rise and Threatened Maritime Entitlements: Applying an Exception Rule to Manage an Exceptional Situation
Signe Veierud Busch 309

14 Integrating Climate Change in the Governance of Areas beyond National Jurisdiction
Christian Prip 336

15 The Law of the Sea and Its Institutions: Today's Hermeneutic Approach and Some Suggestions for an Ocean-Centred Governance Model
Margherita Paola Poto 354

16 **The Law of the Sea as Part of the Climate-Change Regime Complex**
Ingvild Ulrikke Jakobsen, Elise Johansen and Philipp Peter Nickels 374

Bibliography 386

Index 421

Contributors

Nigel Bankes is Professor of Law and Chair of Natural Resources Law at the University of Calgary, Canada. From 2013 to 2019 he also served as Adjunct Professor at the K. G. Jebsen Centre for the Law of the Sea (JCLOS), UiT The Arctic University of Norway.

Alan Boyle is Emeritus Professor of Public International Law at Edinburgh Law School, University of Edinburgh. His publications include *International Law and the Environment* (with Catherine Redgwell) (4th ed., forthcoming) and *The Making of International Law* (with Christine Chinkin) (Oxford University Press, 2007). He is a barrister and practises international law from Essex Court Chambers, Holborn, London.

Signe Veierud Busch is Associate Professor at the Norwegian Centre for the Law of the Sea (NCLOS), UiT The Arctic University of Norway. She teaches law of the sea and academic writing at the Faculty of Law at UiT The Arctic University of Norway; has headed the JCLOS research project on Climate Change and the Law of the Sea (CCLOS); and is currently leading one of NCLOS's five main research programmes. Busch is also head of the Joint Nordic Master Programme in Environmental Law (NOMPEL). Her main research interests are climate change and the law of the sea, maritime limits and boundaries, and dispute settlement.

Robin Kundis Craig is the James I. Farr Presidential Endowed Professor of Law at the University of Utah[,] S. J. Quinney College of Law in Salt Lake City, Utah, where she specializes in ocean and coastal law and climate change. She has authored or edited 11 books, including *Comparative Ocean Governance: Place-Based Protections in an Era of Climate Change* (Edward Elgar, 2012), as well as over 100 articles and book chapters. Craig is an elected member of the American Law Institute and the American College of Environmental Lawyers, is a member of the IUCN World Commission on Environmental Law and was chosen to participate in the Papahanaumokuakea Marine National Monument programme for marine educators in 2010. Her work on marine and climate change issues has been quoted in *National Geographic*, *The Atlantic*, *The New York Times* and many other distinguished news outlets.

Irene Dahl is Associate Professor at NCLOS, Faculty of Law, UiT The Arctic University of Norway. She is one of two academic leaders of the course 'Norwegian Laws and Regulations on Marine Resources', in the Master's Programme in Law Studies, and has taught and published on international law of the sea, fisheries law and aquaculture law.

Ingvild Ulrikke Jakobsen is Professor at NCLOS, Faculty of Law, UiT The Arctic University of Norway; Deputy Dean for Research at the Faculty of Law; and co-leader of NCLOS. She has taught and published extensively within the fields of international and national environmental law and the law of the sea. Jakobsen has broad experience as research project leader. In addition to serving as Vice-Dean and co-leader of NCLOS, she headed a main research programme at JCLOS (2013–2015) and has been involved as partner in several projects funded by the Norwegian Research Council. Jakobsen has also headed the academic LLM Programme in Law of the Sea. Her main research interests are within international environmental law and the law of the sea.

Elise Johansen is Associate Professor at NCLOS, Faculty of Law, UiT The Arctic University of Norway. She has published widely on international law of the sea, climate law and environmental law. She teaches courses in the law of the sea and in environmental law in Norway and the US. She has headed several NCLOS research programmes and is currently leading one of five main research programmes at NCLOS. She is currently co-editor (with Professor Nele Matz Lück and Senior Research Fellow Øystein Jensen) of *The Law of the Sea: Normative Context and Interactions with other Legal Regimes* (Routledge, forthcoming, 2020).

Erik J. Molenaar has been affiliated with the Netherlands Institute for the Law of the Sea (NILOS) at Utrecht University since 1994 and currently holds the position of Deputy Director. In 2006 he also worked at UiT The Arctic University of Norway in Tromsø, where he is currently a professor at NCLOS. After having completed his PhD on 'Coastal State Jurisdiction over Vessel-Source Pollution' (1998), Molenaar expanded his research into the field of international fisheries law and international law relating to the

Arctic and the Antarctic. He is the author or editor of over 100 publications; has participated in diplomatic conferences and other intergovernmental meetings – including the annual meetings of several regional fisheries management organizations; and has been involved in international litigation work as well as many consultancies.

Maria Madalena das Neves is Associate Professor at the Faculty of Law at UiT The Arctic University of Norway and also a researcher at NCLOS. She is currently the academic director of the LLM Programme in Law of the Sea at UiT. Further, das Neves teaches and conducts research on the law of the sea, energy and climate change law, and international and EU trade law.

Philipp Peter Nickels is Research Fellow and PhD candidate at NCLOS, Faculty of Law, UiT The Arctic University of Norway. His research interests include public international law, the law of the sea and international environmental law.

Margherita Paola Poto is Researcher at NCLOS, UiT The Arctic University of Norway. Her research interests include ocean governance, climate change and indigenous law, comparative administrative law, environmental law, Arctic governance and the role of non-state actors, as well as food safety, security and sovereignty in the Arctic and beyond. She is currently exploring integrated research methodologies for tackling complex problems in law and beyond, with a focus on indigenous methodologies, intra-comparative analysis and intersectionality.

Christian Prip is Senior Policy Analyst at the Fridtjof Nansen Institute (FNI) in Lysaker, Norway, and is also affiliated with the Norwegian Centre for the Law of the Sea (NCLOS). He has published a large number of articles, book chapters and reports related to the management of biodiversity and natural resources at the global, regional (Arctic) and national levels. He has extensive experience with evaluation and consultancy in this field. Further, Prip has more than twenty years of experience as a negotiator on international environmental policy and law in various forums, for the government of his native Denmark and for the European Union when Denmark held the EU Presidency. From 2005 to 2007, he chaired the Subsidiary Body on Scientific, Technical and Technological Advice (SBSTTA) under the Convention on Biodiversity.

Henrik Ringbom is based in Finland and holds part-time professorships in three universities in the Nordic countries: at the NCLOS (UiT The Arctic University of Norway), at the Scandinavian Institute of Maritime

Law (University of Oslo) and at the University of Turku in Finland. He is also Adjunct Professor (docent) at Åbo Akademi University in Turku, Finland. His previous work experience includes serving as Head of Unit for Marine Environment, Training and Statistics at the European Maritime Safety Agency (EMSA) in Lisbon (2007–2012) and as Administrator at the Maritime Safety Unit of the European Commission in Brussels (1997–2003). Ringbom has published widely in the field of European and international shipping and environmental law, and is the author of *The EU Maritime Safety Policy and International Law* (Brill, 2008), editor of *Jurisdiction over Ships* (Brill, 2015) and co-editor of *Autonomous Ships and the Law* (Routledge, forthcoming 2020).

Karen N. Scott is Professor of Law at the University of Canterbury in New Zealand, having previously taught at the University of Nottingham in the United Kingdom, where she headed the School of Law between 2015 and 2018. She is currently President of the Australian and New Zealand Society of International Law (ANZSIL) and is editor-in-chief of *Ocean Development and International Law*. She conducts research and teaching in the fields of public international law, law of the sea and international environmental law. Karen has published over seventy journal articles and book chapters in these areas, and is the co-editor, with Donald R. Rothwell, Alex Oude Elferink and Tim Stephens, of the *Oxford Handbook on the Law of the Sea* (Oxford University Press, 2015; paperback edition, 2017). She is currently co-editor (with Professor David VanderZwaag) of the *Edward Elgar Research Handbook on Polar Law* (forthcoming, 2020).

Colin Summerhayes, an emeritus associate of the Scott Polar Research Institute at the University of Cambridge, UK, is a marine geologist and oceanographer with expertise in the role of climate in forming marine sediments and in interpreting the history of climate from sedimentary records. He served as Director of the Natural Environment Research Council's Institute of Oceanographic Sciences Deacon Laboratory (1988–1995), with responsibility for managing the United Kingdom's major research programmes on the role of the oceans in climate change. Further, he served on the UNESCO Intergovernmental Oceanographic Commission as Director of the Global Ocean Observing System, established to provide the ocean component of the UN Global Climate Observing System, which detects changes and trends in global climate and provides advice to the UN Framework Convention on Climate Change. Summerhayes was also Executive Director of the Scientific Committee on

Antarctic Research (SCAR). His most recent major publication is *Earth's Climate Evolution* (Wiley, 2015; 2nd ed., 2020). He is a member of the Anthropocene Working Group.

Davor Vidas is Research Professor in International Law at FNI, Norway, and Honorary Visiting Professor in the School of Geography, Geology and the Environment at the University of Leicester, UK. He initiated, and is the Chair of, the Committee on International Law and Sea Level Rise of the International Law Association (ILA, 2012–2022) and is a member of the Anthropocene Working Group at the International Commission on Stratigraphy. During the past twenty-five years, he has initiated and headed several major research projects on international law and interdisciplinary approaches to ocean issues, including the international research project 'Climate Change and Sea-Level Rise in the Anthropocene: Challenges for International Law in the 21st Century' (Research Council of Norway, 2014–2019). Professor Vidas is the founding editor-in-chief of the journal monograph series Brill Research Perspectives in the Law of the Sea and of a popular science book series Anthropocene (published by Skolska knjiga, Zagreb).

Mark Williams is Professor of Palaeobiology at the School of Geography, Geology and the Environment at the University of Leicester, UK. He has previously worked for the British Antarctic Survey as a polar scientist and was a long-term member of the PRISM paleoclimate group of the United States Geological Survey. Professor Williams has been a member of the Anthropocene Working Group since its formation in 2009 (and was its first Secretary). He specializes in studying the degree and rate of past environmental change and using this to inform the present. With Jan Zalasiewicz, he has co-authored three books – *The Goldilocks Planet* (2012), *Ocean Worlds* (2014) and *Skeletons: The Framework of Life* (2018), all published by Oxford University Press – and is, with J. Zalasiewicz, C. Waters and C. Summerhayes, a co-editor of *The Anthropocene as a Geological Time Unit: A Guide to Scientific Evidence and Current Debate* (Cambridge University Press, 2019). Professor Williams holds a PhD from the University of Leicester.

Jan Zalasiewicz was formerly Chair of the Anthropocene Working Group of the International Commission on Stratigraphy. He is Emeritus Professor of Palaeobiology at the School of Geography, Geology and the Environment at the University of Leicester, UK, and was formerly a field geologist and biostratigrapher at the British Geological Survey. He is a member (formerly

Chair) of the Stratigraphy Commission of the Geological Society of London and is currently serving as Chair of the Subcommission on Quaternary Stratigraphy. His main research interests lie in the analysis of palaeoenvironments using evidence from sedimentary strata (mudrocks in particular) and from fossils (graptolites in particular), and in the study of the Anthropocene concept and its geological validity. In addition to the volumes co-authored in 2012, 2014 and 2018 with Mark Williams (see earlier), Professor Zalasiewicz is the author of *The Earth After Us* (2008), *The Planet in a Pebble* (2010), *Rocks: A Very Short Introduction* (2016) and *Geology: A Very Short Introduction* (2018), all published by Oxford University Press. He holds a PhD from the University of Cambridge.

Preface

The K. G. Jebsen Centre for the Law of the Sea (JCLOS) at UiT The Arctic University of Norway was established in 2013 on the initiative of, and partly funded by, Stiftelsen K. G. Jebsen. Throughout the six-year funding period, the research activities of JCLOS spanned a broad range of law of the sea issues, from dispute settlement, maritime delimitation, navigation, marine resource conservation and management to the protection of the marine environment.

When research projects under JCLOS were planned, the impacts of climate change were identified as already posing major challenges to the law of the sea and the governance of the oceans of our planet. The oceans are vital to the earth's climate system, absorbing and storing excess heat and CO_2. The impacts of climate change include warmer oceans, sea-level rise, more acid oceans and pockets of oceans with less oxygen. Climate change threatens marine life and ecosystems, the livelihood of coastal communities and might lead to more severe climatic conditions in the future. Research projects at JCLOS aimed at analysing if and how the current law of the sea addresses the challenges ensuing from these impacts – such as the future status of baselines and maritime boundaries following sea-level rise, or navigation in waters where sea ice is melting and withdrawing. The overall objective of work at JCLOS was to assess how the law of the sea is responding to new and existing challenges.

In line with this objective, the project Climate Change and the Law of the Sea was established, to undertake a comprehensive assessment of whether current law of the sea provides adequate means for mitigating and adapting to the impacts of climate change. Thus the project has studied the flexibility and the limitations of the law of the sea to adapt to the emerging, and continuing, challenges of climate change. This book volume is a result of that research project. The contributing authors provide valuable background and insights into how the law of the sea may contribute in mitigating and adapting to the impacts of climate change.

JCLOS has now been renamed the Norwegian Centre for the Law of the Sea (NCLOS). NCLOS will build on and develop the research from the JCLOS years. Important lessons will be drawn from this and other projects – not least, recognition of the need to integrate knowledge from other legal regimes and disciplines into research on the law of the sea. Today, even more than before, it is essential to understand the complexity of ocean governance, to assess its capacity to meet new and existing challenges – and to offer solutions.

Acknowledgements

The editors would like to thank the exceptional group of scholars who agreed to contribute their expertise to this volume. We could not have asked for a more talented, knowledgeable and reliable group of colleagues. It has indeed been a privilege to work with them.

Further, we wish to thank Ellen Hey, Jason Czarnezki and Dominique Grace, for valuable inputs at the author workshop held in January 2019. Thanks are also extended to Susan Høivik (text editor), Marion Ravna (research assistance) and Endalew Lijalem Enyew (researcher at NCLOS) for their invaluable contributions. We are deeply grateful for their all-important work on the manuscript texts and, not least, for not giving up when faced with varying forms of English and reference styles. Our appreciation also goes to Philipp Peter Nickels, research fellow at NCLOS, for his comments during the final stages of the project and assistance in synthesizing the findings in Chapter 16. Further, this book would not have been possible without the support of NCLOS and its Director Tore Henriksen. Thank you all for believing in and supporting this project.

Finally, we would like to express our gratitude to Cambridge University Press for their cooperation and editorial support.

Elise Johansen, Signe V. Busch and Ingvild U. Jakobsen

Tromsø 2020

International Instruments

1945 Charter of the United Nations, San Francisco, 26 June 1945, 1 UNTS 16.

1945 Statute of the International Court of Justice, San Francisco, 26 June 1945, 33 UNTS 993.

1946 International Convention for the Regulation of Whaling, Washington, 2 December 1946, 161 UNTS 72.

1966 International Covenant on Civil and Political Rights, New York, 16 December 1966, 999 UNTS 171.

1969 Vienna Convention on Law of the Treaties, Vienna, 23 May 1969, 1155 UNTS 331.

1971 Convention on Wetlands of International Importance Especially as Waterfowl Habitat, Ramsar, 2 February 1971, 996 UNTS 245.

1973 International Convention for the Prevention of Pollution from Ships, London, 2 November 1973, 1340 UNTS 184, as Amended by the Protocol of 1978 Relating to the International Convention for the Prevention of Pollution from Ships of 1973, 17 February 1978, 1340 UNTS 61 (MARPOL).

1973 Convention on International Trade in Endangered Species of Wild Fauna and Flora, Washington, DC, 3 March 1973, 993 UNTS 243.

1974 Convention on the Protection of the Marine Environment of the Baltic Sea Area, Helsinki, 22 March 1974, 1507 UNTS 166 (Helsinki Convention).

1974 International Convention for the Safety of Life at Sea, London, 1 November 1974, 1184 UNTS 277, with protocols and regularly amended (SOLAS 74).

1976 Convention for the Protection of the Mediterranean Sea against Pollution, Barcelona, 16 February 1976, (1976) 15 ILM 290.

1978 Convention on Cooperation in the Northwest Atlantic Fisheries, Ottawa, 24 October 1978, 1135 UNTS 369.

1979 Convention on the Conservation of Migratory Species of Wild Animals, Bonn, 23 June 1979, 1651 UNTS 333.

1979 Convention on Long-Range Transboundary Air Pollution, Geneva, 13 November 1979, 1302 UNTS 217.

1980 Convention on the Conservation of Antarctic Marine Living Resources, Canberra, 20 May 1980, 1329 UNTS 47.

1980 Protocol for the Protection of the Mediterranean Sea against Pollution from Land-based Sources and Activities, Athens, 17 May 1980.

1982 United Nations Convention on Law of the Sea, Montego Bay, 10 December 1982, 1833 UNTS 3 (LOSC).

1986 Convention for the Protection of Natural Resources and Environment of the South Pacific Region, Noumea, 25 November 1986, (1987) 26 ILM 38.

1987 The Montreal Protocol on Substances that Deplete the Ozone Layer, Montreal, 16 September 1987, 1522 UNTS 3.

1991 Convention on Environmental Impact Assessment in a Transboundary Context, Espoo, 25 February 1991, 1989 UNTS 309.

1991 Protocol on Environmental Protection to the Antarctic treaty, Madrid, 14 October 1991, 30 ILM 1461.

1992 United Nations Framework Convention on Climate Change, Rio de Janeiro, 9 May 1992, 1771 UNTS 107 (UNFCCC).

1992 Convention on Biological Diversity, Rio de Janeiro, 5 June 1992, 1760 UNTS 69 (CBD).

1992 Rio Declaration on Environment and Development, Rio de Janeiro, 14 June 1992, 31 ILM 874, UN Doc. A/CONF.151/26 (vol. I).

1992 Convention for the Protection of the Marine Environment of the North-East Atlantic, Paris, 22 September 1992, (1993) 2354 UNTS 67 (OSPAR Convention).

1994 Convention on Nuclear Safety, Vienna, 17 June 1994, 1963 UNTS 293.

1994 Agreement Relating to the Implementation of Part XI of the United Nations Convention on the Law of the Sea of 10 December 1982, New York, 28 July 1994, 1836 UNTS 3 (Implementing Agreement).

1995 Agreement for the Implementation of the Provisions of the United Nations Convention on the Law of the Sea of 10 December 1982 Relating to the Conservation and Management of Straddling Fish Stocks and Highly Migratory Fish Stocks, New York, 4 August 1995, 2167 UNTS 3 (UN Fish Stocks Agreement).

1995 FAO Code of Conduct for Responsible Fisheries, Rome, 31 October 1995 (FAO Code of Conduct).

1996 Protocol to the Convention on the Prevention of Marine Pollution by Dumping of Wastes and Other Matter, 7 November 1996, 36 ILM 7.

1997 Kyoto Protocol to the United Nations Framework Convention on Climate Change (Kyoto Protocol), Kyoto, 11 December 1997,2303 UNTS 162.

1999 Protocol Concerning Pollution from Land-Based Sources and Activities to the Cartagena Convention, Oranjestad, 6 October 1999.

1999 Protocol to Abate Acidification, Eutrophication and Ground-level Ozone to the 1979 Convention on Long-Range Transboundary Air Pollution (as amended in 2012) (Gothenburg Protocol), 30 November 1999, 2319 UNTS 81.

2003 Protocol on Strategic Environmental Assessment to the Convention on Environmental Impact Assessment in a Transboundary Context, Kiev, 21 May 2003, 2685 UNTS 140.

2009 Convention on the Conservation and Management of High Seas Fishery Resources in the South Pacific Ocean, Auckland, 14 November 2009, 2899 UNTS 211.

2013 Kiruna Declaration of the Eighth Ministerial Meeting of the Arctic Council, Kiruna (15 May 2013).

2015 Paris Agreement, Framework Convention on Climate Change, Conference of the Parties, Twenty-First Session, Paris, UN Doc. FCCC/CP/2015/10/Add.1, UN Doc. FCCC/CP/2015/L.9 (12 December 2015).

2018 Agreement to Prevent Unregulated High Seas Fisheries in the Central Arctic Ocean, Ilulissat, 3 October 2018. Not in force; text included in the Annex to EU Doc. COM(2018) 453 final, 12 June 2018.

Table of Cases

Anglo-Norwegian Fisheries case [1949] (*Order of November 9th*) ICJ Rep. p. 233.

Corfu Channel (United Kingdom v. *Albania) Merits (Judgment)* [1949] ICJ Rep. p. 4.

South West Africa cases (*Ethiopia* v. *South Africa*; *Liberia* v. *South Africa*), Preliminary Objections (*Judgment*) [1962] ICJ Rep. p. 319.

Northern Cameroons (*Cameroon* v. *United Kingdom*) Preliminary Objections (*Judgment*) [1963] ICJ Rep. p. 15.

North Sea Continental Shelf cases (*Judgment*) [1969] ICJ Rep. p. 22.

Nuclear Tests (*Australia* v. *France*) (*Judgment*) [1974] ICJ Rep. p. 253.

Applicability of the Obligation to Arbitrate under Section 21 of the United Nations Headquarters Agreement of 26 June 1947 (Advisory Opinion) [1988] ICJ Rep. p. 12.

Gabčíkovo-Nagymaros Project (Hungary/Slovakia) (Judgment) [1997] ICJ Rep. p. 7.

Southern Bluefin Tuna (New Zealand v. *Japan; Australia v. Japan)* (Provisional Measures) [1999] ITLOS Rep. p. 280.

Southern Bluefin Tuna Arbitration (*Australia, New Zealand* v. *Japan*) (Jurisdiction and Admissibility) (2000) Arbitral Tribunal constituted under LOSC Part XV, Annex VII.

Reports of International Arbitral Awards vol. XXIII, pp. 1–57.

MOX Plant (Ireland v. *United Kingdom*) (Provisional Measures, Order of 3 December 2001) [2001] ITLOS Rep. p. 95.

Measures affecting the transit and importation of swordfish, WT/DS193 (2002) WTO Annual Report.

Land Reclamation in and around the Straits of Johor (*Malaysia* v. *Singapore*) (Provisional Measures, Order of 8 October 2003) [2003] ITLOS Rep. p. 10.

MOX Plant Arbitration (Ireland v. *United Kingdom)* [2003] PCA Case No. 2002–01.
Reports of International Arbitral Awards, Vol. XXIII pp. 59–151.
Iron Rhine Arbitration (*Belgium* v. *Netherlands*) [2005] PCA Case No. 2003–02.
Reports of International Arbitral Awards Vol. XXVII pp. 35–125.
Pulp Mills on the River Uruguay (*Argentina* v. *Uruguay*) (Provisional Measures) [2006] ICJ Rep. p. 113.
Commission of the European Communities v. *Ireland* (C-459/03) [2006].
Decisions of the Appeals Chamber of the International Criminal Tribunal for Rwanda (Case No. ICTR-97–20-A, Judgment, 20 May 2005 [194]; Case No. ICTR-98–44-AR73(C), Decision, 16 June 2006 [22–23]).
Case concerning the Conservation and Sustainable Exploitation of Swordfish Stocks in the South-Eastern Pacific Ocean (*Chile/European Union*) [2000] ITLOS Rep. 148 and [2009] ITLOS Rep. 2008–2010 p. 13.
Pulp Mills on the River Uruguay (*Argentina* v. *Uruguay*) (*Judgment*) [2010] ICJ Rep. p. 14.
Case C-366/10, *Air Transport Association of America, American Airlines Inc., Continental Airlines Inc., United Airlines Inc.* v. *Secretary of State for Energy and Climate Change* [2011].
Responsibilities and Obligations of State Sponsoring Persons and Entities with Respect to Activities in the Area (Advisory Opinion) [2011] ITLOS Rep. p. 10.
Questions relating to the Obligation to Prosecute or Extradite (*Belgium* v. *Senegal*) (Judgment) [2012] ICJ Rep. p. 422.
Territorial and Maritime Dispute (*Nicaragua/Colombia*) (*Judgment*) [2012] ICJ Rep. p. 624.
The Atlanto-Scandian Herring Arbitration (*The Kingdom of Denmark in respect of the Faroe Islands* v. *The European Union*) [2014] PCA Case No. 2013–30 https://pca-cpa.org/en/cases/25/.
European Union: Measures on Atlanto-Scandian Herring, WT/DS469, terminated on 21 August 2014.
Whaling in the Antarctic (*Australia* v. *Japan*: *New Zealand* intervening) [2014] ICJ Rep. p. 226.
Chagos Marine Protected Area Arbitration (*Mauritius* v. *United Kingdom*) [2015] PCA Case No. 2011–13.
Reports of International Arbitral Awards, Vol. XXXI pp. 359–606.
South China Sea Arbitration (*The Republic of Philippines* v. *The People's Republic of China*) (*Jurisdiction and Admissibility*) [2015] PCA Case No. 2013–19 https://pcacases.com/web/sendAttach/2579.
Request for Advisory Opinion submitted by the Sub-Regional Fisheries Commission (SRFC) (Advisory Opinion) [2015] ITLOS Rep. p. 4.

The Arctic Sunrise Arbitration (*Netherlands* v. *Russia*) (*Merits*) [2015] PCA Case No. 2014–02 https://pcacases.com/web/sendAttach/1438.

Certain Activities carried out by Nicaragua in the Border Area (*Costa Rica* v. *Nicaragua*) and *Construction of a Road in Costa Rica along the San Juan River* (*Nicaragua* v. *Costa Rica*) (*Judgment*) [2015] ICJ Rep. p. 665.

Obligations concerning Negotiations relating to Cessation of the Nuclear Arms Race and to Nuclear Disarmament (*Marshall Islands* v. *United Kingdom*), Preliminary Objections (Judgment) [2016] ICJ Rep. p. 833.

Case *Al-Dulimi and Montana Management Inc.* v. *Switzerland* [GC] App. No. 5809/08 (ECtHR, 2016) https://hudoc.echr.coe.int/eng#{%22appno%22:[%225809/08%22],%22itemid%22:[%22001-164515%22]} .

Certain Activities Carried Out by Nicaragua in the Border Area (Costa Rica v. Nicaragua), Compensation (Judgment) [2018] ICJ Rep. p. 15.

Review Panel established on 25 April 2018 pursuant to the SPRFMO Convention [2018] PCA Case No. 2018–13 https://pcacases.com/web/sendAttach/2400.

4 October 2019 – Case C-733/19, *Kingdom of the Netherlands* v. *Council of the European Union*, European Parliament; action for annulment of Annex V, Part D, points 1 to 5 of Regulation (EU) 2019/1241.

Abbreviations

ABMTs	Area-based Management Tools
ABNJ	Areas Beyond National Jurisdiction
AMAP	Arctic Monitoring and Assessment Programme
ASIL	American Society of International Law
AWG	Anthropocene Working Group
BBNJ	Biodiversity of Areas Beyond National Jurisdiction
CBD	Convention on Biological Diversity
CCAMLR	Commission for the Conservation of Antarctic Marine Living Resources
CCS	Carbon Capture and Storage
CIGI	Centre for International Governance Innovation
CIL	Centre for International Law
CITES	Convention on International Trade in Endangered Species
CMS	Convention on Migratory Species
COP	Conference of Parties
ECtHR	European Court of Human Rights
EEZ	Exclusive Economic Zone
EIA	Environmental Impact Assessment
EMEP	European Monitoring and Evaluation Programme
EOR	Enhanced Oil Recovery
ERUs	Emissions Reduction Units
EU	European Union
ESS	Earth System Science
FAO	United Nations Food and Agriculture Organization
GAIRS	Generally Accepted International Rules and Standards
GESAMP	Group of Experts on the Scientific Aspects of Marine Environmental Protection

GHG	Greenhouse Gas
GSSP	Global Boundary Stratotype Section and Point
IAEA	International Atomic Energy Agency
IAP	Interacademy Panel on International Issues
ICJ	International Court of Justice
ICS	International Commission on Stratigraphy
IDDRI	Institut du Développement Durable et des Relations Internationales
IEA	International Energy Agency
IEAGHG	International Energy Association's Greenhouse Gas Research and Development Program
IGC	Intergovernmental Conference
ILA	International Law Association
IMO	International Maritime Organization
IOC	Intergovernmental Oceanographic Commission
IPCC	Intergovernmental Panel on Climate Change
IRENA	International Renewable Energy Agency
ISA	International Seabed Authority
ITLOS	International Tribunal for the Law of the Sea
IUCN	International Union for Conservation of Nature
LOSC	United Nations Convention on Law of the Sea
MARPOL	International Convention for the Prevention of Pollution from Ships
MPA	Marine Protected Areas
MSP	Marine Spatial Planning
nm	nautical miles
OSPAR	Convention for the Protection of the Marine Environment of the North-East Atlantic
PCA	Permanent Court of Arbitration
PNAS	Proceedings of the National Academy of Sciences
ppm	parts per million
PSSAs	Particularly Sensitive Sea Areas
RAMF	Risk Assessment and Management Framework
RFMOs	Regional Fisheries Management Organizations
SDG	Sustainable Development Goals
SEA	Strategic Environmental Impact Assessments
SEEMP	Ship Energy Efficiency Management Plan
SOLAS	International Convention for the Safety of Life at Sea

SQS	United Nations Subcommission on Quaternary Stratigraphy
UN	United Nations
UNCLOS	United Nations Conference on the Law of the Sea
UNESCO	United Nations Educational, Scientific and Cultural Organization
UNFCCC	United Nations Framework Convention on Climate Change
UNGA	United Nations General Assembly
UNTS	United Nations Treaty Series

1

The Role of the Oceans in Regulating the Earth's Climate

Legal Perspectives

Elise Johansen

. . . all people on Earth depend directly or indirectly on the ocean and cryosphere

Opening Statement, IPCC 2019 Special Report[1]

1.1 INTRODUCTION

Our oceans are already suffering under the impacts of climate change.[2] The 2019 Special Report of the Intergovernmental Panel on Climate Change (IPCC) on the Ocean and Cryosphere paints a troubling picture of the status and prospects of the world's ice and oceans.[3] The earth's climate and the state of the oceans are interdependent. The oceans play a fundamental role in our climate system, through the uptake and redistribution of anthropogenic CO_2 and heat, as well as their crucial involvement in the hydrological cycle.[4]

Despite the critical role that oceans play in climate regulation, international climate law and the law of the sea have developed as two different, largely separate, legal regimes.[5] The United Nations Framework Convention on

[1] Intergovernmental Panel on Climate Change (IPCC), H. O. Pörtner et al. (eds.), *IPCC Special Report: The Ocean and Cryosphere in a Changing Climate: Summary for Policymakers* (2019) (in press) (IPCC SR 2019, *The Ocean and Cryosphere in a Changing Climate*).

[2] Oceans and seas are differentiated by their depth, area and marine life. However, these terms are used interchangeably in this chapter. The term 'the ocean' is used when referring to the seas and oceans as a single dynamic ecosystem.

[3] IPCC SR 2019, *The Ocean and Cryosphere in a Changing Climate*.

[4] The physical interlinkages between the climate and the oceans, and the consequences of climate change for the oceans and coastal areas, are presented in detail by D. Vidas et al., in this volume, Chapter 2, and R. Craig, in this volume, Chapter 3.

[5] See, e.g., S. Oberthür, 'Interactions of the climate change regime with ICAO, IMO, and the EU burden-sharing agreement' in S. Oberthür and T. Gehring (eds.), *Institutional Interaction*

Climate Change (UNFCCC)[6] functions as the framework convention for the UN Climate Regime and establishes the foundations of the regime by defining the principles which guide its development – but there is in the UNFCCC no acknowledgement of the central role of oceans, except as natural sinks.[7] However, one part of emissions control has been delegated to the Law of the Sea Regime: the Kyoto Protocol designates the International Maritime Organization (IMO) as the relevant UN agency for dealing with emissions from maritime transport.[8]

The 2015 Paris Agreement does not contain special provisions regarding the role of oceans.[9] However, the oceans are mentioned in the Preamble – which may be seen as recognition of a need for a stronger focus on oceans and climate issues; indeed, the interlinkages between climate and oceans have been taken up by the UN Climate Regime itself. Increasing attention in climate negotiations has been paid to the oceans as a fundamental element, starting with the discussions at Oceans Day at COP21 in 2015, via the development of the Action Roadmap,[10] to the IPCC decision to devote a special report to the interaction between climate change, the ocean and the cryosphere.[11] However, little attention has been devoted to the relationship and the interaction between the two legal frameworks governing ocean issues and climate change.

The same lack of recognition of the existence and impact of the UN Climate Regime characterizes the Law of the Sea Regime. Climate is not

in Global Environmental Governance (Cambridge, MA: MIT Press, 2006); S. Kopela, 'Climate change, regime interaction, and the principle of common but differentiated responsibility: the experience of the International Maritime Organization' (2014) 24(1) *Yearbook of International Environmental Law*, 70–101.

6 United Nations Framework Convention on Climate Change (UNFCCC), Rio de Janeiro, 9 May 1992, in force 21 March 1994, 1771 UNTS 107.

7 UNFCCC, Art. 4(d).

8 Kyoto Protocol to the United Nations Framework Convention on Climate Change (Kyoto Protocol), 11 December 1997, in force 16 February 2005, 2303 UNTS 162, Art. 2.2.

9 The Paris Agreement, adopted by Decision 1/CP.21 Report of the Conference of the Parties on its twenty-first session, held in Paris from 30 November to 13 December 2015, in force 4 November 2016, Adoption of the Paris Agreement, UN Doc. FCCC/CP/2015/10/Add.1 (12 December 2015), Annex, 21, available at http://unfccc.int/resource/docs/2015/cop21/eng/10a01.pdf.

10 International Expert Working Group on Oceans and Climate, *Toward a Strategic Action Roadmap on Oceans and Climate: 2016 to 2021, Part of the Global Strategic Action Initiative on Ocean and Climate*, B Cicin-San et al. (eds.), October 2016, Policy Recommendations on Oceans and Climate for Consideration at UNFCCC COP 22 and Beyond, 4, available at https://globaloceanforumdotcom.files.wordpress.com/2013/03/strategic-action-roadmap-on-oceans-and-climate-november-2016.pdf.

11 IPCC SR 2019, *The Ocean and Cryosphere in a Changing Climate.*

mentioned in the 1982 Law of the Sea Convention (LOSC),[12] nor was it part of the negotiations that led to the final agreement. Here the explanation is straightforward: climate issues had not yet entered the international environmental agenda when the LOSC was negotiated.[13] Today, the UN Climate Regime interacts with a large number of other international institutions and legal regimes because climate change has a wide range of impacts on the natural environment and society, and many different human activities and sectors of society contribute to the problem. The states parties made a deliberate choice of not referring to any specific legal regime or sector due to the global character of climate change.[14]

The lack of regime interaction presents a twofold dilemma: on the one hand, the LOSC is intended to cover all matters related to the oceans, without expressly referring to climate change; on the other hand, the UN Climate Regime is meant to cover matters related to climate change, which is highly terrestrial and atmospheric in scope, and with very limited application to the oceans. The physical relationship between the oceans and climate is, however, indisputable. While the risks and consequences of climate change regarding the oceans continue to grow, it remains unclear whether the existing international legal framework is capable of properly dealing with these threats.

1.2 THE UN CLIMATE REGIME

The UN Climate Treaty Regime forms the main corpus and the identity of international climate change law.[15] The UNFCCC, adopted in 1992, has almost universal membership today.[16] It serves as a *framework convention* due to its role in setting the governance structure for the international climate regime.[17]

12 United Nations Convention on the Law of the Sea, adopted 10 December 1982, in force 16 November 1994, 1833 UNTS 3.

13 This is not to say that climate change had not been debated or identified as an issue, but it was certainly not a priority, and less was known of the pace and consequences of climate change than today.

14 See D. Bodansky, J. Brunnée and L. Rajamani, *International Climate Change Law* (Oxford University Press, 2017); C. P. Carlarne, K. R. Gray and R. G. Tarasofsky, 'International climate change law: mapping the field' in C. P. Carlarne, K. R. Gray and R. G. Tarasofsky (eds.), *The Oxford Handbook of International Climate Change Law* (Oxford University Press, 2016), 3.

15 P. Cinnamon et al., 'International climate change law: mapping the field' in P. Cinnamon et al. (eds.), *The Oxford Handbook of International Climate Change Law* (Oxford University Press, 2016), 7.

16 There are currently 197 parties to the UNFCCC. Status of Ratification of the Convention; see https://unfccc.int/process-and-meetings/the-convention/status-of-ratification/status-of-ratification-of-the-convention.

17 Bodansky, Brunnée and Rajamani, *International Climate Change Law*, 118.

The long-term objective of the UNFCCC is to stabilize the concentrations of greenhouse gases (GHGs) in the atmosphere at a level that can prevent dangerous anthropogenic interference with the earth's climate system.[18] Incorporated in this objective is also a temporal dimension that allows for a natural period of adaptation. Although the UNFCCC treaty itself is legally binding, the commitments in its various provisions contain few substantive obligations. The parties are, however, obliged to develop national inventories of anthropogenic emissions and removals by sinks of all GHGs (except those controlled by the Montreal Protocol)[19] and to implement measures to mitigate GHG emissions (UNFCCC Article 4(a) and (b)). Furthermore, the parties are obliged to cooperate in, *inter alia*, the development and application of technologies (Article 4(c)), the conservation and enhancement of sinks (Article 4(d)) and preparing for adaptation to the impacts of climate change (Article 4(e)). However, as the wording used in Article 4 describing the duties of the parties is general and rather vague, the UNFCCC stands more like a paper tiger with nothing more than political statements of good intentions. Lacking clear, legally binding commitments,[20] the UNFCCC has not been able to create the necessary changes in state behaviour.[21] However, the parties to the Convention recognize the need to supplement the UNFCCC through other instruments: work on establishing mechanisms and approaches to give substance to the UNFCCC obligations has been an ongoing process since its adoption.

The 1997 Kyoto Protocol was intended to supplement the UNFCCC by establishing internationally negotiated, legally binding, quantitative emissions targets. The Protocol, which entered into force in 2005, established strong emissions targets for Annex I parties. These thirty-eight developed states committed themselves to reduce their overall GHG emissions not controlled by the Montreal Protocol by at least 5 per cent below 1990 levels in the commitment period 2008–2012.[22] The Kyoto Protocol provides for the use of market-based mitigation tools, allowing the parties to achieve their targets in a flexible manner.[23] In Annex B, the Protocol established the

[18] UNFCCC, Art. 2.

[19] The Montreal Protocol on Substances that Deplete the Ozone Layer, Montreal, 16 September 1987, in force 1 January 1989, 1522 UNTS 3.

[20] On the issue of legal character in assessing the significance of climate commitments, see D. Bodansky and S. D. O'Connor, 'The legal character of the Paris Agreement' (2016) 25(2) *Review of European, Comparative & International Environmental Law*, 142–150.

[21] Cinnamon et al., 'International climate change law', 5.

[22] The Kyoto Protocol, Art. 3.

[23] The Kyoto Protocol introduced three market-based mechanisms: (1) clean development mechanism (CDM), (2) joint implementation, (3) emissions trading. The CDM, defined in

quantified emissions limitation and reduction commitments individually for its parties: some were obliged to reduce, while others were allowed to increase their emissions.[24]

After the first commitment period, agreeing on a second commitment period proved challenging. The Kyoto Protocol had a relatively narrow target, to strengthen the mitigation commitments of Annex I parties only – thereby excluding, for example, China and India, two of the world's largest contributors of GHGs – and to cover only six GHGs, without including all GHG-intensive sectors. This was expected to be widened, however. The parties did agree in Durban 2011 to extend the Kyoto Protocol for a second commitment period from 2013 to 2020, which resulted in the adoption of the Doha Amendment to the Kyoto Protocol in 2012.[25] With the extended commitment came an expansion of the list of GHGs that were included, an increase in the collective emissions target (18 per cent below the 1990 level) and restricted possibilities for non-parties to the Doha Amendments to participate in the Kyoto Mechanisms. According to Articles 21 and 22 of the Kyoto Protocol, the Doha Amendment will enter into force when accepted by 144 parties.[26] As of June 2020, only 140 parties had deposited their instruments of acceptance, which makes the Doha Amendment very unlikely to enter into force before the commitment period ends in December 2020.[27]

Article 12 of the Protocol, allows a country with an emissions reduction or emissions limitation commitment under the Kyoto Protocol (Annex B Party) to implement emissions reduction projects in developing countries. Joint implementation mechanisms, defined in Article 6 of the Kyoto Protocol, allow a country with an emissions reduction or limitation commitment under the Kyoto Protocol (Annex B Party) to earn emissions reduction units (ERUs) from an emissions reduction or emissions removal project in another Annex B Party, each equivalent to one tonne of CO_2, which can be counted towards meeting its Kyoto target. Emissions trading, as set out in Article 17 of the Kyoto Protocol, allows countries that have emission units to spare to sell this excess capacity to countries that are over their targets. For definitions of the three market-based mechanisms, see the UN website on climate change, https://unfccc.int/process/the-kyoto-protocol/mechanisms.

24 For example, Norway could increase its quantified emissions limitation and reduction commitments by 101 per cent; Australia by 108 per cent and Iceland by 110 per cent. See N. Oral, 'Ocean acidification: falling between the legal cracks of UNCLOS and the UNFCCC' (2018) 45 *Ecology Law Quarterly*, 9–30.

25 Amendment to the Kyoto Protocol by decision 1/CMP.8 in accordance with Articles 20 and 21 of the Kyoto Protocol, (the Doha Amendment), UN Doc. FCCC/KP/CMP/2012/13/Add.1 (8 December 2012).

26 However, the parties that have already deposited their instruments of acceptance are de facto bound by its obligations due to Decision 1/CMP.8; see Amendment to the Kyoto Protocol pursuant to its Article 3, para. 9.

27 Interactive status of the Doha Amendment to the Kyoto Protocol, United Nation Treaty Collection, available at https://treaties.un.org/Pages/ViewDetails.aspx?src=TREATY&mtdsg_no=XXVII-7-c&chapter=27&clang=_en.

After several years of negotiations, the Paris Agreement was adopted in December 2015. Entry into force proceeded faster than most had dared to hope: the requisite accession of at least fifty-five parties,[28] accounting for 55 per cent of total global emissions, was achieved in early October 2016.[29]

The objective of the Paris Agreement is to strengthen the global response to the threat of climate change.[30] To achieve this, it sets a long-term target for states, of holding the global average temperature increase to 'well below 2°C above pre-industrial levels and pursuing efforts to limit the temperature increase to 1.5°C above pre-industrial levels'.[31] The collective emissions target assumes that the parties will reach the vertex as quickly as possible and then reduce emissions rapidly so that there is a balance between anthropogenic emissions by sources and removals by sinks of GHGs: 'climate neutrality'.[32]

The Paris Agreement has a stronger focus on adaptation and resilience-building compared to the UNFCCC and the Kyoto Protocol.[33] In practice, the UN Climate Regime is concerned mainly with mitigation: adaptation was downplayed in the initial work undertaken to implement and strengthen UNFCCC commitments.[34] However, the IPCC has stressed that 'limitation [of GHG emission] and adaptation strategies must be considered as an integrated package and should complement each other to minimize net costs'.[35] The Paris Agreement calls for stronger adaptation commitments from its states parties by widening the normative framework around adaptation. The Agreement is explicit as to the multilevel nature of adaptation governance and the need for stronger transparency mechanisms for assessing adaptation progress – and has therefore been called 'a

[28] The Paris Agreement, Art. 21(1).

[29] By 20 August 2018, 179 of the 197 parties to the UNFCCC had ratified the Paris Agreement, including both China and Russia. The United States, originally part of the Paris Agreement, later withdrew under the Trump administration. Withdrawal is, however, a four-year process. Any party to the Agreement may withdraw, but only after three years from the date on which the Agreement entered into force for that party (Art. 28(1)). It will then take one year from the notification of withdrawal until the withdrawal takes effect (Art. 28(2)). For the United States, the Paris Agreement entered into force on 4 November 2016, so its withdrawal can be effective as of 4 November 2020 at the earliest.

[30] The Paris Agreement, Art. 2(1).

[31] Ibid., Art. 2(1)(a).

[32] Ibid., Art. 4.

[33] Resilience strengthening is expressly addressed in the Paris Agreement: Articles 2(1)(b), 4(h), 7(1), 9(e) and 10.

[34] Bodansky, Brunnée and Rajamani, *International Climate Change Law*, 135.

[35] IPCC, *Climate Change – The IPCC Response Strategies* (Library of Congress Cataloging-in-Publication Data 1991) [xxvi].

milestone in ongoing efforts to make adaptation an equal priority with mitigation'.[36]

Unlike the Kyoto Protocol, the Paris Agreement applies a bottom-up approach with a very wide margin of discretion: the parties pledge their own nationally determined contributions. The lack of legal obligations for the parties to reach their nationally determined contributions (Article 4(2) uses the words 'with the aim of achieving') and the lack of enforcement mechanisms have resulted in considerable criticism of the Paris Agreement as being 'weak and voluntary' without substantive obligations.[37] Nevertheless, it has taken a major step forward in 'creating a global process of engagement that overcomes many of the Kyoto Protocol's divisions'.[38]

In order to put the Paris Agreement into practice, the parties agreed to develop an operating manual based on the rules of Article 6 of the Paris Agreement, which offers Parties three modalities of voluntary cooperation in the implementation of their NDCs. It was mandated to be finalized by the end of COP24, held in Katowice, Poland, in December 2018. The 'rulebook' should include a set of guidelines on how governments will measure, report on and verify their emissions-cutting efforts. The aim is twofold: (1) to facilitate a functional system which invites the parties to develop strategies and (2) to ensure that the states abide by their commitments. Although some progress was made, countries failed to agree on the rules for voluntary market mechanisms, pushing part of the process onto the 2020 COP25, held in Madrid, November 2020.[39] However, consensus on these issues proved impossible once again, and the adoption of the 'Article 6 rulebook' was deferred to COP26 in Glasgow. The key deadline for measuring the success of the Paris Agreement is 2020, when countries must show they have met their targets for cutting their emissions and must agree to new, much tougher targets.

36 A. Lesnikowski et al., 'What does the Paris Agreement mean for adaptation?' (2017) 17 *Climate Policy*, 825–831.

37 A. M. Slaughter, 'The Paris Approach to global governance' (2015) *Project: Syndicate*, blog available at www.project- syndicate.org/commentary/paris-agreement-model-for-global-governance-by- anne-marie-slaughter-2015–12; R. Falk, 'Voluntary international law and the Paris Agreement' (2016) *Commentary on Global Issues*, blog available at ht tps://richardfalk.wordpress.com/2016/01/16/voluntary-international-law-and-the-paris-agr eement/.

38 C. Streck, P. Keenlyside and M. von Unger, 'The Paris Agreement: a new beginning' (2016) 13 *Journal for European Environmental & Planning Law*, 3–29.

39 COP24 Katowice 2018 United Nation Climate Change Conference, *The Katowice Rulebook – main principles of the document* (6 May 2019), available at https://cop24.gov.pl/news/news-details/news/the-katowice-rulebook-main-principles-of-the-document/.

1.3 THE LAW OF THE SEA

1.3.1 *The Development of the Modern Law of the Sea*

Throughout the entire existence of humans, our relationship with the oceans has been strong. The oceans provide food, jobs and ways of transportation. They influence every human life as a provider of resources and economic opportunities, and as a moderator of the earth's climate, affecting human safety and health. This inextricably interconnected relationship is also reflected in how human activity in the ocean space is regulated.

For centuries, attempts to regulate uses of the oceans were dominated by European practice, developing technologies for using the oceans as maritime highways.[40] Early in the seventeenth century, Hugo Grotius wrote the commissioned work *Mare Liberum* (1609), establishing the doctrine of freedom of the seas. That came to be the dominant principle for ocean governance until today's legal regime, with the LOSC as the cornerstone, was developed in the twentieth century.[41]

The LOSC was negotiated at a time of growing concern over the continued degradation of the marine environment and the overuse of resources. There was also an impetus to shift from having the freedom of the seas as the dominant principle for ocean governance to giving more powers to the coastal states by extending national maritime zones. Embracing the tension between the desire to protect the freedom of the seas, while giving the coastal states increased jurisdiction, and the desire for access to resources and preservation of the marine environment, the LOSC was negotiated as a package deal. The overarching goal was to ensure the peaceful and cooperative uses of the seas.

The LOSC, often referred to as the 'constitution of the oceans', is widely recognized as the general legal framework within which all activities in the oceans and seas are to be carried out.[42] With almost universal participation – to date 168 states parties, including the European Union – and broad geographical and substantial scope, the LOSC is a shining example of the role international law and policy can have in creating and maintaining world order.

[40] D. R. Rothwell and T. Stephens, *The International Law of the Sea*, 2nd ed. (Hart, 2016), 2.

[41] H. Grotius, *The Freedom of the High Seas: Or the Right Which Belongs to the Dutch to Take Part in the Indian Trade*, R. Van Deman Magoffin (tr.), introduction by J. Brown Scott (Oxford University Press, 1916).

[42] On the LOSC as the 'constitution of the oceans', see *'A Constitution of the Oceans': Remarks by Tommy T. B. Koh, of Singapore, President of the Third United Nations Conference on the Law of the Sea* (Montego Bay, Jamaica, 11 December 1982). UN text available at www.un.org/depts/los/convention_agreements/texts/koh_english.pdf.

Like the UNFCCC, the LOSC is a framework agreement, leaving it to other instruments and institutions to carve out the substantive standards for achieving the overarching goals set. Its major substantial contribution has been to provide the jurisdictional framework, thereby minimizing the potential for conflict by providing predictability and stability.

1.3.2 *The LOSC's Regulatory Approach*

The jurisdictional framework is laid out by describing the prescriptive and enforcement powers of the relevant actors, based on whether the actor is a coastal, flag or port state, where the activity takes place (in what maritime zone, or inside/outside national jurisdiction) and the types of activities undertaken (e.g. fishing, navigation, marine scientific research).

The zonal and sectoral architecture of the LOSC forms its regulatory approach to ocean management. The zonal regime reflects that the LOSC bases its regulatory approach on the establishment of maritime zones. The sectoral regulatory regime refers to the distribution of competence to the relevant authorities to prescribe and enforce the LOSC's rules and regulations depending on the type of activity, with different activities assigned separate rights and obligations. Activities are regulated and managed independently of others, and according to the legal category of ocean spaces.

As some maritime zones existed prior to the LOSC, it also represents a codification of already established maritime areas, such as the high seas and the territorial sea, although the LOSC finally settled the debate on the breadth of the territorial sea (12 nautical miles (nm)).[43] Other maritime zones did not exist prior to the adoption of the LOSC, such as the Exclusive Economic Zone (EEZ), which is often referred to as a separate functional zone of a *sui generis* character.[44] The Continental Shelf Regime had its origin in US claims made in the 1950s, when President Truman proclaimed that the natural resources of the subsoil and seabed of the continental shelf appertained to the United States and were thus subject to US jurisdiction and control.[45] With the LOSC, the inherent right of states to a 200 nm continental shelf was established, together with the substantive and procedural rules for establishing an

43 LOSC, Art. 3.

44 R. R. Churchill and A. V. Lowe, *The Law of the Sea*, 3rd ed. (Manchester University Press, 1999), 166.

45 Presidential Proclamation No. 2667 (28 September 1945). See also M. Scharf, *Customary International Law in Times of Fundamental Change: Recognizing Grotian Moments* (Cambridge University Press, 2013), 107–122.

outer continental shelf.[46] A distinct regime for the 'Area' (the seabed and ocean floor and subsoil thereof, beyond the limits of national jurisdiction)[47] was established by LOSC Part XI, which concerns management of the Area and provides for dispute resolution through the Seabed Disputes Chamber. Part XI also establishes the International Seabed Authority (ISA) to oversee a body referred to as 'the Enterprise' in exploration and exploitation of the deep seabed in compliance with the principles of common heritage agreed upon in the LOSC. Part XI and the establishment of the ISA were the primary reasons why the United States chose not to become a party to the LOSC, despite active participation in the three 'Conference on the Law of the Sea' that led to the design and adoption of the LOSC.[48]

The maritime zones closest to land, internal waters and the 12 nm territorial sea are regarded as part of the state's territory where the state enjoys full sovereignty.[49] The only exception is the right of ships of all states to enjoy innocent passage through the territorial sea.[50] In their EEZs, which can be up to 200 nm measured from the baseline, coastal states enjoy sovereign rights over the natural resources and have jurisdiction over certain other activities, including marine scientific research and protection of the marine environment.[51] The same sovereign rights are granted to the coastal states over natural resources, both living and non-living, on and in the continental shelf.[52] The high seas and the Area are beyond national jurisdiction. The high seas are governed by the principle of the freedom of the seas: all states have the right to undertake certain activities such as fishing, marine research and navigation, and no state has the right to assert authority unless this has been expressly granted.[53] Governed by a slightly different regime than that of the high seas, the Area has the status of 'common heritage of mankind'.[54]

46 LOSC, Arts. 76 and 77.
47 Ibid., Art. 1(1)(1).
48 The main concern of the United States was lack of influence over regulatory decisions about the exploitation and exploration of the Area which could constrain US activities and impose financial losses on US businesses involved in exploitation and exploration.
49 LOSC, Art. 2(1).
50 Ibid., Art. 17.
51 Ibid., Art. 56 (1).
52 Ibid., Art. 77(1).
53 Ibid., Arts. 87 and 89.
54 LOSC Part XI, and the Agreement Relating to the Implementation of Part XI of the United Nations Convention on the Law of the Sea 10 December 1982, New York, 28 July 1994, in force 28 July 1996, 1836 UNTS 42.

To summarize, under the LOSC the ocean was divided into multiple maritime spaces with eight basic categories: (1) internal waters, (2) territorial seas, (3) archipelagic waters, (4) the exclusive economic zone, (5) the contiguous zone, (6) the continental shelf, (7) the Area and (8) the high seas. The LOSC distributes the jurisdiction of states through the zonal approach, with multiple jurisdictional zones.[55] Simply put, the further from the coast, the less prescriptive and enforcement jurisdiction the coastal state has. In areas beyond national jurisdiction (ABNJ), the LOSC relies mainly on flag-state jurisdiction and flag-state responsibility to ensure that vessels flying their flag comply with the LOSC's obligations. However, the execution of effective flag-state jurisdiction has proven unrealistic in practice.[56]

Part XII of the LOSC was designed to overcome some of the structural challenges by ensuring the overarching duty to prevent marine pollution, applicable in every maritime zone and for any activity. Part XII is devoted to the protection and preservation of the marine environment and rules concerning the conservation of marine living resources. This has been described as a paradigm shift, as Part XII changed the focus from obligations of responsibility from damage, to general and comprehensive regulation aimed at preventing pollution.[57] It is in Part XII that the LOSC aligns with the core objective of the UN Climate Regime. Several chapters of this book explore the extent to which the LOSC obligation to protect the marine environment is applicable to climate-change causes and effects.

1.3.3 *The Challenging Way Forward for Ocean Governance*

Despite the LOSC objective of establishing a legal order for the seas and oceans within which all activities must be carried out, changing circumstances have

55 Y. Tanaka, *The International Law of the Sea* (Cambridge University Press, 2012), 4, describes the law of the sea as playing a dual role in international relations. The first is the spatial distribution of jurisdiction of States, which is the primary function of international law. The second is the international cooperation, which is a prerequisite for conservation of marine living resources and biological diversity. International cooperation is necessary due to the divergence between the law and nature, which the traditional zonal management approach is not able to address.

56 See G. C. Kasoulides, *Port State Control and Jurisdiction: Evolution of the Port State Regime* (Brill Nijhoff, 1993); R. G. Rayfuse, *Non-Flag State Enforcement in High Seas Fisheries* (Brill Nijhoff, 2004); T. L. McDorman, 'Regional port state control agreements: some issues of international law' (2000) 5 *Ocean and Coastal Law Journal*, 207–225; S. Kopela, 'Port-state jurisdiction, extraterritoriality and the protection of global commons' (2016) 47(2) *Ocean Development and International Law*, 89–130.

57 Y. Tanaka, 'Principles of international marine environmental law' in R. Rayfuse (ed.), *Research Handbook on International Marine Environmental Law* (Edward Elgar, 2015), 35.

challenged the LOSC's capacity to achieve the ambitious goal of settling 'all issues relating to the law of the sea',[58] putting its ability to function as a provider of both stability and flexibility to the test. How the law of the sea is able/unable to deal with change makes it necessary to rethink whether the LOSC's approach to ocean governance can, in fact, ensure sustainable use of the oceans. One area where the LOSC's ability to respond to new challenges is questioned is its use of the zonal and sectoral approach to ocean management, which fails to reflect the inter-connectedness of the global ecosystem. The ocean is a *single dynamic ecosystem* that requires a dynamic and holistic management approach,[59] whereas the zonal and sectoral regime is a management approach based on spatial distribution of rights and obligations, ignoring the interrelationships between marine issues. Tanaka sees this as a serious deficiency in the traditional zonal and sectoral management approach, sought compensated by the LOSC and by general international law through the obligation to cooperate.[60] Some international cooperation and coordination mechanisms have been established, by the LOSC itself and by supplementing agreements, to regulate activities at sea so as to safeguard the common interest of the international community as a whole. The latest example is the ongoing process of negotiating, under UN auspices, a new treaty under the LOSC for the conservation and sustainable use of marine biological diversity in areas beyond national jurisdiction (BBNJ).[61]

Ocean law and governance, like the broader system of modern international law within which it exists, is under increasing pressure from systemic challenges. One example of the latter is climate change, yet another emerging issue that challenges the LOSC's ability to stand the test of time, and requires the ability to adapt as well as 'evolve and develop new standards and institutions within a unified framework'.[62] The LOSC operates in the intersection

58 LOSC, Preamble.

59 K. N. Scott, 'Integrated ocean management: a new frontier in marine environmental protection' in D. R. Rothwell et al. (eds), *The Oxford Handbook of The Law of the Sea* (Oxford University Press, 2015); R. Barnes, 'The Law of the Sea Convention and integrated regulation of the ocean' (2012) 27(4) *The International Journal of Marine and Coastal Law*, 859–866; Y. Tanaka, *A Dual Approach to Ocean Management: The Cases of Zonal and Integrated Management in International Law of the Sea* (Routledge, 2009); B. Cicin-Sain and R. Knecht, *Integrated Coastal and Ocean Management: Concepts and Practices* (Island Press, 1998).

60 Tanaka, 'Principles of International Marine Environmental Law', 4.

61 The Intergovernmental Conference has its own website: www.un.org/bbnj/. See also this volume, Chapter 14.

62 J. Barrett, 'The UN Convention on the Law of the Sea: a living treaty' in J. Barrett and R. Barnes (eds.), *Law of the Sea: UNCLOS as a Living Treaty* (British Institute of International and Comparative Law, 2016), 5.

between stability and the need for change. Approaches to date have involved either dynamic interpretation of the LOSC or developing complementary legal instruments.[63] Recently, legal scholars have questioned how far the dynamic adaptation of the LOSC can go,[64] and whether the LOSC can evolve sufficiently to respond to systemic challenges such as climate change.[65] This book is meant as a contribution to the debate, examining the ability of the LOSC to respond to new and systemic challenges affecting the ocean and its resources, and to interact and supplement the UN Climate Regime.

1.4 THE FOCUS OF THIS BOOK

At the physical level, oceans and climate are closely interconnected. As noted in Chapters 2 and 3 of this book, the impacts of climate change on oceans, and vice versa, are many and severe. From a legal perspective, the importance of the oceans in the UN Climate Regime has gradually been acknowledged, with the 2019 IPCC Special Report on Oceans and Cryosphere and the UNFCCC Conference of the Parties (COP) in December 2019 (the 'blue COP') devoted to the oceans. The contributions to this book examine how the international Law of the Sea Regime recognizes its role in addressing climate change, by exploring how the law of the sea can contribute to achieving the objectives of the UN Climate Regime.

The main objective here is to assess how the Law of the Sea Regime can be interpreted, developed and applied to support the objectives of the UN Climate Regime. The contributing authors examine the interaction between two international legal regimes by assessing how causes primarily dealt with by one regime (the UN Climate Regime) are handled by another (the Law of the Sea Regime), and to see whether 'systemic harmonization' is sufficient to address the gaps and challenges created by the intersection of causes and effects concerning climate and the oceans.[66] Legal scholarship to date has focused mainly on the Law of the Sea Regime and its ability to tackle

63 Either by implementing agreements such as the Fish Stock Agreement and the forthcoming agreement on biodiversity in areas beyond national jurisdiction, or by complementing agreements such as the Convention on Biodiversity.

64 Barrett, 'The UN Convention', 5.

65 See, e.g., Barrett and Barnes (eds.), *Law of the Sea*; International Ocean Institute, Canada (ed.), *The Future of Ocean Governance and Capacity Development* (Brill Nijhoff, 2018).

66 'Systemic harmonization' refers to an approach towards regime interaction based on the new orientation of international courts and tribunals, towards systemic harmonization rather than normative conflict. See, e.g., the European Court of Human Rights Grand Chamber in Al Dulimi; *Al-Dulimi and Montana Management Inc.* v. *Switzerland*, [GC] App. No. 5809/08 (ECtHR, 2016). See also L. A. Sicilianos, 'The European Court of Human Rights facing the

climate-induced challenges by mapping the relevant and applicable rules and regulations and identifying gaps and challenges.[67] There has been less study of the interaction between the UN Climate Regime and the Law of the Sea Regime, and even less using a law-of-the-sea perspective.[68] In this book, we ask: to what degree is the Law of the Sea Regime able to support the main objectives of the UN Climate Regime by supplementing, coordinating, complementing and developing in accordance with the main objectives of the latter?

In assessing the complementing and supporting role of the Law of the Sea Regime, the contributing authors evaluate the possibilities and potential of the Law of the Sea Regime to fill some of the gaps and shortcomings of the UN Climate Regime. Dealing with ocean acidification is one example,[69] the use of the LOSC's dispute resolution system is another.[70] We also examine how the rules and regulations of the Law of the Sea Regime can be interpreted and applied so that they are not only in accordance with the UN Climate Regime's objectives but also strengthen state obligations to deal with the climate crisis. Further, to what degree do the main objectives of the UN Climate Regime inform the interpretation of, and influence the development of, rules and

Security Council: towards systemic harmonization' (2017) 66(4) *International & Comparative Law Quarterly*, 783–804; A. Peters, 'The refinement of international law: from fragmentation to regime interaction and politicization' (2017) 15(3) *International Journal of Constitutional Law*, 671–704.

67 There is extensive research on the impacts on climate change on oceans, mapping the ability of the legal frameworks to respond to these challenges: see, e.g., R. S. Abate (ed.), *Climate Change Impacts on Oceans and Coastal Law* (Oxford University Press, 2015); T. Stephens, 'Warming waters and souring seas: climate change and ocean acidification' in D. R. Rothwell et al. (eds.), *The Oxford Handbook of The law of the Sea* (Oxford University Press, 2015), 777–798; R. Rayfuse, 'Climate change and the Law of the Sea' in R. Rayfuse and S. V. Scott (eds.), *International Law in the Era of Climate Change* (Edward Elgar, 2012), 147–174.

68 There is little literature on the interaction between the UN Climate Regime and the Law of the Sea Regime focusing on the role of the law-of-the sea perspective. See, however, A. Boyle, 'Litigating climate change under Part XII of the LOSC' (2019) *The International Journal of Marine and Coastal Law* 458–481; P. Sands, 'Climate change and the rule of law: adjudicating the future in international law' (2016) 28 *Journal of Environmental Law*, 114–134; A. Boyle and N. Singh Ghaleigh, 'Climate change and international law beyond the UNFCCC' in C. P. Carlarne, K. R. Gray and R. G. Tarasofsky (eds.), *The Oxford Handbook of International Climate Change Law* (Oxford University Press, 2016), 26–54; A. Boyle, 'Climate change, ocean governance and UNCLOS' in J. Barrett and R. Barnes (eds.), *Law of the Sea: UNCLOS as a Living Treaty* (British Institute of International and Comparative Law, 2016), 225–231; Kopela, 'Climate change', 70; A. Boyle, 'Law of the sea perspectives on climate change' (2012) 27 *The International Journal of Marine and Coastal Law*, 831–838; M. Doelle, 'Climate change and the use of the dispute settlement regime of the Law of the Sea Convention' (2006) 37 *Ocean Development & International Law*, 319–337.

69 See this volume, Chapter 5.

70 See this volume, Chapter 4.

regulations appertaining to the law of the sea – for example, by influencing how to balance the different interests incorporated in the Law of the Sea Regime? To achieve 'systemic harmonization' and hence successful interaction between legal regimes, avoiding loss of unity and coherence is an important element in reducing the risk of failure of a legal regime.[71] Thus, the supportive potential of the Law of the Sea Regime is also determined by its ability to avoid incompatibilities which mute the goals of the UN Climate Regime.

The UN Climate Regime has two main strategies for achieving its basic objectives: mitigation of harmful emissions and adaptation to climate change. The assessments offered in this book, of the law of the sea's capacity to support and complement the UN Climate Regime, build on the use of the same two strategies. By covering different topics, aspects and challenges of the current legal regime, we aim to offer an in-depth analysis of the Law of the Sea Regime – its potential and limitations in addressing the fundamental challenges of climate change. To this end and to ensure inner coherence, each chapter offers an analysis of the rules and regulations applicable to the specific topic, including an assessment of the ability to adapt to or address the given situation, in order to identify to what extent the Law of the Sea Regime is able to respond to the climate-change crisis – and whether the available responses are in line with the objectives of the UN Climate Regime.

By identifying the potential and constraints of the Law of the Sea Regime in supporting and complementing the UN Climate Regime in the mitigation of and adaptation to climate change, this book offers a new perspective on the law of the sea and its capacity to evolve so as to respond to systemic challenges, and its potential to adapt and ensure a resilient and sustainable future.

1.5 STRUCTURE OF THE BOOK AND ITS CHAPTERS

This book has four parts. The *Introductory Part I* consists of five chapters that set the stage for the following parts, by describing the main consequences of climate change for the marine environment and providing discussions and analyses of the general framing for marine environmental protection in the LOSC.

Chapter 2 by *Davor Vidas, Jan Zalasiewicz, Mark Williams and Colin Summerhayes* examines the two overarching themes of the book – climate change and the oceans – through the lens of the Anthropocene. The authors start by explaining the content and emergence of the concept of the Anthropocene, and then discuss how it relates to climate change and the

[71] Peters, 'The refinement of international law', 679.

role of the oceans. They discuss whether and how the law of the sea, which emerged in the epoch of the Holocene, can respond to the context and conditions of the new epoch – the Anthropocene. A new epoch implies a change of the context in which international law operates, in turn, requiring comprehensive new responses. The authors argue that the role – and responsibility – of international law scholarship in contributing to the development of international law will become enhanced as the Earth System leaves the generally stable conditions of the Holocene Epoch and enters the new planetary state of the Anthropocene.

Chapter 3 by *Robin Kundis Craig* examines the two general categories of legal and policy responses to climate change: *mitigation*, or actions to reduce global GHG emissions and ultimately reduce the atmospheric concentrations of these gases; and *adaptation*, or actions to enable communities and nations to cope with the climate-change effects that are already occurring or that are unavoidable in the future. The chapter first provides definitions of 'mitigation' and 'adaptation' and an extended examination of how the UNFCCC and the IPCC deal with each facet of climate law and policy. The author then examine the role played by the oceans in climate mitigation and climate adaptation, pointing out that international law indeed creates a duty to protect the oceans.

Chapter 4 by *Alan Boyle* examines the obligations to protect the marine environment as established by Part XII of the LOSC, and discusses its applicability and relevance to climate-change causes and effects. Boyle asks whether the LOSC could assist or offer an alternative legal basis to the Paris Agreement, by assessing the content of the legal obligations embodied in LOSC Part XII and the potential for using the LOSC's Part XV dispute settlement system in climate-change cases. He concludes that LOSC can at best provide a vehicle for compulsory dispute settlement, which is notably lacking in the UNFCCC regime. Beyond that, protecting the oceans from harmful climate change will depend on how states interpret and apply the Paris Agreement – not on giving LOSC Part XII separate, additional effect.

Chapter 5 by *Karen N. Scott* examines the complexity of the ocean acidification regime and assesses whether the applicable international legal regimes, in particular, LOSC Part XII and the obligations to prevent, reduce and control pollution of the marine environment, establish standards that require states to take action to prevent, reduce and control ocean acidification. Scott assesses whether standards under the 1992 UNFCCC comprise 'international standards' for the purposes of LOSC Article 212, and whether this constrains the development of the law of the sea as regards effectively addressing ocean acidification. She argues that the parties to the LOSCs are, in fact, subject to a due diligence obligation under its Part XII; further, that this obligation is not satisfied by merely complying with UNFCCC obligations unless actions taken under the UNFCCC directly address the problem of ocean acidification. Scott holds that this interpretation of the LOSC represents a significant opportunity under the law of the sea to address ocean acidification.

The chapters in Part II – *Mitigation and the Law of the Sea* – discuss the role of the law of the sea regime in achieving the emission targets and the temperature goals of the UN Climate Regime by assessing how and if the law of the sea could contribute to mitigating the effects of climate change by how activities falling within the scope of the LOSC are regulated. Some chapters in Parts II and III concern adaptation as well as mitigation, and could have been placed in either part.

In Chapter 6, *Henrik Ringbom* examines developments in the regulation of GHGs from maritime transport. He begins by charting the institutional relationship between the two main international fora involved, the UNFCCC and the IMO, and briefly assesses the regulatory achievements of the IMO to date, in particular, the recent adoption of an 'initial IMO strategy on reduction of GHG emissions from ships'. He goes on to note that a wide gap still remains between the stated climate ambitions of the IMO and actual emission requirements, and that the battle for governance lead in the field is not over. Ringbom holds that certain developments of recent years give rise – for the first time – to cautious optimism as to the prospect of establishing an adequate governance framework for shipping and GHGs in the coming decades. On the other hand, the urgency of achieving concrete reductions is becoming increasingly obvious, and the question is still open whether recent policy commitments will – or indeed can – be translated to binding emissions reductions from the shipping sector.

Chapter 7 by *Nigel Bankes* studies the relationship between carbon capture and storage (CCS) and the law of the sea. Bankes examines how CCS projects may be regulated under different legal instruments, starting with the Law of the Sea Convention, moving on to the London Dumping Convention and its Protocol, and ending with the treatment of such projects in regional agreements, specifically the Convention for the Protection of the Marine Environment of the North-East Atlantic (OSPAR). He concludes that the LOSC allocates clear and appropriate authority to coastal states to deal with CCS activities. This is less clear in ABNJ, but he concludes that CCS activities might fall under the regime of flag state freedom. The flag-state regime, Bankes points out, is unlikely to provide a secure foundation for capital-intensive CCS operations that require a clear, detailed and precautionary regulatory regime. The analysis in this chapter shows that the LOSC does not itself prohibit CCS activities, but that there are also other global or regional instruments which might have that effect.

Chapter 8 by *Elise Johansen* discusses to what extent the Law of the Sea Regime facilitate the use of ocean fertilization techniques as a mitigating measure. Johansen first examines how ocean fertilization sits within the framework of the LOSC, and then how the London Dumping Regime and the Convention on Biological Diversity have framed ocean fertilization. This chapter shows how ocean fertilization activities are regulated by and fall under several different legal regimes, creating practical and conceptual problems. Johansen argues that, although the LOSC does not directly hinder ocean fertilization activities, today's regulatory challenges represent an obstacle to further exploration of ocean fertilization as a strategy for countering the effects of climate change.

In Chapter 9, *Maria Madalena das Neves* examines to what extent the law of the sea enables or hampers the development of offshore renewable energy projects. She begins with a description of the various forms of offshore renewable energy, discussing their potential role in mitigating climate change. She then identifies key challenges related to the development of offshore renewable energy: competing uses of the oceans and balancing of different interests, impacts to the marine environment and regulatory challenges. Although the law of the sea emplaces certain constraints related to the protection of the marine environment and the rights of other states, it does not hamper the development of offshore energy. On the contrary, das Neves holds, it offers a framework that provides a certain degree of jurisdictional predictability, and facilitates various activities central to offshore energy projects such as navigation, laying of submarine cables, and operation of artificial islands, installations and structures. Nonetheless, she also concludes that additional regulation of the offshore renewable energy industry will be necessary.

Chapter 10 by *Ingvild Ulrikke Jakobsen* examines how use of marine protected areas (MPAs) can function as an effective tool to counter the effects of climate change. Jakobsen first discusses to what extent MPAs may respond to and comply with the requirements that follow from the UN Climate Regime. She then explores to what extent the international obligations to protect the marine environment and to conserve marine ecosystems and biological diversity that follow from the LOSC and the CBD include requirements to establish MPAs for the purpose of mitigation and adaptation to climate change. Next comes an analysis of the legal opportunities and the legal constraints when establishing MPAs for climate purposes within the legal regime of the law of the sea. Jakobsen concludes that the legal regimes relevant for 'climate

MPAs' are not yet sufficiently coordinated to provide an effective legal framework; furthermore, that the LOSC with its zonal and sectoral approach to ocean management may be an obstacle for the establishment and effective management of MPAs. Jakobsen argues that the best way forward would be to build on the positive experiences in regional agreements, and develop a legal framework and practice at the regional level where interlinkages between the global instruments are made, to ensure the use of the MPAs as a response to climate change.

The contributions in Part III – *Adapting to a changing marine environment* – raise the general question whether the law of the sea provides an adequate legal framework for dealing with the impacts of climate change in a timely and flexible manner. Adaptation to impacts of climate change requires a legal regime that can respond quickly to changes. The authors here explore various climate-change-related situations, assessing to what extent the law of the sea can offer strategies for adapting to new circumstances.

Chapter 11 by *Erik J. Molenaar* examines the extent in which climate change has been integrated in the domain of international fisheries law, and whether this domain entitles or requires states to take account of climate change and its impacts in their fisheries management. Molenaar first charts how climate change impacts marine capture fisheries and how marine capture fisheries are able to adapt to the new climate-induced stressors. Then follows a detailed examination of the global component of international fisheries law – in particular, the LOSC and the Fish Stocks Agreement. Molenaar then examines the mitigation component of international fisheries law – a relatively unexplored topic, compared to adaptation. After discussing climate change and regional fisheries management organizations (RFMOs), Molenaar concludes that nothing in the LOSC or the Fish Stocks Agreement constrains the discretion of coastal states and high-seas fishing states to take account of climate-change impacts in fisheries management, or to address the contribution of fishing to climate change. However, the effectiveness of voluntary adaptation and mitigation measures is significantly compromised by the consensual nature of international law, as reflected in the fundamental principle of *pacta tertiis*. Furthermore, he argues, the extent to which RFMOs integrate climate change into their management processes is highly significant, given their role as the pre-eminent institutions of international fisheries law. Here he notes the lack of political support and insufficiently wide mandates of RFMOs, and how these are perceived by their members, as reasons why climate-change mitigation has remained unexplored territory for RFMOs.

In Chapter 12, *Irene Dahl* focuses on the impact of climate change on aquaculture, noting the gap in the international regulation of aquaculture. She discusses to what degree international law, and especially the law of the sea, provides a framework for adaptive responses by coastal and other states to the effects of climate change. Using Norwegian aquaculture law and policy as examples of implementation of international norms and guidelines, she asks which approaches or measures, deriving from the Paris Agreement and FAO instruments, commit or request states to implement in order to make aquaculture more resilient to climate change. Dahl concludes that the Paris Agreement imposes relevant global goals and obligations applicable to national aquaculture law and policy, including the obligation to enhance adaptive capacity, strengthen resilience and reduce vulnerability to climate change. The Paris Agreement may serve as a first step in this direction; also relevant are FAO's guidelines as regards complying with the Paris Agreement. However, Dahl argues that the vagueness of the Paris Agreement and the inherent 'soft law' character of FAO instruments should encourage the international community to start a process on adoption of a binding legal instrument.

Chapter 13 by *Signe Veierud Busch* examines one of the main consequences of climate change, namely sea-level rise, and identifies and discusses possible approaches for *how* to adapt the Law of the Sea to moderate the consequences of sea-level rise. Busch takes stock of and analyses the latest developments in discussion of sea-level rise as threatening maritime limits, including the work of the ILA Committee, and explores whether the *exception rules* in the LOSC can be utilized as a starting point for adapting the Law of the Sea to unavoidable climate change. She argues that the ILA Committee has employed an overly narrow approach for addressing the problems in the law of baseline; as a result, the ILA resolution proposes a solution which does not really solve the problem, but shifts it to another segment within the law of the sea. Busch concludes that, although the LOSC does not offer a permanent solution to *all* consequences of sea-level rise on maritime limits and entitlement, wider application of its existing provisions can provide a good short-term response to the threat of sea-level rise on the maritime entitlements of vulnerable coastal states.

The chapters of Part IV – *Exploring the Future of Ocean Governance* – aim to widen the scope when assessing the role and function of the LOSC as the legal framework within ocean management must operate. The authors challenge the LOSC as the normative framework, pointing to the need to include climate change in the new UN agreement under development addressing

ABNJ and in designing a new comprehensive approach to ocean governance, and finally in addressing the current regulatory gaps identified in Parts II and III.

Chapter 14 by *Christian Prip* focuses on ABNJ and how science is gradually discovering knowledge of marine life not previously known, and with that also knowledge about the stressors on the marine ecosystems in areas previously beyond human impact. Prip discusses the extent to which LOSC and other legal instruments address the impacts of climate change in ABNJ and contribute to mitigation endeavours. He then analyses the negotiations in the intergovernmental conference on an international legally binding instrument under the United Nations Convention on the Law of the Sea on the conservation and sustainable use of marine biological diversity of areas beyond national jurisdiction (BBNJ), asking whether this process may provide an opportunity to fill the gaps identified. Next, he discusses the role of Environmental Impact Assessments as a particularly important legal tool for addressing the impacts of climate change on ABNJ. Prip concludes that the BBNJ process is an opportunity to incorporate concerns for climate-change-induced impacts into the legal framework.

In Chapter 15, *Margherita Paola Poto* examines the factors of fragmentation that characterize the institutional structure of the law of the sea, beginning with the law of the sea's normative system and its implementing measures, and its exponential growth in norms, institutions and tools since 1982. Analysing the provisions of LOSC Part XII and the ensuing agreements which, under the LOSC umbrella, have sought to regulate climate change, she finds elements of a deterministic approach in the law of the sea. She then explores alternative solutions that could offer simplification and efficiency, and ultimately an effective change 'from the inside-out'. Drawing on holistic and integrated approaches among indigenous peoples, Poto offers reflections on the interconnectedness of humankind and nature, and concludes that a broader and more comprehensive approach to ocean governance is sorely needed – one that can shift the focus to climate and the oceans in their reciprocal interconnectedness and in relation to human communities: a truly ocean-centred perspective.

In Chapter 16 *Elise Johansen, Ingvild Ulrikke Jakobsen and Philipp Peter Nickels* identify and synthesize the findings of the chapters, and offer some answers to the overall research question of this book.

2

Climate Change and the Anthropocene

Implications for the Development of the Law of the Sea

Davor Vidas, Jan Zalasiewicz, Mark Williams and Colin Summerhayes*

In December 2015, the 21st Conference of Parties (COP21) to the UN Framework Convention on Climate Change invited the Intergovernmental Panel on Climate Change (IPCC) to provide a special report on the impacts of global warming of 1.5°C above pre-industrial levels and related global greenhouse gas emission pathways.[1] In October 2018, the IPCC issued a Special Report on the impacts of global warming of 1.5°C above pre-industrial levels.[2] This was the first IPCC report to employ the concept of the *Anthropocene* in its climate-change assessments – referring to it as the 'overarching context' and a 'boundary concept' that provides the 'unifying lens' through which to acknowledge 'profound, differential but increasingly geologically significant human influences on the Earth system as a whole'.[3]

Major challenges, also as regards inter-state relations regulated by international law, stem from the relevance of (climate) change on a geological time scale, as represented by the Anthropocene, and its increasing co-occurrence with the politically relevant time span. Thus far, international law has

* All authors of this chapter are members of the Anthropocene Working Group. Prof. Davor Vidas, Fridtjof Nansen Institute, Prof. Jan Zalasiewicz, University of Leicester, Prof. Mark Williams, University of Leicester, Dr. Colin Summerhayes, University of Cambridge.

1 This invitation was contained in the decision on the adoption of the Paris Agreement. See para. 21 in 'Adoption of the Paris Agreement', Framework Convention on Climate Change, Conference of the Parties, Twenty-first session, Paris, 12 December 2015, UN Doc. FCCC/CP/2015/L.9.

2 IPCC, V. Masson-Delmotte et al. (eds.), *Global warming of 1.5°C: An IPCC Special Report on the Impacts of Global Warming of 1.5°C above Pre-industrial Levels and Related Global Greenhouse Gas Emission Pathways, in the Context of Strengthening the Global Response to the Threat of Climate Change, Sustainable Development, and Efforts to Eradicate Poverty* (2018), available at www.ipcc.ch/sr15/ (IPCC SR 1.5 (2018)). This report was the first publication issued in the IPCC's Sixth Assessment Report (AR6) cycle, which is due to be completed in the first half of 2022.

3 Ibid., 'Chapter 1: Framing and Context', 49–91, at 49, 52–54.

addressed changing issues in inter-state relations by drawing on and building upon accumulated experience from the past, in order to achieve the ultimate objective of facilitating the avoidance of conflicts and the maintenance of peace. The change has been understood primarily in its political context, against the background of the generally stable natural conditions of the Earth System over the course of several millennia, including most of the twentieth century. With the profound change of natural, Earth-System conditions – the characteristic of the Anthropocene – it is becoming increasingly necessary to anticipate future developments not only in their political context, but also on the basis of well-founded scientific predictions, to be able to formulate legal options for unprecedented circumstances in which international law will need to regulate relations between states and other subjects of international law in the coming decades of the twenty-first century (and beyond).

This chapter relates the two overarching themes of the book – climate change and the ocean – through the lens of the Anthropocene and explores the impact on the development of the law of the sea within a broader framework of international law, including the climate-change regime. We explain the emergence and the content of the Anthropocene concept, initially in the natural sciences and then in geology, as a proposed epoch in the history of the Earth (Section 2.1). We then relate the Anthropocene to climate change and the role of the oceans (Section 2.2). Finally, in Section 2.3 we discuss the development of international law of the sea in the context of the conditions of two different epochs: the Holocene, in which this law emerged; and the Anthropocene, to which it would now need to start responding. We argue that the role – and responsibility – of international law scholarship in contributing to the development of international law will become enhanced as the Earth System leaves the generally stable conditions of the Holocene Epoch and enters the new planetary state of the Anthropocene.

2.1 THE CONCEPT OF THE ANTHROPOCENE

2.1.1 *Its Origins and Development in the Natural Sciences*

When the Anthropocene was offered as a concept, improvised on the spur of the moment by Paul Crutzen at a meeting of the Scientific Committee of the International Geosphere-Biosphere Programme, held in Cuernavaca, Mexico, in 2000,[4] it crystallized a general feeling that had been growing for some time:

4 P. Crutzen, 'We aren't doomed' (interview with C. Schwägerl) in N. Möllers, C. Schwägerl and H. Trischler (eds.), *Welcome to the Anthropocene: The Earth in Our Hands* (Deutsches Museum, 2014), 30–36, at 32. As Crutzen explained (ibid., at 32), after his intervention at the

that human-caused environmental impacts may be changing fundamental processes of our planet, of a scale and permanence that rivalled some of the great changes of the geological past, changes that had been reflected by geologists in the formal divisions – Carboniferous, Jurassic, Pleistocene, and so on – of the geological time scale.

This concept had been mooted, in one form or other, from the earliest days of organized geology.[5] However, the science of geology had also been seeking to establish the immensity of both the Earth's age – now measured at over 4.5 billion years – and of the huge scale of its processes, such as the opening and closure of oceans, where events like massive asteroid impacts or sustained volcanic eruptions were becoming more clearly established as drivers of Earth processes. The human impact seemed tiny and fleeting in comparison, so ideas such as the 'anthropozoic' were long disregarded or disdained by the geological community.

Crutzen's intervention came not from within the geological community, but from the Earth System Science (ESS) community, which focused more on very recent Earth history, and made extensive use of observational data, recorded by scientific instruments in real time, rather than ancient 'proxy' evidence, fossilized within rock strata.[6] Crutzen's comparison was with the Holocene Epoch: the geological time unit (within which we still, formally, live) that represents the interglacial phase – the latest of many such climate phases of the Ice Ages – which began 11,700 years ago.[7] Once global

IGBP congress, he found out that the term 'Anthropocene' had been used previously by a limnologist of the University of Michigan, Eugene Stoermer. Upon Crutzen's invitation, they together published the first, brief paper about the Anthropocene: P. J. Crutzen and E. F. Stoermer, 'The "Anthropocene"' (2000) 41 *Global Change Newsletter*, 17–18.

5 Buffon's 1778 scientifically based Earth history is arguably the first such comprehensive account; see Comte de Buffon, *The Epochs of Nature*, J. Zalasiewicz, A.-S. Milon and M. Zalasiewicz (trs.) (University of Chicago Press, 2018): the last of Buffon's seven epochs of Earth time was marked by 'human assistance' to natural processes. Later, similar ideas resurfaced sporadically in the mid- and late nineteenth century and subsequently, as in Stoppani's 'anthropozoic era' of 1873; see A. Stoppani, *Corso di Geologia*, Vol. II, *Geologia stratigrafica* (G Bernardoni e G Brigola, 1873).

6 The two approaches, ESS-based and geological, differ in emphasis, methodology and philosophy, but are complementary and essentially in agreement as regards the nature of the Anthropocene; see: W. Steffen et al., 'Stratigraphic and Earth system approaches in defining the Anthropocene' (2016) 8 *Earth's Future*, 324–345; also J. Zalasiewicz et al., 'Petrifying Earth process: the stratigraphic imprint of key Earth System parameters in the Anthropocene' (2017) 34 *Theory, Culture & Society*, 83–104.

7 The base of the Holocene Epoch as starting 11,700 (±99) years before year 2000 was ratified in 2008 by the International Union of Geological Sciences; see M. Walker et al., 'Formal definition and dating of the GSSP (Global Stratotype Section and Point) for the base of the Holocene using the Greenland NGRIP ice core, and selected auxiliary records' (2009) 24 *Journal of Quaternary Science*, 3–17.

temperature and then sea level stabilized, some 11,000 and 7,000 years ago, respectively, there ensued a period of considerable stability for the Earth System. This provided the foundations for the growth of settled human civilization and, eventually, the establishment of territorially based nation states and the borders between them. The observed relative stability of land–sea geography came to be seen as essentially permanent, not least given the experience of all preceding generations extending back to the dawn of recorded history.

Crutzen argued that anthropogenic change had become so far-reaching that we could no longer be said to be living in the stable state of the Holocene Epoch, which, therefore, must be recognized as having ended. He quickly – and prominently – developed this logic in print,[8] noting that human impacts, escalating since industrialization, were fundamentally changing the Earth's landscape, ocean/atmospheric chemistry and the biosphere.

Crutzen was a highly respected scientist, a Nobel laureate in chemistry (1995) for his research on the destruction of the ozone layer, working within the large and highly active ESS community, which soon began to use the Anthropocene term and concept as de facto reality.[9] Subsequent work by members of that community detailed the range and scale of anthropogenic change, noting, in particular, the 'Great Acceleration' in many key processes linked to population growth, industrialization and globalization since the mid-twentieth century.[10]

2.1.2 *The Anthropocene Concept in Geology*

Although used matter-of-factly since the beginning of the 2000s, as if it were already established geologically, the Anthropocene had been subjected to none of the extensive analysis and bureaucratic decision-making processes that need to be applied by the geological community to establish its formal

[8] P. J. Crutzen, 'Geology of mankind' (2002) 415 *Nature* 23. Crutzen's first article on the Anthropocene, published in 2000, was co-authored with the limnologist Eugene Stoermer (see 4) who had, independently, been using the same concept in his teaching and research during the 1990s.

[9] For example, M. Meybeck, 'Global analysis of river systems: from Earth System controls to Anthropocene syndromes' (2003) 358 *Philosophical Transactions of the Royal Society*, 1935–1955; and W. Steffen et al., *Global Change and the Earth System: A Planet under Pressure* (Springer, 2004).

[10] See, initially, W. Steffen, P. J. Crutzen and J. McNeill, 'The Anthropocene: are humans now overwhelming the great forces of nature?' (2007) 36 *Ambio* 614–621. This thesis is further elaborated in W. Steffen et al., 'The trajectory of the Anthropocene: the Great Acceleration' (2015) 2 *The Anthropocene Review*, 81–98.

status; even today it has remained informal. It was only in 2006 that the Geological Society of London's Stratigraphy Commission, noting the increasing use of the 'Anthropocene' in scientific publications, initially considered it as a potential formal addition to the geological time scale.[11] As a national body, it had no power of international decision, but it could initiate a geological study of the Anthropocene. The type of evidence it cited in a paper published two years later included the rise in atmospheric CO_2 levels and incipient global warming/ocean acidification, changes to terrestrial erosion and sedimentation patterns and extinctions/species migrations associated with land use change.[12] The cautious conclusion based on this generalized and preliminary review was that the concept seemed to have merit in geological terms, and should be investigated further.[13]

This soon led to an invitation from the Subcommission on Quaternary Stratigraphy (SQS), the relevant component body of the International Commission on Stratigraphy (ICS) that oversees the geological time scale, to establish a new study group – the Anthropocene Working Group (AWG) – to examine the question formally. The AWG has been active since 2009; its uniquely multidisciplinary membership (reflecting the overlap of historical and geological time, and natural and anthropogenic process, in the Anthropocene) has been gathering, analysing, discussing and publishing evidence on this question since then.[14]

A few peculiarities of formal geological time should be noted. It is a *time* framework, within which all Earth phenomena must be accommodated. As many of these phenomena are highly variable in time and space, the boundaries of the time framework need to be synchronous.[15] As all systematic evidence of Earth history prior to human written records is held within rock strata, the timescale has a dual nature, and so includes both material (strata)

11 J. Zalasiewicz et al., 'The geological Anthropocene: born in Burlington House' (December 2017/January 2018) 27 *Geoscientist*, 16–19.

12 J. Zalasiewicz et al., 'Are we now living in the Anthropocene?' (2008) 18(2) *GSA Today*, 4–8.

13 Ibid.

14 For example, M. Williams et al. (eds.), 'The Anthropocene: a new epoch of geological time?' (2011) 369 *Philosophical Transactions of the Royal Society* A, 833–1112 (thematic issue on the Anthropocene); C. N. Waters et al., *A Stratigraphical Basis for the Anthropocene* (Geological Society of London, 2014); J. Zalasiewicz et al. (eds.), *The Anthropocene as a Geological Time Unit: A Guide to the Scientific Evidence and Current Debate* (Cambridge University Press, 2019).

15 That is, it must represent the same time instant, as far as is possible, all around the world. The purpose of synchronous geological time boundaries is to provide a temporal framework that helps geologists to order and analyze the complex record of Earth history across time and space.

and time components.[16] Definition may be by a chosen time boundary (a 'Global Standard Stratigraphic Age') but is preferably and most typically made by a carefully chosen physical reference point within strata – a 'Global Boundary Stratotype Section and Point' (GSSP), more commonly known as a 'golden spike'. Therefore, for the Anthropocene to be recognized as a formal geological time unit, it must be defined so as to be synchronous worldwide, must be definable as both a time unit and a material unit made of recent strata, its hierarchical level must be decided, and candidates for a suitable 'golden spike' must be located and analysed in detail: those are essentially the ingredients of any formal proposal in stratigraphy. Such a proposal on formalization then needs to be put to a vote, initially by the AWG itself in order for a proposal to be made to stratigraphic decision-making bodies – the SQS and ICS, successively, for their approval – and finally ratified by the International Union of Geological Sciences (IUGS). Approval of the proposal at each of those instances requires a supermajority of 60 per cent of delivered votes (provided that a quorum of 60 per cent has been attained).

Evidence gathered by the AWG since it began its work in 2009 led in 2016 to the interim conclusions and recommendations.[17] According to the interim conclusions, firstly, the Anthropocene is 'geologically real': it represents a distinctively new and rapidly (and in many aspects, irreversibly) changing Earth System in which the changes are reflected in an array of new components that characterize recent strata worldwide – including industrially sourced fly ash particles, plastics, persistent organic pollutants, concrete debris, altered carbon and nitrogen isotopes and the remains of many invasive species.

Second, many of these changes cluster around the mid-twentieth century, which hence emerged as the optimal time level at which to seek to place the beginning of the Anthropocene. This is in full recognition of many thousands of years of detectable human impacts on the environment from late Pleistocene and through Holocene times, from the extinction of megafaunal species to local and regional perturbations associated with the spread of farming. However, these early impacts occurred within an Earth System where fundamental factors such as the carbon, nitrogen and phosphorus cycles, global climate and sea level were essentially stable, or showed only

[16] For instance, the Jurassic System is made up of all the rocks and fossils that formed during the exactly parallel Jurassic Period, when dinosaurs roamed, volcanoes erupted, and so on. The geological time scale is also hierarchical, with larger units enclosing smaller ones. The Jurassic Period/System, for instance, is within the Mesozoic Era/Erathem, and is subdivided into epochs/series and these, in turn, into ages/stages.

[17] J. Zalasiewicz et al., 'The Working Group on the Anthropocene: summary of evidence and interim recommendations' (2017) 19 *Anthropocene*, 55–60.

minor fluctuations against a generally stable background. The Anthropocene represents a clear departure from this stability. The Earth during the Holocene may be regarded as having been in a sustainable state from a human perspective, in which successive generations inherited fundamentally the same kind of planet. In the Anthropocene, in contrast, stable planetary conditions cannot be sustained, and each future generation seems set to live on an Earth in which the boundary conditions of climate, sea level and biosphere will be evolving, for at least several centuries and millennia to come.

Third, the changes associated with the transition from background Holocene to Anthropocene conditions are at least as great as those from the Pleistocene to the Holocene epochs, and greater than the temporary climate fluctuations used to mark the formal subdivisions of the Holocene.[18] The Anthropocene is hence considered, conservatively, by the AWG as a unit of epoch/series status. Its formalization would end the Holocene, as Crutzen originally hypothesized.

Fourth, it was agreed to propose a definition of the Anthropocene in classical geological terms, using a physical reference level, GSSP (or 'golden spike'). The extensive selection, sampling and analytical work required is now underway,[19] but will take several years to accomplish. There was less agreement as to the primary marker, from among the wide range of possibilities, for defining the Anthropocene, but artificial radionuclides (plutonium, enhanced radiocarbon), scattered globally by atmospheric thermonuclear bomb tests since the mid-twentieth century, have found most favour thus far, as these provide the sharpest and most nearly synchronous signal within strata.

On 20 May 2019, following ten years' study of the issues involved, members of the AWG held a binding vote on two key questions: (1) should the Anthropocene be treated as a new formal unit of the geological time scale, conventionally defined by a GSSP ('golden spike')?; and (2) should the beginning of the Anthropocene be defined by a stratigraphic signal around

[18] Following a longstanding informal tripartite subdivision, the Holocene has recently been formally subdivided – on the basis of temporary climate perturbations – into three parts of roughly equal temporal duration, with the respective boundaries around 8236 and 4250 years ago (before 2000 CE). The logic was set out in M. J. C. Walker et al., 'Formal subdivision of the Holocene Series/Epoch' (2012) 27 *Journal of Quaternary Science*, 649–659. Formal ratification of this subdivision is set out in M. J. C. Walker et al., 'Formal ratification of the Holocene Series/Epoch (Quaternary System/Period): two new Global Boundary Stratotype Sections and Points (GSSPs) and three new stages/subseries' (2018) 41(4) *Episodes* 213; this subdivision was ratified by the IUGS Executive Council on 14 June 2018.

[19] C. N. Waters et al., 'Palaeoenvironmental archives and their differing suitabilities for candidate Global Boundary Stratotype Sections and Points (GSSPs) for the Anthropocene' (2018) 178 *Earth-Science Reviews*, 379–429.

the mid-twentieth century? Both questions received a majority of 88 per cent votes in favour,[20] thereby setting the formal framework for the next stage in the decision-making process towards potential inclusion of the Anthropocene in the geological time scale.

2.2 CLIMATE CHANGE, THE OCEANS AND THE ANTHROPOCENE

2.2.1 *The Scope of the Anthropocene: A Wide Spectrum of Change*

The Anthropocene is sometimes conflated in general discussions with climate change, but its span is considerably wider,[21] and its relation to climate change and directly associated effects, such as sea-level rise, is not simple. Many of the clearest, most advanced and most characteristic signals of the Anthropocene[22] – the landscape and biota transformed by urbanization and agriculture, the proliferation of plastics and persistent organic pollutants, the radionuclide signal – have only indirect links with climate. Indeed, these changes in themselves could serve as a basis for defining a new geological time unit, even if they took place against a background of long-term climate stability.

Compelling evidence has accumulated in recent decades: it has been confirmed that climate warming has begun, and that considerably more warming is in store (see Sections 2.2.2 and 2.2.3). This has wider significance, as the influence of climate change far exceeds the immediate effects of rising global average temperatures and the melting of polar and mountain ice in raising sea levels.

Climate change impacts profoundly on the biosphere, not only on land but even more so in the oceans, because of narrower thermal tolerances of marine than terrestrial organisms. The geographic ranges of marine organisms are already changing because of warming, especially at high latitudes.[23] These changes are produced as a result of climatic effects on

20 See the webpage of the Anthropocene Working Group at http://quaternary.stratigraphy.org/working-groups/anthropocene/, accessed 25 September 2019.

21 Libby Robin observes that the Anthropocene concept was 'conceived in the context of climate change', even though it 'concerns global changes in population, economics, and ecological systems as much as the atmospheric changes associated with climate change'; see L. Robin, 'A future beyond numbers' in N. Möllers, C. Schwägerl and H. Trischler (eds.), *Welcome to the Anthropocene: The Earth in Our Hands* (Deutsches Museum, 2014), 19–24, 19.

22 C. N. Waters et al., 'The Anthropocene is functionally and stratigraphically distinct from the Holocene' (2016) 351 *Science*, 137.

23 See, e.g., M. Edwards, 'Sea life (Pelagic Ecosystems)', in T. M. Letcher (ed.), *Climate Change: Observed Impacts on Planet Earth*, 2nd edn. (Elsevier, 2016), 167–182.

temperature and salinity, which have been driving marine organisms generally towards higher latitudes.

Moreover, there are already signs that warmer oceans are becoming less well oxygenated (so far, by some 2 per cent),[24] which will further constrain the living space of marine species and organisms. These effects are acting on marine populations that have already been heavily modified by other forms of Anthropocene-related change, such as intense fishing pressure, pollution and the proliferation of many invasive species. These phenomena were pervasively altering the marine realm already in the last century, although the uniquely climate-driven changes have remained modest.

There is also the 'other carbon dioxide problem' – of ocean acidification – the scale of which was realized relatively late.[25] An influential modelling study indicated that, as a result of anthropogenic CO_2 emissions, ocean pH could drop by 0.7 units over the next few centuries, which could be a greater change than has occurred over the past 300 million years.[26] Over the past 100 years, the mean global surface pH of the oceans has already decreased from around 8.2 to below 8.1.[27] The CO_2 produced by anthropogenic processes first dissolves in the surface waters of the oceans, where it produces carbonic acid. As a result (the pH scale being logarithmic), surface waters now include about 26 per cent more hydrogen ions than in pre-industrial times.[28] Increasing dissolved CO_2 in seawater leads to chemical reactions that reduce the availability of carbonate ions for calcifying organisms to build their skeletons, and hence build carbonate-based landmasses such as atolls and marine platforms (like that of the Florida coast and the Bahamas). It has been estimated that a doubling of pre-industrial CO_2 in the atmosphere could result in a 40 per cent reduction in coral reef calcification,[29] with significant impacts on corals observed in experimental studies,[30] and potentially catastrophic losses for coral reefs if seawater pH

24 D. Breitburg et al., 'Declining oxygen in the global ocean and coastal waters' (2018) 359 *Science*, 46.

25 K. Caldeira and M. E. Wickett, 'Anthropogenic carbon and ocean pH' (2003) 425 *Nature*, 365.

26 Ibid.

27 S. Birchenough, P. Williamson and C. Turley, 'Future of the sea: ocean acidification', Government Office for Science, 2017, available at www.gov.uk/go-science.

28 IPCC, *Climate Change 2014: Synthesis Report. Contribution of Working Groups I, II and III to the Fifth Assessment Report of the Intergovernmental Panel on Climate Change* (Core Writing Team, R. K. Pachauri and L. A. Meyer (eds.)) (IPCC, 2014).

29 O. Hoegh-Guldberg et al., 'Coral reefs under rapid climate change and ocean acidification' (2007) 318 *Science*, 1737–1742.

30 For example, S. Comeau et al., 'Ocean acidification accelerates dissolution of experimental reef communities' (2015) 12 *Biogeosciences*, 365–372.

should drop below 7.8 – which occurs at atmospheric levels of 750 parts per million (ppm) CO_2, thus within the range of climate scenarios for 2100.[31] The potential loss of biodiversity to the oceans is colossal, as corals provide environments for millions of species.[32] They also protect coastlines from flooding and offer physical platforms for terrestrial biota, including humans.

As the impacts of acidification on coral reef systems intensify and are combined with the effects of elevated sea-surface temperatures, this produces coral bleaching (expelling of the symbiotic algae on which corals rely) and heat-induced coral death on reefs, such as those of the Great Barrier Reef during 'marine heat waves',[33] which are a growing feature of the emerging climate state.[34] These types of heat stresses, rare and local prior to the 1980s, have become widespread due to anthropogenic global warming during the past few decades.[35] Predictions of future climate change using IPCC scenarios RCP4.5 and RCP8.5 indicate that most coral reef systems will experience severe bleaching by the mid- to late twenty-first century.[36]

2.2.2 *Relating Climate Change to the Anthropocene*

We are dealing with a system where there are considerable leads and lags between climate drivers and their effects. Climate drivers such as levels of atmospheric greenhouse gases like carbon dioxide and methane are already well outside the norms of the Holocene Epoch (the past 11,700 years). Indeed, levels are now greater than at any time in the Quaternary – the past some 2.6 million years of the 'Ice Age' – and are approaching those of the Pliocene Epoch, some 3 million years ago, when global mean surface temperatures were some 2–3°C higher than those of the mid-twentieth century, and sea level

31 K. E. Fabricius et al., 'Losers and winners in coral reefs acclimatized to elevated carbon dioxide concentrations' (2011) 1 *Nature Climate Change*, 165–169.

32 See, e.g., N. Knowlton, 'The future of coral reefs' (2001) 98 *PNAS*, 5419–5425.

33 T. P. Hughes et al., 'Global warming and recurrent mass bleaching of corals' (2017) 543 *Nature*, 373–377; and T. P. Hughes, K. D. Anderson and S. R. Connolly, 'Spatial and temporal patterns of mass bleaching in the Anthropocene' (2018) 359 *Science*, 80–83.

34 T. L. Frölicher, E. M. Fischer and N. Gruber, 'Marine heatwaves under global warming' (2018) 560 *Nature*, 360–364.

35 T. P. Hughes et al., 'Global warming transforms coral reef assemblages' (2018) 556 *Nature*, 492–496.

36 R. van Hooidonk et al., 'Local-scale projections of coral reef futures and implications of the Paris Agreement' (2016) 6 (39666) *Scientific Reports* 1–8. 'RCP' refers to the IPCC's 'Representative Concentration Pathway' scenarios: see further also in n. 65–67 and the related text.

was some 10–20 m higher.[37] The *speed* of rise of those atmospheric greenhouse gases has been extraordinarily rapid, perhaps without geological precedent.

Carbon dioxide levels in the atmosphere, which remained stable at between 260 and 280 ppm over most of the Holocene, with only minor fluctuations,[38] began to rise in the nineteenth century, reaching ~310 ppm by the mid-twentieth century, then accelerating to the current rate of ~20 ppm/decade,[39] currently reaching the range of ~410 ppm (with a seasonal peak in May 2019 reaching 415 ppm).[40] Thus, some 100 ppm of this rise has occurred in the space of only seventy years or so since the mid-twentieth century: the timespan we ascribe to the Anthropocene so far. This rate is ~100 times faster than the rise from ~180 to ~280 ppm, which took place over some 8,000 years (in geological terms, abruptly), with the ending of the Pleistocene Epoch and the beginning of the Holocene Epoch. Probably (although the constraints are looser) this was an order of magnitude more rapid than the increase at the inception of the Paleocene–Eocene Thermal Maximum – a geologically brief but sharp global warming event, driven by a natural outburst of greenhouse gases that took place about 56 million years ago.[41]

Methane levels have seen a proportionately even greater increase;[42] levels of other greenhouse gases such as nitrous oxide and chlorofluorocarbons have risen as well. These gases intercept the infrared radiation given off by the Sun-warmed surface of the Earth, absorbing this heat and re-radiating it in all directions including back down towards the Earth's surface. Overall, this process helps to keep the atmosphere 33°C warmer than it would be otherwise – and is thus a process conducive to life on Earth, as we know it. When more greenhouse gases are added (as is happening now, due to human activities), then further warming follows.

The increasing concentration of greenhouse gases means that the Earth is now retaining more solar heat – which, in turn, is increasing the levels of

37 See C. P. Summerhayes, *Earth's Climate Evolution* (Wiley-Blackwell, 2015) and references therein; also C. P. Summerhayes, 'Climate', in J. Zalasiewicz et al. (eds.), *The Anthropocene as a Geological Time Unit: A Guide to the Scientific Evidence and Current Debate* (Cambridge University Press, 2019), 200–218. See also K. D. Burke et al., 'Pliocene and Eocene provide best analogs for near-future climates' (2018) 115 (52) *PNAS*, 13288–13293.

38 J. Fluckiger et al., 'High resolution Holocene N_2O ice core record and its relationship with CH_4 and CO_2' (2002) 16 *Global Biogeochemical Cycles* 10–1–10–8, see data at ftp://ftp.ncdc.noaa.gov/pub/data/paleo/icecore/antarctica/epica_domec/dc_co2_hol_flo2.txt.

39 E. W. Wolff, 'Greenhouse gases in the Earth system: A Palaeoclimate perspective' (2011) 369 *Philosophical Transactions of the Royal Society* A, 2133–2147.

40 See www.co2.earth/daily-co2, accessed 25 September 2019.

41 C. Gutjahr et al., 'Very large release of mostly volcanic carbon during the Paleocene-Eocene thermal maximum' (2017) 548 *Nature*, 573–577.

42 Waters et al., 'The Anthropocene'.

the most abundant greenhouse gas, water vapour (H_2O), by increased evaporation, further accentuating the warming. Part of the heat retention is seen in the warming of the atmosphere – the temperature that we 'feel' – where the rise of ~1.1°C since pre-industrial times (and accelerating since the mid-twentieth century) has been convincingly ascribed to anthropogenic warming.[43] This temperature rise cannot be due to any increase in the heat coming from the Sun, because the Earth should be in a cooling phase since 1980 as regards the patterns of sunspot cycles. Nor can the warming relate to changes in the Earth's tectonic or astronomical behaviour (i.e., 'Milankovich cycles', which operate on much longer timescales), or in volcanism (where the most immediate effect is one to two years of minor cooling following major eruptions, as last happened with the 1991 Mount Pinatubo eruption).

Most of the extra heat is being absorbed by the oceans: for the present, this is slowing the rate of atmospheric temperature rise. However, as the oceans have much greater heat storage capacity than does the atmosphere, this additional heat will be released in the decades and centuries to come. Among the various consequences, the pattern and rate of ice melting concern us most here. High-altitude temperate mountain glaciers on land contain only ~1 per cent of the Earth's ice; however, their contribution to sea-level rise is currently proportionately larger, as these glaciers have been retreating almost everywhere in recent decades.[44] It is the major polar ice masses of Antarctica and Greenland, though, holding sufficient water to raise global average sea level by >60 metres if completely melted, that are the prime concern. These ice masses can melt at their surfaces, as air temperatures rise; from underneath, as their bases come into contact with warmer water impinging upon them; and by increased glacier flow, as buttressing ice shelves collapse. All three processes are now underway, and both of the world's major ice sheets – Antarctica and Greenland – have been losing mass in recent decades.[45]

The pattern of acceleration of sea-level rise in this decade indicates a trend of increase.[46] The total rate of rise was, in accordance with IPCC's

43 J. Cook et al., 'Consensus on consensus: a synthesis of consensus estimates on global warming' (2016) 11(4) *Environmental Research Letters*, 1–7.

44 M. Zemp et al., 'Historically unprecedented global glacier decline in the early 21st century' (2015) 61 *Journal of Glaciology* 745–762.

45 See Summerhayes, *Earth's Climate Evolution*; C. P. Summerhayes, 'Ice' in J. Zalasiewicz et al. (eds.), *The Anthropocene as a Geological Time Unit: A Guide to the Scientific Evidence and Current Debate* (Cambridge University Press, 2019), 218–233.

46 R. S. Nerem et al., 'Climate-change-driven accelerated sea level rise detected in the Altimeter Era' (2018) 115(9) *PNAS*, 2022–2025.

assessments, 3.2 mm/year (in the period 1993–2010),[47] and has risen to 3.6 mm/year (in the period 2005–2015).[48] The World Meteorological Organization has estimated the latest rate of sea-level rise at 4 mm/year (based on the ten-year period from 2007 to 2016).[49] The pattern will in future depend on such factors as the levels of greenhouse gas emissions over coming decades,[50] feedbacks from global warming and assorted non-linear effects including those associated with 'tipping points'.[51] One such tipping point may well have been crossed: an already irreversible phase of ice melt that may represent several metres of sea-level rise, driven by positive feedback effects as warming ocean waters increasingly melt the bases of glaciers that flow out into the sea.[52] This is part of a centennial to millennial trend now being set in motion, in which the potential range of near-future pathways of warming and sea-level rise in the Anthropocene will reflect future emissions trajectories.[53]

Current projections indicate a loss of ice equivalent to a sea-level rise of 1.4 to 2.0 metres by 2100, to continue for at least the next 200 years (and more) beyond that.[54] Geology tells us that the last warming of 2–3°C above today's conditions brought sea-level rises of 4–9 metres (during past interglacial periods) and of 10–20 m in the Pliocene (around 3 million years ago). How far can this process go, and how fast is it taking place? A recent assessment has

47 See J. A. Church et al. (eds.), *Climate Change 2013: The Physical Science Basis, Contribution of Working Group I to the Fifth Assessment Report of the Intergovernmental Panel on Climate Change* (Cambridge University Press, 2014), 1137–1216.

48 For the latest IPCC's assessment (of 25 September 2019), see IPCC, *Special Report on the Ocean and Cryosphere in a Changing Climate* (H. O. Pörtner et al. (eds.)), at https://report.ipcc.ch/srocc/pdf/SROCC_FinalDraft_FullReport.pdf, accessed 25 September 2019.

49 See the report *United in Science*, compiled by the World Meteorological Organization under the auspices of the Science Advisory Group of the UN Climate Action Summit 2019, issued on 22 September 2019, at public.wmo.int/en/resources/united_in_science, accessed 23 September 2019.

50 IPCC SR 1.5 (2018).

51 W. Steffen et al., 'Trajectories of the Earth System in the Anthropocene' (2018) 115(33) *PNAS*, 8252–8259.

52 E. Rignot and S. S. Jacobs, 'Rapid bottom melting widespread near Antarctic ice sheet grounding lines' (2002) 296 *Science*, 2020–2023. See also E. Rignot et al., 'Ice-shelf melting around Antarctica' (2013) 341 *Science*, 266–270; and, most recently, E. Rignot et al., 'Four decades of Antarctic ice sheet mass balance from 1979–2017' (2019) 116(4) *PNAS*, 1095–1103.

53 P. U. Clark et al., 'Consequences of twenty-first-century policy for multi-millennial climate and sea-level change' (2016) 6 *Nature Climate Change*, 360–369.

54 The ~130 metre sea-level change around the Pleistocene–Holocene boundary took place over the course of some 13 millennia, between ~20,000 and ~7,000 years ago, because the great ice sheets took so long to melt and adjust to the new temperature regime. It is a complex process, and current ice melt projections are being revised upwards as a consequence of improving understanding of the factors involved: see, e.g., J. L. Bamber Kopp et al., 'Ice sheet contributions to future sea-level rise from structured expert judgement' (2019) 116(23) *PNAS*, 11195–11200.

indicated that the Earth will have a Pliocene-like climate already between 2030 and 2040 (depending on the greenhouse gases emissions scenario) – and, with 'business as usual', an Eocene-like climate (ultimately leading to little or no land ice) by 2150.[55] The latter prospect would, in effect, reverse some 50 million years of overall planetary cooling.

The near-future pattern of sea-level rise – and thus of changes in land/sea geometry – will vary locally and regionally, depending on a number of factors including human-driven subsidence of deltas and coastal plains,[56] a process generally exceeding global sea-level rise in scale and rate thus far. Local sea level is already also changing where the supply of sediment to the coast through major rivers has basically ceased because of large upstream dams. This is causing major deltas (like that of the Nile) to sink, and their coasts to retreat.

Given that much of the coastal landscape has developed over several millennia of the late Holocene to be at or near the generally constant sea level of those times, the first 1–2 metres of sea-level rise will flood proportionally more human-inhabited land, including major coastal megacities and ports, than further sea-level rise beyond that. Even the decimetre-scale sea-level rise of recent decades has produced significant coastal retreat locally,[57] while a 'tipping point' for delta survival is projected to be crossed by the end of the century,[58] necessitating various forms of societal adaptation.[59] The development of new legal frameworks (discussed further below) will be a key element in this upcoming process.

2.2.3 *International Law Relevance of the Change as Represented by the Anthropocene*

Ongoing atmospheric and oceanic processes are already beginning to impact the ice–sea–land interface.[60] A built-in time lag due to the absorption capacity

55 Burke et al., 'Pliocene and Eocene', 15. See further discussion (in Section 2.2.3), in the context of relevance for international law.

56 J. P. M. Syvitski et al., 'Sinking deltas due to human activities' (2009) 2 *Nature Geoscience*, 681–686.

57 J. F. Meeder and R. W. Parkinson, 'SE Saline Everglades transgressive sedimentation in response to historic acceleration in sea-level rise: a viable marker for the base of the Anthropocene?' (2018) 34 *Journal of Coastal Research*, 490–497.

58 R. E. Turner, M. S. Kearney and R. W. Parkinson, 'Sea-level rise tipping point for delta survival' (2018) 34 *Journal of Coastal Research*, 470–474.

59 J. Hinkel et al., 'The ability of societies to adapt to twenty-first-century sea-level rise' (2018) 8 *Nature Climate Change*, 570–578.

60 See Clark et al., 'Consequences of twenty-first-century policy'; see also P. Wadhams, *A Farewell to Ice: A Report from the Arctic* (Allen Lane, 2016).

of the oceans of heat and greenhouse gases from the atmosphere has delayed a more significant sea-level rise so far. However, the key conclusion is already unambiguous: even if various 'mitigating' measures would, *in theory*, suddenly preclude any further emissions, major ice melting in the polar regions is underway and will continue during this and the next several centuries, likely millennia. Instead of relatively stable sea levels as experienced during the course of the past several millennia of the Holocene, we will be facing continuing change, characteristic of the Anthropocene. This will have important consequences for international law as we know it today.

Showing relative stability throughout recent human history, the underlying conditions of the Earth System have been taken as given, and upon that premise our political and international law structures have been created over the past centuries. The relationship of international law to observed geographical features and indeed to the overall geological dimension of the Earth System has generally been confined to the implicit assumption of an undetermined, long-term horizon to current conditions, as an objective circumstance affecting us since time immemorial. Many aspects of international law – the law of the sea included – are based on this understanding of the stability of Earth System conditions. Now, however, it is becoming more widely recognized that the onset of a significant change in the ice–sea–land ratio is already built-in, due to ocean–atmosphere interplay and the delayed thermal response time of the oceans to atmospheric CO_2 build-up.[61]

The question is no longer *whether* we are heading for a change in the relatively stable ice–sea–land conditions as generally experienced over the past six to seven thousand years[62] – a key overall circumstance that has contributed to perceptions of enduring general stability, on which various aspects of international law are based. The increasingly pressing question is now, given recent scientific findings,[63] rather *when*, and at what pace, a profound change in these conditions will happen. The possibility of a major change in the ice–sea balance over the coming decades is no longer a remote and speculative one; this will inevitably result in profound challenges

61 Among several important recent studies, see especially: R. M. DeConto and D. Pollard, 'Contribution of Antarctica to past and future sea-level rise' (2016) 531 *Nature*, 591–596. See also Clark et al., 'Consequences of twenty-first-century policy'; Wadhams, *A Farewell to Ice*.

62 K. Lambeck et al., 'Sea level and global ice volumes from the last glacial maximum to the Holocene' (2014) 111 (43) *PNAS*, 15296–15303.

63 A. Ganopolski, R. Winkelmann and H. J. Schellnhuber, 'Critical insolation-CO_2 relation for diagnosing past and future glacial inception' (2016) 529 *Nature*, 200–203; Clark et al., 'Consequences of twenty-first-century policy'; DeConto and Pollard, 'Contribution of Antarctica'.

for the fundamentals of the normative and intellectual architecture on which the present-day international law (of the sea) is built.

A recent study[64] of the pace and size of that change finds that accelerated rate of change appears to be exceptionally fast on the geological scale, to the extent of becoming societally and politically relevant in a near-term perspective. The study used two of the IPCC's 'Representative Concentration Pathway' scenarios – those of RCP8.5 and RCP4.5 – across several climate simulation models.[65] Under both scenarios and across all models, already between 2030 and 2040 the Earth's climate resembled conditions of the Pliocene, some 3–3.5 million years ago. Under RCP4.5, the climate would thereafter stabilize at mid-Pliocene-like conditions; but, under unmitigated greenhouse gas emissions such as of RCP8.5, the warming would continue, achieving Eocene-like conditions by around 2150, which would 'effectively rewind the climate clock by approximately 50 million years, reversing a multi-million year cooling trend in less than two centuries'.[66] As the authors note:

> Traditional systems for designing infrastructure, mitigating natural hazard risk, and conserving biodiversity are often based on implicit assumptions about climate stationarity and recent historical baselines, which fail to encompass expected trends.[67]

This brings the relevance of the geological dimension also to the international law discourse. Not only are we clearly leaving the stable conditions of the late Holocene Epoch (measured in thousands of years) – we may already be headed outside of the parameters of the Quaternary Period (on the scale of millions of years). The context of the Anthropocene means that the conditions which facilitated the emergence of not only international law but of human civilization as we know it are currently undergoing substantial change, initiated not long ago. Inclusion of the Anthropocene at the top of the geological time scale would also formalize its geological status through a due scientific process in stratigraphy. This confirmed fact of a new epoch, the Anthropocene, with conditions very different from those in the preceding

64 Burke et al., 'Pliocene and Eocene'.

65 RCP8.5 represents a future climate scenario under 'business as usual', while RCP4.5 is a scenario in which greenhouse gas emissions are moderately reduced. As the authors of the study confirm: 'Based on observational data [. . .] we may be somewhere between RCP4.5 and RCP8.5, though if we increase our climate mitigation efforts – like switching to the renewable energy – we could find ourselves closer to the lower end'; see K. A. Tyrrell, 'Humans may be reversing the climate clock by 50 million years', www.Phys.org, 10 December 2018.

66 Burke et al., 'Pliocene and Eocene'.

67 Ibid.

geological time, would become common knowledge, with a wide range of implications, legal ones not least.[68]

2.3 THE INTERNATIONAL LAW OF THE SEA IN THE CONTEXT OF TWO EPOCHS

2.3.1 *Development of the Law of the Sea under Late Holocene Conditions*

The foundations of today's law of the sea are the product of several centuries of often-antagonistic struggles among and between dominant human forces. These forces have produced impressive technological capabilities and made possible the modern way of life in industrialized societies, but they also have contributed substantially towards threatening the stable conditions of the late Holocene – and bringing about our entry into the Anthropocene.

The linkages between the development of the law of the sea and the onset of the Anthropocene Epoch may be seen as twofold.[69] First, there is a linkage of origin. In this connection, it is essential to realize that the legal development started and advanced under the conditions of the general stability of the late Holocene. The ideological foundations of the law of the sea, partly contained in the early seventeenth-century *Mare Liberum* (but also elsewhere prior to this, as witnessed by the *Annales* of Queen Elizabeth I already in the late sixteenth century),[70] involve 'deep-time' origins for the later processes which have ultimately brought about the Anthropocene.[71]

68 As confirmed also in international jurisprudence, whether a fact qualifies as a 'fact of common knowledge' is a legal question. 'Notorious facts' or 'facts of common knowledge' are defined in international jurisprudence as 'universally known facts, such as general facts of history or geography, or the laws of nature. Such facts are not only widely known but also beyond reasonable dispute'; see decisions of the Appeals Chamber of the International Criminal Tribunal for Rwanda (e.g., Case No. ICTR-97–20-A, Judgment, 20 May 2005 [194]; Case No. ICTR-98–44-AR73(C), Decision, 16 June 2006 [22–23]). According to the Rules of the Tribunal, a Chamber 'shall not require proof of facts of common knowledge but shall take judicial notice thereof'; Rule 94(A).

69 This line of argument was introduced in D. Vidas, 'The Anthropocene and the international law of the sea' (2011) 369 *Philosophical Transactions of the Royal Society A*, 909–925, on which this section partly draws.

70 See *Annales Rerum Gestarum Angliae et Hiberniae Regnate Elizabetha*, by William Camden (as published in 1615 and 1625–1627), with the annotations of Sir Francis Bacon, in D. F. Sutton (ed.), University of California, Irvine, web-publication 2000/01, at www.philological.bham.ac.uk/camden, accessed 25 September 2019.

71 For further discussion, see D. Vidas, 'Responsibility for the seas', in D. Vidas (ed.), *Law, Technology and Science for Oceans in Globalisation* (Brill/Martinus Nijhoff, 2010), 3–40, at 17–27.

Second, there may be a renewed linkage in interaction between geology and international law. Geological information has prompted key law-of-the-sea developments since the introduction of the continental shelf in the mid-twentieth century, first as a political concept, and soon thereafter an international law one – conceived, and then codified, in order to facilitate exploitation of natural (hydrocarbon) resources and to maximize economic and strategic gains.

In the post–Second World War political era, a single law-of-the-sea framework eventually emerged, building on developments over several preceding centuries: the 1982 United Nations Convention on the Law of the Sea (LOSC).[72] This legal framework, produced through negotiations during the 1970s and early 1980s, still governs all major issues of the entire ocean space. On the one hand, there is a broad political consensus that the integrity of the legal framework of the LOSC must be maintained.[73] On the other hand, the pace of change is tremendous: population trends, advances in technology, scientific achievements – with resultant uses of, and impacts on, the seas.

The law of the sea, centred on the LOSC, is to some extent flexible and adjustable as a framework for future regulation. It is, however, also deeply rooted in earlier developments and the way of thinking characteristic of what has probably become a remnant of the past epoch, also in geological and not only in political terms. The LOSC rests on the implied assumption of the permanence of the relative stability of the conditions of the late Holocene, in which human history was impacted primarily by changes in economic and political circumstances – against the backdrop of relatively stable natural conditions.

Under those conditions, the law of the sea developed gradually as an exponent of two main driving forces, and the consequences of both are now captured in the LOS Convention. One driving force has been that of territorial appropriation of the seas. In some periods, territorial claims were reduced to a relatively narrow belt of the sea near the coast. In the post–Second World War period, however, the territorial driving force returned in the form of claims for segments of sovereignty – sovereign rights and exclusive jurisdiction – to be extended beyond the outer limits of the

72 United Nations Convention on the Law of the Sea, Montego Bay, 10 December 1982, in force 16 November 1994, 1833 UNTS 397.

73 As of 25 September 2019, LOSC is binding on 168 parties (including the EU). Beyond the EU, several parties to the Convention are non-members of the UN: Cook Islands, Holy See, Niue, and the State of Palestine.

territorial sea.[74] These claims related to fisheries resources in vast areas of the water column, as well as to the natural (primarily hydrocarbon) resources of the continental shelf.[75] As a result, today there are maritime zones in which, although lying beyond the coastal state's (land and maritime) territory,[76] sovereign rights and exclusive jurisdiction of the coastal state apply, mainly in order to secure the exploitation of natural resources.

The other driving force in the development of the law of the sea has been that of economic profit by functional as opposed to territorial access; and of securing strategic gains of naval powers in distant sea areas. Both were promoted by the concept of the 'freedom of the seas' which, initially at the turn of the seventeenth century, came to offer an ideological platform for securing unimpeded international trade for emerging (and thereupon established) maritime powers – with the dual goals of maximizing profits for their economies and increasing their strategic dominance over new territories.[77]

This, in turn, facilitated the development of the forces that were to lead to the Industrial Revolution and eventually, in the course of the twentieth century, to the levels of development that have resulted in ever-greater human impacts on the Earth System. The end of the Second World War in 1945 was also the time when the last 'tectonic change' in the law of the sea began. Out of that war came various new technologies – many of which represented new applications for fossil fuels – and commitments by governments in some industrially advanced countries to subsidize research and development. Only months after the war ended, the United States initiated articulation of the continental shelf as a concept of international law, with geological information playing a crucial role. The final outcomes are still emerging today, three quarters of a century later, through the current process of determining the outer limits of the continental shelf beyond 200 nautical miles, facilitated by the work of the Commission on the Limits of the Continental Shelf.

The law of the sea is today a well-developed legal system, addressing human uses of the seas and oceans, organized through various maritime zones where

74 See, e.g., B. Oxman, 'The territorial temptation: a siren song at sea' (2006) 100 *American Journal of International Law*, 830–851.

75 The claims were contained in two unilateral acts issued by the United States in September 1945: US Presidential Proclamation No. 2667 and No. 2668.

76 In contrast to the EEZ and the continental shelf, the territorial sea is a part of a coastal state's sovereign territory.

77 See especially: M. J. van Ittersum, *Profit and Principle: Hugo Grotius, Natural Rights Theories and the Rise of Dutch Power in the East Indies (1595–1615)* (Brill, 2006).

the rights and duties of states (and the many stakeholders involved) are carefully balanced. The present system of the law of the sea aims at facilitating stable international relations regarding the maritime spaces and their uses, as well as promoting the peaceful settlement of disputes that may arise.

However, we are already living in a profoundly different world – one in which changes in natural parameters, such as climate change and its impact on the oceans and polar regions, are poised to overshadow the importance of any other changes known in recorded human history. The consequences of this newly emerging change, embodied in the onset of the Anthropocene conditions, may become evident in two main directions regarding the law of the sea. First, there already are serious consequences for the biological and chemical conditions of the oceans across various legal maritime zones. Second, there are physical consequences on the horizon, impacting how the limits of maritime zones and boundaries between them will be determined in the foreseeable future – conceivably already in the course of the current century. This takes us outside the envelope of the late Holocene, during which the law of the sea was developed and implicitly came to embody its current parameters, to the ongoing climate change and the new perspectives for the development of the law of the sea under the changing conditions of the Anthropocene. In the twenty-first century, with consequences of human activities reaching a geological scale, a new and different development of the law of the sea will become necessary – in order to respond to changing conditions in the Anthropocene, in which it will become increasingly important to minimize losses rather than maximize profits.

2.3.2 *The Law of the Sea and Climate Change at the Beginning of the Anthropocene*

Human impacts on the marine component of the Earth System, such as those induced by climate change, do not depend primarily on the boundaries between states or the driving forces shaping them. With few exceptions, however, today's rules regulate human impacts on the oceans in terms of just that: the political boundaries of sovereignty and jurisdiction, translated into law. This is what is expressed through the maritime zones and the basic division of jurisdictional competences among coastal and flag states. However, many real concerns are global or transboundary in character: they neither depend on nor can be limited by such divisions. In this respect, climate change may present a serious challenge to the sustainability of the current structure of the law of the sea.

With the exception of changes based on previous experience,[78] negotiators at UNCLOS III (1973–1982) did not foresee substantial changes in coastal geography – certainly not those caused by a major natural phenomenon such as atmosphere–ocean–ice interaction, now recognized as a key factor in the current process of sea-level rise. With rising sea levels, the coastal features determining baselines from which the breadth of the territorial sea is measured would move landward,[79] affecting the limits of various maritime zones. Ultimately, sea-level rise may call into question the entire structure of the maritime zones under today's law of the sea. Notwithstanding our desire to preserve the stability of the law, this will increasingly be confronted by changing facts. Enabling adequate responses will be a highly challenging task, and not solely a legal one – it is an intellectual and political question.

The objective criterion on which maritime zones are based (and baselines determined) relies on a given coastal geography. This serves not only as the basis for the various maritime zones but is also central to the delimitation of maritime boundaries between states. The purpose of those rules of international law of the sea is to maintain certainty and predictability. Sea-level rise threatens to bring increasing uncertainty.

Seeking a solution, most law of the sea experts have so far proposed the development of a new rule of international law that would have the effect of 'freezing' the baselines, or permanently fixing the limits of maritime zones at today's status – by fixing them on a chart, or suchlike.[80] In other words, proposals for legally responding to sea-level rise aim at preserving a static

[78] The 'Bangladesh exception' – Article 7(2) of LOSC – applying primarily to highly unstable coastlines caused by river deltas and the related impact on straight baselines, which is of limited reach and is targeted to specific situations, being caused by changes related to the rivers and not the sea itself. On the negotiating history of Article 7(2) see: S. N. Nandan and S. Rosenne (eds.), *United Nations Convention on the Law of the Sea, 1982: A Commentary*, vol. 2 (Martinus Nijhoff, 1993), 97–101, stating that 'the provisions in paragraph 2 were drafted with the specific case of the Ganges/Brahmaputra River delta in mind' (at 101).

[79] See conclusions of the International Committee on the Baselines under the International Law of the Sea, in 'Baselines under the international law of the sea: committee report', in International Law Association, *Report of the Seventy-Fifth Conference held in Sofia, August 2012* (London: ILA, 2012), 385–428, at 422–426. That report is available also online at ILA webpage, at www.ila-hq.org/en/committees/index.cfm/cid/1028.

[80] See, e.g., D. D. Caron, 'When law makes climate change worse: rethinking the law of baselines in light of a rising sea level' (1990) 17 *Ecology Law Quarterly*, 621–653; A. H. A. Soons, 'The effects of a rising sea level on maritime limits and boundaries' (1990) 37 *Netherlands International Law Review*, 207–232; J. L. Jesus, 'Rocks, new-born islands, sea level rise and maritime space' in J. A. Frowein et al. (eds.), *Verhandeln für den Frieden. Negotiating for Peace: Liber Amicorum Tono Eitel* (Springer, 2003), 579–603; M. Hayashi, 'Sea-level rise and the law of the sea: future options' in D. Vidas (ed.), *The World Ocean in Globalisation* (Brill/Martinus Nijhoff, 2011), 187–206.

legal situation in the face of increasingly dynamic processes of natural change. This illustrates a core dilemma: on the one hand, the natural processes of convergence between conditions of the late Holocene and the early Anthropocene will require responses or transformations in accordance with the needs and purposes of the new situation, rather than the imposition, by analogy or precedent, of static forms developed on the basis of an earlier situation currently undergoing a change. On the other hand, the international legal order will always be in search of stability and, ultimately, solutions to facilitate peace and prevent conflict. This is the core objective that must remain unchanged.

Evolving over centuries and resulting in the current legal framework that emerged in the second half of the twentieth century, the context for the law of the sea was provided primarily by the changing political, economic and technological circumstances – not changes in the overall natural, Earth-System conditions as well. This is a legal system tailored to the circumstances of the late Holocene, implicitly held to remain permanent. With the profoundly different circumstances on the Anthropocene horizon, responding to the challenges for the law of the sea may increasingly involve more than merely amending or adjusting the rules of individual treaties, or adding new ones. The very foundations of this legal system and its current parameters may require re-evaluation at some point. Certain cornerstone concepts of the law-of-the-sea architecture, such as the legal axiom of the law of the sea – the 'land dominates the sea' – will inevitably be challenged by the factual change of increasing proportions, once the sea begins to dominate the land. And this may well happen already in the course of the present century. How well are we equipped to meet this new reality?

2.3.3 *An Anthropocene Horizon for International Law Facing Climate Change*

Scientific findings regarding the horizon of change in the Anthropocene, some of which are described in this chapter, provide a major new context for future tensions in inter-state relations, likely to emerge already in the coming decades of this century. This new context will increasingly require an appreciation of the foreseeable political consequences of climate change, in order to facilitate the avoidance of future conflicts, or at least contribute to diminishing the risk of these. In our view, this understanding of a political mechanism, drawing on well-founded scientific predictions to assist also in the formulation of options for interpretation and progressive development of law, should become the focus of international law scholarship regarding climate change and impacts on the oceans.

International law, as understood today, is implicitly based on the conditions of the late Holocene. That is a system of law providing rules premised on constant political changes in relations between subjects of international law – but against the backdrop of generally stable natural conditions, including those of geography. The relationship of international law with observed geographical features and indeed with the overall geological dimensions of the Earth System has generally been confined to the implicit assumption of an undetermined, long-term horizon to current conditions, understood as a set of objective circumstances existing since time immemorial. Many aspects of international law are based on such an understanding of the stability of Earth-System conditions. On that premise, which recognizes the importance of change caused by political factors – yet on the stable background of a given context of natural circumstances – a huge edifice of international law has been constructed over the centuries. This has remained the state of the architecture of international law thus far. The standard definition of international law as a 'system of legal rules which regulate relations between the subjects recognized within the international community'[81] does not reach the new underlying layer that conditions its continued validity. This is so because today's international law is also a 'system of legal rules resting on foundations that evolved under the circumstances of the late Holocene, assumed to be everlasting'.[82]

Wide-ranging changes in those conditions will challenge the very basis of several key concepts of international law – ranging from the role of objective and predictable criteria for determining the baselines, and consequently, the limits of maritime zones and boundaries in the law of the sea, all the way to the criteria for statehood under international law – and may lead to new kinds of conflicts.

2.3.4 *The Role of International Law Scholarship in the Anthropocene: Five Theses*

Already now, research engagement on international law must start to flow from *two* basic types of challenges now facing this legal discipline – not

[81] See, e.g., J. Andrassy, *Međunarodno pravo* (International Law), 7th edn. by B. Bakotić and B. Vukas (Školska knjiga, 1998), 1.

[82] D. Vidas, 'International law at the convergence of two epochs', in H. N. Scheiber et al. (eds.), *Ocean Law and Policy: 20 Years under UNCLOS* (Brill/Nijhoff, 2017), 101–123, at 105; see also D. Vidas, J. Zalasiewicz and M. Williams, 'What is the Anthropocene – and why is it relevant for international law?', *Yearbook of International Environmental Law* 25 (Oxford University Press, 2016), 3–23.

predominantly one, as hitherto. The one persistent challenge which remains is, as ever, how to respond adequately to the complexities of the world situation in its political, economic and overall societal contexts. Ever since the inception of international law several centuries ago, there has been no essential difference in the *nature* of challenges facing this legal system. Changes in relations in and between the societies, and with states as the primary subjects of international law have remained central in these challenges.

However, international law today faces an entirely new type of challenge, related to the prospects of profound and accelerated change in *natural* circumstances, not only societal ones. In focus here is the Earth-System context, now in transition from the relatively stable natural conditions of the late Holocene to a new planetary state with far less familiar natural conditions. The horizon of challenges for many aspects of international law will shift, incrementally and then profoundly, creating circumstances fundamentally different from any experienced previously. The 'political' and 'natural' sphere of change will become increasingly intertwined.

The lawyer's instinct, or training, is to invoke precedents and search for analogies, seeking to prove or maintain a certain legal situation. However, the phenomenon in question is unprecedented – it has never been experienced since the invention of international law and the development of the territorially centred state. There are no suitable analogies available. The natural processes of convergence between conditions of the Holocene and of the Anthropocene will require a whole range of responses or transformations, including the development of new legal axioms, in line with the needs and contexts of the new situation – rather than responding by analogy or precedent based on earlier conditions no longer valid.

The change of the context in which international law operates will require comprehensive new responses. International law scholarship may prove of utmost importance here, not least owing to the special position accorded to scholarship in the system of international law.[83] Here, we outline five theses for the direction of those responses, and for the new role of the international law scholarship, as we leave the Holocene and enter the Anthropocene:

83 See Art. 38(1)(d) of the Statute of the International Court of Justice, San Francisco, 26 June 1945. On the role of scholarship in the development of international law, see, e.g., S. Sivakumaran, 'The influence of teaching of publicists on the development of international law' (2017) 66 *International and Comparative Law Quarterly*, 1–37; also L. Damrosch et al., 'Scholars in the construction and critique of international law' (2000) 94 *ASIL Proceedings*, 317–320.

1. *The special role and responsibility of international law scholarship*, in view of the growing availability of scientific predictions regarding Earth System change and its consequences. This role is enhanced due to the unique possibilities of foresight offered by natural science findings, on the one hand, and a time horizon for consequences still too often perceived as beyond the reach of political decisions, on the other.
2. *The need for conceptual change in international law*, as we are no longer living in the relative stability of late Holocene conditions, which are increasingly being replaced by change characterizing the Anthropocene. International law will not be able to respond adequately by simply amending some rules or adding new ones: systemic change is necessary.
3. *The need for periodization of proposals for the progressive development of international law*, since in any systemic change it is essential to distinguish options available in a shorter-term perspective from those in the mid- to longer term, to enable adequate responses in a changing factual situation and facilitate conflict avoidance.[84] This distinction also entails an adjustment of methodological approaches.
4. *The need for adjustment in methodological approaches*, not least regarding treaty interpretation: the changing context will necessarily result in greater importance of subsequent practice in the application of treaties as constituting the agreement of the parties regarding interpretation,[85] also to avoid results that may be manifestly absurd or unreasonable.
5. *The unchanged overall objective of international law:* to contribute to the maintenance of international peace and security. This ultimate objective has been codified in the major constitutive instruments of international law, such as the 1945 Charter of the United Nations,[86] the 1969 Vienna Convention on the Law of Treaties,[87] and the 1982 UN

[84] Regarding the application of this approach in recent international law scholarship, see the 2018 Report of the ILA Committee on International Law and Sea Level Rise. The Committee decided to divide its work into two main phases: in the first phase (until 2018), it examined priority areas in a relatively shorter-term perspective and adopted recommendations regarding these, while in the second phase (from 2019) the Committee will be studying issues of international law prompted by the mid- and longer-term predictions of sea-level rise. See further in D. Vidas, D. Freestone and J. McAdam (eds.), *International Law and Sea Level Rise: Report of the International Law Association Committee on International Law and Sea Level Rise* (Brill, 2019), especially at 13–14 and 41–42.

[85] For the work of the International Law Commission on subsequent practice in relation to treaty interpretation, see UN Docs A/71/10, A/73/10, and A/CN.4/175.

[86] Charter of the United Nations, San Francisco, 26 June 1945, 1 UNTS 16.

[87] Vienna Convention on the Law of Treaties, Vienna, 23 May 1969, in force 27 January 1980, 1155 UNTS 331.

> Convention on the Law of the Sea. This is considered the constant and stable objective of international law, providing the main criterion regarding any change of conceptual approaches, periodization of proposed measures and methodological adjustments.

Applying the above hypotheses across the various areas of international law – including the law of the sea – will necessarily be characterized by *anticipation*. Anticipatory approaches are not new in international law: they have been applied in the development of the law of the sea in some of its most important milestones since the end of the Second World War – as with the emergence of new concepts of the continental shelf since 1945,[88] and the seabed beyond national jurisdiction as the common heritage of mankind, since 1967.[89] This anticipatory approach has drawn on geological information (regarding petroleum sources of the continental shelf, and the seabed manganese nodules and strategic minerals, respectively). In both cases, the anticipation was fuelled by potential future economic gains, or their redistribution, and the related strategic implications. By contrast, the anticipatory approach proposed here, while also drawing on geological information (now related to the consequences of the use of hydrocarbons, not securing access to them and their exploitation and use), is profoundly different: the ultimate purpose is not to contribute to the maximization of profits but to the minimization of losses, and the avoidance of future conflicts.

Regarding the potential conceptual change, some entrenched concepts of international law may receive different meaning in the new light of the Anthropocene circumstances, as against their usual meaning in the conditions of the Holocene. One example is the concept of *inherent rights*, which has different meanings in different areas of international law – meanings which, although differing, have not yet come into collision. In the law of the sea, the coastal state has an inherent right to the continental shelf (i.e. its resources);[90] in the sphere of human rights, the right to life is an inherent right;[91] and regarding the rights of states, the right to self-defence has been codified as an

[88] See US Presidential Proclamation No. 2667, Policy of the United States with Respect to the Natural Resources of the Subsoil and Sea Bed of the Continental Shelf (Washington, DC, 28 September 1945), 10 *Federal Register* 12303.

[89] See the famous speech by Arvid Pardo at the UN General Assembly, in UN Doc. A/C.1/PV (1 November 1967), 115 and 116.

[90] *North Sea Continental Shelf* cases, 19.

[91] For example, Art. 6 of the 1966 International Covenant on Civil and Political Rights, New York, 16 December 1966, 999 UNTS 171: 'Every human being has the inherent right to life.'

inherent right.[92] Under the conditions of the Anthropocene, might those different meanings of inherent rights start to impact on each other and come into conflict? The horizon of consequences of climate change indicates that such conflicts may well emerge in the course of the coming decades.

2.4 CONCLUDING REMARKS

Our planet is in the process of leaving the relatively stable natural conditions of the late Holocene. We are encountering the increasingly unstable conditions of a new planetary state – the Anthropocene – marked by emerging and accelerated changes in natural, Earth-System conditions: climate change and its impacts, including the interplay with the oceans, are among key manifestations of this major ongoing change. While all this is leading to changes in the history of the *Earth* that might still prove moderate in terms of deep geological time, it very probably represents the onset of the biggest change for the history of the *World* – our political world, as humans have created it over the course of several millennia and especially in recent centuries, culminating (after the tragedies of two world wars, and many other wars as well) with the United Nations and other international institutions established in the twentieth century. The implicit assumption of relatively stable natural conditions, present through millennia and centuries (including most of the twentieth century), is built into foundations of the political and legal structures surrounding us today – but this is what will, already in the coming decades of this century, progressively lose its factual basis.

The distinction introduced by the Anthropocene is in that, within politically relevant time, changes of geological proportions are already underway. On this background, we hold that it is a *responsibility* of international law scholarship to engage more actively in contributing not only to interpretation but also to facilitating options for the development of international law, to enable us to meet the challenges to inter-state relations and human rights that will arise, more and more rapidly, under the changing conditions of the Anthropocene. This is an entirely new perspective on the development of international law and the role of international law scholarship; it may well encounter reluctance and resistance. However, given the evidence now available, and given the pace of change and the horizons ahead, this perspective must be grasped and taken into account as a matter of urgency.

92 See Art. 51 of the Charter of the United Nations.

3

Mitigation and Adaptation

Robin Kundis Craig*

The ocean is the subject of the Law of the Sea Convention (LOSC),[1] but it also plays a critical role in mediating climate – and climate change. As a result, to understand how LOSC can legally support the UN Climate Regime – the overall goal of this book – one must first understand the roles that the ocean plays in climate change, particularly with respect to the Climate Regime's two foci, climate change mitigation and climate change adaptation. As Chapter 2 described, anthropogenic climate change is the result of humans burning fossil fuels since the Industrial Revolution, resulting in increased concentrations of greenhouse gases (GHGs) in the atmosphere that are accelerating the planet's heat retention. The Intergovernmental Panel on Climate Change (IPCC) reported in 2014 that the planet has been warming since at least 1850, and the last thirty years are likely the hottest thirty-year period in the Northern Hemisphere in a millennium or more.[2] The strong scientific consensus conclusion is that climate change is well underway, including in the ocean.

Indeed, the ocean has been absorbing large quantities of anthropogenic carbon dioxide (CO_2), dampening some of the global climate change that would have already occurred had all that gas remained in the atmosphere. At the same time, the ocean is also already reacting to climate change by warming and expanding, contributing to sea-level rise and worsening coastal storms. In other words, the ocean is also already playing significant roles in simultaneously mitigating climate change and making climate change adaptation necessary.

* This research was made possible, in part, through generous support from the Albert and Elaine Borchard Fund for Faculty Excellence. The author may be reached at robin.craig@law.utah.edu.

1 UN Convention on Law of The Sea, Montego Bay, 10 December 1982, in force 16 November 1994, 1833 UNTS 397.

2 IPCC, *Climate Change 2014: Synthesis Report* (2014), 40 (hereinafter 2014 IPCC Synthesis Report).

This chapter provides basic background information on mitigation and adaptation and begins the discussion of how LOSC is relevant to both facets of the UN Climate Regime. Section 3.1 begins by providing basic definitions for both mitigation and adaptation. It then explores both the incorporation of mitigation and adaptation into the United Nations Framework Convention on Climate Change (UNFCCC)[3] and the IPCC's perspective on these two types of responses to climate change. Section 3.2 examines the role of the ocean with respect to the world's climate generally, including both its specific role in climate change mitigation and the adaptation responses that climate change and CO_2 impacts on the ocean are making necessary. This chapter ends in Section 3.3 with an overview of how the parties' duties under LOSC promote, and arguably even require, implementation of the UN Climate Regime with respect to both mitigation and adaptation.

3.1 CLIMATE CHANGE MITIGATION, CLIMATE CHANGE ADAPTATION, AND THEIR RELATIONSHIP

IPCC's periodic reports are the most widely accepted statements of the evolving scientific understandings of climate change and its impacts, and in September 2019 the IPCC published its focused report on the ocean and the cryosphere (ice).[4] While the consensus-generating process that the IPCC employs often means that each report's conclusions can be fairly conservative, these reports nevertheless offer a common terminology for and understanding of climate change and its impacts that provide excellent starting points for policy discussions – especially in the context of linking LOSC to the UN Climate Regime. As such, this section presents the IPCC's definitions of climate change mitigation and adaptation, summarizes its conclusions and recommendations regarding legal and policy strategies for each, and discusses how the IPCC's conclusions dovetail with the UNFCCC.

3.1.1 *Climate Change Mitigation*

In general, climate change mitigation refers to efforts to reduce global GHG emissions (especially anthropogenic GHG emissions) and to reduce the

[3] UN Framework Convention on Climate Change, Rio de Janeiro, 9 May 1992, in force 21 March 1994, 1771 UNTS 107.

[4] IPCC, *The Ocean and Cryosphere in a Changing Climate* (2019) (hereinafter 2019 IPCC Ocean Report).

overall atmospheric concentrations of GHGs, especially CO_2.[5] Mitigation strategies take a variety of forms. For example, one terrestrial strategy involves planting trees either to replace (reforestation) or create (afforestation) forests in order to increase CO_2 uptake through photosynthesis; a variation on this strategy is to keep forests from being cut down in the first place (i.e., prevent deforestation). Another prominent mitigation strategy is to reduce human consumption of fossil fuels, whether by increasing the fuel economy of gasoline-powered vehicles or by switching electricity generation from fossil fuels to wind power, geothermal power, solar power, and nuclear power.

As a legal matter, mitigation policy tends to encourage the world's nations to pursue global governance. Specifically, given the global scale of climate change, mitigation efforts require some form of coordinated international response to be effective in staving off the worst impacts of climate change, especially if global equity and justice are to remain coequal considerations. As the IPCC has noted, 'Climate change has the characteristics of a collective action problem at the global scale, because most GHGs accumulate over time and mix globally, and emissions by any agent (...) affect other agents. Cooperative responses, including international cooperation, are therefore required to effectively mitigate GHG emissions and address other climate change issues.'[6]

The global community has acknowledged this governance reality through the UN Climate Regime – the UNFCCC and its many protocols. Chapter 1 provided an overview of this regime. Here it is enough to emphasize that, while the Convention does not explicitly define 'mitigation', Article 2 frames the UNFCCC's goal in climate change mitigation terms: 'The ultimate objective of this Convention and any related legal instruments that the Conference of the Parties may adopt is to achieve (...) stabilization of greenhouse gas concentrations in the atmosphere at a level that would prevent dangerous anthropogenic interference with the climate system.' Thus, the UNFCCC has always been, and operates primarily as, an international framework to encourage (and occasionally mandate) cooperative international climate change mitigation efforts.

Nevertheless, the UNFCCC's general mitigation objective requires translation into specific targets in order to effectively shape climate change law and policy. The international community usually expresses these ultimate mitigation goals either as a temperature goal (e.g., keep global average warming to

5 2014 *IPCC Synthesis Report*, 76 ('Mitigation is the process of reducing emissions or enhancing sinks of greenhouse gases (GHGs), so as to limit future climate change.').

6 Ibid.

less than 1.5°C or 2°C) or as an atmospheric GHG concentration goal (e.g., 350 or 450 parts per million (ppm) of CO_2-equivalents or lower). The first UNFCCC follow-on agreements, however, sought to achieve progress towards mitigation without precisely deciding on the target.[7]

Establishing the world's ultimate mitigation goals has been a highly contested process. As the IPCC demonstrates, however, the 1.5°C/350 ppm or 2°C/450 ppm pairings have emerged as the most prominent of the possible targets. In 2014, the IPCC reported that keeping atmospheric concentrations below 450 ppm is likely (66–100 per cent[8]) to keep average warming below 2°C.[9] Achieving that goal, however, requires significant climate change mitigation achievements within this century.[10] Goals of keeping the global average temperature increase to 1.5°C or less and/or of reducing atmospheric concentrations of CO_2-equivalents back down to 350 ppm[11] require even more ambitious climate change mitigation efforts,[12] as the IPCC most recently emphasized in its 2018 Special Report.[13]

The strenuous mitigation policies that the world needs in order to avoid the worst impacts of climate change could potentially transform industrialized societies. Specifically, because most anthropogenic GHG emissions derive from the energy and land-use sectors, '[m]itigation can involve fundamental changes in the way that human societies produce and use energy services and land'.[14] At their most vigorous, therefore, climate change mitigation strategies

7 United Nations Climate Change, *Kyoto Protocol: Targets for the first commitment period*, available at https://unfccc.int/process/the-kyoto-protocol, accessed 3 December 2018; United Nations Climate Change, *The Paris Agreement*, UN Doc. FCCC/CP/2015/10/Add.1, Annex (12 December 2015), available at https://unfccc.int/process-and-meetings/the-paris-agreement/the-paris-agreement, accessed 19 November 2018.

8 2014 IPCC Synthesis Report, 37, Box Introduction 2.

9 Ibid., 81.

10 Ibid., 82 ('Scenarios that are likely to maintain warming at below 2°C are characterized by a 40 to 70% reduction in GHG emissions by 2050, relative to 2010 levels, and emissions levels near zero or below in 2100.').

11 Bill McKibben and the grassroots organization 350.org are two of the most visible proponents of the 350 ppm goal, but many developing nations, particularly Pacific Island nations, support it, as well. B. McKibben, 'Remember this: 350 parts per million', *The Washington Post*, 28 December 2007, available at www.washingtonpost.com/wp-dyn/content/article/2007/12/27/AR2007122701942.html; *About* 350, https://350.org/about/, accessed 16 November 2018; *About 350 Pacific*, https://350pacific.org/about/, accessed 16 November 2018.

12 2014 IPCC Synthesis Report, 83.

13 IPCC, *Global Warming of* 1.5°C (2018) (hereinafter 2018 IPCC 1.5°C Report), 6, 14, noting that, if emissions rates do not change, the planet will likely achieve the 1.5°C global average warming between 2030 and 2052, and that modelling indicates that anthropogenic CO_2 emissions must decline to 45 per cent below 2010 levels by 2030 and reach net zero by 2050 to avoid overshooting the 1.5°C goal.

14 2014 IPCC Synthesis Report, 83.

could require significant overhauls of the world's fossil-fuel-based economies, threatening dislocations from the *status quo* that often engender strong resistance or avoidance responses.

The chapters in Part II of this book explore the marine realm's potential contributions to climate change mitigation and the role of the law of the sea in regulating those efforts. For example, marine transportation, like all other facets of the transportation sector, contributes significant emissions of GHGs, which treaties governing marine air pollution are beginning to address. Offshore renewable energy development is already helping to transition the world away from fossil fuels, but the marine versions of geoengineering – the use of technology to artificially cool the planet or, probably more productively, remove GHGs from the atmosphere[15] – may also become important components of a global mitigation strategy. Both of these engineering developments in the ocean are subject to the law of the sea.

Given the potentially high economic costs of the kind of climate change mitigation that the IPCC indicates is warranted, investing in such mitigation efforts acknowledges the fundamental and severe risks that climate change poses to the planet and all life on it – that is, that climate change is not a global problem that we can simply learn to live with.[16] In particular, the IPCC noted in 2014 that '[t]he risks associated with temperatures at or above 4°C include severe and widespread impacts on unique and threatened systems, substantial species extinction, large risks to global and regional food security, consequential constraints on common human activities, increased likelihood of

[15] Ibid., 88 Box 3.3 ('Geoengineering refers to a broad set of methods and technologies operating on a large scale that aim to deliberately alter the climate system in order to alleviate the impacts of climate change. Most methods seek to either reduce the amount of absorbed solar energy in the climate system (Solar Radiation Management, SRM) or increase the removal of carbon dioxide (CO_2) from the atmosphere by sinks to alter climate (Carbon Dioxide Removal, CDR).'); K. Fuentes-George, 'Consensus, certainty, and catastrophe: the debate over ocean iron fertilization' *The New Security Beat*, 3 May 2017, available at www.newsecuritybeat.org/2017/05/consensus-certainty-catastrophe-ocean-iron-fertilization-debate/, noting that 'geoengineering refers to large-scale environmental interventions that "use or affect the climate system (e.g., atmosphere, land, or ocean) globally or regionally and/or . . . cross national boundaries." For critics, geoengineering comes with a specific set of flaws that make it more problematic than other kinds of environmental intervention.'

[16] In 2014, the IPCC made this point emphatically, see 2014 IPCC Synthesis Report, 77:

> Without additional mitigation efforts beyond those in place today, and even with adaptation, warming by the end of the 21st century will lead to high to very high risk of severe, widespread and irreversible impacts globally (*high confidence*). Mitigation involves some level of co-benefits and of risks due to adverse side effects, but these risks do not involve the same possibility of severe, widespread and irreversible impacts as risks from climate change, increasing the benefits from near-term mitigation efforts.

triggering tipping points (critical thresholds) and limited potential for adaptation in some cases."[17] In the IPCC's opinion, therefore, the risks that climate change poses to both human societies and ecosystems warrant a significant mitigation response – and soon.[18]

3.1.2 *Climate Change Adaptation*

While humans cannot live with the worst potential climate change futures, we *are* going to have to live with some climate change, because the world has passed the point where mitigation can avoid all climate change impacts. While the GHGs vary in both their warming potential and their duration in the atmosphere, from a law and policy perspective CO_2 is generally considered the most important anthropogenic GHG because of its connection to fossil fuel use.[19] It is also the most important GHG with respect to impacts on the ocean, as Chapter 2 made clear. Anthropogenic CO_2 remains in the atmosphere for a century or so,[20] with the result that the planet is stuck with some amount of climate change in the near future. As the IPCC emphasized in 2014, 'Human influence on the climate system is clear, and recent anthropogenic emissions of greenhouse gases are the highest in history. Recent climate changes have had widespread impacts on human and natural systems.'[21] Among other impacts, '[t]he atmosphere and ocean have warmed, the amounts of snow and ice have diminished, and sea level has risen.'[22]

As a result, human societies and their laws must cope with – adapt to – the changes that climate change is already imposing, including in the ocean. As the IPCC defines it, climate change adaptation 'is the process of adjustment to actual or expected climate and its effects in order to either lessen or avoid harm or exploit beneficial opportunities'.[23] The United Nations Climate Change Program provides a similar but more expansive definition:

> Adaptation refers to adjustments in ecological, social, or economic systems in response to actual or expected climatic stimuli and their effects or impacts. It

17 Ibid.

18 Ibid. See also generally 2018 IPCC 1.5°C Report.

19 2014 IPCC Synthesis Report, 44 ('Carbon dioxide is the largest single contributor to radiative forcing over 1750–2011 and its trend since 1970.'), 45 (describing the importance of anthropogenic CO_2 emissions to climate change).

20 Ibid., 45 ('About 40% of these anthropogenic CO_2 emissions have remained in the atmosphere (880 ± 35 Gt CO_2) since 1750. The rest was removed from the atmosphere by sinks, and stored in natural carbon cycle reservoirs.').

21 Ibid., 40.

22 Ibid.

23 Ibid., 76.

> refers to changes in processes, practices, and structures to moderate potential damages or to benefit from opportunities associated with climate change. In simple terms, countries and communities need to develop adaptation solution and implement action to respond to the impacts of climate change that are already happening, as well as prepare for future impacts.[24]

As these definitions indicate, therefore, adaptation is, in essence, all of the acts, strategies, and policies that allow human communities to live with the impacts of climate change. Adaptation serves an important role in maintaining functional human societies, because appropriate adaptation 'can contribute to the well-being of current and future populations, the security of assets and the maintenance of ecosystem goods, functions and services now and in the future'.[25]

Because the effects of climate change on the ocean and coastal communities can vary considerably from location to location, adaptation responses can include a wide range of activities and policies, as the chapters in Part III will explore in greater detail. Adaptation to sea-level rise may prompt coastal armouring and retreat, freshwater conservation and drinking water diversification, or migration of farmland inland in response to salt contamination. Warming seas and changing species ranges may require reliance on different marine fisheries, reduced fishing effort, or more investment in aquaculture. Sea-level rise and warming water together may necessitate increased disaster preparedness to deal with coastal storms and improvements in public health measures to address new and resurgent diseases and other health risks. Ocean acidification may make some forms of aquaculture, such as shellfish aquaculture, more difficult. A special consideration is protecting marine biodiversity in a changing ocean, for which marine protected areas (MPAs) and marine spatial planning are increasingly important tools.

As these examples illustrate, adaptation measures operate at a range of scales (e.g., household, municipal, regional, national).[26] These activities, moreover, can generate their own effects, from the relatively minor to the absolutely transformational.[27] Indeed, the IPCC encourages transformational adaptation in some circumstances, noting that '[t]ransformations in economic, social, technological and political decisions and actions can enhance adaptation and

24 United Nations Climate Change, *What Do Adaptation to Climate Change and Climate Resilience Mean?*, available at https://unfccc.int/topics/adaptation-and-resilience/the-big-picture/what-do-adaptation-to-climate-change-and-climate-resilience-mean, accessed 21 November 2018.

25 2014 IPCC Synthesis Report, 79.

26 Ibid., 76, 79.

27 Ibid., 76.

promote sustainable development.'[28] However, transformational adaptation also often demands new governance:

> Transformational adaptation can include introduction of new technologies or practices, formation of new financial structures or systems of governance, adaptation at greater scales or magnitudes and shifts in the location of activities. Planning and implementation of transformational adaptation could reflect strengthened, altered or aligned paradigms and consequently may place new and increased demands on governance structures to reconcile different goals and visions for the future and to address possible equity and ethical implications: transformational adaptation pathways are enhanced by iterative learning, deliberative processes, and innovation.[29]

The world's nations are still developing their conceptualizations of and approaches to climate change adaptation. As the IPCC observed in 2014, even in the last decade or two, adaptation has evolved 'from a dominant consideration of engineering and technological adaptation pathways to include more ecosystem-based, institutional and social measures'.[30] These newer and broader approaches to adaptation allow policymakers to consider multiple values (including ethics, fairness, and environmental values) simultaneously and to incorporate risk, uncertainty, and trade-off analyses into adaptation planning.[31] Scenario planning has also emerged as a prominent tool in adaptation planning, allowing planners and governance entities to consider several possible futures simultaneously and to give preference to 'no regrets' strategies that produce benefits regardless of the exact climate change future that unfolds.[32]

Because much adaptation is local or regional in scale, there is a limit to how effectively international law can address adaptation. Instead, national and local laws are the more natural loci for adaptation policies, tailored to national and local threats, physical and ecological circumstances, and cultural and financial realities.[33] Nevertheless, the UNFCCC and its protocols do address climate change adaptation. For example, under Article 4(1) of the

28 Ibid., 80.

29 Ibid.

30 Ibid., 79.

31 Ibid.

32 For example, S. S. Moore, N. E. Seavy and M. Gearhart, *Scenario Planning for Climate Change Adaptation: A Guidance for Resource Managers* (2013), available at ipclimatechange.trg-learning.com/wp-content/uploads/2013/11/Moore_et_al_2013_Scenario_Planning_for_Climate_Adaptation.pdf.

33 2014 IPCC Synthesis Report, 80 ('Adaptation planning and implementation at all levels of governance are contingent on societal values, objectives and risk perceptions.').

Convention, all Parties, regardless of development status, explicitly agree to '[c]ooperate in preparing for adaptation to the impacts of climate change', including explicitly through coastal management. More extensively, at the 2010 Conference of the Parties in Cancun, Mexico (COP 16),[34] the parties to the UNFCCC adopted the Cancun Adaptation Framework.[35] Acknowledging 'that adaptation is a challenge faced by all Parties, and that enhanced action and international cooperation on adaptation is urgently required to enable and support the implementation of adaptation actions aimed at reducing vulnerability and building resilience in developing country Parties',[36] the Framework invites all Parties to enhance their work on climate change adaptation, including through science development, prioritizing and implementing adaptation actions, programmes, and policies, vulnerability assessments, disaster preparedness, and a variety of other techniques.[37] It also requests that developed countries aid developing nations in adapting.[38] The Framework further established an Adaptation Committee[39] and a work programme 'to consider (...) approaches to address loss and damage associated with climate change impacts in developing countries that are particularly vulnerable to the adverse effects of climate change'.[40]

3.1.3 *Pursuing Adaptation and Mitigation Simultaneously*

When policymakers first identified climate change as a problem, there was some concern that diverting any resources to adaptation would detract from efforts to mitigate, and perhaps solve, the climate change problem. Now, however, almost everyone acknowledges that the climate change impacts that are already occurring make the simultaneous pursuit of adaptation and mitigation necessary.[41] Indeed, the IPCC reported in 2014 that '[a]daptation and mitigation are two complementary strategies for responding to climate

34 Chief Executives Board for Coordination, United Nations, *UNFCCC: Cancun Adaptation Framework*, available at www.unsystem.org/content/unfccc-cancun-adaptation-framework, accessed 21 November 2018.

35 Conference of the Parties, *Report of the Conference of the Parties on its sixteenth session, held in Cancun from 29 November to 10 December 2010: Addendum: Part Two: Action taken by the Conference of the Parties at its sixteenth session*, UN Doc. FCCC/CP/2010/7/Add.1 (15 March 2011), 4–7, available at unfccc.int/resource/docs/2010/cop16/eng/07a01.pdf.

36 Ibid., 4, 11.

37 Ibid., 4–5, 14.

38 Ibid., 5, 18.

39 Ibid., 5–6, 20.

40 Ibid., 6, 26.

41 2014 IPCC Synthesis Report, 78.

change', and 'oth adaptation and mitigation can reduce and manage the risks of climate change impacts'.[42] Failure to mitigate, for example, will lead to intolerable risks that exceed most nations' capacity to adapt,[43] while failure to adapt can leave populations vulnerable even to mitigated climate change.

Notably, however, there can be trade-offs between adaptation and mitigation with respect to specific actions or policies.[44] Moreover, the pursuit of climate change mitigation and adaptation can also create trade-offs with the pursuit of sustainable development goals – although climate change itself also poses a significant risk to the attainability of those goals.[45] The IPCC thus encourages policymakers to pursue strategies that produce co-benefits – that is, actions that achieve mitigation, adaptation, and perhaps other goals simultaneously.[46] 'Examples of actions with co-benefits include (i) improved air quality (...); (ii) enhanced energy security, (iii) reduced energy and water consumption in urban areas through greening cities and recycling water; (iv) sustainable agriculture and forestry; and (v) protection of ecosystems for carbon storage and other ecosystem services.'[47]

3.2 THE OCEAN AND CLIMATE CHANGE

The ocean plays complex roles in climate change, making the linking of climate change law and policy to the law of the sea critical. As a practical matter, the UN Climate Regime simply cannot ignore the ocean. The ocean is always an important element of planetary climate systems, and the effects of increased heat on the ocean can help to propel climate 'weirding' in a variety of ways, some of which can be surprising. For example, significant Arctic Ocean ice melt in the summer appears to subject the east coast of Canada and the United States to exceptionally severe winters, the so-called 'Polar Vortex'.[48] The ocean also absorbs large amounts of heat and anthropogenic CO_2, slowing the impacts of climate change on the rest of the planet. Those dampening services come with costs, however, and the ocean is itself changing in response to climate change, as discussed in Chapter 2, propelling the need for certain kinds of climate change adaptation. As a result, the law of the sea

42 Ibid., 76.
43 Ibid., 80.
44 Ibid., 91, Box 3.4.
45 Ibid., 90.
46 Ibid.
47 Ibid.
48 B. Berwyn, 'Ice loss and the polar vortex: how a warming Arctic fuels cold snaps', Inside climate NEWS, 28 September 2017, available at insideclimatenews.org/news/27092017/polar-vortex-cold-snap-arctic-ice-loss-global-warming-climate-change.

must be cognizant of climate change and what it means for marine resource use and party nations' obligations. This section reviews the many interactions between the ocean and climate change as the necessary foundational understanding that must inform how the UN Climate Regime and the law of the sea can work together with respect to climate change mitigation and adaptation.

3.2.1 *The Ocean's Role in Planetary Climate*

Climate is perhaps most easily understood as the result of the atmosphere's and the ocean's combined efforts to redistribute heat from the Earth's equator to the poles. What happens at the atmosphere–ocean interface, therefore, is critical to climate, climate change, and the ecosystem services provided by every ecosystem on Earth. This section reviews the basic processes of the atmosphere and the oceans, emphasizing their roles in climate regulation and other ecosystem services and paying particular attention to atmospheric–oceanic interactions.

The atmosphere is the layer of gases that envelopes the Earth, held in place by Earth's gravity. In composition, the atmosphere is roughly 78 per cent nitrogen (N_2), 21 per cent oxygen (O_2), 1 per cent argon, and 0.04 per cent CO_2, with trace amounts of several other gases.[49] In addition, the atmosphere contains a varying amount of water vapour. Typically, water makes up about 0.25 per cent of the entire atmosphere but accounts for 1 to 4 per cent of the air near the Earth's surface.[50] The exact concentration of water in any particular location plays an important role in determining weather, precipitation, and humidity.

The ocean, in turn, covers approximately 71 per cent of the Earth's surface and is in continuous contact with the atmosphere. At this ocean–atmosphere interface, the two systems directly exchange gases, water and water vapour, particles, and energy, both kinetic and in the form of heat.[51] The most important point for climate and climate change, however, is that ocean–atmosphere interactions go both ways: the atmosphere affects the ocean and its processes, but the ocean also affects the atmosphere and its processes. At the most basic of physical and chemical levels, therefore, climate change and the ocean are intertwined, and, therefore, their regulatory regimes should be, as well.

Gas and chemical exchanges between the ocean and the atmosphere are important to life processes around the world. The phytoplankton in the

49 Wikipedia, *Atmosphere of Earth*, en.wikipedia.org/wiki/Atmosphere_of_Earth, accessed 3 December 2018.

50 Ibid.

51 J. Kraynak and K. W. Tetrault, *The Complete Idiot's Guide to the Oceans* (Alpha Books, 2003), 18.

ocean produce half of the world's oxygen and are the basis of many food webs. However, phytoplankton growth in the ocean is generally limited by lack of iron, an essential nutrient.[52] Most available iron reaches the ocean through wind-borne dust from the desert,[53] another important atmosphere–ocean interaction.

Gas and chemical exchanges between the atmosphere and ocean are also important to climate change processes. For example, phytoplankton 'produce a chemical that affects the formation of clouds, which influence the amount of the sun's energy the earth retains'.[54] In addition, evaporation of water from the ocean contributes to the concentration of water vapour in the atmosphere, supporting the greenhouse effect and contributing to weather and precipitation patterns throughout the world.[55] Indeed, '[e]vaporation of ocean water is about six times as much globally as evapotranspiration on land'.[56]

Most importantly, the ocean is the world's largest carbon sink, giving it a direct and important role in regulating climate[57] and tying it directly to climate change mitigation. At least three ocean processes affect CO_2 concentrations in the atmosphere. First, CO_2 dissolves directly into seawater.[58] Second, various animal species in the ocean use CO_2 to make their calcium carbonate shells.[59] Finally, phytoplankton extract CO_2 from the atmosphere during photosynthesis[60] and 'are responsible for converting 30 to 50 percent of the CO_2 in the atmosphere back into oxygen'.[61]

Beyond CO_2 interactions, some of the most important atmosphere–ocean interactions with respect to climate involve currents. As Al Gore reported in *An Inconvenient Truth*, 'scientists say that the world's climate is best understood as a kind of engine for redistributing heat from the Equator and the tropics to the poles'.[62] Such redistribution arises because the regions

52 T. D. Jickells et al., 'Global iron connections between desert dust, ocean biochemistry, and climate' (2005) 308 *Science*, 67–71.
53 Ibid.
54 Kraynak and Tetrault, *The Complete Idiot's Guide*, 88.
55 S. E. Alexander, S. H. Schneider and K. Lagerquist, 'The interaction of climate and life' in G. C. Daily (ed.), *Nature's Services: Societal Dependence on Natural Ecosystems* (Island Press, 1997), 71–82 71, 73.
56 Ibid.
57 F. Pearce, *With Speed and Violence: Why Scientists Fear Tipping Points in Climate Change* (Beacon Press, 2007), 86.
58 Alexander, Schneider and Lagerquist, 'The interaction of climate and life', 76.
59 Ibid.
60 Kraynak and Tetrault, *The Complete Idiot's Guide*, 87.
61 Ibid., 88.
62 A. Gore, *An Inconvenient Truth: The Planetary Emergency of Global Warming and What We Can Do About It* (Rodale, 2006), 149.

surrounding the equator absorb far more solar energy than the polar regions. 'The redistribution of heat from the Equator to the poles drives the wind and ocean currents, like the Gulf Stream and the jet stream.'[63]

In the ocean, water circulates in both surface currents and in three-dimensional, globe-spanning, interconnected currents.[64] Prevailing winds drive ocean surface currents,[65] which account for 13 to 25 per cent of all ocean water movement.[66] Near the equator, the trade winds push seawater from east to west; farther north and south, both the winds and the ocean surface currents move from west to east.[67] Moreover, the Coriolis effect applies to ocean surface currents, and the earth's rotation deflects ocean currents clockwise in the northern hemisphere and counterclockwise in the southern hemisphere.[68]

In contrast, the more three-dimensional ocean currents are driven by differences in temperature and salt concentration (salinity) and hence are known as the thermohaline circulation.[69] Nevertheless, while not wind-driven, this circulation still depends upon the ocean's interactions with the atmosphere. As Peter Ward has described it:

> When there are warm surface areas and cold surface areas of the ocean, cold water spontaneously flows toward the warm, and vice versa. But more than surface currents accomplish this. Cold seawater is denser than warm water of the same chemistry and thus sinks. Saline water is denser than less saline water of the same temperature and also sinks. In the heat of the tropical sun, water rapidly evaporates, making the surface saltier and thus denser. In the arctic, the melting of ice adds water to the sea, making it fresher. All of these factors create seawater bodies of different temperature and salinity that want to mix with others of different values, and in so doing produce conveyer currents throughout the world's oceans.[70]

As these powerful ocean currents redistribute heat, they also 'stir[] up nutrients, transport[] food, mix[] salt- and freshwater, and even influence[]much of the weather and climate that we experience across continents'.[71] Thus, ocean currents play a large role in determining long-term climate patterns.

63 Ibid.
64 Kraynak and Tetrault, *The Complete Idiot's Guide*, 13.
65 Wikipedia, *Prevailing Winds*, en.wikipedia.org/wiki/Prevailing_winds, accessed 3 December 2018.
66 Kraynak and Tetrault, *The Complete Idiot's Guide*, 13.
67 Ibid., 13–14.
68 Ibid., 14.
69 Ibid.
70 P. C. Ward, *Under a Green Sky: Global Warming, the Mass Extinctions of the Past and What They Can Tell Us About Our Future* (Smithsonian Books/Harper Collins, 2007), 123.
71 Kraynak and Tetrault, *The Complete Idiot's Guide*, 10–11.

The ocean can store far more heat than the atmosphere, and it transports this heat throughout the world in both the surface and thermohaline currents.[72] Heat transported north in the Gulf Stream, for example, keeps eastern Europe temperate, while the occasional appearance of the strong El Niño current brings warm water to Peru and Ecuador and changes weather patterns throughout the world.[73] Excess heat, however, produces ocean storms, and '[w]hen oceans have stored vast amounts of energy, typically near the equator during the summer months, they frequently release this energy in dramatic and sometimes very destructive ways through the creation of hurricanes (in the Atlantic Ocean), typhoons (in the Pacific Ocean), and cyclones (in the Indian Ocean)'.[74]

Importantly for both humans and ecosystems, the oceanic thermohaline 'conveyer system in its present configuration has (...) been stable for a significant amount of the time that humans have had agriculture, and this stability has allowed both predictability of crop yields in Europe and Asia, as well as the biologically more important stability of ecosystems'.[75] In other words, stable thermohaline circulation patterns produce predictable climates and predictable ecosystem services, including water and food supply.

Finally, the interaction of wind, surface currents, and the thermohaline circulation are also important to ocean food supplies because they produce upwellings of bottom nutrients in specific and predictable places around the globe. Upwellings occur when the Coriolis effect deflects a surface current as it approaches a coast. As a result, '[d]eep nutrient-rich water rises up to replace the water carried away from the coast, causing an upwelling'.[76] Because upwellings are nutrient-rich, they support plankton blooms and high concentrations of marine plants and animals, including commercially important species of fish.[77] Upwellings regularly occur off the coasts of California, Chile, and South Africa,[78] and these highly productive areas of the ocean traditionally have supported '20% of global fishery yield'.[79]

72 Ibid., 17.

73 Ibid., 18.

74 Ibid.

75 Ward, *Under a Green Sky*, 153; see also Gore, *An Inconvenient Truth*, 149 ('These currents have followed much the same pattern since the end of the last ice age 10,000 years ago, since before the first human cities were built.').

76 Kraynak and Tetrault, *The Complete Idiot's Guide*, 15.

77 Ibid., 16.

78 Ibid.

79 F. Chan et al., 'Emergence of Anoxia in the California Current Large Marine Ecosystem' (2008) 319 *Science*, 920.

3.2.2 *The Ocean's Role in Climate Change Mitigation*

The UNFCCC explicitly recognizes that the ocean is important to climate change mitigation. Under Article 4(1), all Parties to the Convention, regardless of development status, agree to '[p]romote sustainable management, and promote and cooperate in the conservation and enhancement, as appropriate, of sinks and reservoirs of all greenhouse gases', including explicitly the ocean and marine and coastal ecosystems. The ocean actually serves as two kinds of mitigating sink – but it is also becoming its own source of GHG emissions, especially of methane.

3.2.2.1 The Ocean as a Heat Sink

As global average temperatures rise as a result of the atmosphere trapping more heat because of increased GHG concentrations,[80] the ocean has been acting as a massive global heat sink. According to the IPCC in 2019,

> It is virtually certain that the global ocean has warmed unabated since 1970 and has taken up more than 90% of the excess heat in the climate system (*high confidence*). Since 1993, the rate of ocean warming has more than doubled (likely). Marine heatwaves have very likely doubled in frequency since 1982 and are increasing in intensity (*very high confidence*).[81]

In contrast, 'only about 1% [of the excess heat has been] stored in the atmosphere'.[82] While ocean warming is greatest at the surface, it now extends at least 3,000 meters down, probably reaching the bottom of most parts of the ocean.[83] Moreover, the rate of heat uptake in the ocean is increasing, and the Southern Ocean has taken up the highest percentage of anthropogenic heat.[84] The IPCC also projects that ocean warming will continue throughout the twenty-first century,[85] and in 2019 it attributed 84–90 per cent of the marine

80 National Aeronautics and Space Administration (NASA), *What Are Climate and Climate Change?*, available at www.nasa.gov/audience/forstudents/5–8/features/nasa-knows/what-is-climate-change-58.html, accessed 3 December 2018.

81 2019 IPCC Ocean Report, SPM-8.

82 2014 IPCC Synthesis Report, 40. According to the International Union for the Conservation of Nature (IUCN), 'More than 93% of the enhanced heating since the 1970s due to the greenhouse effect and other human activities has been absorbed by the ocean, even affecting the deep ocean.' See International Union for the Conservation of Nature (IUCN), D. Laffoley and J. M. Baxter (eds.), *Explaining Ocean Warming: Causes, Scale, Effects, and Consequences* (2016), p. 17, available at portals.iucn.org/library/node/46254.

83 2014 IPCC Synthesis Report, 40.

84 2019 IPCC Ocean Report, SPM-9.

85 2014 IPCC Synthesis Report, 60.

heat waves that have occurred between 2006 and 2015 to 'anthropogenic temperature increase'.[86] While in 2014 the IPCC could observe no trend for the world's thermohaline current,[87] by 2019 it concluded that that current was likely weakening.[88]

The ocean's absorption of anthropogenic heat comes at a cost, even though it has mitigated the full impacts of anthropogenic GHG emissions. For instance, the increased heat content of the ocean affects its role in weather and climate, which in turn is altering the salinity of many parts of the ocean:

> It is very likely that regions of high surface salinity, where evaporation dominates, have become more saline, while regions of low salinity, where precipitation dominates, have become fresher since the 1950s. These regional trends in ocean salinity provide indirect evidence for changes in evaporation and precipitation over the oceans and thus for changes in the global water cycle (*medium confidence*).[89]

At the same time, the dissolved oxygen content of the ocean is decreasing, especially along coasts and in several areas of the open ocean. In particular, the ocean's oxygen minimum zones appear to be expanding,[90] perhaps by as much as 8 per cent in volume.[91]

3.2.2.2 The Ocean as a Carbon Dioxide Sink

In addition to absorbing anthropogenic heat, the ocean also absorbs CO_2 – enough to make it the world's largest carbon sink for CO_2 gas.[92] In terms of climate change mitigation, therefore, the ocean is important because it absorbs the CO_2 that humans 'prematurely' returned to the atmosphere from buried fossil fuels and sequesters it in slower carbon cycle component processes. As the United States' National Aeronautics and Space Administration (NASA) has explained, since the Industrial Revolution, the ocean has absorbed more CO_2 from the atmosphere than it has released to the atmosphere.[93] 'Over millennia, the ocean will absorb up to 85 percent of the extra carbon people have put into

86 2019 IPCC Ocean Report, SPM-9.
87 2014 IPCC Synthesis Report, 40.
88 2019 IPCC Ocean Report, SPM-9.
89 2014 IPCC Synthesis Report, 40.
90 Ibid., 41.
91 2019 IPCC Ocean Report, SPM-10.
92 Pearce, *With Speed and Violence*, 86.
93 National Union for the Conservation of Nature (IUCN), Aeronautics and Space Administration, Earth Observatory, H. Riebeek, *The Carbon Cycle* (2011), available at earth observatory.nasa.gov/Features/CarbonCycle/.

the atmosphere by burning fossil fuels.'[94] Currently, however, winds, currents, and ocean temperatures limit how fast the ocean can take CO_2 out of the atmosphere.[95] At the beginning of the 21st century, the ocean and land ecosystems (mostly plants) were absorbing about half of the anthropogenic emissions of CO_2[96] – roughly 25 per cent by land plants and 25 per cent by the ocean.[97] In 2006, oceanographers at the United States' National Oceanic and Atmospheric Administration (NOAA) estimated that '[o]ver the past 200 years the oceans have absorbed 525 billion tons of carbon dioxide from the atmosphere, or nearly half of the fossil fuel carbon emissions over this period'.[98] The ocean continues to uptake about 22 million tons of CO_2 per day.[99]

As with heat absorption, however, the ocean's absorption of CO_2 comes with a price – ocean acidification. Absorbed CO_2 reacts chemically to reduce the ocean's pH, a phenomenon known as 'ocean acidification'. According to the IPCC, 'Since the beginning of the industrial era, oceanic uptake of CO_2 has resulted in acidification of the ocean; the pH of ocean surface water has decreased by 0.1 (*high confidence*), corresponding to a 26% increase in acidity, measured as hydrogen ion concentration.'[100] As of 2019, more than 95 per cent of the ocean's surface has probably already experienced a drop in pH that exceeds natural variability,[101] meaning that anthropogenic emissions of CO_2 are already pushing ocean chemistry into new realities.

3.2.2.3 The Ocean as a Potential Source of Methane

While CO_2 is the GHG that receives most of the legal and policy attention, other GHGs exist and can be important contributors to climate change.

94 Ibid.

95 Ibid.

96 See P. M. Cox et al., 'Acceleration of global warming due to carbon-cycle feedbacks in a coupled climate model' (2000) 408 *Nature*, 184.

97 'The Ocean Carbon Cycle' *Harvard Magazine*, November–December 2002, available at harvardmagazine.com/2002/11/the-ocean-carbon-cycle.html. Some scientists, however, conclude that the ocean's absorption contribution is even greater: 'Over the past two hundred years, the oceans have taken up ~40% of the anthropogenic CO_2 emissions', see R. E. Zeebe et al., 'Carbon Emissions and Acidification' (2008) 321 *Science*, 51, 52. A more recent summary report published in *Science* declares that the global ocean has 'captured 28% of anthropogenic CO_2 emissions since 1750, leading to ocean acidification', see J. P. Gattuso et al., 'Contrasting futures for ocean and society from different Anthropogenic CO_2 emissions scenarios' (2015) 349 *Science*, 45, 46.

98 R. A. Feely et al., *Carbon Dioxide and Our Ocean Legacy* (NOAA, 2006), 1, available at www.pmel.noaa.gov/pubs/PDF/feel2899/feel2899.pdf.

99 Ibid.

100 2014 IPCC Synthesis Report, 41.

101 2019 IPCC Ocean Report, SPM-9.

Methane, for example, stays in the atmosphere a much shorter time than CO_2 – approximately twelve years[102] compared to, potentially, centuries or millennia for CO_2[103] – but, pound for pound, methane has twenty-five times the warming capacity of CO_2 over the course of a century.[104] While humans contribute 60 percent of the global methane emissions,[105] the ocean may be increasing its contribution of this GHG.

Normally, '[o]cean-produced methane represents around 4 percent of the total that's discharged into the atmosphere', and recent research suggests that much of this oceanic contribution may result from an enzyme common in marine microbes.[106] However, the deep parts of the ocean also sequester vast amounts of methane, including in a large pool in the oxygen minimum zones of the Pacific Ocean[107] and in methane hydrates – ice-trapped concentrated methane – in the colder waters of the Arctic Ocean and other places. If released to the atmosphere as a result of ocean warming or other changes, this ocean-derived methane could potentially drive climate change quite rapidly. In particular, scientists actively debate whether release of methane from the dissociation (breakdown) of methane hydrates – an event that appears to have occurred before in Earth's history, with dramatic climatic impacts and resulting extinctions – is likely.[108] However, the Arctic is already spewing methane into the atmosphere: new video released in October 2019 showed huge methane bubbles 'violently

102 United States Environmental Protection Agency (US EPA), *Overview of Greenhouse Gases: Methane Emissions*, available at www.epa.gov/ghgemissions/overview-greenhouse-gases#methane, accessed 24 November 2018.

103 US EPA, *Overview of Greenhouse Gases: Carbon Dioxide Emissions*, available at www.epa.gov/ghgemissions/overview-greenhouse-gases#carbon-dioxide, accessed 24 November 2018.

104 US EPA, *Overview of Greenhouse Gases: Methane Emissions*.

105 Ibid.

106 Massachusetts Institute of Technology, 'Researchers establish long-sought source of ocean methane' *Science Daily*, 7 December 2017, www.sciencedaily.com/releases/2017/12/171207141635.htm, summarizing D. A. Born et al., 'Structural basis for methylphosphonate biosynthesis' (2017) 358 *Science*, 1336.

107 I. Johnston, 'Source of world's biggest pool of underwater greenhouse gas discovered by scientists' *The Independent*, 28 February 2017, available at www.independent.co.uk/environment/underwater-greenhouse-gas-pacific-ocean-hawaii-source-bacteria-discovered-methane-qmul-a7598051.html.

108 Compare, e.g., J. Bohannon, 'Weighing the climate risks of an untapped fossil fuel' (2008) 319 *Science*, 1753; V. Krey et al., 'Gas hydrates: entrance to a methane age or climate threat?' (2009) 4 *Environmental Resources Letters*, 034007; A. L. Mascarelli, 'A sleeping giant?' (2009) 3 *Nature Climate Change*, 46–49; G. Whiteman, C. Hope and P. Wadhams, 'Climate science: vast costs of Arctic change' (2013) 499 *Nature*, 401–403 (all presenting the dissociation of methane hydrates as a real threat), with C. D. Ruppel and J. D. Kessler, 'The interaction of climate change and methane hydrates' (2017) 55(1) *Reviews of Geophysics*, 126–168, urging greater caution in methane hydrate predictions for a number of reasons.

boiling' in the East Siberian Sea, part of the Arctic Ocean, as a result of the melting permafrost at the sea's bottom, generating methane concentrations nine times greater than the global average.[109]

3.2.3 *The Ocean's Role in Driving Climate Change Adaptation*

The ocean's absorption of heat and CO_2 has slowed the pace of global warming, both giving humanity more time to mitigate climate change and delaying more general pressures to adapt to climate change's terrestrial impacts. Nevertheless, the warming and acidification of the ocean create a number of follow-on consequences within marine environments that require their own adaptation responses. This section provides a brief survey of how the ocean's interaction with GHGs and global warming is accelerating the need for certain kinds of climate change adaptation[110] – topics that the chapters in Part III will explore in greater detail.

3.2.3.1 Changing Weather Patterns and Coastal Storms

A warming ocean means that ocean currents are changing.[111] Changing currents, in turn, affect weather patterns,[112] and one of the most common ocean-related predictions for climate change are increased numbers of increasingly severe coastal storms. For example, in 2014, the IPCC concluded that 'it is virtually certain that intense tropical cyclone activity has increased in the North Atlantic since 1970'.[113]

While scientists continue to have difficulty asserting that anthropogenic climate change *caused* a particular coastal storm event,[114] they can now statistically determine that climate change is making storms more severe.[115] In 2014, moreover, the IPCC concluded with very high confidence

109 K. Gander, 'Video shows sea "violently boiling" with methane bubbles in Siberia as Arctic permafrost thaws', *Newsweek*, 30 October 2019, available at www.newsweek.com/video-sea-boiling-methane-bubbles-siberia-arctic-permafrost-thaws-1468686.

110 See generally R. K. Craig, 'Oceans and coasts' in M. Burger and J. Gundlach (eds.), *Climate Change, Public Health, and the Law* (Cambridge University Press, 2018), 204–240.

111 2014 IPCC Synthesis Report, 41.

112 IUCN, *Explaining Ocean Warming*, 359.

113 2014 IPCC Synthesis Report, 53.

114 Ibid.

115 For example, M. D. Risser and M. F. Wehner, 'Attributable human-induced changes in the likelihood and magnitude of the observed extreme precipitation during hurricane Harvey' (2017) 44(24) *Geophysical Research Letters*, 12,457–12,464.

that '[i]mpacts from recent climate-related extremes, such as heat waves, droughts, floods, [and] cyclones (...), reveal significant vulnerability and exposure of (...) many human systems to current climate variability'.[116] In addition, '[d]irect and insured losses from weather-related disasters have increased substantially in recent decades, both globally and regionally'.[117]

While preparing for coastal storms usually comes under the heading of disaster preparedness, increasing numbers of increasingly severe coastal storms blends disaster preparedness into climate change adaptation. In addition, rising seas make the impacts of these storm events worse. Indeed, the exacerbation of storm surge is the most immediate and significant consequence of sea-level rise, and 'extreme sea levels (for example, as experienced in storm surges) have increased since 1970, being mainly the result of mean sea level rise'.[118] Storm surge, among other impacts, can have significant implications for coastal food security, as Chapter 12 explores in more depth, and the law of the sea is relevant to how coastal nations can exploit marine food supplies.

3.2.3.2 Sea-Level Rise and Inundation

Sea-level rise, of course, prompts its own adaptation responses, as well. Indeed, as Chapter 13 explores in detail, sea-level rise is perhaps the most widely recognized and debated ocean-related climate change adaptation driver. Sea levels are rising as a result of both warming air, which melts glaciers and other terrestrial ice, and the warming ocean itself, which expands with increased temperature.[119] In addition, changes in ocean salinity can affect sea-level rise, and 'regional sea-level changes due to salinity were much larger than had been previously assumed – up to one-quarter of the size of the coincident sea-level changes due to temperature variations and the resulting thermal expansion of the water'.[120] Both increasing and decreasing salinity are important to sea-level rise: 'Whereas in the Pacific Ocean a freshening, or salinity reduction, has led to a density drop that augments thermally driven sea-level rise, in the Atlantic an increase in salinity has boosted density, acting against the sea-level rise due to temperature.'[121]

116 2014 IPCC Synthesis Report, 53.
117 Ibid.
118 Ibid.
119 Ibid.
120 J. Cartwright, 'Salinity changes affect sea level more than scientists thought', Environmental Research News, 9 February 2015.
121 Ibid.

Between 1901 and 2010, global average sea-level rose about 0.19 meters, and the rate of sea-level rise is increasing;[122] between 2006 and 2015, sea level was rising at a rate of 3.6 millimetres per year, a rate 'unprecedented over the last century'.[123] Ice sheet and glacier melt now contribute more to sea-level rise than ocean warming, and anthropogenic forcing has been the major cause of sea-level rise since 1970.[124] The IPCC projects that sea-level rise will accelerate throughout the twenty-first century, although it will not be uniform in all locations.[125] As a result, sea-level rise adaptation, like many climate change adaptation problems, depends on the exact coastal location: 'Since 1993, the regional rates [of sea-level rise] for the Western Pacific are up to three times larger than the global mean, while those for the Eastern Pacific are near zero or negative.'[126]

3.2.3.3 Changing Ocean Conditions and Marine Biodiversity

Humans depend on ocean ecosystems for a variety of services, including storm sheltering, food, and recreation. These ecosystem services are quite valuable (if rarely monetized): In 1997, Robert Costanza and several colleagues estimated that the world's ecosystem services were worth US$16 to US$54 *trillion* each year,[127] and about 63 per cent of that total – about US$20.9 trillion – comes from marine environments.[128] Loss of these ecosystem services as a result of climate change, in turn, demands adaptation.

Ocean warming affects all levels of marine biodiversity and ecosystem function, from microorganisms[129] and plankton[130] to sea turtles[131] and marine mammals.[132] In addition, ocean warming is negatively affecting most marine and coastal plants, including seaweeds,[133] seagrasses,[134] and mangroves.[135] A variety of marine ecosystems are changing in response to ocean warming,

122 2014 IPCC Synthesis Report, 42.
123 2019 IPCC Ocean Report, SPM-10.
124 Ibid.
125 2014 IPCC Synthesis Report, 62.
126 Ibid., 42.
127 R. Costanza et al., 'The value of the world's ecosystem services and natural capital' (1997) 387 *Nature*, 253–260.
128 Ibid., 259.
129 2014 IPCC Synthesis Report, 57.
130 Ibid., 75.
131 Ibid., 289.
132 Ibid., 303.
133 Ibid., 88.
134 Ibid., 121.
135 Ibid., 135.

including intertidal rocky habitats,[136] coral reefs,[137] and deep sea/open ocean ecosystems.[138] 'Observation so far suggest fishes have shifted their ranges by 10s to 100s of [kilometres] as the ocean has warmed', and '[o]cean warming is modifying the seasonality of occurrence of biological events such as spawning and migration. This affects fish because of mismatch in the timing of availability of their prey.'[139] In the Arctic, '[s]ub-Arctic species will expand northward and compete with the Arctic species'.[140]

In addition, the salinity changes occurring in the ocean affect species survival and biodiversity as well as sea-level rise. Species are generally adapted to live within certain salinity ranges, and salt concentrations outside that range will affect growth, reproduction, and survival.[141]

Warming also increases ocean stratification, and, as a result, the ocean's dissolved oxygen content is decreasing.[142] This phenomenon appears to be most significant for the tropics, although it is occurring in many coastal and open ocean regions.[143] Recent research indicates that the ocean's overall dissolved oxygen content has decreased by over 2 per cent since 1960, with some areas near mid-depth oxygen-minimum zones losing 4 per cent per decade over the same period.[144] Decreased oxygen is referred to as 'hypoxia', and the ocean's hypoxic zones are increasing and expanding.[145] Non-air-breathing marine animals (fish, shellfish, zooplankton, but not marine mammals or sea turtles) need dissolved oxygen to survive, and so hypoxia represents a threat to ocean nutrient cycles, marine biodiversity, fisheries, and coastal economies.[146] At the extreme, hypoxia creates ocean 'dead zones' where no animal life can exist.[147]

136 Ibid., 147.
137 Ibid., 178.
138 Ibid., 199.
139 Ibid., 240.
140 Ibid., 322.
141 NOAA Ocean Service, *Salinity*, oceanservice.noaa.gov/education/kits/estuaries/media/supp_estuar10c_salinity.html, accessed 17 July 2017.
142 2014 IPCC Synthesis Report, 41.
143 Ibid.
144 S. Schmidtko, L. Stramma and M. Visbeck, 'Decline in global oceanic oxygen content during the past five decades' (2017) 542 *Nature*, 335.
145 2014 IPCC Synthesis Report, 53, fig. 1.12.
146 Schmidtko, Stramma and Visbeck, 'Decline in global oceanic oxygen', 335; L. Stramma et al., 'Expansion of oxygen minimum zones may reduce available habitat for tropical pelagic fishes' (2011) 2 *Nature Climate Change*, 33–37; R. J. Diaz and R. Rosenberg, 'Spreading dead zones and consequences for marine ecosystems' (2008) 321 *Science*, 926, 926–929; R. Vaquer-Sunyer and C. Duarte, 'Thresholds of hypoxia for marine biodiversity' (2008) 105 *PNAS*, 15452, 15452–15457.
147 'Hypoxia occurs when DO [dissolved oxygen] falls below ≤2 ml of O_2/liter, at which point benthic fauna show aberrant behavior – for example, abandoning burrows for exposure at the sediment-water interface, culminating in mass mortality when DO declines below 0.5 ml of

Finally, ocean acidification already demands adaptation responses, and this demand is likely to increase over time, as Chapter 5 explores in more detail. Ocean acidification most directly affects marine creatures with shells,[148] but pervasive changes to ocean pH can affect other species, as well. For example, fisheries in Alaska – and the communities who depend upon those fisheries – are at significant risk because of ocean acidification.[149] Moreover, ocean acidification will continue into the twenty-first century, and under the worst scenarios ('business as usual') could decrease the ocean's pH by another 0.30 to 0.32 units, an increase in acidity of 100–109 per cent.[150] Thus, most immediately, ocean acidification demands adaptation in the fisheries and shellfish aquaculture industries located in ocean acidification hotspots.[151]

Ultimately, however, ocean acidification – especially in combination with the other stressors to marine life – may demand massive adaptation efforts in fisheries and biodiversity management. For instance, ocean acidification can subtly damage ocean ecosystems, such as interfering with chemical signalling among ocean species.[152] More importantly, according to some scientists, ocean acidification threatens a mass extinction event, and 'the current rate of (mainly fossil fuel) CO_2 release stands out as capable of driving a combination and magnitude of geochemical changes potentially unparalleled in the last ~300 [million years] of Earth history, raising the possibility that we are entering an unknown territory of marine ecosystem change'.[153]

As a result of all of these impacts, climate change and ocean acidification are already affecting marine ecosystems around the globe.[154] Overall, the IPCC concluded in 2019 that:

> Since about 1950 many marine species across various groups have undergone shifts in geographical range and seasonal activities in response to ocean warming, sea ice change and biogeochemical changes, such as

O_2/liter.' Diaz and Rosenberg, 'Spreading dead zones', 926. Research indicates that 'the number of coastal sites where hypoxia has been reported has increased with an exponential growth rate of 5.54% [per year] over time.' Vaquer-Sunyer and Duarte, 'Thresholds of hypoxia', 15452.

148 2014 IPCC Synthesis Report, 51.

149 J. T. Mathisa et al., 'Ocean acidification risk assessment for Alaska's fishery sector' (2015) 136 *Progress in Oceanography*, 71–91.

150 2014 IPCC Synthesis Report, 62.

151 R. K. Craig, 'Dealing with ocean acidification: the problem, the Clean Water Act, and state and regional approaches' (2015) 90 *Washington Law Review*, 1627–1654.

152 T. D. Wyatt, J. D. Hardege and J. Terschak, 'Ocean acidification foils chemical signals' (2014) 346 *Science*, 175–176.

153 B. Hönisch et al., 'The geological record of ocean acidification' (2012) 335 *Science*, 1058–1063, 1062.

154 2014 IPCC Synthesis Report, 50 fig. 1.11(a).

> oxygen loss, to their habitats (high confidence). This has resulted in shifts in species composition, abundance and biomass production of ecosystems, from the equator to the poles. Altered interactions between species have caused cascading impacts on ecosystem structure and functioning (medium confidence). In some marine ecosystems species are impacted by both the effects of fishing and climate changes (medium confidence).[155]

The impacts most relevant to human well-being and to law include changes in marine species richness, changes in regional species abundance, impacts on large non-fish marine species (such as marine mammals), and changes in fishery yields.[156] All of these impacts on marine ecosystems and marine biodiversity challenge both the law of the sea and the UN climate change regime to work towards effective marine adaptation policies. As Chapter 5 discusses in more detail, ocean acidification is likely to plague the ocean for millennia, demanding both new legal and new technological innovations. Chapter 14, in turn, explores the emerging legal and policy responses to changes in those areas of the ocean that are beyond nation jurisdiction, the high seas. Finally, Chapters 11 and 12 examine humanity's future food security in the face of a changing ocean, exploring adaptation responses in marine fisheries regulation and marine aquaculture, respectively.

3.3 LOSC'S ROLE IN FACILITATING CLIMATE CHANGE MITIGATION AND ADAPTATION

As Chapter 1 noted, LOSC is not a climate change convention. In fact, the terms 'global warming' and 'climate change' do not appear in its provisions. Nevertheless, LOSC can aid and support party nations' efforts at climate change mitigation and adaptation in three major ways: (1) by clarifying specific nations' jurisdiction over parts of the ocean, and hence clarifying which nations can act where with respect to both marine-related climate change mitigation efforts and climate change adaptation efforts; (2) by reinforcing the UN climate regime's duty to mitigate through specific duties to conserve and protect the ocean; and (3) by providing ocean-specific mechanisms to facilitate the UN climate regime's duty to cooperate towards effective adaptation. This section explores each of these three facets of LOSC in turn.

155 2019 IPCC Ocean Report, SPM-12.

156 2014 IPCC Synthesis Report, 52, fig. 1.12.

3.3.1 *LOSC Establishes Areas of National Jurisdiction and International Cooperation*

Knowing which nations and other entities have decision-making authority with respect to specific regions of the ocean is a key element of both marine-focused mitigation efforts and marine-focused adaptation efforts, and LOSC supplements the UN climate regime in this sense by clarifying most of the rules regarding ocean jurisdiction. As Chapter 1 laid out in more detail, much of LOSC establishes the boundaries of and rules for coastal nations' jurisdiction over a variety of areas along their shores – the territorial sea extending from the coastal baseline out to 12 nautical miles (Articles 2–32), the contiguous zone from 12 to 24 nautical miles from the baseline (Article 33), international straits (Articles 34–45), the exclusive economic zone extending to 200 nautical miles from the baseline (Articles 55–75), and the continental shelf extending 200 to 350 nautical miles below the water column (Articles 76–85). These jurisdictional provisions give a party coastal nation broad control over extractive activities in its territorial sea, its Exclusive Economic Zone (EEZ), and on its continental shelf and thus help to define for the UN climate regime which nation has authority to act where in the ocean in pursuit of climate change policies. Thus, under LOSC, a party coastal nation might choose *not* to develop any offshore oil and gas in its continental shelf (Article 81), reducing the total supply of fossil fuels on the market – the marine equivalent of the 'leave it in the ground' impulse on land[157] – and instead to promote offshore renewable energy development in its EEZ (Articles 56(1)(b)(i), 60), as is common in Europe and Scandinavia and as explored in more detail in Chapter 9. In addition, LOSC gives jurisdiction over The Area – the seabed more than 200 nautical miles from coastal baselines – to the International Seabed Authority (Articles 133–191), which clearly has jurisdiction to consider mitigation issues. With respect to adaptation, control over the territorial sea under LOSC gives coastal nations fairly plenary authority on how to adapt to sea-level rise, and the choice of pursuing coastal retreat, coastal armouring, and/or restoration of coastal wetlands, mangroves, and other coastal ecosystems generally remains with individual coastal nations, as explored in Chapter 13. Jurisdictional authority through LOSC over the territorial sea and EEZ also gives coastal nations authority to manage changing coastal fisheries (e.g., Articles 61–62, explored further in Chapter 11), to pursue

157 See, e.g., LINGO.org, *History of the idea*, http://leave-it-in-the-ground.org/lingo-history/, accessed 3 December 2018; B. McKibben, 'Why we need to keep 80% of fossil fuels in the ground', 350.org, 16 February 2016, available at 350.org/why-we-need-to-keep-80-percent-of-fossil-fuels-in-the-ground/.

offshore aquaculture (preferably the more benign forms) (Chapter 12), and to establish MPAs and engage in marine spatial planning to promote marine biodiversity in the face of changing ocean conditions (Chapters 10 and 14).

3.3.2 *LOSC and Climate Change Mitigation*

For all of the reasons discussed in Section 3.2, climate change and ocean acidification pose direct threats to the integrity of the ocean and its ecosystems. The IPCC's most recent reports make clear that the ocean is increasingly suffering from the impacts of climate change even as it buffers the impact of global warming. Research published in *Nature* in April 2019 indicates that climate change warming is affecting marine species and ecosystems about twice as badly as it is affecting terrestrial species and ecosystems,[158] and the IPCC concluded in 2018 that the ocean would be a primary beneficiary of achieving the more stringent 1.5°C mitigation goal, emphasizing that 'limiting global warming to 1.5°C is projected to reduce risks to marine biodiversity, fisheries, and ecosystems, and their functions and services to humans, as illustrated by recent changes to Arctic sea ice and warm-water coral reef ecosystems'.[159] LOSC creates a number of conservation and environmental protection duties that, in light of these climate change impacts, certainly support and arguably *require* the extension of the UN climate mitigation regime to the ocean.

Article 192 of LOSC states decisively that 'States have the obligation to protect and preserve the marine environment', which should include protecting the ocean from climate change through mitigation. The right to exploit marine resources is explicitly subject to this duty (Article 193), and the duty extends to 'all sources of pollution to the marine environment', including release of 'harmful' substances from land-based sources and 'pollution' from ocean-based sources (Article 194(3)).

The connection between LOSC and the UN climate regime is strongest when it comes to regulating 'harmful substances' released from land-based sources. While LOSC does not define 'harmful substance', GHGs would qualify under any reasonable definition, given the many impacts of climate change on ocean systems – physical, chemical, and biological. Under LOSC, party nations must take measures that minimize these releases 'to the fullest

158 M. L. Pinsky et al., 'Greater vulnerability to warming of marine versus terrestrial ectotherms' (2019) 569 *Nature*, 108–111.

159 2018 IPCC 1.5°C Report, 10. See also ibid., 10–11 (listing more benefits to the ocean of achieving the 1.5°C goal).

extent possible' (Article 194(3)), providing a direct connection between LOSC and the UN climate regime's focus on land-based sources of GHGs, such as fossil-fuel fired power plants.

LOSC also requires party nations to minimize pollution of the marine environment 'to the fullest possible extent' (Article 194(3)). Under the Article 1(4) of the Convention, 'pollution of the marine environment' is:

> the introduction by man, directly or indirectly, of substances or energy into the marine environment, including estuaries, which results or is likely to result in such deleterious effects as harm to living resources and marine life, hazards to human health, hindrance to marine activities, including fishing and other legitimate uses of the sea, impairment of quality for use of sea water and reduction of amenities.

Under this definition, GHGs and climate change would qualify as 'pollution of the marine environment', as several environmental scholars have argued.[160]

Once parties accept that marine pollution includes GHG emissions and climate change, LOSC imposes a myriad of pollution control duties on parties that effectively implement the UN climate change mitigation regime in the ocean. Most directly related to the UNFCCC and its protocols, 'States shall adopt laws and regulations to prevent, reduce and control pollution of the marine environment from land-based sources, including rivers, estuaries, pipelines and outfall structures, *taking into account internationally agreed rules, standards and recommended practices and procedures*' (Article 207(1), emphasis added). Arguably, LOSC even requires its parties to participate actively in the UN climate change mitigation regime for land-based sources, because 'States, acting especially through competent international organizations or diplomatic conference, shall endeavour to establish global and regional rules, standards and recommended practices and procedures to prevent, reduce and control pollution of the marine environment from land-based sources', and those '[l]aws, regulations, measures, rules, standards and recommended practices and procedures (…) shall include those designed to minimize, to the fullest extent possible, the release of (…) harmful (…) substances (…) into the marine environment' (Article 207(3)(5)). Thus, it seems clear that compliance with LOSC's land-based pollution minimization provisions requires parties to fully implement the UN climate change mitigation regime – if not more.

160 For example, S. A. Alabi, 'Using litigation to enforce climate obligations under domestic and international law' (2012) 6 *Carbon & Climate Law Review*, 555–598; M. Doelle, 'Climate change and the use of the dispute settlement regime of the Law of the Sea Convention' (2006) 37 *Ocean Development & International Law*, 319–337.

However – and again accepting that 'pollution of the marine environment' under LOSC includes GHG emissions and climate change – LOSC both adds obligations to engage in climate change mitigation and clearly extends climate change mitigation duties to activities in the ocean. For example, party nations must, 'as far as practicable, (…) observe, measure, evaluate and analyse, by recognized scientific methods, the risks or effects of pollution of the marine environment' (Article 204(1)), making the analysis of climate change impacts on the ocean mandatory. In addition, parties must undertake 'those [measures] necessary to protect and preserve rare or fragile ecosystems as well as the habitat of depleted, threatened or endangered species and other forms of marine life' (Article 194(5)) and 'cooperate, to the extent possible, in eliminating the effects of pollution and preventing or minimizing the damage' (Article 199), imposing obligations to halt and reverse climate change impacts on marine ecosystems.

More specifically, parties must act individually and through international institutions to prevent, reduce, control, and minimize pollution of the marine environment from marine-based technologies (Article 196(1)); from seabed activities, artificial islands, installations, and structures (Article 208); from vessels (Article 211); and, perhaps most relevant, 'from or through the atmosphere' (Article 212). Moreover, these rules must be enforceable and enforced (Articles 213, 214, 217–220, 222). Given the documented impacts of climate change on fragile marine ecosystems such as coral reefs[161] and the Arctic Ocean,[162] as well as more pervasive impacts on marine life, these LOSC provisions arguably mandate pervasive climate change mitigation efforts both at sea and on land, including GHG emissions reduction requirements from land-based sources (e.g., fossil–fuel-fired power plants), marine installations (e.g., offshore oil and gas drilling), and marine shipping. Indeed, as Chapter 6 explores in more detail, a ship's passage through another nation's territorial sea is not innocent (and hence can be prohibited) if the ship engages in 'any act of wilful and serious pollution contrary to this Convention' (Article 19(2)(h)). Moreover, the coastal state can regulate innocent passage for 'the preservation of the environment of the coastal State and the prevention, reduction and control

[161] For example, K. E. Carpenter et al., 'One-third of reef building corals face elevated extinction risk from climate change and local impacts' (2008) 321 *Science*, 560–563; T. P. Hughes et al., 'Climate change, human impacts, and the resilience of coral reefs' (2003) 301 *Science*, 929–933.

[162] For example, Union of Concerned Scientists, *Arctic Climate Impact Assessment* (2008), available at www.ucsusa.org/global_warming/science_and_impacts/impacts/arctic-climate-impact.html, accessed 13 May 2019.

of pollution thereof' (Article 21(1)(f)). However, Article 24 prevents the coastal nation from unilaterally imposing requirements that effectively block the right of innocent passage or that discriminate among nations, with the result that it is better for the nations to agree upon GHG emissions standards for ships, such as through the International Maritime Organization (IMO).

In addition to pollution control duties, LOSC also imposes a myriad of conservation duties that extend throughout the ocean and that reinforce climate change mitigation obligations under both the UN climate regime and LOSC's pollution control provisions. For example, in their EEZs, coastal nations have jurisdiction over environmental protection (Article 56(1)(b)(iii)) and a duty to 'ensure through proper conservation and management measures that the maintenance of the living resources in the exclusive economic zone is not endangered by over-exploitation' (Article 61(2)). With respect to the high seas, under Article 117, '[a]ll States have the duty to take, or to cooperate with other States in taking, such measures for their respective nationals as may be necessary for the conservation of the living resources of the high seas', and under Article 119 they must 'maintain or restore populations of harvested species at levels which can produce the maximum sustainable yield, as qualified by relevant environmental and economic factors'. Articles 65 and 120 create a duty to conserve marine mammals throughout the ocean. These conservation duties both underscore Article 192's general duty to 'protect and preserve the marine environment' and, given climate change impacts on marine living resources, strengthen the argument that compliance with LOSC duties requires full implementation (if not more) of the UN climate change mitigation regime.

Finally, LOSC creates a number of entities, such as the International Seabed Authority, that could also play important roles in climate change mitigation and adaptation, as Chapter 15 explores in more detail. For example, the International Seabed Authority has a duty 'to prevent, reduce and control pollution of the marine environment from activities in the Area' (Article 209(1)), which arguably mandates GHG emission controls on the vessels and other machines engaged in deep seabed mining – a duty that the Authority can enforce (Article 215). The Authority could also use its mandates to protect the environment (see also Article 145) to ensure that deep seabed mining activities do not disturb pockets of deep-sea methane or methane hydrates in ways that release the methane to the atmosphere, ensuring that human mining activities do not accidentally release the ocean's reservoirs of this potent GHG.

3.3.3 *LOSC and Climate Change Adaptation*

As noted earlier, the UN climate change regime is still evolving with respect to nations' collective duties regarding climate change adaptation; instead, adaptation is generally proceeding at national and local levels in response to more localized climate change impacts. In this sense, as Section 3.3.1 laid out, for coastal nations LOSC's delineation of management and regulatory jurisdiction and authority is a critical component of more localized climate change adaptation strategies in response to sea-level rise and worsening coastal storms, discussed further in Chapter 13, and in promotion of local food security, discussed further in Chapter 12.

With regard to climate change adaptation at the international level, the UNFCCC and its protocols most clearly create a duty for the world's nations to cooperate. Given the global nature of the ocean, this duty to cooperate will be especially important to ocean adaptation, particularly in terms of dealing with climate change impacts to individual marine species, marine biodiversity, and wild capture fisheries. LOSC and its protocols promote such international cooperation in the ocean, and hence LOSC can directly help to implement the UN climate change adaptation regime in the ocean. For example, most generally, under Article 197:

> States shall cooperate on a global basis and, as appropriate, on a regional basis, directly or through competent international organizations, in formulating and elaborating international rules, standards and recommended practices and procedures consistent with this Convention, for the protection and preservation of the marine environment, taking into account characteristic regional features.

Thus, LOSC reinforces the UN climate change regime's emphasis on cooperative adaptation and could become quite helpful in inducing nations to act in concert to manage changing fisheries and to protect living marine resources as those species themselves adapt to climate change impacts.

As noted in Section 3.2, climate change is already requiring adaptation in fisheries, and LOSC's duties of cooperation are most pervasive with respect to marine fisheries, as Chapter 11 explores in more detail. Thus, under Article 63(1), 'Where the same stock or stocks of associated species occur within the exclusive economic zones of two or more coastal States, these States shall seek, either directly or through appropriate subregional or regional organizations, to agree upon the measures necessary to coordinate and ensure the conservation and development of such stocks.' Similarly, under Article 63(2), 'Where the same stock or stocks of associated species occur both within the exclusive economic zone and in an area beyond and adjacent to the zone, the coastal

State and the States fishing for such stocks in the adjacent area shall seek, either directly or through appropriate subregional or regional organizations, to agree upon the measures necessary for the conservation of these stocks in the adjacent area.' Articles 66 and 67 extend the duty to cooperate to anadromous and catadromous fish, as well.

The duty to cooperate with respect to fisheries management also extends into the high seas. Within LOSC itself, Article 64 provides with respect to highly migratory species:

> The coastal State and other States whose nationals fish in the region for the highly migratory species listed in Annex I shall cooperate directly or through appropriate international organizations with a view to ensuring conservation and promoting the objective of optimum utilization of such species throughout the region, both within and beyond the exclusive economic zone. In regions for which no appropriate international organization exists, the coastal State and other States whose nationals harvest these species in the region shall cooperate to establish such an organization and participate in its work.

The 1995 Fish Stocks Agreement further explicating LOSC extends this cooperation imperative to highly migratory fish like tuna and straddling stocks (Articles 2 and 5), encouraging nations to create Regional Fishery Management Organizations (RFMOs) to manage these species throughout most of their ranges (Articles 8–12). While RFMOs have not (yet) been as effective as one might hope,[163] increasing changes to fisheries and potential fisheries may make this mechanism and others like it increasingly important in a climate change era. Thus, for example, the nations most interested in the emerging possibility, as sea ice decreases, of new fisheries opening in the Arctic Ocean entered into the Agreement to Prevent Unregulated High Seas Fisheries in the Central Arctic Ocean in October 2018, agreeing to prohibit commercial Arctic Ocean fisheries for at least sixteen years, until much more was known about how to manage them sustainably.[164]

Importantly, however, the LOSC duty to cooperate applies to more than just fisheries. For example, within EEZs, 'the coastal State and competent

[163] For example, S. Cullis-Suzuki and D. Pauly, 'Failing the high seas: a global evaluation of regional fishery management organizations' (2010) 34 *Marine Policy*, 1036–1042.

[164] NOAA Fisheries, 'U.S. signs agreement to prevent unregulated commercial fishing on the high seas of the central Arctic Ocean', 3 October 2018, available at www.fisheries.noaa.gov/international/international-affairs/us-signs-agreement-prevent-unregulated-commercial-fishing-high-seas-central-arctic; V. Schatz, A. Proelss and N. Liu, 'The 2018 Agreement to Prevent Unregulated High Seas Fisheries in the Central Arctic Ocean: a primer', EJIL Talk!, 26 October 2018, available at www.ejiltalk.org/the-2018-agreement-to-prevent-unregulated-high-seas-fisheries-in-the-central-arctic-ocean-a-primer/.

international organizations, whether subregional, regional or global, shall cooperate to' avoid over-exploitation of marine resources (Article 61(2)). In addition, Article 65 provides that 'States shall cooperate with a view to the conservation of *marine mammals* and in the case of cetaceans shall in particular work through the appropriate international organizations for their conservation, management and study.' Most generally, pursuant to Article 118, 'States shall cooperate with each other in the conservation and management of living resources in the areas of the high seas.' A new convention to extend such cooperation to biodiversity in the high seas – areas of the ocean beyond any one nation's jurisdiction – embodies the impulse to cooperate to protect a changing ocean as the Arctic Ocean fisheries agreement and is the subject of Chapter 14.

* * *

LOSC is thus directly relevant to both climate change mitigation and climate change adaptation, providing both the jurisdictional authority to address climate change in and next to the ocean and additional international law duties that reinforce the UN climate regime. Indeed, if LOSC's provisions are broadly interpreted from a climate change perspective, they could require party nations to implement fully the UN climate regime, and perhaps even to engage in more climate change mitigation than the Paris Agreement currently requires, for the sake of marine environments. Chapter 4 develops this discussion further, more comprehensively examining the role of LOSC's environmental protection requirements in a climate change era.

4

Protecting the Marine Environment from Climate Change

The LOSC Part XII Regime

Alan Boyle

4.1 INTRODUCTION

The 1982 UN Convention on the Law of the Sea (LOSC)[1] was intended to provide 'a legal order for the seas and oceans which will facilitate international communication, and will promote the peaceful uses of the seas and oceans, the equitable and efficient utilization of their resources, the conservation of their living resources, and the study, protection and preservation of the marine environment'.[2] It establishes a global framework for the rational exploitation and conservation of the sea's resources and the protection of the marine environment, while also recognizing the continued importance of freedom of navigation and other traditional freedoms of the seas. The LOSC was designed to be comprehensive in scope and universal in participation; in these respects, it has been largely successful. On many issues it has also been treated as customary international law by courts, international organizations, and non-parties.[3] The LOSC is referred to in Agenda 21 of the 1992 Rio Conference Report as providing 'the international basis upon which to pursue the protection and sustainable development of the marine and coastal environment and its resources'.[4] Chapter 17 of Agenda 21 introduces several new elements,

[1] United Nations Convention on Law of the Sea, Montego Bay, 10 December 1982, 1833 UNTS 3, Preamble.

[2] An earlier version of this chapter with a focus on litigation appears in A. Boyle, 'Litigating climate change under Part XII of the LOSC' (2019) 34 *International Journal of Marine and Coastal Law*, 458–481.

[3] See, e.g., *Territorial and Maritime Dispute (Nicaragua/Colombia) (Judgment)* [2012] ICJ Rep. 624, paras. 114–118, 138–139, 177, 182; A. Roach, 'Today's customary international law of the sea' (2014) 45 *Ocean Development and International Law*, 239–259.

[4] 1992 UN Conference on Environment and Development: Agenda 21, Ch 17, para. 17.1, in *Report of the UN Conference on Environment and Development* I, UN Doc. A/CONF 151/26/

including an emphasis on integrated and precautionary approaches to protection of the marine and coastal environment. The focus is no longer principally on the control of sources of marine pollution, but more broadly on the prevention of environmental 'degradation' and the protection of marine ecosystems. Protection of the exclusive economic zone is linked with sustainable development of coastal areas and sustainable use of marine living resources.

Agenda 21 thus illustrates how 'a more conceptually sophisticated' focus on protection of the marine environment has evolved from Part XII of the LOSC.[5] As one former International Tribunal for the Law of the Sea (ITLOS) judge observes: 'It is hard to conceive of the development of modern law of the sea and the emerging international law of the environment in ocean-related matters outside the close association and interplay between UNCLOS and Agenda 21.'[6] This perspective has been reinforced by subsequent state practice, regional agreements, and case law.[7] The twenty-year review of the Agenda 21 reaffirmed 'the importance of the conservation and sustainable use of the oceans and seas and of their resources for sustainable development' and committed states 'to effectively apply an ecosystem approach and the precautionary approach in the management, in accordance with international law, of activities having an impact on the marine environment'.[8]

The UN's Sustainable Development Goals (SDGs) reflect similar concerns.[9] Three of the goals are relevant here. The first commits states to take 'urgent action' to deal with climate change and its impacts.[10] At least in form they have now done so by adopting the 2015 Paris Agreement.[11] The second addresses

rev.1 (12 August 1992), 3. The same point is reiterated in UNGA Res 66/288 (2012), Annex, para. 158.

5 R. Falk and H. Elver, 'Comparing global perspectives: The 1982 UNCLOS and the 1992 UNCED' in D. Vidas and W. Østreng (eds.), *Order for the Oceans* (Kluwer, 1999), 145–56, 153.

6 A. Yankov, 'The Law of the Sea Convention and Agenda 21: Environmental Implications' in A. Boyle and D. Freestone (eds.), *International Law and Sustainable Development* (Oxford University Press, 1999), 271–96, 272. Yankov also chaired the committee which drafted Part XII of LOSC. See also UNGA Res 47/191 (1992), para. 4 (c) which recognizes that Agenda 21 'is a dynamic programme that could evolve over time'.

7 See especially *South China Sea Arbitration (The Republic of Philippines* v. *The People's Republic of China)* (Merits) [2016] PCA Case no. 2013–19, paras. 939–49, 956–66, 970, 983–93.

8 UNGA Res 66/288 (2012), Annex, para. 158.

9 UNGA Res 70/1 (2015), Annex.

10 SDG 13.

11 Paris Agreement, Paris, 12 December 2015, UN Doc. FCCC/CP/2015/L.9, Annex.

conservation and sustainable use of the oceans and marine resources.[12] In aiming to reduce marine pollution 'of all kinds', land-based sources and ocean acidification are specifically identified as priorities.[13] The third SDG aims to conserve and sustainably manage terrestrial ecosystems such as forests and wetlands, combat desertification, and halt loss of biodiversity.[14] All three SDGs are, of course, inter-linked. None of this adds anything new to international environmental policy or law, but it does serve to reaffirm existing commitments within the context of a process whose outcomes the UN will review in due course.[15]

UN policy and ocean science thus recognize that climate change is one of the major challenges facing the marine environment.[16] Unless the Paris Agreement brings real reductions in greenhouse gas (GHG) emissions, the harmful impacts on the entire marine environment can only increase.[17] The consequences for low-lying states and states dependent on fisheries for their food will be severe. The LOSC was negotiated at a time when climate change was not yet part of the international agenda. Nevertheless, the LOSC was never meant to be a static or immutable legal regime,[18] and it is capable of further evolution through amendment,[19] the incorporation by reference of generally accepted international rules and standards,[20] and the adoption of

12 SDG 14.

13 The targets include: '(1) By 2025, prevent and significantly reduce marine pollution of all kinds, in particular from land-based activities, including marine debris and nutrient pollution; (2) By 2020, sustainably manage and protect marine and coastal ecosystems to avoid significant adverse impacts, including by strengthening their resilience, and take action for their restoration in order to achieve healthy and productive oceans; (3) Minimize and address the impacts of ocean acidification, including through enhanced scientific cooperation at all levels.'

14 SDG 15.

15 UNGA Resolution 70/1 (2015), paras. 72–91.

16 UN Secretary General, *Oceans and Law of the Sea: Report of the Secretary General to the General Assembly*, UN Doc. A/72/70 (2017); GESAMP, *Reports and Studies No 71: Protecting the oceans from land-based activities etc* (2001); GESAMP, *Reports and Studies No 91: Pollution in the Open Oceans 2009–2013* (2015); IMO, *Third Greenhouse Gas Study* (2015).

17 IPCC, *Global warming of 1.5°C: Summary for Policymakers* (2018); CBD, *Technical Series no. 46: Scientific Synthesis of the Impacts of Ocean Acidification on Marine Biodiversity* (2009) 9; IPCC, *5th Assessment Report: Climate Change 2013: The Physical Science Basis: Summary for Policy Makers* (Cambridge University Press, 2013).

18 See J. Barrett, 'The UN Convention on the Law of the Sea: a "living treaty"?' in J. Barrett and R. Barnes (eds.), *The Law of the Sea: UNCLOS as a Living Treaty* (British Institute of International and Comparative Law, 2016), 3–40.

19 Articles 312–314. However, no such amendments have yet been adopted.

20 See especially Articles 21(2), 119, 207–12. In most cases these global standards are derived from IMO regulatory Conventions.

implementing agreements and soft law.[21] It must be interpreted and applied with subsequent developments in international law and policy in mind.[22] There is thus a potential for interaction with the 1992 UN Framework Convention on Climate Change (UNFCCC)[23] climate change regime.

The question at the heart of this book is whether that interaction contributes to reinforcing the climate regime, or whether the LOSC in some way constrains the effective adoption of the mitigation and adaptation strategies elaborated in particular by the 2015 Paris Agreement. So far as climate change mitigation strategies are concerned the answer given by this chapter is a positive one: LOSC Part XII requires states to take the measures necessary to protect the marine environment from the harmful effects of anthropogenic climate change and to that extent it reinforces the Paris Agreement and may provide opportunities for litigating climate change that are not available within the UNFCCC regime.

So far as adaptation to counter the effects of climate change is concerned the relevance of the LOSC is less clear.[24] The LOSC does not specifically require states to adapt to adverse changes in the marine environment, but nor does the UNFCCC. At the same time, both the UNFCCC and the Paris Agreement recognize the importance of adaptation as part of a response to climate change.[25] Provided states do not violate Article 195 by transferring damage or hazards from one area to another, or one type of pollution into another, there is no reason to see the LOSC as an obstacle to adaptation.[26] The more difficult question is whether by funding adaptation and climate resilience in small-island or low-lying states GHG-emitting states might find a way of scaling back on their mitigation obligations under LOSC Part XII and the Paris Agreement.[27] Those obligations are reviewed in the following sections of this chapter.

4.2 CLIMATE CHANGE MITIGATION OBLIGATIONS UNDER PART XII

The scientific evidence shows clearly that anthropogenic GHG emissions have caused marine pollution. There is both an introduction of 'substances

21 See, e.g., 1995 Agreement relating to the Conservation and Management of Straddling Fish Stocks and Highly Migratory Fish Stocks (UN Fish Stocks Agreement), New York, 4 August 1995, 2167 UNTS 3, and related FAO Codes of Conduct and International Plans of Action.

22 Vienna Convention on the Law of Treaties, Vienna, 23 May 1969, 1155 UNTS 331, Article 31(3)(c), and see, in particular, the *South China Sea Arbitration* (Merits).

23 UN Framework Convention on Climate Change, Rio de Janeiro, 9 June 1992, 1771 UNTS 107.

24 See R.K. Craig, this volume, Chapter 3 and S. Busch, this volume, Chapter 13.

25 UNFCCC, Article 4(1); Paris Agreement, Articles 7–10.

26 But see the discussion of ocean fertilization in E. Johansen, this volume, Chapter 8.

27 See the carefully worded provisions of Articles 9 and 10 of the Paris Agreement.

or energy' to the marine environment and a likelihood of the 'deleterious effects' required by Article 1(1)(4). The surface ocean absorbs around one quarter of the carbon dioxide (CO_2) emitted to the atmosphere, at increasingly rapid rates,[28] resulting in progressive acidification of seawater. Other GHGs do not have this effect. Reducing CO_2 deposition is thus crucial to saving the marine environment.[29] The sea also absorbs over 90 per cent of the excess heat ('energy') generated by global warming, resulting in higher ocean temperatures, melting ice shelves in the polar seas, loss of coral reefs and other vulnerable marine species, alterations in the distribution of marine species, and ultimately sea-level rise.[30] The science shows that acidification and warming of the oceans cannot easily be reversed and that they are, in that sense, 'persistent'.[31] Their toxic effects include depleted fish stocks, coral bleaching, and loss of marine biodiversity and ecosystems. Climate change thus degrades the marine environment and causes economic loss to coastal communities dependent for their livelihood on fishing. Other damage to coastal states includes sea-water intrusion affecting freshwater aquifers and inundating coastal areas, causing disruption of family life for those who live on affected coastlines. Sea-level rise may in extreme cases result in internal displacement of populations or even wholesale abandonment of islands or territory. These harmful, toxic, and persistent effects more than satisfy the test for marine pollution established by Article 1 of the LOSC. Thus, in principle, Part XII applies to climate change insofar as it has or is likely to have deleterious effects on the marine environment.

The core of Part XII is the obligation set out in Article 192 'to protect and preserve the marine environment'. According to the *South China Sea Arbitration*, Article 192 'extends to "protection" of the marine environment from future damage and "preservation" in the sense of maintaining or improving its present condition'.[32] It thus covers both current and future impacts.

The 'marine environment' for this purpose includes 'rare and fragile ecosystems as well as the habitat of depleted, threatened, or endangered

28 CBD, *Technical Series no 46*, 9.

29 D. Currie and K. Wowk, 'Climate change and CO_2 in the oceans and global oceans governance' (2009) 3 *Carbon & Climate Law Review*, 387–404; T. Stephens, 'Warming waters and souring seas' in D. Rothwell et al. (eds.), *Oxford Handbook on the Law of the Sea* (Oxford University Press, 2015), 778–786.

30 See IPCC, *Special Report on the Ocean and Cryosphere in a Changing Climate* (2019).

31 IPCC, *Climate Change 2014: Synthesis Report* (2014) 62.

32 *South China Sea Arbitration* (Merits), para. 941; see generally A. Proelss (ed.), *United Nations Convention on the Law of the Sea: A Commentary* (Beck, 2017), 1277–1314 and references cited there.

species and other forms of marine life'.[33] The ITLOS has confirmed that 'living resources and marine life are part of the marine environment'.[34] Later treaties, notably the 1992 Convention on Biological Diversity (CBD)[35] and the 1995 UN Agreement on Straddling and Highly Migratory Fish Stocks, suggest that, consistently with the objects and purposes of the LOSC, Part XII should also be interpreted to cover protection of marine biodiversity in general.[36] A similar conclusion was reached by the arbitral tribunal in the *Chagos Arbitration* when it held that 'Article 194 is … not limited to measures aimed strictly at controlling pollution and extends to measures focused primarily on conservation and the preservation of ecosystems'.[37] In the *Chagos* and the *South China Sea* cases, the ecosystems in question were coral reefs. Thus the 'marine environment' referred to in Part XII has been broadly defined in the subsequent treaty practice and in the jurisprudence of LOSC tribunals.

The content of Article 192 'is informed by the other provisions of Part XII and other applicable rules and principles of international law'.[38] Article 194 is the most important of these. Articles 194(1) and (2) require states to take 'all the measures that are necessary to prevent, reduce and control pollution of the marine environment from any source' and to ensure that 'activities' within their jurisdiction and control do not cause pollution damage to other states or their environment. Article 194(3) reiterates that the measures taken shall deal with 'all sources' of marine pollution, including inter alia 'the release of toxic, harmful or noxious substances, especially those which are persistent, from land-based sources, from or through the atmosphere or by dumping'. Although anthropogenic GHG emissions are not specifically listed here, it is entirely plausible to include them within Article 194 when they cause or are likely to cause marine pollution. The focus of Article 194 is clearly on mitigation of polluting effects on the marine environment rather than on promoting adaptation.

33 Article 194(5).

34 *Request for Advisory Opinion submitted by the Sub-Regional Fisheries Commission (SRFC)* (Advisory Opinion) [2015] ITLOS Rep. 4 (*Fisheries Advisory Opinion*), 4, para. 216.

35 Convention on Biological Diversity, Rio de Janeiro, 5 June 1992, 1760 UNTS 79.

36 See *South China Sea Arbitration* (Merits), para. 945. Although the tribunal does not use the words 'biological diversity', the potential loss of biodiversity in the South China Sea was the key element of the damage to the marine environment predicted by the expert evidence and accepted by the tribunal. See 1992 Convention on Biological Diversity; 1995 UN Fish Stocks Agreement.

37 *Chagos Marine Protected Area Arbitration (Mauritius* v. *United Kingdom)* [2015] PCA Case no. 2011–3 (*Chagos Arbitration*), para. 538.

38 *South China Sea Arbitration* (Merits), para. 941.

A significant proportion of marine pollution already comes from land-based sources that generate airborne depositions of pollutants at sea, and it has never been suggested that this is excluded from the LOSC. If there were any doubt about this, reference could also be made to Article 207 on land-based sources of marine pollution and Article 212 on pollution from or through the atmosphere. Article 207 establishes a general framework for the regulation of pollution from 'rivers, estuaries, pipelines and outfall structures',[39] but, following Agenda 21, regional treaties have expanded its scope to include pollution from 'point or diffuse inputs from all sources on land', whether these are waterborne, airborne, or come directly from the coast.[40] On this view Article 207 would potentially cover coal-fired power stations or other land-based activities which generate GHG emissions that pollute the marine environment. Article 212 would similarly cover CO_2 emissions from ships or aircraft, although it might be argued that it goes no further than that.[41] For the purposes of this chapter it will be assumed that airborne emissions from land-based sources, including GHG emissions, fall under Article 207 rather than Article 212, but it makes little or no difference either way which Article is relied upon.[42] Taken together, Articles 194, 207, and 212 appear to cover all airborne and land-based sources of marine pollution comprehensively, including those currently generating CO_2 emissions and other GHGs.

Examples of such sources would include smelters, steel mills and other industrial installations that emit CO_2, power generators that use oil or coal, and large-scale forest burning for agricultural or development purposes (i.e. not accidental). This does not mean that corporate polluters would be responsible under the LOSC, or that the contribution of each plant would have to be

39 For the drafting history of Article 207, see M. Nordquist (ed.), *United Nations Convention on the Law of the Sea: A Commentary* (Nijhoff, 1991), vol. IV, 125–134.

40 See, e.g., Convention for the Protection of the Marine Environment of the North-East Atlantic, Paris, 22 September 1992, (1993) 2354 UNTS 67 (OSPAR Convention), Article 2; Convention on the Protection of the Marine Environment of the Baltic Sea Area, Helsinki, 22 March 1974, 1507 UNTS 166 (Helsinki Convention), Article 3; 1980 Protocol for the Protection of the Mediterranean Sea against Pollution from Land-Based Sources and Activities, Athens, 17 May 1980 (Mediterranean Protocol), Article 1; 1999 Protocol Concerning Pollution from Land-Based Sources and Activities to the Cartagena Convention, Oranjestad, 6 October 1999, Article 1.

41 On Article 207 see Proelss, *United Nations Convention on the Law of the Sea*, 1277–1314 and references cited there. On aviation emissions see International Civil Aviation Organization Resolution A37-19 (October 2010). On emissions from ships see 1973/78 International Convention for the Prevention of Pollution from Ships, 1340 UNTS 184 (MARPOL), Annex VI; J. Harrison, *Saving the Oceans through Law* (Oxford University Press, 2017), 260–267.

42 Harrison, ibid., 255–257, relies on Article 212 rather than 207.

quantified. Part XII of the LOSC does not address private parties directly, but it does make state parties responsible for regulating and controlling the risk of marine pollution resulting from the activities of the private sector. Fundamentally, this is an obligation of due diligence – states must take the measures necessary to prevent or minimize harmful pollution, including environmental impact assessment, regulation and use of best available technology, application of the precautionary principle or approach, and enforcement.[43] On that basis states have an obligation to control and reduce GHG emissions from any source likely to pollute the marine environment or cause marine pollution damage to other states.

The standard of conduct set by Articles 194 and 207 is very general – 'prevent, reduce and control' – and this neither implies that all pollution must be prevented,[44] nor that anthropogenic GHG emissions must cease immediately, or even eventually. Mitigation in this context does not mean cessation, at least not initially. Measures that gradually reduce marine pollution by lowering emissions over a period of time would be sufficient. The UNFCCC would be relevant when interpreting and applying the LOSC to marine pollution caused by GHG emissions.[45] In particular, Article 2 of the UNFCCC talks about *stabilizing* GHG concentrations at a level that would prevent 'dangerous anthropogenic interference with the climate system'. It does not talk about eliminating GHG emissions altogether. It envisages a timescale 'sufficient to allow ecosystems to adapt naturally to climate change, to ensure that food production is not threatened and to enable economic development to proceed in a sustainable manner'. It does not talk about immediate results, although the longer meaningful action is delayed the more immediate the results will have to be. At the same time, given the scientific uncertainty and the risk of serious and irreversible harm to the marine environment posed by climate change, the measures taken must be adequately precautionary. Article 3(3) of the UNFCCC says that parties 'should' take precautionary measures to anticipate, prevent, or minimize climate change and mitigate its effects. Plainly, if there is evidence of a risk of serious or irreversible risk to the marine environment, interpreting the

43 ILC, *Articles on Prevention of Transboundary Harm, Article 3 and commentary*, UN Doc. A/56/10 (2001), 391–395, paras. (7)–(17); *Pulp Mills on the River Uruguay (Argentina* v. *Uruguay) (Judgment)* [2010] ICJ Rep. 14 (*Pulp Mills* case), paras. 197 and 223; *Responsibilities and obligations of States with respect to activities in the Area* (Advisory Opinion) [2011] ITLOS Rep. 10 (*Advisory Opinion with Respect to Activities in the Area*), paras. 115–120.

44 See *Pulp Mills* case, ibid., para. 187; *Advisory Opinion with Respect to Activities in the Area*, ibid., paras. 110–111.

45 In accordance with Article 31(3) of the 1969 Vienna Convention on the Law of Treaties.

LOSC by reference to the precautionary principle or approach would strengthen the argument for saying that something must be done to reduce GHG emissions. The question is: what?

The most obvious answer is to argue that the 2015 Paris Agreement[46] sets a standard for giving effect to LOSC Articles 192, 194, and 207 – that with respect to GHG emissions affecting the marine environment it indicates the 'necessary measures' and constitutes the generally accepted international rules or standards referred to in those Articles. This argument thus presents a clear pathway through which non-compliance with the Paris Agreement by a specific state or states could be litigated in LOSC proceedings based on non-compliance with the obligations elaborated in Part XII.

The possible counterargument is that Article 207 is notably reticent in its reference to international rules and standards and is drafted in terms which may appear to give no specific content to the underlying obligation of due diligence. In this case states need only 'tak[e] into account' internationally agreed rules and standards on land-based sources of marine pollution.[47] In negotiating this Article states wished to preserve for themselves as much freedom of action as possible in balancing environmental protection measures against the needs of their own economies, where land-based activities generate much of the most harmful pollution. For this reason, Article 207(4) explicitly allows account to be taken of 'characteristic regional features, the economic capacity of developing states and their need for economic development'.[48]

How, if at all, might this wording affect the argument that the Paris Agreement constitutes the 'necessary measures' and generally accepted rules and standards referred to in Articles 194 and 207? If it does so, would it then follow that states are not bound to implement the Paris Agreement but need only take it into account, an arguably lesser requirement of limited significance? Contrast, for example, the Articles on pollution from dumping, seabed

46 This is its full title. The Paris Agreement is in form, albeit not by name, a protocol to the 1992 UNFCCC, with which it shares the same institutional features. It was adopted by decision of the parties to the UNFCCC and only parties to the UNFCCC may become parties to the Paris Agreement. It entered into force on 21 November 2016. See generally D. Bodansky, 'The Paris Climate Change Agreement: a new hope?' (2016) 110 *American Journal of International Law*, 288–319, 306.

47 Articles 207(1) and (5). See also 3rd UN Conference on the Law of the Sea (UNCLOS III), *Official Records*, ii (1974) 317, paras. 20 (Canada) and 328 (China), and c.f. Kenyan draft Articles, UN Doc. A/CONF.62/C 3/42 (1974) and 10-power draft, UN Doc. A/CONF.62/C 3/L 6 (1974) ibid., iii, 245, 249; and Proelss, *United Nations Convention on the Law of the Sea*, 1378–90 and references cited there.

48 See also Mediterranean Protocol, Article 7(2); Protocol for the Protection of South-East Pacific against Pollution from Land-based Sources, Quito, 22 July 1982 (Quito Protocol), Article 6.

activities and ships (Articles 208–211) all of which require that national laws 'shall be no less effective than' or shall give effect to generally accepted international rules and standards.[49] MARPOL annexes, the environmental rules established by the International Seabed Authority and the 1996 London Dumping Convention are thus a mandatory minimum standard for flag states or states licensing or sponsoring seabed activities;[50] they cannot simply be 'taken into account' and then ignored in the way that Article 207 might seem to suggest.

Important though this contrast may be, Article 207 is not quite as empty as it looks. First, Article 207(5) requires parties to ensure that their national laws are 'designed to minimise, to the fullest possible extent, the release of toxic, harmful or noxious substances, especially those which are persistent, into the marine environment'.[51] As we noted earlier, deposition of CO_2 and energy into the oceans is harmful and potentially toxic to marine life and ecosystems and will be persistent. Given its effects on the marine environment, states arguably have to do something significant about climate change if they are to comply with Article 207(5).

Second, Article 207 is weak only when the international standards are ones to which the state concerned is not otherwise a party; where in other words those standards become applicable only by virtue of participation in the LOSC. In that context the point is that Article 207 does not make compliance with internationally agreed standards mandatory. States retain their freedom of action to stay outside the orbit of international agreements as intended by the drafters. But where a state is already a party to binding international agreements, such as the Paris Agreement, Article 207 cannot have the effect of weakening that commitment, nor can it plausibly be argued that Article 207(4) trumps the Paris Agreement. In this context, 'taking into account' the Paris Agreement for parties to that agreement can only mean applying its provisions and taking any other measures that may be necessary to prevent, reduce, and control marine pollution. Any other view of Article 207(1) and (4) would make nonsense of participation in the Paris Agreement (or any other agreement on land-based sources of marine pollution) and undermine the emphasis that international tribunals have placed on cooperation in

[49] Articles 208(3), 209(2), 210(6) and 211(5).

[50] Annexes I–VI to the 1973/78 MARPOL Convention; 1996 Protocol to the London Dumping Convention, 7 November 1966, in force 24 March 2006, 36 ILM 7; ISBA Regulations on: Prospecting and Exploration for Polymetallic Nodules, Doc ISBA/19/C/17 (2013); Cobalt-rich Ferromanganese Crusts, ISBA/18/A/11 (2012); Polymetallic Sulphides, ISBA/16/A/12/rev 1 (2010).

[51] See to the same effect Article 194(3)(a).

implementing Part XII.[52] So we are back to the previous conclusion: that with respect to mitigation of climate change the Part XII obligations of parties to the LOSC are defined principally by the Paris Agreement, whether we base that argument on Article 194 or Article 207, or a combination of the two. The only proviso is that this reasoning works only for parties to the Paris Agreement.[53]

4.3 THE PARIS AGREEMENT

The Paris Agreement sets out a new agenda for implementing the UNFCCC and the UN SDGs post-Kyoto.[54] First, it seeks to hold global temperature increases to 'well below' 2°C and if possible below 1.5°C.[55] It achieves this objective principally by committing all states parties to 'prepare, communicate and maintain successive nationally determined contributions' to meeting the agreement's temperature goal.[56] Second, it seeks to enhance adaptation and climate resilience, inter alia by promoting low CO_2 emissions development.[57] It achieves this objective mainly through provision for cooperation and capacity building and by reiterating the UNFCCC's provisions on financing.[58] There is thus an implicit assumption in the Paris Agreement that sustainable development requires low CO_2 emissions development and a cap on global temperature increases.

The Paris Agreement retains the controversial concept of common but differentiated responsibilities on which the UN climate regime has until now been based,[59] but in a very different form. Unlike the Kyoto Protocol, *all* parties to the Paris Agreement – not just the developed states parties – are

52 *South China Sea Arbitration* (Merits), paras. 946, 985; *Land Reclamation in and around the Straits of Johor (Malaysia* v. *Singapore) (Provisional Measures, Order of 8 October 2003)* [2003] *ITLOS Rep.* 10, para. 92; *MOX Plant (Ireland* v. *United Kingdom) (Provisional Measures, Order of 3 December 2001)* [2001] *ITLOS Rep.* 95, para. 82; *Southern Bluefin Tuna (New Zealand* v. *Japan; Australia* v. *Japan) (Provisional Measures)* [1999] *ITLOS Rep.* 280, para. 78.

53 Whether it would work for a state that ratifies the Paris Agreement and then withdraws is a more difficult question that will not be addressed here.

54 The commitments of developed state parties to reduce GHG emissions under the 1997 Kyoto Protocol expired in 2012 without having achieved any reduction in global GHG emissions against the 1990 baseline.

55 Article 2.

56 Articles 3 and 4. See also Article 5 on conservation of carbon sinks (i.e. forests).

57 Articles 2 and 7.

58 Articles 6, 7, and 9.

59 Preamble, Third recital. See generally L. Rajamani, *Differential Treatment in International Environmental Law* (Oxford University Press, 2006), especially Ch. 6; L. Rajamani, 'Ambition and differentiation in the 2015 Paris Agreement: interpretative possibilities and underlying politics' (2016) 65 *International and Comparative Law Quarterly*, 493–514.

expected to 'prepare' some level of contribution to ensuring that GHG emissions peak as soon as possible and thereafter reduce rapidly so as to stabilize in the second half of the century.[60] The precise contribution for each party has not been agreed in advance, but will be determined unilaterally by each party in accordance with its capabilities. Developed states will still take the lead,[61] but developing states – notably China, the world's biggest GHG emitter, and India, the world's third biggest – are no longer exempt from making any emissions reductions, as they were under the Kyoto Protocol. In essence the unilaterally determined commitment of each party reflects the underlying obligation of due diligence which underpins LOSC Part XII and the whole of international environmental law.[62] However, the understanding in the Paris Agreement is that reductions in GHG emissions are to increase progressively, insofar as each country's circumstances allow, 'on the basis of equity, and in the context of sustainable development and efforts to eradicate poverty'.[63] The obligation is thus evolutionary in character, and located within the global temperature objective set out in Article 2.[64] The Paris Agreement does at least reflect reality: it recognizes that climate change is not caused only by developed states and that it cannot meaningfully be addressed by simplistic ideas of historical responsibility. China and India must play their part in the overall reduction of GHG emissions. This development is an important milestone in the evolution of the UNFCCC regime.

Will the Paris Agreement be more successful than the Kyoto Protocol at reducing GHG emissions? On the positive side the UN climate regime for the first time has a clear and verifiable objective defined by reference to global

60 Article 4.

61 Article 4(4).

62 Thus, in the *Pulp Mills* case at para. 101 the ICJ noted that 'the principle of prevention, as a customary rule, has its origins in the due diligence that is required of a State in its territory. It is 'every State's obligation not to allow knowingly its territory to be used for acts contrary to the rights of other States' (*Corfu Channel (United Kingdom* v. *Albania) Merits (Judgment)* [1949] ICJ Rep. 4, p. 22)'. See also *ILC Report* (2000), UN Doc. A/55/10, para. 718: 'the special rapporteur was of the opinion that "all appropriate measures" and "due diligence" were synonymous'; *Pulp Mills* case, paras. 197, 204, and 223; *Advisory Opinion with Respect to Activities in the Area*, paras. 110–120, 131–135, and 145–149; *Certain Activities Carried Out by Nicaragua in the Border Area (Costa Rica* v. *Nicaragua)* and *Construction of a Road in Costa Rica along the San Juan River (Nicaragua v. Costa Rica) (Judgment)* [2015] ICJ Rep. 665, paras. 104, 153, and 168; *Fisheries Advisory Opinion*, para. 129; *South China Sea Arbitration* (Merits), paras. 744–757.

63 Articles 3 and 4(3).

64 On the legal implications of that objective, see L. Rajamani and J. Werksman, 'The legal character and operational relevance of the Paris Agreement's temperature goal' (2018) 376 (2119) *Philosophical Transactions of the Royal Society A*, 1–14.

temperatures. This may not be an obligation of result,[65] but it provides an important context for interpreting the obligations of conduct set out in Articles 3–5 of the Paris Agreement. Equally importantly, all the principal GHG emitters, including the United States, share a common commitment to reducing GHG emissions, even if their individual contributions will still vary and be nationally determined. On the negative side, based on commitments made so far, global temperatures will continue to rise well beyond 2°C unless states progressively and significantly keep reducing their emissions.[66] The Paris Agreement could work, or it might fail entirely.

With that conclusion in mind we might possibly want to argue that compliance with the Paris Agreement is not necessarily enough to satisfy the mitigation requirements of UNCLOS Part XII – that the two agreements are unrelated, and that UNCLOS is the more demanding, especially if interpreted by reference to the precautionary approach or principle and the duty of due diligence referred to earlier. This is an attractive argument insofar as it might set a higher standard for GHG emissions reductions by all parties and address the inadequacy of the Paris Agreement's emissions reduction commitments. If the evidence of serious or irreversible harm to the marine environment is good enough then, surely, we could say that stronger precautionary measures must not be postponed?[67]

Attractive though this may sound, the counterarguments are considerably easier to make. There is first the *lex specialis* problem. Can it plausibly be claimed that the LOSC regulates climate change impacts on the oceans in splendid isolation from the Paris Agreement? Other marine pollution agreements provide the evolutionary content for Part XII obligations, including the 1973/78 MARPOL Convention and the London Dumping Convention. Why should the Paris Agreement be different? Second, the argument that compliance with agreed standards of pollution control is not enough to satisfy the more general duty of due diligence has been tried and, so far, it has not been successful. Ireland made precisely that argument, based on the LOSC, in the *MOX Plant* case.[68] The point was never decided for jurisdictional reasons, but Ireland's case received no support from the European Commission whose job it is to enforce European

65 L. Rajamani, 'The 2015 Paris Agreement: interplay between hard, soft and non-obligations' (2016) 28 *Journal of Environmental Law*, 337–358.

66 UNEP, *The Emissions Gap Report: Are the Copenhagen Accord pledges sufficient to limit global warming to 2°C or 1.5°C? A preliminary assessment* (2010); IPCC, *Global warming of 1.5° C* (2018), *Summary for Policymakers*.

67 Harrison, *Saving the Oceans through Law*, 254.

68 See Ireland's written pleadings in *MOX Plant Arbitration (Ireland* v. *United Kingdom)* [2003] PCA case no. 2002–01.

treaties against Member states.[69] Argentina made a similar argument unsuccessfully before the ICJ in the *Pulp Mills* case.[70] Third, both developed and developing state parties would undoubtedly also point to Article 193 of the LOSC, which refers to their 'sovereign right to exploit their natural resources pursuant to their environmental policies and in accordance with their duty to protect and preserve the marine environment'. This would be interpreted as a reference to the right to sustainable development, in accordance with the case law of the ICJ.[71] Fundamental to the ICJ's case law is the balancing of interests that must take place when environmental matters are involved.

Taking all these points into account, it seems very likely that any tribunal would view reduction of GHG emissions as an exercise in balancing continued economic development against environmental protection, and that it would be reluctant to require more of states than they have agreed to under the Paris Agreement, or under Article 2 of the UNFCCC, which refers to enabling 'economic development to proceed in a sustainable manner'.[72] This approach would not be helpful to states trying to argue that compliance with the Paris Agreement is insufficient to fulfil LOSC obligations. It might be possible to argue that Articles 194 and 207 require states to take further action or adopt additional measures that do not fall within the ambit of the Paris Agreement; much will depend on the context in which the question arises, but that merely leads us back to the problems inherent in applying Article 207.[73] The more convincing conclusion is that although LOSC Part XII requires states to implement the Paris Agreement, it does not require them to go beyond it. But that leaves open the key question: What does the Paris Agreement require and how far does it take us towards the objective of holding down global temperature increases? Given the open-ended and evolutionary commitments of parties to the Paris Agreement, it seems unnecessary to suggest that 'going beyond' the Paris Agreement might be required; the terms of the Agreement

69 As the European Court of Justice (ECJ) subsequently made clear, that court had exclusive jurisdiction over a dispute involving two EU Member states and a treaty to which the EU is a party and in respect of which it has competence: Ireland had thus violated the duty of co-operation under EU law by bringing Annex VII proceedings. See *Commission of the European Communities* v. *Ireland* (C-459/03) [2006].

70 See *Pulp Mills* case. Argentina's argument applied not to the LOSC but to obligations under the 1975 Statute of the River Uruguay, but the essential point is the same.

71 *Gabčíkovo-Nagymaros Project (Hungary/Slovakia) (Judgment)* [1997] ICJ Rep. 7, para. 140; *Iron Rhine Arbitration (Belgium/Netherlands)* [2005] PCA Case no. 2003–02, paras. 58–9; *Pulp Mills on the River Uruguay (Argentina* v. *Uruguay) (Provisional Measures)* [2006] ICJ Rep. 113, para. 80 and *Pulp Mills* case *(Merits)*, para. 177.

72 See also references to 'the economic capacity of developing states and their need for economic development' in LOSC, Article 207(4).

73 See Section 4.2.

are surely wide enough to sustain whatever level of due diligence is necessary to deliver the objective set out in Article 2.

To understand what LOSC Part XII requires from states parties we must, therefore, first understand what the Paris Agreement requires from them. A detailed examination of that question is beyond the scope of this article,[74] but two points of importance are relevant here. First, although it contains 'a mix of hard, soft and non-obligations between which there is dynamic interplay',[75] the Paris Agreement is not soft law if by that we mean that it is not legally binding; on the contrary it is a binding treaty, governed by the Vienna Convention on the Law of Treaties, ratified and in force for 179 states.[76] Even the United States remains a party until its notice to quit takes effect in 2020; of the non-parties only Russia is one of the top GHG emitters.[77] Thus, on any realistic view of what 'generally accepted international rules and standards' means for the purposes of LOSC Part XII, the Paris Agreement would appear to fall within that category.[78]

Second, although the measures required from each party under the Paris Agreement are to be determined unilaterally by that party, even within the terms of the Agreement they must be 'ambitious', 'represent a progression over time', and be taken with a view to achieving the purpose of the Agreement.[79] On this wording we can conclude that doing little or nothing is not an option for significant GHG-emitting states. Moreover, although subject to heavy caveats, Article 4 also commits the parties to 'prepare, communicate and

74 But see generally D. Klein et al. (eds.), *The Paris Agreement on Climate Change* (Oxford University Press, 2017); Bodansky, 'The Paris Climate Change Agreement'; Rajamani, 'Ambition and differentiation in the 2015 Paris Agreement'; and the now extensive literature on the Paris Agreement.

75 Rajamani, 'The 2015 Paris Agreement', 352.

76 By February 2019 the Agreement had 185 parties. The 13 non-parties included Iran, Iraq, Russia and Turkey. See D. Bodansky, 'The legal character of the Paris Agreement' (2016) 25 *Review of European Comparative & International Environmental Law*, 142–150; Rajamani, 'The 2015 Paris Agreement', 337ff.

77 Russia generates 7.53 per cent of global GHG emissions and is the fourth largest emitter. Iran and Turkey with a combined contribution of 2.54 per cent are the only other significant non-parties to the Paris Agreement but neither of these states is a party to LOSC: see Decision 1/CP.21, UN Doc. UNFCCC/CP/2015/10 (29 January 2016), Annex I.

78 On the meaning of this phrase see B. Oxman 'The duty to respect generally accepted international standards' (1991–1992) 24 *New York University Journal of International Law and Politics*, 109–160; E. Molenaar, *Coastal State Jurisdiction over Vessel-Source Pollution* (Kluwer, 1998) Ch. 5; P. Birnie, 'The status of environmental "soft-law": trends and examples with special focus on IMO norms' in H. Ringbom (ed.), *Competing Norms in the Law of Marine Environmental Protection* (Kluwer, 1997), 31–58; J. Harrison, *Making the Law of the Sea* (Cambridge University Press, 2011), 171–179 and other references cited there.

79 Article 3.

maintain successive nationally determined contributions' which 'aim to reach global peaking of greenhouse gas emissions as soon as possible . . . and to undertake rapid reductions thereafter in accordance with best available science'. Again, this language is not consistent with doing little or nothing: instead it builds upon existing commitments in the UNFCCC.[80]

Although the wording of these Articles is deliberately open-textured,[81] it is consistent with an evolutionary obligation of due diligence, including the one contemplated by LOSC Part XII. Although it remains 'within the discretion of each Party to determine nationally the level of its ambition, including the extent to which the pathways implied by its NDC will be a credible contribution to the temperature goal',[82] if the question arises what measures are 'ambitious' enough to constitute the 'necessary measures' required by the LOSC, a comparison could be made with the best performers in a similar situation. Comparison with other nations' laws and practices in controlling environmental risks was at the core of two ICJ cases – *Pulp Mills*[83] and *Aerial Spraying*.[84] In both cases it was possible to identify what standard of environmental protection should be expected from the respondent states in the exercise of their due diligence obligations even without agreement on more detailed and specific international rules and standards.[85] There is no inherent reason why the same approach could not work for climate change when necessary. Establishing the case that a state is failing to comply with its obligations under the Paris Agreement would not be easy, because the nature of those obligations is deliberately left open to question by the wording of the Agreement, but that is why the system of compulsory settlement of disputes set out in Part XV of the 1982 LOSC is significant in this context.

4.4 THE LOSC AND CLIMATE DISPUTES

The importance of LOSC Part XV for climate disputes is that it may offer a mechanism for compulsory dispute settlement by ICJ, ITLOS, or arbitration

80 In particular, Articles 4(1)(a) and (b).

81 See Rajamani's account of the phraseology used in Articles 3 and 4 in Rajamani, 'The 2015 Paris Agreement', 355–356.

82 Rajamani and Werksman, 'The legal character', 7.

83 See *Pulp Mills* case.

84 This case settled without a judgment. For pleadings see *Aerial Herbicide Spraying* case *(Ecuador* v. *Colombia)* ICJ. See also A. E. Boyle, 'Transboundary Air Pollution and International Law', in S. Jayakumar et al. (eds.), *Transboundary Pollution: Evolving Issues of International Law and Policy* (Ashgate, 2015), 233–259.

85 In the *Pulp Mills* case the parties accepted that the highest national standards for pulp mills were those established by the EU, which Uruguay had adopted.

that is simply not available within the climate regime. However, the political challenge in litigating against the states that are responsible for most of the current GHG emissions should not be underestimated. Some of the small island developing states have already thought about it and backed away. Many are heavily dependent economically on the states they might otherwise want to sue. There is always the risk that litigation might impede negotiations, although the experience is usually the other way round – it pressurizes the reluctant to compromise.[86] But litigation is expensive, and might fail, so there are risks. Successful litigation also has risks: the unsuccessful respondent state might opt out of the LOSC or more likely it would opt out of the Paris Agreement. But no state has so far opted out of the LOSC even after losing a case: even China did not do so following the *South China Sea* case. Exiting either treaty would not alter the binding force of a judgment against that state, nor would opting out of the Paris Agreement alter the climate-related obligations of states parties under LOSC Part XII, which do not depend on continued participation in the Paris Agreement but on that Agreement's role in defining the content of 'necessary measures' and 'generally accepted international rules and standards' for the purposes of Part XII.

There is, moreover, a good argument for saying that disputes concerning climate-related impacts on the marine environment are within compulsory jurisdiction under lOSC Part XV. The most persuasive basis is simply that Articles 286 and 288 cover any dispute concerning interpretation and application of the LOSC unless excluded by Articles 297 or 298.[87] Neither Article excludes a dispute concerning interpretation and application of Articles 192, 194, 207, or 212. Does it matter that there is also a dispute concerning the UNFCCC and the Paris Agreement? Could it be argued that there is no LOSC dispute in such cases? One view is that there can be a LOSC dispute even if there is also a dispute under other treaties. Both the *MOX Plant* case and the *South China Sea Arbitration* observe that there may be parallel obligations under other treaties but accept that there is still a distinct dispute under the LOSC.[88] There may in other words be multiple disputes under different treaties, each subject to its own dispute settlement regime.

86 See, in particular, the *MOX Plant* and *Aerial Herbicide Spraying* cases.

87 See *South China Sea Arbitration* (Jurisdiction and Admissibility) [2015] PCA Case no. 2013–19, paras. 174–8. Article 297(1)(c) as interpreted and applied to the marine environment in the *Chagos Arbitration* is limited to 'coastal states' and is too narrow to cover a climate change case.

88 *MOX Plant* case (Provisional Measures), paras. 48–52; *South China Sea Arbitration* (Jurisdiction and Admissibility), para. 177.

Even if both these cases are wrong to generalize in this way (but why should they be?), a LOSC climate change case is different because it focuses on the 'necessary measures' and 'generally accepted international rules and standards' required by Part XII. In that sense there really is a dispute about interpreting and applying the LOSC. It does not matter whether the necessary measures, rules or standards are in MARPOL annexes or in the Paris Agreement – Articles 192, 194, and 207–212 can only be interpreted and applied by reference to other binding agreements or soft law. In effect evolutionary external rules are incorporated in LOSC Part XII and have to be litigated under the LOSC if they are to be litigated at all. Any other view would extract almost all disputes concerning the marine environment from LOSC Part XV because the content of most of the key obligations is defined by other treaties or soft law, few of which make any provision for compulsory jurisdiction.

Another way of putting the same question is to ask: 'Does Article 14 of the UNFCCC trump the LOSC?' Article 14 provides for compulsory conciliation of a UNFCCC dispute, which for this purpose includes a dispute concerning the Paris Agreement.[89] Although LOSC Part XV provides compulsory jurisdiction over a LOSC dispute, it is residual, in the sense that it defers to other options the parties have explicitly chosen – that is the point of Articles 281 and 282.[90] Could we argue that the parties to a climate-related marine environment dispute must first use the UNFCCC conciliation procedure and that in accordance with Article 281 there is LOSC compulsory jurisdiction *only* if UNFCCC conciliation fails to settle the dispute? That is a possible argument, but Article 14 conciliation is for UNFCCC disputes. A LOSC climate dispute, even if the issues overlap substantially with the Paris Agreement, is not the same dispute. One case interprets and applies the UNFCCC by reference to the Paris Agreement. The other case interprets and applies the LOSC by reference to the Paris Agreement. These look like two different cases. The *Swordfish* cases are the best analogy – an LOSC case and a WTO case simultaneously, but each concerned with quite different legal issues before separate tribunals.[91]

89 Article 24 of the Paris Agreement provides that 'The provisions of Article 14 of the Convention on settlement of disputes shall apply *mutatis mutandis* to this Agreement.'

90 *South China Sea Arbitration* (Jurisdiction and Admissibility), para. 224, which refers to 'the overall design of the Convention as a system whereby compulsory dispute resolution is the default rule and any limitations and exceptions are carefully and precisely defined in Section 3 of Part XV'.

91 See *Case concerning the Conservation and Sustainable Exploitation of Swordfish Stocks in the South-Eastern Pacific Ocean (Chile/European Union)* [2000] ITLOS Rep. 148 and [2009] ITLOS Rep. 2008–2010 13; *Measures affecting the transit and importation of swordfish,*

A similar question arose in the *South China Sea* case with respect to the Convention on Biological Diversity.[92] Although the case concerned inter alia impacts on marine biodiversity and endangered species, which could, respectively, have been subject to disputes under the CBD and the Convention on International Trade in Endangered Species of Wild Fauna and Flora,[93] the arbitral tribunal nevertheless held that there was also a LOSC dispute because Article 194(5) included impacts on biodiversity, ecosystems, and endangered species. The tribunal ruled that only an express exclusion of LOSC Part XV would fall within Article 281 and, in that respect, it declined to follow the *Southern Bluefin Tuna Arbitration*,[94] which had held that an implied exclusion was sufficient.[95] As there is nothing expressly about exclusion of LOSC Part XV in the UNFCCC or the Paris Agreement, Article 281 cannot come into play with respect to a climate-related dispute concerning the marine environment. On that view UNFCCC Article 14 no more excludes compulsory jurisdiction over a LOSC dispute about climate impacts than the Convention for the Conservation of Southern Bluefin Tuna[96] excludes Part XV jurisdiction over a LOSC dispute about conservation of tuna. Thus, if the *South China Sea* case is correct, a LOSC climate case can proceed independently of any potential UNFCCC conciliation.

Three other potential problems need to be addressed, however, before initiating any climate case under the LOSC. First, there is the question of standing to sue: can any state bring proceedings for non-compliance with Part XII of the LOSC or only an injured state? Here the answer appears straightforward. The ICJ judgment in *Belgium* v. *Senegal* provides clear authority for the proposition that all parties to *erga omnes* treaties have a collective and individual interest in ensuring compliance.[97] This was also the assumption of the

WT/DS193 (2002) WTO Annual Report, 109. The dispute was eventually settled without a hearing.

92 *South China Sea Arbitration* (Jurisdiction and Admissibility), paras. 281–289, 317–321.

93 Convention on International Trade in Endangered Species of Wild Fauna and Flora, Washington, DC, 3 March 1973, 993 UNTS 243.

94 *Southern Bluefin Tuna Arbitration (Australia, New Zealand* v. *Japan)* (Jurisdiction and Admissibility) (2000) Arbitral Tribunal constituted under LOSC Part XV, Annex VII.

95 *South China Sea Arbitration* (Jurisdiction and Admissibility), paras. 221–226, 246–247 and 281–289.

96 See A. E. Boyle, 'The Southern Bluefin Tuna Arbitration' (2001) 50 *International and Comparative Law Quarterly*, 447–452.

97 *Questions relating to the Obligation to Prosecute or Extradite (Belgium* v. *Senegal) (Judgment)* [2012] ICJ Rep. 422, paras. 68–70. See also C. Tams, *Enforcing Obligations* Erga Omnes *in International Law* (Cambridge University Press, 2005); B. Simma, 'From bilateralism to community interest in international law' (1994) 250 *Recueil des Cours*, 293–301.

Court's judgment in the *Whaling* case.[98] Not all 'environmental' treaties will fall into this category, but the *South China Sea Arbitration* shows that the duty to protect the marine environment under Part XII of the LOSC does so.[99] Thus any party to the LOSC can bring proceedings alleging non-compliance with Part XII whether or not its own rights are in issue.

Second: is there a dispute? Contentious cases are not requests for an advisory opinion; whoever sues must show that there is a dispute with the respondent state.[100] That question cannot be answered in the abstract, but the *Marshall Islands* case against the United Kingdom failed because the respondents had no reason to think there was a dispute with the Marshall Islands when the case was filed.[101] Much will turn on whether there have previously been negotiations, protests, or other diplomatic contacts between the parties on the issues supposedly in dispute. It is important, therefore, that any state wishing to litigate should demonstrate that the issue has at least been raised with the other state in diplomatic contacts, *notes verbales*, protest notes, and so on, and that the parties 'hold clearly opposite views' on the legal or factual questions which form the subject matter of the dispute.[102]

Third, some level of preliminary diplomatic contact is also required by Articles 279 and 283. Article 279 calls on the Parties to 'seek a solution' to a dispute through any of the means listed in the UN Charter,[103] including negotiations. However, 'a State Party is not obliged to pursue procedures under Part XV, Section 1, of the Convention when it concludes that the possibilities of settlement have been exhausted'.[104] Article 283 sets out an obligation to exchange views concerning settlement of the dispute by negotiation or other peaceful means prior to the commencement of Part XV

98 *Whaling in the Antarctic* (*Australia* v. *Japan*: *New Zealand* intervening) [2014] ICJ Rep. 226. Australia claimed to be upholding the collective interest of all parties to the International Convention for the Regulation of Whaling, see oral pleadings, CR 2013/18, 28, para. 19 (Burmester).

99 *South China Sea Arbitration* (Merits), paras. 939–93.

100 See, e.g., *Applicability of the Obligation to Arbitrate under Section 21 of the United Nations Headquarters Agreement of 26 June 1947* (Advisory Opinion) [1988] ICJ Rep. 12, para. 35; *Nuclear Tests (Australia* v. *France) (Judgment)* [1974] ICJ Rep. 253, para. 55; *Northern Cameroons (Cameroon* v. *United Kingdom)* Preliminary Objections *(Judgment)* [1963] ICJ Rep. 15, at 27; *South West Africa* cases *(Ethiopia* v. *South Africa; Liberia* v. *South Africa), Preliminary Objections (Judgment)* [1962] ICJ Rep. 319, at 328.

101 *Obligations concerning Negotiations relating to Cessation of the Nuclear Arms Race and to Nuclear Disarmament (Marshall Islands* v. *United Kingdom), Preliminary Objections (Judgment)* [2016] ICJ Rep. 833, para. 57.

102 Ibid., paras. 37–41.

103 Charter of the United Nations, San Francisco, 26 June 1945, 1 UNTS 16.

104 *Land Reclamation* case, para. 47; see also *South China Sea Arbitration* (Jurisdiction and Admissibility), para. 350.

proceedings. In the *Chagos Marine Protected Area Arbitration* the arbitrators held that 'Article 283 requires that a dispute have arisen with sufficient clarity that the Parties were aware of the issues in respect of which they disagreed (...). Once a dispute has arisen, Article 283 then requires that the Parties engage in some exchange of views regarding the means to settle the dispute'.[105] However, Article 283 'does not require the Parties to engage in negotiations regarding the subject matter of the dispute'.[106] Thus, consultations on the means of settlement will suffice. These could be negotiation, arbitration, ITLOS, and so on. Provided these limited preliminaries are satisfied, Article 283 is not a meaningful objection to jurisdiction. Although often pleaded, it has never been invoked successfully.

Essentially, a case asking a court or tribunal to interpret and apply the LOSC would most likely be about non-compliance with LOSC pollution control obligations by one or more states. If successful such a case should result in an order to do whatever has not been done – as would surely have happened in *Pulp Mills* had Argentina won that case.[107] So if the problem is a failure to take measures required under the Paris Agreement to reduce GHG emissions then a court could make an appropriate order. Quite what an appropriate order might be will depend on the facts at the time and on how the Paris Agreement is interpreted, but it could include an order to communicate a 'nationally determined contribution' of sufficient ambition to comply with Article 4.

An order for compensation for damage to coastal states would, of course, require proof of damage and valuation of loss, and here the recent *Border Activities* case provides an important precedent because it involves compensation for environmental damage, including the costs of environmental restoration and lost environmental services.[108] A climate damage case would, however, also raise large questions about causation, knowledge of risk, joint liability, and the inter-relationship with the UNFCCC regime, including the loss and damage mechanism agreed in 2013.[109] Article 8 of the Paris Agreement reaffirms that mechanism in terms which are far removed from any assertion or

105 *Chagos Arbitration*, paras. 382–383.

106 *The Arctic Sunrise Arbitration (Netherlands* v. *Russia)* (Merits) [2015] PCA case no. 2014–02, para. 151. See also *South China Sea Arbitration* (Jurisdiction and Admissibility), paras. 332–333.

107 See Argentina's final submissions in *Pulp Mills* case, para. 24.

108 *Certain Activities Carried out by Nicaragua in the Border Area (Costa Rica* v. *Nicaragua), Compensation Owed by the Republic of Nicaragua to the Republic of Costa Rica* (ICJ Judgment of 2 February 2018).

109 Decision 2/CP.19 UN Doc. FCCC/CP/2013/10/Add.1 (31 January 2014) Warsaw international mechanism for loss and damage associated with climate change impacts, 6.

acceptance of responsibility for past or future damage resulting from climate change.[110] On any of these grounds a claim for compensation for historical damage predating the Paris Agreement would most likely fail. But in principle compensation for future damage could be a possible remedy in the right case, which would have to be one focused on coastal state losses resulting from the breach of LOSC Part XII provisions discussed in the previous sections of this chapter. Thus, if major GHG emitters cannot be persuaded to take their obligations under LOSC Part XII and the Paris Agreement seriously, injured states may eventually have some additional recourse to compensation. Prevention would obviously be the better solution, however.

4.5 CONCLUSIONS

The relationship between the LOSC and climate change is not clear-cut, despite its obvious importance. What does seem arguable is that in the context of LOSC Part XII the Paris Agreement sets out the 'necessary measures' and 'generally accepted international rules and standards' for protecting and preserving the marine environment from the deleterious effects of GHG emissions and climate change, whether through acidification or warming of seawater, or sea-level rise. It is thus an evolutionary element in defining the content of Articles 192, 194, 207, and 212 of the LOSC in the same way that the London Dumping Convention and the MARPOL Convention also provide evolutionary content for Articles 210 and 211. As such it addresses mitigation of GHG emissions rather than adaptation to their harmful effects.

It is characteristic of most environmental regulatory treaties that they build upon the due diligence obligation and require parties to take increasingly stronger measures or apply international rules and standards.[111] Once those measures, rules, or standards are agreed on, it is very difficult to sustain the argument that the due diligence obligation has a separate and, if necessary, a more onerous character. Due diligence inevitably represents a compromise between what is possible and what is economically acceptable – a compromise fatally reflected in the UNFCCC, the Kyoto Protocol, and the Paris Agreement. Reformulating that problem in terms of the precautionary principle or approach does not change things. The UNFCCC already

[110] UNFCCC Decision 1/CP.21, UN Doc. FCCC/CP/2015/10/Add.1 (13 December 2015), para. 51, states that 'Article 8 of the Agreement does not involve or provide a basis for any liability or compensation'. See generally Klein et al., *The Paris Agreement*, p 224–238.

[111] See, for example, 1982 LOSC, Articles 194, 207–212; Convention on Nuclear Safety, Vienna, 17 June 1994, 1963 UNTS 293, Articles 6–19.

acknowledges the applicability of the precautionary approach,[112] but that has not resulted in states going any faster or any further. They can legitimately say that what has been agreed represents their adoption of a precautionary approach. Is any international court likely to disagree? Thus, the focus under Part XII has to be on what states have actually agreed rather than on what they should have agreed in some ideal scenario.

At best the LOSC provides a vehicle for compulsory dispute settlement notably lacking in the UNFCCC regime. Part XV procedures could be invoked by any state party if another party's failure to implement the Paris Agreement constitutes non-compliance with its LOSC Part XII obligations. Beyond that, protecting the oceans from harmful climate change will depend on how states interpret and apply the Paris Agreement, not on giving Part XII of the LOSC some separate and additional effect.

112 UNFCCC Article 3(3).

5

Ocean Acidification

Karen N. Scott*

5.1 INTRODUCTION

Ocean acidification refers to the lowering of ocean pH as a consequence of changes in ocean chemistry arising from increased levels of carbon dioxide (CO_2) being drawn down into the oceans from the atmosphere[1] and is a problem concurrent with, rather than a consequence of, climate change. Although we now have a good understanding of the processes of ocean acidification, we know far less about the potential impact of a change in ocean pH on species and ecosystems. Research does indicate, however, that ocean acidification may have significant detrimental impacts on calcifying organisms and reef ecosystems for example,[2] and some attempts have been made to quantify its implications for the blue economy.[3]

* This is an amended version of a paper that was originally published in the *International Journal of Marine and Coastal Law*. The author is grateful to Brill Nijhoff for permission to reproduce it here. The author acknowledges the helpful comments on this paper made by Professor Alan Boyle and other participants at a workshop on *The Law of the Sea and Climate Change: Part of the Solution or Representing Constraints* held at the K. G. Jebsen Centre for the Law of the Sea (JCLOS), UiT The Arctic University of Norway, Trømso, 28–29 January 2019. Any errors remain the responsibility of the author alone.

1 R. E. Zeebe et al., 'Carbon emissions and acidification' (2008) 321 *Science*, 51–52.

2 See the literature cited in Section 5.2.

3 See, e.g., L. Rodrigues, J. van den Bergh and A. Ghermandi, 'Socio-economic impacts of ocean acidification in the Mediterranean Sea' (2013) 38 *Marine Policy*, 447–456; A. Speers et al., 'Impacts of climate change and ocean acidification on coral reef fisheries: an integrated ecological-economic model' (2016) 128 *Ecological Economics*, 33–43; J. Ekstrom et al., 'Vulnerability and adaptation of US shellfisheries to ocean acidification' (2015) 5 *Nature Climatic Change*, 207–214; A. Punt et al., 'Evaluating the impact of ocean acidification on fishery yields and profits: the example of red king crab in Bristol Bay' (2014) 285 *Ecological Modelling*, 39–53; D. Narita and K. Rehdanz, 'Economic impact of ocean acidification on shellfish production in Europe' (2017) 60 *Journal of Environmental Planning and Management*, 500–518; L. Mathis et al., 'Ocean acidification risk assessment for Alaska's fishery sector' (2015) 136 *Progress in Oceanography*, 71–91.

Until very recently, ocean acidification was largely ignored by the climate change regime established under the auspices of the 1992 United Nations Framework Convention on Climate Change (UNFCCC),[4] despite its principal cause being CO_2 emissions. Simultaneously, however, ocean acidification is also not directly addressed by instruments regulating the law of the sea and marine pollution in particular. Bridging and, to a very limited extent, filling the gaps between these regimes are an increasing number of soft commitments and targets such as Sustainable Development Goal 14.3 adopted in 2015.[5] Although ocean acidification is an issue that is subject to a classic regime complex – parallel but functionally overlapping instruments – this chapter will focus on one part of that regime complex: the law of the sea. It will explore the various obligations under Part XII of the 1982 United Nations Convention of the Law of the Sea (LOSC)[6] to prevent, reduce and control pollution of the marine environment, and assess the extent to which these obligations appropriately address ocean acidification. Part XII of LOSC constitutes a framework agreement, which notably draws on and incorporates external standards in respect of pollution prevention and control. This chapter analyses whether the standards developed under the UNFCCC regime, in particular, comprise 'international standards' for the purposes of Article 212 of LOSC, and whether this operates as a 'constraint' on the development of the law of the sea. This chapter argues that LOSC Parties are in fact subject to a due diligence obligation under Part XII of the Convention to prevent, reduce and control ocean acidification, and that this obligation is not satisfied by simply complying with their obligations under the UNFCCC, unless those actions also deliberately address ocean acidification. This interpretation of Part XII of LOSC represents a significant opportunity under the law of the sea to address ocean acidification. Pollution prevention comprises just one part of the ocean acidification regime complex, and in the penultimate section of this chapter the question of whether and to what extent ocean acidification should be factored into decision-making associated with marine planning, fisheries management and area-based protection will be briefly assessed. These questions are developed in more detail elsewhere in this volume. Finally, this chapter concludes with more general observations on the opportunities and constraints of the law of the sea in responding to ocean acidification.

4 1992 United Nations Framework Convention on Climate Change (UNFCCC), Rio de Janeiro, 9 May 1992, 1771 UNTS 107.

5 UNGA Res 70/1 (21 October 2015).

6 1982 United Nations Convention on the Law of the Sea (LOSC), Montego Bay, 10 December 1982, 1833 UNTS 3.

5.2 OCEAN ACIDIFICATION

Ocean pH was remarkably stable, at approximately 8.2 for over 800,000 years,[7] until the onset of the Industrial Revolution in the eighteenth century. Over the last 200 years ocean pH has decreased by 0.1 pH units,[8] the equivalent of an increase in ocean acidity of about 30 per cent.[9] Ocean acidification is not an impact of climate change per se but a consequence of a common cause: an excess of CO_2 in the atmosphere, subsequently absorbed by the oceans.[10] Atmospheric concentrations of CO_2 have risen from approximately 280 ppm in 1750 to over 400 ppm today.[11] The oceans are the most important sink for CO_2, storing 50 times more CO_2 than the atmosphere,[12] and approximately half of all anthropogenic fossil-fuel emissions since the beginning of the Industrial Revolution.[13] Today around 30 per cent of all anthropogenic CO_2 is drawn down into the oceans annually[14] and about half of this is stored in the upper 10 per cent of the oceans.[15] Although CO_2 is the primary cause of ocean acidification, it is not the only cause. Other greenhouse gases such as SO_x, NO_x and NH_3 are now known to contribute to its cause,[16] and land-based runoff, primarily from agriculture, may also have significant localized impacts on ocean pH.[17]

A decrease in ocean pH causes a decrease in the saturation of calcium carbonate ($CaCO_3$) in seawater, and $CaCO_3$ is the principal compound in the

7 C. Turley and J. Gattuso, 'Future biological and ecosystem impacts of ocean acidification and their socioeconomic-policy implications' (2012) 4 *Current Opinion in Environmental Sustainability*, 278–286.

8 V. Rérolle, C. Floquet and M. Mowlem, 'Seawater-pH measurements for ocean-acidification observations' (2012) 40 *Trends in Analytical Chemistry*, 146–157.

9 S. Dupont and H. Pörner, 'A snapshot of ocean acidification research' (2013) 160 *Marine Biology*, 1765–1771.

10 S. Doney et al., 'Ocean acidification: the other CO_2 problem' (2009) *Annual Review of Marine Science* 169–192, 170.

11 World Meteorological Organization (WMO), *Greenhouse Gas Bulletin*, No. 12 (24 October 2016), available at library.wmo.int/doc_num.php?explnum_id=3084.

12 M. Rhein et al., 'Observations: ocean' in T. F. Stocker, et al. (eds.), *Climate Change 2013: The Physical Science Basis. Contribution of Working Group I to the Fifth Assessment Report of the Intergovernmental Panel on Climate Change* (Cambridge University Press, 2013), 255, 260 (hereinafter IPCC Fifth Assessment Report).

13 Group of Experts of the Regular Process, *First Global Integrated Marine Assessment: World Ocean Assessment I* (2016), available at www.un.org/Depts/los/woa, Ch 5, 17 (hereinafter, WOA I).

14 IPCC Fifth Assessment Report, 260.

15 WOA I, Ch 5, 17.

16 K. Hunter et al., 'Impacts of anthropogenic SOx, NOx and NH3 on acidification of coastal waters and shipping lanes' (2011) 38 *Geophysical Research Letters*, L13602.

17 W. Cai et al., 'Acidification of subsurface coastal waters enhanced by eutrophication' (2011) 4 *Nature Geoscience*, 766–770.

shells and skeletons of many marine species.[18] The effect of ocean acidification is global but highly variable in terms of its regional impacts. Research suggests that its impact is greatest at the surface of the oceans,[19] and higher latitude regions such as the Arctic and Antarctic are especially vulnerable as CO_2 is absorbed more easily at lower water temperatures.[20] The exposure of polar ecosystems to ocean acidification is compounded by the low energetic cost adaptation of species that allows them to survive at low temperatures, but which reduces their capacity to adapt to fast-changing environmental conditions.[21] Species most at risk from ocean acidification are calcifying organisms such as pteropods,[22] shelled molluscs[23] and coral reef ecosystems.[24] Moreover, lower ocean pH levels has also been linked to the phenomenon of coral bleaching,[25] which is primarily caused by an increase in ocean temperatures.[26] The impact of a lower ocean pH on fish species is under-researched, but some experiments indicate that low pH levels may damage key organs in the larvae of yellowfin tuna[27] and slow the development of embryos and larvae.[28] Research has also found evidence that some fish

18 B. Hönisch et al., 'The geological record of ocean acidification' (2012) 335 *Science*, 1058–1063, 1059.

19 G. G. Tarling et al., 'Effects of acute ocean acidification on spatially-diverse polar pelagic foodwebs: insights from on-deck microcosms' (2016) 127 *Deep-Sea Research II*, 75–92.

20 Ibid., 76.

21 P. Thor et al., 'Seawater pH predicted for the year 2100 affects the metabolic response to feeding in Copepodites of the Arctic Copepod *calanus glacialis*' (2016) *PLOS One*; P. Matson, T. Martz and G. Hofmann, 'High-frequency observations of pH under the Antarctic sea ice in the southern Ross Sea' (2011) 23 *Antarctic Science*, 607–613, 612.

22 J. Orr et al., 'Anthropogenic ocean acidification over the twenty-first century and its impact on calcifying organisms' (2005) 437 *Nature*, 681–686; N. Bednaršek et al., 'Pteropods on the edge: cumulative effects of ocean acidification, warming, and deoxygenation' (2016) 145 *Progress in Oceanography*, 1–24.

23 J. Ekstrom et al., 'Vulnerability and adaptation of US shellfisheries to ocean acidification' (March 2015) 5 *Nature Climate Change*, 207–214.

24 O. Hoegh-Guldbert et al., 'Coral reefs under rapid climate change and ocean acidification' (2007) 318 *Science*, 1737. For example, calcification of the Great Barrier Reef has decreased by around 21 per cent between 1988 and 2003. See Doney et al., 'Ocean acidification', 175.

25 K. R. N. Anthony et al., 'Ocean acidification causes bleaching and productivity loss in coral reef builders' (2008) 105 (45) *PNAS*, 17442–17446; P. L. Jokiel et al., 'Ocean acidification and calcifying reef organisms: a mescocosm investigation' (2008) 27 *Coral Reefs*, 473–483.

26 See O. Hoegh-Guldberg, 'Climate change, coral bleaching and the future of the world's coral reefs' (1999) 50 *Marine Freshwater Research*, 839–866.

27 A. Frommel et al., 'Ocean acidification has lethal and sub-lethal effects on larval development of yellowfin tuna, *Thunnus albacares*' (2016) 482 *Journal of Experimental Marine Biology and Ecology*, 18–24.

28 K. Verkaik, J. Hamel and A. Mercier, 'Impact of ocean acidification on reproductive output in the deep-sea annelid *Ophryotrocha sp.* (Polychaeta: Dorvilleidae)' (2017) 137 *Deep-Sea Research II*, 368–376.

become less predator adverse,[29] and less able to distinguish between predator and non-predator odours[30] or to sense predators.[31] More generally, ocean acidification reduces the capacity of the ocean to absorb CO_2, jeopardizing the long-term function of the ocean as a CO_2 sink.[32]

It is predicted that without a significant decrease in the emission of CO_2 (and other greenhouse gases) ocean pH could decrease to between 7.9 and 7.7 by 2100.[33] Information on the likely impact of increased ocean acidification on ecosystems and species is limited by the fact that research to date is based primarily on laboratory experiments, often assuming very high levels of CO_2 emissions beyond even worst-case scenarios,[34] limited mesocosms, and observations drawn from historic high pH environments.[35] Research to date indicates that impacts will be variable with substantial differences in the way species,[36] including corals, respond.[37] For example, in some experiments phytoplankton do not appear to be particularly affected by pH changes of the order predicted[38] and indeed, are capable of adapting to a higher CO_2 environment.[39] Even some species of coral[40] and Antarctic sea urchins[41] have been found to be resilient to pH changes. In one experiment for example, one

29 P. Munday et al., 'Selected mortality associated with variation in CO_2 tolerance in a marine fish' (2013) *Ocean Acidification*, 1–5.

30 T. Branch et al., 'Impacts of ocean acidification on marine seafood' (2013) 28 *Trend in Ecology and Evolution*, 178–186, 180.

31 P. Munday et al., 'Replenishment of fish populations is threatened by ocean acidification' (July 2010) 107 *PNAS*, 12930–12934.

32 Rérolle, Floquet and Mowlem, 'Seawater-pH measurements', 146.

33 Turley and Gattuso, 'Future biological and ecosystem impacts', 278.

34 For example, in the experiment carried out by Munday et al. in which the authors demonstrated a dramatic decrease in the survival of larval fish an assumption of CO_2 levels of between 700 and 850 ppm was made. See Munday et al., 'Replenishment of fish populations', 32.

35 Turley and Gattuso, 'Future biological and ecosystem impacts', 278.

36 I. E. Hendriks, C. M. Durart and M. Álvarez, 'Vulnerability of marine biodiversity to ocean acidification: a meta-analysis' (2010) 86 *Estuarine, Coastal and Shelf Science*, 157–164, 161.

37 J. Kavousi et al., 'Colony-specific investigations reveal highly variable responses among individual corals to ocean acidification and warming' (2015) 109 *Marine Environmental Research*, 161–165; J. Kavousi et al., 'Colony-specific calcification and mortality under ocean acidification in the branching coral *Montipora digitata*' (2016) 119 *Marine Environmental Research*, 161–165; J. M. Pandolfi, S. R. Connolly and D. J. Marshall, 'Projecting coral reef ruptures under global warming and ocean acidification' (2011) 333 *Science*, 418–422.

38 T. Eberlein et al., 'Effects of ocean acidification on primary production in a coastal North Sea phytoplankton community' (2017) 12(3) *PLoS ONE*, e0172594.

39 K. Lohbeck, U. Riebesell and T. Reusch, 'Adaptive evolution of a key phytoplankton species to ocean acidification' (2012) 5 *Nature Geoscience*, 346–351.

40 P. Edmunds and A. Yarid, 'The effects of ocean acidification on wound repair in the coral *Porites* spp.' (2017) 486 *Journal of Experimental marine Biology and Ecology*, 98–104.

41 E. Jones et al., 'Ocean acidification and calcium carbonate saturation states in the coastal zone of the West Antarctic Peninsula' (2017) 139 *Deep-Sea Research II*, 181–194, 188.

group of copepod species actually increased in biomass by around 30 per cent under elevated CO_2 conditions, whereas another species decreased in biomass under the same conditions.[42] Some experiments have even found positive impacts as a consequence of ocean acidification, such as an increase in the capacity of seagrasses to sequester CO_2[43] and even a reduction in the release of (N_2O) into the atmosphere.[44] However, the fact that individuals may demonstrate resilience to lower ocean pH does not rule out other negative impacts relating to range, behaviour or ecosystem function,[45] and an absence of identified impacts over the short term does not mean that there are no longer-term impacts which have yet to be observed by scientists.[46] Moreover, although it is known that there is significant spatial variability in the drawdown of CO_2,[47] pH dynamics are more generally poorly understood.[48] Furthermore, limitations in scientific knowledge about ocean ecosystems more generally impact on the ability to know or even to predict the consequences of greater ocean acidity. For example, the majority of coral species are actually found below a depth of 50 metres, and these ecosystems are generally under-monitored so the impacts of a lower ocean pH on these species are simply not known.[49]

5.3 THE OCEAN ACIDIFICATION REGIME COMPLEX

Ocean acidification is not directly regulated by any one global regime. The causes of ocean acidification, on the other hand, are indirectly managed – to a greater or lesser extent – by several regimes with a mandate to manage

42 J. Taucher et al., 'Influence of ocean acidification plankton community structure during a winter-to-summer succession: an imaging approach indicates that copepods can benefit from elevated CO_2 via indirect food web effects' (2017) 12(2) *PLoS ONE*, e0169737.

43 S. Garrard and N. Beaumont, 'The effect of ocean acidification on carbon storage and sequestration in seagrass beds; a global and UK context' (2014) 86 *Marine Pollution Bulletin*, 138–146.

44 A. Rees et al., 'The inhibition of N_2O production by ocean acidification in cold temperature and polar waters' (2016) 127 *Deep-Sea Research II*, 93. N_2O is approximately 300 per cent more potent than CO_2 as a greenhouse gas.

45 S. Widdicombe and J. Spicer, 'Predicting the impact of ocean acidification on benthic biodiversity: what can animal physiology tell us?' (2008) 366 *Journal of Experimental Marine Biology*, 187–197, 188.

46 J. Godbold and M. Solan, 'Long-term effects of warming and ocean acidification are modified by seasonal variation in species responses and environmental conditions' (2013) 368 *Philosophical Transactions B the Royal Society*, 20130186.

47 Jones et al., 'Ocean acidification', 182.

48 Matson, Martz and Hofmann, 'High-frequency observations', 607.

49 J. Roberts and S. Cairns, 'Cold-water corals in a changing ocean' (2014) 7 *Current Opinion in Environmental Sustainability*, 118–126, 124.

atmospheric and oceans pollution, and the conservation of biodiversity. The 1992 UNFCCC provides the global framework for managing emissions of greenhouse gases as well as adaptation to climate change. The 1982 LOSC requires Parties to address pollution of the oceans in Part XII of the Convention. The 1992 CBD imposes broad obligations on Parties to conserve biological diversity. At the regional level soft targets or recommendations have been developed within Arctic and Antarctic regimes and, more specifically, binding targets have been adopted under the auspices of the 1999 Protocol to Abate Acidification, Eutrophication and Ground-level Ozone (1999 Acidification Protocol)[50] to the 1979 Convention on Long-Range Transboundary Air Pollution (LRTAP),[51] in Europe and North America.

Ocean acidification is thus governed by a 'regime complex', which may be defined as functionally overlapping parallel regimes and institutions that are non-hierarchical but which nevertheless affect one another's sphere of operations.[52] In order for a regime complex to be effective, meaningful connections and linkages must be created between regimes in order to create a coherent network of regulatory control. Notably, it is soft law norms and targets that are developing within the interstices between regimes, and which are simultaneously connecting and developing a mandate within those regimes in order to address changing ocean pH. There are, however, significant structural limitations in relying on non-binding instruments as a foundation for a binding regime.

5.3.1 *Aims and Aspirations: Interstitial Soft Law Norms and Ocean Acidification*

Instruments that *directly* address ocean acidification are thus far largely non-binding and aspirational in nature. The United Nations General Assembly (UNGA), in Sustainable Development Goal (SDG) 14.3 adopted in 2015, for example, urges all States to 'minimise and address the impacts of ocean acidification, including through enhanced scientific cooperation at

[50] 1999 Protocol to Abate Acidification, Eutrophication and Ground-level Ozone to the 1979 Convention on Long-Range Transboundary Air Pollution (as amended in 2012) (Gothenburg Protocol), 30 November 1999, 2319 UNTS 81.

[51] 1979 Convention on Long-Range Transboundary Air Pollution (LRTAP), Geneva, 13 November 1979, 1302 UNTS 217.

[52] See further K. J. Atler and S. Meunier, 'The politics of international regime complexity' (2009) 7 *Perspectives on Politics*, 13–24; T. Gehring and B. Faude, 'The dynamics of regime complexes: microfoundations and systemic effects' (2013) 19 *Global Governance*, 119; and K. Raustiala and D. G. Victor, 'The regime complex for plant genetic resources' (2004) 58 *International Organisation*, 277–309.

all levels'.[53] SDG 14.3 builds on UNGA Resolution 66/288 *The Future We Want* (2012), which called for collective action to prevent further ocean acidification and to take steps to promote ecosystem resilience.[54] Ocean acidification has been identified as an issue of serious concern in UNGA resolutions adopted annually on the oceans and the law of the sea since 2007,[55] and the 2017 UN Secretary General's Report on *Oceans and the Law of the Sea* was devoted to the threats climate change and ocean acidification pose to the oceans, emphasizing synergies between and the need to deliberately connect instruments with mandates relating to climate change, the oceans and sustainable development.[56] The eighteenth meeting of the United Nations Open-ended Informal Consultative Process on Oceans and the Law of the Sea held in May 2017 focused on 'the effects of climate change on oceans',[57] and ocean acidification was recognized as one of many cumulative threats to the ocean environment.[58] The meeting also emphasized the importance of strong inter-agency coordination, and advocated the use of UN Oceans to promote coordination and coherence of UN agencies with oceans-related mandates.[59]

Soft obligations relating to ocean acidification have also been developed by the Parties to the 1992 CBD in Target 10 of the 2010 Aichi Biodiversity Targets, which calls on States to minimize the impacts of climate change or ocean acidification on coral reefs and other vulnerable ecosystems so as to maintain their integrity and ecosystem function by 2015.[60] Despite the risks posed by ocean acidification being highlighted in several CBD decisions on ocean and coastal biodiversity[61] and in the two synthesis reports on ocean

53 UNGA Res. 70/1 (15 September 2015).

54 UNGA Resolution 66/288 (27 July 2012) para. 166.

55 For example, in UNGA Res. 71/257 (23 December 2016), ocean acidification was noted as an issue of serious concern and states were urged to take global and regional action to combat its impacts (see the preamble and paras. 186, 187 & 189).

56 Report of the Secretary General, *Oceans and the Law of the Sea*, UN Doc. A/72/70 (6 March 2017).

57 *Report on the Work of the United Nations Open-ended Informal Consultative Process on Oceans and the Law of the Sea at Its Eighteenth Meeting*, UN Doc. A72/95 (16 June 2017). In 2013 ocean acidification comprised the topic for the fourteenth United Nations Open-ended Informal Consultative Process on Oceans and the Law of the Sea. See *Report of the work of the United Nations Open-ended Informal Consultative Process on Oceans and the Law of the Sea at Its Fourteenth Meeting*, UN Doc. A68/159 (17 July 2013).

58 Ibid., para. 21.

59 Ibid., paras. 112–114.

60 Decision X/2 (2010) *Strategic Plan for Biodiversity 2011–2020*, Annex.

61 See. e.g., Decision XII/23 (2014) *Ocean and Coastal Biodiversity* paras. 6, 10.

acidification published in 2009 and 2014,[62] it is clear that the goal in Target 10 has not been met.

At the regional level, more attention has been paid to date to the impacts of climate change rather than ocean acidification per se by regional fisheries management organizations (RFMOs) and regional seas conventions. An important exception to this is the Arctic Council, which commissioned the Arctic Ocean Acidification Assessment in 2013.[63] The Council noted, with concern, the potential impacts of ocean acidification on marine life and people in the Arctic, and formally recognized that CO_2 emissions reductions are the only effective way of mitigating ocean acidification. It requested that Member States take action to monitor and assess Arctic Ocean acidification, as well as mitigating and adapting to its impacts.[64] Most recently, ocean acidification was noted as a challenge across the Commonwealth in the 2018 Commonwealth Blue Charter – 'Shared ocean, shared values',[65] and an Action Group on Ocean Acidification was established under the leadership of New Zealand in order to improve understanding of the impact and drivers of ocean acidification and mitigation, adaptation and resilience measures.[66]

Finally, it is worth noting that soft targets and processes for collaboration and capacity building have also been developed by scientific and other non-governmental organizations. One hundred and twenty-two scientists adopted the Monaco Declaration in 2008 urging States to develop plans to cut emissions drastically, and to improve communication between policymakers and scientists in order to improve understanding of the impacts of ocean acidification.[67] The Global Network of Scientific Academies (IAP) adopted a statement on ocean acidification in 2009, and recommended that CO_2 should be reduced by 50 per cent below 1990 levels by 2050. The statement also advocated action to reduce other stressors on ocean

62 Secretariat of the Convention on Biological Diversity, S. Hennige, J. M. Roberts and P. Williamson (eds.), *An Updated Synthesis of the Impacts of Ocean Acidification on Marine Biodiversity*, Montreal, Technical Series No. 75 (2014); Secretariat of the Convention on Biological Diversity, *Scientific Synthesis of the Impacts of Ocean Acidification on Marine Biodiversity*, Montreal, Technical Series No. 46 (2009).

63 Arctic Monitoring and Assessment Programme (AMAP), AMAP Assessment 2013, *Arctic Ocean Acidification* (2013).

64 2013 Kiruna Declaration of the Eighth Ministerial Meeting of the Arctic Council, Kiruna (15 May 2013).

65 2018 Commonwealth Blue Charter: Shared Values Shared Oceans, para. 17, available at bluecharter.thecommonwealth.org/.

66 See further at bluecharter.thecommonwealth.org/action-groups/ocean-acidification/.

67 Monaco Declaration, adopted at the Second International Symposium on the Ocean in a High CO_2 World (Monaco, 6–9 October 2008), available at www.iaea.org/nael/docrel/MonacoDeclaration.pdf.

ecosystems.[68] The Ocean Acidification International Coordination Centre based in Monaco and supported by the International Atomic Energy Agency (IAEA) was established in 2012 in order to support capacity building and communication of science associated with ocean acidification.[69] Furthermore, the Global Ocean Acidification Observing Network was established shortly thereafter in order to improve understanding of global ocean acidification conditions, ecosystem responses to ocean acidification and to acquire and exchange data and knowledge necessary to optimize modelling for ocean acidification and its impacts.[70]

5.3.2 *The Law of the Sea and Ocean Acidification*

The law of the sea operates within the framework of LOSC. Part XII of the Convention addresses the marine environment, and creates a general obligation on all States to protect and preserve the marine environment,[71] and to take individually or jointly all necessary measures to 'prevent, reduce and control pollution of the marine environment from any source'.[72] Anthropogenic sources of CO_2 can be classified as 'pollution' which, for the purposes of LOSC, is defined as substances or energy introduced directly or indirectly into the marine environment that results in or is likely to result in deleterious effects as to harm living resources and marine life.[73] Whether introduced directly (as a consequence of CO_2 sequestration) or indirectly (through 'natural' draw-down from the atmosphere or from ocean fertilization activities), there is little doubt that the impact of CO_2 on marine life can be described as deleterious. The broad obligation to prevent, reduce and control marine pollution under Article 194 of the Convention is developed in subsequent provisions within LOSC on a sectoral basis: land-based sources;[74] the atmosphere;[75] offshore activities;[76] dumping;[77] and vessel-source

68 Interacademy Panel on International Issues (IAP), *IAP Statement on Ocean Acidification* (2009), available at www.interacademies.net/File.aspx?id=9075.
69 See www.iaea.org/services/oa-icc.
70 See www.goa-on.org/about/goals.php and Global Ocean Acidification Observing Network, JA Newton Feely et al., *Requirements and Governance Plan*, 2nd edn., (2015), available at www.goa-on.org/documents/general/GOA-ON_2nd_edition_final.pdf.
71 LOSC, Arts. 192 and 193.
72 LOSC, Art. 194(1).
73 LOSC, Art. 1(4). For a detailed discussion of Part XII of LOSC and climate change see A Boyle, this volume, Chapter 4.
74 LOSC, Art. 207.
75 LOSC, Art. 212.
76 LOSC, Arts. 208 and 209.
77 LOSC, Art. 201.

pollution.[78] Rather than providing for detailed regulation within the Convention, LOSC uses the novel device of incorporating standards developed under external instruments, and applies those standards to Convention Parties. Those standards, however, are highly variable ranging from detailed binding obligations in respect of vessel source pollution to soft recommendations associated with land-based sources. Unsurprisingly, there are no standards relating directly to ocean acidification itself.

Since 1982, marine environmental protection under the auspices of LOSC has developed to encompass a much broader toolbox than the control of pollution. It now includes general principles such as precaution and environmental impact assessment, as well as specialist tools such as spatial and integrated planning and area-based protection. All of these principles and tools are relevant to a greater or lesser extent to ocean acidification.

5.3.2.1 Atmospheric Pollution Prevention and Ocean Acidification

As the dominant source of ocean acidification is an excess of CO_2 in the atmosphere, subsequently drawn down into the ocean, Article 212 of LOSC, which addresses pollution from or through the atmosphere, is directly applicable. The inclusion of atmospheric pollution within LOSC was advocated during negotiations in 1973, and LOSC is consequently one of the first global treaties that recognized atmospheric pollution as a source of marine pollution.[79] States Party to LOSC are under an obligation to adopt laws or regulation to prevent atmospheric pollution of the marine environment in respect of territory under their sovereignty or in respect of their registered vessels or aircraft.[80] In contrast to LOSC obligations relating to vessel source pollution or dumping, however, States need only *take into account* internationally agreed rules, standards and recommended practices.[81] Moreover, States need only *endeavour* to establish global and regional rules controlling such pollution.[82] Finally, States shall 'take other measures as may be necessary to prevent, reduce and control such pollution',[83] a reference to non-binding measures.[84]

78 LOSC, Art. 211.
79 K. Bartenstein, 'Article 212' in A. Proelss (ed.), *United Nations Convention on the Law of the Sea: A Commentary* (Beck/Hart, 2017), 1445.
80 LOSC, Art. 212(1).
81 Ibid.
82 LOSC, Art. 212(3).
83 LOSC, Art. 212(2).
84 Bartenstein, 'Article 212', 1449.

Whereas instruments regulating dumping and vessel-source pollution were already in place prior to the adoption of LOSC, and thus references to international standards implicitly referenced these instruments, this was not the case for atmospheric pollution. Nevertheless, adopting a teleological approach to treaty interpretation, the reference to 'internationally agreed rules', and so on, in Article 212 can be interpreted as a reference to the 1992 UNFCCC and its associated instruments and other measures. However, although the overall aims of the UNFCCC, as articulated in Article 2 of the Convention,[85] is clearly supportive of the objective as stipulated in Article 212 of LOSC, the focus of the UNFCCC is largely on the atmosphere as opposed to the hydrosphere. This is demonstrated by the definition of climate change itself within the UNFCCC: 'a change of climate which is attributed directly or indirectly to human activity that alters the composition of the *global atmosphere* and which is in addition to natural climate variability observed over comparable time periods.'[86] Substantively, in addressing emissions under the 1997 Kyoto Protocol, Annex I Parties have the flexibility of choosing from a 'basket' of six (now seven)[87] greenhouse gases in order to meet the global commitment of a reduction in greenhouse gas emissions of 5 per cent below 1990 levels,[88] but no specific targets have been set in respect of CO_2, the principal cause of ocean acidification. Even greater flexibility is afforded to the Parties to the 2015 Paris Agreement,[89] which does not specify an emissions reduction target, but instead, requires States to determine their own commitments at the national level designed to meet the Agreement's overarching objective to limit global temperature rise to 2°C with the aim of limiting the rise to 1.5°C.[90] Although both the Kyoto Protocol and the Paris Agreement encourage the enhancement of CO_2 sinks, both instruments focus on forest and other land-based sinks, and essentially ignore the capacity of the ocean as

85 'The ultimate objective of this Convention and any related legal instruments that the Conference of the Parties may adopt is to achieve, in accordance with the relevant provisions of the Convention, stabilization of greenhouse gas concentrations in the atmosphere at a level that would prevent dangerous anthropogenic interference with the climate system. Such a level should be achieved within a time frame sufficient to allow ecosystems to adapt naturally to climate change, to ensure that food production is not threatened and to enable economic development to proceed in a sustainable manner.' See UNFCCC, Art. 2.

86 UNFCCC, Art. 1(1) (emphasis added).

87 The list of greenhouse gases under the 1997 Kyoto Protocol was amended in Doha in 2012. See Decision 1/CMP.8 (2012) *Amendment to the Kyoto Protocol Pursuant to Its Article 3, paragraph 9 (the Doha Amendment)*.

88 Kyoto Protocol, Art. 3(1).

89 Paris Agreement, UN Doc. FCCC/CP/2015/10/Add.1, Annex (12 December 2015) (in force 4 November 2016).

90 Paris Agreement, Art. 2.

a sink.[91] Most importantly, although the Paris Agreement has set a target in respect of temperature rise (which may or may not be sufficient to avoid serious harm to the oceans), it has not established an equivalent target in respect of ocean pH.

Despite these deficiencies, the climate regime is evolving to pay greater attention to the relationship between climate and the oceans, both in terms of impact and in respect of mitigation. It is notable that 70 per cent of the 161 States that have submitted nationally determined contributions (NDCs) pursuant to Article 4(2) of the 2015 Paris Agreement refer specifically to marine issues.[92] Fifty NDCs address ocean mitigation of climate change in addition to adaptation,[93] and actions taken to mitigate climate change, in particular, CO_2 emissions, will directly or indirectly address ocean acidification. At the 2016 UNFCCC Conference of the Parties (COP 22), the ocean was designated as one of nine Global Climate Action Events, and the Global Ocean Acidification Observing Network (GOA-ON), a collaborative network of institutions undertaking research on ocean acidification processes in order to inform policy development was established.[94] The States Party to the UNFCCC (along with other stakeholders, including UN Oceans) also adopted *A Strategic Action Roadmap on Oceans and Climate: 2016–2021* setting out six policy recommendations relating to the role of the oceans in the climate, mitigation, adaptation, displacement, financing and capacity development.[95] In 2017, at COP 23, the *Oceans Pathway Partnership* was launched, endorsing a two-track strategy to increase the consideration of oceans within UNFCCC processes and to increase action in priority areas impacting or impacted by oceans and climate change.[96] Prospects for developing measures under the UNFCCC which are focussed on ocean acidification have, therefore, improved and, as LOSC is undoubtedly an evolving or 'living'

91 UNFCCC, Art. 4(2)(a) and Kyoto Protocol, Art. 4(2)(a).

92 N. D. Gallo, D. G. Victor and L. A. Levin, 'Ocean commitments under the Paris Agreement' (2017) 7 *Nature Climate Change*, 833.

93 Ibid., 834.

94 See UNFCCC, *Global Climate Action Event: Oceans* (12 November 2016), available at unfccc.int/files/paris_agreement/application/pdf/gcaoceansprogramme.pdf.

95 B. Cicin-Sain et al., *Toward a Strategic Action Roadmap on Oceans and Climate: 2016–2021*, Washington, DC: Global Ocean Forum (2016), available at: https://globaloceanforumdotcom.files.wordpress.com/2013/03/strategic-action-roadmap-on-oceans-and-climate-november-2016.pdf.

96 See COP23 website, *The Ocean Pathway*, available at https://cop23.com.fj/the-ocean-pathway.

treaty,[97] such future measures will be relevant for the interpretation and application of Article 212 of the Convention.

At the regional level the only instrument adopted thus far that directly addresses ocean acidification through emissions is the LRTAP 1999 Acidification Protocol, which applies to Europe and North America. The objective of the Protocol is to control and reduce emissions of sulphur, nitrogen oxides, ammonia, volatile organic compounds and particulate matter which cause adverse effects on health and the environment, including acidification.[98] The Protocol requires Parties to establish critical loads for acidity,[99] which are defined as 'the maximum amount of acidifying deposition an ecosystem can tolerate in the long term without being damaged' and which in the long term 'will not cause adverse effects to the structure and functions of ecosystems'[100] and obligations to reduce emissions are set out in Annex II. This is important in the context of local ocean acidification, but notably provides no obligations to reduce CO_2 more generally, which, as noted earlier, is the principal cause of ocean acidification.

Finally, Article 212(1) also refers to atmospheric pollution emitted from vessels and aircraft.[101] In respect of ship-source atmospheric pollution binding regulation was adopted in 1997 when Annex VI was added to the 1979/83 MARPOL.[102] Annex VI sets standards relating to the emission of sulphur oxide (SO_x) and nitrogen oxide (NO_x) and subsequent amendments have strengthened those emissions standards,[103] addressed ship energy-efficiency more generally[104] and designated four Emission Control Areas (ECAs) where emission standards are higher.[105] By virtue of Article 211(2) of LOSC these standards

97 See discussion and references below in Section 5.4.

98 1999 Protocol to Abate Acidification, Eutrophication and Ground-level Ozone, Article 2.

99 Ibid.

100 1999 Protocol to Abate Acidification, Eutrophication and Ground-level Ozone, Annex I. Methodologies for establishing critical loads are set out in Annex 1 and vary according to location (European Monitoring and Evaluation Programme (EMEP) Parties and Parties in North America).

101 See further, H Ringbom, this volume, Chapter 6.

102 International Convention for the Prevention of Pollution from Ships, London, 2 November 1973, 1340 UNTS 184, as Modified by the Protocol of 1978 relating thereto, 17 February 1978, 1340 UNTS 61 (MARPOL 73/78).

103 Resolution MEPC.132(53) (adopted on 22 July 2005).

104 For example, all ships must develop a Ship Energy Efficiency Management Plan (SEEMP). See Resolution MEPC.203(62) (adopted on 15 July 2011).

105 These comprise the Baltic Sea area (SO_x only); the North Sea area (SO_x only); the North American area (SO_x, NO_x and PM); and the United States Caribbean Sea area (SO_x, NO_x and PM).

constitute the minimum to be applied by flag States to vessels within their registries.

5.3.2.2 Land-based Pollution Prevention and Ocean Acidification

Land-based run off from agriculture and from industrial sources makes a minor contribution to ocean acidification overall, but may have significant impact in some local, coastal locations. The obligation on Parties to LOSC to address land-based sources of pollution is expressed in similar terms to their obligation in respect of atmospheric pollution. Article 207 requires Parties to generally prevent, reduce and control land-based sources of pollution, and to take other measures as may be necessary for this task.[106] Parties are encouraged to harmonize policies on a regional basis and to adopt global binding standards and recommended practices taking into account regional features and the needs of developing countries.[107] There is no obligation to adopt, at a national level, agreed international standards, but Parties must *take into account* international standards, recommendations and practices when developing national rules.[108] In contrast to atmospheric pollution, there are no globally binding standards regulating land-based sources of marine pollution. Instead, the 1995 Global Programme for Action (GPA)[109] establishes soft, non-binding targets to limit the release of land-based pollutants, including nutrients, which can exacerbate local sources of acidification. Ocean acidification resulting from land-based activities was expressly identified as a threat to vulnerable developing States in the 2006 Beijing Declaration on the GPA.[110] At the regional level, binding targets in respect of land-based sources of pollution have been adopted in areas such as the Mediterranean[111] and North East

[106] LOSC, Arts. 207(1) and (2).

[107] LOSC, Arts. 207(3) and (4).

[108] LOSC, Art. 207(1).

[109] See UN Environment Programme website, *Addressing Land-Based Pollution*, available at www.unep.org/gpa/.

[110] 2006 Beijing Declaration on furthering the implementation of the Global Programme of Action for the Protection of the Marine Environment from Land-based Activities, adopted at the Intergovernmental Review Meeting on the Implementation of the Global Programme of Action for the Protection of the Marine Environment from Land-based Activities, Second session, Beijing, 16–20 October 2006, UN Doc. UNEP/GPA/IGR.2/7 (23 October 2006), Annex V.

[111] 1996 Protocol for the Protection of the Mediterranean Sea against Pollution from Land-Based Sources and Activities, Athens, 17 May 1980, in force 18 May 2006 (as amended in 1996), available at http://wedocs.unep.org/bitstream/handle/20.500.11822/7096/Consolidated_LBS96_ENG.pdf?sequence=5&isAllowed=y.

Atlantic,[112] but these are similarly more focused on localized pH abatement as opposed to addressing ocean acidification more generally.

5.3.2.3 The Dumping Regime and Ocean Acidification

Of indirect application to ocean acidification is Article 210 and the dumping regime in respect of the sequestration of CO_2, which if released into the marine environment may inadvertently lead to localized if not a more general change in ocean pH, and ocean fertilization, which is deliberately designed to increase the uptake of CO_2 by the oceans in order to mitigate climate change. As both issues are dealt with in detail elsewhere in this volume,[113] only a brief overview will be provided here.

Parties to LOSC are obliged to apply global rules and standards in respect to activities that constitute dumping at sea to their territory and to vessels registered under their jurisdiction.[114] It is accepted that the international standards are provided by the 1972 London Convention[115] and 1996 Protocol to the London Convention.[116] It is unclear, however, whether Article 210 refers to either the 1972 Convention or the 1996 Protocol or, possibly, to both. The 1996 Protocol adopts a different approach to managing dumping as compared to the 1972 Convention, essentially introducing a presumption against dumping subject to limited exceptions. Moreover, rules relating to both CO_2 sequestration and ocean fertilization have been developed under the auspices of the Protocol rather than the Convention. Nevertheless, only fifty-one States have ratified the Protocol to date, and LOSC itself provides no mechanism which expressly recognizes the standards developed in one instrument over another. Furthermore, although the definition of dumping in LOSC[117] is broad enough to encompass the sequestration of CO_2 below the sea bed or in the water column (provided sequestration takes place from a ship or platform), it clearly does not extend to ocean fertilization or other geoengineering activities that cannot constitute 'disposal' or 'placement . . . contrary to the aims of' LOSC. It is unlikely, therefore, that Article 210 of LOSC can be relied on to apply the

112 1992 Convention for the Protection of the Marine Environment of the North East Atlantic (OSPAR Convention), Paris, 22 September 1992, (1993) 2354 UNTS 67, Annex I.

113 See E. Johansen, this volume, Chapter 8 and N. Bankes, this volume, Chapter 7.

114 LOSC, Arts. 210(1) and (6).

115 1972 Convention for the Prevention of Marine Pollution by Dumping from Ships and Aircraft (London Convention), London, 29 December 1972, 1046 UNTS 138.

116 1996 Protocol to the London Convention on the Prevention of Marine Pollution by Dumping of Wastes and Other Matter, 7 November 1996, 36 ILM 7.

117 LOSC, Art. 1(5).

ocean fertilization regime as developed under the 1996 Protocol to all LOSC Parties.

Nevertheless, States Party to the 1996 Protocol will be bound by the regime governing ocean fertilization, once it enters into force. The formal legal basis for regulating ocean fertilization – and potentially other marine geoengineering activities – was created in 2013 through formal amendment to the Protocol.[118] The deliberate transfer of CO_2 from the atmosphere to the oceans in an effort to mitigate climate change – ocean fertilization – risks reducing ocean pH, and thus may exacerbate ocean acidification. Although geoengineering is expansively defined under the 2013 amendment,[119] the Protocol has, for the time being, restricted its regulatory mandate to geoengineering activities that involves the placement of matter into the sea from vessels, aircraft or offshore structures for the purposes of ocean fertilization; activities that are most closely related to dumping. Protocol Parties are not permitted to place any matter in the marine environment for ocean fertilization purposes unless the activity constitutes legitimate scientific research, accords with the detailed Assessment Framework set out in Annex 5 of the Protocol, and is authorized under a permit.[120] As of 2019, however, only five States have ratified the 2013 amendment to the 1996 Protocol (Estonia, Finland, the Netherlands, Norway and the United Kingdom). Therefore, globally, ocean fertilization activities are for practical purposes governed by the more generally applicable rules of the dumping regime, the principles on the prevention of pollution and harm to the marine environment as set out in Part XII of LOSC, and the general principles of international environmental law including precaution, the no harm principle (and due diligence), and process obligations such as environmental impact assessment.[121]

Of less direct relevance to ocean acidification is the regulation of sub-seabed CO_2 sequestration under the Protocol.[122] In order to mitigate any

118 Resolution LP.4(8) *on the Amendment to the London Protocol to Regulate the Placement of Matter for Ocean Fertilization and Other Marine Geoengineering Activities* (adopted on 18 October 2013). This followed the more general declaration in 2008 that ocean fertilization fell within the jurisdiction of the Protocol. See Resolution LP.1 *on the Regulation of Ocean Fertilization* (31 October 2008).

119 *London Protocol*, Art. 1(5)*bis* (amendment not yet in force) defines geoengineering as 'a deliberate intervention in the marine environment to manipulate natural processes, including to counteract anthropogenic climate change and/ or its impacts, and that has the potential to result in deleterious effects, especially where those effects may be widespread, long lasting or severe'.

120 *London Protocol*, Art. 6*bis* and Annex 4 (amendment not yet in force).

121 See K. N. Scott, 'International law in the Anthropocene: responding to the geoengineering challenge' (2013) 34 *Michigan Journal of International Law*, 309–358, 333–350.

122 The disposal or sequestration of CO_2 in sub-seabed geological formations is now expressly permitted following an amendment to the 1996 Protocol in 2006. See 1996 London Protocol, Annex I, paras. 1.8 and 4 as inserted by Resolution LP.1(1) (2006) *on the Amendment to Include*

risks of contamination, the Protocol requires Parties to comply with a detailed risk assessment and management framework when undertaking sub-seabed disposal activities, and must actively consider the nature of the disposal site, processes associated with disposal and potential impacts on biodiversity and habitats when carrying out an environmental impact assessment prior to disposal.[123] The Protocol was further amended in 2009 so as to permit the export of CO_2 within streams for disposal provided that an agreement or an arrangement has been entered into by the countries concerned confirming and allocating permitting responsibilities between the States in accordance with the Protocol.[124] Direct disposal of CO_2 in the water column, which would have implications for ocean pH is not permitted under the Protocol. In theory, sub-seabed CO_2 sequestration should not contribute to ocean acidification provided the CO_2 remains contained.

5.3.2.4 An Independent Obligation to Prevent, Control and Mitigate Ocean Acidification?

The common theme – or constraint – to have emerged from the previous analysis is that whilst all States are subject to a general, mandatory obligation to 'prevent, reduce and control pollution of the marine environment' from atmospheric, land-based and other sources, that obligation appears to have little substance in the absence of associated external globally binding standards. In the context of ocean acidification, there are either no globally binding standards (in the case of land-based pollution), or those standards are not particularly well suited to ocean acidification (as in the case of atmospheric pollution). The question, therefore, arises whether States can be required to take action to address ocean acidification beyond their commitments under the climate regime in order to meet their obligations under Part XII of LOSC,

CO_2 Sequestration in Sub-seabed Geological Formations in Annex 1 to the London Protocol (in force 20 February 2007).

123 See the *Risk Assessment and Management Framework for CO_2 Sequestration in Sub-seabed Geological Structures* (CS-SSGS), adopted at the 28th Consultative Meeting of Contracting Parties under the London Convention and the 1st Meeting of Contracting Parties under the London Protocol (30 October–3 November 2006), LC/SG-CO2 1/7, annex 3. Additional guidelines were adopted in 2012, see 2012 *Specific Guidelines for the Assessment of Carbon Dioxide for Disposal into Sub-seabed Geological Formations* (adopted 2 November 2012), LC 34/15, annex 8.

124 London Protocol, Art. 6(2) as inserted by Resolution LP.3(4) *on the Amendment to Article 6 of the London Protocol* (adopted on 30 October 2009) (amendment not yet in force). See D. Langlet, 'Exporting CO_2 for sub-seabed storage: the non-effective amendment to the London Dumping Protocol and its implications' (2015) 30 *International Journal of Marine and Coastal Law*, 395–417.

in particular, under Articles 192 and 194 of the Convention. There is little doubt that there is no general obligation to refrain from all activities likely to cause ocean acidification, and any obligation under Part XII of LOSC is one of due diligence.[125] The issue is, therefore, whether this due diligence obligation has been met where States comply with their Kyoto/Paris commitments, or whether compliance with UNFCCC regime obligations is insufficient to discharge their LOSC obligations.

On the one hand, it might be argued that the UNFCCC regime provides the *lex specialis* in respect of atmospheric pollution, and it would be unreasonable to expect States to go beyond their climate commitments, particularly when LOSC provides no additional guidance or standards on what would be required to comply with due diligence in this context.[126] On the other hand, if it is demonstrated that UNFCCC commitments are clearly insufficient to 'prevent, reduce and control' pollution leading to ocean acidification, it would seem anachronistic to argue that compliance with those standards constitutes 'due diligence' in this context. As discussed earlier, although the UNFCCC regime is increasing its focus on oceans issues, ocean acidification remains largely overlooked, in contrast to climate change. The UNFCCC regime does not provide specific targets in respect of CO_2 emissions and does not set a pH stabilization goal. It is up to individual States to determine how they are going to contribute to limiting global temperature rise to 2/1.5°C, and while any action taken may also, incidentally, mitigate ocean acidification (where, for example, the action is aimed at reducing CO_2 emissions), it is entirely possible that States are able to comply with their obligations under the UNFCCC without addressing ocean acidification. Therefore, it is argued here that the due diligence obligation under LOSC to 'prevent control and reduce' pollution of the marine environment caused by ocean acidification is not met by merely meeting UNFCCC commitments, except where those commitments also expressly relate to ocean acidification. This conclusion would appear to be supported by SDG 14.3 and other non-binding resolutions and decisions, that call upon States to take specific action in respect of ocean acidification distinct from and beyond their obligations under the UNFCCC regime, implicitly recognizing that UNFCCC obligations do not adequately address ocean acidification. These goals and targets, albeit expressed in non-binding

125 *Responsibilities and Obligations of States with Respect to Activities in the Area* (Order of 18 May 2010) [2010] ITLOS Rep. 10, 39, paras. 115–223.

126 See A. Boyle, 'Climate change, ocean governance and UNCLOS' in J. Barrett and R. Barnes (eds.), *Law of the Sea: UNCLOS as a Living Treaty* (BIICL, 2016), 211–231, 222. See also A. Boyle, this volume, Chapter 4.

form, also arguably inform the content of the due diligence obligation under LOSC to address ocean acidification.

5.3.2.5 Considering Ocean Acidification in the Context of Area Conservation and Fisheries Management

The final mechanism through which the law of the sea may contribute to addressing ocean acidification is the incorporation of ocean acidification into decision-making associated with integrated and marine spatial planning, environmental impact assessment, fisheries management and area protection at the state and regional level. The integration of ocean acidification into these planning and decision-making processes may lead to measures designed to reduce or mitigate ocean acidification (such as managing land runoff), or to measures intended to enhance the resilience of species or ecosystems so that they are able to more robustly withstand the impacts of a changing ocean pH. To date, however, climate change is only slowly being recognized as a factor to be considered in marine and fisheries decision-making, and ocean acidification has barely registered on the agenda of policymakers. For example, in the North East Atlantic, the OSPAR Commission merely encourages Parties to gather baseline data on pH levels for monitoring purposes.[127] Similarly, the 2013 Kiruna Declaration of the Eighth Ministerial Meeting of the Arctic Council also focuses on monitoring and assessment. In the Baltic Sea region, Recommendation 35/1 (2014), which sets out targets and the regulatory framework for establishing a system of MPAs, expressly refers to ocean acidification, but its impacts are not fully integrated into ocean planning processes.[128] It is beyond the scope of this chapter to provide a detailed overview of such measures,[129] but one or two examples relating to fisheries management and the designation of marine protected areas (MPAs) will be drawn on here to illustrate the potential of integrating ocean acidification considerations into decision-making and management processes, and the challenges in doing so.

First, in fisheries management, the impact of ocean acidification on target stocks and indeed the wider ecosystem is a relevant factor for decision-makers

127 OSPAR Commission, *JAMP Guidelines for Monitoring Chemical Aspects of Ocean Acidification*, HASEC 14/14/1, Annex 6 (2014). See also OSPAR Commission and ICES, *Final Report to OSPAR of the Joint OSPAR/ ICES Ocean Acidification Study Group* (SGOA) (2014).

128 HELCOM Recommendation 35/1, *System of Coastal and Marine Baltic Sea Protected Areas (HELCOM MPAs)* (2014).

129 But see K. N. Scott, 'Integrated oceans management and climate change' in J. McDonald, J. McGee and R. Barnes, (eds.), *Research Handbook on Climate Change, Oceans and Coasts* (Edward Elgar, *forthcoming* 2020).

setting catch limits or adopting conservation measures.[130] To date, regional fisheries management organizations (RFMOs) have paid little attention to ocean acidification, and climate change more generally is in the early stages of being actively considered as part of decision-making. One example of a more robust approach, however, was adopted by the Commission for the Conservation of Antarctic Marine Living Resources (CCAMLR), which expressly recognized the threat posed by ocean acidification in 2009, and urged the Commission to consider the impacts of both climate change *and* ocean acidification in its decision-making.[131] In 2015 an Intersessional Correspondence Group (ICG) was established in order to develop approaches to integrate the consideration of climate change impacts into the work of the Commission, with the particular task of making recommendations as to how the Commission can use information relating to climate change in its decision-making under Article II of the Convention, and how the Commission can consider climate change impacts across its agenda.[132] However, at the 2018 CCAMLR Meeting, the ICG proposal to adopt a Climate Change Response Work Program (CCRWP) to further these goals[133] failed to gain consensus, with two States expressing concerns that it duplicated work in other forums.[134] Moreover, a separate initiative developed by Australia, Norway and the United Kingdom, which proposed a mechanism to communicate the nature and implications of known and potential climate change impacts in papers submitted to the Commission and Scientific Committee,[135] was also rejected by the two same States.[136] A number of members nevertheless committed to including climate impact statements in papers on a voluntary basis.[137] Given that CCAMLR characterizes itself as a conservation-focused rather than traditional RFMO, and that ocean acidification is known to have a disproportionate impact at the Poles, the challenges evident in creating meaningful policy within CCAMLR do not bode well for the integration of ocean acidification consideration into fisheries management more generally.

130 See further E. J. Molenaar, this volume, Chapter 11.

131 Commission for The Conservation of Antarctic Marine Living Resources (CCAMLR), Resolution 30/XXVIII, *Climate Change* (2009).

132 CCAMLR, *Report of the Thirty-fourth Meeting of the Commission*, CCAMLR-XXXIV (Hobart, Australia, 19–30 October 2015) para. 7.12.

133 CCAMLR, *Report of the Thirty-seventh Meeting of the Commission*, CCAMLR-XXXVII (Hobart, Australia, 22 October–2 November 2018) paras. 8.7–8.10.

134 Ibid., para. 8.11.

135 Ibid., paras. 8.1–8.6.

136 Ibid., para. 8.3.

137 Ibid., para. 8.5.

The second area where ocean acidification should be considered as part of planning processes is in the context of area-based protection.[138] Designating MPAs may constitute a useful tool in protecting ecosystems vulnerable to ocean acidification, such as coral reefs, by minimizing other threats, including fishing, extraction activities and tourism. The Great Barrier Reef Park is a high profile example of an MPA adapted through re-zoning in order to respond to ecosystem changes caused by climate change.[139] Just as importantly, MPAs may be established as climate change refugia; areas where change is likely to be gradual or where the pristine nature of the ecosystem makes them particularly resilient to change and the MPA supports the maintenance of that pristine ecosystem.[140] It is, however, important to acknowledge the limitations of using MPAs as a tool to try to address ocean acidification. The most significant limitation is the deployment of a static place-based measure within a dynamic three-dimensional environment where ocean acidification is likely to change the nature of the ecosystem. Understanding variability in dispersal and connectivity is a key component of MPA network planning,[141] and MPAs need to be part of a network to spread risk[142] and of sufficient scale to protect ecosystem function.[143] The challenges in responding to this criteria have been recently demonstrated by experience gained through designating MPAs in the North East Atlantic, where it was found that area-based measures 'are by and large, not focused on areas where species and habitats are expected to be sharply impacted by' climate change and ocean acidification, and where there is low overlap between hotspots of change and current and planned MPAs.[144]

138 For further discussion of this issue, see I. U. Jakobsen, this volume, Chapter 10.

139 See Great Barrier Reef Marine Park Authority, *Great Barrier Reef Climate Change Adaptation Strategy and Action Plan (2012–2017)* (2012).

140 B. J. Harvey et al., 'Ecosystem-based management of coral reefs under climate change' (2018) 8 *Ecology and* Evolution, 6354–6368, 6361.

141 M. A. Coleman et al., 'Anticipating changes to future connectivity within a network of marine protected areas' (2017) 23 *Global Change Biology*, 3533–3542, 3534. See also M. H. Carr et al., 'The central importance of ecological spatial connectivity to effective coastal marine protected areas and to meeting the challenges of climate change in the marine environment' (2017) 27 *Aquatic Conservation Marine Freshwater Ecosystems*, 6–29; and J. Monzón, L. Moyer-Horner and M. Baron Palamar, 'Climate change and species range dynamics in protected areas' (2011) 61 *BioScience*, 752–761.

142 B. D. Keller et al., 'Climate change, coral reef ecosystems, and management options for marine protected areas' (2009) 44 *Environmental Management*, 1069–1088, 1070.

143 E. McLeod et al., 'Designing marine protected area networks to address the impacts of climate change' (2009) 7 *Frontiers in Ecology and the Environment*, 362–370, 363 and 365.

144 A. M. Queirós et al., 'Solutions for ecosystem-level protection of ocean systems under climate change' (2016) 22 *Global Change Biology*, 3927–3936, 3932.

5.4 CONCLUDING OBSERVATIONS: CONSTRAINTS AND OPPORTUNITIES

Ocean acidification has traditionally played a 'Cinderella' role compared to climate change more generally, and has been described as being relegated to little more than a 'footnote'[145] within the UNFCCC regime until recently. This has created a significant structural constraint impeding an effective response in that neither the climate nor the law of the sea regimes directly address ocean acidification, or indeed provide a clear set of tools to do so. Ironically, the framework arrangement of LOSC, which in other contexts relies successfully on the incorporation of external standards and the application of those standards to LOSC Parties, arguably operates as an impediment or constraint in relation to ocean acidification. On the assumption that the UNFCCC regime and commitments made under the Kyoto Protocol and Paris Agreement, respectively, represent 'international standards' for the purposes of Article 212 of LOSC, Convention Parties could argue that compliance with their commitments under these instruments constitutes compliance with their obligations to address pollution under LOSC. While attempts have been made within multiple fora to bridge the climate – oceans regimes, and to adopt targets associated with ocean acidification, all are non-binding and ultimately, there is little evidence that they are able to create obligations separate from and additional to commitments under the UNFCCC regime. Ultimately, although the 2015 Paris Agreement has established an overarching goal limiting temperature rise, there is no comparable goal under the Agreement or under any other binding instrument limiting pH change.

On the other hand, the law of the sea is a dynamic body of law and LOSC, in particular, is a living instrument, which has been described as able to 'grow and adapt to changing circumstances'.[146] The evolution of Part XII of LOSC from a set of obligations focused on pollution to a modern conception of marine conservation that expands on those obligations to include precaution, environmental impact assessment and area-based protection as well, demonstrates the vitality of the Convention.[147] Consequently, it is argued here that

[145] J. Ekstrom and B. Crona, 'Institutional misfit and environmental change: a systems approach to address ocean acidification' (2017) 576 *Science of the Total Environment*, 599–608.

[146] *Request for an Advisory Opinion Submitted by the Sub-Regional Fisheries Commission (SRFC)* (Advisory Opinion of 2 April 2015) [2015] ITLOS Rep 4, Separate Opinion, Judge Lucky, para. 18.

[147] See further J. Barrett and R. Barnes (eds.), *Law of the Sea: UNCLOS as a Living Treaty* (BIICL, 2016); D. Moeckli and N. D. White, 'Treaties as "Living Instruments"' in M. J. Bowman and D. Kritsiotis (eds.), *Conceptual and Contextual Perspectives on the Modern Law of Treaties* (Cambridge University Press, 2018), 136–171.

the law of the sea should be interpreted and adapted to address ocean acidification irrespective of developments (or a lack thereof) under the UNFCCC. Returning to the argument made earlier,[148] Parties to LOSC are subject to a due diligence obligation to take all measures to prevent, reduce and control pollution from any source[149] and, in particular, from or through the atmosphere,[150] and to protect and preserve rare or fragile ecosystems such as coral reefs.[151] The UNFCCC provides no *lex specialis* in respect of CO_2 emissions limits or a pH change target, and it is acknowledged that even full compliance with the 2015 Paris Agreement is unlikely to prevent or reduce ocean acidification. It is consequently disingenuous to argue that action under the Paris Agreement, in the absence of any specific consideration of the causes and impacts of ocean acidification, would constitute a due diligence approach a State Party's obligations under Part XII of LOSC.

Identifying the next steps, which logically follow from this conclusion, is, however, not straight forward. Although LOSC provides for a conference of the Parties,[152] this does not traditionally deal with substantive matters and, in contrast to the UNFCCC, COP cannot create obligations for the States Party to the Convention or adopt resolutions interpreting individual provisions. Amendment is in theory possible[153] but, in practice, unfeasible. A range of processes have been created in order to develop in practical terms the law of the sea, and to provide a forum for discussion and debate, but these do not in of themselves have a mandate to create binding obligations or even soft recommendations. Even UN Oceans, which is an interagency collaboration mechanism on ocean and coastal issues within the UN system, and which has taken on a policy leadership role in relation to oceans and climate, including organizing a number of joint events with the UNFCCC, has no mandate to developing binding rules.

One option is the adoption of a UN General Assembly resolution, which actually sets out a target for a reduction in CO_2 emissions and/or a global pH change limit (which may or may not be feasible from a scientific perspective). However, a General Assembly resolution is not binding – although it may be persuasive, as the example of bottom trawling and driftnet fishing demonstrate – and the General Assembly may be reluctant to engage in an area perceived to be under the jurisdiction of the UNFCCC. An alternative is the

148 See Section 5.3.2.4.
149 LOSC, Art. 194(1).
150 LOSC, Art. 212(1).
151 LOSC, Art.194(5).
152 LOSC, Art. 319(2).
153 LOSC, Arts. 312 and 313.

negotiation of an instrument or 'agreement' pursuant to LOSC on ocean acidification, or more sensibly, ocean acidification and climate change, but this is similarly unrealistic given that global negotiations for an agreement on biodiversity beyond national jurisdictions were initiated in 2018, and it is unlikely that States will have the appetite to initiative a set of parallel negotiations.

Ultimately, the most pragmatic and, in many ways coherent, way forward is the development of binding targets and measures under the UNFCCC regime, in conjunction with relevant maritime organizations such as UN Oceans, to be applied consistently by Parties subject to obligations under both regimes. Meanwhile, if States are to comply with their due diligence obligation to prevent, reduce and control pollution arising from ocean acidification under Part XII of LOSC, they need to take action that targets ocean acidification in addition to or at least as part of their measures designed to address climate change. The 2015 Paris Agreement already provides a mechanism for the development of such measures, under the NDC process, whereby States themselves determine national actions that will contribute to achieving the overall aims of the Agreement. In addition, reducing ocean acidification comprises the target of a series of soft law instruments such as SDG 14.3, and these instruments were described earlier as performing an interstitial role, linking the regimes of application to the climate and the oceans. It might be argued that individual state action on ocean acidification, in pursuit of these soft law goals as well as States' due diligence obligation under Part XII of LOSC, can perform a similar interstitial role, linking and connecting the UNFCCC and LOSC in matters of climate change and ocean acidification.

6

Regulating Greenhouse Gases from Ships

Some Light at the End of the Funnel?

Henrik Ringbom

6.1 INTRODUCTION

Developing standards for reducing greenhouse gas (GHG) emissions from ships involves various challenges of a technical, regulatory and political nature. The main role of the 1982 UN Convention on the Law of the Sea (LOSC)[1] here, as with the prevention of pollution from ships more generally, is to ensure that a uniform set of standards applies across the globe. *What* those standards should be is up to other institutions to decide: the LOSC does not specify which institution(s) should be in charge, or even whether there is an obligation for any institution to act in this field.[2] However, pressure from multiple directions has been mounting on the international maritime community to achieve significant reductions in GHG emissions from shipping. The perspective taken in this chapter is mainly an institutional one, focusing on the inter-relatedness and interaction between different legal regimes in a matter which still struggles to find its regulatory format. Despite the appeals in the LOSC for global solutions to regulate shipping, the prospect of regional rules still looms in the background as a legal alternative. However, recent developments have increasingly shifted the focus to the division of responsibilities between certain key global institutions involved in the regulation of GHGs and their mutual roles and responsibilities.

GHG emissions from shipping consist almost exclusively of CO_2 emissions linked to fuel combustion. International maritime transport accounts for some

1 United Nations Convention on Law of The Sea, Montego Bay, 10 December 1982, in force 16 November 1994, 1833 UNTS 397.

2 But see the discussion on the relationship between climate change and the general environmental obligations laid down in LOSC Part XII in A. Boyle, this volume, Chapter 4.

2–3 per cent of total anthropogenic GHG emissions worldwide, and is growing faster than the global average.[3] To achieve an equal contribution to other sectors in achieving the climate goals (50 per cent probability of attaining the 2°C limit to global temperature rise), shipping emissions must be reduced by 50 per cent from 2012 levels by 2050 and reach zero emissions by 2080.[4] However, even dramatic improvements in fuel efficiency in ships would not achieve overall reductions in the cumulative emissions from ships. Due to estimated increases in world trade, total emissions are projected to rise by 50–250 per cent by 2050.[5]

For more than two decades, the reduction of GHGs from shipping has been on the agenda of the main international regulatory body for shipping, the International Maritime Organization (IMO), but few requirements have been agreed to date. Discussions have been marked by a persistent divide within the organization as to what international body should be in charge of the matter and what principles should govern the regulation.

Certain developments in recent years give rise to some cautious optimism concerning the establishment an adequate governance framework for shipping and GHGs in the coming decades. The adoption of the Paris Agreement in 2015,[6] combined with developments at the IMO, offer prospects of smoother institutional interaction and convergence on several divisive issues. On the other hand, the urgency of achieving concrete reductions has become increasingly obvious, and the question is still open as to whether recent policy commitments will – or even can – be translated into binding emissions reductions from the shipping sector.

[3] See, e.g., the International Maritime Organization (IMO), *Third IMO GHG Study* (2014), that estimated international shipping emissions in 2012 to be 796 million tonnes, or about 2.2 per cent of global total anthropogenic CO_2 emissions. The report is available in IMO Doc. MEPC 67/INF.3 and at https://gmn.imo.org/wp-content/uploads/2017/05/GHG3-Executive-Summary-and-Report_web.pdf. A summary is available in IMO Doc. MEPC 67/6, Annex. An earlier IMO study from 2009 had estimated the percentage to be around 2.7, see IMO, *Second IMO GHG Study* (2009), available at www.imo.org/en/OurWork/Environment/PollutionPrevention/AirPollution/Documents/SecondIMOGHGStudy2009.pdf. See also B. Martinez Romera, 'The Paris Agreement and the regulation of international bunker fuels' (2016) 25(2) *Review of European Community & International Environmental Law*, 215–227, at 215–216, with further references.

[4] See J. Scott et al., 'The promise and limits of private standards in reducing greenhouse gas emissions from shipping' (2017) 29 *Journal of Environmental Law*, 231–262, 234.

[5] Ibid.

[6] Paris Agreement, UN Doc. FCCC/CP/2015/L.9, Annex (12 December 2015).

6.2 THE COMPETENT FORUM AND APPLICABLE PRINCIPLES

6.2.1 *LOSC and the Global Setting*

Unlike the case of several other topics addressed in this book, the law of the sea does not dominate discussions on reducing GHGs from shipping. The LOSC offers considerable flexibility for different types of regulatory solutions for existing and future challenges relating to shipping, for environmental or other purposes. The main significance of the LOSC when it comes to regulating shipping lies in its distribution of authority between flag and coastal states, and between states and international institutions.[7] Typically, for shipping, rules are to be adopted by a 'competent international organization' or 'general diplomatic conference', and will normally gain jurisdictional weight only once they are 'generally accepted' or 'generally applicable' on a worldwide basis. As long as the rules and standards are adopted by the IMO or another competent global body, and meet the requirements of general acceptance,[8] they will form part of the set of rules which flag states must require of their ships, irrespective of the sea area, and which coastal states may implement and enforce with respect to foreign ships, subject to certain safeguards.[9] The actual content of the requirements matters less, as far as jurisdiction is concerned.

If the rules do *not* meet these criteria – if they have been agreed solely at national or regional level – only those (flag) states that have formally endorsed the rules will be bound by them. The jurisdiction of coastal states will essentially be limited to prescribing standards for their territorial sea which do not concern the construction, design equipment or manning of ships;[10] and

[7] See, e.g., D. R. Rothwell and T. Stephens, *The International Law of the Sea*, 2nd edn. (Hart, 2016) at 228–244 and 376–386.

[8] See, e.g., the Final Report of the International Law Association's Committee on Coastal State Jurisdiction relating to Marine Pollution over Vessel-Source Pollution (2000), available at www.ila-hq.org/en/committees/index.cfm/cid/12. In practice, the achievement of 'general acceptance' is eased by the fact that the key IMO conventions, including the International Convention on the Prevention of Pollution from Ships (MARPOL), London, 2 November 1973, 1340 UNTS 184, are very widely ratified today and include the 'tacit acceptance' procedure (in Article 16), under which an amendment becomes applicable to all parties to the MARPOL, unless they specifically opt out from the amendment. See also J. Harrison, 'Recent developments and continuing challenges in the regulation of greenhouse gas emissions from international shipping' in A. Chircop, S. Coffen-Smout and M. McConnell (eds.), 27 (2013) *Ocean Yearbook*, 359–84, also available at https://papers.ssrn.com/sol3/papers.cfm?abstract_id=2037038.

[9] In particular LOSC Articles 21, 94 and 211 and, as regards safeguards, Articles 223–233. See also Y. Tanaka, 'Regulation of greenhouse gas emissions from international shipping and jurisdiction of states' (2016) 25(3) *Review of European Community & International Environmental Law*, 333–346.

[10] LOSC, Articles 21(2), 211(5).

port state jurisdiction will have to be based on jurisdiction under general international law, outside the jurisdictional regime outlined in the LOSC.[11] Clearly, the coverage and impact of such rules would be significantly lower than with widely accepted global rules. Moreover, any non-global initiatives in this area are bound to lead to serious political and legal controversies which will complicate their adoption and reduce their legitimacy.

6.2.2 *The Competent Global Forum*

Since the first discussions on climate change in the early 1990s there has been uncertainty as to which global body (and treaty regime) should govern GHG emissions from shipping. While it is well established that emissions from *domestic* shipping form part of a state's national emissions and are subject to national inventories, reports and reduction commitments under the United Nations Framework Convention on Climate Change (UNFCCC),[12] the regulatory position of *international* shipping has been subject to controversy from the outset,[13] and is still not fully clarified.

The question of forum has important substantive implications because of the question of what principles should underlie the regulation. The climate change regime and IMO have emphasized very different principles for how the responsibility for addressing climate change should be allocated between states. Whereas the climate change regime from the outset adopted the 'common but differentiated responsibility' (CBDR) approach, signifying greater responsibility for developed states,[14] international shipping has

[11] H. Ringbom, 'Global problem – regional solution? International law reflections on an EU CO_2 emissions trading scheme for ships' (2011) 26 *The International Journal for Marine and Coastal Law*, 613–641.

[12] See Articles 4(1)(a) and 12 of the UN Framework Convention on Climate Change (UNFCCC), Rio de Janeiro, 9 June 1992, 1771 UNTS 107 and Article 7 of the Kyoto Protocol to the UNFCCC (Kyoto Protocol), Kyoto, 11 December 1997, 2303 UNTS 162, referring to 'anthropogenic emissions by sources ... of greenhouse gases not controlled by the Montreal Protocol'. See also IPCC, *Revised 1996 IPCC Guidelines for National Greenhouse Gas Inventories* (1996).

[13] Among the early documents, see, e.g., UN Doc. A/AC.237/34 (15 July 1993) *Note by the Secretariat: Matters Relating to Commitments, Methodologies for Calculation/Inventories of Emissions and Removals of Greenhouse Gases*. See also Decision 2/CP.3, UN Doc. FCCC/CP/1997/7/Add.1 (25 March 1998), para. 4, in which the UNFCCC Subsidiary Body for Scientific and Technological Advice (SBSTA) was 'urged to further elaborate on' the inclusion of emissions from international maritime transport and aviation in the overall GHG inventories of the parties.

[14] Article 3(1) of the UNFCCC provides that the parties 'should protect the climate system for the benefit of present and future generations of humankind, on the basis of equity and in accordance with their common but differentiated responsibilities and respective capabilities.

traditionally been based on the principle of equal treatment and non-discrimination on the basis of nationality.[15]

6.2.3 *UNFCCC*

The ultimate goal of the UNFCCC is, in its own words, to 'achieve ... stabilization of greenhouse gas concentrations in the atmosphere at a level that would prevent dangerous anthropogenic interference with the climate system'.[16] According to the principles listed in Article 3, climate policies should 'comprise all economic sectors'; specific reference to efforts to reduce emissions from transport is made in Article 4(1)(c). These provisions represent the legal foundation for the activities of the UN climate regime in the field of international shipping.

The UNFCCC started to address GHG emissions from ships in 1995 in recognition of the growing volume of such emissions and their impact on climate change. At the first meeting of the Conference of the Parties, the UNFCCC Subsidiary Body for Scientific and Technological Advice (SBSTA) was tasked with considering how to deal with international emissions from shipping and aviation. It mooted eight options for the allocation of shipping's emissions to states, but there was no agreement with respect to any of these options.[17]

6.2.4 *The Kyoto Protocol*

In view of the difficulties linked to allocating responsibility for internationally mobile emissions, international shipping and aviation emissions were explicitly excluded from the Kyoto Protocol in 1997. Article 2(2) of the Protocol called for Annex I states to

Accordingly, the developed country Parties should take the lead in combating climate change and the adverse effects thereof'.

15 For example, MARPOL Article 5(4). See also Article 1(c) of the 1948 Convention on the International Maritime Organization, Geneva, 6 March 1948, 289 UNTS 3, and the general non-discrimination clause in LOSC Article 227.

16 UNFCCC, Article 2.

17 The eight options were (1) no allocation; (2) allocation to parties in proportion with their national emissions; (3) allocation based on where the bunker fuels were sold; (4) based on the nationality of the transporting company or the ship's state of registry; (5) based on the country of departure or destination of the ship; (6) based on the state of departure or destination of the cargo or passengers; (7) based on the country that owns the cargo or nationality of passengers; or (8) based on where the emission is generated. See UN Docs. FCCC/CP/1995/7/Add.1 (6 June 1995), at p. 16; and UNFCCC/SBSTA/1996/9/Add.2 (26 June 1996).

> pursue limitation or reduction of emissions of greenhouse gases not controlled by the Montreal Protocol from aviation and marine bunker fuels, working through the International Civil Aviation Organization and the International Maritime Organization, respectively.

This solution was the outcome of lengthy deliberations on how best to cover international bunker fuels.[18] It came to represent a way 'to lessen the need for the climate regime to be proactive in the controversial policy issues surrounding allocation and control options'.[19]

The full policy implications of this provision have been subject to controversy over the years;[20] here we may note that it neither grants the IMO exclusive authority to regulate emissions from shipping (in the sense that it would preclude action by other institutions to engage in this matter) nor imposes an obligation of result on the IMO to arrive at reduction measures.

The clause may have met the political needs within the climate regime at the time, but it did not have much effect in terms of reducing emissions from shipping. The IMO started discussing the matter seriously immediately following the adoption of the Kyoto Protocol in 1997. However, as noted in Section 6.4, it was not until 2011 that the first (and so far only) regulatory measures were adopted.

The main issue of contention has been whether the formula in Article 2(2) of the Kyoto Protocol limits the options available to the IMO. Given that this Article is addressed to Annex 1 states only, the question arises as to whether any regulatory solution by the IMO should also be based on a differentiation between Annex 1 and non-Annex 1 countries, or whether the reference includes no such restrictions.[21] It also seems clear that, in the absence of a hierarchical relationship between the two institutions, and indeed the absence of hierarchy in international law more generally, IMO's mandate to act in the field derives not from the Kyoto Protocol,

18 See S. Oberthür, 'Institutional interaction to address greenhouse gas emissions from international transport: ICAO, IMO and the Kyoto Protocol' (2003) 3(3) *Climate Policy*, 191–205; and Centre for International Governance Innovation, A. Chircop, M. Doelle and R. Gauvin, Special Report, *Shipping and Climate Change: International Law and Policy Considerations* (2018) (hereinafter CIGI Report), 11.

19 F. Yamin and J. Depledge, *The International Climate Change Regime: A Guide to Rules, Institutions and Procedures* (Cambridge University Press, 2004), 85.

20 See, e.g., S. Kopela, 'Climate change, regime interaction, and the principle of common but differentiated responsibility: the experience of the International Maritime Organization' (2014) 24(1) *Yearbook of International Environmental Law*, 70–101, 75–77.

21 The general legal view, including that taken by the IMO Legal Affairs Division, is that measures may be taken with respect to all states without contravening the Kyoto Protocol. See Kopela, 'Climate change', 73–78, and Harrison, 'Recent developments'.

but from its own constituent instrument and other conventions and rules adopted by its membership.[22]

However, the IMO has pointed out that the specific reference to the organization in the Kyoto Protocol shows that the climate change regime acknowledges the competence of the UN specialized agencies as the natural forum for negotiating sector-specific GHG emission reductions, given their expertise and experience in regulating other environmental matters, including air emissions.[23]

Just how the CBDR principle could apply in international shipping in practice is not obvious. If requirements followed ships' flag states, their effectiveness would be reduced by the ease by which ship operators can choose their flag state, side-stepping their obligations by a simple change of flag. Some three quarters of the world's tonnage is registered outside the (developed) countries listed in Annex I of the UNFCCC,[24] and that share would probably increase significantly if a future regime covered only ships flying the flag of Annex I states. Differentiating on the basis of the ship's nationality (flag) is therefore not a practical option for regulating shipping, while linking reduction obligations to other states based on the place of destination or true ownership is fraught with other, more practical difficulties – for example, as regards rule evasion and the challenges of gathering reliable data. However, that differentiation between developed and developing states might be done in other forms – perhaps by allocating potential revenues to developing countries for financing mitigation and adaptation measures, or through 'rebate mechanisms', or through technical assistance.

6.2.5 *The Paris Agreement*

Given the lack of regulatory progress at the IMO, and the increasing efforts aimed at reaching agreement on a successor to the Kyoto Protocol, the idea of including international bunker fuels within the climate regime resurfaced in 2007 and remained contentious in the international climate discussions for

22 See, e.g., Article 1(a) and 15(j) of the Convention on the International Maritime Organization. Resolution A.963(23) (4 March 2004), which entrusted the IMO to work with GHG emissions in 2003, established a series of other relevant provisions in IMO instruments and the LOSC, providing a mandate for the IMO to act in this field.

23 See, e.g., IMO's web page on the historic background on air pollution from ships, at www.imo.org/en/OurWork/Environment/PollutionPrevention/AirPollution/Pages/Historic-Background-.aspx.

24 For example, MEPC 60/WP.5 (22 March 2010). See also Kopela, 'Climate change', 93.

many years.[25] The matter remained uncertain until the very end of the negotiations of the Paris Agreement. Draft texts had occasionally included provisions on shipping, notably the 90-page negotiation text from February 2015, which included a reference to the need for 'global sectoral emission reduction targets' for international aviation and shipping and to the need for all parties to work through the IMO (and the International Civil Aviation Organization, ICAO) to develop global policy frameworks for achieving such targets.[26]

These options were maintained in subsequent negotiation texts, but were eventually deleted from the drafts presented at COP 21 in Paris.[27] Some less controversial texts, on the parties' need to pursue the limitation or reduction of emissions by international bunker fuels at IMO and ICAO, resurfaced during the negotiations in Paris and were retained in the draft text as late as three days before the closure of the COP meeting, but also these were eventually removed.[28]

Thus, the Paris Agreement includes no reference to the obligation of the shipping sector to contribute to the goals of the Agreement, or to any particular responsibilities of the IMO in this respect. The omission of such references was essentially due to the policy of eliminating provisions in the draft that were highly contentious and divisive but not essential for the Agreement as a whole.[29]

It has been held that the failure to include a specific reference to shipping and aviation represents a 'missed opportunity', and that including it would have resolved a long-standing problem for the climate regime, while also enhancing equity in the scheme and in the use of potential revenues from international bunker fuels.[30] On the other hand, shipping remains linked to

25 Including international bunker fuels within the climate regime featured as one aspect of the Bali Action Plan, Decision 1/CP.13, UN Doc. FCCC/CP/2007/6/Add.1 (14 March 2008). In the end, however, the question of international bunker fuels was the only item in the Action Plan that was closed without a decision text or follow-up process, nor was there a conclusion in the subsequent negotiations on this topic leading up to the Doha meeting in 2012, Decision 1/CP.18, UN Doc. UNFCCC/CP/2012/8/Add.1 (28 February 2013). For more, see Martinez Romera, 'The Paris Agreement', 217.

26 UN Doc. FCCC/ADP/2015/1 (25 February 2015), para. 40. The same text included as one option that the two sectoral organizations could adopt a levy scheme to provide financial support for the Adaptation Fund and, in doing so, 'to take into consideration the needs of developing countries, particularly the LDCs, SIDS' (para. 116.5).

27 See Martinez Romera, 'The Paris Agreement', 219–220, with further references.

28 UNFCCC *Draft Paris Outcome*, Proposal by the President, 9 December 2015, 15:00, available at http://unfccc.int/resource/docs/2015/cop21/eng/da01.pdf.

29 Martinez Romera, 'The Paris Agreement', 220.

30 Ibid., 219.

the climate regime, through Article 4(1) of the UNFCCC, and could be taken up in the SBSTA or another forum.

Experience with the Kyoto Protocol model shows that a formulation that explicitly delegates such a task to the IMO is no guarantee for regulatory results or even clarity about the governing principles.[31] The solution adopted in the Paris Agreement – no mention of shipping at all – will probably serve the interests of future climate regulation of maritime transport better than a Kyoto Protocol-type exclusion clause. It maintains effective pressure on the IMO to act, without emplacing specific targets as to the outcome.[32] Accordingly, neither including nor excluding shipping emissions in the global climate framework represents a convenient compromise which may prove significant in the future, in particular if trust in the IMO's capabilities for addressing the matter were to erode.

More importantly, the approach taken in the Paris Agreement includes several elements likely to influence discussions on shipping in the longer term. Here we may note: the establishment of global climate stabilization goals, rather than prescriptive emissions reduction requirements;[33] the bottom-up approach under which countries will determine their own contributions on an individual and successive basis; and the softening of the CBDR principle to include all states in mitigation efforts.[34] These elements offer a clear target, and clarify that no state or group of states is exempt from making emissions reductions; at the same time, there is flexibility for tailor-made solutions to deal with specific issues. All these elements are likely to ease the tensions that have troubled negotiations at the IMO over the past decades.

31 The Kyoto Protocol and its sharp division between developed and developing states has been held to be at the root of IMO's problems in finding a regulatory solution: see, e.g., A. Chrystostomou and E. Vagslid, 'Climate change: a challenge for IMO too' in R. Asariotis and H. Benemara (eds.), *Maritime Transport and the Climate Change Challenge* (Earthscan, 2012), 81. See also Kopela, 'Climate change', 75–111, 89–94.

32 The solution has also been interpreted by Martinez Romera, 'The Paris Agreement', 225–226 as legitimizing unilateral action by states or regions as the sole effective means, while Scott et al., 'The promise and limits', 255, note industry concerns that not specifically tasking the IMO to address the matter might increase the risk of regional regulatory action in the field.

33 The Paris Agreement identifies a target of global temperature increase above pre-industrial levels of 'well below 2°C', with the aim of limiting the increase to 1.5°C.

34 Paris Agreement, 3rd recital, Article 2(2) and several paragraphs of Article 4. See also L. Rajamani, 'Ambition and differentiation in the 2015 Paris Agreement: interpretative possibilities and underlying politics' (2016) 65 *International Journal of Comparative Law Quarterly*, 493–514; D. Bodansky, 'The Paris Climate Change Agreement: a new hope?' (2016) 110(2) *American Journal of International Law*, 288–319, notes 60–62.

6.3 REGULATORY DEVELOPMENTS AT THE IMO

6.3.1 *Introduction*

GHGs have been discussed more or less continuously in the IMO ever since the late 1990s, but with greater intensity and focus on reduction requirements in the past decade.[35] Some technical rules for newly built ships were adopted in 2011, coupled with operational measures of a voluntary nature. Market-based measures were discussed in the same period, but proved so difficult that the discussions were suspended in May 2013. A new policy framework for the future was agreed in 2018 in the form of an 'initial strategy', to be complemented by a more developed strategy in 2023.[36] In addition, a data collection scheme intended to form the basis of any future regulatory measure has been approved, but not yet put into operation.[37] These measures are briefly reviewed further.

6.3.2 *The EEDI*

The first requirement aimed at reducing CO_2 emissions from shipping concerned the design of ships.[38] It introduced minimum standards of energy efficiency for new ships, in the form of an index – the attained Energy Efficiency Design Index (EEDI) – which is based on the amount of fuel (and CO_2 emissions) that the ship burns (and emits), at a given reference speed taken at 75 per cent of the Maximum Continuous Rating (MCR) of its main propulsion power under maximum cargo/loading capacity.[39] The required EEDI sets a minimum energy-efficiency level per capacity mile (tonne mile) for different ship types and size segments. The requirement for energy efficiency performance is to be made more stringent every five years, so that ships will gradually become more energy efficient. Under the scheme, ships built in

35 For an overview, see CIGI Report, 36–48.

36 See IMO Resolution MEPC.304(72) (13 April 2018), *Initial IMO Strategy on Reduction of GHG Emissions from Ships*.

37 Additionally, the IMO has commissioned three comprehensive studies on the extent of GHG emissions from shipping, including projections for the future, in 2000, 2012 and 2014. These studies represent the main scientific basis for action in the field, and represent state-of-the art science on the matter. The 2014 study, *Third IMO GHG Study*, is currently being updated.

38 IMO Resolution MEPC.203(62) (15 July 2011), introducing a new chapter 4 to MARPOL Annex VI, which entered into force on 1 January 2013.

39 MARPOL, Annex VI, chapter 4, regulations 19–21. See also the 2014 *Guidelines on the Method of Calculation of the Attained Energy Efficiency Design Index* (EEDI) for new ships, IMO Doc. MEPC 66/21 (25 April 2014), Annex 5.

2025 will be 30 per cent more energy efficient than those built in 2014. The reduction factors and reference line values which form the basis of the energy efficiency requirements are also to be reviewed subject to technical developments.[40]

The technical requirements introduced by the EEDI are entirely goal-based in the sense that they leave the technical decisions on how to achieve the necessary reductions to ship designers. The EEDI value could be reduced either by reducing engine power, fuel consumption or the carbon factor of fuel, or by increasing the deadweight or speed of the ship (without affecting fuel consumption). The principal technical options available today include slimmer hull design, lightweight construction materials, more efficient engines, alternative fuels or complementary energy sources, such as solar or wind power (e.g. serving auxiliary and backup systems).

The rule applies to all ships, of the covered twelve ship types ordered or having undergone major conversions as from 2017.[41] Each ship shall carry a certificate indicating its EEDI value,[42] to be issued by its flag state and checked by port-state control, irrespectively of flag.[43] A series of supplementary guidelines have been adopted to assist in the calculation of the index values and reference lines, and for implementing the scheme more generally.[44]

In view of the scope of the requirement it is clear that the EEDI can have only a limited impact on reducing emissions from ships in the short term. Since the measure covers only new ships (or major conversions), a significant time lag for its impact on global emissions is inevitable. As ships normally have a commercial life of some thirty years, it will take several decades before all ships have been built to EEDI standards. In addition, the reference lines have

[40] The EEDI originally covered only the largest and most energy-intensive segments of the world merchant fleet: tankers, bulk carriers, gas carriers, general cargo ships, container ships, refrigerated cargo carriers and combination carriers. In 2014, Marpol Annex VI was amended to extend the scope of EEDI to LNG carriers, ro-ro cargo ships (vehicle carriers), ro-ro cargo ships; ro-ro passenger ships and cruise passenger ships having non-conventional propulsion.

[41] In 2011 seven ship types were included (bulk carriers, gas carriers, tankers, container ships, general cargo ships, refrigerated cargo ships and combination carriers), which were thought to cover 70 per cent of the total shipping emissions. In 2014, five new ship types were added (LNG carriers, vehicle carriers, ro-ro cargo ships, ro-ro passenger ships and cruise passenger ships with non-conventional propulsion systems), bringing the percentage up to an estimated 85 per cent. However, the regime applies only to new ships and to ships above 400 gross tonnage.

[42] MARPOL, Annex VI, Regulation 19. See also 2014 *guidelines on survey and certification of EEDI*, Resolution MEPC.254(67) as amended by IMO resolution MEPC.309(73).

[43] MARPOL, Annex VI, Regulation 10(5).

[44] See IMO's web page on energy efficiency measures, at www.imo.org/en/OurWork/Environment/PollutionPrevention/AirPollution/Pages/Technical-and-Operational-Measures.aspx.

been set quite conservatively, so many existing ships will satisfy the EEDI requirements for several decades to come. The implication for certain categories of ships is that, unless the requirements are further strengthened, even ships ordered in the coming decade can be designed according to today's energy-efficiency practices.[45] However, for certain ship types, the requirements concerning implementation dates were strengthened in May 2019.[46]

6.3.3 *The SEEMP*

Reducing fuel consumption (and CO_2 emissions) from ships is not only – or even mainly – a function of how ships are designed. The ways in which they are operated entail significant reduction potentials. It has been estimated that a single operational measure based on slow steaming may reduce bunker consumption by up to 59 per cent.[47] Other mechanisms for achieving better energy efficiency include improved voyage planning, more frequent cleaning of the hulls (underwater parts of the ship), ship/fleet energy management policies, planned engine maintenance, etc. It has been estimated that, by combining various operational measures and using only existing technologies, GHG emissions from shipping could be reduced up to 75 per cent.[48] Such measures would also provide benefits in the form of fuel savings.

In order to include the operation of ships, including existing ships, in the regulatory framework, the IMO developed in parallel with the EEDI an obligation for all ships to have a ship energy efficiency management plan (SEEMP) on board.[49] Through the SEEMP, the shipowner, operator or charterer, is to aim at improving that ship's energy efficiency through planning, monitoring, implementation and improvement. The IMO also proposed that an energy efficiency operational indicator (EEOI) could be used as a monitoring tool to measure improvements over time.[50]

45 IMO Doc. MEPC 74/WP.8 (16 May 2019), *Report of the Working Group on Air Pollution and Energy Efficiency*, para. 39 and Annex 9.

46 IMO Doc. MEPC 74/18, *Final Report*. The amendment brings forward the entry-into-force date of phase 3 to 2022 (from 2025), for several ship types, and tightens the requirements by up to 50 per cent for large container vessels.

47 A. Wiesmann, 'Slow steaming: a viable long-term option?' (2010) *Wärtsilä Technical Journal*, 49–55, 50. See also CIGI Report, 59. However, some estimates fail to note that in such cases more ships would be needed to perform the work.

48 *Second IMO GHG study*, 54 and 58.

49 MARPOL, Annex VI, Regulation 22.

50 The EEOI is a simple calculating tool that indicates the ratio between CO_2 emissions and transport work (cargo carried × distance). See also IMO Doc. MEPC.1/Circ. 684 (17 August 2009).

However, in terms of normative impact, the SEEMP is of limited value. While the SEEMP urges ship operators at each stage of the plan to consider new technologies and practices when seeking to optimize the performance, it does not require any specific type of reduction or even monitoring method to be used. Simply having a management plan on board is sufficient to meet Marpol requirements.[51]

6.3.4 *Market-Based Measures*

It is widely acknowledged that existing measures are far from sufficient to meet the climate goals set by the IMO. Indeed, a study commissioned by the IMO in 2010 indicated that, because of the projected growth in trade, GHG emissions from international shipping would increase, even with the implementation of the EEDI and the SEEMP.[52] The third main group of measures discussed at the IMO concerns market-based measures (MBMs), that is, economic incentives for ship operators to reduce their bunker fuel consumption.[53] The proposed measures range from various forms of 'levies' or 'carbon taxes' on bunker fuel to efficiency-credit trading programs and fully fledged 'cap and trade' emission trading schemes where emissions rights can be sold and purchased on the market.

MBMs were originally put forward as an option in the first IMO GHG Study from 2000 and have been discussed since 2003, in greater depth from 2006.[54] In contrast to the (partial) progress made on technical and operational measures, MBMs have proven very difficult. IMO members have been deeply divided on whether and how to include such measures, and whether, in that

51 MARPOL, Annex VI, Regulations 22(2), requires only that the management plan 'shall be developed taking into account guidelines adopted by the [IMO]'. This refers in particular to the 2016 *Guidelines for the Development of a Ship Energy Efficiency Management Plan* (SEEMP), IMO Resolution MEPC.282(70) (28 October 2016).

52 *Full Report of the Work Undertaken by the Expert Group on Feasibility Study and Impact Assessment of Possible Market-Based Measures*, IMO Doc. MEPC 61/INF.2 (31 October 2011). See also Y. Shi, 'Reducing greenhouse gas emissions from international shipping: is it time to consider market-based measures?' (2016) 64 *Marine Policy*, 123–134.

53 The Organisation for Economic Co-operation and Development (OECD) defines market-based measures more narrowly, by stating that they 'seek to address the market failure of "environmental externalities" either by incorporating the external cost of production or consumption activities through taxes or charges on processes or products, or by creating property rights and facilitating the establishment of a proxy market for the use of environmental services'. See stats.oecd.org/glossary/detail.asp?ID=7214. See also H. N. Psaraftis, 'Market-based measures for greenhouse gas emissions from ships: a review' (2012) 11(2) *World Maritime University Journal of Maritime Affairs*, 211–232.

54 IMO's web page on market-based measures, www.imo.org/en/OurWork/Environment/PollutionPrevention/AirPollution/Pages/Market-Based-Measures.aspx.

case, this should be a system for the shipping sector alone or might be made applicable in other sectors as well; and on whether and how the system should accommodate the CBDR principle.

Seven main types of MBMs have been proposed to date. These are a GHG Fund;[55] a port state levy;[56] an 'Efficiency Incentive Scheme';[57] a 'Ship Efficiency and Credit Trading' scheme;[58] a global emissions trading system;[59] a system based on penalties on trade and development;[60] and a rebate mechanism for market-based instruments.[61] Following the conclusion of the energy-efficiency measures in 2011, IMO decided in 2012 to discuss these seven groups with a view to narrowing down a more limited range of options. However, the topic proved so divisive that it was decided to suspend discussions in 2013,[62] and they have not yet resumed. MBMs are not expected to be adopted in the short term, due mainly to concerns regarding possible extra costs for the shipping industry.[63]

6.3.5 *Mandatory Data Collection System*

In 2016, the global data collection system for maritime transport was adopted to address the absence of reliable ship emissions data and to facilitate the development of further regulatory measures.[64] Starting from 2020, the IMO data collection system requires all ships above 5,000 gross tonnage to collect consumption data for each type of fuel oil they use, as well as additional, specified, data including proxies for transport work. These data are reported by owners to the flag state on a yearly basis. Flag states issue a 'Statement of Compliance' to the ships that have been reported in accordance with the

55 IMO Doc. MEPC 60/4/8 (19 December 2009) (Cyprus, Denmark, the Marshall Islands, Nigeria and IPTA).

56 IMO Doc. MEPC 60/4/40 (15 January 2010) (Jamaica).

57 IMO Doc. MEPC 60/4/39 (15 January 2010) (World Shipping Council).

58 IMO Doc. MEPC 60/4/12 (14 January 2010) (United States).

59 IMO Docs (15 January 2010) MEPC 60/4/22 (Norway), MEPC 60/4/26 (UK) and MEPC 60/4/41 (France).

60 IMO Doc. MEPC 60/4/10 (13 January 2010) (Bahamas).

61 IMO Doc. MEPC 60/4/55 (29 January 2010) (IUCN).

62 IMO Doc. MEPC 65/22 (24 May 2013), 44.

63 See Y. Shi and W. Gullett, 'International regulation of low-carbon shipping for climate change mitigation: development, challenges and prospects' (2018) 49(2) *Ocean Development and International Law*, 134–156, 140.

64 IMO Resolution MEPC.278(70) (28 October 2016) introducing a new Regulation 22A to MARPOL Annex VI, including two new appendices. See also Resolution MEPC.293(71) (7 July 2017) and IMO Press Briefing on the amendments, available at www.imo.org/en/MediaCentre/PressBriefings/Pages/04MARPOLamendments.aspx.

requirements, and subsequently transfer the data, in aggregated form, to an IMO Ship Fuel Oil Consumption Database. The IMO then produces an annual report to its Marine Environment Protection Committee (MEPC), summarizing the data collected.

This data collection system was preceded by the adoption of a regional EU Regulation on 'monitoring, reporting and verification' (MRV) in 2015. As discussed in Section 6.4.4, there are certain differences between the systems and it seems likely, despite ongoing efforts to align them, that some differences will persist.

6.3.6 *2018 IMO Initial Strategy*

Following the adoption of the Paris Agreement in 2015, the IMO came under significant pressure to demonstrate its capacity to deal efficiently with emissions from shipping. In 2016 it adopted a roadmap for developing a 'Comprehensive IMO strategy on reduction of GHG emissions from ships';[65] an 'initial strategy' was adopted in 2018,[66] to be replaced by a comprehensive strategy in 2023. Even if it is not a binding instrument, the strategy sets certain important goals for the organization in dealing with GHGs from ships, while also suggesting a common approach to some of the previously contentious issues.

Under the overarching vision of the initial strategy, 'IMO remains committed to reducing GHG emissions from international shipping and, as a matter of urgency, aims to phase them out as soon as possible in this century'.[67] The strategy envisages a reduction in carbon intensity of international shipping (to reduce CO_2 emissions per transport work, as an average across international shipping), by at least 40 per cent by 2030, pursuing efforts towards 70 per cent by 2050, compared to 2008, and that total annual GHG emissions from international shipping should be reduced by at least 50 per cent by 2050 compared to 2008. Significantly, it is also acknowledged that the Paris Agreement temperature goals form part of the levels of ambition that direct the strategy[68] and that both non-discrimination and the CBDR principles represent guiding principles for the strategy.[69]

The initial strategy also includes a list of candidate short-, mid-, and long-term further measures, with possible timelines, to be revised as appropriate as

65 IMO Doc. MEPC 70/18/Add.1 (28 October 2016), Annex 11. See also IMO Doc. MEPC 70/7/8 (19 August 2016).
66 Rothwell and Stephens, *The International Law of the Sea*.
67 *Initial IMO Strategy*, para 2.
68 Ibid., para. 3.1.3.
69 Ibid., para. 3.2.1.

additional information becomes available. The short-term measures (to be agreed between 2018 and 2023) include further improvement of the EEDI and SEEMP tools for improving energy efficiency, along with a series of measures to stimulate the adoption of innovatory technologies. Five mid-term measures (2023–2030) are listed, one of which is 'new/innovative emission reduction mechanism(s), possibly including Market-based Measures (MBMs), to incentivize GHG emission reduction'.[70]

While reaching consensus on these goals and principles is highly significant in light of the earlier divisions in IMO, the initial strategy is still very far from producing any emission reductions from shipping. The document is an expression of objectives, not actions, in a legally non-committing format, and includes no concrete actions in the form of reduction measures to be undertaken. In reality, existing technologies may not be sufficient to achieve the longer-term reduction goals.[71] Moreover, even if the reduction goals expressed in the initial strategy were achieved, that would not be sufficient to meet the climate goals of the Paris Agreement, let alone those of the latest report of the Intergovernmental Panel on Climate Change (IPCC).[72] Finally, it may be noted that some less-transparent accounting techniques built into the strategy reduce its actual level of ambition.[73]

6.3.7 *Assessment*

The regulation of GHGs from shipping is the most politically divisive matter ever discussed at the IMO. The division on fundamental principles has deadlocked progress for more than a decade, and has contributed to casting

70 Ibid., para. 4.8.3. The only candidate longer-term measures (beyond 2030) listed in para. 4.9 are to 'pursue the development and provision of zero-carbon or fossil-free fuels to enable the shipping sector to assess and consider decarbonization in the second half of the century' and to 'encourage and facilitate the general adoption of other possible new/innovative emission reduction mechanism(s)'.

71 See, e.g., Transport & Environment, Position Paper, *Initial IMO GHG strategy* (2018), available at www.transportenvironment.org/sites/te/files/publications/2018_03_TE_position_paper_IMO_Initial_GHG_strategy.pdf, at 4.

72 According to para. 3.1 of the Initial IMO Strategy, reviews should take into account updated emissions estimates and the reports of IPCC. On the availability of technology, see, e.g., Transport & Environment, *Initial IMO GHG strategy*, at 1–4, and International Workshop on Greenhouse Gas Emissions and Shipping, Singapore, *Workshop Report* (13–14 November 2018) (Singapore Report), available at https://cil.nus.edu.sg/wp-content/uploads/2019/01/Greenhouse-Gas-Emissions-and-Shipping-Workshop-Report.pdf, paras. 16, 72.

73 Notably, the year selected as the reference year for the reduction requirements, 2008, was by far the peak year for shipping CO_2 emissions to date; it was lower in the following years, due to the general downturn in world trade. See Third IMO GHG Study, and CIGI Report, 47.

doubt on the organization's ability to deal with the matter at all. Even if shipping is generally thought to involve greater opportunities for cutting emissions through technical and operational measures than, for example, aviation,[74] there are as yet no requirements which concern the operation of ships or otherwise target shipowners beyond the ship design stage.

That the IMO has had difficulties in agreeing on further measures is due to several reasons. Apart from the technical and scientific complexities surrounding GHGs and climate change, the fact that the concerns involved extend beyond shipping has entailed a series of additional challenges for the organization.

First, uncertainty about the share of shipping in the global problem, and hence what would constitute a 'fair' mechanism for addressing it, given the fact that shipping is largely a function of global trade, has contributed to a certain reluctance to adopt far-reaching rules in the field. Fears have repeatedly been expressed that shipping will be a funding source, or 'milch cow', for financing climate-mitigation measures in other sectors.

Second, deliberations at the IMO have clearly been affected by politically delicate discussions underway in parallel in other UN bodies on climate change, notably the UNFCCC. Linking the available shipping solutions to a broader political agenda, e.g. on the role and relevance of the CBDR principle more generally, has fragmented the debate and impaired affected the prospects of finding consensus-based solutions. An exacerbating factor is that some of the principles that have governed negotiations in the UNFCCC are manifestly difficult to apply in shipping.

Finally, some of the IMO's own traditions and procedures have proven difficult in dealing with a matter fraught with so many uncertainties. For example, the IMO tradition has been that a new regulation should not be introduced unless there is a 'compelling need' for it, and having regard to its cost implications.[75] Another tradition is not to extend new technical rules to existing ships, but to include a 'grandfather clause' limiting the application of new rules to future ships, to avoid retrofitting needs and the accompanying uncertainty for ship operators.

74 See, e.g., Martinez Romera, 'The Paris Agreement', 216, and CIGI Report, 57.

75 The principle that applied for decades, that 'proposals for new conventions or amendments to existing conventions be entertained only on the basis of clear and well-documented compelling need and having regard to the costs to the maritime industry and the burden of the legislative and administrative resources of Member States' (IMO Resolution A.777(18) (4 November 1993), para. 4), has since been moderated through IMO Resolution A.1103(29) (26 November 2015), providing in Annex, para. 1.1 that 'before considering the introduction of new regulation, there is a need to establish, in advance, if the administrative requirement can be met by other means'.

Generally speaking, the IMO regulatory process tends to work best when it deals with challenges that can be resolved by technical means, preferably for new ships only, based on a level playing field covering all ships, by solutions to be implemented by engineers, approved by classification societies, certified by flag states and verified by port-state control. This is the typical way for IMO to approach issues in its conventions. Implementation is essentially delegated to naval architects and engineers, leaving it to shipowners, operators and states to ensure that the required equipment/certificate is in place, knowing that all other operators will be subject to identical requirements. Of the measures discussed for GHG reduction, only the EEDI fits this description, which can at least in part explain why agreeing on the EEDI has been so much easier within the IMO, despite its huge technical complexity compared to the proposed operational measures.

In the case of operational and market-based measures, this setting is different. For such measures, emission reductions necessarily entail changes in the way ships are operated, or at least a higher price tag for maintaining the status quo. They also imply a wide range of methods to ensure compliance, forcing ship operators individually to find the mechanism that fits their particular needs. This in turn requires more effort on the part of ship operators, and increases the costs as well as the prospect of different solutions – all of which are effects that the IMO has traditionally sought to avoid in its regulations.

Operational and market-based measures, or any combination of them, have no precedents in existing IMO Conventions, and will necessarily involve several difficult regulatory challenges. In shifting the focus from technology to operations, for example, it becomes necessary to establish the responsible party, the scope of the measure and how to avoid various jurisdictional concerns linked to implementing operational rules that need to be specified in geographical terms. Such a shift also involves important challenges in terms of monitoring and enforcement mechanisms. Furthermore, some of the measures discussed will require establishing new institutions, principles governing the use of funds, or legal challenges in relation to international taxation.

All such challenges are surmountable, and the IMO certainly seems better placed than any other (global or regional) body to deal with them. A key concern, however, remains: bar a massive switch to nuclear fuel in shipping (which seems unlikely for various reasons),[76] none of the technologies or fuels

[76] In addition to high investment and operating costs, there are technical concerns with nuclear propulsion of commercial ships. See, e.g., S. Hirdaris et al., 'Considerations on the potential use of Nuclear Small Modular Reactor (SMR) technology for merchant marine propulsion' (2014) 79 *Ocean Engineering*, 101–130, who conclude that further maturity of nuclear technology and the development and harmonization of the regulatory framework are necessary. That

that exist today, could meet the longer-term reduction goals set forth in the strategy, in view of the projected increase in maritime transport. Reducing total GHG emissions from international shipping by at least 50 per cent by 2050 'whilst pursuing efforts towards phasing them out' simply does not seem feasible without significant technological breakthroughs in the field of engines and fuels. Currently no such technologies are available for large-scale use by international shipping.[77] On the other hand, without pressure in the form of additional costs for fuel combustion, as under operational and market-based measures, there would be even fewer incentives for the industry to invest in developing such alternative technologies.

6.4 POST-PARIS PRESSURES ON THE IMO

6.4.1 *General*

Apart from the commitments undertaken by the IMO itself, the organization is under external pressure from many directions to produce tangible results in the form of concrete emissions-reduction requirements. Those pressures range from implicit or explicit policy pressures and legal challenges by other intergovernmental institutions, to commercial pressure by progressive industry parties. The key external institutional pressures are briefly reviewed further.

6.4.2 *The Global Climate Regime*

Even if the solution adopted in the Paris Agreement is widely considered to consolidate the IMO's position as the international body in charge of regulating GHG emissions from ships,[78] there has been no express pronouncement to that effect. As noted earlier, the non-hierarchical nature of international law complicates the imposition of mandates or other regulatory directions between international treaty regimes or institutions.[79] Moreover, in view of the solution adopted in the Paris Agreement not to refer to international bunker fuels at all, there is nothing to prevent the UNFCCC regime from re-engaging itself in the matter if the IMO fails to deliver what is perceived as an

said, concerns related to climate change have clearly served to increase interest in nuclear propulsion for commercial ships. See, e.g., S. Kraemer, 'Why now is the time for nuclear cargo shipping', Clean Technica, 28 January 2017, available at cleantechnica.com/2017/01/28/now-time-nuclear-cargo-shipping/.

77 See, e.g., presentation by Prof. Lam in the Singapore Report, paras. 30–36.

78 See, e.g., Martinez Romera, 'The Paris Agreement', 221, 224: the CIGI Report, 45.

79 See text at note 22.

effective scheme within reasonable time. A parallel climate regime for shipping within the UNFCCC could be developed on the basis of existing provisions, and would not require any amendment of its existing mandate.[80]

The 1992 UNFCCC, which remains the main framework convention for the regulation of climate change, has not changed and remains applicable. As noted earlier, the Convention refers to measures addressing 'all greenhouse gases not controlled by the Montreal Protocol', the contribution by 'all economic sectors', and even includes certain references to transport in some of the key provisions.[81] Moreover, even the Kyoto Protocol's express request for the IMO to pursue emissions reductions did not amount to an exclusive mandate for that organization. The absence of a similar clause in the Paris Agreement strengthens the argument that responsibility for the matter is shared – or at least not specifically apportioned – between the two regulatory regimes.

More importantly, the Paris Agreement itself includes all GHG emissions within its long-term mitigation goals. The aim is 'to strengthen the global response to the threat of climate change' by containing the increase of temperature within the limits referred to in Article 2(1)(a).[82] In order to achieve those goals, 'Parties aim to reach global peaking of greenhouse gas emissions as soon as possible . . . so as to achieve a balance between anthropogenic emissions by sources and removals by sinks of greenhouse gases in the second half of this century'.[83] It seems clear that allowing the emissions of shipping to increase by a factor of two or more until 2050[84] would jeopardize the climate goals set by the Paris Agreement, and would therefore not be consistent with the Agreement.

Nor would the reference in the LOSC to a single 'competent international organization' as regards ship-source pollution constitute a limit in this regard. The wording is commonly understood as referring to the IMO, but there is no limitation to that effect in the LOSC itself.[85] The climate change regime could

80 See also A. O'Leary and J. Brown, 'Legal bases for IMO climate change measures', Report by Environmental Defense Fund (Columbia Law School, 2018), available at columbiaclimatelaw.com/files/2018/06/OLeary-and-Brown-2018-06-IMO-Climate-Measures.pdf.

81 Section 6.2.3.

82 Paris Agreement, Article 2(1).

83 Paris Agreement, Article 4(1).

84 T. Smith et al., *CO_2 Targets, Trajectories and Trends for International Shipping* (2015), summarized at www.ucl.ac.uk/bartlett/energy/publications/2015/may/co2-targets-trajectories-and-trends-international-shipping, Table 3. See also Scott et al., 'The promise and limits', 235.

85 The use of the word 'organization' in the singular in some parts of LOSC that deal with ship-source pollution (e.g. Article 211(1) does not preclude that several organizations may be competent for different aspects of the topic (note e.g. the division of competence between the IMO and ILO on different aspects of regulation of seafarers)). Note also that the reference is frequently coupled with the phrase 'or general diplomatic conference' (e.g. Article 211(2)). This addition

very well be the organization competent for regulating GHG emissions from shipping, in view of its better understanding of the global challenge underlying the need for regulation. Nor is there anything in the LOSC to preclude sharing of competence for a given matter between two or more organizations.

In more practical terms, however, shifting the regulatory initiative to the UNFCCC would require some preparation. The only body within the climate regime that addresses international bunker fuel emissions is the SBSTA, and its involvement is currently limited to progress reporting by ICAO and IMO.[86] The mitigation tools offered by the Paris Agreement – the national pledges – are not well suited for dealing with emissions caused by international shipping; and the UNFCCC framework offers fewer opportunities for adopting amendments that apply worldwide within a few years (unlike the IMO's tacit acceptance procedure) and includes no tools for ensuring a workable monitoring and enforcement regime.

It now seems widely accepted, also within the climate change regime, that the IMO is the body best most suited for addressing GHG emissions from ships.[87] Regulatory measures, such as the EEDI, and implementation tools, such as the data collection system, have strengthened the IMO's position in this respect in the past few years, and at present the organization appears to feel little pressure from the UNFCCC.[88] The debate on the appropriate regulatory forum may be more settled than it has been for decades, but continued consensus will depend on the IMO achieving concrete emissions reductions from the shipping sector in the next few years.

6.4.3 *The Aviation Sector*

The regulatory achievements of the ICAO since the conclusion of the Paris Agreement have brought increased pressure to bear on the IMO, as aviation

was made precisely to preclude a monopoly for a single organization. See, e.g., H. B. Robertson, 'Navigation in the Exclusive Economic Zone' (1984) 24(4) *Virginia Journal of International Law*, 866–915, 899; D. Bodansky, 'Protecting the Marine Environment from Vessel-Source Pollution' (1991) 18 *Ecology Law Quarterly*, 719–777, 772. In conclusion, 'general acceptance' of a given standard seems more important than the forum in which it has been adopted. See also S. Rosenne, 'The International Maritime Organization interface with the Law of the Sea Convention' in M. Nordquist and J. Moore (eds.), *Current Maritime Issues and the International Maritime Organization* (Martinus Nijhoff, 1999), 251–268, 263; L. Sohn, 'Managing the law of the sea: Ambassador Pardo's forgotten second idea' (1997) 36 *Columbia Journal of Transnational Law*, 285–305 295; and Y. Shi, 'Are greenhouse gas emissions from international shipping a type of marine pollution?' (2016) 113 *Marine Pollution Bulletin*, 187–192.

86 Martinez Romera, 'The Paris Agreement', 224.

87 Ibid., 221.

88 Singapore Report, para. 47.

and shipping have been deemed similarly situated as regards the nature and magnitude of emissions,[89] growth scenarios, international dimension, problems in accommodating state-based solutions and in differentiating among various categories of states. The two industries, with their respective organizations, have traditionally been treated in parallel in the international climate negotiations.

While aviation, generally speaking, has greater difficulties than shipping in achieving emissions reductions by technical or operational measures,[90] there has been some with respect to market-based measures. In 2016, the ICAO Assembly adopted a resolution on establishing the 'Carbon Offsetting and Reduction Scheme for International Aviation' (CORSIA).[91] Participation in the pilot phase (2021–2023) and the first phase (2024–2026) is voluntary,[92] but the second phase (2027–2035) will be mandatory for all states, based on certain economic parameters which permit differentiation on the basis of the economic capabilities of states to contribute.[93]

CORSIA is route-based and thereby treats all airlines on the same routes in the same way. It covers only routes between two participating countries. Operators are to estimate their CO_2 emissions for these voyages and report to their countries. Until 2030 the required offsets will be calculated on the basis of the growth factor for the whole industry, rather than individually for each operator. The scheme will be reviewed every third year from 2022; the longer-term intention is to serve as a vehicle to assist the industry, through offsetting, to achieve the aspirational goal of carbon-neutral growth from 2020.[94]

In 2017 a supplementary measure to support CORSIA was adopted in the form of an amended Annex 16, Volume III, to the Chicago Convention on

89 While aviation's share of CO_2 emissions is usually estimated to lie at around 2 per cent, the climate impact is larger, due inter alia to the release of certain other GHGs and because most CO_2 emissions occur at high altitude, amplifying their effect. A more accurate figure for measuring climate effect, the global anthropogenic radiative forcing, has been estimated to lie at around 3.5 per cent. See CIGI Report, 57 with further references.

90 For an overview, see CIGI report, 58–59.

91 ICAO Resolution 39-3. See also Convention on International Civil Aviation, Chicago, 7 December 1944, 15 UNTS 295, Annex 16, Environmental Protection, International Standards and Recommended Practices, Vol. IV, Carbon Offsetting and Reduction Scheme for International Aviation, 1st edn, 27 June 2018, effective on 22 October 2018.

92 Despite the voluntary nature of the system, states have shown great interesting in participating. By 6 May 2019, eighty states, representing 76.63 per cent of international aviation activity, had opted to participate. See www.icao.int/environmental-protection/CORSIA/Pages/state-pairs.aspx.

93 The parameters are linked to the size and share of the country's revenue by tonne kilometre; certain categories of developing countries are specifically excluded.

94 ICAO Resolution 39-3, para. 4.

Civil Aviation. The new rules impose new CO_2 standards for new aircraft, as from 2020, depending on the type and size of the aircraft.[95] Aircraft that do not meet these standards are to be phased out by 2028.

The environmental effects of CORSIA remain to be seen. The scheme will enter its pilot phase in 2021, but individual reduction obligations – the only true incentive for air operators to reduce their emissions – will apply only from 2030. Nevertheless, it is already clear that establishing CORSIA has contributed to a convergence of regimes governing international and national emissions, and that many arguments about the impossibility of finding solutions for international bunker fuels have weakened along the way. This clearly increases pressure on the IMO to prepare regulatory measures, notably in the field of MBMs.

6.4.4 *Unilateral Regional Action (the EU)*

In addition to the global pressures on the IMO, its work on GHGs has from the outset been marked by tensions with the EU regarding format and pace. The EU has taken a very broad interest in climate policy more generally, with limited sympathy for the special needs of shipping. The absence of emissions reduction rules for shipping has repeatedly been indicated as a concern for the EU, more recently coupled with the observation that shipping is the only sector *not* expressly addressed by an EU emissions reduction objective or specific mitigation measures.[96] Warnings have been voiced that specific EU rules may be introduced in this area, if satisfactory global rules cannot be established at the IMO.[97]

Yet, at least at policy level, the starting point for the EU has always been that it will act in the field of GHG and shipping only if global regulation fails.[98] What the EU expects from the global regime in terms of reduction standards has not been specified; and earlier deadlines for when global measures must be in place to satisfy the EU have been postponed. Both aspects serve to undermine the threat element of the EU's position. Most recently, the EU has agreed to postpone its threat of unilateral action, to allow the IMO time to make concrete its initial strategy.[99] The current EU deadline for IMO

95 For details, see www.icao.int/Newsroom/Pages/ICAO-Council-adopts-new-CO2-emissions-standard-for-aircraft.aspx.

96 See, e.g., Proposal COM(2019) 38 final, amending Regulation 2015/757, 1.

97 See, e.g., third recital of Directive 2009/29 amending Directive 2003/87/EC.

98 See, e.g., the European Commission's strategy as reflected in COM(2013) 479 final.

99 Recital No 4 of Directive 2018/410, amending Directive 2003/87, reads: 'The adoption of an ambitious emission reduction objective as part of this initial strategy has become a matter of urgency and is important for ensuring that international shipping contributes its fair share to

measures that 'duly contribute' to achieving the climate goals of the Paris Agreement is accordingly set to 2023.[100]

Regarding substance, the current EU climate strategy for shipping is based on three steps:[101]

(1) monitoring, reporting and verification of CO_2 emissions;
(2) GHG reduction targets for the shipping sector; and
(3) further measures, including MBMs in the medium to long term.

The first step has already resulted in EU regulation: the MRV Regulation was adopted in 2015.[102] The EU Regulation and the IMO's global data collection system are largely similar regarding data to be included in the report, but there are significant differences between the two systems, notably in relation to the scope (global/regional reach, coverage of port emissions), the calculation of cargo carried, transparency of data, and the process for verifying data submitted by shipowners.[103] Where the IMO data collection system places the responsibility for monitoring and reporting on the flag state, the EU system is based on independent verification of the data by accredited third parties and on port-state jurisdiction in the sense that it covers only those ships which call at a port of the EU.[104]

An EU proposal to align the two systems has been presented by the European Commission,[105] but even if approved in the proposed form, it would not amount to full harmonization between the regional and global

the efforts needed to achieve the objective of well below 2 °C agreed under the Paris Agreement. The Commission should keep this under regular review, and should report at least once a year to the European Parliament and to the Council on the progress achieved in the IMO towards an ambitious emission reduction objective, and on accompanying measures to ensure that the sector duly contributes to the efforts needed to achieve the objectives agreed under the Paris Agreement. Action from the IMO or the Union should start from 2023, including preparatory work on adoption and implementation and due consideration being given by all stakeholders.'

100 See previous note.

101 COM(2013) 479 final.

102 EU Regulation 2017/757. In preambular para. 34 it is considered that the EU MRV system also should serve as a model for the implementation of a global system. See also Delegated Regulation 2016/2071 (amendment of Regulation), Delegated Regulation 2016/2072 (on verification and accreditation activities) and Implementing Regulations 2016/1972 (on templates) and 2016/1928 (on the definition of cargo carried for certain ship categories).

103 See, e.g., J. Dufour, 'EU MRV vs. IMO fuel consumption data collection system', Verifavia Shipping, 2 December 2016, available at www.verifavia-shipping.com/shipping-carbon-emissions-verification/press-media-eu-mrv-vs-imo-fuel-consumption-data-collection-system-155.php; COM(2019) 38 final.

104 EU Regulation 2017/757, Article 2(1).

105 In COM(2019) 38 final it is proposed, inter alia, to harmonize the use of certain key definitions to ensure that same entities are in charge of monitoring and reporting obligations

regimes.[106] It is thus unlikely that all differences will be removed even once an alignment measure has been adopted by the EU. The more probable outcome of a forthcoming alignment is therefore largely harmonized reporting procedure – but, apart from that, the parallel regimes look set to continue.

As to the second step, the strategy sets no specific reduction targets for shipping at EU level. The strategy discusses global reduction targets set by the UNFCCC and general targets set by the EU, but mentions no specific targets for shipping. Indeed, it is pointed out that shipping is the only industry sector and transport mode which is not covered by legislation to contribute to the EU general CO_2 reduction targets.[107]

The main focus of the EU strategy is accordingly on reduction measures (third step). As measures linked to strengthening the requirements linked to the EEDI and SEEMP need to be taken at the IMO, there is no regional alternative available, even if the IMO should fail to deliver such measures by 2023.[108] By contrast, as regards MBMs, the EU has been quite open about its readiness to implement such a scheme on a regional level, if necessary. The EU strategy highlights both a compensation fund and an ETS as potential MBMs for shipping; but, given the inclusion of aviation in the regional ETS,[109] it is not far-fetched to assume that a preferred option for the European Commission would be to include shipping in an ETS. Whether

under the two regimes. Alignment is also made relating to the calculation of distance and cargo, as well as the reporting period and the minimum requirements for monitoring plans. Alignment between the EU and (a future) IMO reporting schemes was already foreseen in Article 22 of the MRV Regulation (Regulation 2015/757).

106 Under the Commission's proposal, the MRV system will be revised in order for the EU to take '*appropriate account*' of the IMO's global data collection system 'with a view to allow for streamlining and reducing administrative effort for companies and administrations as possible [*sic*], while preserving the objectives of the EU MRV Regulation'. See COM (2019) 38 final, 2.

107 COM(2013) 479 final, 7.

108 Among the other measures listed in para. 4.7 of the IMO initial strategy, new operational measures on the basis of new indicators have found support at the EU level. For an example, see IMO Doc. MEPC 66/4/6.

109 The ETS Directive (2003/87) was amended by Directive 2008/101 to include aviation within the scope of the EU ETS as from 2012. However, due to strong protests from third countries, it was decided to postpone application of this amendment for flights between the EU and third countries. Intra-EU flights thus remain included in the ETS, but inclusion of flights to and from third countries will depend on progress made at the ICAO, notably with CORSIA. See, e.g., the European Commisions web page on reducing emissions from aviation, at ec.europa.eu/clima/policies/transport/aviation_en. The application of EU rules to non-EU countries raised legal concerns, too, but in Case C-366/10, *Air Transport Association of America, American Airlines Inc., Continental Airlines Inc., United Airlines Inc.* v. *Secretary of State for Energy and Climate Change* [2011], the Court of Justice of the European Union considered that the extension did not amount to a breach of international law. See, e.g., S. Bogojevic, 'Legalising environmental leadership: a comment on the CJEU's ruling in

that also means that a global ETS is the preferred option for the EU for a global market-based measure is not clear, however.

The EU can be criticized for not indicating more precisely what it wants the IMO to achieve or providing any guidance on what it considers to be sufficient as an output. The approach provides great flexibility for the EU to decide on its actions in the future, but is not a very helpful stance from the perspective of the international maritime community. It gives the impression that the EU wants to place pressure on the IMO without being certain about what the consequences of failure would be – which in itself serves to reduce part of that pressure.

That said, the EU has certainly been a significant driver in this field at global level to date and a power behind many of the actions of the IMO. The EU has been more vocal than any other source of pressure and has played a major role in advancing the global data collection system at IMO. In addition, the EU and the European Maritime Safety Agency undertake a significant amount of behind-the-scenes work to support, for example, fact-finding and capacity-building measures and by supplying data to member states and others, contributing to studies, developing methodologies, and so on.[110]

6.4.5 *Assessment*

The previous review indicates that the challenge facing the IMO – to turn its initial strategy into concrete regulatory tools and reductions – is under significant pressure from several directions. From an IMO perspective the GHG file involves an unusually broad range of international institutions and other players with an interest in designing a future regulatory regime. It also involves a wider than usual set of governance mechanisms applied to bring about the change.

The three institutions discussed earlier exercise different kinds of pressures on the IMO. Most effective among them is probably the UNFCCC regime. Action through the global climate regime and the Paris Agreement framework can provide a real alternative to the IMO if the regulatory efforts there should come to a halt. The necessary mandate to take action is already in place; from an institutional point of view would be nothing extraordinary in the global climate change institution taking the lead here, rather than the global

C-366/10 on the inclusion of aviation in the EU Emissions Trading Scheme' (2012) 24(2) *Journal of Environmental Law*, 345–356.

110 See, e.g., 'EC funding gives green light to ambitious IMO energy-efficiency project', Press Release by IMO of 12 January 2016, available at www.imo.org/en/MediaCentre/PressBriefings/Pages/01-2016-MTCC-.aspx.

shipping institution. While it is true that decades of relative inaction in the field within UNFCCC has reduced its chances of claiming exclusive authority over the file, its action could be more specified by covering only certain aspects. UNFCCC could, for example, be entrusted with setting the regulatory goals for international shipping, for example, in the form of a sectoral reduction target, leaving the modalities of achieving the target to the IMO.[111]

Involving the UNFCCC regime in regulation of shipping would place the focus on the climate change perspective, bringing the environmental aspects to the forefront. Inconveniences caused to the shipping industry or the practicalities of trade would probably receive less attention. While not ideal from a shipping perspective, this option represents a real safety valve available if negotiations at the IMO should lose momentum or ambition. Given the nature and urgency of the climate change challenge, no organization should be entrusted with a mandate that could be (ab)used for postponing meaningful measures. An institutional fallback regime with its specific point of departure in environmental demands and the relationship to commitments undertaken by other industries is a valuable mechanism for complementing the primary mandate of the IMO and for exercising some healthy pressure on it to proceed with the urgency entailed in the nature of the challenge. It is also the only one of the regulatory institutions discussed here for which support may be found in LOSC.[112]

The EU has gradually lost some of its potential to exercise such pressure. The very explicit threat of regional action in the field has no doubt served as a trigger for several achievements of the IMO, and that pressure has not disappeared. However, the adoption of the Paris Agreement has opened the door for other mechanisms for handling stalemates at IMO. In addition, the EU's unclear policy positions (including its inability to specify the conditions on which acceptance of global measures would be based), combined with repeated postponements of the critical cut-off dates in question, has reduced the credibility of the EU to serve as the key challenger to the IMO in this matter.

In addition come several legal considerations which weaken the case for regional action in a field so global as climate change and shipping. That the LOSC fails to specify a role for regional organizations for regulating shipping does not mean that the EU is toothless in jurisdictional terms, as port-state

111 See also, in this sense, the CIGI Report, 92.

112 This support presumes that the UNFCCC is regarded as the competent international organization to address climate change for shipping, and that that its rules meet the standard of general acceptance (see Sections 6.2.1 and 6.4.2). By contrast, regional or non-governmental action has no explicit role in the LOSC provisions that address regulation of shipping.

jurisdiction offers opportunities to regulate ships of any nationality that enter EU ports. However, regional action necessarily entails more limited coverage than a global solution. Moreover, various other legal uncertainties (notably in relation to the law of the sea, general international law and, possibly, international trade law) are more likely to be raised by regional action in this field.[113] Such concerns can be reduced or eliminated if action is taken at the global level, whether by the IMO or by another global organization.

The pressure exercised by the ICAO is more psychological in nature. The most recent advancements in aviation represent a model for what can be achieved, not least with respect to MBMs. While the solutions agreed for aviation may not be suitable or even workable for shipping, given the many features that distinguish the two modes of international transport, their adoption at ICAO does dilute one of the key defences used by the IMO to postpone regulatory action, in particular relating to MBMs. Even at this early pre-implementation stage, the very presence of CORSIA illustrates that there are solutions for, inter alia, linking international transports to reduction commitments made by other sectors, and for combining the principle of non-discrimination with privileged treatment of states with greater needs. Through the mitigation measures agreed in recent years, ICAO has essentially highlighted that what is really lacking at the IMO is political willingness on the part of states to take effective regulatory measures.

However, the IMO is not particularly receptive to such pressures. It is widely, and rightly so, considered to be the body that is best placed to take effective measures to reduce GHGs from shipping. Recent developments – notably, the adoption of the data collection system – have strengthened the impression that this is the body in charge and best informed to lead discussions, and indeed the only global body that has been active in the field thus far. The broad agreement on the initial strategy has provided more time and directions for elaborating specific emissions reduction measures without interference from others.

The bigger question is whether the IMO will be capable of delivering specific measures by the key target date of 2023. The credibility of both the IMO and the EU as actors on climate change and shipping will be at stake, and neither institution can afford further postponement of effective IMO measures.

6.5 CONCLUDING OBSERVATIONS

Despite the broad range of activities, at the IMO and elsewhere, aimed at curbing GHG emissions from shipping, very little has been accomplished in

113 Ringbom, 'Global problem'.

terms of legally binding emission reductions. The only rules with some normative implications that have been adopted to date relate to ship design – but, given the threshold levels and timing of their introduction, and their applicability to new ships only, even those rules are set to remain almost without effect for many years to come.

The past few years have seen several important developments that could indicate a shift towards a better regulatory climate in the field. In particular, the adoption of the Paris Agreement and subsequent developments at the IMO have removed some of the longstanding difficulties that have beset the regulation of GHGs from international shipping. And that may give reason for optimism with respect to regulatory progress in the future.

The institutional battle has entered a period of consolidation and relative 'truce' since the adoption of the Paris Agreement in 2015 and with the unanimous approval of the initial IMO strategy. The regime currently provides for 'dynamic stability', with the IMO clearly positioned in the driving seat. The truce will not last forever, however. At the latest, it will come to an end if the IMO fails to deliver significant regulatory results by 2023.

In addition to the jurisdictional considerations flowing from the law of the sea, there are more practical arguments to favour a dominant role for the IMO in this field. It is clearly the international body with the greatest technical knowledge and experience of regulating shipping, including the challenges of workable implementation and enforcement mechanisms. The IMO is also the only body considered legitimate in the view of the targets of regulation – the ship operators.

With respect to guiding principles as well, the shift made in the Paris Agreement towards a more nuanced form of differentiation between states has paved the way for convergence between the two competing principles, so problematic for work at the IMO. There now seems to be a good basis for continuing the IMO tradition of regulating ships without differentiation to their flag in this field. The objectives of the CBDR principle remain relevant – but the principle may be expected to feature mainly in the form of allocation of revenues to developing countries for financing mitigation and adaptation measures, or through technical assistance, while playing a limited role (if any) in the design of technical, operational or market-based measures as such. This is indeed a welcome development, and a condition for an effective regulatory regime in shipping.

As to timing, the Paris Agreement and the initial strategy are based on the premise that measures and commitments should be reviewed and updated every five years, and the processes seem aligned. In the longer run, this can pave the way for a development, which would seem natural, whereby international shipping could be introduced as a separate international sector under the Paris Agreement.

Whereas the Paris Agreement is neutral as to the measures to be taken to achieve the targets, the IMO has indicated a range of potential measures to be studied in the short, mid, and long term. Given the current state of technical development, it seems inevitable that technical and operational measures will need to be complemented by market-based measures if the stated goals for shipping are to be achieved. The type of MBM remains as open a question as ever, and is not advanced in any of the instruments agreed.

The development of workable operational and market-based measures that actually serve to reduce emissions and/or produce sufficient offsets for compensating for them in other sectors will be the ultimate test of the IMO's capability to regulate GHGs. By setting itself ambitious goals, the IMO has secured another period of regulatory calm that should last at least until 2023, at which point all pressures seem poised to converge.

The main challenge is the difficulty of achieving the long-term reduction goals to which the IMO has committed itself, or the Paris climate goals, without a large-scale shift to technologies that are not yet available in shipping. Success will depend on some form of technological breakthrough, notably in the area of alternative fuels. The current mismatch between goals and technologies has made clear both the urgent need to take measures to reduce emissions by means of existing technologies and to provide financial incentives for ship operators to reduce emissions. This can be achieved only by strengthening the legal requirements in all categories of measures: technical, operational *and* market-based. MBMs include the additional advantage of generating funds which may be specifically earmarked for advancing research and development, thereby supporting the shift towards more energy-efficient technologies. This, too, appears to be a condition for meeting the longer-term climate goals set by the Paris Agreement and the IMO's initial strategy.

In terms of international law, the dynamism between the key institutions involved in regulating GHG from shipping calls into question a perception deeply rooted within the international maritime community: that the IMO enjoys some kind of legal monopoly for regulating international shipping. The LOSC provides for no such a monopoly. It highlights the importance of global, generally applicable, rules for shipping but does not identify any particular institution to be in charge of various aspects. The solution adopted in the Paris Agreement, in contrast to that in the Kyoto Protocol, highlights the continued interest and concern of the global climate regime in measures for reducing emissions from shipping. In addition, international law offers other avenues, including for regional rule-making in this field, even in the absence of an explicit mention of such jurisdiction in the LOSC.

We may reasonably conclude that the regime set out in the LOSC has helped to avoid the proliferation of national and international law-making initiatives to curb GHGs from shipping. However, pressure is now mounting on the IMO to agree and implement tangible reduction measures within the next few years. Close involvement by other global institutions, regional bodies or non-governmental actors may not be foreseen in the LOSC, but if the work of the IMO fails to meet expectations, it is only natural – and entirely consistent with the law of the sea – that they should assume a greater role in setting the standards for GHG emissions reductions from shipping.

7

Carbon Capture and Storage and the Law of the Sea

Nigel Bankes*

7.1 INTRODUCTION

Carbon capture and storage (CCS) is a recognized technology for mitigating greenhouse gas (GHG) emissions, in particular, carbon dioxide (CO_2).[1] CCS involves the capture of CO_2 at large final emitters,[2] the compression and transportation of the CO_2 to a storage destination and its injection under pressure through an oilfield-type well into the pore space of suitable geological formations, where it will remain forever.[3] The main storage targets are depleted oil and gas reservoirs and saline aquifers; the latter are much more significant in terms of volume.

This chapter examines the relationship between CCS and the law of the sea and considers the extent to which the law of the sea facilitates or poses an obstacle to the adoption of CCS activities in marine areas. Section 7.2 provides a brief discussion of CCS focusing on the disposal or storage part of the value chain, as well as the injection of CO_2 as part of enhanced oil recovery (EOR) operations (CO_2/EOR). Section 7.3 examines how CCS projects and CO_2

* I acknowledge with thanks helpful comments on an earlier draft from Karen Scott and Elise Johansen; any remaining errors are my responsibility.

1 Intergovernmental Panel on Climate Change (IPCC), *Special Report on Carbon Capture and Storage* (IPCC, *Special Report*) (2005). A particularly useful policy-oriented study is the report prepared by the International Energy Association's greenhouse gas research and development program (IEAGHG), *Interaction of CO_2 Storage with Subsurface Resources* (2013) (*IEAGHG Interaction Report*), available at http://ieaghg.org/docs/General_Docs/Reports/2013–08.pdf.

2 Such large final emitters may include power plants (coal or natural gas) and a range of industrial facilities including cement operations and a variety of hydrocarbon processing facilities.

3 R. S. Haszeldine et al., 'Negative emission technologies and carbon capture and storage to achieve the Paris Agreement commitments' (2018) 376 *Philosophical Transactions of the Royal Society* A, 1–23, 7; IPCC, *Special Report*.

/EOR projects may be regulated under the law of sea (and, in particular, the Law of the Sea Convention (LOSC[4])) while Section 7.4 examines how CCS and CO_2/EOR projects fall to be regulated under the London Dumping Convention (LC)[5] or the Protocol which succeeds the Convention (LP or London Protocol).[6] Section 7.5 deals with the treatment of such projects in regional agreements specifically the Convention for the Protection of the Marine Environment of the North-East Atlantic (OSPAR Convention).[7] Section 7.6 concludes.

None of the treaties listed earlier contemplated CCS or the possible use of CCS as a GHG mitigation measure at the time that they were adopted. While there has been no suggestion that the LOSC needs to be amended to accommodate CCS activities, the parties to both the LP and the OSPAR Convention reacted expeditiously to amend these instruments to accommodate CCS activities. In doing so, the parties recognized that, since the health of the oceans was being impaired by acidification due to elevated concentrations of CO_2 in the atmosphere, and further recognized that CCS is one of a portfolio of options for reducing atmospheric CO_2, it would be appropriate to facilitate CCS operations in marine spaces (subject to appropriate terms, conditions and safeguards) for those jurisdictions that chose to pursue this option. In both cases, the Parties to those treaties emphasized that CCS should not be considered as a substitute for other measures to reduce CO_2 emissions.[8]

The chapter is only concerned with geological sequestration of CO_2 in the seabed. It does not examine proposals to dispose of CO_2 in the water column or *on* the seabed or schemes for ocean fertilization.[9]

4 United Nations Convention on the Law of the Sea, Montego Bay, 10 December 1982, 1833 UNTS 397.

5 Convention on the Prevention of Marine Pollution by Dumping of Wastes and Other Matter, London, 29 December 1972, in force 30 August 1975, 1046 UNTS 138.

6 1996 Protocol to the Convention on the Prevention of Marine Pollution by Dumping of Wastes and Other Matter, 7 November 1966, in force 24 March 2006, 36 ILM 7.

7 1992 Convention for the Protection of the Marine Environment of the North-East Atlantic, Paris, 22 September 1992, 2354 UNTS 67.

8 See the Preamble to Resolution LP.1(1) amending Annex I of the London Protocol. Similar sentiments were expressed by contracting Parties and others during the adoption of amendments to OSPAR: see Meeting of the OSPAR Commission, Ostend, 25–29 June 2007, Summary Record, 2.10 (discussed in Section 7.5.1).

9 For discussion of these ideas see K. N. Scott, 'The day after tomorrow: ocean CO_2 sequestration and the future of climate change' (2005) 18 *Georgetown International Environmental Law Review*, 57–108. Part II of this excellent and comprehensive article covers geological sequestration in marine areas, Part III addresses direct injection of CO_2 into the water column and Part IV deals with ocean fertilization.

7.2 CARBON CAPTURE AND STORAGE AND CO_2 INJECTION AS PART OF ENHANCED OIL RECOVERY

As noted earlier, CCS is a recognized technology for mitigating GHG emissions, in particular, CO_2.[10] Although CCS technology has not been adopted as quickly, or on as widespread a basis as had been expected a decade ago,[11] many countries identify a role for CCS projects (or as part of negative emission technologies including CO_2 capture from the air) in their Nationally Determined Commitments under the Paris Agreement.[12] The EU, for example, continues to reference CCS as part of its 2030 climate and energy policy framework.[13]

7.2.1 *Carbon Capture and Storage*

CCS projects may be implemented onshore or offshore. Two important offshore examples are the Sleipner and Snøhvit projects on the Norwegian continental shelf. Both projects involve the separation and capture of CO_2 from produced natural gas[14] and both inject CO_2 into saline formations. Sleipner commenced operations in 1996 and Snøhvit in 2008.[15] Both

[10] This section draws on N. Bankes, 'The use of sub-seabed transboundary geological formations for the disposal of carbon dioxide' in C. Banet (ed.), *The Law of the Seabed: Access, Uses, and Protection of Seabed Resources* (Brill, 2020), 397–430.

[11] Haszeldine et al., 'Negative emission technologies' 1, 7; S. Haszeldine and N. S. Ghaleigh, 'Geological factors for legislation to enable and regulate storage of carbon dioxide in the deep subsurface' in I. Havercroft, R. Macrory and R. Stewart (eds.), *Carbon Capture and Storage: Emerging Legal and Regulatory Issues*, 2d edn. (Hart Publishing, 2018), 5–31; D. Langlet, 'Exporting CO_2 for sub-seabed storage: The non-effective amendment to the London Dumping Protocol and its implications' (2015) 30 *International Journal of Marine and Coastal Law*, 395–417, exploring at 395–397 some of the pros and cons of CCS.

[12] 2015 Paris Agreement under the United Nations Framework Convention on Climate Change, UN Doc. FCCC/CP/2015/L.9 (12 December 2015); and on negative emission technologies, see Haszeldine et al., 'Negative emission technologies' 1, 7.

[13] A policy framework for climate and energy in the period from 2020 to 2030, COM(2014) 15 final, 22 January 2014 (15, section 4.3 of the policy). For a fairly recent summary of approaches to the adoption of CCS in Europe, see Report from the Commission to the European Parliament and the Council on Implementation of Directive 2009/3/EC on the Geological Storage of Carbon Dioxide, COM(2017) 37 Final, 1 February 2017.

[14] Natural gas (methane, CH_4) may be contaminated with a significant percentage of CO_2 requiring processing in the field to produce pipeline quality gas. The separated CO_2 may then be reinjected.

[15] The Sleipner project is located 240 km west of Stavanger. Processing and injection occur at the production site. The Snøhvit project involves production from three separate fields in the Barents Sea. The gas is piped to shore to a processing and LNG facility where the CO_2 is separated and then piped back to the field for injection. See Carbon Sequestration Leadership Forum, Technical Group, *Final Report from Task Force on Technical Barriers and R &*

projects were initiated in response to a carbon tax imposed by the government of Norway.

There are pros and cons associated with selecting an offshore disposal site. Positive aspects include: sediments of continental shelves frequently contain large volumes of high-quality storage; in many cases prior oil and gas exploration provides a good geological understanding of the offshore; there is typically a single owner (the state); there is minimal conflict with freshwater aquifers (a major potential concern with onshore sites); the absence of resident populations and communities thereby minimizing or avoiding NIMBY (not in my back yard) objections; there is frequently an existing pipeline and production/injection infrastructure;[16] there are likely fewer legacy wells offshore than onshore to serve as possible pathways to surface; it may be easier and cheaper to apply monitoring techniques and seismic imaging offshore.[17] The principal disadvantages of offshore sites are the elevated costs and risks of offshore operations as well as concerns for the marine environment in the unlikely event of leakage.[18] A 2013 study by the International Energy Agency (IEA) concluded that CO_2 storage is not likely to take place in the near future at onshore locations in the five countries surrounding the North Sea and that the North Sea is a much more promising option both for those countries 'and indeed for many other nearby European countries'.[19]

D Opportunities for Offshore, Sub-Seabed Geologic Storage of CO_2, CSLF-T-2015–06, 20 October 2015 (CSLF, *Offshore Geologic Storage*), available at www.cslforum.org/publications/documents/riyadh2015/tg_OffshoreSubSeabedStorageTaskForceFinalReport-Riyrhadh1115.pdf, 8–9.

16 See, for example, the proposed Acorn project off the NE coast of Scotland which proposes to make use of legacy oil and gas assets as the basis for a CO_2 transportation and storage network, at https://pale-blu.com/category/acorn/; similarly see also the Northern Lights project proposed by a consortium of Equinor, Shell and Total, at www.equinor.com/en/news/statoil-shell-total-co2-storage-partnership.html

17 This section relies on CSLF, *Offshore Geologic Storage*, 2 and 5.

18 Ibid., 6.

19 *IEAGHG Interaction Report*, 37–38. There have been a number of regional-scale European studies of offshore storage options. These studies include *One North Sea, A study into North Sea* CO_2 *Cross-border Transport and Storage*, see Elements Energy Limited, Final Main report for the Norwegian Ministry of Petroleum and Energy and the UK Foreign and Commonwealth Office on behalf of the North Sea Basin Task Force (2010), available at www.ccsassociation.org/docs/2010/OneNorthSea.pdf. Chapter 6 deals with legal and regulatory issues; *Carbon Capture and Storage in the Skagerrak/Kattegat Region*, Final Report (2102), available at www.globalccsinstitute.com/publications/ccs-baltic-sea-region-bastor-2-work-package-4-legal-and-fiscal-aspects. Most of the legal analysis in these reports is concerned with the EU's CCS Directive and the LP.

Injection sites should be carefully characterized and located so as to ensure adequate and efficient storage capacity[20] as well as geological containment with appropriate trapping mechanisms.[21] Upon injection the CO_2 will migrate within the target formation as a plume of CO_2. The CO_2 will be buoyant relative to the brine in the reservoir and will thus rise and spread laterally when trapped under cap-rock formations. Injection will also elevate pressure conditions within the reservoir. The pressure effect of injection will initially be localized at the injection site, but the resulting pressure front will extend beyond the actual CO_2 plume (in some cases as far as 100 km[22]) and slowly dissipate throughout the target formation. Once injection comes to an end, the CO_2 plume may continue to migrate within the target formation moving upwards and laterally (because of the buoyancy of the plume).[23] Migration will continue at a slow rate for centuries. The environmental risks associated with sub-sea sequestration activities can be minimized by careful site selection. The risks include induced seismicity and possible loss of containment resulting in locally elevated pH levels in the water column.[24]

7.2.2 CO_2 *Storage and Enhanced Oil Recovery*

Enhanced oil recovery using carbon dioxide (CO_2/EOR)[25] is a tertiary recovery technique for enhancing recovery of petroleum from some reservoir

20 S. Bachu, 'Review of CO_2 storage efficiency in deep saline aquifers' (2015) 40 *International Journal of Greenhouse Gas Control* 188–202. 'Storage efficiency' refers to the fact that not all available pore space will be accessed by CO_2 in the same way as not all estimated hydrocarbon reserves will be producible.

21 The literature refers to six trapping mechanisms which may operate cumulatively and over different time scales: (1) structural and stratigraphic trapping, (2) hydrodynamic traps (CO_2 entrained in groundwater), (3) residual gas trapping, (4) solubility trapping, (5) mineral trapping, (6) adsorption trapping, see *IEAGHG Interaction Report*, 7.

22 *IEAGHG Interaction Report*, 67.

23 Bachu, 'Review of CO_2 storage', 198.

24 Scott, 'The day after tomorrow', 64.

25 This section draws on a number of sources including the Report Prepared for the Carbon Sequestration Leader Forum (CSLF) Technical Group by the CSLF Task Force on the Technical Challenges in the Transition from CO_2–EOR to CCS (2013) (CSLF, CO_2/EOR Technical Report), available at www.cslforum.org/publications/documents/CO2-EORtoCCS_FinalReport.pdf; P. Marston et al., 'Carbon dioxide infrastructure: pipeline transport issues and regulatory concerns – past, present and future' (2015) 52 *Rocky Mountain Mineral Law Foundation Journal*, 275–313, especially 278–286; N. Bankes and E. Brennan, 'Enhanced oil recovery and the geological sequestration of carbon dioxide' (2013) a paper prepared for Natural Resources Canada, available at www.law.ucalgary.ca/files/law/final_june7_enhanced-oil-recovery-and-the-geological-sequestration-of-carbon-dioxide.pdf.

types.[26] Primary production (using the original pressure conditions in the reservoir) may result in the recovery of between 10 and 20 per cent of the original oil in place.[27] Waterflooding operations and other secondary recovery techniques may double the recovery rate. CO_2/EOR operations may allow the recovery of an incremental 5–15 per cent of the original oil in place and in some cases as much as an additional 25–40 per cent. CO_2/EOR operations involve the injection of liquid or supercritical CO_2 into the producing formation where the CO_2 interacts with the oil remaining in the pores of the formation.[28] The combined fluids (oil, CO_2 and brine) flow towards the low-pressure point of the producing well. Not all of the CO_2 injected will be produced with the oil, some will remain permanently contained within the reservoir. Industry experience with EOR projects suggests that up to 90–95 per cent of purchased CO_2 will eventually become 'incidentally trapped' (i.e. stored) within the reservoir over the life of the project.[29]

While CO_2/EOR operations may be relatively small scale, they offer significant advantages when compared with saline projects. The most important advantage is that the incremental oil recovery provides a source of revenue to offset the expenses incurred in capturing the CO_2.[30] There may also be other non-carbon advantages for CO_2/EOR operations. For example, the use of CO_2 /EOR will extend the producing lives of reservoirs and mature basins thereby maintaining employment, deferring reliance on other sources of petroleum and contributing to the social aspect of sustainable development.[31]

Despite those prospects, there are very few offshore CO_2/EOR projects due to the limited availability of CO_2 and the cost of converting existing

26 Not all fields are suitable for CO_2/EOR operations or even for CO_2 storage in a depleted reservoir. For an accessible account of relevant considerations see *IEAGHG Interaction Report*, 12.

27 Marston et al., 'Carbon dioxide infrastructure', 279.

28 Ibid., 281. Emphasis in original, references omitted.

29 Marston et al., 'Carbon dioxide infrastructure', 283, referring to various sources including CSLF, CO_2/EOR, Technical Report and Global CCS Institute, 'The Global Status of CCS: 2012', 147.

30 The CSLF Technical Group report, summarizes the advantages as follows: (1) it enables CCS technology improvement and cost reduction; (2) it improves the business case for CCS demonstration and early movers; (3) it supports the development of CO_2 transportation networks; (4) it may provide significant CO_2 storage capacity in the short-to-medium-term, particularly if residual oil zones (ROZ) are produced; (5) it enables knowledge transfer, bridging the experience gap and building and sustaining a skilled CCS workforce; and (6) it helps gaining public and policy-makers acceptance. See CSLF, CO_2/EOR Technical Report, 1 and 58.

31 Scottish Carbon Capture and Storage, CO_2 *Storage and Enhanced Oil Recovery in the North Sea: Securing a Low Carbon Future for the UK* (2015) at 2, available at www.sccs.org.uk/images/expertise/reports/co2-eor-jip/SCCS-CO2-EOR-JIP-Report-SUMMARY.pdf.

infrastructure.[32] The only significant offshore CO_2/EOR project is the Lula Project, which is located on Brazil's continental shelf in very deep waters approximately 300 km off the coast of Rio de Janeiro. The project commenced operations in 2013.[33]

7.3 THE TREATMENT OF CCS PROJECTS AND CO_2/EOR PROJECTS UNDER THE LAW OF THE SEA CONVENTION

This part of the chapter examines the treatment of CCS projects and CO_2 /EOR projects under the terms of the LOSC. There are two main lines of enquiry: first, the authority to conduct CCS operations in marine areas, and, second, the obligations or responsibilities of the coastal state engaged when conducting CCS operations in marine areas.

7.3.1 *The Authority to Conduct CCS Operations in Marine Areas*

As noted in Section 7.2, CCS operations involve the capture of CO_2 at large final emitters (whether on land or at sea), compression and then transport, typically by pipeline but potentially by other modes including ships, and then injection through wells drilled into appropriate geological formations. All of these activities when carried out at sea fall under the authority of the relevant coastal state or states, whether they occur in internal waters, the territorial sea, the exclusive economic zone, the continental shelf or any archipelagic waters as relevant. The sovereignty of the coastal state extends to its internal waters, its territorial sea and any archipelagic waters.[34] Sovereignty allows the coastal state to regulate all aspects of these activities. While the LOSC describes the coastal state's rights with respect to both the continental shelf and the EEZ as sovereign rights,[35] or sovereign rights and jurisdiction[36] rather than full sovereignty, the rights accorded by the Convention still afford the coastal state all necessary authority to permit and regulate CCS activities in these maritime zones. The next few paragraphs support that claim.[37]

In the case of the EEZ, Article 56(1)(a) of the LOSC affords the coastal state

[32] CSLF, *Offshore Geologic Storage*, at 14. The only significant offshore CO_2/EOR project is the Lula Project, Brazil, ibid. at 11.

[33] For the Lula EOR project fact sheet, see https://sequestration.mit.edu/tools/projects/lula.html.

[34] LOSC, Article 2.

[35] LOSC, Article 77.

[36] LOSC, Article 56.

[37] See Scott, 'The day after tomorrow', 65–74; B. Milligan, 'Planning for offshore CO_2 storage: law and policy in the United Kingdom' (2014) 48 *Marine Policy*, 162–171, 163–164; D. Langlet,

> sovereign rights for the purpose of exploring and exploiting, conserving and managing the natural resources, whether living or non-living, of the waters superjacent to the seabed and of the seabed and its subsoil, and with regard to other activities for the economic exploitation and exploration of the zone, such as the production of energy from the water, currents and winds.

Thus, the coastal state's EEZ rights include rights pertaining to the subsoil of the seabed. While CCS projects involve the injection of new substances into the subsoil rather than production from the subsoil, the pore space of the subsoil is itself as much a resource as are the hydrocarbon or other contents of pore space. Exploratory wells and seismic are required to appropriately characterize the structure of target formations and the pore space within those formations. These activities may all be regulated by the coastal state.

Article 56(1)(b) adds that the coastal state has jurisdiction for 'the establishment and use of artificial islands, installations and structures', while Article 56(3) confirms that the rights of the coastal state 'with respect to the seabed and subsoil shall be exercised in accordance with Part VI'. Part VI is that part of the LOSC dealing with the continental shelf. Additionally, Article 60 confirms that in its EEZ the coastal state has the 'exclusive right to construct and to authorize and regulate the construction, operation and use of' inter alia 'installations and structures for the purposes provided for in Article 56 and other economic purposes'. In exercising its rights in the EEZ, the coastal state shall have 'due regard to the rights and duties of other States'. The leading decision on the 'due regard' obligation is the Award of the tribunal in the *Chagos Arbitration*, which indicates that what due regard requires in any particular case is highly contextualized and that

> the extent of the regard required by the Convention will depend upon the nature of the rights held by [the other State], their importance, the extent of the anticipated impairment, the nature and importance of the activities contemplated by the [coastal State], and the availability of alternative approaches. In the majority of cases, this assessment will necessarily involve at least some consultation with the rights-holding State.[38]

The LOSC describes the rights of the coastal state with respect to the continental shelf as exclusive 'sovereign rights for the purpose of exploring it and

'Transboundary dimensions of CCS: EU law problems and prospects' (2014) *Carbon & Climate Law Review*, 198–207, 201; D. Langlet, 'Safe return to the underground? The role of international law in subsurface storage of carbon dioxide' (2009) 18 *Review of European Community and International Environmental* Law, 286–304, 201–292.

38 *Chagos Marine Protected Area (Republic of Mauritius* v. *United Kingdom)* (Award) [2015] PCA Case no. 2011–3 para. 519.

exploiting its natural resources'.[39] The shelf itself is defined as the 'seabed and subsoil' of the submarine areas beyond the territorial sea to the outer edge of the continental margin or at least up to 200 nm.[40] The shelf consists of 'the seabed and subsoil of the shelf, the slope and the rise. It does not include the deep ocean floor with its oceanic ridges or the subsoil thereof'.[41]

The continental shelf beyond 200 nm (where applicable) is known as the extended continental shelf and paragraphs 4–9 of Article 76 together with Annex II provide the rules for establishing the outer limits of a coastal state's shelf.[42]

Article 60 deals with the exclusive right of the coastal state 'to construct and to authorize and regulate the construction, operation and use of' inter alia 'installations and structures for the purposes provided for in Article 56 and other economic purposes'. While located in Part V (dealing with the EEZ) it applies *mutatis mutandis* to installations and structures on the continental shelf[43] and 'The coastal State shall have the exclusive right to authorize and regulate drilling on the continental shelf for all purposes'.[44] The exercise of the rights of the coastal state 'must not infringe or result in any unjustifiable interference with navigation and other rights and freedoms of other States as provided for in this Convention'.[45] In sum, there is no doubt as to the authority of the coastal state to exclusively regulate all aspects of CCS activities on its shelf, including its extended shelf. This would include pipelines serving injection facilities on the shelf of the coastal state,[46] although a proposal to build a CO_2 pipeline that would transit through the continental shelf of a coastal state would be entitled to the benefit of Article 79. Article 79 provides that all states are entitled to lay pipelines on the continental shelf and that the coastal state cannot impede that activity '[s]ubject to its right to take reasonable measures for the exploration of the continental shelf, the exploitation of its natural resources and the prevention, reduction and control of pollution from pipelines'.[47] Delineation of the course of such a pipeline is, however, subject

39 LOSC, Article 77.
40 LOSC, Article 76(1).
41 LOSC, Article 76 (3).
42 The details of these provisions do not concern us here. For an overview see J. Mossop, *The Continental Shelf beyond 200 Nautical Miles: Rights and Responsibilities* (Oxford University Press, 2016), 67–80.
43 LOSC, Article 80.
44 LOSC, Article 81.
45 LOSC, Article 78(1). There is presumably little difference between this and the obligation of due regard.
46 LOSC, Article 79(4).
47 LOSC, Article 79(2).

to the consent of the coastal state[48] and any state laying a pipeline 'shall have due regard to cables or pipelines already in position'.[49]

Article 82 of the LOSC requires the coastal state to share revenues attributable to the exploitation of the non-living resources of any extended continental shelf with the international community, but this obligation is only triggered by 'production'. Hence, while a CCS operation no doubt constitutes the exploitation of the non-living resources of the shelf,[50] Article 82 would be inapplicable to a saline CCS operation.[51] The obligation would, however, apply to production from an EOR operation that was also storing CO_2 at least for so long as there was continuing hydrocarbon production from the site.

All activities in the Area (the seabed and ocean floor and subsoil thereof beyond the limits of national jurisdiction) are subject to Part XI of the LOSC and the Implementing Agreement.[52] The LOSC defines 'Activities in the Area' as 'all activities of exploration for, and exploitation of, the resources of the Area'[53] and Article 137 vests 'All rights in the resources of the Area ... in mankind as a whole on whose behalf the Authority shall act.' Part XI, however, defines 'resources' narrowly to mean 'all solid, liquid or gaseous mineral resources in situ in the Area at or beneath the seabed, including polymetallic nodules'.[54] As a result, some take the view that CCS activities in areas beyond national jurisdiction would effectively fall outside Part XI and would instead be governed by traditional high seas freedoms and flag state jurisdiction.[55] While there is textual support for this conclusion in the definition of resources,

48 LOSC, Article 79(3).

49 LOSC, Article 79(5). See D. Langlet, 'Transboundary transit pipelines: reflections on the balancing of rights and interests in light of the Nord Stream project' (2016) 63 *International and Comparative Law Quarterly*, 977–995; and G. Haver and H. C. Bugge, 'Transboundary chains for CCS: allocation of rights and obligations between the state Parties within the climate regime' (2007) 5 *Journal for European Environmental & Planning* Law, 367 at 371–372.

50 *Accord*, Haver and Bugge, ibid., at 371.

51 For a more extended discussion of different possible interpretations see Mossop, *The Continental Shelf*, 150; Mossop too concludes that 'carbon storage in not the sort of "exploitation of the non-living resources" anticipated by the Convention'. Scott, 'The day after tomorrow', 67, is more equivocal suggesting that 'It is unclear whether this provision should apply to the exploitation of the capacity to store CO_2 beneath the seabed and if so how such a payment should be calculated.'

52 LOSC, Article 134; Agreement relating to the implementation of Part XI of the United Nations Convention on the Law of the Sea of 10 December 1982, adopted 28 July 1994, entered into force 28 July 1996, available at www.un.org/Depts/los/convention_agreements/convention_overview_part_xi.htm.

53 LOSC, Article 1(1)(3).

54 LOSC, Article 133(a).

55 See Langlet, 'Safe return to the underground?', 292, in note 83. Langlet also refers to Haver and Bugge, 'Transboundary chains', 371, but they do not seem to refer expressly to the situation beyond the limits of national jurisdiction.

it seems entirely inconsistent with both the philosophy behind the common heritage concept and the security needs of any CCS project. The 'free-for-all' ideas associated with high seas freedoms are completely inimical to the exclusivity required to develop and operate a storage facility.[56]

7.3.2 *The Obligations and Responsibilities of Coastal States for CCS Operations in Marine Areas*

Part XII of the LOSC deals with the protection and preservation of the marine environment.[57] Article 208 establishes that all states including coastal states have the obligation to protect and preserve the marine environment generally, and specifically the obligation to do so while exploiting their natural resources.[58] Article 194 provides additional guidance with respect to pollution but also requires states to take measures necessary 'to protect and preserve rare or fragile ecosystems as well as the habitat of depleted, threatened or endangered species and other forms of marine life'.[59]

Article 208 imposes specific obligations on coastal states with respect to seabed activities and installation and structures under their jurisdiction. These obligations are directly relevant to CCS operations in marine areas. Article 208(1) obliges a coastal state to adopt laws and regulations as well as other necessary measures 'to prevent, reduce and control pollution of the marine environment' from seabed activities. 'Such laws, regulations and measures shall be no less effective than international rules, standards and recommended practices and procedures.'[60] Thus, a coastal state must adopt appropriate rules dealing with drilling and injection activities associated with CCS operations, much as it must in relation to conventional oil and gas operations. In doing so, it must pay specific attention to the drilling and completion requirements for injection wells for acidic gases such as CO_2.[61] Similarly, all states have the

56 One possible way ahead would be to have the parties to the LOSC through the International Seabed Authority adopt an agreed interpretation of 'resources' for the purposes of Part XI so as to clarify that it includes geological sequestration activities. However, the characteristics and relative remoteness of the Area may well mean that it is ill-suited geologically and economically for storage projects and thus unlikely ever to be a target for CCS operations.

57 Other chapters in this volume discuss Part XII in more detail. See, in particular, Boyle, in this volume, Chapter 4. See also Scott, 'The day after tomorrow', 68–74.

58 LOSC, Articles 192 and 193.

59 LOSC, Article 194(5). *South China Sea Arbitration (The Republic of the Philippines and the People's Republic of China)* Award [2016] PCA Case no 2013–19 paras. 939–945.

60 LOSC, Article 208(3).

61 Domestic jurisdictions typically develop special rules for such wells. See, e.g., the rules developed by the Environment Protection Agency in the United States for Class VI wells,

responsibility to conduct assessments of proposed activities at least where they 'have reasonable grounds for believing that planned activities under their jurisdiction or control may cause substantial pollution of or significant and harmful changes to the marine environment'.[62]

While all of these obligations are important, most academic commentary on CCS activities in ocean space has concentrated on the question of dumping both under the terms of the LOSC and under the terms of the London Convention (LC) and London Protocol (LP) and regional agreements such as the OSPAR Convention[63] since all are more specific than the LOSC. The following section, therefore, examines how the dumping provision in the LOSC may apply to CCS activities before turning to these different instruments.

7.3.3 *CCS Operations and Dumping under the LOSC*

The LOSC treats dumping as a form of pollution. Article 210 of the LOSC obliges all states 'to adopt laws and regulations to prevent, reduce and control pollution of the marine environment by dumping' and to provide that such laws always require state authorization for any dumping.[64] National laws, regulations and measures shall be no less effective than the global rules and standards and states shall endeavour to establish (and then re-examine from time to time) global and regional rules, standards and recommended practices and procedures to prevent, reduce and control dumping. Dumping within the territorial sea or the EEZ 'or onto the continental shelf' requires the express prior approval of the coastal state. It is, therefore, evident that Article 210 deals with the regulation of dumping rather than the prohibition of dumping.[65]

Insofar as the LOSC treats dumping as a form of pollution, it is important to assess whether the injection of CO_2 into subsea geological formations constitutes pollution and/or dumping for the purposes of the LOSC. Both terms are

that is, wells used for geologic sequestration: https://www.epa.gov/uic/class-vi-wells-used-geologic-sequestration-co2

62 LOSC, Article 206.

63 For examples of the academic commentary see R. Purdy and R. Macrory, *Geological Carbon Sequestration: Critical Legal Issues* (Tyndall Centre for Climate Change Research 2004), Working Paper 45, 18–26; Scott, 'The day after tomorrow'; C. Armeni, 'Legal developments for carbon capture and storage under international regional marine legislation' in I. Havercroft, R. Macrory and R. B. Stewart (eds.), *Carbon Capture and Storage: Emerging Legal and Regulatory Issues* (Hart Oxford, 2011), 145–159.

64 LOSC, Article 210, paras. 1 and 5; Article 216 deals with enforcement obligations in relation to dumping.

65 Langlet, 'Safe return to the underground?', 292.

defined in the LOSC. The definition of pollution emphasizes such things as 'harm to living resources and marine life' and 'impairment of quality for use of sea water and reduction of amenities', which might suggest that the definition is concerned with pollution of the water column or the surface of the seabed rather than the subsoil itself.[66] 'Dumping' so far as relevant means 'any deliberate disposal of wastes or other matter from vessels, aircraft, platforms or other man-made structures at sea'.[67] It is unclear whether 'at sea' should be interpreted as including disposal into a sub-seabed geological formation or whether this term should be confined to the water column and the surface of the seabed.[68] Langlet concludes that reasonable arguments can be made both ways.[69] In addition, it should be noted that dumping does not include 'the disposal of wastes or other matter incidental to, or derived from the normal operations of … platforms or other man-made structures at sea and their equipment'.[70] This would serve to exclude from the definition the injection of CO_2 separated from offshore production of natural gas as in the Sleipner project. Neither is it dumping if matter is 'placed' 'for a purpose other than the mere disposal thereof, provided that such placement is not contrary to the aims of this Convention'. While some have speculated that this might serve to except CO_2 sequestered for climate mitigation purposes, the better view seems to be that the overall purpose is still disposal even if motivated by other considerations.[71]

While these represent considerable interpretive challenges in relation to CCS activities it is more important to consider if and the extent to which CCS activities have been dealt with in the LC and the LP, especially given the importance that Article 210 of the LOSC attaches to the elaboration of 'global and regional rules, standards and recommended practices and procedures to prevent, reduce and control' dumping.[72] The LP completely replaces the LC for

66 LOSC, Article 1(1)(4).

67 LOSC, Article 1(1)(5).

68 Langlet, 'Exporting CO_2', 402.

69 Ibid. See also Scott, 'The day after tomorrow', 75 discussing the issue in the context of the similar language in the LC.

70 Ibid.

71 For more detailed discussion, see Scott, 'The day after tomorrow', 77 referencing Purdy and Macrory, *Geological Carbon Sequestration*, 23.

72 LOSC, Article 210(4). See E. J. Molenaar, 'The 1996 Protocol to the 1972 Convention' (1997) 12 *The International Journal of Marine and Coastal Law*, 396, 402–403 noting that LC standards may become binding on non-parties to the LC through Article 210(4) of the LOSC. While this is likely the case for the LC, some doubt if the Protocol has yet reached the threshold of establishing a set of 'global rules and standards'; see, e.g., Langlet, 'Exporting CO_2', 402–403. As of 30 August 2018 there are fifty parties to the LP: see LC 40/2, Status of the London Convention and Protocol, 31 August 2018.

those states that become a Party to the Protocol,[73] and as a result, the LP with its more restrictive regime for dumping at sea is and will become more important.[74]

7.4 THE TREATMENT OF CCS IN THE LONDON CONVENTION AND THE LONDON PROTOCOL

Neither the LC nor the LP as originally drafted expressly referred to CCS or CO_2 disposal.

7.4.1 *The Treatment of CCS in the London Convention*

The LC[75] preceded the adoption of the LOSC by a decade and yet commentators generally consider that the LC provides a regulatory elaboration of the LOSC with respect to dumping.[76] The definition of dumping in the LOSC was largely borrowed from the LC which similarly applies to dumping 'at sea' and also expressly provides that 'The disposal of wastes or other matter directly arising from, or related to the exploration, exploitation and associated off-shore processing of sea-bed mineral resources' is not covered by the LC.[77] Much as with the LOSC it is also clear that the LC does not apply to either CO_2/EOR operations or even an operation such as Sleipner that involves the separation of CO_2 from produced natural gas and its reinjection.[78]

The LC bans the dumping of substances listed in Annex I.[79] As of 1996 Annex I has included industrial waste which refers to 'waste materials generated by manufacturing or processing operations'.[80] The dumping of wastes listed in Annex II requires a prior special permit and the dumping of all other wastes requires a prior general permit.[81] It follows from this that the treatment

73 LP, Article 23: 'This Protocol will supersede the Convention as between Contracting Parties to this Protocol which are also Parties to the Convention.'

74 See Armeni, 'Legal developments'; and T. Dixon, S. McCoy and I. Havercroft, 'Legal and regulatory developments on CCS' (2015) 40 *International Journal of Greenhouse Gas Control* 431–448.

75 Molenaar, 'The 1996 Protocol', 397, reminds us that the parties to the Convention agreed in 1992 to refer to the Convention as the London Convention rather than the 'London Dumping Convention' to avoid the suggestion that the Parties to the agreement formed a 'dumping club'.

76 Langlet, 'Exporting CO_2', 403.

77 LC, Article III(1)(c).

78 Snøhvit is more difficult since in that case a shore-based facility separates the CO_2 from the methane and the CO_2 is then piped back to the field for reinjection.

79 LC, Article IV(1)(a).

80 LC, Annex I at para. 11.

81 LC, Article IV(1)(b) and (c).

of CO_2 captured from large final emitters and transported to the offshore for injection purposes turns on whether the CO_2 can be said to be 'generated by manufacturing or processing operations'. In some cases the classification can readily be made but in other cases it may be more difficult. CO_2 separated from the processing of natural gas would appear to be industrial waste within the meaning of the LC but CO_2 produced as a result of the generation of electricity from a carbon fuel may not be.[82] In sum there is some uncertainty as to applicability of the LC to different streams of CO_2. The position is clearer under the LP.[83]

7.4.2 *The Treatment of CCS in the London Protocol*

The LP adopts a 'prohibited unless permitted' model for dumping with the result that dumping of substances is prohibited unless the waste stream is listed in Annex I of the Protocol.[84] In addition, the Protocol defined dumping to include 'any storage of wastes or other matter in the seabed and the subsoil thereof from vessels, aircraft, platforms or other man-made structures at sea'.[85] Since CO_2 was not listed as a permitted waste stream, it was thus clear that the text as originally adopted prohibited geological storage of CO_2 in subsea geological formations.[86] The text would not prohibit the injection of CO_2 as part of a CO_2/EOR operation[87] nor the injection of CO_2 as part of the offshore processing of a natural gas stream,[88] but the effective prohibition of pure CO_2 disposal operations was generally considered to be 'an unwitting legal barrier to CCS deployment, based on the assumption that the Protocol had been adopted without CCS in mind'.[89]

82 See Purdy and Macrory, *Geological Carbon Sequestration*, 21 and Scott, 'The day after tomorrow', 77–78.

83 Accord, Purdy and Macrory, *Geological Carbon Sequestration*, 22 (with some qualifications) and Scott, 'The day after tomorrow', 78.

84 LP, Article 4.

85 LP, Article 1(4)(1)(3). 'Dumping' does not include placement for a purpose other than mere disposal (Article 1(4)(2)(2)).

86 Langlet, 'Exporting CO_2', 405; Armeni, 'Legal developments', 148.

87 See both the 'other than mere disposal' provision in LP Article 1(4)(1)(3) and also Article 1(3) which provides that 'The disposal or storage of wastes or other matter directly arising from, or related to the exploration, exploitation and associated off-shore processing of seabed mineral resources is not covered by the provisions of this Protocol.'

88 Ibid. Article 1(3) certainly addresses the scenario of the Sleipner operation, but in the case of Snøhvit the gas stream is subject to onshore processing before the CO_2 is separated and shipped back to the platform.

89 Armeni, 'Legal developments', 148. See also T. Dixon et al., 'International marine regulation of CO_2 geological storage: developments and implications of London and OSPAR' (2009) 1 *Energy Procedia* 4503–4510.

As a result, the first meeting of the Parties to the Protocol agreed to adopt an amendment to Annex 1 of the Protocol to list 'Carbon dioxide streams from carbon dioxide capture processes for sequestration' subject to the caveat that such streams 'may only be considered for dumping' if the operation meets three conditions. First, the disposal must be into a sub-seabed geological formation (i.e. it does not cover CO_2 disposal into the ocean itself). Second, the waste stream must consist 'overwhelmingly of carbon dioxide' but 'may contain incidental associated substances derived from the source material and the capture and sequestration processes used'. This would allow a combined waste stream from a gas processing facility that included other acid gases such as hydrogen sulphide along with the CO_2. Third, no wastes or other matter can be added 'for the purpose of disposing of those wastes or other matter'.[90] Amendments to Annex I enter into force for each Contracting Party no later than 100 days following adoption except for any Party that makes a declaration to the contrary within that period.[91] Accordingly, this amendment entered into force for all Parties in 2006.[92]

As a result of the amendment, a contracting Party may issue a permit for the sub-seabed disposal of a CO_2 waste stream that meets these requirements. However, a Party may only issue a permit after having complied with the requirements of Annex 2 of the Protocol.[93] Annex 2 requires such things as a waste prevention audit, consideration of different waste management options, characterization of the waste, criteria for the selection of dumping sites and assessment of the potential effects of dumping activities. Perhaps more importantly (and certainly more pertinent than the general provisions of Annex 2) the Parties to the Protocol have also adopted two sets of technical guidelines for CO_2 operations: the Risk Assessment and Management Framework (RAMF) for CO_2 Sequestration in Sub-seabed Geological Structures,[94] and the Specific Guidelines for the Assessment of Carbon Dioxide for Disposal into Sub-seabed Geological Formations. The Specific Guidelines were first adopted in 2007. An amended version that addresses transboundary migration of stored CO_2 was adopted in November 2012.[95]

90 LP, Annex 1, paras. 1(8) and 4.
91 LP, Article 22.
92 LC 40/2.
93 LP, Article 4(1).
94 RAMF Guidelines, Adopted at the joint session of the 28th Consultative Meeting of Contracting Parties under the LC and the 1st Meeting of Contracting Parties under the LP, 30 October–3 November 2006.
95 Adopted 2 November 2012, LC 34/15, annex 8 (Specific Guidelines, 2012). As guidelines the documents provide guidance to the Parties but their use is not obligatory, Dixon et al., 'International marine regulation', 4506.

The RAMF aims to provide generic guidance to the Parties in order to help them characterize the risks to the marine environment associated with an offshore CCS project and in order to collect the necessary information to develop a management strategy to address uncertainties and residual risks. The RAMF contemplates a six-stage process: (1) problem formulation, (2) site selection and characterization, (3) exposure assessment, (4) effects assessment, (5) risk characterization and (6) risk management.[96]

Finally, the Parties also agreed to adopt an understanding to the effect that the injection of CO_2 for enhanced oil recovery purposes does not engage the Protocol.[97]

That still left one outstanding obstacle within the Protocol to the adoption of CCS in marine areas. This is Article 6 which prohibits the export of wastes 'to other countries for dumping or incineration at sea'. The Parties identified two potential implications of this prohibition for geological sequestration of CO_2: export and migration (or 'migration-as-export'). 'Export' refers to the export of CO_2 from one country for disposal in the jurisdiction of another country. It was agreed that this activity was subject to the prohibition of Article 6, that the problem could not be resolved by way of an agreed interpretation, and that it could only be resolved by means of an amendment. An amendment to provide an exception for the export of CO_2 for geological sequestration was adopted in 2009[98] but is still a long way from formally entering into force.[99] According to the International Energy Agency and others this represented a considerable obstacle to the adoption of offshore CCS in some regions (e.g. Western Europe).[100]

The amendment would add an additional paragraph to the prohibition on export in Article 6 so as to provide that notwithstanding the prohibition, an export of a CO_2 waste stream for disposal may occur provided that 'an agreement or arrangement' has been entered into by 'the countries concerned'.[101] The agreement or arrangement must include a 'confirmation

96 RAMF Guidelines.

97 See International Maritime Organization (IMO) webpage, Carbon Capture and Sequestration www.imo.org/en/OurWork/Environment/LCLP/EmergingIssues/CCS/Pages/default.aspx.

98 Resolution LP.3(4) adopted 30 October 2009.

99 As of 31 August 2018 only five parties had ratified the amendment: Norway, Netherlands, UK, Iran and Finland, LC 40/2. The amendment will not enter force until two-thirds of the Contracting Parties have indicated their acceptance (LP, Article 21).

100 IEA, *Carbon Capture and Storage and the London Protocol: Options for Enabling Transboundary CO2 Transfer* (2011). This IEA working paper as the title suggests explores six different options that Parties might consider pending the entry into force of the amendment. Langlet, 'Exporting CO_2', 411–417 provides a critique of the more significant options.

101 LP, Article 6(1) (not yet in force, but, as noted further, now subject to provisional application).

and allocation of permitting responsibilities' consistent with the Protocol 'and other applicable international law'; and, where the export is to a non-contracting Party, steps must be taken to include provisions that ensure that there is no derogation from the obligations of Parties to 'protect and preserve the marine environment'. The Parties have also adopted a guidance note on the requirements for an agreement or arrangement that meets the requirements of Article 6.2.[102]

The Parties eventually addressed the issue of delayed entry into force at the 14th Meeting of the Contracting Parties in October 2019 where they agreed to adopt a resolution on the provisional application of the amendment.[103] The original amendment did not allow for provisional application, but the parties concluded that they could take advantage of Article 25(1) of the Vienna Convention on the Law of Treaties which contemplates that a treaty may be provisionally applied pending its entry into force either where the treaty itself so provides or where 'the negotiating States have in some other manner so agreed'. The Parties concluded that a resolution of the contracting parties adopted by consensus could provide the necessary agreement.[104]

The migration-as-export scenario arises when CO_2 is injected into a shared geological structure in State A and the CO_2 plume migrates (either intentionally or unintentionally) from State A to State B (or to an area beyond national jurisdiction). The Parties concluded that such a migration does *not* constitute an export within the meaning of Article 6 (and adopted a resolution to that effect).[105] It is, therefore, a form of disposal that can in principle be brought within the ambit of the Annex 1 amendment discussed earlier. However, the Parties agreed that it required special consideration under the Specific Guidelines for the Assessment of Carbon Dioxide for Disposal into Sub-seabed Geological Formations. The amended version of the Guidelines which addresses the migration scenario was adopted in November 2012.[106] The Guidelines (2012) address geological waste disposal of CO_2 generally but also contain a number of more specific provisions dealing with disposal into

102 Guidance on the Implementation of Article 6(2) on the Export of CO_2 streams for disposal in sub-seabed geological formations for the purposes of sequestration (2013). Attached as Annex 6 to the Report of the 35th Consultative Meeting of Contracting Parties to the LDC and the Eighth Meeting of the Contracting Parties to the PLDC, 21 October 2013, LC 35/15.

103 Resolution LP.5(14) on the Provisional Application of the 2009 Amendment to Article 6 of the London Protocol, adopted 11 October 2019.

104 For a more detailed examination see N. Bankes, 'Provisional application of an amendment to the London Protocol to facilitate collaborative CCS projects' (10 December 2019), available at ABlawg, http://ablawg.ca/wp-content/uploads/2019/12/Blog_NB_Article6.pdf.

105 Resolution LP.3(4), 30 October 2009, Recital 12.

106 Adopted 2 November 2012, LC 34/15, annex 8 (Specific Guidelines, 2012).

geological formations where there is potential for transboundary movement of injected CO_2. The general provisions address such matters as waste prevention audits, consideration of waste management options, the chemical and physical properties of the waste stream (i.e. proper characterization of the waste stream), an action list (a screening tool to determine whether a material is considered acceptable for dumping), site selection and characterization, assessment of potential effects (a risk assessment and an impact hypothesis), monitoring and risk management, and permit and permit conditions.[107] The more detailed provisions dealing with the transboundary situation are discussed elsewhere.[108]

In conclusion, the Parties to the LP, recognizing that CCS may contribute to mitigating GHG emissions, have reacted quickly to the concern that the LP as adopted posed a serious obstacle to applying the technology in an offshore environment. The Parties identified two particular obstacles: the failure to list CO_2 waste streams on the permitted disposal list of Annex 1, and the prohibition on exports. The Parties have adopted amendments to deal with both issues along with appropriate guidance documents. While the amendment to Annex I resolved the waste stream issue the amendment to the prohibition on exports has yet to enter into force although the resolution adopted at the LP meeting in 2019 now permits provisional application of the amendment.

7.5 REGIONAL CONVENTIONS

The LC and LP are both global regimes that expand upon some of the more general provisions pertaining to dumping in Article 210 of the LOSC. However, in addition to these global instruments it is also necessary to examine regional and regional seas instruments that may also pose obstacles or otherwise regulate CCS activities in marine areas, especially where such regimes may be more restrictive than the global regime. The next section focuses on the OSPAR Convention as an example.

107 For more detailed discussion see Dixon et al., 'International marine regulation', at 434. See also IEAGHG, Review of Project Permits under the London Protocol – An Assessment of the Proposed P18-4 CO_2 Storage Site, Report: 2016/TR4, May 2016. The project involves injection and storage into the P18-4 field which is a near-depleted natural gas field located approximately 20 km off the Dutch Coast. The report involves an analysis of the Netherlands permitting exercise to test compliance with the Specific Guidelines. It does not contain an assessment of potential transboundary issues presumably because the storage complex was a confined rather than an open complex.

108 See Bankes, 'The use of sub-seabed' and Dixon et al., 'International marine regulation', 433–436.

7.5.1 *The OSPAR Convention*

The OSPAR Convention is a regional seas convention extending to the 'maritime area' of the North-east Atlantic, the North Sea and adjacent Arctic Waters.[109] 'Maritime area' is defined in terms of the internal waters and the territorial seas of the Contracting Parties as well as adjacent areas under the jurisdiction of the coastal state (i.e. EEZ and continental shelf), and the high seas within the Convention area including for each zone 'the bed of all of those waters and its sub-soil'.[110] According to one of the Convention's technical working groups, the term 'sub-soil' is evidently intended 'to cover all underground strata below the seabed'.[111] Consequently, it seems clear that the OSPAR regime is intended to apply to more than just the water column and the ocean floor and that the implications of this broad definition of 'maritime area' have to be carried through into the other definitional and substantive provisions of the Convention. Thus 'pollution' includes the introduction of substances into the maritime area[112] and dumping includes deliberate disposal of 'wastes or other matter' into the maritime area.[113]

The operative Articles of the Convention include both a 'general obligation' (Article 2) as well as a series of specific obligations with respect to pollution from land-based sources (Article 3 and Annex I), pollution by dumping or incineration (Article 4 and Annex II) and pollution from offshore sources (Article 5 and Annex III). The general obligation is described (in part) as the duty to 'take all possible steps to prevent and eliminate pollution and shall take the necessary measures to protect the maritime area against the adverse effects of human activities so as to safeguard human health and to conserve marine ecosystems' and to that end 'adopt programmes and measures' and 'harmonise ... policies and strategies all informed by both the precautionary principle and the polluter pays principle'. Furthermore, in implementing the Convention the Parties

109 For the background to the OSPAR Convention and an overview of its main provisions see L. de La Fayette, 'The OSPAR Convention comes into force: continuity and progress' (1999) 14 *The International Journal of Marine and Coastal* Law, 247–295.

110 OSPAR, Article 1(a).

111 Report from the Group of Jurists and Linguists on Placement of Carbon Dioxide in the OSPAR Maritime Area (2004). OSPAR 04/23/1-E, Annex 12 at para 12, note 9 (GJL Report). Accord, Scott, 'The day after tomorrow', 80; for possible counter arguments see Purdy and Macrory, *Geological Carbon Sequestration*, 28–29.

112 OSPAR, Article 1(d).

113 OSPAR, Article 1(f). In common with the LC, the LP and the LOSC dumping under OSPAR does not include placement of a matter other than for the purpose of disposal, see OSPAR Article 1(g)(ii); nor does it include the disposal of wastes derived from the 'normal' operation of offshore installations, OSPAR Article 1(g)(i).

agreed to define for the purposes of programmes and measures, best available techniques and best available practice.[114]

The multiple regimes within the Convention presented considerable complexity when it came to assessing how sequestration activities should be either prohibited or regulated depending upon whether the waste stream originated from onshore or from an offshore installation and depending on whether injection activities involved an offshore platform or vessel and depending as well on the purpose of any injection activities (experiment, climate change mitigation or pure disposal).[115] Further investigation[116] suggested that whereas geological sequestration of CO_2 originating from an offshore installation would not be prohibited by the Convention,[117] a scenario in which CO_2 was captured onshore and then transported by pipeline to an installation for injection and sequestration would be prohibited.[118]

In response to this the contracting Parties, by consensus, ultimately agreed to adopt four measures designed to deal with the disposal of CO_2 in the maritime area covered by the OSPAR Convention.[119] These were: (1) amendments to Annexes II and III to permit CO_2 sequestration activities under each of the dumping Annex and the Annex on pollution from offshore sources; (2) a decision prohibiting the storage or disposal of CO_2 into the water column or the seabed;[120] (3) a decision setting out how regulatory actions including permitting should be taken with respect to CCS;[121] and (4) a set of guidelines on risk assessment and management of CO_2 streams for CCS (FRAM).[122] The measures were adopted as a package to address the concerns of those who wished to ensure that CCS operation should be subject to robust regulatory requirements.[123]

114 OSPAR, Article 2(3).

115 See GJL Report para. 32. For other discussions of these complexities see Purdy and Macrory, *Geological Carbon Sequestration*, 27–35 and Scott, 'The day after tomorrow', 79–85.

116 Ibid and see, in particular, the Appendix to the report.

117 This follows from Article 5 (pollution from offshore sources) and Annex III, Article 3. Article 3(1) provides that 'Any dumping of wastes or other matter from offshore installations is prohibited' but Article 3(2) provides that 'This prohibition does not relate to discharges or emissions from offshore sources.'

118 This conclusion follows from the same provisions, ibid.

119 Meeting of the OSPAR Commission, Ostend, 25–29 June 2007, Summary Record [2.10].

120 OSPAR Decision 2007/1 to Prohibit the Storage of Carbon Dioxide Streams in the Water Column or on the Sea-bed, ibid. Annex 5.

121 OSPAR Decision 2007/2 on the Storage of Carbon Dioxide Streams in Geological Formations, ibid. Annex 6.

122 OSPAR Guidelines for Risk Assessment and Management of Storage of CO2 Streams in Geological Formations including a framework for Risk Assessment and Management of Storage of CO2 Streams in Geological Formations (FRAM), ibid. Annex 7.

123 Ostend Meeting Summary Record, 25–29 June 2007, paras. 2.1–2.10.

The amendments to the Annexes closely followed the amendments to Annex I to the LP discussed earlier, but they also included an additional condition to the effect that CO_2 streams from CO_2 capture are 'intended to be retained in these formations permanently and will not lead to significant adverse consequences for the marine environment, human health and other legitimate uses of the maritime area'.[124]

As noted earlier, two of the four measures took the form of 'decisions'.[125] The first decision reaffirmed that the disposal of CO_2 in the water column or on the seabed was prohibited, whereas Decision 2007/02 was designed to prescribe the use of the Guidelines as part of permitting, authorizing or regulating any geological sequestration activity and further prescribing that 'A decision to grant a permit or approval shall only be made if a full risk assessment and management process has been completed to the satisfaction of the competent authority and that the storage will not lead to significant adverse consequences for the marine environment, human health and other legitimate uses of the maritime area.'[126] The FRAM guidelines are the functional equivalent of RAMF guidelines adopted by the Parties to the LP with some refinements.[127] Since decisions under the OSPAR Convention are legally binding, Parties are required to use these guidelines in making decisions with respect to offshore CCS activities.

In sum, much as with the LP regime, the Parties to the OSPAR Convention have taken steps to facilitate geological sequestration of CO_2 within the maritime area provided such activities meet certain minimum standards and proceed in accordance with a set of guidelines on risk assessment and management.

7.6 CONCLUSIONS

As demonstrated in Chapter 1 of this volume, elevated GHG emissions and the concentrations of such gases in the atmosphere pose a threat to ocean health. Human activities on the ocean also provide additional sources of anthropogenic GHG emissions. These activities include navigational activities (see Chapter 6) as well as oil and gas exploration, processing and production activities. But the ocean may also provide GHG mitigation options including

124 OSPAR. Annex II, Article 3(2)(f) and Annex III, Article 3(3).

125 Subject to an opt-out procedure, decisions adopted by the Commission are legally binding on Parties 200 days after adoption. OSPAR, Article 13(2) and de La Fayette, 'The OSPAR Convention', 257.

126 OSPAR, Decision 2007/02, s. 3.1.

127 Dixon et al., 'International marine regulation', 4507.

forms of marine geoengineering (see Chapter 8) as well as geological sequestration or CCS, the focus of this chapter.

While CCS still has important advocates including the International Energy Agency it has yet to be adopted on a large scale. The principal reasons for this slow uptake are economic, but if capture costs fall and/or the price of carbon rises, or there is a perceived need to achieve negative emissions, then CCS may become much more attractive. It is thus important to have in place the appropriate legal and regulatory measures to allow CCS to be conducted in a safe and environmentally sensitive way. In many cases, especially with respect to land-based CCS activities, this legal and regulatory framework will principally be domestic but in marine areas international law plays a more significant role. Consequently, it is important to assess whether we have in place an appropriate legal and regulatory framework for offshore CCS operations.

The analysis in this chapter demonstrates that the LOSC clearly allocates to coastal states the exclusive prescriptive authority to decide to engage in CCS operations in marine areas and that this authority extends beyond the territorial sea, throughout the EEZ, and, where there is an extended continental shelf, out to the maximum limits of the extended shelf as provided for in Article 76 of the LOSC. This is both a clear and appropriate allocation of authority given the overall resource allocation regime effected by the LOSC.[128] Beyond the limits of national jurisdiction (i.e. within the Area), the text of the Convention seems to suggest (counter intuitively) that CCS activities might fall within the regime of flag state freedoms. Such a regime is unlikely to provide a secure foundation for capital intensive CCS operations that demand a clear, detailed and precautionary regulatory regime.

While coastal states clearly play the dominant role with respect to possible future offshore CCS activities, international law also imposes obligations and responsibilities with respect to the conduct of those activities. The relevant instruments include both global and regional agreements dealing with environmental protection (but especially dumping activities) that may constrain coastal state discretion either to undertake CCS activities or to influence or prescribe the terms and conditions of those activities. The analysis in this chapter demonstrates that LOSC does not itself prohibit CCS activities, but it also demonstrates that other global or regional instruments might have that effect, absent amendment. For example, the LP as originally adopted clearly prohibited most offshore CCS disposal activities (as opposed to CO_2/EOR). Similarly, the OSPAR Convention also prohibited most forms of offshore

[128] Accord, Haver and Bugge, 'Transboundary chains', 371.

CCS activities. Given the potential mitigation benefits of offshore CCS operations, states Parties have responded by seeking to amend the relevant agreement to allow CCS activities (or to clarify that certain activities such as CO_2/EOR are permitted without amendment). The amendments or clarifications adopted to date have tended to emphasize that: the disposal target must be a geological sequestration site; the waste stream must consist overwhelmingly of CO_2 with no additional wastes added; and disposal should be subject to regulatory permitting on the basis of prescribed or recommended risk assessment and management protocols. In addition, the background discussion to the amendments has noted that CCS is simply one mitigation option in a portfolio of options and that it must not be adopted as a substitute for other mitigation measures.

In key cases it has proven to be relatively easy to adopt regulatory fixes where a global or regional regime may have inadvertently precluded consideration of the CCS option, but in one case it has proven to be more challenging. Where the necessary changes can be made by amending an annex, the amending procedures are typically such that amendments can be easily adopted and enter into force automatically (perhaps subject to an opt-out entitlement). This has been the case for example for the sequestration amendments to the LP and to the OSPAR Convention. By contrast, amending the 'no export of waste for dumping' rule in the LP proved to be much more difficult because the rule is contained in the body of the treaty rather than in an annex. As such, this amendment is subject to a more demanding amendment and entry into force procedure. While the no-export rule does not preclude a coastal state from adopting CCS for its own emissions, it does present an obstacle to a group of coastal states that might seek to establish a carbon disposal network of pipelines and disposal sites to achieve economies of scale, or to take advantage of optimal storage sites. It is also an obstacle for land-locked states that may have no suitable onshore storage sites. Seen in this light, the recent adoption of a resolution by the parties of the LP to deal with the provisional application of the amendment to Article 6 represents a creative and welcome solution that should allow like-minded states to explore collaborative opportunities for offshore CCS activities that involve transboundary movement of CO_2.

8

Ocean Fertilization

Elise Johansen

8.1 INTRODUCTION

Despite the predicted and already felt consequences of climate change, our dependence on fossil fuels shows no signs of wavering. According to the Climate Transparency's *Brown to Green Report 2018*, 15 of the G20 nations reported a rise in emissions in 2017.[1] In order to meet the goals of the Paris Agreement,[2] large-scale extraction of carbon dioxide (CO_2) seems imperative.[3] This was acknowledged by the IPCC in its Fifth Assessment Report (2014), where the Synthesis Report contained a brief discussion of the present and potential future role and limitations of geoengineering technologies.[4] In the 2018 IPCC report on the implications of exceeding 1.5°C, the mitigation strategies presented all rely on CO_2 removal, in varying amounts.[5]

1 Climate Transparency, *Brown to Green Report – The G20 Transition to a Low-Carbon Economy 2018*, available at www.climate-transparency.org/g20-climate-performance/g20report2018.

2 The Paris Agreement, adopted by Decision 1/CP.21 Report of the Conference of the Parties at its twenty-first session, held in Paris from 30 November to 13 December 2015, entered into force 4 November 2016, Adoption of the Paris Agreement, UN Doc. FCCC/CP/2015/10/Add.1, Annex, 21, available at http://unfccc.int/resource/docs/2015/cop21/eng/10a01.pdf.

3 See D. Keith, *A Case for Climate Engineering* (MIT Press, 2013).

4 Intergovernmental Panel on Climate Change (IPCC), *Climate Change 2014: Synthesis Report. Contribution of Working Groups I, II and III to the Fifth Assessment Report of the Intergovernmental Panel on Climate Change*, Core Writing Team R. K. Pachauri and LA Meyer (eds.), IPCC, Geneva, 15.

5 Intergovernmental Panel on Climate Change (IPCC), *Global Warming of 1.5°C, an IPCC Special Report on the Impacts of Global Warming of 1.5°C above Pre-industrial Levels and Related Global Greenhouse Gas Emission Pathways, in the Context of Strengthening the Global Response to the Threat of Climate Change, Sustainable Development, and Efforts to Eradicate Poverty* (IPCC SR 1.5 2018), available at www.ipcc.ch/pdf/special-reports/sr15/sr15_draft.pdf.

Geoengineering, or climate engineering, can be defined as deliberate large-scale interventions in the Earth's systems to counteract climate change.[6] Geoengineering is an umbrella term that covers a diverse set of proposed techniques, including ocean fertilization.[7] Of the marine geoengineering techniques discussed to date – such as carbon storage in the ocean, ocean pumping, enhancing ocean alkalinity and increasing ocean albedo – ocean fertilization is the most tested and most deployed.[8] This chapter examines the relationship between ocean fertilization and the law of the sea, asking whether and how the law of the sea regime facilitates ocean fertilization techniques for climate change mitigation.

'Ocean fertilization' refers to adding iron or other nutrients, such as volcanic ash, phosphate and urea, into the ocean in areas with low biological productivity in order to stimulate phytoplankton growth. Stimulating biological production in the ocean requires light and a range of essential elements or nutrients, including large amounts of carbon (C), nitrogen (N) and phosphor (P).[9] Planktonic (drifting) micro-organisms fix carbon by photosynthesis.[10] In theory, the resulting phytoplankton draw down atmospheric CO_2 and then die, falling to the ocean bed and sequestering carbon. Ocean fertilization is hence a technique for

6 Common to all definitions of geoengineering is the component requirement of intent and the scale of the environmental intervention; see D. Bodansky, 'May we engineer the climate?' (1996) 33 *Climactic Change*, 309–321. The Royal Society defines geoengineering as 'deliberate large-scale intervention in the Earth's climate system, in order to moderate global warming'. J. Shepherd et al., The Royal Society Report on Geoengineering (The Royal Society Report) (2009) *Geoengineering the climate: Science, governance and uncertainty* (Report 10/09) 1, available at https://royalsociety.org/~/media/Royal_Society_Content/policy/publications/2009/8693.pdf.

The IPCC defines geoengineering as 'a broad set of methods and technologies that aim to deliberately alter the climate system in order to alleviate the impacts of climate change'. IPCC Expert Meeting on Geoengineering, 20–22 June 2011, Meeting Report available at www.ipcc.ch/pdf/supporting-material/EM_GeoE_Meeting_Report_final.pdf.

7 Geoengineering techniques can be divided into two broad categories: (1) reducing the levels of carbon dioxide and other greenhouse gases from the atmosphere and sequestering them (greenhouse gas removal), and (2) exerting a cooling influence on Earth by reducing the amount of sunlight absorbed by Earth (solar radiation management). See A. M. Hubert, *Code of Conduct for the Responsible Geoengineering Research* (2017), available at https://ce-conference.org/system/files/documents/revised_code_of_conduct_for_geoengineering_research_2017.pdf.

8 GESAMP, P. W. Boyd and C. M. G. Vivian (eds.), GESAMP No. 98, *High Level Review of a Wide Range of Proposed Marine Geoengineering Techniques* (2019) (GESAMP 2019), ch 5.

9 Royal Society Report.

10 The Intergovernmental Oceanographic Commission, D. W. R. Wallace et al., *Ocean Fertilization: A Scientific Summary for Policy Makers* (2010), 2, available at unesdoc.unesco.org/ark:/48223/pf0000190674.

accelerating the natural, continuous and ongoing process described as the ocean's biological pump.[11] The intention is to enhance the growth of microscopic marine plants on a scale large enough not only to increase the uptake of atmospheric carbon by the ocean significantly but also to remove it from the atmosphere for long enough to provide global climatic benefit. Simply put, the objective of ocean fertilization is to mitigate climate change by putting some of the carbon into a 'hidden' reservoir, where it cannot reach the atmosphere.

To date scientists have conducted at least thirteen ocean fertilization experiments.[12] The potential effectiveness of ocean fertilization as a climate change mitigation measures is, however, still disputed.[13] Science is not able to provide clear evidence as to the role of the added iron (or other nutrients) compared to other factors (such as light, seasonality or oxygen production), or to the 'export and fate' of the extra carbon.[14] The effects of stimulating the ocean's biological pump have been questioned, as research has indicated that most of the CO_2 absorbed by phytoplankton blooms would be released back into the atmosphere when the phytoplankton decompose.[15] Although this is one of the few geoengineering techniques to have been developed beyond the theory stage, lack of scientific certainty as to the mitigating effects makes ocean fertilization highly debatable.

From a legal perspective there are also many uncertainties in relation to ocean fertilization activities. No international treaty regime or bodies are devoted to ocean fertilization or geoengineering activities in general. That does not mean that ocean fertilization takes place in 'a regulatory Wild West or a legal black hole'.[16] Ocean fertilization falls under several spheres of

11 G. Jeffries, 'Time for a new international legal regime for ocean fertilization in the high seas?' (Master's Thesis LLM in Law of the Sea, UiT – The Arctic University of Norway, 2017), 9, available at https://munin.uit.no/bitstream/handle/10037/12501/thesis.pdf?sequence=2&isAllowed=y.

12 Geoengineering Monitor, *Ocean Fertilization (Technology Factsheet)* (2018), available at www.geoengineeringmonitor.org/2018/05/ocean-fertilization/. See also M. Branson, 'A green herring: how current ocean fertilization regulation distracts from geoengineering research' (2014) 54 *Santa Clara Law Review*, 163–200.

13 GESAMP 2019, Chs 5.1–5.3.

14 Jeffries, 'Time for a new international legal regime', 10. See also K. N. Scott, 'Regulating ocean fertilization under international law: the risks' (2013) 2 *Carbon and Climate Law Review*, 108–116, 110, especially references in footnote 22.

15 P. Williamson, 'Emissions reduction: scrutinize CO_2 removal methods', in *Nature: International Weekly Journal of Science* (10 February 2016), available at www.nature.com/news/emissions-reduction-scrutinize-co2-removal-methods-1.19318.

16 K. N. Scott, 'International law in the Anthropocene: responding to the geoengineering challenge' (2013) 34 *Michigan Journal of International Law*, 309–358, 330.

international law, including environmental law, climate law and the law of the sea. Ocean fertilization is a measure deployed to solve one particular problem (excess greenhouse gases [GHGs] in the atmosphere) that might create other problems (pollution of the marine environment). It is both a potential fixer and creator of environmental threats, depending on the legal regime involved. That an activity is governed by and relevant under different legal regimes is neither a novel nor a unique situation. Legal fragmentation is to some extent unavoidable.[17] Interaction involving several international legal regimes is one way of ensuring that the objectives of different regimes are met and potential conflicts avoided by ensuring effective implementation of rules and efficient institutional operation of regimes.[18] But is regime interaction through systemic harmonization able to provide sufficient responses to interconnected environmental problems?[19] As Scott points out, the greatest challenge for the law of the sea in the 21st century may be 'responding to interconnected environmental systems through disconnected political and legal institutions'.[20]

Ocean fertilization is, at the global level, presented as a possible contributor to the reduction of GHGs in the atmosphere. Since such activity takes place in the ocean space, the law of the sea will play an important role in how, and to what extent, ocean fertilization techniques are further developed and deployed, by providing the legal framework. As noted in the 2019 GESAMP report on *High Level Review of a Wide Range of Proposed Marine Geoengineering Techniques*, in order for ocean fertilization techniques to be developed into a well-functioning and well-used tool, a coordinated framework for proposing and assessing marine geoengineering activities should be developed.[21] Furthermore: 'it is essential that the process of evidence-based

[17] International Law Commission, Report of the Study Group (2006), *Fragmentation of International Law: Difficulties Arising from the Diversification and Expansion of International Law*, finalized by M. Koskenniemi, Doc. A/CN.4/L.682, 11.

[18] S. Kopela, 'Climate change, regime interaction, and the principle of common but differentiated responsibility: the experience of the International Maritime Organization' (2014) 24:1 *Yearbook of International Environmental Law*, 70–101, 72.

[19] The phrase 'systemic harmonization' refers to an approach towards regime interaction based on the new posture of international courts and tribunals of being oriented towards systemic harmonization rather than towards normative conflict. See, e.g., the European Court of Human Rights Grand Chamber in *Al-Dulimi*; Case *Al-Dulimi and Montana Management Inc.* v. *Switzerland* [GC] App. No. 5809/08 (ECtHR, 2016) para. 140. See also L. A. Sicilianos, 'The European Court of Human Rights facing the Security Council: towards systemic harmonization' (2017) 66:4 *International & Comparative Law Quarterly*, 783–804; A. Peters, 'The refinement of international law: from fragmentation to regime interaction and politicization' (2017) 15:3 *International Journal of Constitutional Law*, 671–704.

[20] K. N. Scott, 'Marine geoengineering and the law of the sea' in R. C. Beckman et al. (eds.), *High Seas Governance: Gaps and Challenges* (Brill Nijhoff, 2018), 34, 35.

[21] GESAMP 2019, 14.

assessment takes place in parallel with ongoing efforts to devise research governance structures, since both are inextricably linked in the marine geoengineering debate and the development of policy.'[22]

This chapter asks whether the law of the sea, in the broadest understanding of the term, provides such a framework. Before analysing how ocean fertilization techniques are dealt with by the Law of the Sea Regime, it begins by charting how marine geoengineering techniques in general, and ocean fertilization in particular, sit within the UN Climate Change Regime (Section 8.2). It then assesses ocean fertilization within the framework of the 1982 Law of the Sea Convention (LOSC) (Section 8.3),[23] before discussing how other conventions, mainly those regulating marine dumping and the Convention on Biological Diversity (CBD),[24] have framed ocean fertilization (Section 8.4). The purpose of examining the how and why of different regulatory approaches to ocean fertilization activities is to identify the potential environmental and socio-economic aspects entailed in divergent legal approaches. If one regime views ocean fertilization as pollution while another does not, or the harm threshold is interpreted differently, that not only creates legal uncertainties that could slow down future investments in ocean fertilization techniques, but also undermines the frameworks developed to ensure a process that provides opportunities for effective, transparent scientific review. (The latter is further discussed in Section 8.5 of this chapter, which examines the legal consequences of the different regulatory approaches.) The chapter ends with some concluding remarks (Section 8.6).

8.2 THE UN CLIMATE CHANGE REGIME AND OCEAN FERTILIZATION

The main objective of the UN climate change treaty regime, consisting of the 1992 United Nations Framework Convention on Climate Change (UNFCCC),[25] the 1997 Kyoto Protocol[26] and the 2015 Paris Agreement,[27] is to 'stabilize greenhouse gas concentrations in the atmosphere at a level that

[22] Ibid.

[23] 1982 United Nations Convention on the Law of the Sea (LOSC), Montego Bay, 10 December 1982, in force 16 November 1994, 1833 UNTS 397.

[24] 1992 Convention on Biological Diversity (CBD), Rio de Janeiro, 5 June 1992, 1760 UNTS 69.

[25] 1992 United Nations Framework Convention on Climate Change (UNFCCC), Rio de Janeiro, 9 June 1992, 1771 UNTS 107.

[26] Kyoto Protocol to the United Nations Framework Convention on Climate Change (Kyoto Protocol), Kyoto, 11 December 1997, in force 16 February 2005, 2303 UNTS 162.

[27] The Paris Agreement, adopted by Decision 1/CP.21 Report of the Conference of the Parties at its twenty-first session, held in Paris from 30 November to 13 December 2015, entered into force

would prevent dangerous anthropogenic interference with the climate system'.[28] In the 2015 Paris Agreement this is specified as holding global average temperature increase to 'well below 2°C above pre-industrial levels and pursuing efforts to limit the temperature increase to 1.5°C above pre-industrial levels'.[29]

In order to achieve these objectives, the international community has accepted that a range of mitigation and adaptation measures must be implemented.[30] The UNFCCC definition of 'mitigation' includes national policies and measures 'limiting anthropogenic emissions of greenhouse gases and protecting and enhancing greenhouse gas sinks and reservoirs'.[31] The Kyoto Protocol calls for the promotion of research and implementation of 'advanced and innovative sound technologies' – which could be interpreted as including geoengineering techniques.[32] However, it is not yet clear whether ocean fertilization activities fall under this criterion. This uncertain legal status is evident from a review of the use of market-based mechanisms introduced by the Kyoto Protocol, which created what is now known as the 'carbon market'. Offsets from ocean fertilization projects are not included in any carbon markets and cannot be traded on regulated carbon markets such as the European Union Emission Trading Scheme (EU ETS) or the Chicago Climate Exchange (CCX).[33] This shows both that regulatory requirements are needed if carbon offsets through ocean fertilization activities are to be part of the carbon market, and that such activities have not been clearly defined or categorized in international climate law.[34]

The Paris Agreement builds upon the Kyoto Protocol's use of market mechanisms, but CO_2 removal was not specifically discussed in Paris. However, the acceptability of including geoengineering techniques as a mitigation option is indicated in the reference to the use of 'sinks'.[35] The definition of 'sinks' broadly encompasses 'any process, activity or mechanism which removes a greenhouse gas, an aerosol or a precursor of a greenhouse gas

4 November 2016, Adoption of the Paris Agreement, UN Doc. FCCC/CP/2015/10/Add.1, Annex, 21, available at http://unfccc.int/resource/docs/2015/cop21/eng/10a01.pdf.

28 UNFCCC, Art. 2.

29 Paris Agreement, Art. 2(1)(a).

30 D. Freestone and R. Rayfuse, 'Ocean iron fertilization in international law' (2008) 364 *Marine Ecology Progress Series*, 227–233.

31 UNFCCC, Art. 4(2)(a).

32 Kyoto Protocol, Art. (2)(1)(a)(iv).

33 C. Bertram, 'Ocean iron fertilization in the context of the Kyoto Protocol and the post-Kyoto process' (2010) 38 *Energy Policy*, 1130–1139, 1135.

34 Ibid.

35 Paris Agreement, Art. 4(1).

from the atmosphere'.[36] Article 5 of the Paris Agreement addresses sinks and reservoirs specifically, obliging the parties to 'conserve and enhance' sinks and reservoirs. This wording might be interpreted as an intention to limit sinks and reservoirs to natural processes. However, Craik and Burns argue, 'this would not preclude the use of CDR [CO_2 removal] approaches that seek to amplify natural sink processes, including ... ocean iron fertilization'.[37]

Although the Paris Agreement does not clearly mandate or otherwise authorize the use of geoengineering technologies, the structure of and especially the bottom-up architecture of the Agreement provides for the possibility of factoring geoengineering techniques into the Paris commitment.[38] The Paris Agreement's bottom-up approach, where the parties pledge their own determined nationally contributions, leaves considerable discretion to the various states on how to contribute.[39] Craig and Burns point out that this allows states to identify and include geoengineering measures in their nationally determined contributions, 'since removals of CO_2 are expressly contemplated as an element of mitigation under Article 4'.[40]

However, use of geoengineering techniques may continue to sit uncomfortably even within the climate regime, due the need to develop and fine-tune the science involved in the key technologies, such as developing reliable accounting methodologies, including addressing issues of permanence that arise in relation to carbon sequestration.[41] In addition, as within the Law of the Sea Regime, any action taken should be balanced against other interests, especially environmental concerns. This is expressed in the preamble to the Paris Agreement, 'Noting the importance of ensuring the integrity of all ecosystems, including oceans, and the protection of biodiversity.'

However, the main function of geoengineering measures is to mitigate climate risk. The primacy of the main objectives of the Paris Agreement, expressed as temperature targets and long-term goals of climate neutrality, is implicit in the Preamble, which recognizes 'that Parties may be affected not only by climate change, but also by the impacts of the measures taken in response to it'. International climate change law seems to recognize that

36 UNFCCC, Art. 1(8).

37 Centre for International Governance Innovation (CIGI), A. N. Craik and W. C. G. Burns, Special Report, *Climate Engineering under the Paris Agreement: A Legal and Policy Primer* (2016) (CIGI Report 2016), available at www.cigionline.org/sites/default/files/documents/GeoEngineering%20Primer%20-%20Special%20Report.pdf.

38 Ibid., 7.

39 See A. Savaresi, 'The Paris Agreement: a new beginning?' (2016) 34:1 *Journal of Energy & Natural Resource Law*, 16–26, 20–21.

40 CIGI Report 2016, 6.

41 Ibid., 9.

conventional forms of mitigation and adaptation alone will be insufficient to avert serious climate change, and that the cost entailed in employing geoengineering techniques is a price that the regime is willing to pay.

8.3 OCEAN FERTILIZATION AND THE LOSC

For activities that take place in the ocean space, the natural starting point for identifying applicable rules and regulations is the LOSC. The LOSC was intended to govern all ocean issues by establishing a 'legal order for the seas and oceans', striving to attain a balance between the interests of multiple actors, including the global interest of protecting the marine environment.[42] Despite the ambition of governing all activities in the ocean space, geoengineering techniques were not mentioned in the discussions during the negotiations leading to the adoption of the LOSC. There are hence no provisions of direct application to geoengineering, in general, or ocean fertilization specifically within the LOSC, making ocean fertilization subject to a myriad of principles, concepts and rules of various LOSC categories. Many are highly relevant but none is sufficient on its own, which prompts the question of whether the legal framework offered by LOSC can fill the gaps by adapting its existing principles and rules to the new situation, or must develop a new regime designated to regulate ocean fertilization.

As a 'negative' emissions technology, ocean fertilization presents opportunities for meeting the climate goals of the Paris Agreement, advantageous for all. As such, ocean fertilization could serve as a tool in line with the obligations embodied in LOSC Part XII to protect and preserve the marine environment by limiting GHG emissions and their negative effects on the ocean. The assumption of ocean fertilization as an 'environmentally friendly' tool is, however, challenged by the possible negative effects of adding iron sulphate or other nutrients to the marine environment. The positive effects must be viewed against the possible negative effects of this activity when interpreting the rights and obligations of LOSC Part XII. However, the LOSC is built on the concept of state sovereignty, giving states sovereign rights to explore and exploit the resources within their maritime zones.[43] In that regard, ocean fertilization represent an opportunity for coastal states, or flag states if deployed

42 LOSC, Preamble, Third Recital.

43 LOSC, Arts. 2, 49, 56 and 77. See also the provisions on marine scientific research in LOSC Part XIII, Articles 245 and 256, granting to coastal states exclusive jurisdiction in managing marine scientific research in their waters. On the high seas, marine scientific research is categorized as a 'freedom of the high seas', which must be carried out in accordance with LOSC Part XIII. On the latter, see Scott, 'Marine geoengineering', 47–48.

on the high seas, to meet their obligations under the Paris Agreement by factoring it into their nationally determined contributions – provided a method for quantifying the negative emission is developed. This makes ocean fertilization activities a potential resource for the coastal or flag state, with the LOSC serving as a protector of both the environment and the rights of coastal states to explore and exploit their marine resources. The perspective from which ocean fertilization is viewed and legally categorized is central to how the regulatory framework for this activity can be best designed. To this we now turn.

Protection of the marine environment is the focus of LOSC Part XII, which describes the responsibility of states to prevent, reduce and control marine pollution. LOSC Article 196 requires the parties to 'take all measures necessary to prevent, reduce and control pollution of the marine environment resulting from the use of technologies under their jurisdiction or control'. The wording makes the definition of *pollution* in Article 1(4) an important qualifying term for LOSC obligations. A literal understanding of Article 196 and its reference to pollution means that ocean fertilization activities at or above the threshold of harm established by Article 1(4) cannot be executed at all, or must be carried out in a way that lowers the negative effects to the tolerated level (e.g. by reducing the amount of nutrients used or changing location). The first question in relation to how ocean fertilization activities are treated in the LOSC is hence whether this activity qualifies as *pollution*.

Pollution is defined in Article 1(1)(4) as:

> [T]he introduction by man, directly or indirectly, of substances or energy into the marine environment, including estuaries, which results or is likely to result in such deleterious effects as harm to living resources and marine life, hazards to human health, hindrance to marine activities, including fishing and other legitimate uses of the sea, impairment of quality for use of sea water and reduction of amenities.[44]

The definition relates both to the origin and location of pollution (first part) and to the effects that qualify as pollution (second part). As to the first part, it could be argued that adding iron sulphate or other nutrients to the ocean involves a 'substance' that is 'introduced by man'. However, it could be questioned whether certain ocean fertilization techniques, such as pipes used in the water column to stimulate the transfer of nutrients from deep-water columns towards the surface, would involve an 'introduction'.[45]

44 LOSC, Art. 1(1)(4).

45 K. N. Scott, 'Geoengineering and the marine environment' in R. Rayfuse (ed.), *Research Handbook on International Marine Environmental Law* (Edward Elgar, 2015), 451–472.

As to the second part of the definition, what makes an activity 'pollution' is not the nature of the substance introduced, but its potential deleterious effects.[46] The definition of 'pollution' offers no guidance as to what would amount to 'deleterious effect' other than the examples in the end of the provision, which give little guidance on what the threshold actually is. 'Harm to living resources and marine life' could mean anything from an algae bloom putting pressures on other species and forcing them to move, to the extinction of a species or disruption of entire ecosystems. The term 'harm' does not indicate the level of effect that cannot be tolerated. This shows how broad, general terms can create legal uncertainties unless complemented or specified by other instruments or institutions. Adding iron sulphate to the ocean in one region could mean an increase in plankton productivity, which might reduce the yields of fisheries elsewhere. Such risks have resulted in the near-universal rejection of ocean fertilization as a climate intervention, through bodies such as the CBD. However, it can also be argued that the effects are *not* deleterious, as the effects of ocean fertilization activities are no different from the natural biological ocean pump, and because stimulating biological productivity by adding nutrients has a net positive effect.[47] It is hence not possible to state categorically that ocean fertilization is always pollution, or that it never crosses the pollution threshold. Without any specifying criteria or direct reference to ocean fertilization in LOSC, it must be decided on a case-by-case basis whether a given activity crosses the harm threshold established by LOSC Article 1(4).

Even if an ocean fertilization activity is not categorized as pollution, it must still, as any other activity carried out in the ocean space, meet the obligations of precaution and due diligence. The general obligation in Article 192 to protect and preserve the marine environment is general and comprehensive: it includes protection of everything from individual species to habitats and large ecosystems, and is not limited to protection from pollution.[48] The general obligation laid down in Article 192 is specified through the subsequent provisions and sections of Part XII, supplemented by key principles of international environmental law such as the precautionary principle, the no-harm rule and the obligation to act with due

[46] R. Abate and A. Greenlee, 'Sowing seeds uncertain: ocean iron fertilization, climate change, and the international environmental law framework' (2010) 27 *Pace Environmental Law Review*, 555–598.

[47] Ibid., 573–574.

[48] D. Czybulka, 'Article 192, mn 3' in A. Proelss (ed.), *United Nations Convention on the Law of the Sea: A Commentary* (C H Beck, 2017), 1287.

diligence.[49] While the two latter principles are expressed in LOSC Articles in various forms, the precautionary principle is nowhere enunciated in the LOSC. However, the significance of the precautionary principle for marine governance has been confirmed and its application developed through international case law,[50] making it part of the LOSC obligation to act 'with precaution and due diligence'.

For ocean fertilization activities, a precautionary approach would imply a process that ensures that the potential risks have been identified, weighed and remedied to be below the harm threshold. This would include applying an environmental impact assessment (EIA), in line with the obligations in LOSC Article 206 and the general requirement to conduct EIAs as developed in international environmental law.[51]

Assuming that an ocean fertilization activity can be characterized as 'pollution', the next question is whether this qualifies as dumping, which LOSC Article 210 sees as a form of pollution.[52] Dumping is defined in Article 1(1)(5) of the LOSC – not to signal that it differs from pollution, but to facilitate regulation through specific rules and regimes.[53] According to Article 210, states shall 'adopt laws and regulations to prevent, reduce and control pollution of the marine environment by dumping'. The 1972 Convention on the Prevention of Marine Pollution by Dumping of Wastes and Other Matter (London Convention) and the 1996 Protocol to the London Convention (London Protocol) form the 'global rules and standards' referred to in LOSC Article 210.

The relevant part of LOSC Article 1(5)(a) describes dumping as 'any deliberate disposal of wastes or other matter from vessels, aircraft, platforms or other man-made structures at sea'. This description fits the main elements of most ocean fertilization activities, as it concerns 'matter' to be deliberately disposed of at sea. However, Article 1(5) (b)(ii) underlines that dumping does *not* include 'placement of matter for a purpose other than the mere disposal thereof, provided that such placement is not contrary to the aims of this

49 See, e.g., the South China Sea Arbitration, where the obligation to ensure prevention of harm was phrased as an obligation of conduct, to be carried out with due diligence. *South China Sea Arbitration (The Republic of Philippines* v. *The People's Republic of China)* (Award) [2016] PCA Case No. 2013-19, para. 944.

50 See, e.g., *Responsibilities and Obligations of State Sponsoring Persons and Entities with Respect to Activities in the Area* (Advisory Opinion) [2011] ITLOS Rep. 10, para. 135; *Pulp Mills on the River Uruguay* (Argentina v. Uruguay) (Judgement) [2010] ICJ Rep. 14, para. 164.

51 Scott, 'Marine geoengineering', 44.

52 LOSC, Art. 210 Pollution by dumping.

53 LOSC, Art. 1(5)(a)(i) defines dumping as: 'any deliberate disposal of wastes or other matter from vessels, aircraft, platforms or other man-made structures at sea'.

Convention'. Ocean fertilization activities fit this description of what is exempted from the dumping definition, as the purpose of such activities is to sequester CO_2 and not the mere disposal of the nutrients used to get this effect. According to the LOSC, then, ocean fertilization does not constitute dumping – yet the international dumping regime has mandated itself to regulate this activity. The next section examines recent initiatives to supplement the LOSC in regulating ocean fertilization activities, starting with the international London Dumping Regime.

8.4 RESPONDING TO THE GAPS AND CHALLENGES

The 1972 Convention on the Prevention of Marine Pollution by Dumping of Wastes and Other Matter (London Convention) and the 1996 Protocol to the London Convention (London Protocol) provides rules and standards that pertain to ocean fertilization.[54] Article 1 of the London Convention presents the main objective of the regime when obliging the contracting parties to 'take all practicable steps to prevent the pollution of the sea by the dumping of waste and other matter'.

The London Convention forbids dumping of substances listed in its Annex I. However, the later London Protocol turned the regulation around, forbidding the dumping of wastes and other matter, except for those on a prescribed list, which may be assessed and granted permits for dumping.[55] This 'reverse list' of substances makes the dumping regime stricter, and represents full embracement of the precautionary principle.[56]

Sparked by the active interests in this activity by both scientists and private operators, the contracting parties set about constructing a regulation on ocean fertilization.[57] Having confirmed their belief 'that the scope of work of the London Convention and Protocol included ocean fertilization',[58] in 2008 the contracting parties adopted 'Resolution LC-LP. 1 (2008) On the Regulation of Ocean Fertilization'.[59] This resolution

54 Convention on the Prevention of Marine Pollution by Dumping of Wastes and Other Matter, London, 29 December 1972, in force 30 August 1975, 1046 UNTS 138 (London Convention). 1996 Protocol to the Convention on the Prevention of Marine Pollution by Dumping of Wastes and Other Matter, 1972, 7 November 1966, in force 24 March 2006, 36 ILM 1 (London Protocol).

55 The London Protocol supersedes the London Convention as between contracting parties to both legal instruments. London Protocol, Art. 23.

56 London Protocol, Art. 3.

57 Jeffries, 'Time for a new international legal regime', 18–19.

58 IMO Doc LC/29/17, 0.2.3.2.

59 IMO Doc LC 30/16. Resolution LC-LP.1 is included in Annex 6.

defined ocean fertilization as 'any activity undertaken by humans with the principle intention of stimulating primary productivity in the oceans', and reaffirmed the belief that ocean fertilization fell within the scope of the London Convention and Protocol.[60] However, the same wording as used in the LOSC to describe what is exempted from being defined as dumping is used by the London Convention and Protocol: dumping does not include 'placement of matter for a purpose other than the mere disposal thereof, provided that such placement is not contrary to the aims of the Convention or Protocol'.[61] It is hence not quite clear whether the international dumping regime views ocean fertilization as a form of dumping, or regards this activity as falling under its scope by developing a new regime that broadens the original mandate.

The 2008 resolution stated that ocean fertilization for non-scientific purposes is subject to and contrary to the London Convention and Protocol.[62] 'Legitimate scientific research', by contrast, involves 'placement of matter for a purpose other than mere disposal' and may be permitted on a case-by-case basis if conducted in accordance with the Assessment Framework adopted by the contracting parties in 2010.[63] Pursuant to this Framework, parties must undertake environmental assessments, emplace monitoring procedures and facilitate adaptive management.[64] The Assessment Framework has been criticized for its scope and its content, inter alia for failing to provide incentives for the necessary scientific research on risk analysis by raising bureaucratic barriers to research experiments.[65] Nevertheless, the Framework is described as a 'model of precautionary and adaptive management', offering both procedural and substantive environmental requirements.[66]

Neither the 2008 nor the 2010 resolution is legally binding, but a legally binding resolution to regulate ocean fertilization was adopted in 2013. This resolution amends only the London Protocol, and adds a new Article 6*bis*:

> Contracting Parties shall not allow the placement of matter into the sea from vessels, aircraft, platforms or other man-made structures at sea for marine

60 Resolution LC-LP.1, para. 1, footnoting that 'conventional aquaculture, or mariculture, or the creation of artificial reefs' fell outside this definition.
61 London Convention, Art. III(1)(b).
62 Ibid.
63 Assessment Framework for Scientific Research Involving Ocean Fertilization, IMO Doc LC 32/15. The Assessment Framework is included in Annex 6.
64 Scott, 'Regulating ocean fertilization', 351.
65 Branson, 'A green herring', 186.
66 Scott, 'Regulating ocean fertilization', 351.

geoengineering activities listed in Annex 4, unless the listing provides that the activity or the sub-category of an activity may be authorized under a permit.[67]

A new Annex V adds the Assessment Framework for matter that may be considered for placement under Annex 4. The resolution stipulates that only ocean fertilization activities 'constituting legitimate scientific research taking into account [the] specific [2010] assessment framework' can be considered for a permit.[68] The amendments will enter into force sixty days after two thirds of forty-eight contracting parties have deposited instruments of acceptance of the amendment with IMO.[69] That has not yet happened, as of this writing.

The Director of the IMO Marine Environment Division, Dr Stefan Micallef, proclaimed the adoption of the 2013 amendment as 'a true testament to the fact that the London Protocol continues to be among the most advanced international regulatory instruments addressing human activities in the marine environment and there is no doubt that this much-awaited amendment will be appreciated by other international bodies'.[70] This is discussed further in Section 8.5.

Like the London Dumping Regime, the CBD has recognized the need to discuss how to approach ocean fertilization in the marine environmental context. The CBD provides a global legal framework for action on biodiversity. The governing body of the Convention, the Conference of the Parties (COP), meets every two years, or as needed, and advances implementation of the Convention through its decisions. The objectives of the CBD are to conserve biodiversity, encourage the sustainable use of its components, and to ensure fair and equitable sharing of the benefits arising from the utilization of genetic resources.[71] Thus it complements and specifies the Part XII LOSC obligations to protect the marine environment.

With few exceptions, the same approximately195 states are parties to both the UNFCCC and the CBD.[72] Climate change, and the related phenomenon

67 The Amendment to the London Protocol to Regulate the Placement of Matter for Ocean Fertilization and other Geoengineering Activities (19 October 2013) Resolution LP.4(8) (amendment not yet in force), Art. 6*bis*(1).

68 Resolution LP.4(8), Annex 4.1.3.

69 London Protocol, Art. 21(3).

70 IMO, Press Briefing to 35th Consultative Meeting of Contracting Parties to the Convention on the Prevention of Marine Pollution by Dumping of Wastes and Other Matter, 1972 (London Convention) 8th meeting of Contracting Parties to the 1996 Protocol thereto (London Protocol), *Marine Geoengineering Including Ocean Fertilization to Be Regulated under Amendments to International Treaty* (18 October 2013), available at www.imo.org/en/MediaCentre/PressBriefings/Pages/45-marine-geoengieneering.aspx#.XQp1r1wzY2x.

71 CBD, Art. 1.

72 Williamson, 'Emissions reduction'.

of ocean acidification, are additional drivers of the main direct drivers of biodiversity loss – which are habitat loss, over-exploitation of harvested species, pollution (including from excess nutrients), and the introduction of invasive alien species.[73] Successful deployment of geoengineering techniques, helping to limit future temperature increase, would be of benefit for biodiversity as well.[74] Nevertheless, the CBD regime sees all forms of ocean fertilization activities as contrary to the aims of the Convention and has rejected ocean fertilization as a climate intervention.[75]

With Decision IX/16, a moratorium was emplaced as regards ocean fertilization activities. This moratorium will remain until there is an 'adequate scientific basis on which to justify such activities, including assessing associated risks, and a global, transparent and effective control and regulatory mechanisms in place for these activities'.[76] The sole exception concerns small-scale scientific studies within coastal waters that can justify the need to gather specific scientific data.[77]

However, Decision IX/16 also notes the 'legal analysis [of ocean fertilization governance] occurring under the auspices' of another legal instrument, and urges parties to act in accordance with the outcome of that process.[78] This is a reference to the development of the international London Dumping Regime as described earlier. Although Decision IX/16 is not legally binding, it strongly recommends the parties to the CBD to follow the development of the London Dumping Regime. Both the Assessment Framework and the legally binding resolution of the London Dumping Regime were adopted after Decision IX/16 of the COP. Williamson and Bodle argue that the London Protocol amendment, once it enters into force, 'will strengthen the regulatory framework for ocean fertilization activities and provide a framework for the further regulation of other marine geoengineering activities'.[79] Although these instruments might satisfy the demand for 'global, transparent and effective control and regulatory mechanisms', the lack of 'adequate scientific basis' might be considered as still existing. Nevertheless, the CBD COP has invited the parties to

73 P. Williamson and R. Bodle, *Update on Climate Geoengineering in Relation to the Convention on Biological Diversity: Potential Impacts and Regulatory Framework* (2016) Technical Series No. 84. Secretariat of the Convention on Biological Diversity, Montreal, 94.

74 Ibid.

75 COP to the CBD at its Ninth Meeting, 19–30 May 2008, IX/16 Biodiversity and Climate Change, UNEP/CBD/COP/DEC/IX/16, 9 October 2008, [C.4].

76 Ibid.

77 Ibid.

78 Jeffries, 'Time for a new international legal regime', 17, referring to Decision IX/16, [C.4] and [C.2.].

79 Williamson and Bodle, *Update on Climate Geoengineering*, 14.

the London Protocol to ratify this amendment and other governments to apply measures in line with this amendment, as appropriate.[80]

8.5 THE RIGHT RESPONSE?

The analysis in Sections 8.2 and 8.4 of this chapter has shown that the current legal regime applicable to ocean fertilization suffers from several normative overlaps and gaps. Ocean fertilization is defined and approached differently by the various legal regimes. Furthermore, existing applicable law is too general, and many of the applicable legal instruments do not refer to ocean fertilization or were negotiated without ocean fertilization or geoengineering techniques in mind. The result is a legal regime faced with several problems, including how to deal with competing regulatory approaches.[81] That might mean that opportunities to mitigate climate change by ocean fertilization techniques could be slowed down, even abandoned.

One of the main problems is how to balance the differing interests of the LOSC, UNFCCC, the CBD and the London Convention and Protocol. Although ocean fertilization is not specifically mentioned, it is in line with the climate-change regime's main objectives to view this geoengineering technique as a mitigation measure. The most recent IPCCC reports presuppose the use of CO_2 removal measures if success in decelerating the negative emission spiral is to be achieved.[82] However, as shown earlier, with ocean fertilization activities the crux of the problem is that in reducing the scale of one problem (climate change), other new problems may be created (polluting the marine environment causing, for example, loss of biodiversity or disruption of ecosystems). Indeed, 'each CDR technology implemented at a scale contemplated to meet the Paris Agreement goals is accompanied by significant environmental, social and economic costs'.[83] Other legal regimes and instruments must supplement the climate regime to ensure protection of other rights, obligations and interests, including the protection of the marine environment. And here we must ask: is the applicable legal framework to ocean fertilization, and geoengineering in general, equipped to address the 'complex interplay of environmental, ethical social, and legal concerns' associated with the deployment of geoengineering techniques?[84]

80 Ibid., 88, referring to CBD COP decision XII/20.
81 See Jeffries, 'Time for a new international legal regime', 30–31 where he identifies seven problems with the current legal regime.
82 Intergovernmental Panel on Climate Change (IPCC), *Global Warming of 1.5°C*.
83 Williamson and Bodle, *Update on Climate Geoengineering*, 5.
84 Hubert, *Code of Conduct*, 4.

As regards the LOSC and the London Dumping Regime, the complex interplay is evident. Dumping is defined in the same way, but ocean fertilization is categorized differently. According to the LOSC, ocean fertilization does not constitute dumping. It may be a form of pollution if the activity, decided on a case-by-case basis, approaches the harm threshold. That the parties to the London Dumping Regime deem themselves competent to develop a regulatory framework for ocean fertilization under its (dumping) regime adds to the complexity and uncertainty as to how ocean fertilization is to be treated under international law. It is not clear whether they do this because ocean fertilization is categorized as dumping or because they consider it part of their (broader) mandate. The question remains: how to solve the problem of norm collision and coordinate two subfields of international law?

At first sight, this would seem to create an incompatibility of legal definitions, possibly resulting in conflicting legal obligations. Can reliance on regime interaction through systemic harmonization provide guidance on balancing different interests based on today's patchwork of overlapping and partly competing laws and regulations? Or will be necessary to improve the current regime?

The relation of the LOSC to other conventions and international agreements is spelled out in its Articles 311 and 237, which state that LOSC provisions are without prejudice to the specific obligations assumed by states under special conventions and agreements concluded previously, as long as they are carried out in ways that do 'not affect the enjoyment by other States Parties of their rights' (Article 311(2)) and are 'consistent with the general principles and objectives of this Convention' (Article 237(2)). LOSC Part XII applies to ocean fertilization activities as a potential pollutant. The relationship between the LOSC and the London Dumping Regime is hence regulated by Article 237, which is more flexible than Article 311 as regards allowing the LOSC and its Part XII to be supplemented not only by obligations concluded previous to the LOSC but also in furtherance to it.

While Article 311 (2) requires that the agreement in question to be 'compatible', Article 237 only mentions consistency with the 'general principles and objectives' of the LOSC. The question is whether the London Dumping Regime is being 'consistent' the with LOSC's general principles and objectives in categorizing ocean fertilization as 'dumping'. Here I hold that the answer is *yes*. Placing ocean fertilization under the London Dumping Regime does not change the basic characteristics of how this activity is viewed. Dumping is a form of pollution, according to both LOSC Part XII and the definition of dumping in the London Protocol, which refers to the disposal of waste and other matter into the sea.[85] The main objective of the London Dumping Regime is, according to Article 1 of the London Convention, to promote the effective control of all sources of marine pollution and to take all practicable steps to prevent sea pollution caused by dumping of wastes and other matter – an objective clearly in line with the general principles and objectives of the LOSC.

However, ocean fertilization does fall under the LOSC definition of 'marine scientific research'. Ocean fertilization activities have not yet developed beyond the level of research and into actual climate change mitigation, meaning that in addition to Article 237, Article 311 applies in the regulation of the relationship between LOSC and the London Dumping Regime.[86] In areas beyond national jurisdiction, marine scientific research is categorized as a 'freedom of the high seas' to be carried out in accordance with LOSC Part XIII.[87] Within their maritime zones, coastal states have exclusive rights to regulate, authorize and conduct marine scientific research,[88] as long as this takes place in compliance with the rules and principles of the LOSC, including its Part XII obligations.[89] But is it in accordance with Article 311(2) and its 'compatible' requirement to restrict a coastal state's possibility to undertake ocean fertilization activities by requiring a permit which only considers ocean fertilization activities that constitute 'legitimate scientific' activity?[90] According to LOSC Article 240, marine scientific research 'shall be conducted in compliance with all relevant regulations adopted in conformity with this Convention including those for the protection and preservation of the marine environment'. This general reference to regulations other than those of LOSC has allowed the London Dumping Regime to adopt restrictions on ocean fertilization activities, especially since the objective of the regulations is to protect the marine environment.

The relationship between the LOSC and the London Dumping Regime is hence not a case of conflict of norms, but how to deal most effectively with an emerging, previously unregulated, activity. By adopting a regulatory regime for ocean fertilization activities, the London Dumping Regime has addressed a gap in the law of the sea and created a 'pre-emptive regulatory regime that endorses and implements a highly precautionary approach'.[91] But, we must ask, is the London Dumping Regime the appropriate forum

85 London Protocol, Art. 1(4).
86 Scott, 'Marine geoengineering', 47.
87 LOSC, Art. 87(1)(f).
88 LOSC, Art. 245 and 246.
89 LOSC, Art. 230.
90 Resolution LP.4(8), Annex 4.1.3.
91 Scott, 'Marine geoengineering', 50.

for providing a global regulatory framework for this activity? It can be argued that another approach to manage ocean fertilization is needed. First, there are practical problems with the current London Dumping Regime regarding its applicability. Only forty-eight states are parties to the London Protocol; moreover, the amendment on ocean fertilization is not in force as it has been accepted by only one state.[92] The low endorsement of the London Protocol, and even lower for the amendment, make it difficult to argue that these regulations have become binding on all LOSC parties through the rule of reference included in LOSC Article 210.[93] Jeffries deems it 'largely unlikely that a regime potentially implemented with the support of only 32 States [the number of States necessary for the amendments to the London Protocol to become legally binding] will be a widely accepted and workable regime on a global basis'.[94] Here he cites the relative low adherence to the London Convention and Protocol by states already parties to the regime.[95] Over a thirty-three-year period, only 55.6 per cent of the state parties complied with the London requirement to report dumping activities in areas under their jurisdiction and control.[96]

Another problem with the London Dumping Regime is the reliance on flag-state jurisdiction, which is a consequence of the sectoral and zonal approach of the LOSC. States have jurisdiction over ocean fertilization activities in their maritime zones and over vessels and aircrafts flying their flag,[97] which leaves ocean fertilization activities on the high seas subject solely to flag-state jurisdiction. This represents a considerable gap in the current legal regime relating to ocean fertilization, as reliance on flag-state jurisdiction has historically not resulted in high rates of compliance. Scott identifies a third challenge with placing ocean fertilization activities under the London Dumping Regime, noting that the London Protocol and its Meeting of the Parties is not the proper forum, nor has it demonstrated any initiative, to discuss broader ethical and moral issues associated with ocean fertilization, including its relation to the climate regime and its potential function as a emissions-reducing measure.[98]

92 Ibid.

93 This is questionable even for the London Convention and Protocol itself. See Freestone and Rayfuse, 'Ocean iron fertilization', 311; Scott, 'Regulating ocean fertilization', 353; Jeffries, 'Time for a new international legal regime', 26.

94 Jeffries, 'Time for a new international legal regime', 25.

95 Ibid.

96 G. Wilson, 'Murky waters: ambiguous international law for ocean fertilization and other geoengineering' (2014) 49 *Texas International Law Journal*, 507, 545–46.

97 London Protocol, Art. 10(1)(2)(3).

98 See K. N. Scott, 'Engineering the "mis-Anthropocene": international law, ethics and geoengineering' (2015) 29 *Ocean Yearbook*, 61–84.

This shows that states should think carefully before choosing in what forum and at what level a regulatory gap should be addressed. The initiative of the parties to the London Protocol is admirable for taking regulatory action when needed. However, the desired effect is difficult to achieve. The low adherence to the London Protocol not only makes it difficult to create regulations that represent global standards – it also undermines global responses to global issues, as it can result in states becoming unwilling to discuss the subject elsewhere. If it is believed that ocean fertilization is a matter dealt with under the London Dumping Regime, that could lower the impetus to put it on the agenda in other forums. For that reason, legal scholars such as Bodansky, Scott and Hubert have noted the need to develop truly global responses. They discuss various options for how to address geoengineering, including ocean fertilization: addressing geoengineering within the climate change regime,[99] addressing geoengineering within the proposed international instrument on the conservation and sustainable use of marine biological diversity beyond national jurisdiction (BBNJ),[100] addressing geoengineering within a designated UNGA resolution,[101] developing a stand-alone instrument on geoengineering (binding or non-binding),[102] and developing mechanisms for better coordination of related instruments and institutions.[103]

Improved coordination between the climate regime, the LOSC, the London Dumping Regime and the CBD could, in fact, provide normative solutions to the regulatory gaps confronting ocean fertilization activities. The CBD has encouraged its parties to follow the development of the London Dumping Regime, and, with its almost universal participation, has the potential to create the endorsement and legitimacy necessary for recognition and further building on these standards as global international standards.

8.6 CONCLUSIONS

Considerable uncertainty attends the development and implementation of key technologies of ocean fertilization, which will require significant research

99 See Bodansky, 'May we engineer the climate?', 318; A. Lin, 'Geoengineering governance' (2009) 8 *Issues in Legal Scholarship*, 1–24, 22; Scott, 'Regulating ocean fertilization', 355; Branson, 'A green herring', 191.

100 Scott, 'Marine geoengineering', 53–54. See also Jeffries, 'Time for a new international legal regime'.

101 Scott, 'Marine geoengineering', 54–56.

102 See Hubert, *Code of Conduct*; R. Rayfuse et al., 'Ocean fertilisation and climate change: the need to regulate emerging high seas uses' (2008) 23 *International Journal of Marine and Coastal Law*, 297–326, 320; and Wilson, 'Murky waters', 555.

103 Scott, 'Marine geoengineering', 52.

and financial support. In addition to uncertainty as to the effectiveness of ocean fertilization, the international legal regime for this geoengineering technique has been described as 'unclear',[104] 'contradictory'[105] and with certain 'inherent limits'.[106] The LOSC treats ocean fertilization as 'pollution': LOSC Part XII, including and supplemented by the general principles of international environmental law, provides a regulatory framework for ocean fertilization. The London Dumping Regime opens for scientific ocean fertilization activities if conducted in line with the procedures set out in the Assessment Framework. The CBD, by contrast, takes the opposite point of departure and has emplaced a moratorium on ocean fertilization activities. The climate regime views ocean fertilization activities as being in line with its own main objectives and as a necessary component for achieving the goals of the UNFCCC and the Paris Agreement. This demonstrates the challenge of the fragmented character of international law, especially in respect of cross-cutting and global issues.

Although the UN Climate Change Regime views ocean fertilization as a mitigation measure, it is the Law of the Sea Regime's categorization of ocean fertilization as pollution that had set the premises for a regulatory approach. As ocean fertilization is an activity carried out in the ocean space and affecting the marine environment, it must adhere to the assigned limits of the LOSC Part XII obligations. Hence, as to competing definitions of ocean fertilization activities in the Law of the Sea Regime and the UN Climate Change Regime, it is not a question of choosing one over the other, but of acknowledging that two or more alternatives exist concurrently.

Attaining the 2°C target will involve a mixture of emissions reductions and GHG removals. Ocean fertilization has the potential to become a vital technology for achieving the emissions target. This makes developing and applying ocean fertilization techniques important in the context of the UN Agenda for Sustainable Development – and not only in relation to Sustainable Development Goal (SDG) 13, which urges action to combat climate change, but also SDG 14, on ensuring sustainable use of the oceans.[107]

This chapter has examined to what extent the Law of the Sea Regime serves to facilitate the use of ocean fertilization techniques as a mitigating measure. The answer is *not very much*. Ocean fertilization activities are regulated by and fall under several different regimes, creating practical and conceptual

[104] Abate and Greenlee, 'Sowing seeds uncertain', 597.

[105] Freestone and Rayfuse, 'Ocean iron fertilization', 230.

[106] Scott, 'Regulating ocean fertilization', 357.

[107] United Nations, *Transforming Our World: the 2030 Agenda for Sustainable Development* (2015), available at https://sustainabledevelopment.un.org/post2015/transformingourworld.

problems. Regulatory challenges represent an obstacle to the further exploration of ocean fertilization as a strategy for countering the effects of climate change. There is a pressing need for more 'concerted and coherent action'.[108] One way of achieving that is to ensure better coordination among the legal regimes involved.

108 Scott, 'Marine geoengineering', 56.

9

Offshore Renewable Energy and the Law of the Sea

Maria Madalena das Neves[*]

9.1 INTRODUCTION

The oceans are increasingly seen as the answer to a myriad of challenges facing humankind.[1] One such challenge relates to balancing the imperative need to mitigate the effects of climate change against the need to ensure energy security – ensuring access to sufficient energy resources at reasonable prices for the foreseeable future and without major disruptions.[2] Energy is indispensable for the socio-economic development of countries and the welfare of their citizens. Meeting the high levels of global energy demand to sustain such development will require continued efforts to develop energy production. However, the levels of energy production and consumption from fossil fuels are also key factors in aggravating pollution and climate change. This has led to increasing pressure to reduce the exploitation of hydrocarbons in the seabed, and to step up the development of offshore renewable energy technology to harvest the energy potential of the sea – as a resource, as with wave, tidal and thermal energy, or as an area for developing other resources, like offshore wind and solar power. Whereas the possibility of exploiting the renewable power from the oceans as an alternative to fossil fuels was recognized in the 1970s (because of high petroleum prices at the time), the impetus for exploring this potential in view of climate-change con-

* The author thanks Elise Johansen and Nigel Bankes for helpful comments on an earlier draft. Any remaining errors are the sole responsibility of the author.

1 Organisation for Economic Co-operation and Development (OECD), *The Ocean Economy in 2030* (2016).

2 N. Bankes and S. Trevisanut (eds.), *Energy from the Sea: An International Law Perspective on Ocean Energy* (Brill Nijhoff, 2015).

cerns started in the 1990s.[3] Today, the potential of the oceans as a source of renewable energy,[4] and of offshore renewable energy in mitigating climate change in the long term, are widely acknowledged.[5] However, the further development of energy activities at sea adds to the problem of the competing uses of maritime space, and accentuates the need to balance and articulate the interests of the different users of the seas (states, offshore energy investors, fishers, shippers, etc.) and the need to protect the marine environment from the deleterious effects of various activities.

Section 9.2 describes various forms of offshore renewable energy and their potential role in mitigating climate change; Section 9.3 identifies key challenges related to the development of offshore renewable energy; Section 9.4 examines the relevant provisions of the United Nations Convention on the Law of the Sea (LOSC),[6] with references other legal instruments underpinning the development of offshore renewable energy projects; and Section 9.5 draws conclusions on the extent to which the law of the sea enables or obstructs such projects.

9.2 OFFSHORE RENEWABLE ENERGY AND ITS ROLE IN MITIGATING CLIMATE CHANGE

As discussed in previous chapters of this book, there is an urgent need to implement measures that can significantly reduce anthropogenic greenhouse gas (GHG) emissions. With energy-related emissions accounting for most of global CO_2 emissions,[7] it has become imperative to tackle the problems of energy demand (reducing energy demand through, for instance, increases in energy efficiency) and energy production (gradually substituting fossil fuels for cleaner forms of energy).[8] UN Sustainable

3 See D. Leary and M. Esteban, 'Climate change and renewable energy from the ocean and tides: calming the sea of regulatory uncertainty' (2009) 24 *The International Journal of Maritime and Coastal Law*, 617–651, 618.

4 See, for example, UNGA Res. 71/257 *Oceans and The Law of the Sea* (20 February 2017), para. 278; UNGA Report on the work of the United Nations Open-ended Informal Consultative Process on Oceans and the Law of the Sea at its thirteenth meeting, UN Doc. A/67/120 (2 July 2012).

5 See, for example, Intergovernmental Panel on Climate Change (IPCC), Special Report, *Renewable Energy Sources and Climate Change Mitigation* (2012 Edition), 497–533.

6 1982 United Nations Convention on the Law of the Sea, Montego Bay, 10 December 1982, UNTS 397.

7 International Energy Agency, *Global Energy CO2 Status Report 2017*, OECD/IEA (2018).

8 This chapter focuses exclusively on the second problem – energy demand; increased energy production in cleaner forms, specifically from offshore renewable sources.

Development Goals 7 (affordable clean energy)[9] and 13 (climate action)[10] emphasize this necessity.[11]

In its 2018 *World Energy Outlook*, the International Energy Agency (IEA) noted the rapid increase in the use of renewable energy, and its potential to contribute towards offsetting rising energy demand and reducing the need for fossil-fuel use – although a scenario free of fossil fuels is still quite far into the future.[12] In another report, the IEA noted that achieving the long-term climate goals identified in its Sustainable Development Scenario will require increasing the share of low-carbon energy sources[13] to 1.1 percentage points annually, corresponding to five times the growth recorded during 2017.[14] Moreover, within these low-carbon energy sources, the use of renewable sources must expand at an average of 700 TWh per year – an 80 per cent increase in relation to 2017 values.[15]

The International Renewable Energy Agency (IRENA) similarly underlines that, in order to achieve the decarbonization goals of the 2015 Paris Agreement, states and stakeholders must decrease energy-related emissions by around 3.5 per cent per year until and post-2050; and increase the share of renewables at least sixfold – from 15 per cent of the total primary energy supply recorded in 2015, to two-thirds by 2050.[16]

Covering some 71 per cent of the earth's surface, the oceans and seas contain considerable power-generating capacity. The Intergovernmental Panel on Climate Change (IPCC) has estimated the theoretical potential of the world's oceans at 7400 EJ per year, although only a portion of that will be feasible in light of currently available technologies and costs.[17] The IEA projects that the oceans have the potential to generate 20,000–80,000 TWh per year.[18] If

[9] Goal 7 calls for states to 'ensure access to affordable, reliable, sustainable and modern energy for all', UNGA Res. 70/1, *Transforming Our World: the 2030 Agenda for Sustainable Development*, A/RES/70/1 (2015).

[10] Goal 13 calls for states to 'take urgent action to combat climate change and its impacts', UNGA Res. 70/1.

[11] UNGA Res. 70/1.

[12] International Energy Agency, *World Energy Outlook 2018*, OECD/IEA (2018).

[13] 'Low-carbon energy sources' refers to sources of power production that emit lower amounts of CO_2 as compared with power produced from conventional sources, that is, fossil fuels. The term 'low-carbon energy sources' encompasses nuclear power as well as renewables.

[14] International Energy Agency, *Global Energy CO2 Status Report 2017*, 4.

[15] Ibid.

[16] International Renewable Energy Agency, *Global Energy Transformation: A Roadmap to 2050*, IRENA (2018), 9–10; and International Renewable Energy Agency, *Global Energy Transformation: A Roadmap to 2050*, IRENA (2019 Edition), 22.

[17] IPCC, *Special Report on Renewable Energy Sources and Climate Change Mitigation* (2011), 87.

[18] IEA, Energy Technology Network, 'Ocean: pilots, projects and potentials' (2015) available at web.archive.org/web/20150522054948/http://www.iea.org/techinitiatives/renewable energy/ocean/, accessed 5 January 2019.

technically and practically feasible, this would still be significant, considering the global electricity demand of approximately 17,500 TWh per year.[19]

The significance of renewable energy, including offshore renewable energy, is recognized in the context of the climate-change legal framework.[20] In particular, offshore renewable projects qualify to operate within the Clean Development Mechanism under the Kyoto Protocol to the United Nations Framework Convention on Climate Change (UNFCCC).[21]

Tidal and current power, wave power, ocean thermal energy conversion and salinity gradients are the key forms of ocean-power resources; wind and solar power can be implemented in the vast offshore areas of our planet. Also important are geothermal energy from submarine geothermal sources and bioenergy from marine biomass such as algae.[22]

Tidal power derives from the changing gravitational pull of the moon and sun on the seas and oceans, and is influenced by factors such as the earth's rotation, the topography of the ocean floor, and the temperature and salinity of the water. The kinetic energy in tides and currents can be harnessed through turbines installed in underwater tidal energy convertors (such as horizontal and vertical axis, oscillating hydrofoil, venturi, Archimedes screw, and tidal kite) fixed to the seabed. Tidal energy can also be harnessed in barrages. Major tidal projects in operation or pilot stages include the Swansea Bay Tidal Lagoon in Wales (320 MW capacity),[23] the La Rance Tidal Power Station in France (240 MW capacity),[24] the Sihwa Lake Tidal Power Station in Korea (254 MW capacity),[25] the MeyGen Tidal Stream Project in Scotland (under construction, up to 398 MW capacity),[26] the Jiangxia Pilot Tidal Power Plant

19 Ibid.

20 E. Johansen, this volume, Chapter 1, provides an explanation of the legal framework concerning climate change.

21 1997 Kyoto Protocol to the United Nations Framework Convention on Climate Change, Kyoto, 11 December 1997, 2303 UNTS 162.

22 For an overview of existing and planned projects for offshore renewable energy see, for example, International Energy Agency/Energy Technology Network – Ocean Energy Systems (IEA-OES), Annual Report, *An Overview of Ocean Energy Activities in 2018* (2018), available at report2018.ocean-energy-systems.org/documents/OES-Annual-Report-2018/, accessed 18 January 2020.

23 See www.tidallagoonpower.com/projects/swansea-bay/, accessed 20 June 2019.

24 See www.edf.fr/en/the-edf-group/industrial-provider/renewable-energies/marine-energy/tidal-power, accessed 20 June 2019.

25 See http://english.kwater.or.kr/eng/tech/sub01/sub02/patentPage.do?s_mid%3D1207, accessed 20 June 2019.

26 See https://simecatlantis.com/projects/meygen/, accessed 20 June 2019.

in China (4.1 MW capacity),[27] and the Annapolis Tidal Station in Canada (20 MW capacity).[28]

Wave power consists of kinetic energy existing in the movement of ocean waves, caused by winds on the surface of the ocean. It can be harnessed through floating or buoy systems, fixed structures, or submerged structures that use the rise and fall of waves to drive hydraulic pumps, via oscillating water column or body devices, overtopping, and tapered channels. Wave-power projects are currently operating or under development, inter alia, in waters under the jurisdiction of Australia, China, Indonesia, Italy, New Zealand, Norway, Portugal, Spain, Sweden, the United Kingdom, and the United States.[29] Still, the costs of wave power remain higher than other forms of offshore renewable energy such as tidal power and offshore wind power, making it necessary to engage larger investors and utility companies.[30]

At present, projects involving tidal and wave power are located either in internal waters or in the territorial sea. While it is possible to expand such projects further out to sea, the technological and commercial feasibility of such expansion still needs to be fully demonstrated.[31]

Ocean thermal energy conversion (OTEC) produces electricity from the temperature difference between warm surface waters and cold deep waters. Tropical areas of the globe offer the best conditions for the deployment of this technology. OTEC plants can be located on land or offshore via fixed or floating installations. These plants are connected to pipes that carry cold water from the depths as well as warm water into the plant, for thermal conversion. As yet, OTEC plants are mostly at the experimental stage, but have the potential to provide stable base-load power. The largest operational plant is the Makai Ocean Thermal Energy Conversion Power Plant located in Hawaii (0.1 MW capacity).[32] The success of this plant will be instrumental in expanding knowledge and in bolstering the commercialization of larger-scale ocean thermal conversion plants. The location of existing OTEC power projects is also confined to areas within the national jurisdiction of states.

Salinity gradients draw energy from differences in salt concentration between fresh and salt water, via pressure-retarded osmosis or reversed electro-

27 See https://tethys.pnnl.gov/annex-iv-sites/jiangxia-pilot-tidal-power-plant, accessed 20 June 2019.

28 See https://tethys.pnnl.gov/annex-iv-sites/annapolis-tidal-station, accessed 20 June 2019.

29 See more information on wave projects in IRENA, *Wave Energy: Technology Brief* (2014); and International Energy Agency/Energy Technology Network, *An Overview of Ocean Energy Activities in 2018*.

30 Ibid.

31 See also D. Greaves and G. Iglesias, *Wave and Tidal Energy* (Wiley, 2018), 458.

32 For further information, see www.makai.com/ocean-thermal-energy-conversion/, accessed 20 June 2019. There are plans to expand and build a 10 MW plant.

dialysis. Estuaries where fresh water flows from rivers to the sea offer excellent locations for the installation of salinity gradient plants. This technology, which is still in the research and development phase, was initially tested in Norway (0.010 MW capacity) and the Netherlands (0.050 MW capacity).[33]

Offshore wind power is based on the same premises as onshore wind: the kinetic energy from wind is converted into mechanical power via the use of wind turbines. With higher and more constant wind speeds, and to some extent less visual impact as onshore wind farms (reduced 'not in my back yard' effect depending how far wind farms are from shore), offshore areas can offer prime conditions for wind-power generation. Offshore wind installations can also be larger and, therefore, produce more energy. In general, installed offshore wind-power capacity is located in areas within national jurisdiction (territorial sea and exclusive economic zone), at shallow depths up to 60 meters, using fixed installations. However, new technological developments such as floating wind farms will gradually allow offshore wind energy to expand to areas beyond national jurisdiction and to greater depths. Offshore wind power is the most mature form of offshore renewable energy, with several projects already under operation and development around the world. Belgium, Denmark, Germany, the Netherlands, Norway, and the United Kingdom have been taking the lead. Outside Europe, China has been investing heavily in offshore wind development. Walney Extension, the world's largest offshore wind farm to date, is located in the United Kingdom, in the Irish Sea. It comprises eighty-seven turbines with a total capacity of 659 MW and maximum height of 195 m, covers an area of 145 km^2 and provides electricity to nearly 600,000 households.[34]

Offshore solar energy will harness the power of the sun through technologies such as concentrating solar power and photonic technology used in floating solar plants.[35] This solution is still in the initial stages, however. There are already some examples of operating floating solar plants – for example, in Chile, China, and Portugal – these are located in inland bodies of water. Other examples of 'offshore' solar plants consist of plants installed on

33 For more information on salinity gradient projects, see IRENA, *Salinity Gradient Energy: Technology Brief* (2014); and International Energy Agency/Energy Technology Network, *An Overview of Ocean Energy Activities in 2018*.

34 See https://walneyextension.co.uk/About-the-project, accessed 20 June 2019.

35 For detailed explanations of the forms of offshore renewable resources and corresponding harnessing technology referred to in this paragraph, see, inter alia, S. P. Neil and M. Reza Hashemi, *Fundamentals of Ocean Renewable Energy: Generating Electricity from the Sea* (Elsevier, 2018); IPCC, *Special Report on Renewable Energy Sources and Climate Change Mitigation* (2011), 87–103; as well as ocean energy definitions available at www.irena.org/ocean and at www.oceanenergycouncil.com, accessed 3 January 2019.

land in areas reclaimed from the sea, as with the Kagoshima Nanatsujima Mega Solar Power Plant in Japan. Solar-power plants entirely designed as offshore floating plants are still limited to pilot projects such as those in the Netherlands[36] and in Norway.[37]

Bioenergy derives from marine biomass such as algae and seaweed which can be processed into biofuels such as biodiesel and bioethanol. While there are several projects for producing bioenergy from algae on land, there have been few research projects on offshore bioenergy. One exception is the project of the US National Aeronautics and Space Administration (NASA) on an offshore membrane enclosure for growing algae and subsequent production of fuel.[38]

Geothermal energy derives from the heat or thermal properties within the Earth.[39] Commercial production of onshore geothermal energy is an established technology, not least in Iceland, New Zealand, and the Philippines, but the use of submarine geothermal energy is still at a very incipient stage of development. The few research projects include the Marsili Project in Italy, which is exploring a submarine volcano mountain in the Tyrrhenian Sea;[40] the project in the Gulf of California conducted by the National University of Mexico concerning a submarine power plant located over a hydrothermal vent;[41] and the offshore geothermal project of North Tech Energy in Icelandic waters.[42]

As yet, offshore renewable energy represents only a small share of overall global renewable energy production, with an approximate installed offshore capacity of only 19 GW, about 90 per cent of which is located in Europe.[43] Wind power is the most advanced and developed form of offshore clean energy, followed by wave and tidal power.[44] The other forms are either at experimental or pre-commercialization stages. Nonetheless, with technological development, reduction of costs and increasing investments, offshore

36 For more information on the Dutch project, see https://oceansofenergy.blue/press-release-1-new-consortium-builds-first-offshore/, accessed 20 June 2019.

37 For more information on the Norwegian project, see https://oceansun.no/, accessed 20 June 2019.

38 For more information, see www.nasa.gov/centers/ames/pdf/638200main_OMEGA_FactSheet_final.pdf, accessed 20 June 2019.

39 World Energy Council, *World Energy Resources 2016*, 603.

40 For more information, see www.eurobuilding.it/marsiliproject/, accessed 20 June 2019.

41 G. Hiriart et al., 'Submarine geothermics: hydrothermal vents and electricity generation' in *Proceedings of World Geothermal Congress* (2010).

42 For more information, see www.nte.is/offshore-geothermal/, accessed 20 June 2019.

43 IRENA, *Offshore Innovation Widens Renewable Energy Options: Opportunities, Challenges and the Vital Role of International Co-operation to Spur the Global Energy Transformation*, Brief to G7 Policy Makers (2018).

44 Ibid.

renewable energy can become paramount in decarbonization efforts, also because of the negligible level of emissions from renewable energy production. IRENA estimates that offshore renewables may expand to 128 GW of installed capacity by 2030 and 521 GW by 2050.[45] Consequently, offshore renewable energy has enormous potential within the context of climate-change mitigation.

9.3 CHALLENGES ASSOCIATED WITH DEVELOPING OFFSHORE RENEWABLE ENERGY

The development of offshore renewable energy faces numerous challenges: technological capability (generating units, interconnection with land); investment and economic viability of technological solutions; capacity-building and technology transfer, particularly as regards developing countries; competing uses of the oceans; balancing of different interests; impacts on the marine environment; and regulatory challenges.[46] This section examines the last three challenges, which although treated separately, are highly interrelated.

9.3.1 *Competing Uses of the Oceans and Balancing of Different Interests*

The seas and oceans are subjected to increasing competition for the use of their spaces. With such vast areas of seas and oceans, one might think that there is ample space to accommodate all sorts of marine activities – but reality is different. It is precisely because of the overlapping and conflicting uses of the seas and oceans areas that concepts such as marine spatial planning (MSP), integrated ocean management, area-based management, and others have emerged, shifting (or attempting to shift) from the laissez faire, or ad hoc, and sectoral self-serving management of marine activities to more holistic approaches.

Offshore renewable energy uses a range of technical solutions. These technologies involve using infrastructures above sea level, in the water column, or on the seafloor; anchoring systems to the seafloor; in some cases pipes/pipelines; electricity subsea cables connecting the generating units to the onshore grid; and subsea electricity interconnectors in the case of transnational projects. Shipping activity to ensure the installation, maintenance,

[45] Ibid.

[46] See UN Doc. A/67/120 (2 July 2012), 9–12 for a discussion of opportunities and challenges related to the development of offshore renewable energy.

and decommissioning of these infrastructures/systems will be a necessary element in all this.

Furthermore, offshore renewable energy solutions may encounter and even collide with other marine uses (possibly forcing the displacement of other existing activities), including offshore hydrocarbon activities, fishing and aquaculture, navigation/shipping,[47] laying of submarine cables and pipelines related to other activities (communications and hydrocarbons respectively), sea tourism, and marine scientific research. As offshore renewable energy activities move to deeper waters and waters beyond national jurisdiction, account must be taken of deep seabed mining activities. Although not all areas will be suitable for the deployment of offshore renewable energy installations, some level of overlap can be expected with other activities – giving rise to the question of how to balance the various activities. Should or can primacy be given to offshore renewable energy, considering its potential vital role in climate-change mitigation?

Furthermore, because of pressures on the marine environment, it will also be necessary to expand the creation of marine protected areas and the designation of particularly sensitive sea areas. In such areas, perhaps the establishment of offshore renewable energy installations may be more limited, or ruled out altogether. Lack of transparency and uncertainty concerning the potential areas for establishment of offshore renewable energy or the criteria for balancing the various interests at stake might delay or discourage investments, as such uncertainty entails greater risks and costs as regards developing offshore renewable energy.[48]

9.3.2 *Impacts to the Marine Environment*

Because the amount of installed offshore renewable energy is still limited, with most forms still in the initial stages of development, it is not possible to grasp and document fully the environmental impacts of these technologies, the cumulative effect in particular.[49] However, within the context of climate

47 The possible conflicts with navigation/shipping do not relate exclusively to potential area conflicts, for example, placement of renewables infrastructure in or close to navigation lanes, but may also involve interference with navigation instruments, radar and radio in the case of offshore wind turbines where the rotation of the blades creates electromagnetic waves.

48 Young, for example, also notes the discouraging effects of uncertainties surrounding offshore renewable energy and competing uses of the oceans. M. Young, 'Building the blue economy: the role of marine spatial planning in facilitating offshore renewable energy development' (2015) 30 *The International Journal of Marine and Coastal Law*, 148–174, 157.

49 See similarly M. A. Shields, 'An introduction to marine renewable energy', in M. A. Shields and A. I. L. Payne (eds.), *Marine Renewable Energy Technology and Environmental Interactions* (Springer, 2014), 1–3, 3.

change and in terms of GHG emissions, the impacts of offshore renewable energy seem relatively negligible, especially when compared to fossil fuels. This is because offshore clean-energy solutions are emissions-free, for most their lifecycle. The emissions related to offshore renewable energy derive from the production of components, transport of those components to location, installation of technological solutions on site, and decommissioning. However, even these are not significant compared to the fossil-fuel emissions from conventional power generation.

Another matter is to what extent offshore renewable energy pollutes the marine environment. Various environmental impacts may occur during the construction, installation, operation, maintenance, and decommissioning phases. The environmental impacts most commonly associated with offshore renewable energy include disruption of migration paths of fish and marine mammals due to vibrations, noise, changes in water flows, and electromagnetic fields of submarine electricity cables; disruption of bird migration paths, especially with offshore wind turbines; loss of bird, fish and marine mammal life due to collisions with the various types of installations and due to the electromagnetic fields generated by submarine electricity cables; habitat disturbance or destruction during the construction phase; and release of polluting substances during construction, operation and decommissioning phases or resulting from potential vessel collisions with the installations.[50]

Offshore wind, in particular, but also wave and tidal power, are the sectors that offer the most concrete evidence, having now been subject to many environmental impact assessments (EIAs) and strategic environmental assessments (SEAs), and other scientific studies. Examination of EIAs and scientific reports conducted thus far indicates that the impacts caused by offshore renewable energy are not sufficient to cause significant damage to the marine environment.[51] That is, if there are adequate technological/engineering

[50] See, for example, UN Division for Ocean Affairs and the Law of the Sea, Office of Legal Affairs (ed.), Other marine based energy industries, *The First Global Integrated Marine Assessment: World Ocean Assessment* (Cambridge University Press, 2017), 353–362.

[51] See, for example, Statoil, *The Hywind Scotland Pilot Park Environmental Statement* (2015), available at file:///C:/Users/mne021/Downloads/Statoil-Environmental%20Statement%20April%202015.pdf; Norwegian Water Resources and Energy Directorate, *Offshore Wind Power in Norway: Strategic Environmental Assessment*, English summary available at http://publikasjoner.nve.no/diverse/2013/havvindsummary2013.pdf and full assessment in Norwegian available at http://publikasjoner.nve.no/rapport/2012/rapport2012_47.pdf; International Energy Agency, Ocean Energy Systems Initiative, *2016 State of the Science Report: Environmental Effects of Marine Renewable Energy Development around the World* (2016), available at https://tethys.pnnl.gov/sites/default/files/publications/Annex-IV-2016-State-of-the-Science-Report_HR.pdf; WWF-Norway, *Environmental Impacts of Offshore Wind Power Production in the North*

solutions in place; if the project location has been carefully selected; and if planning, operational and monitoring strategies are designed and implemented so as to minimize the potential impacts indicated earlier. In some instances, offshore renewable energy installations could actually enhance marine habitats in the post-construction phases, for example, by providing artificial reefs.[52] Nonetheless, it is not possible to generalize from the apparently positive results of certain offshore renewable energy projects conducted in specific locations to the entire offshore renewable energy sector and to all projects irrespective of location. The authorization and development of each project must be anchored in proper SEAs, EIAs, and taking into consideration the precautionary approach as well as the principle of prevention.

9.3.3 *Legal and Regulatory Challenges*

Because most offshore renewable energy technologies are still in their infancy, the legal and regulatory frameworks are limited, and have not been specifically designed to address the challenges involved (wind power being a partial exception). Moreover, as offshore projects move further out to sea or involve transboundary aspects,[53] states must face additional challenges of designing regulatory frameworks that accommodate the intricacies of each form of offshore renewable energy, the environmental aspects, and cross-border cooperation.

From an investment perspective, legal certainty and predictability can be decisive for attracting energy investors to develop offshore renewable projects.[54] Uncertainty as to which state has jurisdiction over a given maritime

Sea: A Literature Overview (2014), available at http://awsassets.wwf.no/downloads/wwf_a4_report___havvindrapport.pdf; Danish Energy Authority, *Offshore Wind Farms and the Environment: Danish Experiences from Horns Rev and Nysted* (2006), available at https://naturstyrelsen.dk/media/nst/Attachments/havvindm_korr_16nov_UK.pdf; and UN Division for Ocean Affairs and the Law of the Sea, *The First Global Integrated Marine Assessment*. All these websites accessed 20 June 2019.

52 UN Division for Ocean Affairs and the Law of the Sea, *The First Global Integrated Marine Assessment*, 357.

53 For example, an offshore wind farm located in the EEZ of State A will provide electricity to both State A and State B through submarine electricity cables which will have to be laid both on the continental shelves of State A and State B and interconnectors.

54 On the relationship between legal certainty and offshore energy investments see, for example, S. Trevisanut and N. Giannopoulos, 'Investment protection in offshore energy production: bright sides of regime interaction' (2018) 19 *The Journal of World Investment & Trade*, 790–827; and G. Goettsche-Wanli, 'Sustainable production of offshore renewable energy: a global perspective' in M. Kotzur et al. (eds.), *Sustainable Ocean Resource Governance: Deep Sea Mining, Marine Energy and Submarine Cables* (Brill Nijhoff, 2018), 10.

area may not necessarily preclude the development of offshore renewable energy projects,[55] but it certainly adds to the risks and costs of such projects.

9.4 LOSC AND OTHER KEY LEGAL INSTRUMENTS REGULATING OFFSHORE RENEWABLE ENERGY

There is no specific legal framework regulating offshore renewable energy. Instead, we find a plethora of legal instruments that regulate different aspects of the lifecycle of offshore energy installations/structures – mainly development, deployment, operation, and decommissioning. Within public international law, several key legal instruments – especially the LOSC – are central regarding offshore renewable energy.[56] As offshore renewable energy installations/structures are still in areas within national jurisdiction, the intricacies related to the licensing of and conduct of offshore renewable energy projects are generally covered in domestic legislation; with EU member states, also by EU law. Domestic legislation, and EU law (where applicable), may be decisive in regulating offshore renewable energy.[57] However, the following subsections focus on the instruments of international law, the LOSC, in particular.

9.4.1 *Offshore Renewable Energy in the Context of the LOSC*

The preamble of the LOSC states that the Convention establishes a legal order for the seas and oceans that aims to promote the peaceful uses of the oceans, the equitable and efficient use of resources, and the conservation and preservation of living resources and the marine environment.[58] The significance of the LOSC as regards offshore renewable energy is immediately evident. The LOSC provides for the use of the ocean's resources in the various maritime zones, including offshore energy resources. It also imposes conditions on that use, by requiring states to take into consideration other competing uses of the

55 The offshore hydrocarbons industry provides some examples of activities being conducted in marine disputed areas between different states, even in the absence of joint development agreements. Scrutiny of some of these instances makes clear the enormous risks and added costs involved (for instance, the Tullow's TEN field, in the previously disputed area between Ghana and Côte d'Ivoire, where some activities took place before the maritime boundary was finally set by ITLOS judgment).

56 Section 4.2 notes other key legal instruments relevant for offshore renewable energy.

57 See H. K. Müller, 'Legal bases for offshore grid development under international and EU law: why national regimes remain the determining factor' (2013) 38(5) *European Law Review*, 618–637.

58 LOSC, Preamble.

seas and the rights of other states, and by obliging them to preserve and protect the marine environment. For the various maritime zones, and activities occurring in them, the LOSC outlines the freedoms, rights, and duties of states. Here the LOSC offers at least some degree of jurisdictional certainty in relation to the development of offshore renewable energy.[59] But, while it is true that the LOSC affords renewable energy developers some clarity in terms of ascertaining which state has jurisdiction (and which type of jurisdiction) in the various maritime zones, closer examination of the relevant provisions of the LOSC is needed in order to determine if it does indeed provide a clear framework to facilitate the development of offshore renewable energy. Here it should be noted that, apart from one reference in Article 56 to the coastal state's sovereign rights over 'production of energy from the water, currents and winds', there are no specific provisions in the LOSC dealing expressly or exclusively with offshore renewable energy. This lacuna has triggered proposals for the negotiation of an additional protocol on energy to the LOSC,[60] or the renegotiation of the LOSC altogether, to better accommodate issues related to the development and deployment of offshore renewable energy technologies.[61] Regardless, there can be no doubt that the broad wording of the LOSC and its framework nature encompass all forms of offshore renewable energy.

9.4.1.1 Costal-state Jurisdiction over Offshore Renewable Energy

As per LOCS Article 2, the sovereignty of the coastal state extends beyond its internal waters to its territorial sea, including the corresponding air space, seabed, and subsoil. Thus, in internal waters and in the territorial sea, the coastal state has the exclusive right to exploit its offshore renewable resources and to regulate all related aspects. However, this sovereignty of the coastal state is limited by the obligation not to hamper the passage of foreign-flagged vessels exercising their right of innocent passage.[62] The main issue is then to ensure that the emplacement of offshore renewable energy installations does not hamper the right of innocent passage. Here we may conclude, using the analogy of the placement of offshore hydrocarbons installations/structures, that the coastal state may indeed deploy as many such installations/structures

[59] See also Leary and Esteban, 'Climate change', 617–651.

[60] See, inter alia, M. Tsamenyi and M. Herriman, 'Ocean energy and the law of the sea: the need for a protocol?' (1998) 29(1) *Ocean Development & International Law*, 3–19.

[61] See, for example, F. Galea, 'A legal regime for the exploration and exploitation of offshore renewable energy' (2011) 25 *Ocean Yearbook*, 101–129.

[62] LOSC, Article 24.

as it sees fit, provided they do not unreasonably hinder or prevent the right of innocent passage and the coastal state's obligations to protect the marine environment (see Section 9.4.1.3).[63] Furthermore, the coastal state may, under Article 22, require that foreign vessels in innocent passage use sea lanes and traffic separation schemes to ensure safety of navigation.[64] The rule of sovereignty limited by the right of innocent passage also applies in internal waters that were not considered as such before being enclosed by straight baselines,[65] and in archipelagic waters.[66] In straits used for international navigation, other states enjoy the right of transit passage,[67] or, where the strait does not qualify for application of the transit regime, the right of innocent passage.[68] States bordering the strait must not impede or hamper transit or innocent passage.[69] A coastal state bordering a strait and considering the development of offshore renewable energy projects must take great care in selecting the location for such projects, and the width of safety zones required. Projects located in a strait used for international navigation are likely to encounter greater opposition from other states, given the possibility of interference with international navigation.[70]

Article 56(1)(a) specifically grants the coastal state sovereign rights to explore and exploit the natural resources of its EEZ, including 'activities for the economic exploitation and exploration of the zone, such as the production of energy from the water, currents and winds'.[71] The use of the term 'such as' indicates that the types of energy production indicated in the provision are not exhaustive. Consequently, this provision also makes other forms of offshore energy production, such as bioenergy, solar and geothermal, subject to the sovereign rights of the coastal state. Further, according to Article 56(1)(b), the coastal state also has jurisdiction over 'the establishment and use of artificial islands, installations and structures'.[72] Article 60 builds on the latter provision,

63 In this regard, Leary and Esteban, 'Climate change', 633. On this problem in relation to offshore petroleum infrastructures, see H. Esmaeili, *The Legal Regime of Offshore Oil Rigs in International Law* (Ashgate, 2001), 73.

64 For example, the United Kingdom and the Netherlands both proposed to the IMO traffic separation measures to ensure safety of navigation and of the integrity of offshore energy activities. M. A. Castelos, 'Marine renewable energies: opportunities, law, and management' (2014) 45 *Ocean Development & International Law*, 221–237, 226.

65 LOSC, Article 8(2).

66 LOSC, Articles 49 and 52.

67 LOSC, Article 38.

68 LOSC, Article 45.

69 LOSC, Articles 44 and 45.

70 Galea, 'A legal regime', 112.

71 LOSC, Article 56(1)(a).

72 LOSC, Article 56(1)(b).

and underlines the exclusive right of the coastal state to construct, authorize, and regulate the construction, operation, and use of artificial islands, installations, and structures in its EEZ.[73] The coastal state may also designate safety zones around artificial islands, installations, and structures in order to ensure the integrity of the latter as well as safe navigation. Given these provisions, there can be no doubt that the coastal state has exclusive authority for undertaking or authorizing the development of offshore renewable energy projects. Nonetheless, the coastal state is limited by its obligation to show due regard for the rights and duties of other states in its EEZ,[74] in particular, their rights of navigation, overflight, laying of submarine cables and pipelines, and other related internationally lawful uses of the sea.[75] The freedom of other states to lay submarine cables and pipelines is also relevant here, as it facilitates their ability to participate in transboundary offshore energy projects. Finally, the coastal state is also precluded from placing in its EEZ artificial islands, installations, or structures and safety zones in areas where they might cause interference to recognized sea lanes that are essential to international navigation.[76]

Activities on the continental shelf, or that involve drilling on the continental shelf, fall under the sovereign, and exclusive, right of the coastal state.[77] It is thus clear that any offshore renewable energy project involving activity, drilling on, or placement on, the continental shelf falls under the purview of the coastal state. LOSC Article 60 on artificial islands, installations, and structures applies *mutatis mutandis* to the continental shelf. Activities on the extended continental shelf are a different matter, however. In exercising its sovereign rights over the continental shelf, the coastal state must not infringe or unjustifiably interfere with navigation or other rights and freedoms of other states in the waters and airspace superjacent to the continental shelf.[78] This includes the right of other states to lay submarine cables and pipelines on the continental shelf.[79] LOSC Article 82 requires coastal states to share with the international community any revenues from production deriving from the exploitation of non-living resources of the continental shelf beyond 200 nm.[80] Although this provision was drafted with mineral resources in mind, it could

73 LOSC, Article 60(1).
74 LOSC, Article 56(2).
75 LOSC, Article 58(1).
76 LOSC, Article 60(7).
77 LOSC, Articles 77 and 81.
78 LOSC, Article 78.
79 LOSC, Article 79(1).
80 LOSC, Article 82(1).

become relevant regarding geothermal energy produced on the extended continental shelf.

LOSC Article 87(1) prescribes that the high seas are open to all states, with enjoy freedom to engage in various activities. Article 87(1), provides a non-exhaustive list of activities (use of the term inter alia), making express reference to the freedom to lay submarine cables and pipelines,[81] and to the freedom to construct artificial islands and installations.[82] These two freedoms are key components for offshore renewable projects. We may conclude that Article 87, albeit not referring expressly to energy as Article 56 did, also incorporates the freedom to conduct offshore renewable energy projects in the high seas. It has been suggested that Article 89 could prevent the development of offshore renewable energy projects in the high seas.[83] That is because offshore renewable energy projects might occupy high seas area for a considerable time, and Article 89 establishes that a state may not 'validly purport to subject any part of the high seas to its sovereignty'.[84] However, such reading of Article 89 in relation to offshore renewable projects seems dubious, not least because Article 87 expressly allows for the construction and deployment of such installations and artificial islands (which also have a more permanent nature) including their respective safety zones. From a strictly *de lege ferenda* perspective, we might anticipate a debate similar to the one on marine genetic resources on the high seas: namely, whether offshore renewable energy in the high seas should remain the privilege of developed states with the financial and technological means to pursue such activities, or whether it should be conducted for the benefit of all mankind. Notwithstanding, it seems that, regarding the high seas, a state is limited only by the obligation to show due regard for the interests of other states exercising their high-seas freedoms or for activities undertaken in the Area,[85] and by its obligation to protect the marine environment. In relation to the latter, it should be noted that negotiations for an international legally binding instrument under the LOSC on the conservation and sustainable use of marine biological diversity of areas beyond national jurisdiction could have implications for the development of renewable energy projects in the high seas.[86]

81 LOSC, Article 87(1)(c).

82 LOSC, Article 87(1)(d). The Area, as defined in Article 1(1) of the LOSC, encompasses 'the seabed and ocean floor and subsoil thereof, beyond the limits of national jurisdiction'.

83 See, for example, N. J. Lund, 'Renewable energy as a catalyst for changes to the high seas regime' (2010) 15(1) *Oceans and Coastal Law Journal*, 108–109.

84 LOSC, Article 89.

85 LOSC, Article 87(2).

86 Section 4.1.3 further examines this issue as well as the obligations to protect the marine environment prescribed in Part XII of the LOSC.

In the Area, the rights to resources are vested in mankind as a whole and are administered by the International Seabed Authority.[87] Article 133(a) defines as 'resources' of the Area 'all solid, liquid or gaseous mineral resources in situ in the Area at or beneath the seabed, including polymetallic nodules'. This raises the issue of whether Part XI of the LOSC and its implementing agreement[88] apply to offshore renewable energy activities in the area, particularly the development of submarine geothermal energy. Interestingly, during the negotiations of the LOSC in UNCLOS III, initially proposed definitions of 'resources' included 'liquid or gaseous substances such as petroleum, gas, condensate, helium, nitrogen, carbon dioxide, water, steam, hot water, and also sulphur and salts extracted in liquid form in solution'.[89] Water, steam, and hot water are pertinent in the context of submarine geothermal energy production. However, these proposals to include 'water, steam, hot water' in the definition of resources of the Area were rejected.[90] The final text of the LOSC includes only the simplified version 'all solid, liquid or gaseous mineral resources'. The emphasis is on 'mineral' resources in their various forms, so it can be posited that the wording of Article 133 does not encompass resources such as water, steam or hot water.

9.4.1.2 Balancing Different Interests under the LOSC

As shown in Section 9.3.1 earlier, the increasing pressure and competition for ocean space might trigger conflicts between offshore renewable energy and other activities, particularly in relation to large offshore renewable energy projects requiring the use of large marine areas[91] (such as offshore wind). Conflicts with other marine uses/rights of other states and uncertainty as to how such conflicts can be solved could pose difficulties for states and deter some investors. States need to balance their rights with the rights of other states, but also as regards the various activities under their jurisdiction. To what extent and how does the LOSC balance and conciliate the different competing rights of states and their different activities? Difficulties

87 LOSC, Article 137.

88 Agreement Relating to the Implementation of Part XI of the United Nations Convention on the Law of the Sea of 10 December 1982, New York, 28 July 1994, 1836 UNTS 3.

89 UNCLOS III, Informal Single Negotiating Text (Part I), UN Doc. A/CONF.62/WP.8/PART I (1975), OR IV, 137–138 (Article 1); and UNCLOS III, Informal Composite Negotiating Text (Revision 1), UN Doc. A/CONF.62/WP.10/Rev.1 (1979), OR VIII, 73 (Article 133).

90 In the second text revision of 1980, the terms 'water, steam, and hot water' were no longer included in the text. See UNCLOS III, Informal Composite Negotiating Text (Revision 2), UN Doc. A/CONF.62/WP.10/Rev.2 (1980), OR VIII, 75 (Article 133).

91 Not only for the installations/structures themselves but also the safety zones around them.

experienced in negotiating the LOSC and its 'package deal' nature necessarily led to including in the final text several compromises between the different states. Furthermore, nowhere does the LOSC expressly establish a hierarchy of competing interests that could clearly answer the question of what activity – fishing, navigation, marine scientific research, offshore energy, and so on – should prevail in case of competition for the same maritime space.

Instead, the negotiating states chose to accommodate compromises in the LOSC by using terms like 'due regard' in Articles 56(2), 58(3), and 87(2) of the LOSC. These provisions oblige a state exercising or discharging its rights, duties, and freedoms in the EEZ or in the High Seas to have due regard for the rights, duties, and freedoms of other states in those same maritime zones. However, as an open-textured[92] and indeterminate concept, its application will necessarily be unpredictable.[93] In the present context, it requires a state considering authorizing or undertaking offshore renewable energy activities to reflect on what it must do to ensure compliance with its due regard obligations. Several decisions by international tribunals have clarified the content of due regard, to some extent.[94] In the *Chagos MPA Arbitration*, the Arbitral Tribunal concluded that there was no 'universal rule of conduct' in relation to due regard.[95] This entails that 'due regard' must be assessed on a case-by-case basis. Moreover, the Tribunal noted that the ordinary meaning of 'due regard' indicates that a state must have 'such regard for the rights [of another state] as is called for by the circumstances and by the nature of those rights'.[96] The Tribunal went on to note that the LOSC 'does not impose a uniform obligation to avoid any impairment of [another state's] rights; nor does it uniformly permit [a state] to proceed as it wishes by merely noting such rights'. The determination of the extent of the obligation of due regard will 'depend upon the nature of the rights held by [a state], their importance, the extent of the anticipated impairment, the nature and importance of the activities contemplated by [the other state], and the availability of alternative approaches'.[97] Finally, the Tribunal emphasized that due regard involves

92 J. Gaunce, 'On the interpretation of the general duty of "due regard"' (2018) 32 *Ocean Yearbook*, 27–59, 28.

93 Gaunce, 'On the interpretation', 27–59; and L. B. Sohn et al., *Cases and Materials on the Law of the Sea*, 2nd edn. (Martinus Nijhoff, 2014) 79.

94 See, for example, *Chagos Marine Protected Area Arbitration (Mauritius* v. *United Kingdom) (Chagos MPA Arbitration)* [2015] PCA Case No. 2011–03, Award of 18 March 2015; and *The Republic of the Philippines* v. *the People's Republic of China (South China Sea Arbitration)* [2016] PCA Case No. 2013–19, Award of 12 July 2016.

95 *Chagos MPA Arbitration*, para. 519.

96 Ibid.

97 Ibid.

good faith,[98] and requires some degree of consultation[99] between the relevant states that 'need not continue indefinitely or 'until the other party is happy'.[100] The Tribunal in the *South China Sea Arbitration* endorsed this interpretation.[101]

In practical terms, this means that a state interested in offshore renewable energy activities in the EEZ or in the high seas must at least take into consideration the rights of other relevant states by engaging in consultations with them. It also means that a state must consider and discuss possible alternatives, particularly concerning the location of intended projects, so that it can minimize objections from other states. This may prove challenging. Consider, for example, an offshore renewable energy project in the high seas where the rights of all other state parties to the LOSC might be affected. How can the proponent state fulfil the duty to engage in consultations, considering the potential number of affected states? Must the state consult with *all* other states? Does the state need to discuss this in global or regional fora?[102] As yet, this has not been problematic for activities in the high seas. However, as offshore renewable energy projects are of a different nature and entail the deployment of installations/structures as well as the establishment of safety zones over long periods, states could begin to raise objections. As Gaunce points out, 'due regard encompasses not only a mutual duty bilaterally between competing states to balance their activities but also a duty to the interests of the international community'.[103]

For offshore renewable energy activities in the territorial sea, the coastal state must take into consideration its duty not to hamper innocent passage, as explained earlier, and other rules of international law that may be applicable.[104] This has implications for the location of offshore installations/structures and of submarine cables and pipelines. In short, the coastal state must balance the exercise of its sovereignty and authority to approve offshore renewable energy projects with the specific right of navigation that the LOSC grants to other states.

Apart from the aspect of balancing the different rights of states, it is also important to ascertain to what extent the LOSC offers guidance for managing

98 Ibid., para. 520.

99 Ibid., para. 519.

100 Ibid., para. 531.

101 *South China Sea Arbitration*, para. 742.

102 Lund, for example, has proposed the creation of an international regulatory or oversight body to assess offshore renewable energy projects and ensure they comply with international law. See Lund, 'Renewable energy', 124.

103 Gaunce, 'On the interpretation', 59.

104 In this regard, see *Chagos MPA Arbitration*, para. 514.

and balancing the various marine and coastal activities. As noted, the LOSC does not expressly create a hierarchy of activities nor does it prescribe specific ways in which to articulate them. Still, in its preamble, the LOSC acknowledges that 'the problems of ocean space are closely interrelated and need to be considered as a whole'.[105] Read together with LOSC Part XII,[106] which requires states to adopt laws, regulations, and measures to prevent, reduce, and control pollution of the marine environment, and to cooperate in these matters, this part of the preamble facilitates the adoption of integrated ocean management approaches and of management tools such as MSP.[107] Although there is no generally accepted definition of 'integrated ocean management', it can be broadly understood as

> an attempt to respond to the deficiencies of a fragmented/zonal approach to ocean management by offering a holistic approach that allows coordinated and comprehensive management of the different activities and interests related to the sea.[108]

There is also no agreed definition of MSP, but it can be defined as a process that is concerned with

> analyzing and allocating parts of the three-dimensional marine space to specific uses, to achieve ecological, economic, and social objectives that are usually specified through the political process. MSP is place-or area-based and can provide a practical approach to long-term ecosystem-based management. MSP should be comprehensive and adaptive, and resolve conflicts among multiple uses and the ecosystem.[109]

An integrated ocean management approach and other holistic management tools thus have a strong environmental and socio-economic focus offering important guidance and some predictability as to the articulation of different

105 LOSC, Preamble.

106 Discussed in more detail in Section 4.1.3.

107 On the relationship between the LOSC and integrated regulation of the oceans, see, for example, R. Barnes, 'The Law of the Sea Convention and the integrated regulation of the oceans' (2012) 27 *The International Journal of Marine and Coastal Law*, 859–866. On the relationship between the LOSC and integrated coastal zone management and marine spatial planning see, inter alia, N. Oral, 'Integrated coastal zone management and marine spatial planning for hydrocarbon activities in the Black Sea' (2008) 23 *The International Journal of Marine and Coastal Law*, 453–476.

108 E. Johansen, 'Norway's integrated ocean management: a need for stronger protection of the environment?' (2018) 32 *Ocean Yearbook*, 239–263, 242, with an account of other definitions of integrated ocean management in 242–243.

109 C. Ehler and F. Douvere, *Visions for a Sea Change*, Report of the first international workshop on Marine Spatial Planning, Intergovernmental Oceanographic Commission and Man and the Biosphere Programme, IOC manual and guides no. 48 (Paris: UNESCO, 2007), 24.

marine activities. This is because they imply a shift in management approaches from sector-based to integrated area-based management. MSP is particularly important in the context of articulating offshore renewable energy activities with other uses. If well designed and based on meaningful stakeholder participation, a marine spatial plan could enable spaces to be allocated for the competing activities, avoiding conflicts between the different uses and protecting the marine environment. In addition, such a plan would contribute sound decision-making, with predictability as to licensing of activities, thus offering clarity to investors/stakeholders.[110]

9.4.1.3 Protection and Preservation of the Marine Environment and Offshore Renewable Energy

A final aspect central in assessing to what extent the LOSC hampers or enables offshore renewable energy concerns the obligations prescribed in Part XII concerning the protection and preservation of the marine environment. This is perhaps the aspect of the LOSC that may pose an obstacle to investors, since protection of investments and environmental protection often clash. This may occur when the state changes the initial conditions of the investment, by adopting subsequent, more stringent environmental regulations that significantly affect the value of the investment or make it altogether inviable.[111] LOSC Part XII also points clearly towards constraining of states' rights to authorize or engage in offshore renewable energy activities. In effect, as Article 193 confirms, states must exercise the sovereign right to exploit their natural resources in accordance with the general duty to protect and preserve the marine environment as expressed in Article 192.

Several decisions of international tribunals have expounded on the content of the general obligation of protection and preservation prescribed by Article 192. The latter applies to all maritime zones;[112] includes living marine resources and biodiversity within the concept of marine environment;[113] encompasses a positive obligation for states to adopt measures to protect and

110 F. Maes, 'The international legal framework for marine spatial planning' (2008) 32 *Marine Policy*, 797–810, 798.

111 In this respect see, inter alia, E. Whitsitt and N. Bankes, 'The evolution of international investment law and its application to the energy sector' (2013) 51(2) *Alberta Law Review*, 207–147, 213; and Trevisanut and Giannopoulos, 'Investment protection', 813–815.

112 *Request for Advisory Opinion Submitted by the Sub-Regional Fisheries Commission*, ITLOS Reports 2015, para. 120.

113 *Southern Bluefin Tuna Case Between Australia and Japan and Between New Zealand and Japan*, Provisional Measures, Order of 27 August 1999, ITLOS Reports 1999, 280; and *South China Sea Arbitration* para. 945.

preserve the marine environment;[114] encompasses a negative obligation whereby states have the duty not to harm the marine environment;[115] and imposes a due diligence obligation whereby states must not only adopt preventive/protective measures but also exercise vigilance and enforce said measures.[116] The content of Article 192 is further informed by Article 194, which contains more specific obligations for the state concerning the prevention, reduction, and control of pollution of the marine environment: states must take all measures to prevent, reduce, and control pollution from any source;[117] and must also take all measures to ensure that activities under their jurisdiction or control do not cause transboundary damage.[118] As underlined in the *Chagos Arbitration*, 'Article 194 is [. . .] not limited to measures aimed strictly at controlling pollution and extends to measures focused primarily on conservation and the preservation of ecosystems.'[119] Amongst the measures that states must take to minimize to the fullest possible extent the pollution of the marine environment, Article 194(3)(d) specifically mentions measures concerning 'pollution from other installations and devices operating in the marine environments' – clearly significant for offshore renewable energy installations/structures. If the latter are considered to fall under the category of 'technologies', which seems quite plausible, then also Article 196 must be taken into consideration, as it reinforces the obligation of states to take all measures to 'prevent, reduce and control pollution of the marine environment resulting from the use of technologies under their jurisdiction or control'.

The remaining substantive provisions of Part XII are also relevant concerning offshore renewable energy, particularly Articles 208 and 211. Article 208 obliges states to establish rules and measures concerning prevention, reduction, and control pollution from seabed activities and from installations and structures; Article 211 obliges states to adopt rules and standards to prevent, reduce, and control pollution from vessels. As explained in Section 9.2, offshore renewable energy technologies will entail deploying some form of fixed or floating installations/structures at sea, and will require transport and servicing by use of vessels. Although those provisions do not refer specifically to pollution from submarine cables and pipelines, which will be essential for deployment of offshore renewable energy, these are still encompassed by the general obligation of Article 192, and could also be considered as falling under

114 *South China Sea Arbitration*, paras. 941–942.
115 Ibid.
116 Ibid. para. 944.
117 LOSC, Article 194(1).
118 LOSC, Article 194(2).
119 *Chagos MPA Arbitration*, para. 538.

the concept of 'installations and structures' specifically addressed by Article 208. The provisions on enforcement (Articles 214, 217, 218, and 220) are also highly important. Provisions concerning pollution by dumping (Articles 210 and 216) could become relevant – but it must be underlined that, in offshore renewable energy activities, the disposal of wastes or other materials incidental to the normal operations of the support vessels or of the installations/structures do not constitute 'dumping'.[120]

In addition, the LOSC prescribes the obligation to monitor the risks of effects of pollution,[121] the obligation to publicize reports concerning the risks or effects of pollution of the marine environment,[122] and the obligation for the state to conduct an EIA before authorizing any activities that could cause significant harmful changes to the marine environment.[123] All these obligations are relevant for the development of offshore renewable activities. However, Article 206 concerning EIA is relatively limited. It obliges states to conduct EIAs for activities under their jurisdiction only as far as practical, and only when they have reasonable grounds to believe that such activities may cause substantial pollution or significant harmful changes to the marine environment. Furthermore, Article 206 does not indicate what the content and criteria of the EIA should be. This gives rise to the question of whether a state could avoid conducting a proper EIA by arguing that it reasonably believes that offshore renewable energy will not pose major threats to the marine environment (as Section 9.3.2 suggests). The answer here must be negative. The actual impact of the various offshore renewable energy technologies can only be ascertained via EIAs; moreover, Article 206 must be read in conjunction with customary international law and other relevant instruments which are more nuanced regarding EIAs.[124] Furthermore, by conducting an EIA in relation to a given activity the state is fulfilling, to some extent, its general obligation of due diligence.

From the earlier discussion, it is clear that LOSC Part XII does not preclude the development of offshore renewable energy projects if the state has adopted the necessary measures to mitigate potential environmental hazards, to monitor activities, and to enforce applicable environmental

120 LOSC, Article 1(5)(b)(i).
121 LOSC, Article 204.
122 LOSC, Article 205.
123 LOSC, Article 206.
124 See Trevisanut and Giannopoulos, 'Investment protection', 812; *Certain Activities Carried Out by Nicaragua in the Border Area (Costa Rica* v. *Nicaragua)* and *Construction of a Road in Costa Rica Along the San Juan River (Nicaragua* v. *Costa Rica) (Judgement)* [2015] ICJ Rep. 665; and *Pulp Mills on the River Uruguay (Argentina* v. *Uruguay)* [2010] ICJ Rep. 14, paras. 203–204.

regulations. What the provisions of Part XII constrain is a state's unbridled support for exploiting offshore renewable resources at the expense of the marine environment, or the lowering of environmental rules and standards in order to attract investments in offshore renewable energy. This is indeed an appropriate limitation which should prevent negative trade-offs between climate-change mitigation via offshore renewable energy and the health of the marine environment. Moreover, the stringency of LOSC Part XII, increasingly demonstrated in recent cases heard by international tribunals, sends a clear message to investors in the offshore renewable energy sector – into their expectations, costs, and risk assessments they must factor the possibility of changes as technology develops and environmental standards become increasingly rigorous.

Finally, concerning the protection and preservation of the marine environment from offshore renewable energy activities, it is important to note the international legally binding instrument under the LOSC on the conservation and sustainable use of marine biological diversity of areas beyond national jurisdiction currently being negotiated.[125] If and when approved, this instrument will have repercussions for the development of offshore renewable activities on the high seas, specifically as to the interaction between offshore renewable energy and the conservation of marine biological diversity, as well as area-based management tools, EIAs, capacity building and the transfer of marine technology.

9.4.2 *Other Key Legal Instruments Regulating Offshore Renewable Energy*

There is a plethora of binding and non-legally binding global and regional legal instruments that are relevant in the context of offshore renewable energy. This section briefly describes only the key legal instruments that are pertinent to the offshore renewable energy sector and that further complement the LOSC regime.

As noted in Section 9.4.1, when the LOSC was negotiated and concluded, offshore renewable energy was not yet a concern – which explains why the text of the LOSC does not expressly mention this activity, except for a brief reference in Article 56. Moreover, the LOSC, as a framework convention regulating all aspects concerning the seas and oceans, does

[125] A draft of the text of this instrument is available at www.un.org/bbnj/sites/www.un.org.bbnj/files/draft_text_a.conf_.232.2019.6_advanced_unedited_version_corr.pdf, accessed 3 July 2019.

provide the basis for the regulation of offshore energy renewable activities but, understandably, does not regulate these activities in detail. However, the LOSC was designed to be a dynamic instrument, capable of evolving and adapting to new developments.[126] This dynamism was inserted in the LOSC by the possibility of amendment, the conclusion of implementing agreements, and the incorporation, by reference, of generally accepted international rules and standards (GAIRS). With no amendments to the LOSC or the negotiation of an offshore energy implementing agreement in sight, incorporation by reference of GAIRS has been relevant when it comes to offshore energy. LOSC Articles 60 and 80 require states to take into account GAIRS when removing abandoned or disused installations or structures. Here it is important to refer to the Guidelines and Standards for the Removal of Offshore Installations and Structures in the Continental Shelf and in the Exclusive Economic Zone, adopted by the International Maritime Organization (IMO) in 1989.[127] LOSC Articles 60 and 80 further prescribe that states can adopt safety zones only around artificial islands, installations and structures exceeding a distance of 500 meters as authorized by GAIRS. The 2010 IMO Guidelines for Safety Zones and Safety of Navigation around Offshore Installations and Structures are relevant and applicable to offshore renewable energy projects.[128] Another example is Article 211, which refers to GAIRS in relation to the prevention, reduction and control of pollution from vessels. As vessels will support offshore renewable energy activities, this provision also opens the door to the application of other IMO instruments, such as the International Convention for the Prevention of Pollution from Ships (MARPOL).[129]

While such instruments have assisted in providing additional guidance to states and investors, it must be stressed that, as Redgwell noted, some gaps

[126] A. Boyle, 'Further development of the Law of the Sea Convention: mechanisms for change' (2005) 54(3) *International and Comparative Law Quarterly*, 563–584.

[127] IMO, *Guidelines and Standards for the Removal of Offshore Installations and Structures in the Continental Shelf and in the Exclusive Economic Zone*, IMO Assembly Res. A.671(16) (19 October 1989).

[128] IMO, *Guidelines for Safety Zones and Safety of Navigation around Offshore Installations and Structures*, IMO Doc. SN.1/Circ.295 (7 December 2010). IMO had adopted guidelines on the same topic in 1989; however, these concerned only installations and structures used for the exploitation of resources on the continental shelf.

[129] 1973 International Convention for the Prevention of Pollution from Ships, London, 2 November 1973, 1340 UNTS 184, as modified by Protocol of 1978 relating to the International Convention for the Prevention of Pollution from Ships of 1973, 17 February 1978, 1340 UNTS 61.

remain concerning the regulation of offshore energy,[130] notably in relation to submarine electricity cables and the regulation of offshore installations.[131]

In addition, LOSC Article 237 recognizes that states may conclude other agreements in furtherance of the general principles of the LOSC concerning the protection and preservation of the marine environment. This opens the way for complementing the LOSC with other global and regional instruments also relevant in the context of offshore renewable energy. Cases in point include the Convention on Biological Diversity (CBD),[132] the London Convention on Dumping (London Convention)[133] and Protocol (1996 Protocol),[134] the Convention on Conservation of Migratory Species of Wild Animals (CMS Convention),[135] the Convention on Wetlands of International Importance especially as Waterfowl Habitat (RAMSAR Convention),[136] the Convention on Environmental Impact Assessment in a Transboundary Context (Espoo Convention)[137] and the Protocol on Strategic Environmental Assessment,[138] the International Convention for the Regulation of Whaling (IWC Convention),[139] the Convention for the Protection of the Marine Environment of the North-East Atlantic (OSPAR Convention),[140] and the Convention for the Protection of the Marine Environment and the Coastal Region of the Mediterranean (Barcelona Convention).[141]

130 C. Redgwell, 'Mind the gap in the GAIRS: the role of other instruments in LOSC regime implementation in the offshore energy sector', in N. Bankes and S. Trevisanut (eds.), *Energy from the Sea: An International Law Perspective on Ocean Energy* (Brill, 2015), 59.

131 Ibid.

132 1992 Convention on Biological Diversity, Rio de Janeiro, 5 June 1992, 1760 UNTS 69.

133 1972 Convention on the Prevention of Marine Pollution by Dumping of Wasters and Other Matter, London, 29 December 1972, 1046 UNTS 138.

134 1996 Protocol to the Convention on the Prevention of Marine Pollution by Dumping of Wastes and Other Matter, 7 November 1996, 36 ILM 7.

135 1979 Convention on the Conservation of Migratory Species of Wild Animals, Bonn, 23 June 1979, 1651 UNTS 333.

136 1971 Convention on Wetlands of International Importance especially as Waterfowl Habitat, Ramsar, 2 February 1971, 996 UNTS 245.

137 1991 Convention on Environmental Impact Assessment in a Transboundary Context, Espoo, 25 February 1991, 1989 UNTS 309.

138 2003 Protocol on Strategic Environmental Assessment to the Convention on Environmental Impact Assessment in a Transboundary Context, Kiev, 21 May 2003, 2685 UNTS 140.

139 1946 International Convention for the Regulation of Whaling, Washington, 2 December 1946, 161 UNTS 72.

140 1992 Convention for the Protection of the Marine Environment of the North-East Atlantic, Paris, 22 September 1992 (1993) 2354 UNTS 67.

141 For a more detailed account, see S. McDonald and D. L. VanderZwaag, 'Renewable ocean energy and the international law and policy seascape: global currents, regional surges' (2015) 29 *Ocean Yearbook*, 299–326; and Goettsche-Wanli, 'Sustainable production', 8–75.

In relation to the specific aspect of environmental regulation of offshore energy, Giannopoulos maintains that the LOSC, together with complementary hard and soft law instruments, does have the ability to 'fill the current legal gaps and strengthen the international legal standards for the regulation of this environmentally sensitive sector'.[142] Although an energy investor would find it more convenient to have all aspects concerning the regulation of offshore renewable energy dealt with in a single legal instrument, a thorough 'due diligence' survey of the legal framework applicable to the sector should provide enough information to proceed with specific renewable energy projects. Regarding the remaining regulatory gaps, investors should seek to clarify and secure the conditions for their investments with the state that is licensing or controlling the offshore renewable energy activity.

9.5 CONCLUSIONS

This chapter has described the potential role of offshore renewable energy in mitigating climate change, particularly taking into consideration the ocean's energy-generating capacity in light of global energy-consumption levels. Studies seem to indicate that the various forms of offshore renewable energy have only limited impacts on the marine environment, and that there are possible ways to mitigate the impacts identified. However, offshore renewable energy has yet to be adopted on a large scale. It still represents a small share within the global energy mix, because the overall challenges identified in this chapter constrain the swift development and implementation of offshore renewable energy technologies. There is a pressing need to address the technological and financial challenges so pivotal to increasing the share of offshore renewables. This will require supporting innovation, research, and development; fostering capacity building and transfer of technology; and reducing costs so as to make offshore renewable energy cost-competitive against other resources. Continued work towards a deeper understanding of the environmental impacts, including cumulative impacts, of the specific forms of offshore renewable energy and developing mitigation strategies is essential. Finally, there must be a legal and regulatory framework that provides legal predictability and stability.

This chapter has shown that the LOSC does regulate key aspects underpinning offshore renewable energy activities, not least by providing some degree

142 N. Giannopoulos, 'Global environmental regulation of offshore energy production: searching for legal standards in ocean governance' (2018) *Review of European, Comparative and International Environmental Law*, 1–15.

of certainty in relation to state jurisdiction over offshore renewable energy projects. It also gives states considerable discretion to pursue or authorize such projects in areas within their jurisdiction. However, there are limitations related to the LOSC as an overarching framework regulating all aspects concerning the oceans; the compromises introduced in its text to accommodate the differing interests, rights, and duties of states; and the general obligation imposed on states to protect the marine environment. The LOSC does not regulate all aspects concerning offshore renewable energy: it needs to be complemented by a range of binding and non-legally binding instruments. The fact that the LOSC does not provide a clear hierarchy of rights or of competing interests could complicate the balancing of offshore renewable energy projects with other uses of the seas. The LOSC does open the way to the use of management tools that can aid in achieving rational use of marine space, and proper consideration of the different uses and of the marine environment – but ultimately it depends on the states whether those tools, such as MSP, are properly designed and implemented. Concerning the obligation to protect the marine environment enshrined in LOSC Part XII, this chapter has also noted that to a certain degree the LOSC emplaces constraints on states. That, however, is amply justified by the need to prevent negative trade-offs between the use of offshore renewable energy to mitigate GHG emissions and the health of the marine environment.

The overall conclusion is hence that the law of the sea, and the LOSC, in particular, does not preclude the development of offshore renewable energy. On the contrary, it provides a basic legal framework that enables and is supportive of such activities.[143] That is not to say additional regulation of the offshore renewable energy industry or the creation of a proper international institutional setting is unnecessary – especially if or when offshore renewable energy activities move to areas beyond national jurisdiction.

[143] For a similar conclusion see, for example, Gabriele Goettsche-Wanli, who points out that the LOSC 'creates an enabling legal environment for economic activities, such as the production of offshore renewable energy, including by providing for universally agreed limits for maritime zones and the peaceful settlement of disputes, as well as facilitating safety of navigation, the laying of submarine cables and pipelines and the operation of artificial islands, installations and structures'. See Goettsche-Wanli, 'Sustainable production', 10.

10

Marine Protected Areas and Climate Change

Ingvild Ulrikke Jakobsen

10.1 INTRODUCTION

Marine protected areas (MPAs) and other area-based management tools (ABMTs) are recognized worldwide as important tools for conservation of marine biodiversity.[1] Establishing protected areas is one of the key measures set out in the Convention on Biological Diversity (CBD)[2] Article 8 (a). According to the Aichi Target 11 adopted under the CBD, states have committed themselves to, by 2020, conserve 10 per cent of coastal and marine areas by establishing

> effectively and equitable managed, ecologically representative and well connected systems of protected areas and other effective area-based conservation measures.[3]

This commitment is reinforced by the international community through the Sustainable Development Goals (SDG), in particular, SDG 14.[4] A new international instrument is currently negotiated under the UN auspices, which could fill the legal gaps in the conservation and sustainable use of marine

1 ABMTs include MPAs and broader spatial conservation measures such as marine spatial planning, closure of fisheries, and so on. See 'Revised draft text of an agreement under the United Nations Convention on the Law of the Sea on the conservation and sustainable use of marine biological diversity of areas beyond national jurisdiction', Note by the President, Art. 1(3) (hereinafter draft treaty), available at www.un.org/bbnj/sites/www.un.org.bbnj/files/revised_draft_text_a.conf_.232.2020.11_advance_unedited_version.pdf.

2 Convention on Biological Diversity (CBD), 5 June 1992, in force 29 December 1993, 1760 UNTS 79.

3 The Aichi targets are available at www.cbd.int/sp/targets/.

4 See the UN website on SDGs at sustainabledevelopment.un.org/sdgs. It follows from SDG 14.5 that states should: 'By 2020, conserve at least 10 per cent of coastal and marine areas, consistent with national and international law and based on best available scientific information.'

biodiversity in areas beyond national jurisdiction (ABNJ). The use of MPAs and other ABMTs is also identified as one of the four key elements in the ongoing negotiations for a new legally binding treaty on long-term conservation and sustainable use of biological diversity in areas beyond national jurisdiction (BBNJ).[5]

MPAs are a well-recognized measure for conservation and sustainable use of marine biodiversity. This chapter focuses on the use of MPAs as a potential contribution to dealing with the problems of climate change. MPAs do not directly address the release of greenhouse gases, but recent years have seen growing awareness of MPAs as an effective tool in fighting the severe threats of climate change.[6] Through the establishment of MPAs, the total pressures on marine ecosystems may be controlled. The removal of other stressors will strengthen marine ecosystems, making them more adaptive and resilient in the face of climate change. This effect of protection and conservation of marine ecosystems is recognized also in SDG 14.2, with the follow target for the international community:

> By 2020, sustainably manage and protect marine and coastal ecosystems to avoid significant adverse impacts, including by strengthening their resilience, and take action for their restoration, to achieve healthy and productive oceans.

Marine ecosystems may also have a mitigation function, as they absorb large amounts of global carbon emissions. Networks of MPAs may be established and managed so that habitats and species that are important as carbon stores are protected against human activities.[7] MPAs may thus serve as a mitigation and adaptation measure simultaneously: this chapter discusses both aspects.[8] Additionally, MPAs may serve as a tool to address ocean acidification, which is an effect of CO_2 emissions.[9]

This chapter investigates to what extent MPAs are addressed or identified as a potential tool or a strategy for adaptation and mitigation within the UN

5 On the negotiations, see www.un.org/bbnj/.

6 C. M. Roberts et al., 'Marine reserves can mitigate and promote adaptation to climate change' (2017) 114 *Proceedings of the National Academy of Sciences of the United States of America*, 6167–6175. See also F. Smiard, D. Laffoley and J. M. Baxter (eds.), *Marine Protected Areas and Climate Change: Adaptation and Mitigation Synergies, Opportunities and Challenges* (International Union for Conservation of Nature, 2016).

7 F. Quemmerais-Amice and J. Baxter, 'Executive Summary' in Smiard, Laffoley and Baxter (eds.), *Marine Protected Areas and Climate Change*, 14.

8 See R. K. Craig, this volume, Chapter 3.

9 See K. Scott, this volume, Chapter 5.

Climate Change Regime. How might this tool respond to and comply with requirements that follow from various climate-change instruments, in particular, the United Nations Convention on Climate Change Conservation (UNFCCC)[10] and the Paris Agreement,[11] and contribute to achieving their objectives? Furthermore: to what extent do international obligations to protect the marine environment and to conserve marine ecosystems and biological diversity that follow from the United Nations Convention on the Law of the Sea (LOSC)[12] and the CBD include requirements to establish MPAs for mitigation and adaptation to climate change? As these obligations were not adopted with climate change in mind, I also examine whether they are adequate for addressing the use of MPAs as a response to climate-change effects.[13]

The main legal framework is provided by the LOSC. Often referred to as the constitution of the oceans, it aims at establishing a comprehensive legal order for the oceans. Whereas the LOSC is flexible and considered to be capable of dealing with emerging problems, we must ask: to what extent has the LOSC the potential to respond to new threats and provide adequate solutions for dealing with them?[14] More concretely, here I assess how and to what extent the LOSC provides for or limits the use of MPAs as a tool for mitigation and adaptation and thus contributes to the achievement of the objectives of the UN Climate Change Regime.

The questions raised in this chapter are complex, as they involve analyses of three legal regimes: climate change law, international environmental law and the law of sea.[15] These legal regimes are not entirely overlapping as to objectives or obligations. It is necessary to examine their uses of MPAs to clarify the intersection of the different legal instruments and regimes. Could the various

[10] United Nations Framework Convention for Climate Change, adopted 9 May 1992, in force 21 March 1994, 1771 UNTS 107 (UNFCCC).

[11] The Paris Agreement, 12 December 2015, in force 4 November 2016, UN Doc. FCCC/CP/2015/L.9, Annex.

[12] United Nations Convention on the Law of the Sea (LOSC), London, 10 December 1982, in force 16 November 1994, 1833 UNTS 397.

[13] See A. Trouwborst, 'International nature conservation law and the adaptation of biodiversity to climate change: a mismatch?' (2009) 21(3) *Journal of Environmental Law*, 419–442, on whether international conservation law adequately facilitates the adaptation of species and ecosystems to climate change.

[14] Similar questions are raised by C. Kojima, 'Climate change and protection of the marine environment: food security, evolutionary interpretation, and the novel application of dispute settlement mechanisms under the United Nations Convention on the Law of the Sea' in N. Craik et al. (eds.), *Global Environmental Change and Innovation in International Law* (Cambridge University Press, 2018), 138–157, at 144.

[15] On the meaning of definitions of the term 'legal regime', see M. A. Yong, 'Introduction: the productive friction between regimes' in M. Yong (ed.), *Regime Interaction in International Law: Facing Fragmentation* (Cambridge University Press, 2012), 1–20.

regimes and relevant legal instruments be coordinated and read together as an effective legal framework for using MPAs for mitigation and adaptation to climate change?

10.2 THE CONCEPT OF MPAs

10.2.1 *Definitions*

There are many types and definitions of MPAs. One widely used definition is that provided by the International Union for Conservation of Nature (IUCN):

> A clearly defined geographical space, recognised, dedicated and managed, through legal or other effective means, to achieve the long-term conservation of nature with associated services and cultural values.[16]

Protected area is defined in the CBD 'as a geographically defined area which is designated or regulated and managed to achieve specific conservation objectives'.[17] The CBD Conference of the Parties (COP) has endorsed a definition of MPAs based on the IUCN definition:

> 'Marine and Coastal Protected Area' means any defined area within or adjacent to the marine environment, together with its overlying waters and associated flora, fauna, and historical and cultural features, which has been reserved by legislation or other effective means, including custom, with the effect that its marine and/or coastal biodiversity enjoys a higher level of protection than its surroundings.[18]

At the regional level, the OSPAR Convention has defined MPAs as:

> an area within the maritime area for which protective, conservation, restorative or precautionary measures, consistent with international law have been instituted for the purpose of protecting and conserving species, habitats, ecosystems or ecological processes of the marine environment.[19]

Three core elements or requirements as to what constitutes an MPA may be identified or deduced from these definitions. An MPA is a *geographically defined area*; it has a *conservation purpose or objective*, and *protective measures to regulate*

[16] International Union for Conservation of Nature, G. Kelleher (ed.), *Guidelines for Marine Protected Areas* (1999), available at www.iucn.org/sites/dev/files/import/downloads/mpaguid.pdf

[17] CBD, Art. 1.

[18] The definition is endorsed by the COP in Decision VII/5, UN Doc. UNEP/CBD/COP/DEC/VII/5 (13 April 2004), para. 10.

[19] OSPAR Commission, 'OSPAR Recommendations 2003/3 on a Network of Marine Protected Areas', Summary record OSPAR 03/17/1-E, Annex 9, para. 1.1.

human measures are adopted therein. However, none of these definitions reflects the use of MPAs as a response to the effects of climate change.

10.2.2 *MPAs versus Other ABMTs*

Various international legal instruments and policy instruments encourage or require the use of MPAs and other ABMTs.[20] There is globally an increasing emphasis today on the use of MPAs and other ABMTs for the protection of the marine biodiversity, as shown by the commitment of the international community to protect 10 per cent of all marine areas by 2020.

The commitments in SDG 14, Aichi target no. 11 and the ongoing BBNJ process with its draft treaty text all provide for the use of a broader set of ABMTs as a means of conserving marine biological diversity. Aichi target 11 refers to 'protected areas and other effective area-based measures . . . '; SDG 14.5 does not mention MPAs explicitly, but encourages states 'to conserve at least 10 per cent of coastal and marine areas, consistent with international and national law'. The draft of the new treaty on BBNJ addresses 'area-based management tools, including MPAs'.[21]

The use of a broader set of spatial area-based conservation measures is emphasized alongside MPAs and as part of MPA networks. However, scientists have pointed out that there must be clear objective for the areas to be protected, and that these must be managed strictly and efficiently, if they are to have mitigation and resilience functions and serve as effective tools for mitigation and adaptation.[22] This chapter therefore restricts the analysis to MPAs and legal questions related to the use of MPAs for climate purposes. That is not to say, however, that also other ABMTs, such as marine spatial planning, closures of fisheries or Particularly Sensitive Sea Areas (PSSAs), can also serve as important measures for protecting the marine ecosystems and preventing the harmful effects of climate change.

10.2.3 *MPAs as a Tool for Mitigation and Adaptation to Climate Change*

MPAs may be adopted for a range of different purposes. They ensure a higher level of protection from environmental impacts of human activities within

20 For an overview of the international legal framework for MPAs see I. U. Jakobsen, *Marine Protected Areas in International Law: An Arctic Perspective* (Brill Nijhoff, 2016), 9–11.

21 Draft treaty, Part 3.

22 C. R. Hopkins, D. M. Bailey and T. Potts, 'Perceptions of practitioners: Managing marine protected areas for climate change resilience' (2016) 128 *Ocean & Coastal Management*, 18–28.

a given geographical area; they may ensure conservation of vulnerable and endangered species, ecosystems or habitats; or set aside as special reference areas. The level of protection may vary from area to area – from strictly protected areas to areas where uses such as sustainable fisheries are allowed. The emphasis on MPAs in international fora must be seen in light of the shift in international law, from the sectoral approach of the LOSC and earlier environmental treaties regulating a particular source of pollution, to more integrated holistic approaches. As MPAs are intended to protect and conserve an ecosystem, a habitat, or a species against potential threats within geographical limits, the tool may be seen as a means of implementing the precautionary principle as well as the ecosystem-based approach.[23]

Together with overfishing and habitat destruction, the impacts of climate change are the most powerful causes of decreases in marine biodiversity. Other important stressors include invasive species and marine pollution.[24] Therefore, strengthening integrated ocean governance and conservation of marine biodiversity (as through the use of MPAs) are increasingly important to ensure resilience in the face of the threats from climate changes and other stressors on the marine environment.[25]

Moreover, the oceans play a fundamental role in regulating the climate, as marine ecosystems sequester carbon and serve as sinks, and healthy oceans and ecosystems are essential for adaptation to climate change. Thus, in addition to their key role for conservation of marine biology, MPAs may be important in helping the oceans to mitigate and adapt to climate change.[26]

Through appropriate management measures to ensure the protection of habitats and species known to be important carbon stores, MPAs can contribute to increased storage of carbon by marine ecosystems.[27] Furthermore, by establishing and implementing appropriate management measures within a specific area that limits and controls other stressors and threats to the marine environment, MPAs may serve as part of an adaptation strategy to climate changes by ensuring resilient ecosystems.[28]

23 See K. N. Scott, 'Integrated oceans management: a new frontier in marine environmental protection' in D. Rothwell et al. (eds.), *The Oxford Handbook of the Law of the Sea* (Oxford University Press, 2015), 462–490; and Jakobsen, *Marine Protected Areas*, 66.

24 R. K. Craig, 'Marine biodiversity, climate change, and governance of the oceans' (2012) 4 *Diversity*, 224–238.

25 Ibid.

26 See Roberts et al., 'Marine reserves', 6168–6169, especially the figure (at 6169) showing how MPAs may help.

27 Quemmerais-Amice and Baxter, 'Executive Summary', 14.

28 Ibid.

However, it is not just enough to set aside an area as an MPA, and then sit back and reap the benefits of adaptation or mitigation of climate-change effects. There are well-known limitations and shortcomings of MPAs as a tool for conservation of marine biological diversity, relevant also when the MPAs are established for the purpose of minimizing the adverse effects of climate change. First and foremost, marine ecosystems transcend jurisdictional boundaries, but the traditional zonal and sectoral approach to ocean management in the LOSC may hinder the establishment of integrated effectively managed MPAs with appropriate protective measures that address the human activities that threaten the objective of conservation. Furthermore, if the level of protection of the MPA is weak, or the protective measures are not enforced, the expected conservation benefits will not be achieved.[29] Recognizing the shortcomings of MPAs, scientific research indicates that MPAs must be effectively and properly managed and designed to mitigate and promote adaptation to climate change.[30]

There is not much practice in the establishment and use of MPAs to address the impacts of climate change. Some design principles and guidelines have been established, but a deeper discussion of these recommendations is beyond the scope and objective of this chapter.[31] Suffice it to note that MPAs which are large, well established, and well enforced have the best conservation benefits, and their effectiveness in supporting climate change adaptation and mitigation hinges on these factors.[32] The importance of adaptive management is also stressed.[33] Another key lesson is that MPAs must be strictly protected in order to promote climate change resilience, also for monitoring the effects of climate change.[34] A further crucial factor: climate considerations must be integrated early in the planning of MPAs as criteria for selection, in the design phase and planning of management measures.[35] Also important are selection of ecosystems/habitats or species that have a mitigation role, and establishing networks of MPAs.[36]

[29] See Roberts et al., 'Marine reserves', 6168.

[30] Ibid.

[31] E. McLeod et al., 'Designing marine protected area networks to address the impacts of climate change' in (2009) 7(7) *Frontiers in Ecology and the Environment*, 362–370; Smiard, Laffoley and Baxter (eds.), *Marine Protected Areas and Climate Change*, Chs. 3 and 4; and Hopkins, Bailey and Potts, 'Perceptions of practitioners'.

[32] Roberts et al., 'Marine reserves', 6172.

[33] Hopkins, Bailey and Potts, 'Perceptions of practitioners', 18.

[34] Ibid.

[35] Ibid., 26.

[36] J. Baxter et al., 'Marine Protected Areas and climate change mitigation: how MPAs can contribute to the reduction of greenhouse gas emissions' in Simard, Laffoley and Baxter (eds.), *Marine Protected Areas and Climate Change*, 41–48.

10.3 MPAs AS A TOOL FOR MITIGATION AND ADAPTATION TO CLIMATE CHANGE IN INTERNATIONAL LAW

10.3.1 *General*

The use of MPAs as a tool or measure for addressing mitigation and adaptation to climate change is not governed by one global instrument. The LOSC, the CBD, the UN Climate Change Regime, as well as regional agreements, are all of relevance. The LOSC Part XII requires states to address pollution of the oceans, including the release of greenhouse gases, and to protect and conserve the marine environment, including fragile ecosystems and rare habitats.[37] The UN Climate Change Regime provides an international legal framework for mitigation of and adaptation to climate change, financial and other means for support as well as international oversight mechanisms to promote implementation, compliance and effectiveness.[38] The CBD imposes obligations to conserve and ensure the sustainable use of biological diversity, including *in situ* conservation by the use of protected areas. Global obligations to protect and conserve the marine environment and the marine ecosystems are implemented at the regional level through regional agreements and frameworks for networks of MPAs, such as the OSPAR Convention,[39] the CAMLR Convention,[40] by initiatives by the Arctic Council, to mention a few.[41]

This, a multitude of regimes, must be analysed in investigating the potential of MPAs as a strategy for adaptation and mitigation, and whether the international law requires or provides for the use of MPAs for this purpose. To be effective, connections and interlinkages between the regimes must be created or identified.[42] In accordance with the principle of systemic interpretation, international treaties must be interpreted and applied in the context of the development of international law.[43] The legal instruments relevant for MPAs as a measure or strategy for mitigation or adaptation may thus be approached

37 See Boyle, this volume, Chapter 4.

38 D. Bodansky, J. Brunnèe and L. Rajamani, *International Climate Change Law* (Oxford University Press, 2017), 11.

39 Convention for the Protection of the Marine Environment of the North-East Atlantic, Paris, 22 September 1992, in force 25 March 1998, 2534 UNTS 67 (OSPAR Convention).

40 Convention on the Conservation of Antarctic Marine Living Resources, Canberra, 20 May 1980, in force 7 April 1982, 1329 UNTS 47.

41 Such as the Framework for a Pan-Arctic Network of Marine Protected Areas Arctic Council, adopted by PAME, Arctic Council (April 2015), available at pame.is/images/03_Projects/MPA/MPA_Report.pdf

42 See Scott, this volume, Chapter 5, Section 5.3.

43 Vienna Convention on the Law of Treaties, Vienna, 23 May 1969, in force 27 January 1980, 1155 UNTS 331 (Vienna Convention), Art. 31(3)(C).

and interconnected through evolutionary interpretation.[44] This section analyses the provisions relevant for MPAs in the UN Climate Change Regime, the LOSC and the CBD, seeking to identify connections and interlinkages or norms that can connect these regimes and provide an effective regime for MPAs adopted for the purpose of mitigation and adaptation to the effects of climate change.

10.3.2 *The UN Climate Change Regime and MPAs*

MPAs are not directly regulated by the UN Climate Change Regime as a measure to minimize greenhouse gases by preserving sinks or to increase the resilience of marine ecosystems to adapt to the effects of climate change. To what extent do the UNFCCC and the Paris Agreement recognize and address the protection and conservation of marine ecosystems by the use of MPAs?

The UNFCCC was adopted as a framework convention in 1992, and established the governance structure for the UN Climate Change Regime.[45] It has broad support (197 parties) and has established a COP responsible for elaborating it further.[46] The UNFCCC has also been further developed and elaborated through the Kyoto Protocol and the Paris Agreement.[47] The ultimate objective of the UNFCCC is, according to Article 2, to achieve

> stabilization of greenhouse gas concentrations in the atmosphere at a level that would prevent dangerous anthropogenic interference with the climate system.

Thus, some climate change is seen as unavoidable, but the concentration of greenhouse gases in the atmosphere must be stabilized to a level that would 'prevent dangerous anthropogenic interference'.[48] The objective or accepted level of greenhouse gas concentrations should be achieved within a timeframe that allows

> ecosystems to adapt naturally to climate change, to ensure that food production is not threatened and to enable economic development to proceed in a sustainable manner.[49]

Hence, the Convention acknowledges as part of its objective the natural capacity of ecosystems to adapt to climate change.

44 Kojima, 'Climate change', 140.
45 Bodansky, Brunée and Rajamani, *International Climate Change Law*, 118.
46 See list of parties at https://unfccc.int/process/parties-non-party-stakeholders/parties-convention-and-observer-states.
47 See E. Johansen, this volume, Chapter 1.
48 Ibid.
49 UNFCCC, Art. 2.

UNFCCC, Article 4, includes general commitments on mitigation and adaptation. The general commitments are very broad and vague with several qualifications, making the legal requirements unclear.[50] The duties are very broad and general, and cover all sectors, but without specifically addressing activities in the oceans or the marine environment.[51] However, it follows from the Preamble to UNFCCC that the parties to the Convention are:

> *Aware* of the role and importance in terrestrial and marine ecosystems of sinks and reservoirs of greenhouse gases.

While the UNFCCC acknowledges the role of marine ecosystems as sinks, it does not impose any requirements for states to establish MPAs, but merely notes that the parties are aware of this function of marine ecosystem, as sinks and reservoirs. Hence, the Convention states in Article 4(1)(d) that the parties shall

> Promote sustainable management, and promote and cooperate in the conservation and enhancement, as appropriate, of sinks and reservoirs of all greenhouse gases not controlled by the Montreal Protocol, including biomass, forests and oceans as well as other terrestrial, coastal and marine ecosystems.

Following this, the UNFCCC requires the parties to promote and cooperate in the conservation of marine ecosystems as sinks of greenhouse gases. This duty is not formulated in strict terms: states are required only to *promote and cooperate* in the conservation of marine ecosystems for this purpose. Neither does the Convention require the parties to protect the marine environment and marine ecosystems per se.[52] However, Article 4(1)(d), read in the context of the Preamble, suggests that the Convention supports the use of MPAs as mitigation measure.

Mitigation and adaptation are acknowledged as equally important strategies within the UN Climate Change Regime. Nevertheless, the UNFCCC includes a few provisions on adaptation.[53] Besides the general obligation in Article 4(1)(b) to adopt national or regional programmes that contain measures to facilitate adequate adaptation to climate change, the UNFCCC specifically addresses adaptation in Article 4(1)(e). This duty does not mention adaption to

50 See Bodansky, Brunée and Rajamani, *International Climate Change Law*, 130–131.

51 See Johansen, this volume, Chapter 1.

52 T. Stephens, 'Warming waters and souring seas: climate change and ocean acidification' in D. Rothwell et al. (eds.), *The Oxford Handbook of the Law of the Sea* (Oxford University Press, 2015), 777–798, 290.

53 Bodansky, Brunée and Rajamani, *International Climate Change Law*, 135.

climate change through the conservation of marine ecosystems or the use of MPAs for this purpose. It follows from Article 4(1)(e) that the parties are obliged to cooperate 'in preparing for adaptation to the impacts of climate change', and more specifically to 'develop and elaborate appropriate and integrated plans for coastal zone management . . . and for the protection and rehabilitation of areas'. Although not specifically mentioned or required, this could include the use of MPAs as part of 'coastal zone management' and as a tool for the 'protection and rehabilitation of areas'. The parties could comply with this duty by cooperating at the regional level in establishing MPAs that strengthen the resilience of marine ecosystems to the unavoidable effects of climate change.

The Convention makes no further reference to the role of the oceans or to marine ecosystems. Hence, the UNFCCC does not directly indicate the conservation of marine ecosystems as a solution for meeting the challenges of climate change, nor does it set out a clear legal duty for the contracting parties to ensure the conservation of marine ecosystems. The Convention has also been criticized for not emphasizing the role of the oceans in mitigating the effects of climate change, or its effects on the marine environment.[54] However, of relevance is Article 3(3), which states that the parties should

> take precautionary measures to anticipate, prevent or minimize the causes of climate change and mitigate its adverse effects.

Furthermore, it follows from the obligation to take precautionary measures that such policies and measures:

> should take into account different socio-economic contexts, be comprehensive, cover all relevant sources, sinks and reservoirs of greenhouse gases and adaptation, and comprise all economic sectors.

Consequently, although the UNFCCC does not set out any clear duties about conserving marine biodiversity or marine ecosystems, or establishing and managing MPAs for the purpose of mitigation or adaptation to climate-change effects, it does underline the importance of marine ecosystems as carbon sinks. Hence, establishing MPAs may serve to ensure conservation of marine ecosystems as sinks, as an appropriate precautionary measure for mitigating the effects of climate change and an application of the precautionary principle as set out in UNFCCC Article 3. Inter-state cooperation in establishing MPAs as an adaptation measure may also serve as a policy or measure for precautionary approach that could minimize adverse effects of climate change.

[54] J. Harrison, *Saving the Oceans through Law* (Oxford University Press, 2017), 253.

The Paris Agreement was adopted in 2015; as of December 2019, 186 states and the EU have ratified or acceded to the instrument.[55] The objective of the Paris Agreement is to enhance implementation of UNFCCC, to 'strengthen the global response to the threat of climate change'.[56] To achieve this, the Paris Convention sets a target for the parties: to hold the increase in the global average temperature 'to well below 2°C above pre-industrial levels and pursuing efforts to limit the temperature increase to 1.5°C above pre-industrial levels'.[57] The general obligation on mitigation is the most important legal obligation here.[58] As per Article 4(2), states shall

> prepare, communicate and maintain successive nationally determined contributions that it intends to achieve. Parties shall pursue domestic mitigation measures, with the aim of achieving the objectives of such contributions.

Compared to the UNFCCC, the 2015 Paris Agreement acknowledges more clearly the importance of the conservation of biological diversity. As noted, marine ecosystems may serve as carbon sinks and thereby mitigate emissions from the carbon they store.[59] Mangrove forests, sea-grass meadows and coral reefs are highlighted as important in this respect and can serve as long-term sinks.[60] Their carbon sequestering services are recognized in the Preamble, which states that the parties to the Agreement

> Recognizing the importance of the conservation and enhancement, as appropriate, of sinks and reservoirs of the greenhouse gases referred to in the Convention,

Furthermore:

> Noting the importance of ensuring the integrity of all ecosystems, including oceans, and the protection of biodiversity . . .

Article 5 specifies the duty of the parties to

> take action to conserve and enhance, as appropriate, sinks and reservoirs of greenhouse gases as referred to in Article 4, paragraph 1 (d), of the Convention, including forests

55 See list of parties to the Paris agreement at en.wikipedia.org/wiki/List_of_parties_to_the_Paris_Agreement
56 Paris Agreement, Art. 2.
57 Ibid., Art. 2(b).
58 Bodansky, Brunée and Rajamani, *International Climate Change Law*, 231.
59 Baxter et al., 'Marine Protected Areas', 42.
60 Ibid.

This reference to forests as an example of a sink or reservoir that the parties shall take actions to conserve and enhance should not be understood to mean that conservation of marine ecosystems is not included in the legal duty. Rather, the wording 'including forests' indicates that also other ecosystems, such as marine ecosystems, are part of the legal duty to conserve or enhance sinks and reservoirs.[61]

The Paris Agreement has a stronger focus on adaptation than UNFCCC, and refers in several provisions to resilience.[62] In Article 7 it is stated that:

> Parties hereby establish the global goal on adaptation of enhancing adaptive capacity, strengthening resilience and reducing vulnerability to climate change, with a view to contributing to sustainable development and ensuring an adequate adaptation response in the context of the temperature goal referred to in Article 2.

This obligation is relevant also for strengthening the resilience of marine ecosystems by using MPAs. The Paris Agreement recognizes the importance of conservation and resilience, but it does not contain specific obligations for states to conserve marine biodiversity and ecosystems as means of responding to the effects of climate change.

Although the Paris Agreement takes a step forward compared to the UNFCCC in acknowledging the role of the oceans in minimizing the effects of climate change, it does not contain specific legal duties for the parties to conserve marine biodiversity by the use of MPAs.

The UN Climate Change Regime provides very little guidance on conservation of marine ecosystems or biological diversity for mitigation and adaptation to climate change.[63] However, the obligations in the Regime open for the use of MPAs for mitigation and adaptation to climate change, and can supplement and support the obligations under the LOSC and the CBD to protect and conserve ecosystems and biological diversity. While the use of MPAs is not mentioned in the obligations of UNFCCC or Paris Agreement, these may still be interpreted and applied so that MPAs as a tool could be recognized and accepted as part of states' nationally determined contribution for complying with the obligations and objectives laid down in the UN Climate Change Regime. Greater recognition has gradually been emerging of the importance

[61] C. Martinez, C. Lefebvre and D. Herr, 'Strengthening the relationship between Marine Protected Areas and ocean protection and measures to deliver climate change adaptation and mitigation' in Simard, Laffoley and Baxter (eds), *Marine Protected Areas and Climate Change*, 20.

[62] See Johansen, this volume, Chapter 1.

[63] Trouwborst, 'International nature conservation law', 430.

of the oceans as a part of the solution to the effects of climate change – more specifically, the importance of conservation of marine biological diversity as a means for mitigation and adaptation to climate change.[64]

10.3.3 *MPAs as a Response to Climate Change under the Obligations to Protect and Conserve the Marine Environment and Marine Biological Diversity*

10.3.3.1 General

The UN Climate Change Regime may, as noted earlier, provide support for the designation of MPAs. The details of how the MPAs are to be managed, where they are to be designated, and so on, follow from international environmental law and the relevant instruments setting out the legal and political framework for MPAs. To clarify the scope and content of state obligations to protect and conserve marine ecosystems and biological diversity by the use of MPAs as a response to the effects of climate change, we must turn to the international regulations dealing specifically deal with protection and conservation of the marine environment and marine biodiversity.

This section analyses the global obligations in the LOSC and the CBD relevant for the establishment of MPAs, to clarify the role of MPAs as a response to climate change. These legal instruments were never developed to address climate change as such.[65] However, recent years have witnessed recognition of the importance of better integration between the areas of law through soft-law norms – such as COP decisions under the CBD, policy reports and the SDG goals.[66] Moreover, environmental principles adopted and elaborated within the international environmental law and the CBD regime – such as the precautionary approach and the ecosystem approach – are of relevance for strengthening the resilience of ecosystems and to adaptation to the unavoidable effects of climate change.[67]

However, is the international legal framework for MPAs adequate to facilitate and contribute to mitigation and adaptation to climate change – and, if so, how? Climate change already has, and will continue to have, significant impacts on biological diversity. Do the obligations to protect and conserve the marine environment and ecosystems provide for the necessary cooperation

64 Smiard, Laffoley and Baxter (eds.), *Marine Protected Areas and Climate Change*, 17.

65 Trouwborst, 'International nature conservation law' (421) refers to international nature conservation law and discusses their adequacy for facilitating the adaptation of species and ecosystems to climate change.

66 Martinez, Lefebvre and Herr, 'Strengthening the relationship', 17–21.

67 Trouwborst, 'International nature conservation law', 426.

between states, as well as the regulations necessary to facilitate enhancing marine ecosystems as sinks and the adaptation of species and ecosystems to climate change?[68]

10.3.3.2 MPAs and the LOSC

The LOSC, with its Part XII on environmental protection, marked an historical milestone when it was adopted in 1982. Unfortunately, these general obligations of states to protect and preserve the marine environment were negotiated at a time when climate change scarcely featured on the political agenda. However – and even though the LOSC is known as 'the constitution of the oceans' – it is not a static legal instrument. It is a dynamic instrument that is capable of adapting to new circumstances and that may be interpreted and implemented in light of later treaties, such as the CBD and the UNFCCC.[69] Let us examine whether the general obligations under LOSC Part XII also cover the duty to protect and conserve marine biological diversity by, for example, the use of MPAs for climate-change mitigation and adaptation. And to what extent do the general obligations provide for such use of MPAs?

According to Article 192, states are under an obligation to protect and preserve the 'marine environment'. While most of the obligations in Part XII relate to marine pollution, the general obligation is not limited to marine pollution. The wording of Article 192 is broad and may cover protection of the marine environment from a wide range of activities, including pollution, climate change, habitat destruction and overfishing.[70] It is clear that conservation of living resources is part of the obligations to protect and preserve the marine environment. This follows from a contextual reading of Articles 192 and 193, as well as case law.[71] Article 194 sets out measures that states shall take to prevent and minimize marine pollution. The heading of Article 194 ('Measures to prevent, reduce and control pollution to the marine environment') could suggest that the provision concerns only activities that lead to marine pollution. However, a contextual interpretation with Article 192, as well as subsequent practice

68 See also similar questions raised in Trouwborst, ibid., 421.

69 See Boyle, this volume, Chapter 4. See also J. Barrett, 'The UN Convention on the Law of the Sea: a living treaty?' in J. Barret and R. Barnes, *Law of the Sea: UNCLOS as a Living Treaty*, (BIICL, 2016), 3–40.

70 Harrison, *Saving the Oceans*, 24. See also Boyle, this volume, Chapter 4.

71 *Southern Bluefin Tuna* cases (*New Zealand* v. *Japan*; *Australia* v. *Japan*) (*Order for Provisional Measures*) [1991] ITLOS Rep. 3 and 4, para. 70.

and case law, indicates that Article 194(5), requiring states to adopt measures 'to protect and preserve rare or fragile ecosystems as well as the habitat of depleted, threatened or endangered species and other forms of marine life', has a broader scope. A broad interpretation of the wording 'marine environment' was also supported by the Arbitral Tribunal in the *Chagos Arbitration*, which stated that Article 194 'is accordingly not limited to measures aimed strictly at controlling the pollution and extends to measures focused primarily on conservation and the preservation of ecosystems'.[72] Moreover, 'marine environment' is an open term, which indicates that it may be interpreted in the light of new legal norms laid down in later treaties, such as the CBD and also the Paris Agreement. The principle of systemic interpretation as per the Vienna Convention Article 31(3)(C) suggests that the broad term 'marine environment' may be interpreted in an 'evolutionary' way in light of new international treaties and norms. Furthermore, the tribunal in the *South China Sea Arbitration* clarifies that the content of Article 192 'is informed by other provisions of Part XII and other applicable rules of international law'.[73] Thus it would appear that the obligation to protect and preserve the marine environment, as per LOSC Article 192, includes a duty to take measures to protect and conserve marine biological diversity.[74]

In light of these analyses, it is reasonable to argue that the duty to protect the marine environment and to protect and conserve marine biological diversity also includes a duty to take mitigation and adaptation measures as a response to the effects of climate change. Article 192 includes a legal *due diligence* obligation to adopt measures to protect and preserve the marine environment against future as well as current threats.[75] The South China Sea Arbitration held that

> This 'general obligation' extends both to 'protection' of the marine environment from future damage and 'preservation' in the sense of maintaining or improving its present condition. Article 192 thus entails the positive obligation to take active measures to protect and preserve the marine environment, and by logical implication, entails the negative obligation not to degrade the marine environment.[76]

72 *Chagos Marine Protected Area Arbitration* (*Mauritius* v. *United Kingdom*) (*Award*) [2015] PCA Case no. 2011–3, para. 538.

73 *South China Sea Arbitration* (*The Republic of Philippines* v. *The People's Republic of China*) (*Award*) [2016] PCA Case No. 2013–19, para. 941.

74 See also Boyle, this volume, Chapter 4.

75 See Harrison, *Saving the Oceans*, 24. See also *South China Sea Arbitration*, para. 945.

76 *South China Sea Arbitration*, para. 941.

That it is a *due diligence* obligation means that states are required to adopt appropriate measures to protect and preserve the marine environment.[77] Hence, the terms 'protection and preservation' of the marine environment cover all activities and threats to the marine environment, as well as a positive duty to take active measures and a negative obligation not to degrade the marine environment.[78] Clearly, the general obligation in Article 192, as elaborated in Articles 194, 207 and 212, includes the duty to take necessary measures to protect the marine environment from pollution from anthropogenic emissions.[79] Following this, it seems reasonable to hold that the obligation to protect and conserve marine biological diversity is not only an obligation to conserve biological diversity in itself: it encompasses the use of conservation measures for protecting ecosystems that play important roles in sequestering and storing carbon (such as mangroves, tidal marshes and seagrass meadows) and thereby serve as measures for climate-change mitigation. Otherwise, if marine ecosystems that store carbon are degraded or threatened by human activities, the effects of climate change are likely to be more serious, and the marine environment could suffer more severe harm. Consequently, actions to protect the marine ecosystems that serve as carbon sinks, thereby mitigating emissions and limiting the effects of climate change, are part of the *due diligence* obligation to protect and conserve the marine environment.

Opinion differs as to whether the general obligations include adaptation measures against climate change. In his chapter in this book, Boyle argues that the role of LOSC as regards adaptation to the effects of climate change is less clear, compared to mitigation. He adds, however, that 'there is no reason to see LOSC as an obstacle against adaptation'. Stephens, on the other hand, argues that the 'LOSC will be highly relevant to policies of adaptation at national, regional and global strategies'.[80]

In my opinion, measures for conservation of marine biological diversity and measures on adaptation to climate change are closely interconnected. Article 192 requires states to take positive steps to protect and conserve marine biological diversity, including the duty to take measures necessary to protect and conserve rare or fragile ecosystems and habitats of depleted, threatened, or endangered species and other forms of marine life, as prescribed in Article 194(5). Measures to protect ecosystems against human activities (for instance, by reducing stress from other activities) could make them more resilient,

77 Ibid., paras. 964 and 974.
78 Harrison, *Saving the Oceans*, 24.
79 See Boyle, this volume, Chapter 4.
80 Stephens, 'Warming waters', 798.

lessening the negative effects of climate change. Thus, conservation measures adopted to comply with the obligations in Articles 192 and 194(5) may serve both as adaptation strategies to reduce the effects of climate change, and as measures for conservation of biological diversity itself. It is also reasonable to interpret the obligations so that states must take conservation measures that are appropriate actions to address impacts of climate change. This could involve reducing stressors, restoring degraded ecosystems, adopting networks of MPAs, or monitoring marine biological diversity in ways that open for more adaptive management of marine resources and ecosystems.[81] Therefore, adaptive measures against climate change could, under Article 194(5), be considered as necessary measures to protect rare or fragile ecosystems.

That also means that failure to take into account climate-change considerations, with respect to mitigation and adaption, could be considered a breach of the obligation to protect and preserve the marine environment.[82]

The content of Article 192 is, as emphasized earlier, informed and interpreted in the light of later treaty practice. The precautionary principle in UNFCCC Article 3(3) is relevant for interpreting the content of the legal obligation in Article 192: the parties must take precautionary measures to 'anticipate, prevent or minimize the causes of climate changes and to mitigate its adverse effects'. However, it is uncertain what this implies for states when implementing the legal duty in Article 192. Establishing MPAs for mitigation or adaptation to climate change, where marine ecosystems are protected from other human activities, may in itself be seen as a precautionary measure for minimizing the effects of climate change and thus an application of this principle.

To sum up, the obligations in the LOSC and the UN Climate Change Regime may be connected though interpretation and implementation. The broad general obligations in Articles 192 and 194(4) may be interpreted to include both mitigation and adaptation measures to minimize the effects of climate change, thereby reinforcing the rather weak obligations under the UNFCCC and the Paris Agreement. Indeed, failure to take action against the impacts of climate change could even be considered a breach of the general obligation in Articles 192 and 194(5).[83] Still, the broad and vague obligations in the UNFCCC and the Paris Agreement do not set clear requirements; states have wide discretion as to what actions to take and how. The obligations to protect and preserve the marine environment and marine ecosystems cannot be interpreted as *requiring*

81 See suggested activities to reduce the impacts of climate change on biodiversity, in Decision X/33 on Biodiversity and Climate Change, UN Doc. UNEP/CBD/COP/DEC/X/33 (29 October 2010), para. 8 (c)–(d).

82 See Kojima, 'Climate change', 149–150.

83 Ibid.

states to adopt a network of MPAs. However, they open up for the use of this measure; and it could be argued, in light of later treaty practice, that this is an appropriate tool for complying with treaty obligations. On the whole, then, the broad environmental obligations in LOSC facilitate and support an approach where MPAs are identified and managed as measures for conservation of biological diversity, and as a strategy for mitigation and adaptation to the effects of climate change.

10.3.3.3 MPAs and the CBD

The objective of the CBD is to ensure sustainable use of its components, with conservation of marine biological diversity and the fair and equitable sharing of the benefits arising from genetic resources. To contribute to achieving this objective, its Article 8 includes several measures for *in situ* conservation, defined in Article 2 as

> the conservation of ecosystems and natural habitats and the maintenance and recovery of viable populations of species in their natural surroundings and, in the case of domesticated or cultivated species, in the surroundings where they have developed their distinctive properties.

Article 8(a) sets out a legal duty for the contracting parties to 'as far as possible and as appropriate', establish 'a system of protected areas or areas where special measures need to be taken to conserve biological diversity'. Although the legal duty is qualified by the wording 'as far as possible and as appropriate', the CBD requires states to protect and conserve the marine biodiversity inter alia by the use of MPAs. The obligation is soft and the qualifier 'as far as possible and as appropriate' weakens the legal obligation, but that does not alter the legal status of the obligation.[84] The obligation for the states to establish MPAs applies pursuant to CBD Article 4(a) in areas within national jurisdiction.

Article 8(a) does not provide any guidance as to what areas should be selected or which human activities should be regulated, or how strict the regulations adopted to protect and conserve the marine biodiversity should be. Article 8(b) leaves it to the states to develop

> guidelines for the selection, establishment and management of protected areas or areas where special measures need to be taken to conserve biological diversity.

[84] Jakobsen, *Marine Protected Areas*, 153.

Hence, the CBD accords broad discretion to states as regards implementing the legal obligation. The obligation of *in situ* conservation is aimed at conserving ecosystems, habitats and species in their natural surroundings. To achieve this, protected areas are (as defined in Article 2) designated to 'achieve specific conservation objectives'. Thus the obligation in Article 8 to ensure *in situ* conservation of biological diversity does not explicitly refer to adaption or mitigation of climate-change effects.[85] However, the measures for *in situ* conservation listed in Article 8 are relevant here.[86] In particular, the duties to establish a system of protected areas (Article 8 (a)) and to promote the protection of ecosystems, natural habitats and the maintenance of viable populations of species in natural surroundings (Article 8 (d)) are relevant in the context of adaptation and mitigation of climate-change effects, by strengthening the resilience of biological diversity.

The CBD does not directly address the use of MPAs as a tool for mitigation and adaptation to climate change, or integrate climate considerations into the obligations on in situ conservation. However, the CBD is a *framework* convention, where the content of the legal duties is further specified and elaborated through several decisions of the COP. Subsequent practice may provide guidance to states in implementing the vague obligations laid down in the Convention. The COP has also served a role in filling gaps such as by adopting decisions and work programmes that address the conservation of marine and coastal biodiversity, ocean fertilization, ocean acidification and underwater noise.[87]

The obligation of *in situ* conservation and to establish MPAs are elaborated through COP Decisions. The CBD COP has also adopted several decisions underlining the connection and synergies between biological diversity and climate change,[88] and has urged the parties to 'enhance the integration of climate-change considerations related to biodiversity in their implementation of the Convention'.[89] Stress has been put on the importance of marine biodiversity to mitigation and adaptation of climate change by: 'Highlighting the role and potential of marine and coastal ecosystems, such as coral reefs and estuaries, and habitats such as tidal salt marshes, mangroves and seagrasses.'[90] Furthermore, by:

85 Trouwborst, 'International nature conservation law', 436.
86 Ibid.
87 Harrison, *Saving the Oceans*, 48.
88 Martinez, Lefebvre and Herr, 'Strengthening the relationship', 19.
89 Decision IX/16, UN Doc. UNEP/CBD/COP/DEC/IX/16 (9 October 2008).
90 Decision X/29, UN Doc. UNEP/CBD/COP/DEC/X/29 (29 October 2010), para. 8(a).

> Enhancing their efforts to increase the resilience of coastal and marine ecosystems, through, *inter alia*, improved implementation, towards achieving the 2012 target of establishing marine protected areas, consistent with international law and based on best scientific information available, including representative networks[91]

States have been encouraged to reduce 'the negative impacts from climate change as far as ecologically feasible, through conservation and sustainable management strategies that maintain and restore biodiversity', not least by 'implement(ing) activities to increase the adaptive capacity of species and the resilience of ecosystems in the face of climate change'.[92] These activities include reducing non-climatic stressors, such as pollution, over-exploitation, habitat loss and fragmentation, and invasive alien species.[93] Also emphasized are the strengthening of protected area networks, integrating biodiversity into wider seascape and landscape management, restoring degraded ecosystems and ecosystem functions, and facilitating adaptive management by strengthening monitoring and evaluation systems.[94]

The importance of protected areas as a response to climate change effects was also recognized in a COP 2011 decision:

> the significant role that protected areas, restored ecosystems and other conservation measures can play in climate-change-related activities[95]

Although these decisions are not legally binding, they play a role in interpreting the obligation of *in situ* conservation in Article 8.[96] This development and practice can also be said to have relevance for the interpretation and application of the LOSC *due diligence* obligation to protect and conserve the marine environment, including rare and fragile habitats and species.[97]

Thus, even though the conservation obligations of the CBD to ensure *in situ* conservation by the use of MPAs do not explicitly mention mitigation or adaptation to climate change as a purpose or objective, these obligations can be reasonably interpreted to cover an obligation to conserve marine ecosystems for this purpose. Still, the broad and vague obligations, also as further elaborated by the COP, do not appear to provide sufficient and

91 Ibid., para. 8(d).
92 Decision X/33, para. 8(c) –(d).
93 Ibid., para. 8(d)(i).
94 Ibid., para. (d)(iii)–(vi).
95 Decision XI/21, UN Doc. UNEP/CBD/COP/DEC/XI/21 (5 December 2012), para. 6(d).
96 For an overview of biodiversity and climate-change decisions, see www.cbd.int/climate/decision.shtml.
97 Harrison, *Saving the Oceans*, 258.

adequate guidance on how to integrate climate considerations, or how to manage and design MPAs to that end. Further clarification is needed. That could take place at the regional level, by elaborating the existing regional frameworks for MPAs and clarifying how MPAs can address the harmful effects of climate change.[98]

10.4 MPAs AS A CLIMATE-CHANGE RESPONSE WITHIN THE LAW OF THE SEA REGIME: OPPORTUNITIES AND OBSTACLES

10.4.1 *Legal Opportunities for Establishing MPAs under the LOSC*

Coastal states enjoy sovereignty in their internal and territorial waters, and therefore have broad competence to establish MPAs for environmental purposes, including as mitigation and adaptation measures.[99] Many of the ecosystems important for carbon sequestration are located along in coastal areas.[100] Coastal states may exercise their sovereignty to establish and manage MPAs aimed at protecting coastal and marine habitats from damage and degradation, for instance by restricting trawling and aquaculture, to ensure that these habitats may continue to serve as carbon sinks.

Similarly, coastal states may establish MPAs in their EEZs for the purpose of conserving and managing living resources or protection of the marine environment, on the basis of their sovereign rights and jurisdiction laid down in LOSC Article 56. Within these MPAs, coastal states may control and restrict human activities to reduce risks of damage and strengthen the resilience of an ecosystem or a habitat. They may take adaptation measures, for instance by regulating fisheries, protecting species that are threatened, and by removing other threats in addition to the impacts of climate change.

Also, coastal states may protect sea-bed ecosystems, for instance by prohibiting trawling. They have sovereign rights to explore and exploit the natural resources of the continental shelf, as per LOSC Article 77. The wording 'exploring and exploiting' is broad enough to include the right of a coastal state to establish an MPA on the continental shelf, where mineral exploitation or extraction of oil and gas resources are not allowed, in order to protect, for instance, ecosystems that play a role in carbon sequestering.

98 According to an IUCN report: 'The cross-sectoral approach of the oceans for better addressing climate change is a critical challenge for the regional frameworks and agreements and more particularly for the Regional Seas Conventions', see Martinez, Lefebvre and Herr, 'Strengthening the relationship', 21.

99 LOSC, Art. 2.

100 Quemmerais-Amice and Baxter, 'Executive Summary', 14.

However, coastal states must respect the rights of other states in their maritime zones. Thus, MPAs adopted within the territorial sea must not violate the right of innocent passage.[101] And other states continue to enjoy the freedom of navigation in the EEZ.[102] In exercising their sovereign rights and jurisdiction to adopt MPAs in their EEZs, coastal states 'shall have due regard to the rights and duties of other States'.[103] Similarly, Article 78(2) states that regulations adopted for MPAs on the continental shelf must not 'infringe or result in any unjustifiable interference with navigation and other rights and freedoms of other States'.[104]

There is currently no clear legal basis for establishing MPAs in ABNJs. The high seas are open to all states, and the principle of the freedom of the high seas applies (LOCS Article 87). As no states enjoy sovereignty or sovereign rights, no states are allowed to define, unilaterally, an area on the high seas as an MPA. Furthermore, states are under a *due diligence* obligation to protect the marine environment, which includes the legal duty to conserve marine biological diversity in all maritime zones, also in an ABNJ. Also, the LOSC requires that states shall cooperate at the global level and, as appropriate, at the regional level in protecting the marine environment.[105] This obligation to cooperate for the protection of the marine environment at global and regional levels creates an opportunity for the states in a given region to enter into an agreement and develop a framework for establishing MPAs in ABNJs within that region. Such an instrument or framework could also include provisions for states to establish MPAs as mitigation and adaptation strategies, by providing criteria for selection of areas as well as management measures or guidelines for the activities to be regulated. To ensure that the establishment of MPAs in ABNJs is consistent with the LOSC, careful consideration must be given to the selection of areas, as well as to how protective measures may be adopted, while ensuring compatibility with the freedoms of the high seas.[106] MPAs adopted on the basis of such agreement are not legally binding for third states, however. Moreover, establishing MPAs in ABNJs requires coordination and cooperation with relevant international bodies such as the International Maritime Organization (IMO) and Regional Fisheries Management Organizations (RFMOs). Most of the MPAs or other ABMTs that have been adopted in ABNJs are sectoral, focusing on either fishing or

101 LOSC, Art. 17.
102 LOSC, Art. 58.
103 LOSC, Art. 56(2).
104 For more on the right to establish MPAs, see Jakobsen, *Marine Protected Areas*, p 18–62.
105 LOSC, Art. 197.
106 Jakobsen, *Marine Protected Areas*, 53.

shipping.[107] However, some cross-sectoral MPAs in ABNJs have been adopted under the OSPAR Convention and the CAMLR Convention.[108]

To sum up: coastal states have the right, and full possibilities, to adopt MPAs within their maritime zones where climate-change considerations related to mitigation and/or adaptation are included.[109] The general obligations in LOSC Part XII are broad enough to cover the establishment of MPAs as a mitigation and adaptation strategy. Establishing MPAs as a measure for limiting the effects of climate change falls within the scope of Articles 192 and 194(5), and the obligations provide for the use of such a tool for complying with them. As for the ABNJ, states may cooperate within a regional agreement and establish MPAs where also climate-change considerations are integrated.

10.4.2 *Establishing MPAs: Legal Constraints and Challenges*

The LOSC, with its traditional zonal approach, has proven insufficient to ensure protection of the marine environment and sensitive habitats, ecosystems and biological diversity.[110] More recent environmental norms and instruments, such as the obligation to conserve biological diversity, and newer global threats such as climate change, require more holistic approaches, where human activities are addressed across jurisdictional boundaries and cumulative effects are also taken into consideration.[111] The general obligations under LOSC Part XII are broad, and do provide for the use of MPAs. However, MPAs must be adopted within the legal regime of the LOSC where states are subject to differing jurisdiction and rights and obligations in their respective maritime zones.[112] The LOSC may therefore represent a legal obstacle to the establishment and management of MPAs.

The process of establishing MPAs in order to achieve Achi target no 11 and SDG no 14 has been too slow. The latest assessment of progress in achieving the Aichi targets by the CBD concludes that even if 10 per cent coverage is reached by the year 2020, the qualitative elements of the target – on establishing ecologically representative and well-connected systems of protected areas and other area-based conservation measures that are effectively and equitably

107 Scott, 'Integrated oceans management', 484.

108 See R. Tiller et al., 'The once and future treaty: towards a new regime for biodiversity in areas beyond national jurisdiction' (2019) 99 *Marine Policy*, 239–242, at 242.

109 Stephens, 'Warming waters', 794–795.

110 Scott, 'Integrated oceans management', 464.

111 See T. Henriksen, 'Conservation and sustainable use of Arctic marine biodiversity' (2010) 1(2) *Arctic Review on Law and Politics*, 249–278, at 250.

112 CBD Article 22(2) states that the obligations should be implemented consistently with the rights and obligations of the law of the sea.

managed – will not be achieved.[113] The jurisdictional boundaries of the LOSC and its traditional zonal and sectoral approach to ocean management could be one explanation here.

Both the loss of biological diversity and the effects of climate change are complex global threats that must be addressed across jurisdictional and institutional and sectoral boundaries. Coastal states, however, must establish MPAs within their national jurisdiction, in accordance with the LOSC and the rights of other states in the respective maritime zones. Under the sectoral specialist approach of the law of the sea, regulations on certain human activities (such as shipping) are adopted by specialist institutions that have legal competence to address only that specific activity and are not mandated to consider the cumulative effects of the human activities. As various institutions may have the competence to regulate activities within the same ocean space, this can lead to problems in coordinating the protective measures and may result in gaps in protecting the marine environment and sensitive ecosystems within a specific area.[114] For instance, a coastal state must turn to the IMO if it wishes to adopt routing measures in order to protect an MPA in its EEZ from operational pollution or the risk of accidental pollution from shipping.

With its sectoral and zonal approach, the LOSC may thus represent legal constraints for the use of MPAs. This is particularly the case for MPAs in ABNJs. As such areas comprise nearly two thirds of the global marine areas, it is crucial to establish MPAs – to ensure conservation of biological diversity, but also as tools for mitigation and adaptation to climate change. While coastal habitats are recognized as serving an important role as carbon sinks, more is now known about carbon sequestration beyond coastal waters and in ABNJs.[115] There is as yet no clear legal basis for adopting MPAs or other ABMTs in ABNJs. However, the draft of the new legally binding treaty does include provisions on the use of MPAs / ABMTs, which may fill this gap.[116]

Still, it remains to be seen what role the new global treaty and its institutions will have, and what responsibility states will have through

[113] L. M. Campbell and N. J. Gray, 'Area expansion versus effective and equitable management in international marine protected areas goals and targets' (2019) 100 *Marine Policy*, 192–199, at 197. See also www.cbd.int/pa/UN-Ocean-Conference/faq-en.pdf .

[114] Harrison, *Saving the Oceans*, 275.

[115] Because the Ocean, *Ocean for Climate* Report (2019), available at www.becausetheocean.org/wp-content/uploads/2019/10/Ocean_for_Climate_Because_the_Ocean.pdf, accessed December 2019. See also Quemmerais-Amice and Baxter, 'Executive Summary', 14.

[116] Draft treaty, Part 3.

regional cooperation and existing regional agreements. Several states have argued that the new treaty should build on existing instruments, and that existing regional and sectorial instruments and organizations should have responsibility for establishing MPAs.[117] Furthermore, according to the draft of the new treaty, the agreement shall be interpreted so as to promote coherence and coordination with other relevant instruments.[118] It seems likely that regional agreements, with their framework for MPAs, will play an important role, also if the states succeed in getting the new treaty adopted. Moreover, there has been some practice of establishing MPAs beyond national jurisdiction, adopted under regional agreements, OSPAR and CAMLR, on which the new treaty can build.[119]

The new treaty does not include climate-change considerations as a central element.[120] The linkages between biodiversity conservation and mitigation and adaptation to climate change are apparently not addressed in the draft, and there are only a few references to climate change. However, climate change is included in the second draft as one of the objectives for the MPAs/ABMTs, to

> rehabilitate and restore biodiversity and ecosystems, including with a view to enhancing their productivity and health and building resilience to stressors, including those related to climate change[121]

Vulnerability to climate change is included in the list of indicative criteria for identification of areas in Annex 1 to the treaty,[122] but habitats that serve carbon sinks are not included. Otherwise, the draft of the treaty fails to clarify the role that MPAs have or could have in dealing with climate change. This is indeed a weakness with the on-going negotiations and the new treaty: today the global community has a unique opportunity to adopt a more integrated treaty for conservation and sustainable use of biological diversity where biodiversity conservation and climate change considerations are connected.

117 On the various approaches the new treaty could take, see E. Druel and K. Gjerde, 'Sustaining marine life beyond boundaries: options for an implementing agreement for marine biodiversity beyond national jurisdiction under the United Nations Convention on the Law of the Sea' (2014) 49 *Marine Policy*, 90–97. See also the draft treaty, Arts 4, 6 and 15.

118 Draft treaty, Art. 4.

119 See E. M. De Santo, 'Implementation challenges of area-based management tools (ABMTs) for biodiversity beyond national jurisdiction (BBNJ)' (2018) 97 *Marine Policy*, 34–43.

120 See C. Prip, this volume, Chapter 14.

121 Draft treaty, Art. 14.

122 Ibid., Annex 1.

10.5 REGIONAL COOPERATION: PART OF THE SOLUTION AND WAY FORWARD?

In view of the zonal and sectoral approach of LOSC, regional cooperation in protecting the marine environment and conserving the marine biological diversity appears to be the key to success in establishing MPAs where climate-change considerations are integrated. The BBNJ process also underlines this, as explained in Section 10.4. Moreover, a regional approach is consistent with the obligation under LOSC Article 197 to cooperate in the protection and preservation of the marine environment.

However, there are today very few networks of MPAs where mitigation of or adaptation to the effects of climate change has been included in the planning, selection or management.[123] Efforts are being made under the Arctic Council, under its working group PAME: the 'Framework for Pan-Arctic Network of Marine Protected Areas' envisages the establishment of MPAs that protect and promote the resilience of biological diversity.[124] To achieve this vision, the Framework specifies 'strengthening ecological resilience' as one of four goals, with corresponding objectives.[125] A further objective of the Framework is to conserve areas 'of high primary productivity that capture and store carbon to mitigate the effect of climate change, such as coastal wetlands'.[126]

The PAME Framework also underlines the important of adaptive and flexible management, so that the MPAs can respond to environmental change, and proposes the use of dynamic MPAs that protect ecologically important areas that move over time, or that include seasonal protective measures.[127] However, the Framework is not legally binding; its success hinges on the efforts of the individual Arctic states, as the network is composed of MPAs established by them within their national waters.[128]

Furthermore, CAMLR has references to adaptation to climate change and to strengthening of ecosystem resilience, as principles of conservation.[129] Its Commission (CCAMLR) adopted a general framework for the establishment of MPAs in 2011. This framework recognizes that MPAs established within CCAMLR aim to 'maintain the ability to adapt in the face of climate change'. The framework includes key criteria for the establishment of MPAs, which

[123] Martinez, Lefebevre and Herr, 'Strengthening the relationship', 21.
[124] PAME, Framework for a Pan-Arctic Network of Marine Protected Areas.
[125] Ibid., 9–10.
[126] Ibid., 10.
[127] Martinez, Lefebvre and Herr, 'Strengthening the relationship', 20.
[128] For an analysis of the Pan-Arctic Framework for Marine Protected Areas, see Jakobsen, *Marine Protected Areas*, 233–243.
[129] CAMLR, Art. II (C).

shall be established to contribute to the achievement of specific objectives, including 'the protection of areas to maintain resilience or the ability to adapt to the effects of climate change'.[130] Two MPAs have been adopted by the CCAMLR: the South Orkney Islands southern shelf in 2009 and the Ross Sea region MPA in 2016.[131] The rationale for establishing the Ross Sea MPA follows from the preamble of the conservation measure, which recognizes that the Ross Sea MPA offer opportunities for the study and understanding of climate-change effects. The Ross Sea MPA has several specific objectives. Concerning climate change, the Ross Sea MPA is 'to provide reference areas for monitoring natural variability and long-term change, and in particular a Special Research Zone, in which fishing is limited to better gauge the ecosystem effects of climate change and fishing'.[132]

These are examples of efforts at integrating climate change into the network of MPAs at the regional level. However, there is a need to enhance these efforts and develop more detailed frameworks for MPAs where climate-change considerations are included.[133]

10.6 CONCLUDING REMARKS

The legal duties to protect and conserve the marine environment and ecosystems, as per the LOSC and the CBD, provide for the use of MPAs, and can also be interpreted to include duties for the states to take conservation measures for the purpose of mitigation of and adaptation to the effects of climate change. The obligations under the UN Climate Change Regime, the LOSC and the CBD are thus mutually supportive. As yet, however, the legal regimes relevant for establishing MPAs where climate-change considerations are integrated are not sufficiently coordinated to provide an effective legal framework. The best way forward would be to build on the positive experiences in regional agreements and develop a legal framework and practice at the regional level, with interlinkages between the global instruments to ensure the use of MPAs as a response to climate change. Criteria for selection of areas, and guidelines

130 CCAMLR, Conservation Measure 91–04 (2011): General framework for the establishment of CCAMLR Marine Protected Areas, available at www.ccamlr.org/en/measure-91–04-2011.

131 CCAMLR, Conservation Measure 91–03 (2009): Protection of the South Orkney Islands southern Shelf; and Conservation Measure 91–05 (2016): Ross Sea region marine protected area. Available at www.ccamlr.org/en/conservation-and-management/browse-conservation-measures.

132 CCMLR, Conservation Measure 91–05 (2016), para. 3. For more on the management of the Ross Sea Region MPA, see J. Jabour and D. Smith, 'The Ross Sea Region Marine Protected Area: can it be successfully managed?' (2018) 32(1) *Ocean Yearbook*, 190–205.

133 Martinez, Lefebvre and Herr, 'Strengthening the relationship', 25.

for planning and management of MPAs where climate considerations are incorporated, could be further developed at the regional level, to provide implementation guidance.

The LOSC, with its zonal and sectoral approach to ocean management, may prove to be an obstacle for the establishment and effective management of MPAs. This may be especially the case with MPAs adopted for the purpose of mitigation of and adaptation to climate change, because scientific studies have shown that such MPAs should preferably be larger areas with strict and effective regulations. Regarding ABNJ there is a fragmented approach to ocean management. That makes it essential to strengthen the cooperation and integration between relevant sectoral institutions to enhance the integrated approach to ocean management, and to facilitate the establishment of MPAs where climate-change considerations and actions to promote mitigation and adaptation are included. However, the legal situation with ABNJs will depend on the outcome of the BBNJ negotiations.

11

Integrating Climate Change in International Fisheries Law

Erik J. Molenaar*

11.1 INTRODUCTION

There is now broad scientific consensus that anthropogenic climate change is occurring, and will continue for the foreseeable future.[1] For those prepared to see and acknowledge it, evidence of climate change is all around us. Such evidence is particularly overwhelming in the Arctic region, where the continuous thinning and receding sea-ice in the Arctic Ocean stands out as especially clear-cut evidence. Ample proof of human-induced climate change also exists in the domain of marine capture fisheries, for instance, with sightings of new species arriving from lower latitudes while 'traditional' fish species leave for higher latitudes.

This chapter examines the extent to which climate change has been integrated in the domain of international fisheries law, and whether this domain entitles or requires states – individually or through regional fisheries management organizations (RFMOs)[2] – to take account of climate change and its impacts in their fisheries management. International fisheries law is the domain (or: 'rule-complex') of international law that relates specifically to the conservation, management and/or development of marine capture fisheries. It consists of substantive norms (e.g. rights, obligations and objectives), substantive fisheries standards (e.g. catch restrictions) as well as institutional

* Work on this chapter was also facilitated by funding from the Netherlands Polar Programme and the Research Council of Norway (project *STOCKSHIFT*). The author is very grateful for comments received from Solène Guggisberg, Eelco Leemans, Florence Poulain, Henrik Ringbom, Wouter Jan Strietman, Osvaldo Urrutia and Ganesan Vethiah on an earlier version.

[1] See D. Vidas et al., this volume, Chapter 2 and R. B. Craig, this volume, Chapter 3.

[2] For the purpose of this chapter, the acronym RFMOs also covers regional fisheries management arrangements (RFMAs). Unlike RFMOs, RFMAs do not establish an intergovernmental organization and are not necessarily created by legally binding instruments.

rules and arrangements (e.g. mandates and decision-making procedures). International fisheries law is part of public international law and can also be seen as a branch or part of the domain of the international law of the sea.

Section 11.2 on 'The Impacts of Climate Change on Marine Capture Fisheries' also examines dispute settlement procedures on climate change and marine capture fisheries. Section 11.3 deals with 'Climate-Change and the Global Component of International Fisheries Law'; Section 11.4 delves into the relatively unexplored topic of 'Marine Capture Fisheries and Climate Change Mitigation'. Section 11.5 covers 'Climate Change and RFMOs'. Some conclusions are offered in Section 11.6.

11.2 THE IMPACTS OF CLIMATE CHANGE ON MARINE CAPTURE FISHERIES

As explained elsewhere in this book,[3] human emissions of carbon dioxide (CO_2) into the Earth's atmosphere have led to the concurrent problems of ocean acidification – as most atmospheric CO_2 is eventually absorbed by the oceans – and climate change. The climate-change-induced impacts most directly relevant for marine capture fisheries are increases in temperature, de-oxygenation and stratification, changing currents, and reductions in salinity (due to increased freshwater inflow caused by melting land-ice), and sea-ice cover. These impacts lead to changes in species productivity and composition, as well as shifts in distribution and abundance (which can lead to 'mismatches' in prey availability for predators),[4] and may even culminate in commercial or actual extinction. Some of these changes are by no means new, because marine ecosystems are highly dynamic. It may well be, however, that these climate-change-induced changes will become more frequent, more profound and possibly less predictable, as well as irreversible at human timescales. As argued by Trathan and Agnew: 'as climate change potentially introduces a greater level of ecosystem uncertainty, successful ecosystem outcomes potentially mean that management practices may need to be more conservative.'[5]

Ocean acidification is expected to be especially problematic for calcium carbonate skeletal maintenance of marine invertebrates such as molluscs and

[3] See Vidas et al., this volume, Chapter 2 and K. N. Scott, this volume, Chapter 5. See also the Intergovernmental Panel on Climate Change (IPCC) Special Report on the Ocean and Cryosphere in a Changing Climate (SROCC), 25 September 2019.

[4] P. N. Trathan and D. Agnew, 'Climate change and the Antarctic marine ecosystem: an essay on management implications' (2010) 22 *Antarctic Science*, 387-398, 390.

[5] Ibid., 388.

crustaceans, and important biological habitats such as coral reefs, as it affects their growth, reproduction and prospects for survival.[6] Moreover, increases in temperature and extreme weather events – such as typhoons and floods – will mean more damage to habitats of critical importance to fish stocks, such as coral reefs (including through coral bleaching), seagrass beds and mangrove forests that function as spawning or nursing areas for fish species.[7] The shifts in species distribution are predominantly towards higher latitudes and deeper waters, at rates of tens to hundreds of kilometres per decade.[8] They are likely to lead to significant regional differences, with the highest positive impacts predicted for the Arctic region and the highest negative impacts predicted for tropical regions.[9] The polar regions will benefit not only from shifts in distribution but also from sea-ice recession, which will allow fishing to commence in new geographical areas.

These climate-change-induced impacts on marine capture fisheries have emerged at a time when fisheries management authorities are already struggling to cope with their 'internal' challenges, for instance: overexploitation; overcapacity; subsidies; illegal, unreported and unregulated fishing; bycatch and discards of target and non-target species; impacts on benthic ecosystems; other unsustainable fishing practices (e.g. large-scale pelagic drift-net fishing; fishing with explosives or cyanide); and abandoned, lost or discarded fishing gear which continue 'ghost fishing'. The need to deal with these internal challenges in conjunction with climate-change-induced impacts and other 'external' challenges (e.g. other sources of marine pollution and invasive alien species) will put additional pressures on the performance of fisheries management authorities, and may even lead to irreversible change when 'tipping points' are exceeded and irreversible 'regime shifts' occur.[10]

6 See Scott, this volume, Chapter 5; Trathan and Agnew, 'Climate change', 388–389; and W. W. L. Cheung et al., 'Modelling future oceans: the present and emerging future of fish stocks and fisheries' in R. Caddell and E. J. Molenaar (eds.), *Strengthening International Fisheries Law in an Era of Changing Oceans* (Hart, 2019), 13–24, section 2.

7 Report of the 18th Meeting of the UN Open-ended Informal Consultative Process on Oceans and the Law of the Sea (ICP Meeting), UN Doc. A/72/95, 16 June 2017, paras. 21, 39. See also 'Impacts of climate change in fisheries and aquaculture: synthesis of current knowledge, adaptation and mitigation options', *FAO Fisheries and Aquaculture Technical Paper* No. 627 (FAO, 2018) (2018 FAO Climate Change Technical Paper), iv–vi.

8 See Cheung et al., 'Modelling future oceans', section 2; SOFIA, *The State of World Fisheries and Aquaculture 2018: Meeting the Sustainable Development Goals* (FAO, 2018) (SOFIA 2018), 131–138.

9 V. W. Y. Lam et al., 'Projected change in global fisheries revenues under climate change' 6 *Scientific Reports* No. 32607, 1, 3; 2018 FAO Climate Change Technical Paper, iv.

10 R. Rayfuse, 'Addressing climate change impacts in regional fisheries management organizations' in Caddell and Molenaar (eds.), *Strengthening International Fisheries Law*, section 1; Trathan and Agnew, 'Climate change', 391.

Changes in the distribution and abundance of species have significant implications in the context of the international law of the sea, which divides the marine environment into coastal state maritime zones, and areas beyond national jurisdiction (ABNJ: the high seas and the international seabed – 'the Area'). Whereas coastal states have exclusive access to fisheries resources in their own maritime zones pursuant to their sovereignty or sovereign rights therein,[11] all states have a right to fish in ABNJ.[12] Significant changes in distribution and abundance between coastal state maritime zones and ABNJ will, therefore, lead to changes relating to access and availability, and thereby undermine intergovernmental arrangements on access and allocation of fishing opportunities. This can also occur between RFMOs, with respect to a fish stock whose distributional range straddles the regulatory areas of RFMOs with competence over the species.[13]

It seems plausible to assume that climate-change-induced changes to species productivity, composition, distribution and abundance will lead to more intergovernmental disputes,[14] and possibly more intergovernmental dispute settlement procedures. So far, however, no dispute settlement procedures on fisheries disputes have been explicitly or exclusively established on account of changes induced by climate change. However, climate change played a role in two cases on Atlanto-Scandian herring (*Clupea harengus*) brought by Denmark in respect of the Faroe Islands against the European Union (EU) under the LOSC[15] and the World Trade Organization (WTO).[16] As both procedures were terminated before the written phase had commenced, however, the exact nature and extent of the role of climate change in them cannot be determined. At any rate, the procedures did not concern the respondent's contribution to climate change. Rather, they centred on the changes in the distribution and abundance of the stocks of Atlanto-Scandian herring and North-East Atlantic mackerel (*Scomber scombrus*), which had led to increased abundance of these species in the maritime zones of the Faroe Islands.

11 Arts. 2, 19(2)(i), 21(1)(d), 49, 56(1)(a) and 77(1) and (4) of the United Nations Convention on the Law of the Sea, Montego Bay, 10 December 1982, in force 16 November 1994, 1833 UNTS 397 (LOSC).

12 Ibid., Arts. 116 and 86.

13 See discussion in Rayfuse, 'Addressing climate change impacts', section 2.

14 See, e.g., J. Spijkers et al., 'Marine fisheries and future ocean conflict' (2018) *Fish and Fisheries*, 798–806; M. L. Pinsky et al., 'Preparing ocean governance for species on the move' 360 *Science*, 1189–1191, 1189; and 2018 FAO Climate Change Technical Paper, iv.

15 For full details, see note 11.

16 *The Atlanto-Scandian Herring Arbitration* (*The Kingdom of Denmark in respect of the Faroe Islands* v. *The European Union*) [2014] PCA Case No. 2013-30; Termination Order of 23 September 2014; *European Union: Measures on Atlanto-Scandian Herring*, WT/DS469, terminated on 21 August 2014.

According to the claimant, as these changes were significant and not merely temporary, the Faroe Islands was entitled to a larger share of the total allowable catch (TAC) for both stocks.[17] Although the claimant was not required to prove that these changes were entirely or partially caused by anthropogenic climate change, it implicitly alluded to the likelihood that they were in part driven by climate change.[18]

Climate change was also not mentioned by Ecuador or any other participants in their written and oral pleadings for the 2nd Review Panel established under the South Pacific Regional Fisheries Management Organisation (SPRFMO) Convention.[19] It is worth noting, however, that no significant catches of Jack mackerel (*Trachurus murphyi*) were made in Ecuador's maritime zones in the years before the establishment of the 2nd Review Panel, unlike the case in some earlier years.[20] Although overfishing of the stock throughout its range was probably one of the main reasons for the decline of the stock's abundance in Ecuador's maritime zones, climate change might have played a role as well, and may perhaps be a contributing factor to the stock's distribution and abundance in the future as well. Admittedly, this is mere speculation. What is clear is that, in the domain of marine capture fisheries, climate-change-induced changes will result in gains and losses, and winners and losers. Some states may be fortunate enough to be 'overall winners' as gains outweigh losses: others may be 'overall losers'. This obviously raises concerns of fairness and equity, in particular if the overall losers have hardly contributed to anthropogenic climate change.

11.3 CLIMATE CHANGE AND THE GLOBAL COMPONENT OF INTERNATIONAL FISHERIES LAW

11.3.1 *The LOSC*

The cornerstone of today's global jurisdictional framework for marine capture fisheries is the LOSC, which divides seas and oceans into maritime zones and

17 See, e.g., J. Spijkers and W. J. Boonstra, 'Environmental change and social conflict: the northeast Atlantic mackerel dispute' (2017) 17 *Regional Environmental Change*, 1835–1851, 1847.

18 Information provided to the author by a government official of the Faroe Islands by email, 18 December 2018.

19 Convention on the Conservation and Management of High Seas Fishery Resources in the South Pacific Ocean, Auckland, 14 November 2009, in force 24 August 2012 www.sprfmo.int; Review Panel established on 25 April 2018 pursuant to the SPRFMO Convention, [2018] PCA Case No. 2018-13, Findings and Recommendations of 5 June 2018.

20 See the SPRFMO Memorandum in the 2nd SPRFMO Review Panel, PCA Case No. 2018-13, Findings and Recommendations, 5, available at https://pca-cpa.org/en/cases/156/.

specifies the basic rights and obligations of states therein. Through various key obligations, the LOSC regulates the exercise of entitlements to fishing that states have in their capacities as coastal or flag states. As noted, coastal states have exclusive access and jurisdiction over fisheries resources in all their relevant maritime zones. The two main entitlements of flag states are the right to fish on the high seas, and access to the surplus of the TAC in the exclusive economic zones (EEZs) of coastal states.[21] The general obligations included in the LOSC have been built upon by a suite of global fisheries instruments, in particular the Fish Stocks Agreement,[22] legally binding and non-legally binding instruments adopted by the Food and Agriculture Organization of the United Nations (FAO), as well as certain (parts of) UN General Assembly (UNGA) Resolutions.

As the LOSC was negotiated during 1973–1982, well before the first studies on the impact of global warming on seas and oceans began to emerge,[23] it is understandable that it does not mention climate change. Whereas the third preambular paragraph of the LOSC ('*Conscious* that the problems of ocean space are closely interrelated and need to be considered as a whole') may be interpreted as recognition of an ecosystem approach *avant la lettre*,[24] it is submitted that a more convincing view is that it refers to the package-deal approach pursued during the negotiations on the LOSC.[25] Arguments linking this preambular paragraph to climate change would therefore be equally unconvincing.

21 LOSC, Arts. 62(2) and 116.

22 Agreement for the Implementation of the Provisions of the United Nations Convention on the Law of the Sea of 10 December 1982 relating to the Conservation and Management of Straddling Fish Stocks and Highly Migratory Fish Stocks, New York, 4 August 1995, in force 11 December 2001, 2167 UNTS 3.

23 A. H. A. Soons, 'An ocean under stress: climate change and the law of the sea', presented at the 2018 Annual Meeting of the Royal Netherlands Society of International Law (KNVIR), available at www.knvir.org/, notes at 75 that these studies began to emerge in the second half of the 1980s.

24 This interpretation seems reflected in the 2005 UNGA 'Oceans Resolution' (No. 60/30, 29 November 2005), which contains a preambular paragraph starting with '*Conscious* [...] as a whole' and continues with 'through an integrated, interdisciplinary and intersectoral approach, and reaffirming the need to improve cooperation and coordination at national, regional and global levels, in accordance with the Convention, to support and supplement the efforts of each State in promoting the implementation and observance of the Convention, and the integrated management and sustainable development of the oceans and seas'. This paragraph has been retained in all Annual UNGA Oceans Resolutions since then.

25 Note the identical wording in the 'Declaration incorporating the "Gentleman's Agreement" made by the President and endorsed by the Conference at its 19th meeting on 27 June 1974', appended to the Rules of Procedure for the negotiations on the LOSC (UN Doc. A/CONF.62/30/Rev.3).

The LOSC pursues a 'zonal' as well as a 'thematic' or 'sectoral' approach. The former is reflected in its Parts II, IV–VII and XI which cover the different maritime zones. Examples of the latter are Part XII, entitled 'Protection and Preservation of the Marine Environment', and Part XIII, entitled 'Marine Scientific Research'. The LOSC does not have separate parts dedicated to fishing, shipping or seabed activities, but covers these human activities under zonal or thematic/sectoral parts. Except for Article 194(5), fishing is exclusively governed by the zonal parts.[26]

Parts II, IV and VI (territorial sea, archipelagic waters and continental shelf) merely confirm the coastal state's sovereignty and sovereign rights over fisheries resources in these maritime zones without imposing any constraints.[27] Conversely, Parts V and VII (EEZ and the high seas) contain rights as well as obligations. As the Area is not excluded from the scope of LOSC Article 86, the rights and obligations relating to high seas fishing laid down in Section 2 of Part VII also apply to the Area.

Pursuant to Paragraphs 1 and 2 of LOSC Article 61, a coastal state is required to avoid overexploitation by setting a TAC and other conservation and management measures, 'taking into account the best scientific evidence available to it'.[28] Paragraph 3 of Article 61 stipulates:

> Such measures shall also be designed to maintain or restore populations of harvested species at levels which can produce the maximum sustainable yield, as qualified by relevant environmental and economic factors, including the economic needs of coastal fishing communities and the special requirements of developing States, and taking into account fishing patterns, the interdependence of stocks and any generally recommended international minimum standards, whether subregional, regional or global.

[26] Art. 194(5) reads: 'The measures taken in accordance with this Part shall include those necessary to protect and preserve rare or fragile ecosystems as well as the habitat of depleted, threatened or endangered species and other forms of marine life.' In its Award in the *Chagos Marine Protected Area* Arbitration (*Mauritius* v. *United Kingdom*) (Award) [2015] PCA Case No. 2011-03, paras. 320, 538 the Arbitral Tribunal held that Art. 194(5) 'is not limited to measures aimed strictly at controlling pollution and extends to measures focussed primarily on conservation and the preservation of ecosystems' – thereby bringing fishing within its range. See also the *South China Sea Arbitration* (*The Republic of Philippines* v. *the People's Republic of China*) (Award) [2015] PCA Case No. 2013-19, paras. 945, 956, 960.

[27] LOSC, Arts. 2, 19(2)(i), 21(1)(d), 49 and 77(1) and (4). Such constraints may nevertheless arise from other sources of international law, including customary international law. One example would be the duty not to cause transboundary harm (*sic utere tuo ut alienum non laedas*). However, this duty would not be immediately relevant in the context of this chapter.

[28] Art. 119(1)(a) of the LOSC uses the slightly different phrase 'on the best scientific evidence available to the States concerned'.

A similar obligation is imposed on high seas fishing states pursuant to LOSC Article 119(1)(a). Both obligations require TACs and other conservation and management measures to be designed to produce the maximum sustainable yield (MSY) 'as qualified by relevant environmental and economic factors'. The two examples of economic factors that are provided ('the economic needs […] developing States') indicate that coastal states and high seas fishing states have a considerable margin of discretion in setting TACs that are above MSY.[29] Even though no examples of environmental factors are provided, the rationale for their inclusion would presumably be to require coastal states and high seas fishing states to set TACs below MSY in case such factors are present. Taking such action would imply foregoing revenue in order to avoid a higher risk of overexploitation. LOSC Articles 61(4) and 119(1)(b) also stipulate that setting TACs below MSY and other measures may be required to avoid undesirable effects on associated or dependent species. Whereas the term 'associated species' is used in the LOSC and the Fish Stocks Agreement to refer to species caught as bycatch with the target species – for instance, in mixed fisheries – the term 'dependent species' is used to refer to species that have a predator–prey relationship with the target species.

It speaks for itself that coastal states and high seas fishing states may also voluntarily set TACs below MSY, for instance, in relation to target prey species with low commercial value in order to optimize food availability for target predator species with high commercial value, which would increase the latter's biomass and thereby allow for higher TACs. Setting TACs below MSY could also maintain or enhance food availability for non-target species (e.g. birds, marine mammals, marine turtles), thereby ensuring or furthering their conservation or preservation.

Similarly, nothing in the LOSC precludes states from applying discretion in setting TACs below MSY based on scientific evidence relating to climate change. However, as most fish stocks are transboundary – that is, their distributional ranges overlap with the maritime zones of more than one coastal state and/or the high seas – such voluntary action is only effective if taken together with all relevant coastal states and/or high seas fishing states. Due to the consensual nature of international law, as reflected in the fundamental principle of *pacta tertiis*, it is not possible to require unwilling states to join a 'coalition of the willing'. Such unwilling coastal or flag states would therefore benefit as 'free riders' from the relinquished catches or other conservation measures agreed by others.

[29] Note also 'discretionary powers for determining the allowable catch' in LOSC Art. 297(3)(a).

Whereas the previous discussion focuses mainly on the size of TACs for target species, this is by no means the only conservation and management measure to be considered in the context of climate change or ocean acidification. Where non-target species or vulnerable benthic marine ecosystems are already under significant pressure due to climate change or ocean acidification, fisheries management authorities should consider all possible measures for reducing, minimizing or avoiding additional pressures from fishing.[30] This may include gear restrictions, bycatch mitigation measures and spatial and/or temporal measures. Marine protected areas (MPAs) and other area-based fisheries management measures can have a dampening effect on climate-change impacts, or serve as 'insurance'.[31] Where such area-based measures are located within the maritime zones of a single coastal state, their effectiveness would not depend on the support of all relevant states as much as TACs would.

However, even though coastal states and high seas fishing states may take account of climate-change impacts in fisheries management, or the contribution of fishing to climate change, they are not necessarily obliged to do so. Arguably, a qualified obligation on climate-change adaptation can to some extent be derived from the qualified obligation relating to 'best scientific evidence available' laid down in LOSC Articles 61(2) and 119(1)(a). However, it seems unconvincing to hold that a similar obligation is constituted by the generic reference to 'relevant environmental factors' in Articles 61(3) and 119(1)(a) – if only because climate change and its impacts on seas and oceans were entirely unknown to those who negotiated the LOSC. For similar reasons, a broad interpretation of the duty of conservation laid down in LOSC Article 117 seems equally unconvincing. It is submitted that Article 117 applies

30 See Trathan and Agnew, 'Climate change', 388, who argue that 'exacerbation of climate impacts should not be allowed to occur through inappropriate management practices'. See also page 393 on non-target species and benthic ecosystems; Report of the 11th (2015) Round of Informal Consultations of States Parties to the Fish Stocks Agreement (ICSP), UN Doc. ICSP11/UNFSA/INF.3, 14 May 2015 para. 51; and Report of the 18th (2017) ICP Meeting para. 36.

31 Further on MPAs, this volume, Chapter 10. See also the Report of the 37th (2018) Annual CCAMLR Meeting, para. 8.17 in which the Antarctic and Southern Ocean Coalition takes the view that MPAs 'can provide climate reference zones and increase ecosystem resilience'; similarly, Report of the 2010 Resumed Fish Stocks Agreement Review Conference, UN Doc. A/CONF.210/2010/7, of 27 July 2010, para. 62; and Arts. 5(b), 14(1)(f) and 16(2)(q) of the 'Draft text of an agreement under the United Nations Convention on the Law of the Sea on the conservation and sustainable use of marine biological diversity of areas beyond national jurisdiction' (UN Doc. A/CONF.232/2019/6, of 17 May 2019). In the view of the author of this chapter, there are no indications that MPAs or other area-based management tools can contribute to climate change mitigation as such. This view is also reflected in the Report of the 37th (2018) Annual CCAMLR Meeting, para. 6.53.

only to fishing on the high seas, and can, therefore, not be interpreted as a general obligation on climate-change mitigation in relation to the impacts on the conservation of the living resources of the high seas of any human activity undertaken anywhere.

Finally, although the discussion in this subsection and the next revolves exclusively around entitlements and obligations to constrain fishing, it should be noted that states may also experience new or enlarged fishing opportunities. This may occur, for instance, in new geographical areas due to receding sea-ice, or in existing fishing areas due to the emergence of new species or to greater abundance of existing species, caused by climate-change-induced shifts in distribution.

11.3.2 *The Fish Stocks Agreement*

The general provisions of the LOSC relating to straddling and highly migratory fish stocks are strengthened, modernized, elaborated and further operationalized by the Fish Stocks Agreement. Just like the LOSC, climate change is not mentioned in this Agreement. This is quite striking, as sufficient support within the international community to commence negotiations on what eventually became the Fish Stocks Agreement materialized during the 1992 United Nations Conference on Environment and Development,[32] which was held after the completion of the negotiations on the UNFCCC.[33] However, as explained in Subsection 11.3.3 it took until 2007 before the impacts of climate change on fisheries were highlighted at the global level (in FAO).

Among the innovations introduced by the Fish Stocks Agreement are the precautionary approach to fisheries management and – *de facto* – the ecosystem approach to fisheries management (EAF). The former is laid down in Articles 5(c) and 6, and Annex II. These provisions are of critical importance in the context of climate change, due to its negative implications for the level or extent of the certainty, reliability and adequacy of scientific information. Under these circumstances, states are required to take more cautious conservation and management measures. Whether the root cause of this is climate change or something else is irrelevant in this regard.

EAF was developed in response to the shortcomings of traditional target-species-oriented fisheries management, for instance, in relation to bycatch of non-target species and impacts on benthic ecosystems. Today, EAF is

[32] See Agenda 21 (Annex II to the Report of the United Nations Conference on Environment and Development, Rio de Janeiro, 3 to 14 June 1992. UN Doc. A/CONF.151/26, available at www.unep.org), paras. 17.49(e).

[33] United Nations Framework Convention on Climate Change, New York, 9 May 1992, in force 21 March 1994, 1771 UNTS 107.

generally accepted within the international community as the preferred approach to fisheries management. Article 5 of the Fish Stocks Agreement is widely regarded as embracing EAF even though it is not explicitly mentioned as such, let alone defined. Article 5 builds on LOSC Articles 61(2), (3) and (4) and 119(1)(a) and (b) by incorporating their text almost verbatim in paragraphs (b) and (e), including the phrases 'best scientific evidence available' and 'as qualified by relevant environmental and economic factors'. Also relevant for EAF are paragraphs (d), (f) and (g), which read:

> (d) assess the impacts of fishing, other human activities and environmental factors on target stocks and species belonging to the same ecosystem or associated with or dependent upon the target stocks;
>
> (f) minimize pollution, waste, discards, catch by lost or abandoned gear, catch of non-target species, both fish and non-fish species, (hereinafter referred to as non-target species) and impacts on associated or dependent species, in particular endangered species, through measures including, to the extent practicable, the development and use of selective, environmentally safe and cost-effective fishing gear and techniques;
>
> (g) protect biodiversity in the marine environment;

As to the relevance of these provisions for climate change, it is clear that, concerning entitlements, they do not affect the discretion of coastal states and high seas fishing states pursuant to the LOSC to set lower TACs and other conservation and management measures in response to climate change. In terms of obligations, however, these provisions are stronger and broader than those in the LOSC. Especially relevant are the obligations to assess the impacts of other human activities and environmental factors included in paragraph (d)[34] and, more indirectly, the obligation to protect biodiversity in the marine environment included in paragraph (g). It seems unlikely that the obligation to 'minimize pollution' (paragraph (f)) was also intended to cover air pollution – thereby requiring climate-change mitigation measures. Rather, it was probably meant to be limited to other forms of vessel-source pollution and pollutants generated by fishing (e.g. packaging materials).[35]

11.3.3 *Actions by Global Bodies*

Whereas this subsection provides an overview of actions by global bodies on climate change and marine capture fisheries in general, Subsection 11.4.4 covers

[34] See also paras. (d) and (g) of Art. 10, which are the related functions of RFMOs.

[35] See notes 91–92 and accompanying text.

those actions by FAO that are specifically aimed at mitigation. The discussion starts with FAO and then turns to the UNGA and various associated bodies.

At its 24th (2007) Session, the FAO Committee on Fisheries (COFI) supported a proposal to undertake a scoping study to identify the key issues in climate change and fisheries, and for FAO to take the lead on informing fishers and policymakers about the likely consequences of climate change for fisheries.[36] This assessment role led to the 2009 FAO Climate Change Technical Paper,[37] its subsequent update – the 2018 FAO Climate Change Technical Paper[38] – and several associated workshops and other outputs.[39] In 2011, COFI recommended members to 'intensify their efforts to assess environmental and anthropogenic factors affecting aquatic ecosystems including changes in migratory patterns of fish species and other adverse impacts including ocean acidification' and to 'consider these in management approaches'.[40] Other roles performed by FAO include providing technical assistance to its members and regional fishery bodies, and raising the profile and awareness of the role of fisheries regarding food security under climate change.[41]

In 2016, FAO adopted a Strategy for FAO's Work on Climate Change[42] and a Strategy for Fisheries, Aquaculture and Climate Change for 2017–2010 for its Fisheries and Aquaculture Department.[43] It has identified various adaptation options – listed under three categories: (1) institutions and management; (2) livelihood adaptation; (3) resilience and risk reduction – and guidance on the four stages – (1) institutional stock-taking and assessment; (2) technical assessment; (3) planning integration; and (4) implementation – in which climate change should be integrated in fisheries management.[44] Whereas some of its guidelines also deal with climate change,[45] FAO has not yet adopted dedicated guidelines on climate change and fisheries.[46]

36 Report of the 24th (2007) COFI Session, para. 76.

37 FAO, 'Climate Change Implications for Fisheries and Aquaculture: Overview of Current Scientific Knowledge', *Fisheries and Aquaculture Technical Paper* No. 530 (FAO, 2009).

38 See 2018 FAO Climate Change Technical Paper, note 7.

39 See the compilation of 'FAO Fisheries and Aquaculture Climate Change Publications' at www.fao.org/fishery/publications/en.

40 Report of the 29th (2011) COFI Session, para. 40a.

41 Ibid., paras. 40f–40g. See also SOFIA 2018, 130–38; FAO Doc. COFI/2018/Inf.23, June 2018.

42 FAO Doc. COFI/2016/Inf.17, April 2016.

43 FAO Doc. COFI/2016/Inf.18, April 2016.

44 SOFIA 2018, 134–36.

45 For example, the 2014 Voluntary Guidelines for Securing Sustainable Small-Scale Fisheries in the Context of Food Security and Poverty Eradication, which deal in Chapter 9 with 'Disaster risks and climate change'.

46 COFI nevertheless requested such guidelines in 2016 and 2018 (Report of the 32nd (2016) COFI Session, paras. 16, 144; and Report of the 33rd (2018) COFI Session, para. 101). A FAO workshop

Relevant actions by the UNGA and associated bodies include those taken in the context of the Annual UNGA 'Sustainable Fisheries' Resolutions, the Rounds of Informal Consultations of States Parties to the Fish Stocks Agreement (ICSPs); and the (Resumed) Fish Stocks Agreement Review Conferences. In addition, reference should be made to the 18th (2017) Meeting of the United Nations Open-ended Informal Consultative Process on Oceans and the Law of the Sea (ICP), on 'The effects of climate change on oceans', which also touched on fisheries.[47]

Only the Annual UNGA Sustainable Fisheries Resolutions and the 'Outcomes' of the (Resumed) Fish Stocks Agreement Review Conference contain encouragements and/or recommendations. Climate-change issues have come up in almost all ICSPs since 2010.[48] Specific mention can be made of some of the key points on strengthening the science–policy interface identified by the chairperson at the 13th (2018) ICSP: namely, that this science–policy interface is critical in the context of climate change, and that the uncertainties regarding the impacts of climate change on fisheries require adaptive management strategies and application of the precautionary approach.[49]

As regards the Annual UNGA Sustainable Fisheries Resolutions, the first reference to climate change appeared in 2007 in the Preamble, merely noting the actions of COFI earlier that year.[50] As regards the (Resumed) Fish Stocks Agreement Review Conferences, climate change is covered for the first time in the 2010 Resumed Fish Stocks Agreement Review Conference.[51] The 2008 UNGA Sustainable Fisheries Resolution not only expresses concern on the implications of climate change in the Preamble, but also contains the following operative paragraph:

> *Urges* States, either directly or through appropriate subregional, regional or global organizations or arrangements, to intensify efforts to assess and address, as appropriate, the impacts of global climate change on the sustainability of fish stocks and the habitats that support them[52]

scheduled for November 2019 aims to develop good practices on climate change and fisheries management (information provided by Florence Poulain (FAO) to the author on 5 June 2019).

47 Report of the 18th (2017) ICP Meeting, paras. 21, 31, 33, 36, 38

48 Report of the 9th (2010) ICSP, UN Doc. ICSP9/UNFSA/INF.4, para. 19; Report of the 11th (2015) ICSP, UN Doc. ICSP11/UNFSA/INF.3, para. 51; Report of the 12th (2016) ICSP, UN Doc. ICSP12/UNFSA/INF.3, para. 28; Report of the 13th (2018) ICSP, UN Doc. ICSP13/UNFSA/ INF.2, paras. 39, 45, 51, 65, 69.

49 Report of the 13th (2018) ICSP, para. 23.

50 UNGA Res. 62/177, 18 December 2007, 4.

51 Report of the 2010 Resumed Fish Stocks Agreement Review Conference, UN Doc. A/CONF.210/2010/7, 27 July 2010, paras. 53, 56, 62, 144, 158, 42.

52 UNGA Res. 63/112, 5 December 2008, para. 3.

Whereas the resolutions between 2009 and 2015 repeat the 2008 text almost verbatim,[53] the Outcome section of the Report of the 2010 Resumed Fish Stocks Agreement Review Conference recommends somewhat more specifically that, 'where possible', climate-change impacts be considered 'in establishing conservation and management measures for straddling fish stocks and highly migratory fish stocks'.[54] This text is retained in Paragraph 4(a) of the Outcome section of the Report of the 2016 Resumed Fish Stocks Agreement Review Conference, and complemented by the following subparagraphs:

> (b) Explore ways to incorporate the consideration of the adverse impacts of climate change and ocean acidification and the uncertainties regarding such impacts on fisheries, including in relation to migration patterns and productivity, in decision-making processes related to the adoption of conservation and management measures, in line with the precautionary approach.
>
> (c) Collaborate closely with other States, regional fisheries management organizations and arrangements, Regional Seas Conventions and Action Plans, scientific organizations, academia and civil society in conducting research to achieve an understanding of the impacts of, and risks associated with, climate change with respect to fish stocks, including the vulnerabilities of individual species to changes in marine ecosystems, with a view to identifying options for reducing such risk and promoting the health and resilience of marine ecosystems, sharing information and identifying and sharing best practices in this regard.[55]

These recommendations are also reflected in the 2016 UNGA Sustainable Fisheries Resolution,[56] albeit in somewhat different wording. The 2017 resolution is essentially similar to that of the previous year, but the 2018 resolution adds new operative paragraphs on climate change – bringing the total number to six – with new elements such as the need to assist developing states, and the importance of the science–policy interface.[57]

[53] From 2010 onwards, the phrase 'in particular the most affected ones' was added to the operative paragraph.

[54] Report of the 2010 Resumed Fish Stocks Agreement Review Conference, 42.

[55] Report of the 2016 Resumed Fish Stocks Agreement Review Conference, UN Doc. A/CONF.210/2016/5, 1 August 2016. See also the discussion in paras. 8, 20, 25, 40–42, 90 and 180.

[56] UNGA Res. 71/123, 7 December 2016, paras. 9, 185.

[57] UNGA Res. 73/125, 11 December 2018, paras. 10, 11, 13, 14, 183, 198.

11.4 MARINE CAPTURE FISHERIES AND CLIMATE-CHANGE MITIGATION

11.4.1 *Introduction*

Some fisheries – small-scale traditional fisheries, in particular – are undertaken by relatively small vessels propelled by peddles and/or sails, but most fishing today relies on combustion engines and fossil fuels that produce emissions of CO_2 and other substances, thereby contributing to climate change and ocean acidification. This is not limited to vessels engaged in fishing as such, but extends to vessels that support such fishing activities, for instance, by transhipping catch or provisioning fishing vessels with fuel, water, food, spare parts or crew members. Account could also be taken of emissions produced after the fish is landed, for instance fish processing, transportation and marketing.[58]

There are many ways of reducing emissions by fishing vessels and fishing-support vessels – for instance, by using alternative means of propulsion (e.g. hybrid-electric engines), alternative or cleaner fuels, more fuel-efficient engines, enhanced hull shapes or reducing the mean speed of vessels. The International Maritime Organization (IMO) already pursues some of these regulatory approaches, but not necessarily very stringently.[59] Moreover, some of these regulations apply only to 'ships engaged on international voyages' (or: in international shipping)[60] or to ships above a minimum tonnage (e.g. 400),[61] thereby excluding all or most fishing vessels.

Significant reductions in emissions by fishing vessels can be achieved through reducing fuel consumption and striving for higher fuel-use intensity (FUI: the quantity of fuel used per quantity of fish landed). This may, for instance, relate to the fishing technique used, where fuel consumption depends, among other things, on the size of the fishing gear, the depth at which the gear is deployed, and whether or not it is in contact with the seabed.

58 According to P. He et al., 'Countering climate change: measures and tools to reduce energy use and greenhouse gas emission in fisheries and aquaculture' in 2018 FAO Climate Change Technical Paper, 585, 586, 'globally, fishing vessels (including inland vessels) consumed 53.9 million tonnes of fuel in 2012, emitting 172.3 million tonnes of CO_2. This is about 0.5 percent of total global CO_2 emissions that year'. These figures do not include emissions after landing.

59 See Ringbom, this volume, Chapter 6.

60 For example, International Convention for the Safety of Life at Sea, London, 1 November 1974, in force 25 May 1980, 1184 UNTS 277, with protocols and regularly amended (SOLAS 74), Reg. I-1(a).

61 For example, International Convention for the Prevention of Pollution from Ships (MARPOL 73/78), London, 2 November 1973, with protocols and regularly amended, Reg. VI-6(1)(a).

As noted by He et al.: 'For towed fishing gears, measures to reduce emissions include multi-rig gear, efficient otter boards, off-bottom fishing, high-strength materials, and large mesh sizes and smaller diameter twines' and the 'use of efficient LED lights can significantly reduce emissions in fisheries that use lights for attracting fish.'[62]

Significant progress towards higher FUI can be made by addressing overcapacity – thereby increasing catch per unit effort[63] – and allowing transfer of catch quotas.[64] Notorious for their low FUI are 'Olympic fisheries', which consist of the fishery's commencement on a given date and time, subsequent regular reporting of the catch, and the fishery's closure once the TAC has been reached or is about to be reached. This mechanism is, for instance, still used in many fisheries regulated by the Commission for the Conservation of Antarctic Marine Living Resources (CCAMLR), as mechanisms using national catch or effort quotas are expected to raise tensions related to the question of sovereignty over Antarctic territory.[65]

11.4.2 *Electric Pulse Trawl Fishing*

The high FUI of the traditional beam trawl fishery in the North Sea has, together with its high impact on benthic ecosystems, been a main driver for the development of electric pulse trawl fishing by Netherlands fishing vessels. This technique uses parallel electrodes in tow direction which emit short electric pulses in order to stimulate flatfish to raise up from the seabed and be caught by the net that follows. Fuel consumption is, on average, 45% lower than with traditional beam trawl gear.[66] Electric pulse trawl fishing was to a limited extent permitted under EU legislation that was in force during 1998–2019.[67] In January 2018, however, the European Parliament called for a ban for this technique,[68] and in April 2019 agreed to ban it from 1 July 2021

62 He et al., 'Countering climate change', 585.

63 Ibid., 601.

64 Ibid., 586, 602–603.

65 Report of the 9th (1977) Antarctic Treaty Consultative Meeting, 7 ('the regime would exclude catch allocation and other economic regulation of harvesting').

66 Information at www.pulsefishing.eu/.

67 Council Regulation (EC) No. 850/98 of 30 March 1998 for the conservation of fishery resources through technical measures for the protection of juveniles of marine organisms (consolidated version), Art. 31a, which constitutes an exception to the prohibition of the use of electric current under Art. 31.

68 See the European Parliament's amendments to EU Doc. COM(2016) 134 final, 11 March 2016, proposal for a Regulation on the conservation of fishery resources and the protection of marine ecosystems through technical measures, laid down in EU Doc. P8_TA(2018)0003.

onwards, while allowing some pulse trawling to continue until then.[69] Subsequently, the Netherlands government decided to challenge this outcome before the European Court of Justice.[70]

In the debate on the advantages and disadvantages of this innovatory fishing technique, the benefit of reduced fuel consumption for climate-change mitigation is acknowledged but plays only a minor role.[71] This also applied to the January 2018 debate at the European Parliament, which mainly devoted attention to the known and potential detrimental effects of electric pulse trawl fishing, and thereby supported the interests of fishers using traditional beam trawl fishing.[72] The focus and thrust of the debate not only means that this new fishing technique has come under significantly more scrutiny than existing fishing techniques, but also that a comparative analysis of the advantages and disadvantages of electric pulse trawl fishing and traditional beam trawl fishing has (conveniently) not been considered.[73]

Although the EU is likely to severely curtail pulse trawling in EU waters in the near future, that will not stop this new fishing technique from being used elsewhere – even by EU fishing vessels or by non-EU fishing vessels using pulse fishing gear that Dutch fishermen felt compelled to sell. Whereas the climate-change benefits of pulse trawling could therefore still materialize elsewhere, there is also a risk of this occurring in a regulatory environment less able and willing to ensure that these benefits are not outweighed by disadvantages, for instance in relation to bycatch and selectivity, especially

69 Position of the European Parliament as laid down in EU Doc. P8_TA-PROV(2019)0381, in particular, recital 12 and Part D of Annex V. This resulted in Regulation (EU) 2019/1241, 20 June 2019 on the conservation of fisheries resources and the protection of marine ecosystems through technical measures, *OJ* 2019, L 198/105.

70 Action brought on 4 October 2019 – Case C-733/19, Kingdom of the Netherlands v. Council of the European Union, European Parliament; action for annulment of Annex V, Part D, points 1 to 5 of Regulation (EU) 2019/1241.

71 See, e.g., the opinion-piece of several Dutch NGOs, 'The time to research electric pulse fishing is now', at www.noordzee.nl/the-time-to-research-electric-pulse-fishing-is-now/. See also the Final Report of the Working Group on Electrical Trawling (WGELECTRA), Doc. ICES CM 2017/SSGIEOM:11. The request by the Netherlands for advice by the International Council for the Exploration of the Sea (ICES) on 'the comparison of the ecological and environmental effects of pulse trawls and traditional beam trawls when exploiting the North Sea sole TAC' made no reference to climate-change benefits either (see ICES Special Request Advice, Greater North Sea Ecoregion, sr.2018.08, published 30 May 2018, available at https://doi.org/10.17895/ices.pub.4379).

72 Debate on 15 January 2018 as transcribed in doc. CRE 15/01/2018–13.

73 See 'Electric "pulse" fishing: why it should be banned' by the NGO BLOOM, in the version of November 2018, available at www.bloomassociation.org/en/our-actions/our-themes/electric-pulse-fishing/.

in species-rich marine ecosystems in tropical regions. Towards the end of 2019, this risk had possibly already materialized as Malaysian authorities had detained a foreign fishing vessel and commenced an investigation on the possible use of electric pulse trawl gear, which is prohibited under Malaysian legislation.[74]

11.4.3 *Heavy Fuel Oil*

Some fuels contribute more to climate change and ocean acidification than others. The use of heavy fuel oil (HFO) is especially harmful in the Polar Regions as it produces higher emissions of black carbon particles, thereby accelerating the warming cycle when these particles land and settle on snow and ice.[75] Following an initiative by the Antarctic Treaty Consultative Meeting in 2005,[76] the Marine Environment Protection Committee (MEPC) of the IMO adopted a ban for all ships on the use and carriage of HFO in the Antarctic Treaty area in 2010.[77]

A ban on the use and carriage of HFO also in Arctic waters is currently under consideration in IMO.[78] Analyses conducted under the auspices of the Arctic Council have shown that 'fishing vessels make up the greatest percentage of vessels operating within the Arctic Region' but are 'more likely to rely upon distillate fuels' rather than HFO.[79] Other analyses nevertheless conclude that fishing vessels are significant contributors to black carbon pollution, with Russia as the largest contributing flag state.[80] In view of the socio-economic impacts that an IMO ban on HFO use in Arctic waters would have on Russian fishing vessels in particular, Russia (and possibly other central Arctic Ocean coastal states) may prefer an exemption for fishing vessels. Such an exemption could also materialize by confining the ban to ships engaged in international shipping.

74 Information provided by Ganesan Vethiah to the author by email, 3 December 2019.

75 See, e.g., www.hfofreearctic.org.

76 ATCM Decision 8 (2005) 'Use of Heavy Fuel Oil'.

77 IMO Res. MEPC.189(60), 26 March 2010, by which a new Chapter 9 was added to Annex I of MARPOL 73/78.

78 Much of the preparatory work is done by the Sub-Committee on Pollution Prevention and Response (PPR). See the draft Report of MEPC 74 (May 2019), IMO Doc. MEPC 74/WP.1, 17 May 2019, paras. 5.66, 10.22–10.25.

79 IMO Doc. MEPC 72/INF, 31 January 2018, paras. 8, 13.

80 See 'Heavy Fuel Oil use in the IMO Polar Code Arctic by Russian-flagged ships, 2015' and other briefings by the International Council on Clean Transportation (ICCT) at https://www.hfofreearctic.org/en/category/publications_en/.

11.4.4 *Actions by FAO and RFMOs*

As noted in Section 11.3, neither the LOSC nor the Fish Stocks Agreement includes obligations on climate-change mitigation in the context of marine capture fisheries. FAO already highlighted the contribution of marine capture fisheries to climate change in the 2009 FAO Climate Change Technical Paper.[81] That same year, COFI supported the conclusion that 'the primary mitigation route for the [fisheries] sector lies in its energy consumption'.[82] Subsequent COFI Sessions in 2011, 2016 and 2018 specifically devoted attention to mitigation, which led to various expert workshops and other output.[83] The mitigation dimension is also explicitly viewed as being part of EAF.[84] It is also noteworthy that in all the actions by the UNGA and associated bodies discussed in Subsection 11.3.3, the mitigation dimension is not mentioned at all.

Despite FAO's attention to climate-change mitigation and fisheries for more than a decade, however, no RFMOs seem to have taken action in this regard. That might be due to lack of political support, but it could also be related to the mandates of RFMOs and how these are viewed by their members. Some measures for reducing emissions by fishing vessels, for instance, on fuel content and efficiency, clearly fall within the mandate of IMO. However, in case of insufficient action by IMO or insufficient compliance with such action, members of RFMOs may advocate that these RFMOs adopt legally binding or non-legally binding instruments among themselves, thereby respecting the principle of *pacta tertiis*. Other members may object to such action on the ground that it undermines the primacy of IMO.[85]

[81] T. Daw et al., 'Climate change and capture fisheries: potential impacts, adaptation and mitigation' in 2009 FAO Climate Change Technical Paper, 107.

[82] FAO, 'Report of the FAO Expert Workshop on Climate Change Implications for Fisheries and Aquaculture, Rome, 7–9 April 2008', *FAO Fisheries Report* No. 870 (FAO, 2008), 12; in conjunction with the Report of the 28th (2009) COFI Session, para. 88. See also FAO Doc. COFI/2009/8, November 2018, para. 15.

[83] See Report of the 29th (2011) COFI Session, para. 40; Report of the 32nd (2016) COFI Session, para. 18; Report of the 33rd (2018) COFI Session, para. 101. See also FAO Docs. COFI/2011/6, October 2010, paras. 24, 27–30, 41; COFI/2018/10/Rev.1, June 2018, paras. 23–24; and the FAO Expert Workshops on Strategies and Practical Options for Greenhouse Gas Reductions in Fisheries and Aquaculture Food Production Systems (2013) and on Greenhouse Gas Emissions Strategies and Methods in Seafood (2012). Links to the Reports of these Workshops and other publications are included in the compilation of 'FAO Fisheries and Aquaculture Climate Change Publications'. See also note 46.

[84] See, e.g., FAO Doc. COFI/2011/6, October 2010, paras. 24, 38

[85] See, e.g., the debate reflected in the Report of the 7th (2019) Annual SPRFMO Meeting, paras. 139–142. Similar debates have taken place in relation to the actions by CCAMLR listed in note 91.

Other measures are clearly outside the mandate of IMO and at first sight within the mandates of RFMOs – for instance, on fishing techniques, overcapacity and practices on the transfer and allocation of fishing opportunities. On closer examination, however, mandates may not necessarily be broad enough to adopt such measures for the purpose of climate-change mitigation. This may, for example, be the case with the NAFO Convention,[86] whose objective is 'to ensure the long term conservation and sustainable use of the fishery resources in the Convention Area and, in so doing, to safeguard the marine ecosystems in which these resources are found'.[87] Members could perhaps argue that measures adopted pursuant to the NAFO Convention must be specifically aimed at the fishery resources and marine ecosystems located in the NAFO Convention Area. That would then preclude climate-change mitigation measures, as these have a wider objective and also benefit fishery resources and ecosystems located outside the NAFO Convention Area.

The objective of the SPRFMO Convention uses similar wording as the NAFO Convention, but also contains the phrase 'through the application of the precautionary approach and an ecosystem approach to fisheries management'.[88] This additional phrase could be seen as supporting the interpretation that measures for climate-change mitigation may be adopted pursuant to the SPRFMO Convention if so required under EAF. An obstacle here is that EAF is not defined in the SPRFMO Convention or by its main decision-making body – the SPRFMO; and that a generally accepted definition is also lacking at the global level. By way of example, reference can be made to the definition of EAF included in the 2013 Basic Regulation of the EU's Common Fisheries Policy (CFP), which reads as follows:

> an integrated approach to managing fisheries within ecologically meaningful boundaries which seeks to manage the use of natural resources, taking account of fishing and other human activities, while preserving both the biological wealth and the biological processes necessary to safeguard the composition, structure and functioning of the habitats of the ecosystem affected, by taking into account the knowledge and uncertainties regarding biotic, abiotic and human components of ecosystems.[89]

86 Convention on Cooperation in the Northwest Atlantic Fisheries – originally named 'Convention on Future Multilateral Cooperation in the Northwest Atlantic Fisheries' – Ottawa, 24 October 1978, in force 1 January 1979, 1135 UNTS 369, as amended; consolidated version available at www.nafo.int.

87 Ibid., Art. II.

88 Art. 2 of the SPRFMO Convention.

89 Art. 4(1)(9) of Regulation No 1380/2013, 11 December 2013. Judging by the wording of this definition, it has also used the definition of EAF developed by FAO and laid down in

Even though climate change does not appear in this definition or elsewhere in the 2013 CFP Basic Regulation, it would be covered indirectly by the phrase 'other human activities' and the text connected to 'knowledge and uncertainties' towards the end. Interestingly, Article 2(3) also requires the CFP to implement EAF 'to ensure that negative impacts of fishing activities on the marine ecosystem are minimized' and to 'endeavour to ensure that aquaculture and fisheries activities avoid the degradation of the marine environment'. Arguably, this would also cover emissions and thereby require climate-change mitigation.

As EAF has evolved gradually, by integrating additional ecosystem considerations in a stepwise fashion, this evolution may at some time in the future culminate in general acceptance among states and within RFMOs that EAF also requires climate-change mitigation. That would be more likely if it becomes generally accepted practice for all regulatory authorities to assume responsibility for the climate-change impacts of the societal sectors or human activities under their purview. In such a scenario, RFMOs would have to follow suit. Which RFMO will take the lead on this remains to be seen. As CCAMLR was given an EAF mandate *avant la lettre*[90] and has also used this mandate to adopt general environmental protection measures (e.g. prohibitions on discarding waste generated by fishing),[91] it might have been expected to pioneer also in this regard. However, as discussed in Section 11.5, the integration of climate-change adaptation in CCAMLR's work has encountered stubborn opposition from two CCAMLR members in recent years. Taking a further step towards climate-change mitigation is, therefore, not something on which consensus among CCAMLR members is likely to emerge in the near future. As SPRFMO's 2019 measures on fishing gear and marine plastic pollution[92] go beyond CCAMLR's general environmental protection measures in certain respects, leadership on climate-change mitigation among RFMOs may well be assumed by SPRFMO. It is also relevant in this regard that

Technical Guidelines for Responsible Fisheries. No. 4 'Fisheries Management'; Suppl. 2 'The Ecosystem Approach to Management' (FAO, 2003), 14.

90 See Art. II(3)(c) of the Convention on the Conservation of Antarctic Marine Living Resources (CAMLR Convention), Canberra, 20 May 1980, in force 7 April 1982, 1329 UNTS 47.

91 CCAMLR Conservation Measure 26-01 (2018) 'General environmental protection during fishing'. Not also that various CCAMLR Resolutions – which are non-legally binding – go well beyond traditional fisheries management (e.g. 20/XXII, 23/XXIII and 28/XXVII).

92 Conservation and Management Measure 17-2019 'on Fishing Gear and Marine Plastic Pollution in the SPRFMO Convention Area'. See also the Report of the 7th (2019) Annual SPRFMO Meeting, paras. 139–142.

SPRFMO can adopt measures by a three-fourths majority,[93] whereas progress in CCAMLR has often been stifled by consensus decision-making.

11.5 CLIMATE CHANGE AND RFMOs

As RFMOs are at present arguably the pre-eminent institutions of international fisheries law, it is no surprise that recent actions on climate change and fisheries by the UNGA and associated bodies (see Subsection 11.3.3) also explicitly call for action on adaptation (but not mitigation) by states through RFMOs.[94]

In her recent study, Rayfuse[95] examines the practices of twelve RFMOs – five tuna RFMOs[96] and seven non-tuna RFMOs[97] – on integrating climate change into their management processes. Her analysis focuses on the extent to which these RFMOs have done this in relation to three key tasks: (1) actively anticipating climate stressors in their scientific research; (2) absorbing the importance of these stressors into their decision-making; and (3) reshaping their management measures to address climate-driven changes. These three tasks are largely similar to the various tasks identified by the 2018 UNGA Sustainable Fisheries Resolution.[98] Rayfuse concludes that a considerable number of the selected RFMOs perform reasonably well on the first task, but only a few RFMOs (notably CCAMLR and NAFO[99]) have taken some modest steps as regards the second and third tasks.

As for CCAMLR, its 37th (2018) Annual Meeting did not produce outcomes that will significantly enhance its performance on climate-change adaptation. Despite the efforts of the intersessional correspondence group on climate change, a revised proposal for a Climate Change Response Work Program for CCAMLR could not be adopted by consensus, due to the lack of support

93 SPRFMO Convention, Art. 16(2)(b).

94 For example, UNGA Res. 73/125, 11 December 2018, paras. 13, 183, 198.

95 Rayfuse, 'Addressing climate change impacts'.

96 The Commission on the Conservation of Southern Bluefin Tuna (CCSBT); the Indian Ocean Tuna Commission (IOTC); the International Commission for the Conservation of Atlantic Tunas (ICCAT); the Inter-American Tropical Tuna Commission (IATTC); and the Western and Central Pacific Fisheries Commission (WCPFC).

97 CCAMLR; the General Fisheries Commission for the Mediterranean (GFCM); the North-East Atlantic Fisheries Commission (NEAFC); the Northwest Atlantic Fisheries Organization (NAFO); the North Pacific Fisheries Commission (NPFC); the South-East Atlantic Fisheries Organization (SEAFO); and SPRFMO.

98 UNGA Res. 73/125, 11 December 2018, para. 13.

99 See note 97.

by China and Russia – as in the previous year.[100] Moreover, a proposal for climate-change impact statements – which would have required working papers and fishery reports to make explicit note of known and potential impacts and, where applicable, propose relevant actions – could also not be adopted due to opposition by the same two members. Many members nevertheless indicated that they would include such impact statements in working papers, on a voluntary basis.[101] Presumably in light of the opposition at the 37th Meeting, no revised proposal on a Climate Change Response Work Program was submitted for the 38th (2019) Annual Meeting. Unfortunately, no other concrete step towards further integrating climate change could be agreed either.[102] Things could of course also have taken a turn for the worse. This was illustrated by the Arctic Council's May 2019 Rovaniemi Ministerial Meeting which, for the first time in its history, did not lead to the adoption of a Ministerial Declaration, due to the Trump Administration's refusal to sign a declaration dealing with climate change.[103]

The first multilateral fisheries instrument to be developed as a direct result of climate change is the CAOF Agreement,[104] which features a qualified and temporary abstention from high seas fishing in the central Arctic Ocean.[105] As the CAOF Agreement is arguably an RFMO[106] – actually: a regional fisheries management arrangement[107] – it is so far the only RFMO to have been negotiated primarily due to climate change.[108]

100 See the Report of the 36th (2017) Annual CCAMLR Meeting, paras. 7.1–7.20, listing China and Russia in para. 7.7; and the Report of the 37th (2018) Annual CCAMLR Meeting, paras. 8.7–8.16.

101 Report of the 37th (2018) Annual CCAMLR Meeting, paras. 8.1–8.5.

102 Report of the 38th (2019) Annual CCAMLR Meeting, version of 25 November 2019, paras. 8.1–8.20.

103 Instead, the meeting adopted the one-page 'Rovaniemi Joint Ministerial Statement 2019', which consists of six very general paragraphs presumably selected from the draft. The draft was converted into a 'Statement by the Chair' and devotes extensive attention to climate change.

104 Agreement to Prevent Unregulated High Seas Fisheries in the Central Arctic Ocean, Ilulissat, 3 October 2018. Not in force; OJ 2019, L 73/3.

105 E. J. Molenaar, 'Participation in the Central Arctic Ocean Fisheries Agreement' in A. Shibata et al. (eds.), *Emerging Legal Orders in the Arctic: The Role of Non-Arctic Actors* (Routledge, 2019), 132, 161–62.

106 Ibid., 162.

107 See note 2.

108 Whereas the first preambular paragraph of the CAOF Agreement recognizes that ice coverage of the high seas portion of the central Arctic Ocean has diminished in recent years, the second paragraph acknowledges that central Arctic Ocean ecosystems are 'changing due to climate change and other phenomena'. The words 'climate change' do not appear elsewhere in the CAOF Agreement.

Climate change is expected to become increasingly challenging to RFMOs. If changes in the abundance and distribution of target species become more frequent, more profound and less predictable, and scientific advice thereby less accurate, this may undermine the ability of RFMOs to respond adequately and in a timely manner. This is especially pertinent in relation to the critical issues of determining the TAC and allocating fishing opportunities. RFMOs must prepare for a more dynamic, less predictable regulatory environment by fully integrating climate change in their EAF to ensure that it becomes more adaptive, pro-active and anticipatory. This might be done by adopting measures on new and exploratory fisheries,[109] and establishing or strengthening mechanisms for coordination and cooperation, or even joint management, with adjacent RFMOs.[110]

As highlighted in Section 11.4, climate-change mitigation is unexplored territory for RFMOs. The various options for increasing fuel-use intensity include addressing overcapacity, allowing quota transfers, phasing out 'Olympic' fisheries and switching to new fishing techniques (e.g. electric pulse trawl fishing).[111] Whereas there are RFMOs that pursue some of these options, this seems to be done exclusively for the purpose of optimizing profit/minimizing costs, not climate-change mitigation.[112]

In the context of the allocation of fishing opportunities within RFMOs, climate change does not seem to have been invoked as an allocation criterion so far.[113] A scenario in which that could occur is that of a coastal state that has essentially not contributed to climate change but is confronted with a decrease in abundance of target species in its maritime zones that is non-temporary as well as attributable to climate change. As such a coastal state is an 'overall loser' on marine capture fisheries, it might take the position that it is entitled to an allocation that compensates for this loss, based on considerations of equity. Such an allocation could be determined on the basis of an agreed pre-climate-change reference period, which would essentially 'freeze' allocations. That would bear some similarity to the proposal of the International Law Association (ILA)'s Committee on

109 See R. Caddell, 'Precautionary management and the development of future fishing opportunities: the international regulation of new and exploratory fisheries' (2018) 33 *International Journal of Marine and Coastal Law*, 199–260.

110 See note 13 and accompanying text.

111 See Sections 11.4.1 and 11.4.2.

112 For example, SPRFMO allows quota transfers, see Conservation and Management Measure 01-2019 'for *Trachurus Murphyi*', para. 9.

113 Some reference to allocation and climate change was nevertheless made during the 18th (2017) ICP Meeting, see Report of 18th (2017) ICP Meeting, paras. 35, 36, 78.

International Law and Sea Level Rise to freeze baselines and limits of maritime zones, meaning that these 'should not be required to be recalculated should sea level change affect the geographical reality of the coastline'.[114] As regards freezing allocations, however, it would also give rise to complex and sensitive issues on access to the maritime zones of coastal states where abundance has increased ('overall winners'), bringing catches and allocations of states back to their level in the agreed pre-climate -change reference period – and if and how the extent to which states have contributed to climate change should be accounted for in all this.

11.6 CONCLUSIONS

This chapter has shown that, notwithstanding the significant current and projected impacts of climate change on marine capture fisheries, climate change has been integrated in international fisheries law only to a limited extent. As regards the global component of international fisheries law, climate change is not mentioned in the LOSC, the Fish Stocks Agreement or any other legally binding instrument. Since 2007, however, the issue of climate change and fisheries has been raised and debated by FAO, the UNGA and associated bodies. This has led, *inter alia*, to various encouragements and recommendations aimed at states, directly or through relevant international bodies, including RFMOs. FAO actions and roles on climate change and fisheries are especially noteworthy, not least given their diversity and their coverage of mitigation, on which no other global bodies or RFMOs seem to have taken any action so far.

Nothing in the LOSC or the Fish Stocks Agreement constrains the discretion of coastal states and high seas fishing states to take account of climate-change impacts in fisheries management – for instance by setting TACs below MSY, or adopting other measures that reduce, minimize or avoid additional pressures exerted by fishing, including gear restrictions, bycatch mitigation measures and area-based fisheries management measures. Likewise, nothing in these two treaties constrains the discretion of such states to address the contribution of fishing to climate change. The effectiveness of voluntary adaptation and mitigation measures is nevertheless significantly compromised by the consensual nature of international law, as reflected in the fundamental principle of *pacta tertiis*. This is especially pertinent in relation to

114 See the Report of this ILA Committee as presented at the ILA's 2018 Conference in Sydney, 19, and ILA Resolution 5/2018; both available at www.ila-hq.org/. See also S. V. Busch, this volume, Chapter 14.

transboundary fish stocks. Strong obligations on adaptation and mitigation would assist in addressing this obstacle. Whereas the LOSC and the Fish Stocks Agreement do not offer these in relation to mitigation, the LOSC contains a qualified obligation on adaptation, and the Fish Stocks Agreement strengthens and expands this as part of the de facto EAF which it embraces.

As RFMOs are arguably the pre-eminent institutions of international fisheries law today, the extent to which they integrate climate change into their management processes is obviously highly significant. RFMOs need to make more progress in this regard, but that often depends on the political support necessary to accept foregoing revenue in order to avoid the higher risk of overexploitation of target species, or additional costs in order to reduce, minimize or avoid impacts on non-target species or vulnerable marine ecosystems. Lack of political support is also likely to be the main reason why climate-change mitigation has remained unexplored territory for RFMOs. In part, this may also be due to insufficiently broad mandates of RFMOs and how these are perceived by their members. For those RFMOs that have embraced EAF within their mandates, the time may come when their members recognize that EAF also requires climate-change mitigation. That may also occur as part of general acceptance that all regulatory authorities must assume responsibility for the climate-change impacts of the societal sectors or human activities under their purview. In such a scenario, RFMOs would have to follow suit.

12

Adaptation of Aquaculture to Climate Change

The Relevance of Temporal International Framework from a Norwegian Perspective

Irene Dahl

12.1 INTRODUCTION

In a book on the law of the sea and climate change, the relevance of the law of the sea for aquaculture may seem questionable: is the law of the sea, in fact, applicable to aquaculture? On the one hand, to a certain degree aquaculture takes place on land territory and/or in fresh waters, and is thereby classified as a land industry. In that case, the relevance of the law of the sea seems quite distant. On the other hand, in Norway and elsewhere, much aquaculture is conducted along the coast – and such installations are subject to coastal state sovereignty in internal waters and the territorial sea (12 nautical miles), according to the 1982 UN Convention on the Law of the Sea (LOSC) Article 2(1).[1] Thus, legislation concerning aquaculture is mainly national law, and is not based on the law of the sea. However, a relevant affiliation of aquaculture may be established to the LOSC: its Article 192 expresses the general obligation of states to protect and preserve the marine environment, and is applicable in all maritime zones. Moreover, several instruments of the Food and Agriculture Organization of the United Nations (FAO) seem to assume a law-of-the-sea perspective on fisheries *and* aquaculture. For example, the introduction to the FAO Code of Conduct for Responsible Fisheries states that fisheries, *including aquaculture*, provide a vital source of food (etc.) throughout the world, for present as well as future generations. 'This Code sets out principles and international standards of behaviour for responsible practices with a view to ensuring the effective conservation, management and development of living aquatic resources, with due respect

[1] United Nations Convention on Law of the Sea, Montego Bay, 10 December 1982, 1833 UNTS 397.

for the ecosystem and biodiversity.'[2] On this background, the law of the sea may be regarded as a legal basis for discussions on the international legal aspects of aquaculture.

Climate change requires states to undertake potentially costly measures to address a long-term, yet quite uncertain threat, and involves virtually every aspect of states' domestic policy.[3] Mitigation measures are critical to avoid worst-case climate-change scenarios. All the same, a certain degree of climate change seems inevitable, as the result of already accumulated greenhouse gases in the atmosphere. 'The time to start preparing for these changes is now, by making adaptation part of a national climate change policy.'[4] Energy, agriculture and transportation are often mentioned as climate-change impacted industries, but also aquaculture has been noted. The FAO recognizes climate change as one of several external forcing factors affecting the global aquaculture sector.[5] Climate change has the potential to impact aquaculture in various ways – impacts on the seasonality of weather patterns, increasing sea levels, warming and the increasing occurrence of extreme events.[6] These impacts may, in turn, affect production and ecology (species composition, production amount and diseases), aquaculture operations (cages and other infrastructure) and economy (adaptation costs).

Climate change has become a growing international concern, as recently shown by the Paris Agreement.[7] Although it does not refer to aquaculture specifically, the Agreement is relevant for aquaculture management. In the Preamble, the parties stress, inter alia, the need for an effective and progressive response to the urgent threat of climate change, the fundamental priority of safeguarding food security, and the particular vulnerabilities of food-production systems.

In addition, FAO has adopted various guidelines and strategies relevant for aquaculture in light of climate change.[8] On the whole, it recognizes

[2] FAO Code of Conduct for Responsible Fisheries, Rome, 31 October 1995 (FAO Code of Conduct).

[3] D. Bodansky, 'The Paris Climate Change Agreement: a new hope?' (2016) 110(2) *American Journal of International Law*, 288–319, 289.

[4] R. K. Craig, 'Stationarity is dead: long live transformation: five principles for climate change adaptation law' (2010) 34 *Harvard Environmental Law Review*, 9–75, 14.

[5] FAO Technical Guidelines for Responsible Fisheries No. 5, Suppl. 4, *Aquaculture development: Ecosystem Approach to Aquaculture* (2010), section 2.2.3.

[6] Ibid., section 2.3.4.2.

[7] Paris Agreement, UN Doc. FCCC/CP/2015/L.9 (12 December 2015), Annex.

[8] (1) FAO Code of Conduct; (2) FAO Technical Guidelines for Responsible Fisheries No. 5, *Aquaculture Development* (1997); (3) FAO Technical Guidelines for Responsible Fisheries No.

ecosystem-based approaches to fisheries and coastal management as necessary to enable critical coastal ecosystems to adapt to the effects of climate change.[9] Regarding ecosystem-based approaches, FAO stresses that both fisheries *and aquaculture* need to be included in national strategies for climate-change adaptation: 'Without careful planning, aquatic ecosystems, fisheries and aquaculture can potentially suffer as a result of adaptation measures applied by other sectors, such as increased use of dams and hydropower in catchments with high rainfall, construction of artificial coastal defences or marine wind farms.'[10] (See Section 12.4.)

This chapter examines how significant elements of the Paris Agreement and FAO instruments may counteract some of the aquaculture impacts of climate change. Climate change relates to aquaculture mainly along two dimensions. The first concerns the effects *from* aquaculture on climate. As this requires measures to reduce emissions from aquaculture activities, it relates to the context of the law of the sea and climate-change mitigation.[11] The second dimension concerns the effects *on* aquaculture, which require an adaptive approach regarding the sector's ability to increase, despite climate-change impacts. In the literature, this aspect is described in terms of how the law of the sea provides a framework for *adaptive responses* by coastal and other states to the effects of climate change.[12]

This chapter focuses on the latter: which approaches or measures, deriving from the Paris Agreement and FAO instruments, are states committed or requested to implement in order to make aquaculture more resilient to climate change? Norwegian aquaculture law and policy are used to exemplify the implementation of international norms and guidelines.

12.2 IMPACTS OF CLIMATE CHANGE ON AQUACULTURE: NORWEGIAN AQUACULTURE

Norway has become the largest exporter of farmed salmon: Export volumes for 2018 were 1.1 million tons at the value of €680 million. Norwegian farmed salmon supplies the world population with 10 million meals each day, and the

5, Suppl. 3, *Aquaculture Development: Genetic Resource Management* (2008); (4) FAO, *Aquaculture Development: Ecosystem Approach to Aquaculture*.

9 FAO, 'Climate change adaptation strategies', available at www.fao.org/fishery/topic/166279/en.

10 Ibid.

11 T. Stephens, 'Warming waters and souring seas: climate change and ocean acidification' in D. R. Rothwell et al. (eds.), *The Oxford Handbook of Law of the Sea* (Oxford University Press, 2015), 777–798.

12 Ibid, 782.

government has expressed the objective of a fivefold increase in production by 2050.[13] However, global climate change seems set to affect conditions in Norwegian coastal waters as well. Scientists at the Norwegian Institute of Marine Research (IMR) have indicated both positive and negative implications of climate change for aquaculture.[14] Among other things, they mention increased rainfall and freshwater runoff into the sea, in turn, reducing salinity and creating a layer of brackish water on the surface. In addition, the combination of wind and tide is likely to cause currents and internal waves; also likely are more frequent and stronger winds.[15] An illustrative example is the storm *Nina* that hit the Norwegian west coast in January 2015. Four aquaculture facilities reported escapees, two of them of an unknown number and the other two approximately 63,000 rainbow trout and 40,000–50,000 salmon unit altogether.[16] Importantly, the suitability of specific locations for various species may change as a consequence of climate change. Another possible impact may be increases in salmon lice,[17] a factor that already poses a significant challenge to Norwegian aquaculture.[18] Scientists have also noted the risk of increased outbreaks of disease. Changes in the local hydrographic conditions may increase the risk, with species resistance decreasing as a consequence of stress.[19] By impacting the ecology, and thereby the economic risks for an industry dependent on ecological circumstances, climate change may lead to the gradual displacement of optimal aquaculture areas for salmon to the northern parts of Norway.

But also in the north, the industry faces risks: significantly warmer oceans are likely to cause more poisonous algae.[20] The recent acute resurgence of algae in some fjords in northern Norway indicates the possible consequences, although a direct link to climate change was not detected regarding this specific incident. In May 2019, several caged-salmon companies reported mass deaths of millions of salmon. According to a scientist at the Norwegian

[13] Meld. St. 16/White Paper (2014–2015), 15.

[14] Ø. Bergh, R. Ingvaldsen and K. A. Mork, 'Fiskeoppdrett i varmere hav'/'Aquaculture in warmer oceans' (2012) 1 2°/C, 36–38.

[15] Ibid.

[16] L. Kvamme, 'Fortviler over rømt fisk'/'Despair over escapees', Bergens Tidende, 14 January 2015, available at www.bt.no/nyheter/okonomi/Fortviler-over-romt-fisk-3280539.html.

[17] Bergh, Ingvaldsen and Mork, 'Fiskeoppdrett i varmere hav'.

[18] Norwegian Institute of Marine Research, ES Grefsrud and T Svåsand, 'Status oppdrett'/'Status aquaculture', *Risikorapport norsk fiskeoppdrett* (2018) 14, available at www.imr.no/filarkiv/2018/02/risikorapport_2018.pdf/nb-no

[19] Bergh, Ingvaldsen and Mork, 'Fiskeoppdrett i varmere hav'.

[20] Norwegian Polar Institute, *The Arctic System: The Sea Is Getting Warmer*, available at www.arcticsystem.no/en/outsideworld/oceancurrents/warmer-ocean.html.

Institute of Marine Research, the algae were likely to spread to surrounding areas and various locations.[21] Total salmon deaths were estimated at 7.5 million.[22] Furthermore, scientists assume that current locations will become suitable for a greater variety of species.[23] Norway, like other significant aquaculture nations, will need to adapt to the circumstances related to climate change.

12.3 INTERNATIONAL REGULATIONS AND GUIDELINES

12.3.1 *Is There a Gap?*

There seems to be a gap in international regulation of aquaculture, as few international agreements apply directly to aquaculture, and international policy in this sector appears underdeveloped. No international treaty specifically addresses the challenges raised by the development of coastal and marine development.[24] This is probably a consequence of the right of coastal states to exploit their natural resources in the maritime zones within their jurisdiction. According to LOSC Article 56, coastal states have sovereign rights in their EEZs; moreover, the territorial sea and coastal waters are viewed as part of the states' territory and are hence subject to coastal-state sovereignty, according to LOSC Article 2. The aquaculture industry is significantly regulated at the national level, as shown by a recently published work that presents a set of national studies of the legal and policy framework for the aquaculture sector in twelve different jurisdictions, including major producers and exporters such as China, India and Norway.[25] As regards climate-change adaptation and the management of marine resources, coastal states can take those adaptive measures deemed appropriate for fisheries located in the EEZ (as well as within the territorial sea) to respond to climate change.[26] On the other hand, a complex mix of international agreements, documents and initiatives has

[21] M. H. Larsen, 'Laksedøden', Norwegian Broadcasting Corporation (NRK), 19 May 2019, available at www.nrk.no/troms/laksedoden_-_-algene-vil-spre-seg-1.14556083.

[22] K. J. Kristoffersen and S. S. Lysvold, '13.000 tonn oppdrettslaks er døde', Norwegian Broadcasting Corporation (NRK), 25 May 2019, available at www.nrk.no/nordland/13.000-tonn-oppdrettslaks-er-dode_-_-vi-snakker-om-dyr_-ikke-_biomasse_-1.14561607.

[23] Ibid.

[24] D. L. VanderZwaag, 'The international law and policy seascape for aquaculture: navigating tangled currents' in N. Bankes, I. Dahl and D. L. VanderZwaag (eds.), *Aquaculture Law and Policy* (Edward Elgar, 2016), 11–32, 11–13.

[25] N. Bankes, I. Dahl and D. L. VanderZwaag (eds.), *Aquaculture Law and Policy* (Edward Elgar, 2016).

[26] Stephens, 'Warming waters', 795.

emerged in favour of promoting sustainable aquaculture.[27] To what extent is international law relevant for Norway and other aquaculture nations when it comes to management and adaptation of aquaculture governance to climate change?

12.3.2 LOSC

As the LOSC establishes the overall rights and responsibilities of states in approving and regulating offshore activities, the Convention and thus the law of the sea in general are relevant for aquaculture. As to the further regulation of aquaculture activities, the LOSC firstly prescribes coastal state rights. Within the internal waters and the 12 nm territorial sea, the right to govern aquaculture is covered by coastal-state full sovereignty.[28] Concerning the 200 nm exclusive economic zones (EEZs), aquaculture operations are probably included in the sovereign rights to exploit and manage natural resources, and are undoubtedly covered by the wording 'other activities for the economic exploitation and exploration of the zone'.[29] And as for the high seas, all states have the right to develop aquaculture projects, according to the principle of freedom of the high seas.[30]

Secondly, some aquaculture-related state responsibilities follow from the LOSC. These fall into two categories: *marine environmental protection* and *international navigation*.[31] As regards the former, the LOSC notes five main areas of state responsibility for protecting the marine environment, including from potential aquaculture operations: (1) the general obligation to protect and preserve the marine environment,[32] (2) various pollution prevention and control responsibilities,[33] (3) environmental impact assessments (EIAs),[34] (4) protection of marine ecosystems and marine species at risk of extinction,[35] and (5) protection from significant and harmful changes caused by non-native species.[36] While areas 1–2 and 4–5 may be applicable to climate-change impacts from aquaculture and thus *mitigation*, the concept of EIA could be seen as applying to assessments of both mitigation and *adaptation*. However,

27 VanderZwaag, 'The international law', 11.
28 LOSC, Arts. 2 and 3.
29 LOSC, Art. 56(1)(a).
30 VanderZwaag, 'The international law', 14.
31 Ibid., 14–16.
32 LOSC, Art. 87(1)(d).
33 LOSC, Arts. 194(1) and (2).
34 LOSC, Art. 206.
35 LOSC, Art. 194(5)
36 LOSC, Art. 196(1).

the wording in Article 206: 'assess the potential *effects* of such activities *on the marine environment*', obviously excludes adaptation assessments.

As regards the second category of aquaculture-related state responsibilities – international navigation – a central question is the extent to which coastal states may regulate shipping activity in the vicinity of aquaculture installations. Climate change may involve the need for regulation and management, for instance, if a coastal state, for reasons of climate change, deems it expedient to locate aquaculture installations in or near a typical route for international navigation. In the territorial sea, ships of all states enjoy the right of innocent passage.[37] However, coastal states are granted broad regulatory powers in order to protect their offshore facilities and installations.[38] In addition, a coastal state may require foreign ships exercising their right of innocent passage to use such sea lanes and traffic separation schemes as it may prescribe for the safety of navigation.[39] Nevertheless, the power of the coastal state in this regard is limited by the obligation not to 'impose on foreign ships requirements that have the practical effect of denying or impairing the right of innocent passage'.[40] Concerning the EEZ, where all states enjoy the freedom of navigation,[41] the coastal state is not empowered to impose designated sea lanes. However, it may establish a measure potentially suitable for protection of aquaculture cages: namely, 'reasonable safety zones around installations and structures'[42] – but such zones shall not exceed a distance of 500 metres around them except as authorized by generally accepted international standards or as recommended by the competent international organization.[43] Consequently, a coastal state may initiate aquaculture in its EEZ with associated safety zones in order to avoid or reduce the impacts of climate change. With respect to Norway, this might entail a massive relocation of aquaculture from the fjords and into the EEZ. However, there is a significant restriction: Norway, as a coastal state, must not establish installations, structures or safety zones which could cause interference with the use of recognized sea lanes essential to international navigation.[44]

Analysis of the relevance of the LOSC as regards aquaculture and adaptation to climate change leaves the impression that the Convention does not

37 LOSC, Art. 17.
38 LOSC, Art. 21(1)(b).
39 LOSC, Art. 22.
40 LOSC, Art. 24(1).
41 LOSC, Art. 58(1).
42 LOSC, Art. 60(4).
43 LOSC, Art. 60(5).
44 LOSC, Art. 60(7).

cover general implications. However, to a certain degree it does restrict the power of coastal states to relocate aquaculture installations, if these hamper international navigation.

12.3.3 *The Paris Agreement*

Although there is no specific treaty dealing with various aspects of aquaculture, the recently adopted Paris Agreement is relevant. It aims to strengthen the global response to the threat of climate change, including by holding the increase in global average temperature to well below 2°C above pre-industrial levels.[45] Moreover, as tools for achieving this aim, the Paris Agreement specifically mentions increasing the ability to adapt to the adverse impacts of climate change and fostering climate resilience.[46] The relevance for aquaculture is supported by the states parties' recognition of the fundamental priority of safeguarding food security and ending hunger, and the particular vulnerabilities of food-production systems to the adverse impacts of climate change.[47] In addition to addressing the common, global aim, the Paris Agreement sets out specific obligations and recommendations for the parties. We return to this in Sections 12.4 to 12.6.

First, some methodical aspects should be noted. The frequent mentions of the Paris Agreement as 'historic', 'a landmark', 'the world's greatest diplomatic success' and 'a big, big deal',[48] leaves an impression of a legally binding instrument with clear obligations on the state parties. Indeed, the Paris Agreement is legally binding, it is globally applicable, and it specifies the same core obligations for all state parties.[49] However, we should recall the general rule of interpretation of treaties, according to which a treaty shall be interpreted in good faith in accordance with the ordinary meaning to be given to the terms of the treaty. The Paris Agreement has some features indicating that the ordinary meaning should prevail. The question of legal form and extent of legal obligations of the Agreement came up during the negotiations:

> In the final phases of the negotiations, states that had concerns over the issue of legal form concentrated on ensuring that particular provisions did not create legal obligations, rather than on depriving the Agreement as a whole of its legal character.[50]

45 Paris Agreement, Art. 2(1)(a).
46 Paris Agreement, Art. 2.
47 Paris Agreement, Preamble.
48 Bodansky, 'The Paris Climate Change Agreement', 289.
49 Ibid., 290.
50 Ibid., 290.

The result was an Agreement that distinguishes between its legal form and the legal character of particular provisions. The prescriptive force of the provisions of the Paris Agreements varies; indeed, many are not formulated as legal obligations.[51] Because 'the Paris Agreement reflects a careful calibration of the prescriptive force of its various provisions', care should be taken regarding an extended interpretation. These methodical aspects are relevant for interpreting the articles of the Paris Agreement concerning aquaculture (see Sections 12.4 to 12.6).

12.3.4 *FAO Instruments*

FAO has stressed that climate change is one of several external forcing factors affecting the global aquaculture sector.[52] It has also noted the increasing world demand for seafood and that capture fisheries are in decline, unable to cover this need. Thus, the FAO member states have expressed the need to further develop aquaculture 'as the only way to bridge [this] gap'.[53] FAO has recognized that, unlike in capture fisheries, existing applicable principles of public international law and treaty provisions provide little guidance on the conduct of aquaculture operations.[54] On the other hand, the organization has adopted several 'instruments of international guidance' – meaning that they are not legally binding – for aquaculture development. They fall into three main categories: (1) FAO Code of Conduct for Responsible Fisheries (FAO Code of Conduct),[55] (2) FAO technical guidelines specific to aquaculture,[56] and (3) various FAO guidelines, reports and documents.[57]

FAO Code of Conduct requests states to establish, maintain and develop an appropriate legal and administrative framework to facilitate the development of responsible aquaculture.[58] The Code addresses aquaculture both through general principles and a specific Article. The main principles that may serve as sources for interpreting aquaculture standards adaptive to climate change are as follows: (1) the principle of *food supply*: fisheries management should

51 Ibid., 296.
52 FAO *Aquaculture Development: Ecosystem Approach to Aquaculture*, section 2.2.3.
53 Ibid., x, 6.
54 Ibid., ix, 12.
55 FAO Code of Conduct.
56 FAO has developed eight technical guidelines specific to aquaculture, including *Aquaculture Development*; *Aquaculture Development: Genetic Resource Management*; and *Aquaculture Development: Ecosystem Approach to Aquaculture*.
57 For an overview of other FAO reports and documents, see VanderZwaag, 'The international law', 16.
58 FAO Code of Conduct, Art. 9(1)(1).

promote the maintenance of the quality, diversity and availability of fishery resources in sufficient quantities for present and future generations,[59] and (2) the *precautionary approach*: states should apply a precautionary approach widely to conservation, management and exploitation of living aquatic resources.[60] The principle of food supply may serve as a request for states to align their aquaculture industry in terms of locations, equipment/cages and the species farmed, with a special focus on climate change in order to promote the supply of fish. On the other hand, the aligning that derives from the principle of food supply is to take place within the frame of the second principle, the precautionary approach. In aligning the regulations on locations, cages, species, and so on, states are to have the objective of protecting the farmed species and of protecting and conserving the marine environment. Hence, adaptation of these elements to climate change should not compromise the objective of protecting and conserving the marine environment. For instance, response to climate change may indicate the need to concentrate aquaculture in a fjord, protected from storms. However, the best scientific evidence available (or the absence of adequate scientific information) may indicate that such concentration will place the marine environment at risk – and is thus to be avoided.

Furthermore, FAO Code of Conduct, Article 9, contains four general measures regarding aquaculture development: (1) responsible development of aquaculture, including culture-based fisheries, in areas under national jurisdiction; (2) responsible development of aquaculture including culture-based fisheries within transboundary aquatic ecosystems; (3) use of aquatic genetic resources for the purpose of aquaculture, including culture-based fisheries; and (4) responsible aquaculture at the production level. The first measure (Art. 9.1) indicates a general recommendation for establishing a legal and administrative framework conducive to the development of responsible aquaculture. The focus on ecological effects from aquaculture, involves requesting states to produce and regularly update aquaculture development strategies and plans to ensure that aquaculture development is ecologically sustainable. The second measure (Art. 9.2) requests neighbouring states to cooperate in the management of aquaculture with regard to transboundary aquatic ecosystems. The third measure (Art. 9.3) requests states to conserve genetic diversity, for example, to minimize adverse genetic, disease and other effects of escaped farmed fish on wild stocks. Finally, Article 9.4 focuses on responsible aquaculture at the production level.

59 Ibid., Art. 6(2).
60 Ibid., Art. 6(5).

The overall impression is that Article 9 refers more to the *impacts from aquaculture* on the environment, than to *adapting aquaculture* to climate change. For instance, 'States should require that the disposal of wastes such as offal, sludge, dead or diseased fish, excess veterinary drugs and other hazardous chemical inputs does not constitute a hazard to human health and the environment.'[61] On the other hand, states should produce and regularly update aquaculture development strategies and plans, as required, to ensure that aquaculture development is ecologically sustainable.[62] It is not clear whether this includes strategies and plans aimed at strengthening adaptation to climate change, in the sense of 'adaptive sustainability'. However, several FAO guidelines are more concrete. After the Code of Conduct was adopted in 1995, FAO has developed a more specific approach to aquaculture and climate change. In the same resolution that adopted the Code of Conduct, FAO was requested to elaborate appropriate technical guidelines in support of the implementation of the Code. These technical guidelines on the ecosystem approach to aquaculture were adopted in 2010.[63] In this document, FAO notes that climate change can affect aquaculture production through changes in the seasonality of weather patterns, rising sea levels, warming and increased extreme events leading to unpredictable production. Hence, 'climate change must be considered as a potentially relevant external element affecting aquaculture sector performance and development, therefore preparedness and adaptive measures must be in place'.[64] It is obvious that FAO recognizes the ecosystem approach as an adequate tool for addressing the challenge of ensuring a sustainable aquaculture sector. The concept is well established in international law regarding natural resource management – but how should it be interpreted in the context of *International Aquaculture Law*?[65]

FAO has defined the ecosystem approach to aquaculture as 'a strategy for the integration of the activity within the wider ecosystem such that it promotes sustainable development, equity and resilience of interlinked social-ecological

61 FAO Code of Conduct, Art. (9)(4)(6).

62 Ibid., Art. (9)(1)(3).

63 FAO, *Aquaculture Development: Ecosystem Approach to Aquaculture*.

64 Ibid., 20.

65 'International Aquaculture Law' is not an established concept in International Law. However, the increasing international focus on aquaculture and the above-mentioned FAO instruments indicate a certain justification of the term. See also VanderZwaag, 'The international law'; S. Wilson, 'Sustainable aquaculture: an organizing solution in international law' (2004) 26(2) *Thomas Jefferson Law Review*, 491–516; H. D. McCoy II, *American and International Aquaculture Law* (Wiley-Blackwell, 2000); and J. Roderburg, 'Marine aquaculture: impacts and international regulation' (2011) 25 *Australian and New Zealand Maritime Law Journal*, 161–179.

systems'.[66] This strategy is divided into three main phases: (1) aquaculture planning process,[67] (2) implementing the ecosystem approach to aquaculture[68] and (3) monitoring and evaluation.[69] (See Sections 12.4 to 12.6.) Furthermore, FAO has addressed climate change in detail in its 2014 circular 'Climate Change Adaptation in Fisheries and Aquaculture'.[70] Although Norway is not included in the compilation of initial examples, the circular contains some guidelines of transfer value.

Before we turn to analysis of concrete adaptation measures, mention should be made of the link between the Paris Agreement and the FAO guidelines. The FAO member states have expressed the importance of developing aquaculture to meet the world's increasing demand for seafood – and the parties to the Paris Agreement recognize the fundamental priority of safeguarding food security and the particular vulnerabilities of food production systems to the adverse impacts of climate change.[71] While the Paris Agreement contains some defined but quite general efforts aimed at boosting states' ability to adapt to adverse impacts of climate change, the FAO guidelines may serve as strategies for significant aquaculture nations in implementing the Paris Agreement in the aquaculture sector.

12.4 PLANNING FOR ADAPTIVE AQUACULTURE

Adaption to climate change is often discussed in terms of providing primarily local benefits – meaning that states have an incentive to adapt regardless of what other states may do.[72] Might international obligations be unnecessary, then?

However, the Paris Agreement operates with the global goal of enhancing adaptive capacity, strengthening resilience and reducing vulnerability to climate change.[73] This common aim is followed by more specific obligations. On the overall level, the parties commit to engage in adaptation planning processes (and implementation).[74] This has been said to be the only adaptation commitment in the entire Agreement.[75] The obligation is on the one

66 FAO, *Aquaculture development: Ecosystem approach to aquaculture*, 2.
67 Ibid., 7–23.
68 Ibid., 23–45.
69 Ibid., 45.
70 FAO, C. Shelton, Fisheries and Aquaculture Circular No. 1088: *Climate Change Adaptation in Fisheries and Aquaculture: Compilation of Initial Examples* (2014).
71 Paris Agreement, Preamble.
72 Bodansky, 'The Paris Climate Change Agreement', 308.
73 Paris Agreement, Art. 7(1).
74 Paris Agreement, Art. 7(9).
75 Bodansky, 'The Paris Climate Change Agreement', 308.

hand quite clear, as each party *shall* engage in such processes. However, the obligation is to a certain degree modified and weakened: parties shall engage *as appropriate* – offering quite wide discretion to states as to the further process and designation of relevant plans. The normative content of this obligation must be further elaborated in order to establish actual obligation of the states parties to engage. Such modification of state obligations in international agreements is not unique to the Paris Agreement. Take, for example, the Convention on Biological Diversity (CBD).[76] It follows from CBD Article 8 (a) that the states 'shall, as far as possible and as appropriate' establish a system of protected marine areas where special measures need to be taken to conserve biological diversity. This qualifier in the CBD has been criticized for making it uncertain whether the states are really committed to do anything.[77] However, some legal scholars take a positive view, stressing that 'the use of these qualifiers provides the states with more options in choosing an effective way to implement their commitments'.[78] Regarding the term 'as appropriate', this phrase may refer to discretion in the manner of implementation, and that the implementation takes place at the national level pursuant to national regulation. Reference is also made to a decision by the High Court of Australia, which interpreted the term 'as far as appropriate' in Articles 4 and 5 of the World Heritage Convention as meaning 'takes account of the difference in legal systems'.[79]

Applied to the interpretation of the Paris Agreement's adaptation commitment, it seems clear that the Agreement does not impose general obligations on the state parties to adapt. The reason is probably that 'since adaptation is in states' self-interest, there is relatively little rationale for imposing obligations on them to adapt'.[80] Nevertheless, the Paris Agreement imposes an obligation on the state parties to include considerations of climate change in their planning processes. On the other hand, precisely how the planning processes are to implement such considerations is largely subject to the states' discretion. However, the Paris Agreement specifies that this *may* include the process of formulating and implementing national adaptation plans and assessment of climate-change impacts and vulnerability, with a view to formulating nationally determined prioritized actions, taking into account vulnerable places and

76 Convention on Biological Diversity, Rio de Janeiro, 5 June 1992, 1760 UNTS 69.

77 I. U. Jakobsen, *Marine Protected Areas in International Law: An Arctic Perspective* (Martinus Nijhoff, 2016), 146–147.

78 Ibid.

79 Ibid, 150–152 with further references.

80 Bodansky, 'The Paris Climate Change Agreement', 308.

ecosystems.[81] In any case, this should be regarded as a normative guideline: states are *requested* to implement it in aquaculture management.

At the planning stage of aquaculture, spatial assessment is of special importance regarding climate-change adaptation. A reasonable interpretation of the measures listed in Article 7.9 of the Paris Agreement is to include assessment of suitable locations where climate-change impacts may be kept to a minimum. This is supported by the view held by FAO, that marine and terrestrial zoning for siting of aquaculture facilities is needed in connection with adapting to rising sea levels.[82] This is elaborated in the FAO list 'Purposes of an adaptation measure and examples of management measures'.[83] In order to reduce exposure to climate hazards, FAO has recommended risk-based zoning, including considering longer-term changes, and site selection for areas to be developed for aquaculture. Furthermore, in order to reduce vulnerability, it recommends farming of species more tolerant to major stressors like temperature, salinity and acidification.[84]

Applied to Norwegian circumstances, relevant reasons for adaptive planning include the changes regarding species' suitability for different areas, more stormy weather and challenging contingencies. Illustrative is farmed salmon, a highly significant species which thrives in quite cold water, but eats less when temperature increases.[85] One strategy may be to move the main salmon aquaculture northwards. However, the algae situation in some fjords in northern Norway is a further problem, illustrating the complexity of adaptive planning. Because of the massive death of salmon in May 2019, and the climate-change-related increased risk of such attacks, the authorities will need to include algae assessments in their adaptation planning processes. Thus, overall strategies should assess and designate which species and areas to prioritize for future aquaculture. Furthermore, the May 2019 algae attack should be acknowledged as an eye-opener concerning the importance of improved contingency planning. If the aquaculture companies in the affected area had received advance warning of the algal bloom, the mass deaths could probably have been prevented, either by temporary termination of feeding to keep the salmon deeper, by use of barriers, or by moving the salmon to other

81 Paris Agreement, Art. 7(9).
82 FAO, Fisheries and Aquaculture Circular No. 1088, 7.
83 FAO, P. B. Bueno and D. Soto, FAO Fisheries and Aquaculture Circular No. 1142: *Adaptation Strategies of the Aquaculture Sector to the Impacts of Climate Change* (2017), 10.
84 Ibid.
85 The Norwegian Environment Agency, The Norwegian Climate Change Adaptation Portal, available at www.klimatilpasning.no/sektorer/fiske-og-havbruk/.

areas/locations.[86] As yet, no operative system has been able to provide such advance warning. However, the Norwegian Institute for Marine Research (IMR) is set to conduct comparative studies of various instruments suitable for immersion, instruments which are also able to recognize pigmentation in the varying algae types. The independent research institute SINTEF, headquartered in Trondheim, and NIVA (Norwegian Institute for Water Research, headquartered in Oslo) are also doing research on the use of satellites for monitoring and alerting of algal blooms. In the near future, it may be possible to distinguish toxic algae from harmless ones, and alert of impending algal blooms.[87] Consequently, adaptation planning processes should include assessments of locations, species and ecological risks such as algal attacks, and contingency plans in cases of such attacks.

Further guidance regarding adaptation planning processes can be found in FAO instruments. The FAO Code of Conduct requests states to produce and regularly update aquaculture development strategies and plans, as required, to ensure that aquaculture development is ecologically sustainable.[88] In a climate-change perspective, sustainability should be interpreted with regard to environmental impacts *from* aquaculture, and *on* aquaculture. Concerning guidelines for relevant principles and content of national plans, the FAO ecosystem approach to aquaculture recognizes that climate change will 'affect the interactions of aquaculture and the ecosystem at all scales and with a temporal dimension adding to uncertainty'.[89] In view of the uncertainty regarding possible future climate-change effects on aquaculture and unknown ecosystem resilience, FAO stresses the importance of applying a precautionary approach, and that time scales are relevant in planning processes.[90] Thus, national plans/strategies concerning aquaculture and adaptation to climate change will need to be revised regularly with regard to actual and potential impacts of climate change.

12.5 IMPLEMENTATION OF ADAPTATION ACTIONS

In addition to planning processes, the Paris Agreement requires the parties to *implement* adaptation actions.[91] On the one hand the obligation is clear: they

86 A. Fenstad, 'Satellitter og maskinlæring kan hindre framtidig fiskedød fra giftalger', Teknisk ukeblad, 22 May 2019, available at www.tu.no/artikler/satellitter-og-maskinlaering-kan-hindre-framtidig-fiskedod-fra-giftalger/465881.

87 Ibid.

88 FAO Code of Conduct, Art. 9(1)(3).

89 FAO, *Aquaculture Development: Ecosystem Approach to Aquaculture*, section 2.2.3.

90 Ibid.

91 Paris Agreement, Art. 7(9).

shall engage. However, parties are not committed to implement actions, only to *engage*. Furthermore, the modifier 'as appropriate', as discussed earlier regarding planning processes, applies to this obligation as well. It could be argued that the objective of the Agreement as such indicates an obligatory element of adaptation to climate change. This is to some extent supported by the wording of Article 7.9, which lists 'implementation of adaptation actions' as one of the elements that may be included in the engagement of the states parties. On the other hand, that adaptation actions *may* be included weakens the degree of obligation. Moreover, the Article nuances the list of measures that *may* be taken to include 'undertakings and/or efforts'. On the whole, then, the normative function of this Article may be questioned: the parties are obliged to engage in the implementation of actions – but all adequate measures, ranging from adaptation actions, undertakings and/or efforts, seem voluntary.

Even though the states parties are not committed to implementing specific adaptation actions, the Paris Agreement may be interpreted as request the states to comply with the obligation to *engage* in the implementation of actions by 'adaptation actions, undertakings and efforts'. The wording indicates a quite wide list of adequate measures. In view of the various possible impacts of climate change at all scales of aquaculture, further interpretation of adaptation actions should be based on relevant objectives of the Paris Agreement. The parties to the Paris Agreement recognize the importance of *averting and minimizing loss and damage* resulting from climate change, such as extreme weather events.[92] Also highlighted is the role of sustainable development in this respect.[93] Reducing loss and damages is important for the industry; consequently the parties are encouraged to focus on risk insurance facilities.[94] However, the aspect of food security may be regarded as a weightier objective. In Article 2(1), the Paris Agreement indicates that the ability to adapt to the adverse impacts of climate change must be boosted, in ways that do not threaten food production.[95]

Furthermore, it follows from the Preamble that the states parties acknowledge the fundamental priority of safeguarding food security and the particular vulnerabilities of food production systems to the adverse impacts of climate change. Consequently, the Paris Agreement requires the parties to give priority to food security in the implementation of adaptation actions. That makes it

92 Paris Agreement, Art. 8(1).
93 Ibid.
94 Paris Agreement, Art. 8(4)f.
95 Paris Agreement, Art. 2(1)b.

relevant also to establish more specific measures for achieving food security from aquaculture as well. Here, the Agreement identifies some areas of facilitation in order to enhance understanding and action, such as early warning systems, emergency preparedness for events that may involve irreversible loss and damage, and resilience of livelihoods and ecosystems.[96] In addition, the parties acknowledge that technology development may contribute to achieving resilience to climate change.[97] It is stressed that accelerating, encouraging and enabling innovation is critical for an effective, long-term global response to climate change and for promoting sustainable development.[98] Here we may note that FAO mentions planned adaptation in fisheries, which, as regards aquaculture, may involve research funding aimed at identifying or developing species resistant to salinity and temperature fluctuations.[99] To increase adaptive capacity, FAO has also recommended improved disease surveillance systems and establishing Aquaculture Management Areas (AMA).[100]

For the case of Norway, with coastlines likely to be exposed to more extreme weather conditions, the guidelines regarding more resistant species and improved technology have significant relevance for the aquaculture authorities. According to the Norwegian Ministry of Fisheries and Coastal Affairs, climate-change impacts on aquaculture will involve mainly the following aspects: the kinds of species that will be suitable along the Norwegian coast if ocean temperature rises, and how changes in the pattern and prevalence of diseases and more extreme weather will affect requirements regarding the designation of aquaculture constructions.[101] An adaptive approach requires that the authorities provide regulations and frameworks adaptive to climate change. As a minimum, the following are necessary: to ensure surveillance and effective treatment of diseases, innovation as to the requirements of various species for water quality and temperature, and that aquaculture constructions are adaptive (see Section 12.4) to current and climatic conditions, to avoid casualties and escapes.

It is indeed interesting that FAO has recommended establishing the AMA concept as a measure to increase adaptive capacity. However, no further

96 Paris Agreement, Art. 8(4).
97 Paris Agreement, Art. 10(1).
98 Paris Agreement, Art. 10(5).
99 FAO, Fisheries and Aquaculture Circular No. 1088, 5.
100 FAO, Fisheries and Aquaculture Circular No. 1142, 10.
101 Fiskeri- og kystdepartementet, *Klimastrategi for Fiskeri- og kystdepartementet*/Ministry of Fisheries and Coastal Affairs, *Climate strategy for the Ministry of Fisheries and Coastal Affairs* (2013), 21.

elaboration seems to have ensued. The concept should be based on assessments of areas most adaptive to climate change, and be developed into applicable guidelines for aquaculture nations. One recently implemented Norwegian measure has the character of designated management areas: the 'traffic light system' (TLS),[102] which divides the Norwegian coast into thirteen production areas. The main premise is that capacity increase of salmon hinges on the amount of salmon lice in the area.[103] The increase potential is to be assessed every second year, whereupon the thirteen production areas are coloured green (increase is basically allowed) or yellow or red (increase is basically not allowed). The objective of TLS is to promote profitability and competitiveness within the frame of environmentally sustainable development. In other words, the objective is not to establish a system for the FAO-based AMA. However, by broadening the scope of environmental indicators to include other relevant factors than salmon lice, Norway's TLS system could have the potential to develop into an AMA system.

12.6 MONITORING AND REPORTING

Adaptation to climate change is at an early stage, globally as well as nationally. It is essential that states systematically gather experience from already-implemented adaptive regulations and policies in order to strengthen long-term adaptation, in general as well as for the aquaculture sector. Concerning follow-up, the Paris Agreement states only that the parties *may include* monitoring, evaluating and learning from adaptation plans, policies, programs and actions in their engagement in adaptation.[104] The parties are thus given some encouragement to assess implemented measures – but the lack of actual treaty obligation may weaken the effectiveness of climate-change adaptation, in the short and the longer term.

Effective reporting mechanisms may also serve as a contribution to a state's effective compliance with international law and policy. The Paris Agreement requires the parties to submit and update periodically adaptation communications, to be recorded in a public registry maintained by the Secretariat of the Agreement.[105] Adaptation communications may include priorities,

102 Forskrift 16. januar 2017 nr. 61 om produksjonsområder for akvakultur av matfisk i sjø av laks, ørret og regnbueørret (produksjonsområdeforskriften)/Regulations 16. January 2017 nr. 61 on production areas for aquaculture of fish in the sea of salmon, trout and rainbow trout (Regulations on production areas).

103 Ibid., § 8.

104 Paris Agreement Art. 7(9)d.

105 Ibid., Art. 7(10–12).

implementation and support needs, plans and actions. However, also this compliance measure appears quite vague: it is up to the parties, 'as appropriate' to submit the relevant data, and communications 'may' contain such data.

12.7 CONCLUDING REMARKS

With its aquaculture, Norway supplies food to an increasing world population. However, climate change will affect conditions also in Norwegian waters. Aquaculture will be affected, and will need to adapt to climate change. LOSC Article 192 emplaces the general obligation on states to protect and preserve the marine environment. From a general legal perspective, this Article, combined with coastal-state sovereignty over internal waters and territorial sea and exclusive and sovereign rights in the EEZ, might serve to establish a relevant affiliation of aquaculture to the law of the sea. However, the sphere of international law as regards environmental impacts from aquaculture and adaptation to climate change is characterized by 'soft law' guidelines.

On the other hand, the Paris Agreement does impose some relevant global goals and obligations, applicable also to Norwegian aquaculture law and policy. Norway is jointly responsible, with all parties to the Agreement, under the global goal on adaptation of enhancing adaptive capacity, strengthening resilience and reducing vulnerability to climate change.[106] As one of the state parties to the Paris Agreement, Norway recognizes the fundamental priority of safeguarding food security and the particular vulnerabilities of food productions systems to the adverse impacts of climate change.[107] Consequently, as a major aquaculture supplier, Norway must work on enhancing the sector's capacity for adaptation. Specifically, the Paris Agreement requires the parties to engage in adaptation planning processes and implementation of actions. Although the binding character of the obligation has been weakened by modifiers, the Agreement does entail a certain degree of commitment. Possible guidelines on how Norway may fulfil this obligation could come from Article 8 of the Paris Agreement, together with FAO instruments – the former focusing on averting and minimizing loss and damage, and the latter on spatial planning and developing species resistant to salinity and temperature fluctuations. The Paris Agreement also imposes certain enforcement measures in order to strengthen implementation – but their character of vagueness and voluntarism seriously undermine the effectiveness of these measures.

106 Ibid., Art. 7(1).
107 Paris Agreement, Preamble.

The international community has, through FAO, indicated that aquaculture should increase in order to cover the world demand for seafood. In addition, FAO has recognized that the need for climate-change adaptation in the aquaculture sector is severe, and increasing. International interest in an adaptive aquaculture calls for international legal measures to meet the challenges. The Paris Agreement may serve as a first step in this direction, and FAO guidelines seem expedient for ensuring compliance with the Agreement. However, given the vagueness of the Paris Agreement, and the inherently soft-law character of the FAO instruments, the international community should embark on the process of getting a *binding legal instrument* adopted. One solution could be an aquaculture agreement that contains measures for reducing the environmental impacts *from* aquaculture and for adapting *to* climate change. As a major aquaculture nation, Norway would appear particularly well suited to initiate such a process.

13

Law of the Sea Responses to Sea-Level Rise and Threatened Maritime Entitlements

Applying an Exception Rule to Manage an Exceptional Situation

Signe Veierud Busch

13.1 INTRODUCTION

The International Panel on Climate Change (IPCC) has delivered several assessment reports, all pointing in the same direction: *sea-level rise is an ongoing and unavoidable consequence of global warming.*

Some of the likely consequences are generally recognized: land territory flooded and rendered uninhabitable, primary industries severely affected, and infrastructure destroyed. Outside academia it is not always equally well known that the geographical extent of maritime entitlement of states will also be severely affected, as a result of moving maritime limits, or that some states may lose entitlement to their entire maritime territory, threatening their very survival. These consequences are the direct result of applying the rules set out in the United Nations Convention on the Law of the Sea (LOSC).

The LOSC is *the* major legal instrument regulating states' access to the living and non-living resources of the water column, the seabed and subsoil. As basis for its distribution of rights and obligations in relation to various uses of the seas, the LOSC contains separate sets of rules for different maritime zones in which coastal states and other states enjoy varying degrees of sovereignty, rights and jurisdiction. Among the overall aims of the Third United Nations Conference on the Law of the Sea (UNCLOS III), which resulted in the LOSC, was to ensure peace, security, cooperation and friendly relations among all nations.[1] Part II of the LOSC, containing the law on baselines,

1 1982 United Nations Convention on the Law of the Sea (LOSC), Montego Bay, 10 December 1982, in force 16 November 1994, 1833 UNTS 3, Preamble, Seventh Recital.

was one of the measures taken with this in mind. However, as a direct result of global warming and sea-level rise, the law of baselines has come under pressure. Continued use of the main rule on drawing of baselines will lead to instability, unpredictability and the emergence of new disputes for many states, resulting in loss of territory and ultimately loss of statehood.

The UN climate-change regime operates with the terms 'mitigation' and 'adaptation' as measures to combat or minimize climate change and its effects.[2] As sea-level rise is deemed unavoidable, this chapter focuses on possible adaptation strategies that can be employed to moderate the consequences experienced. Anticipatory adaptation is preferable, as it is potentially both more effective and less costly than last-minute, emergency adaptation or 'retrofitting'. Still, the suggestions discussed in this chapter probably fall within the category of last-minute adaptation, involving attempts to retrofit the law of baselines to current climate-change challenges.

This chapter identifies and discusses possible approaches to adapting the Law of the Sea to moderate the consequences of sea-level rise. It examines recent developments in discussions on the threat to maritime limits, and whether the *exception rules* in the LOSC can be applied in this situation, as a starting point for adapting the Law of the Sea to unavoidable climate change.

In the following, Section 13.2 provides an introduction to predicted sea-level rise, and gives an account of the current law of baselines. Combined, these two factors result in unstable maritime limits. Section 13.3 discusses the two often-suggested adaptation approaches – maintaining either the baselines or the outer limits of the different maritime zones despite subsequent sea-level rise; and notes how the International Law Association (ILA) Committee on International Law and Sea Level Rise has approached the issue.[3] The ILA Committee has explored the *general rule* on baselines and its interpretation to an exceptional situation, and this chapter comments on the strengths and weaknesses of the chosen approach. In Section 13.4, an alternative adaptation approach is explored: whether it is possible to apply the *exception rules* in the LOSC to this exceptional situation of climate change and sea-level rise.

[2] See E. Johansen, this volume, Chapter 1 for an introduction to the UN climate change regime and a uniform definition of terminology.

[3] In the following also referred to as the ILA Committee on Sea Level Rise.

13.2 SEA-LEVEL RISE AND UNSTABLE MARITIME LIMITS

13.2.1 *Predictions*

The fifth IPCC Report predicts sea-level rise of 26–98 cm by the year 2100.[4] Although this is less than the predictions of the previous report, the IPCC also notes the accelerating *rate* of mean sea-level rise. In its 2019 special report on the Ocean and Cryosphere in a Changing Climate, the estimated mean rise in sea level by the year 2100 is higher and the uncertainty range greater than in the Fifth IPCC Assessment Report:[5] The larger the emission scenario, the greater the associated rise in sea level. Up to the year 2050, the IPCC sees uncertainty in climate-change-driven sea-level rise as being rather low, offering a robust basis for short-term adaptation planning. Global mean sea level (GMSL) is set to rise between 0.17 and 0.40 m.[6] However, the IPCC also points out that 'uncertainty in climate change induced SLR increases substantially due to uncertainties in emission scenarios and the associated climate changes, and the response of the Antarctic ice sheet in a warmer world'.[7] GMSL is projected to rise by 0.29–1.1 m by 2100. However, the IPCC notes that there is a 17 per cent chance that sea-level rise will exceed these figures: indeed, although '[p]rocess-model based studies cannot yet provide this information, [...] expert elicitation studies show that a GMSL of 2 m in 2100 cannot be ruled out'.[8] GMSL will continue to rise for centuries beyond 2100, remaining elevated for thousands of years.[9]

In its 2018 special report on the impacts of global warming of 1.5°C, the IPCC explained the ratio between sea-level rise and its implications for large numbers of people: '[a] reduction of 0.1 m in global sea level rise implies that up to 10 million fewer people would be exposed to related risks, based on population in the year 2100 and assuming no adaptation.'[10] Accordingly, a difference of 10 cm in sea-level rise would affect 10 million people. This

4 IPCC, Core Writing Team, R. K. Pachauri and L. A. Meyer (eds.), *Climate Change 2014: Synthesis Report. Contributions of Working Groups I, II and III to the Fifth Assessment Report of the Intergovernmental Panel on Climate Change* (hereinafter IPCC, 2014) (2014).

5 IPCC, *Special Report on the Ocean and Cryosphere in a Changing Climate* (hereinafter IPCC *SR Ocean and Cryosphere*) (2019), Chapter 4, 4.

6 IPCC *SR Ocean and Cryosphere*, section 4.1.2, 9.

7 Ibid.

8 Ibid.

9 Ibid, section 4.1.2, 10.

10 IPCC, V. Masson-Delmotte et al. (eds.), *Global warming of 1.5°C: An IPCC Special Report on the Impacts of Global Warming of 1.5°C above Pre-industrial Levels and Related Global Greenhouse Gas Emission Pathways, in the Context of Strengthening the Global Response to the Threat of Climate Change, Sustainable Development, and Efforts to Eradicate Poverty*

indicates that a 110 cm rise by the year 2100 will expose more than 110 million people to risks related to sea-level rise. Furthermore:

> [i]ncreasing warming amplifies the exposure of small islands, low-lying coastal areas and deltas to the risks associated with sea level rise for many human and ecological systems, including increased saltwater intrusion, flooding and damage to infrastructure.[11]

These are some of the immediate practical consequences of sea-level rise on coastal states. In addition, several consequences result from, or are reinforced by, the applicable legal regimes. One example is the law of baselines and maritime limits included in the LOSC, as explained in detail in the Section 13.2.2.

13.2.2 *The Law of Baselines and Ambulatory Maritime Limits*

One purpose of baselines is to separate a coastal state's land territory from its maritime territory. The baselines follow the coastline of all coastal states; and LOSC Part II, Section 2, prescribes several alternative methods for the drawing of baselines. The *normal baseline* is the low-water line along the coast,[12] but if the coastline is deeply indented and cut into, or if there is a fringe of islands along the coast in the immediate vicinity, the method of *straight baselines* may be applied.[13] If the coastline is highly unstable due to the presence of a delta or other natural conditions, the LOSC allows the coastal state to draw *deltaic baselines*.[14] The rule on normal baselines is the *main rule*: the rules on straight baselines, including deltaic baselines, are the *exception rules*. The LOSC also provides rules for *archipelagic baselines*,[15] and baselines across river mouths and bays,[16] ports and roadsteads.[17]

The water landward of the baselines is the internal water of the coastal state; the water seaward of the baseline is divided into different maritime zones, with varying degrees for coastal-state rights and obligations. Interestingly, all but one of these maritime zones is measured from the baselines.[18] For example,

(World Meteorological Organization, 2018) 'Summary for policymakers', 6, para. A.1. Available at www.ipcc.ch/sr15/chapter/summary-for-policy-makers/.

11 Ibid., 10, para. B.2.3.
12 LOSC, Art. 5.
13 LOSC, Art. 7.
14 LOSC, Art. 7(2).
15 LOSC, Art. 47.
16 LOSC, Arts. 9 and 10.
17 LOSC, Arts. 11 and 12.
18 The exception is the outer limit of the continental shelf established beyond 200 nm, which is established on the basis of other criteria provided in LOSC Art. 76. See Section 13.4.4.

the territorial sea is not to extend beyond 12 nm from the baselines,[19] while the contiguous zone may not extend beyond 24 nm.[20] The exclusive economic zone (EEZ) is not to extend beyond 200 nm,[21] while the continental shelf extends at least to 200 nm from the baselines even if the continental margin does not extend up to that distance.[22] For the outer continental shelf extending beyond 200 nm, the LOSC provides a 350 nm constraint line, also measured from the baselines.[23]

Accordingly, the location of baselines is of vital importance for the coastal state and other states, in order to determine rights and obligations in relation to navigation, access to living and non-living resources, the laying of submarine cables and pipelines, scientific research and overflight.[24] The baselines and the outer limits of the different maritime zones also contribute to defining the limits of the high seas and the Area, which are negatively defined by the areas subject to national jurisdiction.[25]

When the LOSC was negotiated, the underlying principle was 'the land dominates the sea. In the context of baselines, this means that baselines are to be drawn on the basis of the land territory. This is evident from the main rule: the "normal baseline [...] *is* the low-water line along the coast" (emphasis added)'.[26] The UN Office for Ocean Affairs and the Law of the Sea (DOALOS), defines the low-water line as:

> The intersection of the plane of low water with the shore. The line along a coast, or beach, to which the sea recedes at low water. It is the normal practice for the low-water line to be shown as an identifiable feature on nautical charts unless the scale is too small to distinguish it from the high-water line or where there is no tide.[27]

As the low-water line is also the baseline, the baseline will change if the low-water line changes. Therefore, baselines are often referred to as *ambulatory*.[28]

19 LOSC, Art. 3.
20 LOSC, Art. 33.
21 LOSC, Art. 57.
22 LOSC, Art. 76(1).
23 LOSC, Art. 76(5).
24 LOSC, Arts. 17, 33, 52, 56, 77, 87.
25 LOSC, Art. 1(1).
26 LOSC, Art. 5.
27 United Nations Division for Ocean Affairs and the Law of the (UNDOALOS), *Baselines: An Examination of the Relevant Provisions of the United Nations Convention on the Law of the Sea* (United Nations Publication, 1989), 24.
28 R. Rayfuse, 'Sea level rise and maritime zones: preserving the maritime entitlement of "disappearing" states' in M. B. Gerrard and G. E. Wannier (eds.), *Threatened Island Nations: Legal Implications of Rising Seas and a Changing Climate* (Cambridge University

Although not explicitly mentioned in the LOSC, this follows from the requirement in Article 5 that the low-water line shall be

> marked on large-scale charts officially recognized by the coastal state. Due to navigational safety, such maps must be updated on a regular basis to reflect the reality of the coastline. The updated coastline will also reflect the new normal baseline. For *straight baselines*, the LOSC provides that such baselines 'must not depart to any appreciable extent from the general direction of the coast, and the sea areas lying within the lines must be sufficiently closely linked to the land domain.[29]

This suggests that if the coastline changes, the straight baselines must also be adjusted to follow the general direction of the coast.

However, for *delta baselines*, the LOSC provides that when the baseline is selected along the furthest seaward extent of the low-water line, such a baseline shall remain effective regardless of subsequent regression of the low-water line,[30] 'until changed by the coastal state in accordance with this Convention'. This suggests that delta baselines are less ambulatory than the normal baseline or other straight baselines established in accordance with Article 7(1) – and are also potentially also less vulnerable to sea-level rise. The nature of delta baselines is further discussed in Section 13.4.3 of this chapter.

13.2.3 *New Challenges in an Old Framework*

With the sea-level rise predictions of the IPCC on the one hand, and the law of baselines on the other, it is relatively easy to calculate the potential outcome. If the baselines are to follow the low-water line, and states are to comply with the main rule of the LOSC, sea-level rise will necessitate a landward relocation of the baselines, which in turn will require the coastal states to draw new limits of their maritime zones, all measured from the baselines. When the outer limits of different maritime zones move, the coastal state will suffer loss of territory and entitlements. In areas where the water column and continental shelf between two or more neighbouring states are already subject to a delimitation agreement, or binding judicial decision, the dispute may

Press, 2013), 167–194, 173; L. M. Alexander, 'Baseline delimitations and maritime boundaries' (1982–1983) 23 *Virginia Journal of International Law*, 503–536; C. Schofield, 'Rising waters, shrinking states: the potential impacts of sea level rise on claims to maritime jurisdiction' (2019) 53 *German Yearbook of International* Law, 189–231, 210.

29 LOSC, Art. 7(4).

30 LOSC, Art. 7(2).

resume.[31] Generally, shifting maritime limits may destabilize the oceans, negatively affecting the prospects of maintaining the peaceful uses of the oceans.[32]

Already prior to the entry into force of the LOSC, the IPCC issued its first report describing considerable sea-level rise,[33] and scholars started raising concerns that the rules of baselines in the Convention were poorly developed.[34] In 1990, D.D. Caron, an international judge and arbitrator, and professor of international law, published his concerns about the effect of rising sea levels on the law of baselines, and raised the question of adaptation to climate change. Caron observed that the predicted sea-level rise, as the most probable consequence of global warming, would have potentially disastrous consequences;[35] he also argued that the law of baselines might even aggravate the consequences of climate change.[36] He held that it would be the responsibility of the international community to seek to prevent such change, and to prepare to adapt to the changes likely to occur despite any efforts at prevention. In 2012, the ILA Committee on Baselines similarly observed that 'the existing law of the normal baselines does not offer an adequate solution'.[37] Still, the law of baselines remains unchanged, thirty years after the first concerns were raised.

When the LOSC was negotiated during the 1970s, global warming with dramatic sea-level rise was not a concern; accordingly, the LOSC framework and rules failed to take into account the challenges the world is facing today as

31 Maritime boundary agreements are outside the scope of this chapter and are not be addressed here. See further S. Árnadóttir, 'Termination of maritime boundaries due to a fundamental change of circumstances' (2016) 32(83) *Utrecht Journal of International and European Law*, 94.

32 LOSC, Preamble, Seventh Recital.

33 IPCC, J. T. Houghton, G. J. Jenkins and J. J. Ephraums (eds.), *Climate Change: The IPCC Scientific Assessment, First Assessment Report of the Intergovernmental Panel on Climate Change* (hereinafter IPCC, 1990), (1990) 'Summary for policymakers', XXIX. Available at www.ipcc.ch/site/assets/uploads/2018/03/ipcc_far_wg_I_spm.pdf.

34 D. D. Caron, 'When law makes climate change worse: rethinking the law of baselines in light of a rising sea level' (1990) 17 *Ecology Law Quarterly* 621–653; A. H. A. Soons, 'The effects of a rising sea level on maritime limits and boundaries' (1990) 37 *Netherlands International Law Review*, 207–232; C. Schofield, 'Holding back the waves? Sea level rise and maritime claims' in O. C. Ruppel, C. Roschmann and K. Ruppel-Schlichting (eds.), *Climate Change: International Law and Global Governance: Legal Responses and Global Responsibility* (Nomos, 2013), 593–615 J. McAdam, *Climate Change, Forced Migration, and International Law* (Oxford University Press, 2012); J. G. Stoutenburg, *Disappearing Island States in International Law* (Brill Nijhoff, 2015); Rayfuse, 'Sea level rise and maritime zones'.

35 Caron, 'When law makes climate change worse', 622.

36 Ibid., 623.

37 International Law Association, *Sofia Conference 2012: Report of the Committee on Baselines under International Law of the Sea* (2012), 30–31.

the direct result of climate change. The LOSC was intended to be a dynamic treaty, capable of further evolution – but here it should also be borne in mind that the constant changing of the earth climate differs sharply from 'climate change' and adaptation to climate-change challenges. Regarding sea-level rise, climate change refers to far more than the gradual natural changes under average conditions. Today we are facing greater variations and more rapid rise in sea levels than during the previous two millennia. Although the LOSC might be equipped to handle a foreseen gradual natural change of the earth climate, it may prove unable to adapt to such rapid sea-level rise.[38]

This necessitates reflection on whether the law of the sea is able to adapt to the specific challenges to baselines and maritime limits resulting from climate change and sea-level rise, and which strategies might be applied to adapt to these new circumstances.

13.3 ADAPTING THE LAW OF THE SEA TO SEA-LEVEL RISE: PROSPECTS AND POSSIBILITIES

13.3.1 *Two Approaches*

There are two widely debated approaches that can potentially lessen the consequences of sea-level rise on maritime limits.[39] The first alternative is to make the baselines permanent, instead of ambulatory. That will mean that once the baselines are established along the low-water line in accordance with Article 5, the baseline will not necessarily follow the retracting low-water line when the sea level rises. The internal water landward of the baselines of the affected coastal state will become larger, while the other maritime zones remain unchanged.

[38] IPCC, T. F. Stocker et al. (eds.), *Climate Change 2013, The Physical Science Basis: Contribution of Working Group I to the Fifth Assessment Report of the Intergovernmental Panel on Climate Change* (Cambridge University Press, 2013) 'Sea Level Change', 1139, 1150. Available at www.ipcc.ch/site/assets/uploads/2018/03/WG1AR5_SummaryVolume_FINAL.pdf. See also International Law Association, *Sydney Conference 2018: Report of the Committee on International Law and Sea Level Rise* (hereinafter ILA Sydney 2018 *Conference Report*), 4.

[39] See amongst others Soons, 'The effects of a rising sea level'; Caron, 'When law makes climate change worse', 621–653; C. Schofield and D. Freestone, 'Options to protect coastlines and secure maritime jurisdictional claims in the face of global sea level rise' in M. B. Gerrard and G. E. Wannier (eds.), *Threatened Island Nations* (Cambridge University Press, 2013); S. Sefrioui, 'Adapting to sea level rise: a law of the sea perspective' in G. Andreone (ed.), *The Future of the Law of the Sea: Bridging Gaps Between National, Individual and Common Interests* (Springer Open, 2017) 3–22.

The second alternative is to maintain the existing outer limits of maritime zones, despite subsequent sea-level rise. When all maritime zones are established in accordance with the relevant provisions of the LOSC, they will remain unchanged even if the low-water line and baselines are changed as a result of sea-level rise. If the baseline retracts, this means that the other maritime zones measured from such baseline will become larger than originally described in the LOSC.

For low-lying states which are particularly vulnerable to sea-level rise, the option of making the baselines permanent would maintain stable outer limits of their maritime zones, despite loss of territory and/or basepoints, and allow for stable management of the resources in the EEZ and continental shelf. This would also facilitate the exploration and potential exploitation of areas beyond national jurisdiction.

However, for small island states at risk of partial or complete submergence rendering their land territory *uninhabitable*, the second alternative would seem preferable. LOSC Article 121(3) explicitly states that an uninhabitable island cannot generate an EEZ or continental shelf. However, if such limits are established in accordance with the LOSC *before* the island becomes uninhabitable, the possibility of maintaining the existing outer limits would allow the state to uphold its entitlement to an EEZ and continental shelf. The alternative of freezing baselines around an uninhabitable island would not neutralize Article 121(3), and the state could not maintain the outer limits of its EEZ or continental shelf.

On the other hand, if an island or state is completely submerged, resulting in total loss of baselines, may it maintain the other maritime limits, no longer being based on either land territory or baselines? If so, for how long can maritime zones be maintained if the land territory from which it is measured disappears? These questions concern issues with a relatively long-term perspective, and are beyond the scope of this chapter.

From the perspective of a flag state presumably having interests in the Area, the freedoms of the high seas, or general rights in the EEZ, both of the options noted above may be considered as a threat to the freedoms and common interests in the seas. When sea level rises, both options involve an expansion of the maritime territories subject to national jurisdiction, measured from the low-water line. Although the coastal state will suffer a corresponding loss of land territory, the two options offer either larger internal water or larger territorial sea, EEZ and continental shelf for the coastal state than what follows from the current interpretation of the LOSC. If a coastal state maintains existing baselines or existing maritime zones, it can be argued that the coastal state prevents the high seas from expanding, and territorial seas from becoming EEZ – potentially contrary to global public interest.[40] On the other hand, it can be argued that neither option deprives any other state of its existing maritime space, nor does it encroach upon the high seas or the Area.[41] In addition, the fixing of maritime limits would arguably contribute to stabilizing the oceans and 'the strengthening of peace, security, cooperation and friendly relations among all nations' as per in the LOSC Preamble.

However, both approaches are at odds with current interpretations of LOSC rules. If a state maintains a baseline despite changes in the low-water line, it would ultimately claim a baseline that does not reflect reality – contrary to LOSC Article 5.[42] If a state maintains its existing entitlement to maritime zones despite retreating or lost baselines, the distance between the new baselines and the outer limits of these zones would exceed the 12 and 200 nm distance criterion under the LOSC.[43] Thus, accepting either of these approaches would require changes in the interpretation of LOSC rules.[44] While a relatively unanimous community of legal scholars seems to agree that the way to approach climate-change challenges to maritime limits is to freeze the baselines and boundaries established under the LOSC, they are unable to agree on the procedure for effectuating such modification or expansion of the LOSC.[45]

13.3.2 *Interpreting and Applying a General Rule in an Exceptional Situation*

13.3.2.1 The ILA Committee on International Law and Sea Level Rise

In 2018, the ILA Committee on International Law and Sea Level Rise issued a report on the impacts of sea-level rise on limits of maritime zones. The mandate of the ILA Committee is to 'study the possible impact of sea-level rise and the implications under international law of the partial and complete

40 ILA Sydney 2018, 14.

41 M. Hayashi, 'Sea level rise and the law of the sea: how can the affected states be better protected?' in C. H. Schofield, S. Lee and M.-S. Kwon (eds.), *The Limits of Maritime Jurisdiction* (Brill, 2014), 618–619.

42 ILA Sydney 2018, 13.

43 Ibid.

44 Ibid.

45 Schofield, 'Holding back the waves?', 611; M. Hayashi, 'Sea level rise and the law of the sea: legal and policy options' in *Proceedings of the International Symposium on Islands and Oceans* (Ocean Policy Research Foundation, Tokyo, 22–23 January 2009), 89–90; Rayfuse, 'Sea level rise and maritime zones', 190; A. G. Oude Elferink and D. Freestone, 'Flexibility and innovation in the law of the sea: will the LOS Convention amendment procedures ever be used?' in A. G. Oude Elferink (ed.), *Stability and Change in the Law of the Sea: The Role of the LOS Convention* (Brill, 2005), 169–223.

inundation of state territory, or depopulation thereof, in particular of small island and low-lying states' and to 'develop proposals for the progressive development of international law in relation to the possible loss of all or of parts of state territory and maritime zones due to sea level rise'.[46]

Based on a literature review, the ILA Committee acknowledged the two general approaches *de lege ferenda* for addressing the issue of sea-level rise on maritime boundaries: either by maintaining the existing baselines, or by maintaining the existing defined outer limits of the maritime zones as measured from the baselines. The Committee added that its own proposal regarding the legal consequences of sea-level changes expected in the near future should seek to minimize the proposed changes to the settled law of the sea:[47]

> [T]he most important consideration at this stage was that its proposals should as far as possible attempt to reduce legal uncertainties regarding maritime boundaries and the limits of maritime zones at a time when many coastal states are facing the challenges of sea-level rise and its impacts. In particular, the Committee's proposal should aim to facilitate orderly relations between States and, ultimately, the avoidance of conflict.[48]

On this basis, the ILA Committee undertook a deeper analysis of the two approaches to adaptation, identifying key arguments for and against each of them. They observed that the first option of *maintaining the baselines* despite subsequent changes in the coastline would entail retention of existing entitlements to maritime zones at the widths as prescribed by the LOSC, maintain coastal-state sovereignty over its territory at status quo and consequently shield coastal and island states from *some of* the adverse impacts of climate change. On the other hand, this first option could ultimately mean that the coastal state would maintain its territorial sea and EEZ also where the territory of such zone may have submerged or become uninhabitable.[49] The ILA Committee, therefore, observed that maintaining the baseline despite a changing coastline would be a breach of the main rule that the normal baseline is ambulatory.[50]

The second option – *maintaining the existing outer limits* of all maritime zones – would arguably remove the need for vulnerable states to build artificial structures in order to retain maritime zone entitlement, and allow states to keep their existing zones. In such instances, the baseline would be kept ambulatory in accordance with the law of the sea, but the breadth of the

46 ILA Sydney 2018, 1.
47 ILA Sydney 2018, 13.
48 Ibid.
49 LOSC, Art. 121(3); ILA Sydney 2018, 14.
50 ILA Sydney 2018, 14.

other maritime zones would exceed the limits set by the LOSC.[51] As compared to the first approach, where the ILA Committee observed that maintaining the baselines would shield coastal and island states from *some* of the impacts of climate changes, the ILA noted that the second option would shield coastal states (including island states) from these adverse impacts of climate change.[52] Thus, the latter option might provide a greater shield than the first.

The ILA Committee then explored emerging state practice, noting the important body of regional practice in the Pacific region.[53] The Polynesian Leaders Group[54] seem to prefer to maintain the established baselines, as do the Pacific Island Leaders.[55] The ILA Committee also observed that several Pacific states, such as the Marshall Islands, Kiribati and Tuvalu, have passed new legislation designed to prevent physical changes to their coastlines from impacting on their baseline and maritime zones.[56] Although a new regional practice is certainly developing amongst a group of particularly vulnerable states, the creation of a new rule of customary law will require a pattern of state practice, as well as *opinio juris*.[57] Developing a new rule of customary law is likely to take considerable time, and may, therefore, not be very practical in relation to sea-level rise. As Hayashi observes,

> by the time that a sufficient amount of state practice has accumulated, some island states may have already become submerged, or serious disputes may have arisen – thus is would be too late, even if new rules of international law could emerge.[58]

The ILA Committee also pointed out that if it were to make recommendations regarding the maintenance of maritime entitlements, these should be global and not regional, as they would need to apply to the world community.[59] At

51 Ibid.
52 Ibid.
53 Ibid., 16.
54 Seven Polynesian leaders from French Polynesia, Niue, Cook Islands, Samoa, Tokelau, Tonga and Tuvalu signed the *Taputapuatea Declaration on Climate Change* 16 July 2015, available at www.samoagovt.ws/wp-content/uploads/2015/07/The-Polynesian-P.A.C.T.pdf, accessed 25 June 2019.
55 The leaders of The Federal States of Micronesia, Republic of Kiribati, Republic of the Marshall Islands, Republic of Nauru, Republic of Palau, Independent State of Papua New Guinea, Solomon Islands and Tuvalu signed *The Delap Commitment on Securing Our Common Wealth of Oceans – reshaping the future to take control of the fisheries* in March 2018.
56 ILA Sydney 2018, 17.
57 ILA Sydney 2018, 18.
58 M. Hayashi, 'Sea-level rise and the law of the sea: future options' in D. Vidas and P. J. Schei (eds.), *The World Ocean in Globalization: Climate Change, Sustainable Fisheries, Biodiversity, Shipping, Regional Issues* (Brill Nijhoff, 2011), 200.
59 ILA Sydney 2018, 19.

the time of its report, the Committee did not consider that regional practice in the Pacific had yet constituted international custom.[60]

The ILA Committee then went on to discuss *how* it could present a proposal *de lege ferenda* that coastal and island states should have the option of maintaining their maritime entitlements notwithstanding changes brought by sea-level rise.[61] Here it tried to avoid the exercise undertaken by many scholars before them, which has generally resulted in an examination of the different available procedural options, such as the LOSC amendment procedures, changes through the Meeting of States Parties or a supplementary agreement – without providing a solution.[62] Observing the considerable complexities involved in the many procedural options, the Committee decided 'not to propose any specific option at this point'.[63]

13.3.2.2 Status of ILA Resolution 5/2018

The ILA Committee decided against proposing a specific procedural option for adaptation, but it did propose a *resolution*, adopted by the ILA at its 78th Biennial Conference in Sydney:

> [O]n the grounds of legal certainty and stability, provided that the baselines and the outer limits of maritime zones of a coastal or an archipelagic State have been properly determined in accordance with the 1982 Law of the Sea Convention, these baselines and limits should not be required to be recalculated should sea level change affect the geographical reality of the coastline.[64]

Although reluctant to suggest a procedure for *how* states can change the law of the sea, the Committee suggested a combination of the two approaches presented above: to maintain both baselines *and* outer limits of maritime zones regardless of changing coastlines.

In general, a resolution adopted by the ILA at the Biennial Conference represents the opinion of the ILA concerning the desired development of international law, and may impact those of who are involved in the negotiation of new legal instruments and application of existing rules of international law. The conference reports issued by the ILA attract wide attention, and ILA

60 ILA Committee on International Law and Sea Level rise, *Working Session Report*, Sydney (2018) (hereinafter ILA Sydney 2018 *Working Session Report*), 3.
61 ILA Sydney 2018, 18.
62 ILA Sydney 2018, 18–19.
63 ILA Sydney 2018, 19.
64 ILA, Committee on International Law and Sea Level Rise, *Resolution 5/2018*, Sydney (2018).

resolutions are seen as providing authoritative statements by the most highly qualified publicists of the various nations.[65]

The ILA is a private association, an expert body, known for producing earlier texts codifying key principles of international law, for the benefit of institutions such as the International Law Commission (ILC). Unlike the ILA, the ILC is a permanent, semi-official body of independent experts on international law, established by the UN General Assembly, for the purpose of the progressive development and codification of international law.[66] During its 70th session, the ILC decided to recommend the inclusion of the topic 'sea level rise in relation to international law' in its long-term programme of work, initially in the form of a Study Group.[67] The work of the ILA Committee and its Resolution 5/2018 on sea-level rise and the maintenance of baselines and maritime limits is expected to have great impact on the coming international legal discourse. Most of the ILC's work has resulted in draft conventions that remain subject to further negotiation, adoption and ratification by states,[68] and its consideration of sea-level rise related issues is highly welcomed. However, it should be borne in mind that the ILC tends to proceed rather slowly, which may be a disadvantage as regards the issue of sea-level rise.

The ILA Committee observed that establishing a new rule of customary law will require not only a pattern of state practice, but also *opinio juris:* the acts amounting to a settled practice must be 'carried out in such a way, as to be evidence of a belief that this practice is rendered obligatory by the existence of a rule of law requiring it'.[69] The Committee noted that if its recommendations were discussed and approved by the political organs of the UN, that may well contribute to the development of that *opinio juris*.[70] During the open session at the Sydney Conference, Prof. David Freestone remarked that he

> was aware that a number of Pacific island States were already actively considering taking the findings of the Committee to the floor of the United Nations General Assembly for discussion the result of which, if it were to occur, would inevitably lend the Committee's findings yet more weight.[71]

65 Statute of the International Court of Justice, San Francisco, 24 October 1945, Art. 38(1)(d).
66 Charter of the United Nations, San Francisco, 26 June 1945, 1 UNTS 16, Art. 13(1)(a).
67 UN Doc. A/73/10 (2018), para. 37.
68 A. Boyle and C. Chinkin, *The Making of International Law* (Oxford University Press, 2007).
69 *North Sea Continental Shelf* cases (*Judgment*) [1969] ICJ Rep. 3, para. 77.
70 ILA Sydney 2018 *Conference Report*, 18.
71 ILA Sydney 2018 *Working Session Report*, statement by Prof. David Freestone, 11.

Although the ILA resolution does not have binding effects on states or institutions, it has the potential for impacting on the further process of adapting the law of the sea.

13.3.2.3 Strengths and Weaknesses of ILA Resolution 5/2018

It is highly admirable that the ILA Committee was able to pass a resolution after just four years of study and debate. Resolution 5/2018 is well intended; it reflects emerging state practice, and is in accordance with the views argued by a relatively unanimous body of legal scholars for the past thirty years. During the open session at the Sydney Conference, Freestone, according to the conference report, observed that: '[A]s all [coastal states] had an interest in preserving their maritime entitlements he believed over time there was likely to be considerable support within the international community for the Committee's proposal.'[72]

However, it is less clear *how* the law is to develop. This issue was raised by Captain J. Ashley Roach during the open session at the Sydney conference. While commending the Committee for its work, he also drew attention to the fact that the report did not provide any elaboration on *how* states could freeze the location of their baselines and maritime limits. Therefore, he wondered what options the Committee envisaged for states to obtain such a result.[73] In its 2018 report, the ILA Committee noted that it was aware of 'the fact that its recommendations must have practical utility and clarity for coastal and island states facing the impacts of sea-level rise'.[74] In his reply to Roach, Freestone acknowledged that 'no decision had been made by the Committee as to the actual way (. . .) in which a change in existing customary law might take place', continuing that moving forward on this, the resolution 'would function as both a very important and clear statement on the matter', and that 'numerous options existed'.[75] However, it may be questioned whether the ILA Committee and the recently passed resolution at its current stage provide such 'practical utility and clarity' as desired.[76]

The passing of Resolution 5/2018 marks an important step towards a progressive development of international law, with the ILA giving an authoritative voice to the already widely shared opinion amongst legal scholars, but the observations made by Roach and Freestone highlight

72 ILA Sydney 2018, 8.
73 ILA Sydney 2018, question raised by Captain J. Ashley Roach, 10.
74 ILA Sydney 2018, 15.
75 ILA Sydney 2018, response by Professor David Freestone, 11.
76 ILA Sydney 2018, 15.

important difficulties: it will take *time* to achieve the necessary support within the international community for the Committee's proposal, and the Committee has made no suggestion as to *how* states can maintain their maritime entitlements.

There are also certain practical challenges in the potential implementation of the Resolution that may affect its success in ensuring the maritime entitlement of coastal states, particularly those most vulnerable to rising sea levels. As an underlying premise for a state to maintain its limits, the Resolution requires that the 'baselines and outer limits of maritime zones [. . .] have been *properly determined* in accordance with the [LOSC]' (emphasis added).[77] In practice, this means that states whose limits are subject to disputes with other states, or whose limits are yet to be 'properly determined', will still suffer the consequences of sea-level rise on their maritime territories.

This is particularly problematic in relation to continental shelf limits, where the completion of a submission procedure to the Commission on the Limits of the Continental Shelf (CLCS) is a prerequisite for establishing permanent limits in accordance with Article 76(9).[78] LOSC Article 76(8) prescribes that states with a continental shelf beyond 200 nm shall make documented submissions to the CLCS. Upon the recommendations from the CLCS concerning the location of the outer limit of their continental shelf, the coastal state can establish final and binding limits. Submissions made to the CLCS are queued in the order they are received by the CLCS;[79] forty-five submissions are currently awaiting to be ascribed a sub-commission for consideration, and a total of fifty-seven submissions await CLCS recommendations.[80] The work of the CLCS is time-consuming, and the Commission adopts roughly three to four recommendations per year.[81] As a result of its slow working pace and the overwhelming number of submissions, states may have to wait for ten to twenty years before receiving CLCS recommendations upon which it can establish final, binding and permanent continental shelf limits.[82] In the meantime, the geographical circumstances may change severely for many states with large river deltas and for low-lying island states.

77 ILA, Committee on International Law and Sea Level Rise, *Resolution 5/2018*.
78 See also Section 13.3.5.4.
79 *Rules of Procedure of the Commission on the Limits of the Continental Shelf*, UN Doc. CLCS/40/Rev.1 (17 April 2008), Rule 51 (4).
80 An overview of all submission and the progress of the CLCS consideration procedure is available at www.un.org/Depts/los/clcs_new/commission_submissions.htm.
81 S. Busch, *Establishing Continental Shelf Limits Beyond 200 Nautical Miles by the Coastal State: A Right of Involvement for Other States* (Brill, 2016), 384.
82 Ibid.

Although the wording of the LOSC itself seemingly offers an opportunity for permanent continental shelf limits, with the ILA Committee's resolution similarly pulling in the direction of permanent limits, the requirement of the limits being 'properly determined' may prevent the most vulnerable states, with the most urgent need of stable limits, from employing the opportunity provided by Article 76(9) and suggested in Resolution 5/2018. In worst case, while waiting in line for CLCS consideration, an island state may risk complete loss of territory, or that its island territory is rendered uninhabitable and no longer can generate a continental shelf.[83]

This shows that the challenges resulting from sea-level rise may require a broader action plan than that proposed by the ILA Committee. If the ILA Resolution is to have the desired effect, further examination of the CLCS submission procedure will be necessary, regarding what happens to the maritime entitlements of states in the intermediate period between the time of submission and the CLCS issuing its recommendations. One alternative might involve establishing a 'priority procedure' for states particularly vulnerable to sea-level rise. Another alternative which should be further explored by the ILA Committee in its continued work would be not only to suggest maintaining baselines and maritime limits established in accordance with the LOSC but also to maintain baselines and maritime features documented in submissions awaiting CLCS consideration.

13.4 ADAPTATION BY DEVELOPING THE USE OF EXCEPTION RULES IN THE LOSC

13.4.1 *Introduction*

Whereas the ILA Committee explores the general rule on baselines and its interpretation and application to an exceptional situation, this chapter goes one step further, exploring also the exception rules in the LOSC as basis for adaptation. Most maritime limits provided for in the LOSC are measured from the ambulatory baselines which follow shifts in the coastline.[84] However, there are two instances in which the LOSC makes the baseline somewhat less ambulatory and the maritime limit permanent. These are Article 7(2) on deltaic baselines and Article 76(9) on continental shelf limits, as briefly noted in Section 13.3.2.3. The question now is whether these exception rules

83 LOSC, Art. 121(3).
84 LOSC, Art. 5.

can be subject to wider interpretation and application in order to secure the maritime entitlement of states particularly vulnerable to sea-level rise.

13.4.2 *Ordinary Meaning and Intent of the Parties*

The Vienna Convention on the Law of Treaties provides that treaties shall be interpreted in good faith in accordance with the ordinary meaning to be given to the terms of each treaty in the context and in the light of its object and purposes.[85] Although the Vienna Convention makes no explicit mention of the parties' *intent* when negotiating the treaty, the importance of such intent may be reflected in the 'good faith and purpose' considerations. As to whether the current provisions of the LOSC may be given wider use, the ordinary meaning of the terms, context, object and purpose can serve as guidelines.

The ILA Committee on Sea Level Rise raised the question 'at which point in time it could be considered that sea-level rise, of such magnitude as to impact objective criteria for negotiated boundaries, became a matter which was in the "public domain"'.[86] Although the World Meteorological Organization had hosted the First World Climate Conference already in 1979, Hayashi maintains that 'during the Third UN Conference on the Law of the Sea, there was no widespread recognition of the possible problems of sea-level rise, and negotiators did not anticipate that there would be a significant global regression of coastlines'.[87]

Accordingly, the negotiating parties had no possibility to foresee the ramifications of the law of baselines in combination with sea-level rise, and had no *intent* of providing provisions aimed at securing the entitlement of coastal states in case of sea-level change. However, it is worth investigating whether some provisions in the LOSC may still serve such purpose without going beyond the ordinary meaning of the terms in the treaty in their context and in light of its object and purpose.[88]

13.4.3 *Baselines Surrounding Highly Unstable Coastlines (Article 7(2))*

Article 7(2) provides an alternative to establishing normal baselines in cases where there is a delta or other natural conditions that render the coastline

[85] Vienna Convention on the Law of Treaties (Vienna Convention), Vienna, 23 May 1969, in force 27 January 1980, 1155 UNTS 331, Art. 31.

[86] International Law Association, *Johannesburg Conference 2016, Report of the Committee on International Law and Sea Level Rise* (hereinafter ILA Johannesburg 2016), 17.

[87] Hayashi, 'Sea-level rise and the law of the sea: future options', 194.

[88] Vienna Convention, Art. 31(1).

highly unstable: it provides that baselines established under this provision remain effective notwithstanding subsequent regression of the low waterline.[89] The provision was originally developed for the specific case of the Ganges/Brahmaputra River Delta,[90] but scholars have indicated that it may apply for the impacts of sea-level rise as well.[91] The wording of Article 7(2) is vague:

> (2) Where because of the presence of a delta and other natural condition the coastline is highly unstable, the appropriate points may be selected along the furthest seaward extent of the low-water line and, notwithstanding subsequent regression of the low-water line, the straight baselines shall remain effective until changed by the coastal States in accordance with this Convention.

First of all, it is widely discussed whether Paragraph 2 is subordinate to Article 7(1) on *straight baselines*, and whether the requirements set out in Paragraph 1, of a coastline which is 'deeply indented and cut into, or if there is a fringe of islands along the coast', must be satisfied before Paragraph 2 can be applied to the highly unstable coastline.[92] In its study on baselines, the UN Office for Ocean Affairs and the Law of the Sea[93] stated that 'this paragraph is subordinate to paragraph 1 and is not an alternative to it. In other words, for paragraph 2 to apply, the coastline of the delta must satisfy the conditions set out in paragraph 1'.[94] Several legal scholars have similarly argued that the preliminary geographical

89 The following discussion of Article 7(2) builds partially on S. Busch, 'Sea level rise and shifting maritime limits: stable baselines as a response to unstable coastlines' (2018) 9 *Arctic Review on Law and Politics*, 174–194.

90 'Bangladesh Position on the Question of Baseline', Caracas Session 1974, Reproduced in R. Platzöder (ed.), *Third United Nations Conference on the Law of the Sea: Documents* (Oceana Publications, 1983) vol. IV, 179.

91 L. M. Alexander, 'Alternative interpretation of geographic articles in the 1982 LOS Convention' (Center for Ocean Management Studies, Kingston, University of Rhode Island), 54; Hayashi, 'Sea-level rise and the law of the sea: future options', 194; R. R. Churchill and A. V. Lowe, *The Law of the Sea*, 3rd ed. (Manchester University Press, 1999), 37–38; A. J. Roach and R. W. Smith, 'Straight baselines: the need for a universally applied norm' (2000) 31(47) *Ocean Development & International Law*, 47–80, 51; E. Bird and V. Prescott, 'Rising global sea levels and national maritime claims' (1989) 1 *Marine Policy Reports*, 189; Schofield and Freestone, 'Options to protect coastlines', 159.

92 Bird and Prescott, 'Rising global sea levels', 192; J. A. Roach and R. W. Smith, *Excessive Maritime Claims*, 3rd ed. (Brill, 2012), 67; E. D. Brown, *The International Law of the Sea* (Dartmouth Publishing Company, 1994) vol. I, 27.

93 Currently known as the United Nations Division for Ocean Affairs and the Law of the Sea (UNDOALOS).

94 UNDOALOS, *Baselines*, 24.

requirements in Article 7(1) must be fulfilled before one may proceed to Article 7(2).[95]

In 2014, the ILA Committee on Baselines under the International Law of the Sea acknowledged that there was no single agreed interpretation of Article 7,[96] but argued that the criteria are *not* cumulative:[97]

> The Committee is of the view that Article 7(2) is to be read independently, and not cumulatively, with Article 7(1) and notes the historic basis for this provision is separate and distinctive from the criteria outlined in Article 7(1).[98]

Furthermore: 'any one of these three geographic circumstances will be sufficient for the coastal State to become entitled to use the straight baseline method'.[99] The Committee observed that the objective of adopting Article 7(2) was to lower the threshold for deltaic states to establish baselines which take into account their special challenges.[100] If Paragraph 2 were deemed subordinate to Paragraph 1, requiring delta states to comply with all requirements in both provisions, that would *raise* the threshold for delta states, however.[101]

Also the interpretation of the requirements within Article 7(2) itself has proven troublesome. The paragraph is applicable for states where 'because of the presence of a delta and other natural conditions, the coastline is highly unstable'. It has been debated whether the presence of a delta *and* other

95 W. M. Reisman and G. S. Westerman, *Straight Baselines in International Maritime Boundary Delimitation* (St. Martin's Press, 1992), 101; Roach and Smith, *Excessive Maritime Claims*, 67; A. Bateman and C. Schofield, 'State practice regarding straight baselines in East Asia: legal, technical and political issues in a changing environment', paper prepared for international conference arranged by ABLOS in Monaco (2008), 4, available at www.iho.int/mtg_docs/com_wg/ABLOS/ABLOS_Conf5/Papers/Session7-Paper1-Bateman.pdf; C. Schofield and B. Sas, 'Uncovered and unstable coasts, climate change and territorial baselines in the Arctic' in S. Lalond and T. L. McDorman (eds.), *International Law and Politics of the Arctic Ocean: Essays in Honour of Donat Pharand* (Brill, 2015), 291–414 297.

96 International Law Association, *Washington Conference Report (2014)*, report by the Committee on Baselines under the International Law (hereinafter ILA Washington 2014), para. 60.

97 Ibid., paras. 24–25.

98 Ibid., para. 62. See also ILA, Committee on International Law and Sea Level Rise, *Resolution 5/2018*.

99 Ibid., paras. 24–25. See also M. N. Hoque, *The Legal and Scientific Assessment of Bangladesh's Baseline in the Context of Article 76 of the United Nations Convention on the Law of the Sea* (2005–2006), 76, available at www.un.org/depts/los/nippon/unnff_programme_home/fellows_pages/fellows_papers/hoque_0506_bangladesh.pdf, accessed 26 September 2019.

100 ILA Washington 2014, paras. 24–25.

101 Hoque, *The Legal and Scientific Assessment*, 76.

natural conditions are alternative or cumulative requirements. Although a literal interpretation of 'and' indicates that the requirements may be cumulative,[102] Bird and Prescott observe that while 'the English version and every other official translation except Russia insists on the presence of a delta [, t]he Russian version, like the original draft in the Informal Single Negotiating Text, refers to "deltas *or* other natural conditions"' (emphasis added).[103] Similarly, Churchill and Lowe note that the inclusion of the phrase 'and other natural conditions' 'appears to refer to causes of coastal instability other than deltas'.[104] The ILA Committee on Baselines also uses the terminology 'the presence of a delta *or* other natural conditions' when it lists the instances under which a coastal state can rely upon the method of straight baselines (emphasis added).[105]

Although acknowledging that the original draft of the provision may cause confusion, Stoutenburg maintains that the drafters' intent was to create a 'Bangladesh exception', suggesting that the presence of a delta is required to establish straight baselines subsequent to Article 7(2).[106] However, a similar observation may be made in relation to straight baselines in Article 7(1), often referred to as 'the Norwegian exception'. The system was primarily grounded in the *Anglo-Norwegian Fisheries case*,[107] where the United Kingdom challenged the right of Norway to claim a territorial sea not drawn along the low-water mark, but instead from a series of artificial lines linking the outermost points of the *skjaergaard* (skerry) off the Norwegian coast.[108] Many states have subsequently drawn straight baselines along their coasts, although the system of straight baselines is intended to be limited to exceptional geographic circumstances, and only a 'few States have a coastline that is anywhere near as intended or fringed with islands as that of Norway'.[109]

Although Article 7(1) was initially intended to be an exception rule, it has developed through practice into being applied as one of several main rules for establishing baselines. Therefore, it can be argued that there

102 UNDOALOS, *Baselines*, 24.

103 Bird and Prescott, 'Rising global sea levels', 192; Roach and Smith, *Excessive Maritime Claims*, 192. See also the original draft of the Revised Consolidated Text On Baselines (Provisions 4 to 20 in A/CONF. 62/C.2/WP.1) (9 April 1975), 1, available at www.cia.gov/library/readingroom/docs/CIA-RDP82S00697R000400040004-8.pdf, accessed 26 June 2019.

104 Churchill and Lowe, *The Law of the Sea*, 38.

105 ILA Washington 2014, para. 24.

106 Stoutenburg, *Disappearing Island States*, 133.

107 *Anglo-Norwegian Fisheries* case [1949] (*Order of November 9tth*) ICJ Rep. 233. See also D. R. Rothwell and T. Stephens, *The International Law of the Sea* (Hart Publishing, 2010), 43.

108 M. D. Evans, *International Law* (Oxford University Press, 2014), 655.

109 Churchill and Lowe, *The Law of the Sea*, 38.

should also be room for Paragraph 2, similar to Paragraph 1, to develop further in accordance with international law and state practice, strengthening its position as an independent provision, and encompassing more situations and states than was originally intended.

In an attempt to set aside the vagueness and obscurity in the phrase 'delta and other natural conditions', it can be argued that the decisive requirement in Article 7(2) is not the presence of a delta or other natural conditions, but rather that 'the coastline is highly unstable'. If the *unstable coastline* is the decisive criterion imbedded in Article 7(2), that instability would have to be a result of 'the presence of a delta and other natural conditions'. Prescott and Schofield discuss what would constitute 'natural conditions', noting that the term can be interpreted either as a reference to other coastal landforms or as a reference to the process affecting the size and configuration of deltas. They argue that it should be up to each state to select whether to interpret other natural conditions as landforms or processes.[110] The phrase 'natural condition' is very vague and undefined, and it can certainly be argued that sea-level rise constitutes a natural condition which makes the coastline of low-lying states unstable, thus qualifying for the application of Article 7(2).[111]

As baselines established under Article 7(2) are less vulnerable to sea-level rise, and remain effective regardless of a changing coastline, this exception rule would be well suited for contributing to maintaining the entitlement of vulnerable states exposed to sea-level rise.

13.4.4 *Permanent Continental Shelf Limits (Article 76(9))*

Although not an exception rule per se, the rules applicable to continental shelf limits are still quite exceptional compared to the rules of ambulatory limits that apply to the other maritime zones. LOSC Article 76 describes several distance criteria for the continental shelf measured from the baselines, but it also deviates from the principle of shifting maritime limits, referring to continental shelf limits as 'permanent' – and thereby presumably less vulnerable to sea-level rise. On that basis alone, the rules on permanent continental shelf limits should be explored in the context of sea-level rise.

110 V. Prescott and C. Schofield, *Maritime Political Boundaries of the World* (Brill, 2004), 154.

111 This discussion builds partially on S. Busch, 'Sea level rise and shifting maritime limits: stable baselines as a response to unstable coastlines' (2018) 9 *Arctic Review on Law and Politics*, 174–194.

Paragraph 9 specifically provides that '[t]he coastal State shall deposit with the Secretary-General of the United Nations charts and relevant information [...] *permanently* describing the outer limits of the continental shelf' (emphasis added).[112] This reference to 'permanently describing' has been subject to numerous discussions by legal scholars. There seems to be general agreement that limits so established are unalterable and accordingly not vulnerable to sea-level change.[113]

The provision does not specify if 'permanently established' limits refers only to outer continental shelf limits established pursuant to the CLCS submission procedure described in Article 76(8), or if it applies also to continental shelf limits based on the 200 nm distance criterion in Article 76(1). Neither does it specify whether the 350 nm constraint line is permanently fixed. As the Virginia Commentary observes:

> The expression 'permanently describing' the outer limits indicates that once the outer limits are established they are not to be changed. In this context, it reiterates the provision of the ultimate sentence of paragraph 8, that the limits established by the coastal State on the basis of the recommendations of the Commission on the Limits of the Continental Shelf shall be 'final and binding'.[114]

What can be deduced from the previous statement? It appears to suggest that the permanency requirement is closely linked to the provision on continental shelf limits beyond 200 nm from the baselines. This may well be the meaning of the negotiating parties, as it ensures stable limits between the continental shelf subject to national jurisdiction, and the deep seabed area as the common heritage of mankind. However, also the 200 nm continental shelf limit measured from the baselines constitutes such a limit towards the Area, and the same

112 LOSC, Art. 76(9).

113 International Law Association, Committee on the Outer Continental Shelf, Berlin Conference Paper, *Legal Issues of the Outer Continental Shelf* (2004), 23; International Law Association, Committee on the Outer Continental Shelf, Toronto Conference Paper, *Legal Issues of the Outer Continental Shelf* (2006), 15; T. L. McDorman, 'The Role of the Commission on the Limits of the Continental Shelf: a technical body in a political world' (2002) 17 *The International Journal of Marine and Coastal Law*, 310–324, 315; Soons, 'The effects of a rising sea level', 217; Caron, 'When law makes climate change worse', 635; R. Rayfuse, 'W(h)ither Tuvalu? International law and disappearing states' (2009) *University of New South Wales Faculty of Law Research Series*, Paper 9, 3; Hayashi, 'Sea level rise and the law of the sea: legal and policy options'. See however arguments for the opposite in B. B. Jia, 'Effect of legal issues, actual or implicit, upon the work of the CLCS: suspensive or without prejudice' (2012) 11 *Chinese Journal of International Law*, 107–126, at 114, para. 22.

114 S. N. Nandan and S. Rosenne (eds.), *United Nations Convention on the Law of the Sea 1982: A Commentary* (Martinus Nijhoff, 1993), Vol. II, 882–883, para. 76.18(1).

reasoning is applicable for the ordinary continental shelf limit. Another argument for interpreting Paragraph 9 as applying solely to limits beyond 200 nm is the fact that such limits are established on the basis of geomorphologic criteria, not on the basis of the baseline.

The wording of Article 76(9) may also be read as a continuation of the 'final and binding' requirement included in Paragraph 8, but it should be noted that the reference to 'permanently describing' is included in a separate paragraph in the Article, not as part of paragraph (8). Paragraph (9) makes no distinction between the continental shelf within or beyond 200 nm, but merely refers to 'the outer limits of the continental shelf', a phrase that encompasses all continental shelf delineation limits. In fact, none of the provisions in Article 76, except for paragraph 8, makes any distinction between the 200 nm continental shelf, and the continental shelf beyond such distance – and neither does Article 83 on continental shelf delimitation. That only continental shelf limits beyond 200 nm may be permanently established, while the ordinary 200 nm continental shelf limit will shift apace with ambulatory baselines, would have no legal basis, and seems unjust. Accordingly, the effect of Article 76(9) is that *all* continental shelf limits are permanently established, and will not be affected by sea-level rise and shifting baselines. In practice, this means that when the sea level rises, parts of the seabed previously subject to the territorial sea regime will be subject to the continental shelf regime; and that no part of the Area will be subject to national jurisdiction, as the outer limit remains unaffected.

Although Article 77 provides that the rights of the coastal state over the continental shelf 'do not depend on occupation, effective or notional, or any express proclamation', Article 76(9) seemingly requires certain action before the limits of the continental shelf may be considered as 'permanently established'. Charts and relevant information, including geodetic data, permanently describing such limits must be deposited with the UN Secretary-General. If the coastal state does not deposit charts and relevant information describing the limits, it is submitted that the limit to the extent it is established on the basis of a distance criterion may still be altered.

Article 77 applies also to vulnerable coastal states with a continental shelf limited to 200 nm. As these states are not required to go through the CLCS-submission procedure, and their entitlement exists regardless of any express proclamation, it is not evident that they need to submit charts and information to the Secretary-General in accordance with Article 76(9). However, inherent entitlement is not the same as permanent limits. It is only their entitlement that is made inherent in Article 77, not the geographical extent of such entitlement. The latter is secured by the drawing of specific charts deposited with the Secretary-General. For a state with a continental margin narrower than 200 nm, it is particularly important to take advantage of this opportunity in order to achieve permanency for at least one of its maritime zones. These permanently established continental shelf limits should then remain stable even if the coastline and baselines may change.

For states with a broad continental margin, Paragraph 9 requires that the process of establishing continental shelf limits in accordance with Article 76(8) be completed before the limits may be submitted to the Secretary-General and achieve permanent status. As discussed in Section 13.3.2.3, this will be problematic for several broad-margin states vulnerable to sea-level rise: they are stuck in the CLCS queue, and can expect at least ten to twenty years to pass before they receive recommendations that can create basis for their permanent outer limits.[115]

For particularly vulnerable states, establishing permanent continental shelf limits accordingly becomes a tactical concern. Assuming that the 'permanency' described in Article 76(9) is intended to make the limit unalterable, in order to secure stability and predictability, a state cannot first establish permanent continental shelf limits at 200 nm, and then change these when it receive CLCS recommendations as to the location of the limits beyond 200 nm. Such states must consider whether they are better of securing a permanent 200 nm limit today, or if they dare wait for the CLCS recommendations before they establish permanent continental shelf limits, and risk losing the basis for their entitlement in the meantime. Here it should be noted that this primarily affects states that are either island states at risk of being completely submerged or rendered uninhabitable, or other low-lying states that base their continental shelf limits on the 350 nm constraint line. For other low-lying states, geomorphological factors will determine any entitlement to the shelf beyond 200 nm – and these are unaffected by sea-level rise.[116]

13.4.5 *Summarizing Remarks*

Although the earlier discussions do not provide any definite conclusions, the analysis of LOSC Articles 7(2) and 76(9) offers arguments pulling in the same direction: towards a more strategic application of relevant treaty provisions. These provisions can arguably be used as an immediate

[115] R. Macnab, 'Third-party reactions to continental shelf submissions and their treatment by the Commission on the Limits of the Continental Shelf' in C. R. Symmons (ed.), *Selected Contemporary Issues in the Law of the Sea* (Brill, 2011), 285–304, 301; S. Busch, *Establishing Continental Shelf Limits Beyond 200 Nautical Miles by the Coastal State: A Right of Involvement for Other States* (Brill, 2016), 381–385.

[116] LOSC, Art. 76.

response to sea-level rise, without significantly deviating from their ordinary meaning, object and purpose. Article 7(2) is indeed vague, but that allows some leeway in interpretation. Based on the understanding that baselines established under Article 7(2) are not required to also fulfil the conditions in Article 7(1), particularly vulnerable states with coastlines rendered highly unstable by natural conditions, such as sea-level rise, can certainly argue the need for establishing more long-term baselines that remain effective notwithstanding subsequent changes of the low-water line, with the same underlying reasoning as the Bay of Bengal states when the rule was first negotiated. Moreover, the development of the straight baseline rule, from being an exception rule to becoming almost the new normal, provides a solid argument that there is also room for expanding the scope of application for Article 7(2) as well.

Although this discussion of Article 76(9) on permanent continental shelf limits does not explicitly suggest a re-interpretation of the provision, it does encourage vulnerable states to make deliberate choices in seeking to ensure permanency of their maritime entitlements. To establish permanent continental shelf limits at 200 nm in cases where the continental shelf continues beyond that distance is not optimal, but is at least better than the worst-case scenario.

13.5 CONCLUSIONS: CAN THE LOSC IN ITS CURRENT FORM MITIGATE THE CONSEQUENCES OF SEA-LEVEL RISE?

The major weakness of the LOSC in relation to today's challenge of rising sea levels is the rule of ambulatory baselines, which contributes to loss of territory, relocation of maritime zones, uncertainty and instability. Legal scholars agree that the issue is best addressed by maintaining either the baselines or the outer limits of maritime zones, even if the sea level rises after such limits are established. The ILA Committee has proposed combining these approaches, and freezing baselines and maritime limits when 'they have been properly determined'. Although agreeing that the current main rule of ambulatory baselines and shifting maritime limits is very unfortunate, this author argues that the ILA Committee may well have employed an overly narrow approach for addressing the problems in the law of baselines, by focusing merely on the main rule in Article 5, without analysing the exception rules and other relevant rules on maritime limits – in particular, those relevant for continental shelf limits. The result is that ILA 5/2018 proposes a solution that does not really solve the problem, but (presumably unintentionally) shifts the problem to another segment within the law of the sea. If baselines and maritime limits may be maintained only after having been properly determined, that would mean that several vulnerable low-lying broad-margin states cannot achieve such status until CLCS consideration is delivered, which may take at least ten to twenty years.

On the bright side, this discussion indicates that there exists a certain flexibility in the regime for law of baselines, allowing for a broader interpretation of existing rules without the need to amend the LOSC. Although climate-change considerations were not part of the negotiating parties' intent during UNCLOS III, the stability of oceans and avoidance of new disputes surely lie within the overall purpose of the Convention as set out in its Preamble.

Low-lying coastal states whose coastlines are highly unstable due to sea-level rise should arguably be allowed to establish baselines under Article 7(2) even if they are not delta states, and to maintain such baseline regardless of subsequent sea-level rise. However, this will not afford a solution for small island states at threat of being submerged. Even if baselines have been established subject to Article 7(2), this will not allow a disappearing island to maintain its economic zone and continental shelf as a result of Article 121(3).

Therefore, for a small island state at risk of losing entitlement to their EEZ and continental shelf as measured from one or more islands if such island is rendered uninhabitable, it is advantageous to deposit charts describing the permanent continental shelf limits to the UN Secretary-General in accordance with Article 76(9). For limits drawn along the 200 nm limit, permanency may be achieved at the time of deposit of the continental shelf limits to the Secretary-General, whereas limits based on the existence of a continental margin beyond 200 nm would have to be qualified by the CLCS before such status may be achieved.

For low-lying coastal states, establishing permanent deltaic baselines and permanent continental shelf limits would secure stable maritime limits, including the limits of the territorial sea and EEZ. For a small island state, permanent baselines and continental shelf limits would secure entitlement to both a territorial sea and continental shelf – but, as a result of Article 121(3), would not secure entitlement to an EEZ measured off the island if that island can no longer sustain human habitation or economic life.

Although not providing a permanent solution to *all* the consequences of sea-level rise on maritime limits and entitlement, this wider application of already existing provisions of the LOSC can offer a good short-term response to the threat of sea-level rise as regards the maritime entitlements of vulnerable coastal states.

14

Integrating Climate Change in the Governance of Areas beyond National Jurisdiction

Christian Prip

14.1 CLIMATE CHANGE IN AREAS BEYOND NATIONAL JURISDICTION

As for any other environmental impact on oceans, the impacts of climate change on the marine environment (described in Chapter 2) occur across jurisdictional boundaries.[1] While anthropocentric harm to the marine environment often occurs close to the coast, this is not the case for climate change related impacts often occurring from the atmosphere. High Seas make up 40 per cent of the surface of the planet, comprise 64 per cent of the surface of the oceans and nearly 95 per cent of its volume. Recent research has shown that the remote deep and open oceans host a major part of the world's biodiversity.[2] It is estimated that high seas ecosystems are responsible for almost half of the total biological productivity of the global ocean, and that

[1] United Nations Convention on Law of the Sea (LOSC), Montego Bay, 10 December 1982, in force 16 November 1994, 1833 UNTS 397, distinguishes between two components of areas beyond national jurisdiction: 'the Area' and the 'high seas'. The Area is defined 'as the seabed and ocean floor and subsoil thereof, beyond the limits of national jurisdiction' (LOSC, Art. 1). The Area and its mineral resources have a specific legal status as 'common heritage of mankind' implying that states shall not claim or exercise sovereignty or sovereign rights over any part of the Area or its resources, and that activities in the Area must be conducted for the benefit of mankind as a whole (LOSC, Arts 136, 137 and 140). An International Seabed Authority (ISA) is established as an intergovernmental body to regulate and control all mineral-related activities in the Area.

The High Seas encompass the water column beyond the Exclusive Economic Zones of coastal states and are governed by the traditional freedoms of the sea which include navigation, overflight, fishing, scientific research, laying of submarine cables and pipelines, and construction of artificial islands and other installations permitted under international law (LOSC, Arts 86 and 87).

[2] M. Vierros and S. Arico, 'Governance of Marine Areas Beyond National Jurisdictions', Our World, United Nations University, 14 March 2012.

nearly half a billion of tonnes of carbon (the equivalent of more than 1.5 billion tonnes of carbon dioxide) are captured and stored by high seas ecosystems annually, a value of between 74 and 222 billion US$.[3] Since the adoption of the LOSC in 1982, human activities in areas beyond national jurisdiction (ABNJ) have increased considerably, and climate change with its main stressors, ocean warming deoxygenation and ocean acidification, are expected to compound the impacts on high seas environment.[4] As further discussed in Chapter 2, besides the main climate change stressors, there is evidence of large amounts of the strong greenhouse gas, methane, trapped in the seabed which may be released by human activities.

This chapter discusses if and the extent to which LOSC and other legal instruments address climate change impacts on ABNJ and contribute to mitigation endeavours. Furthermore, it will analyse a current legal process that provides an opportunity to fill out gaps in this regard, namely the negotiations in the Intergovernmental Conference on an international legally binding instrument under the United Nations Convention on the Law of the Sea on the conservation and sustainable use of marine biological diversity of areas beyond national jurisdiction (BBNJ). Finally, the chapter discusses the role of Environmental Impact Assessment (EIA) as a particular important legal tool to address climate change impacts in ABNJ.

14.2 THE LEGAL FRAMEWORK RELEVANT TO CLIMATE CHANGE IMPACTS IN ABNJ

The general duties of states stipulated in LOSC Part XII to protect and preserve the marine environment, also apply to the high seas and the seabed beyond national jurisdiction, the Area. This is an indication that the freedoms of the sea are not absolute rights, but subject to several limitations and corresponding duties. Part XII does not refer to climate change related impacts. This, however, does not imply that climate change induced harmful impacts cannot be considered. As discussed in Chapter 4 of this volume, Part XII in principle applies to climate change insofar as it has or is likely to have deleterious effects on the marine environment. Chapter 3 of this volume describes how this is often the case. In this case, the requirement of states in Article 192 'to protect and preserve the marine environment' includes

3 G. Wright et al., 'The long and winding road continues: towards a new agreement on high seas governance' (2015) Study N°01/16, L'Institut du développement durable et des relations internationales (IDDRI) Paris, France.

4 Wright et al., 'The long and winding road continues'.

preventing and combating climate change. Accordingly, Article 194 which requires states to take all measures necessary to prevent pollution from any source, including from or through the atmosphere, should be interpreted to include prevention of greenhouse gas emissions. Also, Article 207 requiring states to adopt laws and regulations to prevent, reduce and control pollution from land-based sources is relevant for greenhouse gas emissions and applicable to ABNJ.

Essentially, LOSC provisions on protection and preservation of the marine environment, require states to exercise due diligence, as explained in Chapter 4 of this volume. A key component in this context is to conduct EIA as stipulated in Article 206. This provision is further addressed subsequently.

LOSC Articles 117–120 include provisions applicable only to high seas on conservation and management of living marine resources. Besides taking measures directly at harvested species to maintain or restore their populations,[5] States shall take into consideration 'the effects on species associated with or dependent upon harvested species with a view to maintaining or restoring populations of such associated or dependent species above levels at which their reproduction may become seriously threatened'.[6] Specifically important for due diligence in the context of areas that are not under the jurisdiction of any state, states are required to cooperate in the conservation and management of living resources in the high seas.[7] While the general provisions on environmental protection in LOSC, Part XII, should be interpreted to cover protection of living marine resources and biodiversity in general, the articles here should be seen mainly in the context of maintaining commercial fishery and maximize its yields. Marine Capture Fisheries is further addressed in Chapter 11 of this volume.

As regards the Area, Article 145 establishes that states shall take measures to protect the marine environment from harmful effects which may arise from such activities. To this end, the International Seabed Authority (ISA) shall adopt rules and regulations both on the prevention, reduction and control of pollution and other hazards and on the protection and conservation of natural resources of the Area and the prevention of damage to marine flora and fauna.

Environmentally harmful activities in the Area is also covered by Article 209 stipulating that states shall adopt laws and regulations to combat pollution from activities in the Area under their jurisdiction and control and establish

5 LOSC, Art. 119(1)(a).
6 LOSC, Art. 119(1)(b).
7 LOSC, Art. 118.

international regulation to that effect. Requirements for EIA in the Area will be addressed in Section 14.4.

Since the effects of climate change on the deep-sea environment are still not well understood, and since climate change mitigation activities in the oceans are still experimental in character, the LOSC provisions on marine scientific research are also relevant. Article 87 lays down the freedom of scientific research in the high seas subject to the provisions of Part VI on the continental shelf and Part XIII on Marine Scientific Research. Article 257 in Part XIII reinforces this freedom and Article 256 provides a similar freedom of scientific research on the Area. Marine scientific research activities are subject to the marine environmental protection provisions in Part XII.

A number of other international instruments than LOSC are applicable to the protection of the marine environment in ABNJ although they are mostly covering a particular sector or issue, but like LOSC without any explicit reference to climate change.[8]

The Convention on Biological Diversity (CBD) is a comprehensive framework convention laying down three objectives: (1) the conservation of biodiversity; (2) the sustainable use of its components; and (3) the fair and equitable sharing of the benefits arising out of the utilization of genetic resources.[9] Its definition of biodiversity is the diversity of ecosystems, species and genetic diversity.[10] The CBD covers terrestrial as well as marine biodiversity, but its jurisdictional authority over ABNJ is not quite clear.[11] The CBD lays down that in the case of components of biological diversity, its authority is restricted to areas within the limits of national jurisdiction of its Parties, while in the case of 'processes and activities, regardless of where their effects occur, carried out under its jurisdiction or control' it extends to ABNJ.[12] It also includes an obligation for Parties to cooperate in respect of ABNJ.[13] In practice, states have viewed LOSC as the lead legal instrument for biodiversity in ABNJ also on international cooperation as manifested by LOSC hosting the ongoing negotiations

8 Fishing is addressed under the auspices of FAO by different legally binding and non-binding instruments (see this volume, Chapter 11), and shipping is regulated in the framework of IMO by different conventions (see this volume, Chapter 6).

9 Convention on Biological Diversity, Rio de Janeiro, 5 June 1992, 1760 UNTS 69, Article 1.

10 CBD, Art. 2.

11 R. Wolfrum and N. Matz, 'The interplay of the United Nations Convention on the Law of the Sea and the Convention on Biological Diversity' (2000) 4 *Max Planck Yearbook of United Nations Law*, 445–480.

12 CBD, Art. 4(a) and (b).

13 CBD, Art. 5.

towards an international legally binding instrument on biodiversity in ABNJ discussed further. The CBD role in relation to ABNJ has mainly been the identification Ecologically or Biologically Significant Marine Areas (EBSAs) in areas both within and beyond national jurisdiction.[14] Moreover, CBD has adopted guidelines for marine EIAs applying also to ABNJ and climate change impacts and adopted decisions on climate change mitigation activities in the oceans as further described subsequently.

Of other biodiversity-related global instruments applicable in ABNJ are the International Convention on the Regulation of Whaling, the Convention on International Trade in Endangered Species (CITES) the Convention on Migratory Species (CMS) and agreements thereunder on the conservation of albatrosses and petrels and small cetaceans.

Few regional sea instruments with provisions on environmental protection are applicable to ABNJ. These include the Noumea Convention (for the South Pacific),[15] the OSPAR Convention (for the North-East Atlantic),[16] the Barcelona Convention (for the Mediterranean)[17] and the Madrid Protocol (for Antarctica).[18]

In summary, LOSC and the relatively few other legal instruments applicable to marine ABNJ do not include specific provisions to protect the marine environment against the effects of climate change or to contribute to climate change mitigation. However, their more general requirements of states to protect the marine environment, including living resources, could be interpreted to include the well-documented harmful effects of climate change on ABNJ. Very limited attention has so far been given to climate change effects on ABNJ under these instruments. An obvious opportunity to change this situation is the ongoing UN process of negotiating a legally binding instrument on the conservation and sustainable use of marine biodiversity of areas beyond national jurisdiction (BBNJ).

[14] EBSA website, www.cbd.int/ebsa/; D. C. Dunn et al., 'The convention on Biological Diversity's ecologically or biologically significant areas: origins, development, and current status' (2014) 49 *Marine Policy* 137–145, http://dx.doi.org/10.1016/j.marpol.2013.12.002i.

[15] Convention for the Protection of Natural Resources and Environment of the South Pacific Region, Noumea, 25 November 1986, (1987) 26 ILM 38.

[16] Convention for the Protection of the Marine Environment of the North-East Atlantic, Paris, 22 September 1992, (1993) 2354 UNTS 67.

[17] Convention for the Protection of the Mediterranean Sea Against Pollution, Barcelona, 16 February 1976, (1976) 15 ILM 290.

[18] Protocol on Environmental Protection to the Antarctic treaty, Madrid, 14 October 1991, (1991) 30 ILM 1461.

14.3 THE PROCESS OF ENSURING MARINE BIODIVERSITY IN AREAS BEYOND NATIONAL JURISDICTION

14.3.1 *Towards an International Legally Binding Instrument on the Conservation and Sustainable Use of Marine Biodiversity of Areas beyond National Jurisdiction*

The legal framework on the protection of the marine environment in ABNJ, as outlined earlier, is widely viewed as inadequate to meet the environmental pressures of increased human activity mainly in the form of pollution and over-exploitation on marine living resources.[19] The increased awareness on the effects of global warming only reinforces this assumption. First, the obligations of Part XII are very broad. Their structure provides for, and even depends upon, the dynamic evolution of the rules to achieve environmental objectives,[20] and this evolution has yet to take place, for example, in the form of regulatory frameworks for ecosystem-based management, the designation of marine protected areas and minimum standards for EIA. Second, the regulatory framework of ABNJ, actually in place, provides a patchy framework of different agreements and institutions with limited formal cooperation and coherence between their management measures.[21]

The concerns on deficiencies in the regulatory and governance framework have mainly been raised in relation to biodiversity in ABNJ along with growing knowledge and awareness that the high seas and deep ocean beneath them host much more marine life than previously known. For example, underwater seamounts and hydrothermal vents have been found to be unique biodiversity rich ecosystems in ABNJ cradling some of the oldest organisms on the planet.

19 R. Rayfuse and R. M. Warner, 'Securing a sustainable future for the oceans beyond national jurisdiction: the legal basis for an integrated cross-sectoral regime for high seas governance for the 21st century' (2008) 23 (3) *International Journal of Marine and Coastal Law*, 399–421; D. Freestone, 'International governance, responsibility and management of areas beyond national jurisdiction' (2012) 27(2) *The International Journal of Marine and Coastal Law*; K. M. Gjerde, 'Challenges to protecting the marine environment beyond national jurisdiction' (2012) 27(4) *The International Journal of Marine and Coastal Law* 839–847; E. Druel and K. M. Gjerde, 'Sustaining marine life beyond boundaries: options for an implementing agreement for marine biodiversity beyond national jurisdiction under the United Nations Convention on the Law of the Sea' (2013) 49 *Marine Policy* 90–97.

20 A. M. Hubert and N. Craik, 'Towards normative coherence in the international law of the sea for the conservation and sustainable use of marine biological diversity of areas beyond national jurisdiction', The blog of the K. G. Jebsen Centre for the Law of the Sea, 1 February 2018, available at http://site.uit.no/jclos/files/2018/02/JCLOS-Coherence-Blog-Hubert-Craik-v-2.pdf.

21 See this volume, Chapter 15.

With the growing awareness of biodiversity in ABNJ also came awareness of the serious threats to biodiversity caused by the last decades' increasing demand for exploration and exploitation of ABNJ that previously were largely beyond the reach of human activities.[22]

These concerns have led to a process that has elapsed for more than a decade and which may continue for many more years towards an implementing legally binding instrument under LOSC on the conservation and sustainable use of biodiversity in BBNJ. In 2004, United Nations General Assembly established the Ad Hoc Open-ended Informal Working Group to study issues relating to the conservation and sustainable use of biodiversity beyond national jurisdiction. Based on its recommendations, UNGA established a Preparatory Committee which in 2017 came up with substantive recommendations on the elements of a draft text of a legally binding instrument on BBNJ under LOSC. The General Assembly followed up by adopting a resolution to convene an Intergovernmental Conference (IGC) to negotiate the text of an implementing agreement on the conservation and sustainable use of BBNJ.[23] The IGC meet initially for four sessions with one in 2018, two in 2019 and one in 2020.

Since 2011, the discussions in the different UN forums on BBNJ instrument has been focused on a package of four topics: (1) marine genetic resources, including questions on the sharing of benefits, (2) measures such as area-based management tools, including marine protected areas, (3) EIAs and (4) capacity-building and the transfer of marine technology. The General Assembly resolution establishes that the IGC negotiations shall also address this package 'in particular, together and as a whole'.[24]

14.3.2 *Climate Change in the BBNJ Process*

While it has been increasingly acknowledged that climate change is both a direct driver of marine biodiversity loss and exacerbates other drivers, climate change and its impact has played a modest role in the BBNJ process, although the attention has somehow increased in the later phase. The initial Ad Hoc Open-ended Informal Working Group at its second meeting in 2008 identified impacts of climate change among a number of anthropogenic impacts on marine biodiversity beyond national jurisdiction which require

[22] D. J. McCauley et al., 'Marine defaunation: animal loss in the global ocean' (2015) 347 *Science*, 1255641.

[23] UNGA Res. 72/249 (2017).

[24] Ibid.

particular attention and to which the least developed and small island developing states, were particularly vulnerable. At the same meeting, concerns were raised over emerging climate change mitigation activities and their possible impact on ocean biodiversity. These include carbon sequestration and large-scale ocean iron fertilization.[25] The third meeting of the Working Group in 2010 reiterated that human pressures on the marine environment, including as a result of climate change, were increasing and impacting the long-term health, resilience and productivity of marine ecosystems and marine biodiversity.[26] The final report of the Working Group from 2015, with a recommendation to develop a legally binding instrument, does not refer to climate change impacts and how the instrument could address them.[27]

Attention to climate change impacts grew in the four meetings of the Preparatory Committee held in 2016 and 2017 and at the first and second meetings of the IGC in 2018 and 2019. It was introduced that building resilience to the effects of climate change could be a general consideration for decisions made and actions taken under the new instrument, and that decisions should not exacerbate or hasten the adverse impacts of climate change, especially upon Small Island Developing States.[28] It was further acknowledged that the designation of marine protected areas could include consideration of climate change.[29] The thorniest issue in relation to climate change impacts is whether and how cumulative impacts should be included in the EIA procedure laid down by the instrument.[30] These are the effects caused by the combined results of past, current and future activities and which could include climate change effects such as ocean warming, deoxygenation and ocean acidification.[31] (See Chapters 2 and 11.)

25 UN Doc. A/63/79 (2008), with a summary of discussions at the 2nd meeting of the Working Group 28 April to 2 May 2008.

26 See UN Doc. A/65/68 (2010), with a summary of discussions at the 3rd meeting of the Working Group 1 to 5 February 2010.

27 UN Doc. A/69/780 (2015), Annex. Outcome of the Ad Hoc Open-ended Informal Working Group to study issues relating to the conservation and sustainable use of marine biological diversity beyond areas of national jurisdiction and Co-Chairs' summary of discussions.

28 Preparatory Committee established by General Assembly resolution 69/292, 'Chair's streamlined non-paper on elements of a draft text of an international legally-binding instrument under the United Nations Convention on the Law of the Sea on the conservation and sustainable use of marine biological diversity of areas beyond national jurisdiction' (2017), para. 91.

29 Ibid., para. 117.

30 Ibid., para. 162.

31 In the draft text of an agreement prepared by the IGC President for its third meeting in August 2019, cumulative effects are suggested defined as 'impacts on the same ecosystems

There appears to be general support on the view that cumulative impacts could be taken into account, but there is no consensus on whether in that context there should be a specific reference to climate change, ocean acidification, and deoxygenation.[32] A related unresolved issue is whether the instrument should address strategic environmental impact assessments (SEA) which by their nature are likely to include considerations on cumulative effects.[33] These issues are yet to be resolved by the IGC.

Although climate change impact overall has been a marginal topic in the BBNJ process, the instrument, if finalized, may still offer a needed legal framework to fill out existing LOSC provisions in relation to regulation of climate change impacts on marine ABNJ. Obviously, this would be more the case if climate change impacts were explicitly referred to by the instrument, but as discussed above these implicitly fall under LOSC Part XII.

It could be argued that an instrument specifically dealing with biodiversity will only cover a subset of what is needed to protect against climate change impacts in ABNJ – not the marine environment as such. This, however, depends on how the term biodiversity is understood and defined, and this is rather broad in the BBNJ context. Most likely, the understanding of biodiversity in the BBNJ instrument will correspond to the definition of the CBD thereby covering the diversity of ecosystems, species as well as the genetic diversity.[34] Adding to the broad understanding, the instrument like the CBD will address both the conservation and sustainable use of marine biological diversity.[35] Different from the BBNJ context, the CBD in its Article 1 on objectives refers to sustainable use of the 'components' of biodiversity, but there are no indications that the omission of 'components' in the BBNJ context implies another

resulting from different activities, including past, present or reasonably foreseeable activities, or from the repetition of similar activities over time, including climate change, ocean acidification and related impacts'. See UN Doc. A/CONF.232/2019/6, available at undocs .org/a/conf.232/2019/6.

32 UN Doc. A/CONF.232/2019/CRP.1 for the third meeting of the IGC, 19–30 August 2019, 'Drafting proposals submitted by delegations'.

33 Ibid.

34 CBD, Art. 2: 'Biological diversity' means the variability among living organisms from all sources including, inter alia, terrestrial, marine and other aquatic ecosystems and the ecological complexes of which they are part; this includes diversity within species, between species and of ecosystems. There has been an ongoing consensus in the BBNJ process that definitions would need to be consistent with those of other relevant instruments such as the CBD, see Preparatory Committee, 'Chair's streamlined non-paper'.

35 UNGA Res. 72/249 (2017).

understanding of what is to be sustainably used and which could then be everything living.

As for the CBD, the BBNJ instrument is likely to apply an ecosystem approach based on ecosystem-based management. This has been defined in the BBNJ process as 'an integrated approach to management that considers the entire ecosystem, including all stakeholders and their activities, and resulting stressors and pressures with direct or indirect effects on the ecosystem under consideration'. The goal of ecosystem-based management is to maintain or rebuild an ecosystem to a healthy, productive and resilient condition through, inter alia, the development and implementation of cross-sectoral ecosystem-level management plans.[36] In this context, the notion of Ecosystem Services, has also been addressed in the BBNJ process.[37] The *Millennium Ecosystem Assessment* from 2005 defines Ecosystem Services simply as 'the benefits people derive from ecosystems' and groups them into four broad categories: *provisioning*, *regulating*, *supporting* and *cultural*. Climate regulation, and with that the oceans' ability to sequester greenhouse gasses, is classified as a regulating service.[38] With this broad understanding of biodiversity, the instrument would implicitly encompass LOSC Part XII, 'the protection and preservation of the marine environment' regarding ABNJ.

At the time of writing, the negotiations have just only reached the point of text negotiations, and while there seems to be consensus on generally acknowledging climate change to be considered in the conservation and sustainable use of marine biodiversity, more specific coverage of climate change issues have either not been addressed or have been contested. The latter applies to whether and the extent to which climate change impacts should be taken into account when conducting EIAs, a legal tool of particular relevance for addressing climate change impacts.

The following will discuss options for operationalizing and strengthening the current legal framework for conducting EIA in ABNJ through incorporating climate change related impacts. This could be as part of the future BBNJ instrument, or as a distinct instrument under LOSC.[39]

36 Preparatory Committee, 'Chair's streamlined non-paper', paras. 9 and 24.

37 Ibid., paras. 1 and 179.

38 Millennium Ecosystem Assessment, *Ecosystems and Human Well-being: Synthesis* (Island Press, 2005).

39 A. Elferink, 'Environmental impact assessment in areas beyond national jurisdiction' (2012) 27 *International Journal of Marine and Coastal Law*, 449–480.

14.4 THE ROLE OF ENVIRONMENTAL IMPACT ASSESSMENT IN AREAS BEYOND NATIONAL JURISDICTION

14.4.1 *EIA as a Legal Tool to Incorporate Climate Change-Related Impacts in the Protection of ABNJ*

Before providing a rough non-exhaustive overview of the legal framework regarding EIA in ABNJ, it should be noted that EIA is not the only relevant legal tool for addressing climate change induced impacts in ABNJ. Chapters 6 and 11 which address the marine based industries, shipping and marine capture fisheries, and their means to contribute to climate change mitigation and adaptation are relevant for areas within as well as beyond national jurisdiction. The same applies to Chapter 10 on the use of marine protected areas and other area-based management tools as means.

The International Court of Justice (ICJ) in the *Pulp Mills* case has held that EIA may be considered international customary law when an activity may have a significant adverse effect in a transboundary context 'in particular on a shared resource'.[40] Referring to this judgment, the International Tribunal for the Law of the Sea (ITLOS) has stated that it may also apply to activities with an impact on the environment in an area beyond the limits of national jurisdiction, and that the ICJ's references to 'shared resources' may also apply to resources that are the common heritage of mankind.[41] This requirement of customary international law does not extend to the precise scope and content of EIA.[42] This is to be further specified in national and international legal instruments and on which there are diverging views with regard to ABNJ as it has been shown in the BBNJ process. Article 206 of LOSC does not come much closer in terms of scope and content and leaves considerable discretion to individual states and international implementing instruments.[43] The obligation of states is 'as far as practicable' to assess the effects of activities when they 'have reasonable grounds for believing that planned activities under their jurisdiction and control may cause substantial pollution of or significant and harmful changes to the marine environment'. It does not provide details on minimum standards or procedural requirements except that states shall

[40] *Pulp Mills on the River Uruguay (Argentina* v. *Uruguay) (Judgment)* [2010] ICJ Rep. 14, 83, 204.

[41] *Responsibilities and obligations of States with respect to activities in the Area (v)* (Advisory Opinion) [2011] ITLOS Rep. 10, 148.

[42] *Pulp Mills* case, para. 205.

[43] Institut du Développement Durable et des Relations Internationales (IDDRI), E. Druel, *Environmental impact assessments in areas beyond national jurisdiction: identification of gaps and possible ways forward* (2013).

publish their results of the assessments. Also, it leaves it to the discretion of states to decide whether it shall apply solely to project-based EIA or also Strategic Environmental Assessment (SEA), the assessment of strategic policy decisions further 'upstream' in the planning process than EIA, and whether the requirement includes assessment of cumulative environmental effects.[44] These are key outstanding questions in the design of an EIA mechanism under the BBNJ instrument. Related to Article 206 is Article 204 requiring states to monitor the risks or effects of pollution. While many states can be said to have implemented Articles 206 and 204 for areas under their jurisdiction, this is much less the case for ABNJ.[45]

On EIA in the Area, LOSC Article 145 implies a need to assess the impacts of seabed mining activities.[46] This is further specified in the Implementation Agreement on Part XI of the Convention adopted in 1994.[47] On that basis, the ISA has adopted three sets of regulations for the exploration of different types of mineral deposits and recommendations for EIA together referred to as the 'Mining Code'.[48] The ISA has not adopted EIA regulations for other uses of the seabed than mining, and the Mining Code does not refer to cumulative effects.

The CBD includes an obligation 'as far as possible and as appropriate' for both EIA and SEA.[49] The CBD in 2002 adopted a set of guiding principles

44 G. Sander, 'International legal obligations for environmental impact assessment and strategic environmental assessment in the Arctic Ocean' (2016) 31(1) *The International Journal of Marine and Coastal Law* 88–119.

45 Elferink, 'Environmental Impact Assessment'.

46 See J. M. Durden et al., 'Environmental impact assessment process for deep-sea mining in "the Area"' (2017) 87 *Marine Policy*, 194–202.

47 Agreement relating to the implementation of Part XI of the United Nations Convention on the Law of the Sea of 10 December 1982, New York, 28 July 1994, 1836 UNTS 3, Annex, section 1.7.

48 (1) International Seabed Authority, Regulations on Prospecting and Exploration for Polymetallic Nodules in the Area, ISBA/6/A/18 (13 July 2000), amended by ISBA/19/A/9; ISBA/19/A/12 (25 July 2013) and ISBA/20/A/9 (24 July 2014) (Nodules Exploration Regulations), 2014.

(2) International Seabed Authority, Regulations on Prospecting and Exploration for Polymetallic Sulphides in the Area, ISBA/16/A/12/Rev.1 (15 November 2010), amended by ISBA/19/A/12 (25 July 2013) and ISBA/20/A/10 (24 July 2014) (Sulphides Exploration Regulations), 2014.

(3) International Seabed Authority, Regulations on Prospecting and Exploration for Cobalt-rich Ferromanganese Crusts in the Area, ISBA/18/A/11 (27 July 2012), amended by ISBA/19/A/12 (25 July 2013) (Crusts Exploration Regulations), 2013.

(4) International Seabed Authority, Recommendations for the guidance of contractors for the assessment of the possible environmental impacts arising from exploration for marine minerals in the Area, ISBA/19/LTC/8, Kingston, Jamaica, 2013.

49 CBD, Art. 14(1)(a) and (b).

for incorporating biodiversity into EIA and SEA. These were revised and updated 2006[50] and further annotated in 2012 to incorporate marine issues. The guidelines explicitly include ABNJ and the cumulative effects of environmental changes such as climate change and ocean acidification in EIA as so far the only global instrument – albeit it is a soft law instrument.[51] The EIA requirements on dumping of waste and ocean fertilization in accordance with the London Dumping Convention and its Protocol will be addressed further.

Some regional seas conventions that cover ABNJ also include EIA requirements. The most detailed EIA requirements are found in The Protocol on Environmental Protection to the Antarctic Treaty, Madrid Protocol.[52]

An important starting point in relation to any EIA, is to establish a thorough scientific knowledge base on the relevant marine ecosystem to most effectively inform the assessment of the risks or effects of the planned activity. This is all the truer for marine ecosystems in the deeper waters for which ecological data are still generally scarce and even more scarce in terms of risks and effects related to climate change.[53] Thus, the precautionary approach may come into effect when conducting assessments of climate change related impacts. The precautionary approach is not included in the LOSC since it was developed after and then included in Principle 15 of the Rio Declaration as well as in a number of later multilateral and regional environmental agreements. It would therefore be legally applicable and feasible to include this approach in the further operationalization of Article 206 in ABNJ as well as in the implementation of LOSC Part XII as such. This is also acknowledged in the BBNJ process.[54]

The need for new observations and observational tools in remote and deep-sea areas in this field also has implications for technology transfer and capacity building, another of the four topics in the 'BBNJ package' referred to earlier.

[50] Decision VI/7, UN Doc. CBD/COP/DEC/VI/7 (19 April 2002); Decision VIII/28, UN Doc. CBD/COP//DEC/VIII/28 (15 June 2006).

[51] Decision XI/18, UN Doc. CBD/ COP/DEC/XI/18 (5 December 2012) and UN Doc.CBD / COP/11/23 (21 August 2012), para. 31f.

[52] Madrid Protocol, Art. 8 and Annex 1. Other regional seas conventions covering ABNJ with EIA requirements include the Barcelona Convention for the Protection of the Marine Environment and Coastal Region of the Mediterranean (Art. 4(3)(c)) and the Convention for the Protection of Natural resources and Environment of the South Pacific (Art. 16(2)).

[53] Nerus Program, 'Policy brief: Climate change in oceans beyond national jurisdictions', *Neurus Scientific & Technical Briefs on ABNJ Series* (Undated), available at nereusprogram.org/reports/policy-brief-climate-change-in-oceans-beyond-national-jurisdictions/.

[54] Preparatory Committee, 'Chair's streamlined non-paper', para. 103.

In terms of climate change related EIA in ABNJ, two categories can be distinguished: EIA of activities which may have climate change impacts in ABNJ and EIA of climate change mitigation activities in ABNJ.

14.4.2 *EIA of Activities Which May Have Climate Change Impacts in ABNJ*

These impacts may be direct or indirect/cumulative. With respect to direct impacts, it would probably not be any climate change footprint that could come within the threshold for conducting EIA. For example, extraction in the Area of fossil fuels like oil and natural gas and establishment of pipelines to remove it, could most likely not be interpreted as causing 'substantial pollution of or significant and harmful changes to the marine environment' in the understanding of LOSC Article 206, solely because fossil fuels increase the emission of CO_2 to the atmosphere. If, however, extraction, establishment of pipelines and other seabed activities cause risks of disturbing and releasing the pockets of potent greenhouse gasses like methane or methane hydrates in the deep oceans, as described in Chapter 2, this risk of harm to the oceans' function as greenhouse gas reservoirs may well qualify as a trigger for EIA.

In most cases the effects of climate change will be in the form of adding and exacerbating other stressors on the marine environment, but difficult to distinguish from these other stressors. Their combined impact may influence large marine areas and over a long time.[55] This is why the inclusion of cumulative impacts in assessments is particularly important in terms of climate change related impacts. Regarding cumulative impacts, it would be important to introduce and apply SEA as established by the CBD. SEA, by its nature, covers a wider range of activities and over a longer-term span than EIA, and cumulative effects are best anticipated at a strategic level.[56] SEA is commonly seen as being more proactive than EIA.[57]

In practice, considerations for climate change impacts in EIA and SEA would imply that triggering conditions or thresholds should recognize the extent of impacts due to climate change related stressors such as ocean warming, deoxygenation and ocean acidification.[58] A core element of an

55 R. Warner, 'Oceans in transition: incorporating climate-change impacts into environmental impact assessment for marine areas beyond national jurisdiction' (2018) 45 *Ecology Law Quarterly*, 31–52.

56 Elferink, 'Environmental impact assessment'.

57 Decision UNEP/CBD/COP/DEC/VIII/28 (15 June 2006) 'Voluntary Guidelines on Biodiversity-Inclusive Impact Assessment', 27/Add.2 (9 January 2006), Annex II, para. 7.

58 Warner, 'Oceans in transition'.

impact assessment is a baseline study.[59] This study, which addresses the state of the environment and the significance and value of particular species, habitats, ecosystems and ecosystem services within the particular area, should incorporate climate change vulnerability assessment together with considerations on any other projects or activities that may contribute to cumulative impacts.[60] Where an EIA identifies adverse impacts, alternatives and mitigation measures should be considered to prevent biodiversity loss and other harmful effects. This could lead to location of activities away from threatened and fragile ecosystems.[61] According to *Warner*, projects in ABNJ should ideally be flexible enough 'to allow for changes in project structures and operation if environmental conditions alter due to climate change or other adverse impacts'.[62]

14.4.3 *EIA of Climate Change Mitigation Activities in ABNJ*

Here, the activities in question are aimed to mitigate the effects of climate change but may lead to other adverse impacts on the marine environment. Some of these activities are labelled 'geo-engineering'.

With respect to ABNJ, the ability of the oceans to sequester carbon dioxide has been the focus for various schemes for mitigation activities. These include among others, artificial sequestration of carbon dioxide in the water column or seabed, and fertilization of the open ocean with iron or other nutrients to stimulate phytoplankton blooms and thereby enhance the absorption of carbon dioxide in the oceans.[63] Another method is the use of wave driven pumps on the ocean floor to bring up large volumes of nutrient-rich deep ocean water near to the surface with the purpose of enhancing phytoplankton production.[64]

Such types of mitigation activities would easily qualify as subject to case-by-case EIA in a supplementary EIA regime for ABNJ within the framework of LOSC Article 206. However, because of their potential large scale and

59 J. Glasson et al., 'Introduction to Environmental Impact Assessment' 4th ed. (Routledge, 2013).
60 Warner, 'Oceans in transition'.
61 Ibid.
62 Warner, 'Oceans in Transition'.
63 The Intergovernmental Oceanographic Commission, D. W. R. Wallace et al., *Ocean Fertilization: A Scientific Summary for Policy Makers* (2010), available at unesdoc.unesco.org/ark:/48223/pf0000190674.
64 R. M. Warner, 'Preserving a balanced ocean: regulating climate change mitigation activities in marine areas beyond national jurisdiction' (2007) 14 *Australian International Law Journal*, 99–120.

environmental impacts, some of them have individually been subject to international concern, negotiations and precautionary rule-making while still at an experimental stage. Where activities involve the deliberate disposal of waste material at sea, they may fall within the scope of the 1972 Convention on the Prevention of Marine Pollution by Dumping of Wastes and other matters (London Convention) and the 1996 Protocol to the London Convention (London Protocol) under the auspices of IMO.[65] The Protocol, which entered into force in 2006 in principle prohibits dumping of wastes and other matter, if they are not listed in its Annex 1. For dumping of materials listed in Annex 1, stringent rules for impact assessment are set out in Annex 2. In 2006 Annex 1 was amended to include storage of carbon dioxide under but not on or above the seabed.[66] The amendment was supplemented by Specific Guidelines for Assessment of Carbon Dioxide Streams for Disposal into Sub-seabed Geological Formations (lastly amended in 2012)[67] and has provided basis for a precautionary approach to regulation of sub-seabed sequestration. A particular concern for this mitigation activity is the risk of leakage into the sea.[68]

Ocean fertilization will normally be covered by the term 'dumping' and thereby by the London Convention and Protocol. In 2008, the governing bodies of the two instruments adopted a resolution stating that ocean fertilization should not be allowed other than for scientific research given the present lack of knowledge on side effects on marine ecosystems.[69] Those could be unpredictable consequences for global ocean food chains and thereby for the fishery industry caused by changes to phytoplankton and bacterial communities.[70] A subsequent resolution of 2010 further specifies the notion of legitimate scientific research. It guides parties in assessing proposals for ocean fertilization research including detailed provisions for EIA.[71] The resolution to ban ocean fertilization came after a decision by the CBD in

[65] Convention on the Prevention of Marine Pollution by Dumping of Wastes and Other Matter, London, 29 December 1972, in force 30 August 1975, 1046 UNTS 138 (London Convention); 1996 Protocol to the Convention on the Prevention of Marine Pollution by Dumping of Wastes and Other Matter, 7 November 1966, in force 24 March 2006, 36 ILM 7 (London Protocol).

[66] IMO Doc. LC-LP.1/Circ.5.

[67] IMO Doc. I:\LC\29/4.doc.

[68] H. Ringbom and T. Henriksen, 'Governance challenges, gaps and management opportunities in areas beyond national jurisdiction' (Washington, DC: Global Environment Facility – Scientific and Technical Advisory Panel, 2017).

[69] Resolution LC-LP 1, 31 October 2008, on the Regulation of Ocean Fertilization. This resolution is not legally binding.

[70] Ringbom and Henriksen, 'Governance challenges'.

[71] Resolution LC-LP.2, 4 October 2010.

2008 at its COP9 requesting Parties and urging other governments to ensure that ocean fertilization activities do not take place until there is an adequate scientific basis on which to justify such activities, 'including assessing associated risks, and a global, transparent and effective control and regulatory mechanism is in place for these activities'.[72] Moreover, the CBD in 2009 released a scientific synthesis on the impacts of ocean fertilization on marine biodiversity.[73]

The legal framework for regulation of ocean fertilization is further elaborated in Chapter 8. The CBD in 2010, and reaffirmed in 2012 and 2016, has adopted a de facto moratorium on climate-related geo-engineering, however, with the exception of small-scale scientific research studies.[74]

The previous text has demonstrated that the international community has been ready to apply a very strict precautionary approach for mitigation activities that may adversely affect ecosystems in ABNJ either through banning activities until more scientific knowledge has been generated or through development of stringent minimum standards for EIA. The IMO and the parties to the London Convention and Protocol responded quickly to emerging mitigation activities under its jurisdiction.[75] Mitigation activities in ABNJ falling outside the London dumping framework could also warrant a strict precautionary approach and be regulated through an elaborated EIA/SEA instrument under LOSC with specified obligations and minimum standards.

14.5 CONCLUDING REMARKS

Science is gradually revealing knowledge of marine life in ABNJ that was not previously known and with that also knowledge about the stressors on the marine ecosystems in areas that used to be not only beyond national jurisdiction but also largely beyond human impact. Climate change is an additional stressor either directly or by compounding other stressors. These stressors were not known or recognized at the time of the adoption of the LOSC. Therefore, its regime for protecting the marine environment is inadequate in general and

[72] Conference of the Parties to the CBD, Decision UNEP/CBD/COP/DEC/IX/16 (9 October 2008), Biodiversity and climate change, part C, para. 4.

[73] Secretariat of the Convention on Biological Diversity, 'Scientific synthesis of the impacts of ocean fertilization on marine biodiversity' (2009) *CBD Technical Series No. 45*.

[74] Conference of the Parties to the CBD, Decisions UNEP/CBD/COP/DEC/X/33 (29 October 2010), UNEP/CBD/COP/DEC/XI/20 (5 December 2012) and CBD/COP/DEC/XIII/14 (30 November 2018). See also H. Ginzky, 'Marine geo-engineering' in M. Salomon and T. Markus (eds.), *Handbook on Marine Environment Protection* (Springer, 2018), 997–1011.

[75] Ringbom and Henriksen, 'Governance challenges'.

for ABNJ in particular to address climate change concerns and contribute to mitigation efforts. The LOSC does not preclude further development of its regime if its fundamental principles are respected and maintained. It allows for dynamic evolution of its environmental protection regime considering new knowledge including knowledge on climate change impacts. This room for dynamic evolution within the LOSC is not in itself enough to meet the challenges from climate change in ABNJ. The general provisions of LOSC Part XII need to be filled out in more specific legal language. The UNGA initiated process towards an international legally binding instrument on BBNJ is an opportunity to fill the legal gaps and to achieve a more holistic, cross-sectoral and ecosystem-based governance regime of ABNJ. It is also an opportunity to incorporate concerns for climate change induced impacts in the legal framework. However, this issue has received little attention in the process, and at the time of writing when negotiations of legal text have just started, there is no consensus on whether to include considerations for climate change in the instrument.

In relation to climate change considerations, it is particularly important to develop an effective international mechanism for EIA and SEA of activities in ABNJ that have potential harmful impacts on biodiversity – direct and cumulative – that could include climate change related impacts. A soft law instrument already exists with such coverage – the CBD voluntary guidelines on impact assessment – that could help to pave the way.

An EIA/SEA mechanism should also cover the emerging field of using the oceans' ability to sequester carbon dioxide as a tool for climate change mitigation with potential adverse effects for ecosystem functioning. Here, the dumping regime under IMO has paved the way.

15

The Law of the Sea and Its Institutions

Today's Hermeneutic Approach and Some Suggestions for an Ocean-Centred Governance Model

Margherita Paola Poto*

> [O]nce humans began their anthropocentric journey toward feeling superior to non-human forms of life, we also opened the door for similar attitudes toward Nature as a whole [. . .]. This shift from an Indigenous Worldview to what has become our Dominant Worldview may be the foundation for violence against all forms of diversity. Until we learn to understand, respect and reclaim the worldview that operated for most of human history, whether comparing levels of warfare or numbers of fish in the ocean, social/ecological injustices and environmental degradation will continue unabated. We need to return to a more authentic baseline so as to better establish our goals.
>
> (Four Arrows and Narvaez)[1]

15.1 CONCEPTUAL BACKGROUND

This chapter explores the institutional approach to the law of the sea and reflects on how to improve it, in the perspective of a common future in ocean governance.[2] Ocean governance, in the context of climate change, requires

* The author would like to thank Signe, Elise and Ingvild, editors and wonderful colleagues, for their unwavering support and encouragement, and for seeing the potential in the first draft project; Susan Høivik, proofreader and reviewer, for her in-depth comments and corrections, which have greatly improved the manuscript.

[1] Four Arrows and D. Narvaez, 'A more authentic baseline' in N. McCrary and W. Ross (eds.), *Working for Social Justice Inside and Outside the Classroom: A Community of Teachers, Researchers, and Activists* (Peter Lang, 2015), 93–112.

[2] 'Our Common Future' is the original title of the 'Brundtland Report', known for introducing the concept of sustainable development, issued in 1987 by the World Commission on Environment and Development (WCED), available at https://sustainabledevelopment.un.org/content/documents/5987our-common-future.pdf. 'Common future' is an expression that I prefer to 'sustainable development', which contains within itself the dilemma and limits

changes at the ontological, institutional, socio-ecological and system levels.[3] Current strategies for tackling climate change with the means offered by international law and the law of the sea regime have raised critical concerns regarding their adequacy, integration and effectivity in dealing with the challenges posed by environmental threats.[4] Reorienting and restructuring the ontology and the institutional framework of ocean governance towards a more effective ocean-centred system of governance in the context of 'planetary stewardship'[5] is part of the constructive response that this chapter seeks to provide.

Starting from an institutional approach, I show how an extended interpretation of the concept of 'institution', which includes as constituent element the

to growth and progress concerning environmental protection. Implicit in the idea of development is the idea of progress, the assumption that societies move forward in stages, the earlier stages being 'primitive and simple and emotional'. See L. T. Smith, *Decolonizing Methodologies: Research and Indigenous Peoples* (University of Otago Press, 2008). Credit is given to the aboriginal vision of no separation between land, sea and humans. See The South-east Regional Marine Plan Assessment Reports, *Assessment Report: Sea Country: an Indigenous Perspective* (National Oceans Office, 2002), available at www.environment.gov.au/system/files/resources/271c0bfc-34a2-4c6c-9b02-01204ebc0f43/files/indigenous.pdf; J. Korff, *Meaning of Land to Aboriginal People* (2019), available at www.creativespirits.info/aboriginalculture/land/meaning-of-land-to-aboriginal-people.

3 See K. O'Brien and L. Sygna, 'Responding to climate change: the three spheres of transformation' in *Proceedings of Transformation in a Changing Climate* (University of Oslo, 2013), 16–23.

4 For a broad and substantiated analysis on the inadequacy of tackling climate chance through the channel of international (environmental) law see C. Carlarne, 'Delinking international environmental law and climate change' (2014) 4(1) *Michigan Journal of Environmental and Administrative Law*, available at http://repository.law.umich.edu/mjeal/vol4/iss1/1. The author argues that climate change 'is an issue of such scale and complexity that it defies resolution through the constrained channels of an international environmental treaty. It is a challenge rooted in our models of development, capitalism, free trade, and state sovereignty, and we are no more likely to be able to "solve" it with the tools of international environmental law alone than we are likely to be able to solve it using any type of linear approach that ignores the economic and socio-legal realities that shape the field. Yet, we continue to characterize and approach climate change "just like any other international environmental problem"' (4). For a critical overview of the adequacy of the Law of the Sea Convention (LOSC) to deal with climate changes affecting the sea: S. V. Busch, 'Sea level rise and shifting maritime limits: stable baselines as a response to unstable coastlines' (2018) 9 *Arctic Review on Law and Politics*, 174–194, that emphasizes the difficulty for the LOSC to deal adequately with today's challenges of sea-level rise and maritime limits. A different view emerges from Conference Report, *Climate Change and the Law of the Sea: Adapting the Law of the Sea to Address the Challenges of Climate Change* (13–14 March 2018) (Singapore Conference Report), available at https://cil.nus.edu.sg/wp-content/uploads/2018/04/Climate-Change-Law-of-the-Sea-Final-report.pdf.

5 F. Biermann et al., 'Navigating the Anthropocene: improving earth system governance' (2012) 335(6074) *Science*, 1306–1307.

socio-ecological context in which actors and rules are embedded, reaches out to other actors involved in ocean stewardship. It can contribute to the ontology of a model that better responds to climate change by taking into account the challenges of globalization, inclusion and integration of knowledge, and – most importantly – by putting the ocean at the centre of investigation, restoring the connection between oceans and humans.

Such centrality contrasts with the regulatory approach of the law of the sea that emphasizes the sovereign right of the state and state-like organization towards the sea, based on the presumption of the exploitable value of the world's oceans and seas.

To clarify the dichotomy of approaches, the expression 'ocean governance' is used here to refer to the ocean-centred system, while the state-centred system is referred to as 'law of the sea', with a legal ground on the 1982 UN Convention on the Law of the Sea (LOSC).[6] The terms ocean(s), sea(s), and water are used interchangeably in both cases.

The conceptual framework of the law of the sea has been based on the premise of the superiority of humans over nature. This has generated top-down regulatory patterns, with sovereign states at the top level, and exploitable marine resources at the bottom.[7]

The LOSC epitomizes such an approach by stating the obligation for states to protect and preserve the marine environment – and then downgrades this obligation as an ancillary consequence of the sovereign right to exploit natural resources (Part XII).[8] The same logic permeates LOSC implementing measures and the mandates of various institutions of the law of the sea; it remained unchanged even after the regulatory system intersected with the climate-change regulatory framework with the approval of Agenda 21, where an action plan for sustainable development was introduced.[9] Little effort has been made to coordinate the already existing and effective regimes and mechanisms of marine environmental protection. The unchanged focus on the regulation of human activities and the consequent growth of such activities has resulted in a considerable increase in

6 1982 United Nations Convention on the Law of the Sea, Montego Bay, 10 December 1982, 1833 UNTS 397.

7 E. B Weiss, 'The evolution of international environmental law' (2011) 54 *Japanese Yearbook of International Law*, 1–24.

8 N. Oral, 'Implementing Part XII of the 1982 UN Law of the Sea Convention and the role of international courts' (2013) *International Courts and the Development of International Law*, 403–423.

9 See Agenda 21 at https://sustainabledevelopment.un.org/content/documents/Agenda21.pdf.

new and specialized sub-areas and actors at the intersection of the law of the sea and environmental protection.[10]

The proliferation of rules, actors and areas of regulation has exacerbated existing inequalities and imbalances between the actors involved in decision-making, without offering concrete and tangible solutions to the problem of climate change.[11]

The law of the sea consists of top-down measures. By contrast, integral and holistic views on the relationship between oceans and humans have recognized the oceans as an inseparable part of existence. We can find examples of such a vision among indigenous marine communities all over the world.[12] All acknowledge the unconditional value of water, independent of any economic appraisal. Coastal and marine people understand the oceans in terms of connections: between land and sea, earth and sky, day and night; between the spiritual and physical past, present and future; and between knowledge and practice, people and places.[13] Such views have often been considered

10 A. Peters, 'The refinement of international law: from fragmentation to regime interaction and politicization' (2017) 15(3) *International Journal of Constitutional Law*, 671–704.

11 See, for instance, the case of the 1992 Convention on Biological Diversity (CBD), Rio de Janeiro, 5 June 1992, 1760 UNTS 69, frequently mentioned as *the* instrument that introduced and reflected an integrated approach in the protection of marine biodiversity, in coordination with the LOSC regime. R. Wolfrum and N. Matz, 'The interplay of the United Nations Convention on the Law of the Sea and the Convention on Biological Diversity' in J. A. Frowein and R. Wolfrum (eds.), *Max Planck Yearbook of United Nations Law* (Kluwer Law International, 2000), 445–480. The WWF Report *Protecting our Ocean: Europe's Challenges to Meet the 2020 Deadlines* (2019), concludes for the substantial failure of nineteen EU Member States out of twenty-three in complying with the CBD, hinting that the Convention itself has had scarce effectiveness in the protection of the marine environment, see http://d2ouvy59podg6k.cloudfront.net/downloads/protecting_our_ocean.pdf. The scarce level of integration of the CBD has been reported also by the coastal communities of New Zealand, that expressed their concern also on the effects of the Convention on indigenous rights and consultation: Report CBD Response, *Te Ohu Kaimoana's Response to the Secretariat for the Convention on Biological Diversity on the Priorities for Negotiations on a New Framework for Implementing the Convention on Biological Diversity* (2019), at https://teohu.maori.nz/wp-content/uploads/2019/06/Convention-on-Biological-Diversity-Response.pdf.

12 J. Altman and S. Jackson, 'Indigenous land and sea management' in D. Lindenmayer, S. Dovers and S. Morton (eds.), *Ten Commitments Revisited, Securing Australia's Future Environment* (CSIRO, 2014) 207–216; T. A. C. Royal, *Indigenous Worldviews: A Comparative Study: A Report on Research in Progress* (2002), available at https://static1.squarespace.com/static/5369700de4b045a4e0c24bbc/t/53fe8f49e4b06d5988936162/1409191765620/Indigenous+Worldviews.

13 See, for example, G. R. Harmsworth (Te Arawa, Ngāti Tūwharetoa, Ngāti Raukawa) and S. Awatere (Ngāti Porou), 'Indigenous māori knowledge and perspectives of ecosystems' in J. R. Dymond (ed.), *Ecosystem services in New Zealand: Conditions and Trends* (Manaaki Whenua Press, 2013).

liminal or transitory – when not marginalized, ignored or branded as insufficiently objective and non-scientifically testable. And yet, indigenous systems have maintained their own solidity, continually striving to defend and sustain ocean ecosystems. Simply put: indigenous communities in coastal and marine areas are aware of their connection to water and their responsibilities.[14]

15.2 INSTITUTIONS: SYSTEMS OF RULES AND ACTORS EMBEDDED IN SOCIAL RULES

The first step here consists in uncovering the epistemological assumption that the sovereign states, their organizations, and the rules posited by them are the sole relevant model for the law of the sea's institutions. That the term 'law of the sea institutions' is used to denote the measures of solipsistic state-actors emerges clearly from LOCS preparatory conferences and documents,[15] from the letter of the law[16] and from the subsequent literature denouncing the increasing fragmentation of the law of the sea institutional regime, seen as the natural consequence of the 'proliferation of actors'.[17]

This sovereignty discourse on the sea has served to consolidate the principle of superiority of states (and humans) over the sea, in turn creating a scenario where the relationship between institutions and sea becomes unidirectional and essentially non-egalitarian.

A re-reading of the concept of 'institutions' to include structures that are socially embedded, because generated by the interaction of all the actors (beyond the states: collective organizations, individuals and the ocean itself),

[14] Royal, *Indigenous Worldviews*, 353.

[15] For a complete collection of documents, see http://legal.un.org/diplomaticconferences/1958_los/vol1.shtml; for a historical overview: T. Treves, 'Historical development of the law of the sea' in D. Rothwell et al. (eds.), *The Oxford Handbook of the Law of the Sea* (Oxford University Press, 2015), 1–23.

[16] Examples of a state-sovereignty-centred model can be found throughout the LOSC, for instance in the preamble, where it is stated that the Convention aims to contribute to peace, justice and progress for all peoples of the world, and it gives to the states sovereigns the full control of such objective; in Art. 2, where the sovereignty of coastal states on the sea is clearly affirmed in all its extension; in Part XII, as it will be further critically analysed, where the sovereign right of the states is accompanied by a duty to protect the sea.

[17] For a detailed analysis of the institutions in the old law of the sea paradigm, see J. Harrison, 'The Law of the Sea Convention Institutions' in D. Rothwell et al. (eds.), *The Oxford Handbook of the Law of the Sea* (Oxford University Press, 2015), 1–24. Koskenniemi sees the institutional crisis in the international law and law of the sea regimes as being due to a problem of implementation of organs (read: state-actors): International Law Commission, M. Koskenniemi, Report, UN General Assembly, *Fragmentation of International Law: Difficulties Arising from the Diversification and Expansion of International Law* (2006), 247, available at http://legal.un.org/ilc/documentation/english/a_cn4_l682.pdf.

can pave the way for further reflection on the need to rethink the relationship between humans and sea in terms of connectivity, not mere superiority. Such a renewed[18] definition not only expands the horizon of the actors involved and their mutual interactions: it also facilitates the integration of systems of laws that already focus on the connectivity between peoples, knowledge and ecosystems.[19]

The hermeneutic work of adding a dynamic and relational element to the notion of institution is suggested by Hodgson's definition of institutions as 'systems of established and embedded social rules that structure social interactions'.[20]

This approach supports a critical analysis of the system of the law of the sea in the context of interaction with climate change. With the advent of globalization and the environmental law debate, the system of sovereign states reached a tipping point, and erosion began.[21] This took the shape of multilevel[22] and polycentric governance,[23] a system whose components require continuous efforts and strategies towards integration. My argument is that, even though the issue of state sovereignty has been re-discussed in depth by new global actors like environmental NGOs and civil society,[24] the regulation of the seas, when intersecting with the multi-actor net of environmental governance, has remained a fine-meshed system where non-state actors have never served as decision makers.

18 Unfortunately, such reflections on new 'environmental institution building' have been remained unheeded for decades. K. T. Liftin, 'Sovereignty in world ecopolitics' (1997) 41(2) *Mershon International Studies Review*, 167–204, offers a broad spectrum of predictions about the erosion of state sovereignty and the entry of other actors on the global area, foreseeing a 'multidimensional approach to sovereignty' (197) that is still far from being achieved.

19 C. Schreurer, 'The waning of the sovereign state: towards a new paradigm for international law?' (1993) 4 *European Journal of International Law*, 447–471.

20 G. M. Hodgson, 'What are institutions?' (2006) 15(1) *Journal of Economic Issues*, 1–25, 17. The literature on the relationship between sovereignty erosion, institutions, and emerging environmental concerns is immense and covers more than four decades of research. See Liftin, 'Sovereignty in world ecopolitics', for a complete overview until 1997; M. Loughlin, 'The erosion of sovereignty' (2017) *Netherlands Journal of Legal Philosophy*, 57–81 for analysis of the following twenty years.

21 More on this in Section 15.4; Liftin, 'Sovereignty in world ecopolitics'.

22 Specifically concerning water see, inter alia, I. Weibust and J. Meadowcroft, Multilevel Environmental Governance: *Managing Water and Climate Change in Europe and North America* (Edward Elgar, 2014).

23 F. Zelli and H. van Asselt, 'The institutional fragmentation of global environmental governance: causes, consequences, and responses' (2012) 13(3) *Global Environmental Politics*, 1–13.

24 M. P. Poto and L. Fornabaio, 'Participation as the essence of good governance: some general reflections and a case study on the Arctic Council' (2017) 8 *Arctic Review on Law and Politics*, 139–159.

Eventually, the emphasis given to the intrinsic relational-social component of institutions will come to validate the inclusion of established and embedded social rules which, though structuring social interactions, are not regarded yet as institutions in the ocean governance discourse. This step will lead the discourse to a new level (or 'baseline', to echo the wording of Four Arrows and Narvaez),[25] where old and newly defined institutions coexist and cooperate in an integrated manner, to protect the oceans against the adverse effects of climate change.[26]

15.3 LOS RULES

15.3.1 *No Reference to Climate Change in the Original Law of the Sea Regime*

For obvious reasons of temporality, there is in the LOS rules no explicit reference to 'climate change', nor to any specific counteracting measures.[27] The first use of the term in a legal context came after the establishment of two international institutions mandated to deal with and regulate climate change: the Intergovernmental Panel on Climate Change (IPCC) in 1988 and the UN Framework Convention on Climate Change (UNFCCC) in 1992.[28] This does not mean that the phenomenon was nonexistent or studied before the late

25 Four Arrows and Narvaez, 'A more authentic baseline', 93.

26 Central to this chapter have been the writings of Hodgson, 'What are institutions?', 1–25; H. Heclo, 'Thinking institutionally' in R. A. W. Rhodes, S. A. Binder and B. A. Rockman (eds.), *The Oxford Handbook of Political Institutions* (Oxford University Press, 2006), 731–742; Peters, 'The refinement of international law', 671–704; F. Yamin and J. Depledge, *The International Climate Change Regime: A Guide to Rules, Institutions, and Procedures* (Cambridge University Press, 2004).

27 Although climate change was not mentioned in the LOSC, the tension between the sovereign right of the state to exploit its own resources and the responsibility not to harm the environment had been articulated already in 1972, with Principle 21 of the Stockholm Declaration: 'States have, in accordance with the Charter of the United Nations and the principles of international law, the sovereign right to exploit their own resources pursuant to their own environmental and developmental policies, and the responsibility to ensure that activities within their jurisdiction or control do not cause damage to the environment of other States or of areas beyond the limits of national jurisdiction.'

28 M. Hulme, *Why We Disagree about Climate Change: Understanding Controversy, Inaction and Opportunity* (Cambridge University Press, 2009), 3. From being a physical phenomenon, climate change moved to the status of 'political and contested issue'. The establishment of the IPCC and the UNFCCC marked milestones in this new approach, opening the doors to a global debate and more inclusive participation of the various parties involved in the discussion. As Hulme notes, each December since 1995 has witnessed a two-week meeting of the Conference of the Parties (COPs) to the UNFCCC, with emphatic and often agitated participation of politicians, diplomats, business leaders and civil society organizations. Only after the end of Cold War was the context underlying the concept of climate change extended

1980s – only that it was relegated to the meteorological realm, and subsumed under the technical definition of 'climatic changes', encompassing all forms of climatic variabilities, on time scales of more than ten years, with no regard to the underlying causes.[29] At the end of the 1970s, the adjective 'climatic' was reportedly replaced by the noun 'climate', which better expressed the *global* characteristic of the phenomenon, deeply linking changes in the climate to anthropogenic factors.[30] In its new global dimension, 'climate change' finally became associated with human accountability and therefore legal responsibility to protect, and to repair the damage.

The provisions of the LOSC were part of a conceptual and historical framework where solutions to climate change had not yet been theorized, but the logic permeating the law of the sea (actors and rules) remained the same by inertia, also after the 'climate-change season' of reforms. Institutions that invoke permanent sovereignty over natural resources, including the sea, are apparently considered the main (or only) actors capable of tackling environmental problems,[31] including climate change. International environmental governance has failed to implement the idea of non-sovereign 'ecological stewardship',[32] which might better respond to the need of developing a nature-centred system of governance. The response, as described in Section 15.5, must involve recognizing and developing the role of indigenous peoples and marine communities as stewards of the ocean.

15.3.2 *LOSC Part XII: A Critical Reading*

Part XII of the LOSC presents an array of regulatory solutions aimed at mitigating environmental threats.[33] These range from general provisions

from the sphere of meteorology to encompass human causes among the manifestations of the shift from global fears of a nuclear threat to looming environmental catastrophes.

29 Hulme, *Why We Disagree*.

30 Ibid.

31 As L. Guruswamy noted in 'Climate change: the next dimension' (2000) 15 *Journal Land Use & Environmental Law*, 341, criticism has been voiced as to the effectiveness of this framework to address climate change. However, many scholars still argue that the law of the sea regime is equipped to address climate change without major modifications; see the Singapore Conference Report. See also P. Gümplová, 'Restraining permanent sovereignty over natural resources' (2014) 53 *Enrahonar. Quaderns de Filosofia*, 93–114.

32 F. S. Chapin III, G. P. Kofinas and C. Folke (eds.), *Principles of Ecosystem Stewardship: Resilience-Based Natural Resource Management in a Changing World* (Springer, 2009).

33 There is a vast literature on the key role played by Part XII in the protection of the environment. One of the first authors to emphasize the major role played by the LOSC as an environmental treaty is Lakshman Guruswamy, see L. Guruswamy, 'The promise of the

(Section 1), to global and regional cooperation (Section 2), technical assistance and environmental assessments (Sections 3 and 4), measures consequential to land-based activities (Section 5), facilitations (Section 6), as well as enforcement and compliance (Section 9). Some attention is also paid to special regimes (as in the case of ice-covered areas, in Section 8; and exceptionality in case of sovereign immunity, Section 10). A general concluding part in Section 11 alludes to the feature of Part XII in terms of *lex generalis*, and opening the way to specific obligations assumed by the states under special conventions.

However, these provisions need to be contextualized: they are a reflection of their time, anchored in a deterministic way of looking at environmental threats, based on the classical problem–solution pattern and linked to the Westphalian approach[34] that gives precedence to the state actions in any environmental decisions.

Examples of such a state-oriented, deterministic *Leitmotiv* are many in Part XII and will be enumerated and analysed further. Suffice it here to note that there is very little room left for coordinated and integrated actions for protecting the environment, and that states are the sole actors with a major role in decision making. For example, the only reference to joint development of common plans is provided in case of contingencies (see Article 199), whereas the cooperation that is to be pursued on a global basis is purely state-interest-oriented (Article 197).

Part XII starts by generically stating the obligation of a state to protect and preserve the marine environment in Article 192, but then (in Article 193) downgrades such obligation to an ancillary consequence of its sovereign right to exploit natural resources. The right to exploit natural resources does

United Nations Convention on the Law of the Sea (UNCLOS): justice in trade and environment disputes' (1999) 25 *Ecology Law Quarterly*, 189–228, recalls how LOSC, at the time it was signed, was considered by W. Christopher to be the 'strongest and most comprehensive environmental treaty in existence'. He also notes that the LOSC contains several environmental provisions beyond Part XII, namely: Part II, Part V, Part VII, Part IX, Part XI and Part XIII. For more recent literature endorsing the major role of Part XII in defining the environmental scope of the law of the sea, see Oral, 'Implementing Part XII', 403, who holds that the LOSC still represents a 'comprehensive regime for the protection and preservation of the marine environment', with a 'universal codification of the duty [...] to protect and preserve the marine environment'.

34 See R. Grote, 'Westphalian system' (2008) *Max Planck Encyclopedia of Public International Law* (Oxford University Press, 2008), online edition available at www.mpepil.com; B. Teschke, 'Theorizing the Westphalian system of states: international relations from absolutism to capitalism' (2002) 8(1) *European Journal of International Relations*, 5–48; B. Teschke, *The Myth of 1648: Class, Geopolitics and the Making of Modern International Relations* (Verso, 2003).

not imply the state's duty to preserve the sea as a priority in designing and informing decision-making. No, the priority accorded to a state's ocean activities is quite clear in Article 194 (2), where it is stated that necessary measures have to be taken to ensure that such activities do not cause damage to the environment.[35] This kind of logic is an obvious indication of a deterministic pattern in which the state is free to exploit natural resources (the sea being seen as a shareable economic resource, not as a fragile and precious ecosystem), provided it takes measures to limit such exploitation.[36] Had the provision stated that the *oceans* have an inviolable right, then the responsibility of states in case of infringement would have had a significantly different emphasis. Similarly, the provisions in Articles 197–199 reveal a preference for top-down deterministic regulation. Although these provisions allude to a general duty of cooperation at a global and regional level, the initiative to cooperate is described as a unilateral process, whereby it is the states that are asked to take into account characteristic regional features, with no mention of the role of regional levels in such synergy. No reference at all is made to cooperative interactions among different ocean actors.

The same pattern is followed in Section 4 concerning the regulation of monitoring and environmental assessment, where no opportunities for participation or dissent are contemplated, and where the law – even when disciplining activities that go beyond the discretionary powers of the sovereign states (i.e. technical assessments) – does not progress beyond the narrow framing of the states' rights.

Thus, although the need for a more integrated approach to environmental protection has been raised in all the years following the institutional

35 *Contra* Oral, 'Implementing Part XII', 403.

36 Less radical formulations on delimiting the sustainable use of the sea appeared prior to the 1992 UN Conference on Environment and Development in Rio de Janeiro, see https://sustainabledevelopment.un.org/content/documents/Agenda21.pdf. Whereas the doctrine of sustainable development gained acceptance only after the report of the Brundtland Commission in 1987 and the Rio Agenda in 1992, seeds of interest in the optimal use of the natural world can be found in provisions dating back to 1911, when the Convention for the Preservation and Protection of Bering Sea Fur Seals was concluded between Russia, the United States, Great Britain and Canada. The Convention prohibits pelagic sealing activities in the North Pacific Ocean, except for traditional and indigenous sealing, without subordinating such protection to any sovereign right to exploit the natural resources. An example of a more appropriate approach to the balance between human activity and environmental protection is found in the Helsinki Rules on the Uses of the Water of International Rivers, wherein Art. IV reference is made to a 'reasonable and equitable share in the beneficial uses of the water'. For other examples, see T. Kuokkanen, 'Integrating environmental protection and exploitation of natural resources: reflections on the evolution of the doctrine of sustainable development' (2004) 22(3) *Journal of Energy and Natural Resources Law*, 341–356.

consolidation of the law of the sea,[37] it is clear how the LOSC matrix contributed to forging the subsequent implementing measures, tied up in the same conceptual state-sovereignty perspective. Calls for an ocean-centred paradigm system have never been heard: 'inter-*state* cross-boundary cooperation' has been invoked as the sole essential tool to protect marine ecosystems.[38]

15.3.3 *LOSC Implementing Measures: Sectoral and Regional Actors from the Same Matrix Layer*

We now turn to LOSC implementing measures to see how certain recurrent patterns found in the law of the sea framework have their genetic base in the state-centred model emerging from the law of the sea regulation.

The LOSC is considered the pinnacle of the institutional law of the sea framework and the activities of its four main actors:[39]

1. the states parties, or, as a whole, the Conference of the Parties, that are the centre of the institutional framework created by the 1982 Convention (the 'supreme organ');
2. the International Tribunal of the Law of the Sea, as the judicial institutions formed by members appointed by the states parties, and mandated to resolve disputes concerning the law of the sea;
3. the Commission on the Limits of the Continental Shelf, a technical body composed of experts tasked with overseeing the delineation of the continental shelf beyond the 200 nm limit;
4. The International Seabed Authority, an autonomous institution with legal personality, in charge of the supervision of the deep seabed mining regime.

Additional actors have been created at a rather steady pace, the intention being to discipline different sectors of the sea – and ultimately furthering the fragmentation of the system. The environment, the fishery sector, maritime affairs – all have received sectoral and specific protection with the

[37] Gümplová, 'Restraining permanent sovereignty', 93–114, denounces the need for a more integrated framework in environmental governance. On the need for effective integration in marine governance, see K. Grip, 'International marine environmental governance: a review' (2017) 46 *Ambio*, 413–427; and F. Berkes et al. (eds.), *Navigating Social–Ecological Systems: Building Resilience for Complexity and Change* (Cambridge University Press, 2003).

[38] D. Freestone (ed.), *The 1982 Law of the Sea Convention at 30: Successes, Challenges and New Agendas* (Martin Nijhoff, 2013); D. Tladi, *Ocean Governance: A Fragmented Regulatory Framework* (2011), available at http://regardssurlaterre.com/en/ocean-governance-fragmented-regulatory-framework.

[39] Harrison, 'The Law of the Sea', 345.

establishment of ad hoc state-centred authorities and rules. Here we may note the Convention on Biological Diversity, the Convention of Migratory Species; the UN Agreement relating to the Conservation and Management of Straddling Fish Stocks and Highly Migratory Fish Stocks; the International Maritime Organization.[40]

In addition to the proliferation of sectoral institutions have come regional and domestic laws and organizations, such as the Regional Fisheries Organizations, the Regional Seas Conventions, the Marine Protected Areas, to name but a few.[41]

Unsurprisingly, this surge in regional institutions and actors has developed in parallel with the growing focus on integrating them at the national, (sub-) regional and global levels.[42] Moreover, the multiplication of regional actors at sea has not been accompanied by a corresponding shift of focus to an eco-centric and eco-preoccupied system of governance. Regionalism developed as a 'state-led formal institutional-building',[43] rooted in a state (and sub-state)-centric view.

The mainstream perspective focusing on state sovereignty did not change even when the LOSC regulatory system intersected with the institutional framework established to address climate change, because the newly established climate-change system claimed continuity with the LOS provisions (Agenda 21 of the 1992 Rio Conference).[44]

The continuity claim with Part XII is based on the acknowledgement of LOSC as the 'international basis upon which to pursue the protection and sustainable development of the marine and coastal environment and its resources'.[45] Even though the need to shift from the 'control of sources of marine pollution' to a more integrated approach to protecting the marine and coastal environment appeared to broaden the perspective

40 Ibid.

41 For a description of the main regional institutions see UN Environment, *Realizing Integrated Regional Oceans Governance – Summary of Case Studies on Regional Cross-Sectoral Institutional Cooperation and Policy Coherence* (2017). For a complete overview of Regional Sea Programs see R. Billé et al., *Regional Oceans Governance: Making Regional Seas Programmes, Regional Fishery Bodies and Large Marine Ecosystem Mechanisms Work Better Together*, UNEP Regional Seas Report and Studies No. 196 (2016).

42 Billé et al., *Regional Oceans Governance*, 1.

43 T. A. Börzel, 'Theorizing regionalism: cooperation, integration, and governance', in T. A. Börzel and T. Risse (eds.), *Oxford Handbook of Comparative Regionalism* (Oxford University Press, 2016), 1–26; see also T. A. Börzel and V. van Hüllen (eds.), *Governance Transfer by Regional Organizations Patching Together a Global Script* (Palgrave Macmillan, 2015).

44 Available at https://sustainabledevelopment.un.org/content/documents/Agenda21.pdf.

45 Ibid., Ch. 19 [19.1].

angle,[46] the state-oriented perspective remained unchanged in substance. The numerous calls for environmental regulatory measures exacerbated the fragmentation, while the primary focus remained on the regulation of human exploitation of the ocean.[47]

In this sense, 'the universal rhetoric of ecological interdependence' was never translated into effective action.[48]

As explained subsequently, discussion of the 'unshakeable' principle of state sovereignty started with the advent of globalization, but the situation remained substantially unchanged at the level of institutionalization of other actors, and was totally unaffected in the field of marine environmental decision making.

15.4 OPPORTUNITIES OFFERED BY THE EXPANDING EFFECTS OF GLOBALIZATION

Globalization and environmental challenges have offered great opportunities for re-conceptualizing and re-orienting international law and the LOS regime. After the 1992 Rio Declaration,[49] considerations of the protection and preservation of the marine environment moved from a functionalist to a teleological perspective: from being a condition that limited the rights to exploit nature, to the final objective for states to pursue. Moreover, the linear, state-oriented dimension of the protection expanded to embrace a multi-stakeholder approach.

From the function of the state sovereignty to a global common objective, environmental protection helped to provide a new space for actors and their relationships with the sea, in the governance of the oceans. This change was triggered by the inherent but coexisting contradictory terms of globalization, which, while stretching the system almost to the breaking point, emphasized the urgent need to develop checks-and-balances mechanisms.[50] This has been

46 Ibid.

47 P. Birnie, A. Boyle and C. Redgwell, *International Law and the Environment*, 3rd ed. (Oxford University Press, 2009), 386.

48 A. Hurrell and B. Kingsbury (eds.), *The International Politics of the Environment: Actors, Interests, Institutions* (Clarendon Press, 1992), 1.

49 1992 Rio Declaration on Environment and Development, Rio de Janeiro, 14 June 1992, 31 ILM 874, UN Doc. A/CONF.151/26 (vol. I).

50 On the opportunities that globalization offers regarding governance of the global commons, including the ocean, see I. Goldin, *Globalization for Development: Meeting New Challenges*, (Oxford University Press, 2012). For an updated analysis of the expanding institutional structure in environmental governance triggered by awareness of climate change, see M. Di Gregorio et al., 'Multi-level governance and power in climate change policy networks' (2019) 54 *Global Environmental Change*, 64–77.

particularly evident in the development of the concept of 'global governance' and even more in the case of marine environmental governance.[51] Gradually, the scope of ocean governance moved beyond the need to regulate the seas as an inter-state affair, pushing the debate in the direction of defining the oceans as *global commons*.[52] The development of global models of governance (the environmental governance system in particular) was triggered by the expanded vision of reality as a global village, a complex system of relationships involving various levels, actors and objectives. Globalization enriched the phenomenon of regulation and stretched its borders from the government-oriented to the multilevel governance dimension. Both 'government' and 'governance' have their roots in the Latin verb *gubernare*, in turn deriving from the Greek *kybernan*, which meant 'to steer a ship', 'government' has been used mainly to define a territorially based body empowered to make authoritative decisions.

By contrast, 'governance' was initially applied only in the private-sector context, to refer to private companies' strategic operational management of human resources and assets. Transferred to the domain of public law, the term acquired the dimension of 'collective action at local level'.[53] As such, 'governance' has been used to define a multiform system, encompassing 'the direct and indirect roles of formal institutions of local government and government hierarchies, as well as the roles of informal norms, networks, community organizations, and neighbourhood associations in pursuing collective action'.[54]

The expansion of the concept of governance, beyond the boundaries of the private sector, peaked in the 1990s, together with the emerging discussions on climate change:

> Globalization was rendering obsolete the [...] old-fashioned international law built around state sovereignty and strict rules of non-intervention. Bumpy as it might be the road seemed to be leading away from Westphalia – with an expanded role for formal and informal multilateral institutions; a huge increase in the scope, density and intrusiveness of rules and norms made at the international level but affecting how domestic societies are organized; the ever-greater involvement of new actors in global governance; the moves

51 Such attempts can be found in the discussion regarding the Areas Beyond National Jurisdiction; see G. Wright and J. Rochette, 'Regional ocean governance of Areas Beyond National Jurisdiction: lessons learnt and ways forward' (2019) *STRONG High Seas Project*.

52 V. De Lucia, 'Oceans commons, law of the sea and rights for the sea' (2019) 32(1) *Canadian Journal of Law & Jurisprudence* 45–57; see also K. Zou (ed.), *Global Commons and the Law of the Sea* (Brill, 2018).

53 R. Broadway and S. Anwar, *Fiscal Federalism: Principles and Practice of Multilevel Governance* (Cambridge University Press, 2009), 242.

54 Ibid.

> towards the coercive enforcement of global rules; and a fundamental changes in political, legal and moral understandings of state sovereignty and of the relationship between the state, the citizen and the international community.[55]

The 'consciousness-of-the-world-as-a-whole' started to spread, and somehow the antonyms 'central-local territorial dimensions' changed their connotations. Local, national and regional borders were re-configured, in a borderless dimension:

> The impact of globalization and the changing nature of the world political order have raised major questions concerning the role of the nation state and the way in which territory continues to define the spatial extent of sovereignty [. . .]. Notions of a 'borderless world' and political 'de-territorialisation' are seen as signalling a new world order in which the territorial component in world affairs is of much reduced significance.[56]

The effect of globalization on the domain of public law contributed to changing perceptions of the relationships between actors and rules. Before the advent of globalization, law was organized mainly within national boundaries; by contrast, in a global perspective, the regulation of public affairs acquires cross-border characteristics – with the dual effect of supranational systems influencing the national and the local levels, on the one hand, and, on the other hand, of local developments with large-scale repercussions.[57]

In sum, globalization has proven conducive to the proliferation of non-state actors as well as to integrated actions aimed at achieving common global objectives. The change of perspective, from a national to a globally shared dimension, has broken down the territorial boundaries of states and unified the diverse multitude of actors seeking to address common problems, including climate change.[58]

That said, if the global model of governance has contributed to opening up the arena to the participatory rights of non-state actors with a 'Universal Justice

55 A. Hurrell, 'Can the study of global order be de-centred?' (2015) 3 *PRIMO Working Paper*, available at www.primo-itn.eu/PRIMO/wp-content/uploads/2015/07/WorkingPaper-2_Andrew-Hurrell.pdf.

56 D. Newman, 'World society, globalization and a borderless world: The contemporary significance of borders and territory' (2005) 2 *World Society Focus Paper Series*.

57 Poto and Fornabaio, 'Participation', 139–159.

58 As an example of concerted initiative, we may note the effort undertaken by the 1,200 cities, towns and counties that now belong to Local Government for Sustainability, aimed at reducing greenhouse gas emissions on a worldwide basis. See O. R. Young, *On Environmental Governance: Sustainability, Efficiency, and Equity* (Routledge, 2016), 102.

Agenda' (which comprises human rights and environmental protection),[59] the institutional status and decision rights to such actors have not yet been fully developed nor acknowledged.[60] Expanding the concept of 'institution' to comprehend actors' socially embedded rules centred on protection of the environment may make it possible for non-state parties to be recognized as subjects in international law, beyond the rhetoric of mere procedural participation and contributing to re-set the institutional focus towards an environmental-centred agenda.

15.5 ADAPTIVE MODELS WITHSTANDING THE CHANGE

15.5.1 *When Everything Is Interconnected, Sovereignty Shrinks*

Globalization and climate change are the pebbles that strike the frangible point of a state-oriented model that needs to be rediscussed in its foundational structure.[61]

Other actors have developed their rules around a system of ocean governance far from the dogma of sovereignty.[62] Such actors include indigenous marine communities whose cosmologies do not distinguish between land and sea, or even draw a line between sea and humans: sea patterns (waves and particles) correspond to social and human patterns (cycle of ocean tides, seasons, birth, death and rebirth; growing seasons, bird migrations, sunrise and sunset).[63] Such cosmologies help to forge systems of socially embedded rules that place the ocean at the centre of protection.[64]

59 J. von Bernstorff, 'Non-State Actors in law-making and in the shaping of policy: on the legality and legitimacy of NGO participation in international law' (2007), Conference Draft 2007, available at www.kas.de/c/document_library/get_file?uuid=4e2e1560-2408-8bfd-9f85-5dea3e38c200&groupId=252038.

60 Ibid., 11.

61 J. Braudillard sees the problem of saturated social systems as structural and compares them to the formation of a black hole, observing that the phenomenon is already a reality for *global* cities and legal systems in general. See J. Baudrillard, *Hyperreality and Implosion*, Ceasefire Magazine, 10 August 2012, available at https://ceasefiremagazine.co.uk/in-theory-baudrillard-9/, accessed October 2019.

62 J. Altman and S. Jackson, 'Indigenous land and sea management' in D. Lindenmayer, S. Dovers and S. Morton (eds.), *Ten Commitments Revisited: Securing Australia's Future Environment* (CSIRO Publishing, 2014), 207–215.

63 The interconnectedness of nature and human beings is a core belief shared by indigenous peoples around the world: normally it is the elders who are the experts and transmit such knowledge through storytelling, examples, and languages: See G. Cajete, *Native Science: Natural Laws of Interdependence* (Clear Light Publishers, 1999).

64 M. Nursey-Bray, 'Which way? The contribution of indigenous marine governance' (2014) 6 *Australian Journal of Maritime and Ocean Affairs*, 27–40.

One example comes from Oceania, the collective name for the islands of the Central and South Pacific Ocean. Among their marine communities, the Aboriginal peoples of Australia and the Māori of New Zealand (Aotearoa in the Māori language) stand out for their recognition of the centrality of the oceans and the role played by marine communities in protecting them.

The Aboriginal people know Australia as the 'sea country', indicating the sense of a fully cultural and spiritual land-and-seascape relationship. Their perspectives focus on holistic approaches to human stewardship of nature, challenging the Western concepts of land and sea as stocks of resources, rights and commodities. These peoples care communally for their country, respecting its rights, and developing a system of responsibilities to protect them.[65] Mary Graham asserts that Aboriginal relations with land and sea are underpinned by two axioms:[66] the land-sea is the law; and we are not alone in this world. Thus, the land-sea is sacred and the basis of any relationship. The relationship between nature and peoples determines all human relationships and is the pattern for social and therefore institutional relations.

Similar value-sets are shared by the Māori population of New Zealand, who developed a working definition of marine stewardship, *kaitiakitanga*, which can be translated as guardianship, preservation, conservation, fostering, protecting, sheltering.[67] The guardians of the natural world and its domain are the *Papatūānuku* (Mother Earth), the *Ranginui* (Father Sky) and their many children, including *Tangaroa* (the Oceans). Also human beings (*ira tangata*) play a role as *kaitaiki* (caretakers) and have the obligation to nurture and protect the physical and spiritual well-being of the natural systems that surround and support them. *Kaitiaki* are agents that perform the task of active guardianship, and are charged with the responsibility for safeguarding and managing natural resources for present and future generations. Decisions enacted by the *kaitiaki* are based on inter-generational observations and experiential understandings.[68] There is no room for sovereignty, nor for

65 D. Smyth, Report for the Department of Sustainability, Environment, Water, Population and Communities on behalf of the State of the Environment 2011 Committee, *Indigenous Land and Sea Management: A Case Study* (2011), available at citeseerx.ist.psu.edu/viewdoc/download?doi=10.1.1.441.6798&rep=rep1&type=pdf.

66 M. Graham, 'Some thoughts about the philosophical underpinnings of Aboriginal worldviews' (1999) 3(2) *Worldviews: Global Religions, Culture and Ecology*.

67 T. A. C. Royal (ed.), *The Woven Universe: Selected Writings of Rev. Maori Marsden* (Estate of Rev. Maori Marsden, 2003).

68 K. P. Burke and L. Rameka, 'Kaitiakitanga active guardianship, responsibilities and relationships with the world: towards a bio-cultural future in early childhood education', available at researchcommons.waikato.ac.nz/bitstream/handle/10289/11216/Kaitiakitanga%20-%20FINAL.pdf?sequence=11&isAllowed=y.

a separation between human communities and nature: all – humans and non-humans – are connected and committed to the protection of the sea and the land.

Finally, it should be noted that the Māori value system on water is now recognized in the national legislation, the Te Awa Tupua, marking a step forward in the frame of water protection and governance. The Te Awa Tupua (Whanganui River Claims Settlement) Act 2017[69] was approved after the longest-running litigation over Maori land claims in the recorded history of New Zealand. The Whanganui is New Zealand's longest navigable river, stretching from Mount Tongariro in the North Island to the Tasman Sea. The Whanganui River Claims Settlement is founded on two principles: recognizing the health and wellbeing of the river and its status as a legal person 'Te Awa Tupua' ('Te Mana o Te Awa'), and recognizing the relationship of the indigenous Whanganui Iwi in respect of the river ('Te Mana o Te Iwi').[70] The 2017 Act confers legal personality on the river system, offering a precedent in the integration of indigenous knowledge through in the legal culture of New Zealand. This is an innovative approach to protecting the environment, focusing on the centrality of nature and incorporating spiritual values in a way unknown in the environmental law of most Western legal systems.[71]

15.6 TOWARDS INTEGRATION AND CONVERGENCE OF MODELS: A NEW BASELINE

To implement the idea of full institutional recognition of all marine actors (including the ocean itself) in the system of ocean governance, it will probably be necessary to develop a third and new space where old and new paradigms converge to support the oceans and respond effectively to climate threats. A new ontology for ocean governance, one which embraces an ocean-centred paradigm, rather than being state or human-centred, will call for a new legal vocabulary, based on the laws of nature (holism and interconnectedness) and translated into the principles of equality, universality and inalienability as the cornerstones of the ontology.

[69] Te Awa Tupua (Whanganui River Claims Settlement) Act 2017, Public Act 2017 No. 7 (New Zealand). Royal Assent was granted on 20 March 2017. See C. Rodgers, 'A new approach to protecting ecosystems: The Te Awa Tupua (Whanganui River Claims Settlement) Act 2017' (2017) 19(4) *Environmental Law Review*, 266–279.

[70] Ibid.

[71] Ibid.

Holism asserts that the natural world (and consequently, the seas) and human beings have an identical relationship in a level of reality, in which all exist as a part of a unified and indivisible whole. Applied to the oceans, this provides a very strong basis for recognizing the rights of nature and demonstrating the appropriateness of a rights-based regime that involves both nature and humans, founded on equality, universality, inalienability.[72]

First, holism affirms the idea of equality, according to which there is no individualization that can assert or establish any hierarchy, between humans and nature, or among humans.

Second, the fact that nature and individuals are in an equal relationship supports the concept of rights that apply universally, to nature and to humans.

Third, the interconnectedness of humans and nature, deriving from holism, implies that both nature and human rights are inalienable: no aspect of each connected level can be extracted and alienated from one reality to the other.

These three principles could stand as the main pillars of a legal order where the oceans are recognized as a self-regulating system, comprised of physical and human elements. The agency, legal personhood and legal standing of the oceans should be acknowledged, whereby completing and systematizing a process that has already been initiated towards the recognition of the inherent rights of nature.[73]

15.7 CONCLUSIONS

This chapter has pointed out the shortcomings of regulation of the seas that is based on the assumption of supremacy of humans over the oceans. The mainstream system, based on the sovereign right of states to exploit the sea, has overstayed its welcome. Our planet needs alternative systems that place the oceans at the centre of attention. The challenge is to understand how and if we can reverse the pattern, based on acknowledgement of the key role played by the oceans and their communities in helping to deal with climate change – the

[72] A. Dhall, 'On the philosophy and legal theory of human rights in light of quantum holism' (2010) 66(1) *World Futures*, 1–25.

[73] See J. C. Suntrup, 'The legal person and its other: a comparative view on drawing and effacing boundaries in various cultural contexts' (2017) *The Open Journal for the Study of Culture*, 1–24, 3; D. Shelton, 'Nature as a legal person' (2015) *VertigO: La revue électronique en sciences de l'environnement, special issue*, 22; G. Teubner, 'Rights of non-humans? Electronic agents and animals as new actors in politics and law' (2006) 33(4) *Journal of Law and Society*, 497–521; C. Espinosa, 'Interpretive affinities: the constitutionalization of rights of nature, Pacha Mama, in Ecuador' (2015) *Journal of Environmental Policy & Planning* 608–622; C. D. Stone, 'Should trees have standing? Towards legal rights for natural objects' (1972) 45 *Southern California Law Review*, 450–501.

technical problems, by absorbing excess CO_2 in the atmosphere; and relational aspects, by reorganizing social and socio-ecological relationships.[74]

- The opening towards a model of global governance marks a first step in the path towards a holistic approach, by strengthening the participation of non-state actors and by implementing a toolbox of rules that hold us all accountable for the damages caused to the environment.
- The centrality of the protection of the seas marks the second step, with the revitalization of regenerative practices in indigenous and local marine communities who have always understood the importance of paying central attention to the oceans.

Awareness of the interconnectedness of all things restores value to the relationship between nature (water) and peoples. It offers solutions to ocean pandemics, including the loss of biodiversity and climate change, by restoring this essential relationship – which modern classical science and regulatory models have not managed to do. The toolkit for a common blue future is already available: now it is up to us to put it to good use.

74 K. O'Brien, 'The courage to change: adaptation from the inside-out' in S. Moser and M. Boykoff (eds.), *Successful Adaptation: Linking Science and Practice in Managing Climate Change Impacts* (Routledge, 2013); M. Pelling, *Adaptation to Climate Change: From Resilience to Transformation* (Routledge, 2010).

16

The Law of the Sea as Part of the Climate-Change Regime Complex

Ingvild Ulrikke Jakobsen*, Elise Johansen* and Philipp Peter Nickels*

16.1 INTRODUCTION

Climate change has already had severe impacts on the world's oceans; moreover, threats such as rising water temperatures and ocean acidification seem set to increase.[1] Effective regulatory responses are urgently needed to mitigate these adverse effects – or at least to adapt. And yet, '[u]ntil recently, climate change was seen as an "over the horizon" challenge for the law of the sea', as Tim Stephens has pointed out, criticizing responses thus far as a 'wait and see approach'.[2] Against this background, the contributions to this volume have assessed how the Law of the Sea Regime can be interpreted, applied and where necessary developed to support the objectives of the UN Climate Regime.

16.2 THE LAW OF THE SEA AS PART OF THE CLIMATE-CHANGE REGIME COMPLEX

The development of issue-specific areas or 'regimes' of international law, such as the law of the sea or the UN Climate Regime, is one dimension of the

* Professor, PhD in Law, The Norwegian Centre for the Law of the Sea, UIT The Arctic University of Norway.

* Associate Professor, PhD in Law, The Norwegian Centre for the Law of the Sea, UIT The Arctic University of Norway.

* Research Fellow and PhD Candidate at The Norwegian Centre for the Law of the Sea, UIT The Arctic University of Norway.

1 Intergovernmental Panel on Climate Change (IPCC), *Summary of the First Global Integrated Marine Assessment* (2016), available at www.un.org/Depts/los/global _reporting/WOA_RPRO C/Summary.pdf, 7; IPCC, H. O. Pörtner et al. (eds.), *IPCC Special Report on The Ocean and Cryosphere in a Changing Climate* (2019, in press), Summary for Policymakers; see further D. Vidas et al., this volume, Chapter 2, Section 2.2.

2 T. Stephens, 'Warming waters and souring seas: climate change and ocean acidification' in D. R. Rothwell et al. (eds.), *The Oxford Handbook of the Law of the Sea* (Oxford University Press, 2015), 777, 797.

broader phenomenon of the fragmentation of international law.[3] As the International Law Commission (ILC) has noted, the fragmented nature of international law poses 'the danger of conflicting and incompatible rules, principles, rule-systems and institutional practices'[4] – but also has the potential to strengthen 'its responsiveness to the regulatory context'.[5]

While *regime* has been defined variously in international law and international relations scholarship, a 'hybrid definition' describes regimes as 'sets of norms, decision-making procedures and organisations coalescing around functional issue-areas and dominated by particular modes of behaviour, assumptions and biases'.[6] Yet, as Young has aptly noted, '[g]lobal problems [...] do not fit neatly within single regimes'.[7]

Climate change is one case in point: not only the UN Climate Regime but also a multitude of other areas of international law, including the law of the sea, have a bearing on climate-change mitigation and adaptation efforts.[8] One way of conceptualizing such a situation, where more than one single or 'elemental' regime is important for a specific issue, is through the concept of 'regime complex', which Raustiala and Victor define as 'an array of partially overlapping and non-hierarchical institutions governing a particular issue-area'.[9] This has been discussed in the context of climate change in general,[10] as well as in terms of the regulatory framework for ocean acidification.[11]

The fact that more than one *single regime* is relevant for climate-change mitigation and adaptation efforts necessitates taking a closer look at the

3 J. Pauwelyn, 'Fragmentation of international law' in R. Wolfrum (ed.), *Max Planck Encyclopedia of Public International Law* (2006), para. 2, online edition available at https://opil.ouplaw.com/view/ 10.1093/law:epil/9780199231690/law-9780199231690-e1406?rskey=vPn93Q&result=1&prd=EPIL#.

4 International Law Commission, *Fragmentation of International Law: Difficulties Arising from the Diversification and Expansion of International Law, Report of the Study Group of the International Law*, 58th session, UN Doc. A/CN.4/L.682 (13 April 2006), at para. 14.

5 Ibid., at para. 492.

6 M. A. Young, 'Introduction' in M. A. Young (ed.), *Regime Interaction in International Law, Facing Fragmentation* (Cambridge University Press, 2012), 1–19, at 11.

7 M. A. Young, 'Regime interaction in creating, implementing and enforcing international law' in M. A. Young (ed.), *Regime Interaction in International Law, Facing Fragmentation* (Cambridge University Press, 2012), 85–110, at 85.

8 M. A. Young, 'Climate change law and regime interaction' (2011) 2 *Carbon and Climate Change Law Review*, 142–157.

9 K. Raustiala and D. G. Victor, 'The regime complex for plant genetic resources' (2004) 58 *International Organisation*, 277–309, at 279 [emphasis omitted].

10 R. O. Keohane and D. G. Victor, 'The regime complex for climate change' (2011) 9(1) *Perspectives on Politics*, 7–23.

11 K. N. Scott, this volume, Chapter 5, Section 5.3.

interaction between the relevant regimes.[12] Many scholarly contributions on regime interaction have focused on the conflicts, while devoting insufficient attention to the positive synergies arising out of regime interaction.[13] As Young has noted, in addition to conflicting obligations and disputes between different regimes, 'regime interaction occurs during the making, implementation and enforcement of international law'.[14] This is why the contributing authors to this volume have focused not only on assessing the potential for conflicts between the law of the sea and the UN Climate Regime but also on evaluating whether the law of the sea regime is capable of supporting the main objectives of the UN Climate Regime.

16.3 THE ROLE OF THE LAW OF THE SEA IN CLIMATE-CHANGE MITIGATION AND ADAPTATION EFFORTS

16.3.1 *A Framework Convention that Enables New Development*

The United Nations Convention on the Law of the Sea (LOSC)[15] – the central element in the law of the sea regime – cannot be said to be a 'climate-change convention'.[16] It was negotiated back in the 1970s and early 1980s,[17] so terms like 'global warming' and 'climate change' are nowhere to be found in the convention text.[18] However, the LOSC does set out the jurisdictional framework within which ocean-related climate change measures are to be carried out.

The LOSC has been called the 'constitution for the oceans', as it has certain characteristics typical of constitutions – such as comprehensiveness, permanence, timeliness, certainty, and embedded values.[19] Designed to provide predictability and certainty, it also has a built-in flexibility intended to enable

12 M. A. Young, 'Fragmentation, regime interaction and sovereignty' in C. Chinkin and F. Baetens (eds.), *Sovereignty, Statehood and State Responsibility, Essays in Honour of James Crawford* (Cambridge University Press, 2015), 71–89, at 71–72.

13 Young, 'Regime interaction', at 85; S. Oberthür, 'Regime-interplay management, lessons from environmental policy and law' in K. Blome et al. (eds.), *Contested Regime Collisions, Norm Fragmentation in World Society* (Cambridge University Press, 2016), 88–108, at 88.

14 Young, 'Regime interaction', at 91.

15 United Nations Convention on Law of The Sea, Montego Bay, 10 December 1982, in force 16 November 1994, 1833 UNTS 3.

16 See Vidas et al., this volume, Chapter 2.

17 R. K. Craig, this volume, Chapter 3.

18 Vidas et al., this volume, Chapter 2.

19 V. Aiyedogbon et al. (eds.), Report on the Expert Workshop, *Sovereignty, A Shape-Shifting Concept in Ocean Governance?*, Utrecht, 13 June 2019, available at www.uu.nl/sites/default/files/rebo-sovereignty_expert_workshop_programme.pdf

it to adapt to new challenges unknown at the time it was negotiated. New global challenges, such as climate change, have arisen since then, sharpening and challenging this inherent tension between stability and change in the LOSC.

Being a framework convention does, however, provide it with opportunities to evolve with the needs and development of global society. That climate change is not specifically mentioned does not mean that it falls outside the regulatory scope of the convention. On the contrary, the ambition underlying the LOSC was to cover all activities within the ocean space[20] – including the development of new technologies and new needs. Possibilities for using the ocean space for the development of marine renewable energy resources, as well as for deployment of geoengineering techniques to remove excess greenhouse gases (GHGs) from the atmosphere, show how the law of the sea can come to play a vital role in the achieving of the goals of the Paris Agreement.

In Chapter 9 of this volume, das Neves points out that the LOSC 'provides a basic legal framework that enables and is supportive of the development of marine renewable energy resources', by clarifying the rights of states, either in their capacity as coastal states or as part of their freedoms of the high seas, to exploit marine renewable energy. The analyses in Bankes' and Johansen's Chapters 7 and 8 in this volume confirm the flexibility within the law of the sea regime to encompass new activities and changed circumstances, as the LOSC itself does not prohibit the deployment of geoengineering techniques. However, Bankes does point out that other global or regional instruments might have that effect.[21] For example, the London Protocol, as originally adopted, clearly prohibited most offshore carbon capture storage (CCS) disposal activities (as opposed to CO_2/EOR). Similarly, regulatory challenges represent an obstacle to the further exploration of ocean fertilization as a strategy for countering the effects of climate change. In Chapter 8, having shown how ocean fertilization activities are regulated by and fall under several different regimes, creating practical and conceptual problems, Johansen argues the pressing need for more 'concerted and coherent action'.[22]

The need to develop additional regulation is another aspect of the general character of the LOSC as a framework convention. This is relevant for the further development of offshore renewable energy as well as for marine geoengineering techniques. Aquaculture is another example. The international community has, through the FAO, pointed out that aquaculture

[20] LOSC, Preamble.
[21] N. Bankes, this volume, Chapter 7, Section 7.6.
[22] E. Johansen, this volume, Chapter 8, Section 8.6.

should increase in order to cover the world's demand for seafood, as well as recognizing the increasingly severe need for climate-change adaptation in that sector.[23] Furthermore, in Chapter 12 of this volume, Dahl argues the need to develop international measures to ensure and implement the obligations of the law of the sea regime as regards reducing the environmental impacts of aquaculture and adapting to climate change.

16.3.2 *How Flexible Is the LOSC and How Dynamically Can It Be Interpreted?*

The substantive role of the LOSC in the context of climate change is, to some degree, a matter of interpretation. The question of how dynamically it can be interpreted arises not least as regards sea-level rise in connection with baselines. The current main rule of ambulatory baselines and shifting maritime limits, as set out in the Convention, cannot offer solutions to the loss of territory, relocation of maritime zones, uncertainty and instability caused by rising sea levels. In Chapter 13 of this volume, Busch argues that there exists a certain flexibility in the regime for law of baselines, allowing for broader interpretation of existing rules without any need to amend the LOSC.

The question of the flexibility of the LOSC arises also in the context of the obligation of states to reduce emissions and thereby protect the marine environment. Does the Convention provide for more stringent reduction obligations for land-based GHG emissions than the Kyoto Protocol[24] and the Paris Agreement?[25] Here, Boyle concludes that, while the LOSC obliges its states parties to implement the UN Climate Regime, it does not impose more stringent obligations.[26]

However, it is questionable whether the emissions reduction obligations in the Kyoto Protocol and the Paris Agreement 'are appropriate to address the impacts of climate change on the ocean'.[27] In fact, the UN Climate Regime does not deal specifically with ocean acidification.[28] Arguably, the 1992 UN

[23] I. V. Dahl, this volume, Chapter 12, Section 12.7.

[24] Kyoto Protocol to the United Nations Framework Convention on Climate Change, adopted 11 December 1997, entered into force 16 February 2005, 37 ILM 22.

[25] Paris Agreement under the United Nations Framework Convention on Climate Change, adopted 12 December 2015, entered into force 4 November 2016, 55 ILM 743.

[26] Boyle, this volume, Chapter 4, Section 4.3.

[27] K. N. Scott, 'Climate change and the oceans: navigating legal orders' in M. H. Nordquist, J. N. Moore and R. Long (eds.), *Legal Order in the World's Oceans: UN Convention on the Law of the Sea* (Brill 2017), 124–153, 132.

[28] Ibid., 135; Scott, this volume, Chapter 5.

Framework Convention on Climate Change (UNFCCC)[29] provides no *lex specialis* regarding CO_2 emissions limits or a pH change target; indeed, 'it is acknowledged that even full compliance with the 2015 Paris Agreement is unlikely to prevent or reduce ocean acidification'.[30] In this context, Scott (Chapter 5, Section 5.4) argues that, according to one interpretation, the states parties to the LOSC must 'take action that targets ocean acidification in addition to or at least as part of their measures designed to address climate change', if they are to comply with their due diligence obligation to prevent, reduce and control pollution arising from ocean acidification under LOSC Part XII.

16.3.3 *Inherent Obstacles*

The main challenges to the potential of the law of the sea regime to support and enhance the goals of the UN Climate Regime lie in its inherent obstacles to effective marine environmental protection. Among such obstacles are the lack of clarity and the vagueness of the general obligations in Part XII.[31] Furthermore, the LOSC's zonal and sectoral approach to ocean management may prove to be an obstacle for implementing effective measures against the causes and effects of climate change.

Jakobsen (Chapter 10, Section 10.6) argues that establishing effective management of marine protected areas (MPAs) will require a truly integrated approach to ocean management, with MPAs established for the purpose of mitigation of and adaptation to climate change: 'scientific studies have shown that such MPAs should preferably be larger areas with stricter and effective regulations'. Also recognized is the inadequacy of the present regime to protect the marine environment, especially in areas beyond national jurisdiction, which has resulted in the negotiations of an internationally legally binding instrument under the LOSC on the conservation and sustainable use of marine biodiversity in areas beyond national jurisdiction.[32] However, as pointed out by Prip (Chapter 14), at the current stage of negotiations, climate change does not play a major role, and there is

29 United Nations Framework Convention on Climate Change, Rio de Janeiro, 9 May 1992, in force 21 March 1994, 1771 UNTS 107.

30 Scott, this volume, Chapter 5, Section 5.4.

31 R. Churchill, 'The LOSC regime for protection of the marine environment – fit for the twenty-first century?' in R. Rayfuse (ed.), *Research Handbook on International Marine Environmental law* (Edward Elgar, 2015), 3–30. See also Y. Tanaka, *The International Law of the Sea*, 2nd ed. (Cambridge University Press, 2015), Chs. 7–9.

32 UNGA Res 72/249 (24 December 2017).

disagreement on the extent to which climate-change considerations should be reflected in the new treaty.

Climate-change-related impacts on the oceans, such as ocean acidification, threaten fish stocks, thus constituting an additional challenge to the problems of overexploitation, pollution and overcapacity.[33] As Molenaar observes in Chapter 11, the LOSC and the UN Fish Stock Agreement[34] do not restrict the right of coastal states or flag states to incorporate climate-change mitigation and adaptation measures in their fisheries management. However, the LOSC provides only for a 'qualified obligation on adaptation'; the UN Fish Stock Agreement provides for slightly stronger obligations.[35] However, both the LOSC and the UN Fish Stocks Agreement lack any *mitigation* obligations in the context of marine capture fisheries.[36]

To some extent, the challenges entailed in ensuring sustainable global fisheries can be explained by the design and fundamental principles of the law of the sea as well as general international law. By virtue of the *pacta tertiis* principle, states are not bound by treaties without their consent.[37] Molenaar argues that the principle will impede '[t]he effectiveness of voluntary adaptation and mitigation measures'.[38] For example, states which did not consent to measures aimed at reducing GHG emissions from high seas fishing activities would not be obliged to require fishing vessels flying their flag to comply with these measures. Given the constraints of the *pacta tertiis* principle, regional fisheries management organizations (RFMOs) play a key role in the management of transboundary and high seas fish stocks.[39] Thus far, however, RFMOs have inadequately incorporated climate-change considerations, especially

33 E. J. Molenaar, this volume, Chapter 11; see also M. Barange and K. L. Cochrane, 'Impacts of climate change on fisheries and aquaculture: conclusions' in M. Barange et al. (eds.), *Impacts of Climate Change on Fisheries and Aquaculture, Synthesis of current Knowledge, Adaptation and Mitigation Options* (FAO 2018), 611–628, 617.

34 1995 Agreement for the Implementation of the Provisions of the United Nations Convention on the Law of the Sea of 10 December 1982 relating to the Conservation and Management of Straddling Fish Stocks and Highly Migratory Fish Stocks, New York, 4 August 1995, 2167 UNTS 3.

35 Ibid.

36 Ibid.

37 E. J. Molenaar and R. Caddell, 'International fisheries law: achievements, limitations and challenges' in R. Caddell and E. J. Molenaar (eds.), *Strengthening International Fisheries Law in an Era of Changing Oceans* (Hart, 2019), 3–10, 9.

38 Molenaar, this volume, Chapter 11, Section 11.6.

39 See generally, R. Rayfuse, 'Regional fisheries management organizations' in D. R. Rothwell, et al. (eds.), *The Oxford Handbook of the Law of the Sea* (Oxford University Press, 2015), 439–462.

regarding measures aimed at reducing GHG emissions from fishing activities.[40]

Lack of effective regulation of GHG emission from shipping is another indication of the lack of ambition to get the necessary regulations in place. As Ringbom (Chapter 6, Section 6.5) concludes concerning efforts to curb shipping GHG emissions, 'the truth remains that very little has been done so far in terms of legally binding emissions reductions'. While it is true that the International Maritime Organization (IMO) is the international body with the greatest technical knowledge and experience of regulating shipping, and the only body which the targets of regulation (ship operators) recognized as legitimate, the LOSC does not delegate to the IMO any legal monopoly on regulating international shipping. As Ringbom (Chapter 6, Section 6.5) argues, 'if the work of IMO fails to meet their expectations, it is only natural – and entirely consistent with the LOSC – that they should assume a greater role in advancing the matter'. This indicates that the substantial scope of the LOSC is wide enough to admit any issue that has a bearing on the marine environment.

16.3.4 *Complementing the UN Climate Regime*

While the LOSC's substantive role in climate-change mitigation efforts is partly subject to interpretation, Boyle (Chapter 4) argues that the mandatory dispute settlement system provided for in LOSC Part XV, 'could be invoked by any state party if another party's failure to implement the Paris Agreement constitutes non-compliance with its LOSC Part XII obligations'. This is perhaps one of the clearest examples of how the LOSC can both reinforce and strengthen the UN Climate Regime by offering a mechanism for compliance lacking in the Paris Agreement. However, Boyle (Chapter 4, Section 4.5) also observes that so far states have not made use of the LOSC's dispute settlement system in the context of climate change, stressing that 'the political challenge in litigating against the states that are responsible for most of the current GHG emissions should not be underestimated'. In general, Johansen observes that the use of law of the sea-based rights and obligations is almost non-existent in climate litigation.[41]

40 Molenaar, this volume, Chapter 11; see further R. Rayfuse, 'Addressing climate change impacts in regional fisheries management organizations' in E. J. Molenaar and R. Caddell (eds.), *Strengthening International Fisheries Law in an Era of Changing Oceans* (Hart, 2019), 247, 257–267.

41 E. Johansen, 'The role of the law of the sea in climate change litigation' (2020) *The Yearbook of Polar Law*, 141–169.

16.4 THE WAY FORWARD

16.4.1 *New Responses*

The political and legal systems currently in place are premised on the understanding that we are able to predict the responses of natural systems to human activities and offer some predictability and stability in how human activities are governed.[42] However, that is simply no longer the case. If we are to have any hopes of mitigating the worst-case scenarios and adapting to the unavoidable changes brought by climate change, we must recognize that the need for good governance is greater than ever before.

Yes, some responses to climate change have emerged. They must continue across multiple levels and involve multiple actors and sectors, in order to develop and implement international climate change law.[43] As almost all human activities contribute to climate change in some way, 'climate change engages many different areas of international law' – the LOSC not least.[44] The Convention is a flexible instrument, and dynamic interpretation and evolution of its environmental provisions are indeed possible – but more is needed.[45] As the analyses in this book have shown, more specific and detailed regulations must be developed within a range of areas, to address climate change and truly contribute to mitigation and adaptation.

Such new regulations and norms will need to be interactional, so that linkages are created between the various regimes. As pointed out by Scott in Chapter 5, 'for a regime complex to be effective, meaningful connections and linkages must be created between regimes in order to create a coherent network of regulatory control'.[46] The ongoing UNGA process towards a legally binding treaty on BBNJ is, as pointed out by Prip (Chapter 14), one possibility for filling the legal gaps and developing a more integrated cross-sectoral regime that addresses climate-change concerns in areas beyond national jurisdiction. Unfortunately, the importance of addressing climate change has been downplayed in these negotiations. Furthermore, through regional cooperation, and through regional frameworks and agreements, states may develop norms and regulations that connect ocean governance and

42 Vidas et al., this volume, Chapter 2.
43 D. Bodansky, J. Brunnée and L. Rajamani, *International Climate Change Law* (Oxford University Press, 2017), at 30.
44 Ibid.
45 See C. Redgwell, 'Treaty evolution, adaptation and change: is the LOSC "enough" to address climate change impacts on the marine environment?' (2019) 34 *International Journal of Marine and Coastal Law*, 440–457.
46 Scott, this volume, Chapter 5, Section 5.3.

climate-change considerations, thereby addressing the effects of climate change in a more effective way.

In their separate chapters in this volume, Scott, Poto, Vidas, et al., ask whether the system needs to be reformed. In Chapter 15, Poto makes the case for a new ontology of ocean governance: for an ocean-centred paradigm instead of the human-centred paradigm we have today. Similar, in Chapter 2, Vidas and co-authors argue the need for a deep conceptual change in international law: '[I]nternational law will not be able to respond adequately by simply amending some rules or adding new ones: what is necessary is a systemic change.'[47] On the other hand, in Chapter 5, Scott notes that there might be the need for an implementation agreement under the LOSC dealing with climate change – but also points out that, as states are currently involved in the BBNJ negotiations, there is probably not so much interest in negotiating a separate implementation agreement at the same time.[48]

Climate-change law seems set to continue to develop within a regime complex. However, finding truly effective responses to climate change will also require new interactional norms – norms that can set specific targets and measures within areas such as ocean acidification, biodiversity conservation and resilience, binding GHG targets for international shipping, with a regulatory framework for new 'climate-friendly activities', such as developing green energy and marine geoengineering techniques.

16.4.2 *The Significance of Legal Research*

Addressing climate change is a highly complex endeavour. As this systemic challenge may not be fully addressed within one legal regime, legal research will continue to play an important role. Climate change, by its very nature, also changes the context within which international law operates – and that calls for new responses. As pointed out by Vidas and co-authors in Chapter 2, international scholarship may prove of great importance here, given the special position of scholarship in the system of international law. Legal scholarship will have several central roles in the future. First, systemic interpretation of the relevant instruments in light of new practice and changing circumstances is an important task for legal scholars. Through their work, the dynamic interpretation of the LOSC may be developed and the relevant regulations and instruments may be interpreted and read together, in a way that creates linkages between the different regimes. Second, as also noted by

47 Vidas et al., this volume, Chapter 2, Section 2.3.4.
48 Scott, this volume, Chapter 5, Section 5.4.

Vidas and colleagues, we need more interdisciplinary research that takes into account scientific predictions regarding natural circumstances and the effects of climate change. This will require further development of methodological approaches, where the law of the sea is analysed beyond the traditional doctrinal methods, but interpreted and applied in its proper context. Recently, more holistic research has examined entire legal regimes, not only single instruments. This brings us to the third role of legal scholarship: to provide holistic analyses of the interplay between regimes, the interactions between regulations at various levels and involving a range of sectors. Legal scholarship must take responsibility for research aimed not only at revealing the gaps and conflicts resulting from overlaps in regimes and regulations. Professor Sebastian Oberthür, trained as a political scientist and with a strong background in international law, has noted the potential advantages of fragmented governance systems and regime complexes: he argues that regime interplay may in fact enhance synergies and might be the best option for complex and multilevel problems.[49] As climate change is a complex transboundary environmental and societal problem, and difficult to address effectively by means of only one instrument or legal regime, more research is needed on the interplay between the legal regimes. Such research should focus on the coherence and the effectiveness of the regulations and instruments within a given regime complex, as well as whether and how the regime complex allows for the adaptation and flexibility that is necessary to address climate change.[50]

While further (legal) research will play a key role in informing the necessary regulatory responses, it must be stressed that there is first and foremost an urgent need for decisive action on the part of states. Climate changes pose severe threats to the health of the world's oceans – and yet, as Scott observed recently, states have been 'slow to recognize the implications of climate change for the oceans – in contrast to the atmosphere and bio-sphere'.[51]

That being said, there are also grounds for optimism. Here we may note in particular the increasing awareness of the relationship between the ocean and

[49] S. Oberthür, 'Regime-Interplay management, lessons from environmental policy and law' in K. Blome, et al. (eds.), *Contested Regime Collisions: Norm Fragmentation in World Society* (Cambridge University Press, 2016), 88–108, with further references to R. Keohane, D. Victor and E. Ostrom at 91.

[50] See J. van Erp (ed.), *Smart Mixes for Transboundary Environmental Harm* (Cambridge University Press, 2019).

[51] K. N. Scott, 'Legal aspects of climate change' in International Ocean Institute, Canada, *The Future of Ocean Governance and Capacity Development: Essays in Honor of Elisabeth Mann Borgese (1918–2002)* (Brill Nijhoff, 2019), 169–174, at 169.

climate nexus. Recent COP meetings of the UN Climate Regime have paid considerable attention to the role of the oceans, acknowledging that, despite the growing recognition of the work underway concerning ocean and coastal adaptation, there are significant knowledge gaps and needs that remain. And indeed, simple recognizing this is an important step forward.

Bibliography

Abate, R. S. (ed.), *Climate Change Impacts on Oceans and Coastal Law* (New York: Oxford University Press, 2015).

Abate, R., Greenlee, A., 'Sowing seeds uncertain: ocean iron fertilization, climate change, and the international environmental law framework' (2010) 27 *Pace Environmental Law Review*, 555–598.

Aiyedogbon, V., et al. (eds.), Report on the Expert Workshop, *Sovereignty, A Shape-shifting Concept in Ocean Governance?*, Utrecht, 13 June 2019, available at www.uu.nl/sites/default/files/rebo-sovereignty_expert_workshop_programme.pdf.

Alabi, S. A., 'Using litigation to enforce climate obligations under domestic and international law' (2012) 6 *Carbon & Climate Law Review*, 555–598.

Alexander, L. M., 'Baseline delimitations and maritime boundaries' (1982–1983) 23 *Virginia Journal of International Law*, 503–536.

Alexander, L. M., 'Alternative interpretation of geographic articles in the 1982 LOS Convention' (Center for Ocean Management Studies, Kingston, University of Rhode Island, 1990).

Alexander, S. E., Schneider, S. H., Lagerquist, K., 'The interaction of climate and life' in G. C. Daily (ed.), *Nature's Services: Societal Dependence on Natural Ecosystems* (Washington DC: Island Press, 1997), 71–82.

Altman, J., Jackson, S., 'Indigenous land and sea management' in D. Lindenmayer, S. Dovers and S. Morton (eds.), *Ten Commitments Revisited: Securing Australia's Future Environment* (Clayton South VIC: CSIRO Publishing, 2014), 207–216.

Andrassy, J., *Međunarodno pravo* (*International Law*), 7th ed. by B. Bakotić and B. Vukas (Zagreb: Školska knjiga, 1998).

Anthony, K. R. N., et al., 'Ocean acidification causes bleaching and productivity loss in coral reef builders' (2008) 105(45) *Proceedings of the National Academy of Sciences*, 17442–17446.

Arctic Monitoring and Assessment Programme (AMAP), AMAP Assessment 2013, *Arctic Ocean Acidification* (2013). www.amap.no/documents/doc/amap-assessment-2013-arctic-ocean-acidification/881

Armeni, C., 'Legal developments for carbon capture and storage under international regional marine legislation' in I. Havercroft, R. Macrory and R. B. Stewart (eds.), *Carbon Capture and Storage: Emerging Legal and Regulatory Issues* (Oxford: Hart Publishing, 2011), 145–158.

Árnadóttir, S., 'Termination of maritime boundaries due to a fundamental change of circumstances' (2016) 32(83) *Utrecht Journal of International and European Law*, 94–111.

Atler, K. J., Meunier, S., 'The politics of international regime complexity' (2009) 7 *Perspectives on Politics*, 13–24.

Gehring, T., and Faude, B., 'The dynamics of regime complexes: microfoundations and systemic effects' (2013) 19 *Global Governance*, 119–130.

Bachu, S., 'Review of CO_2 storage efficiency in deep saline aquifers' (2015) 40 *International Journal of Greenhouse Gas Control*, 188–202.

Bamber Kopp, J. L., et al., 'Ice sheet contributions to future sea-level rise from structured expert judgement' (2019) 116(23) *Proceedings of the National Academy of Sciences*, 11195–11200.

Bankes, N., 'Provisional application of an amendment to the London Protocol to facilitate collaborative CCS projects' (10 December 2019), available at ABlawg, http://ablawg.ca/wp-content/uploads/2019/12/Blog_NB_Article6.pdf.

Bankes, N., 'The use of sub-seabed transboundary geological formations for the disposal of carbon dioxide' in C. Banet (ed.), *The Law of the Seabed: Access, Uses, and Protection of Seabed Resources* (Brill, 2020).

Bankes, N., Brennan, E., 'Enhanced oil recovery and the geological sequestration of carbon dioxide' (2013) a paper prepared for Natural Resources Canada, available at www.law.ucalgary.ca/files/law/final_june7_enhanced-oil-recovery-and-the-geological-sequestration-of-carbon-dioxide.pdf.

Bankes, N., Dahl, I., VanderZwaag, D. L. (eds.), *Aquaculture Law and Policy* (Cheltenham: Edward Elgar, 2016).

Bankes, N., Trevisanut, S. (eds.), *Energy from the Sea: An International Law Perspective on Ocean Energy* (Leiden: Brill Nijhoff, 2015).

Barange, M., Cochrane, K. L., 'Impacts of climate change on fisheries and aquaculture: conclusions' in M. Barange et al. (eds.), *Impacts of Climate Change on Fisheries and Aquaculture, Synthesis of Current Knowledge, Adaptation and Mitigation Options* (Rome: FAO, 2018), 611–628.

Barnes, R., 'The law of the sea convention and the integrated regulation of the oceans' (2012) 27 *The International Journal of Marine and Coastal Law*, 859–866.

Barrett, J., 'The UN Convention on the Law of the Sea: a living treaty' in J. Barrett and R. Barnes (eds.), *Law of the Sea: UNCLOS as a Living Treaty* (London: British Institute of International and Comparative Law, 2016), 3–41.

Barrett, J., Barnes, R. (eds.), *Law of the Sea: UNCLOS as a Living Treaty* (London: British Institute of International and Comparative Law, 2016).

Bartenstein, K., 'Article 212' in A. Proelss (ed.), *United Nations Convention on the Law of the Sea: A Commentary* (Munchen: Beck/Hart, 2017), 858–881.

Bateman, A., Schofield, C., 'State practice regarding straight baselines in East Asia: legal, technical and political issues in a changing environment', paper prepared for international conference arranged by ABLOS in Monaco (2008), 4, available at www.iho.int/mtg_docs/com_wg/ABLOS/ABLOS_Conf5/Papers/Session7-Paper1-Bateman.pdf.

Baudrillard, J., *Hyperreality and Implosion*, Ceasefire Magazine, 10 August 2012, available at https://ceasefiremagazine.co.uk/in-theory-baudrillard-9/, accessed October 2019.

Baxter, J., et al., 'Marine Protected Areas and climate change mitigation: how MPAs can contribute to the reduction of greenhouse gas emissions' in F. Smiard, D. Laffoley and J. M. Baxter (eds.), *Marine Protected Areas and Climate Change: Adaptation and Mitigation Synergies, Opportunities and Challenges* (Gland: International Union for Conservation of Nature, 2016), 41–49.

Because the Ocean, *Ocean for Climate* Report (2019), available at www.becausetheocean.org/wp-content/uploads/2019/10/Ocean_for_Climate_Because_the_Ocean.pdf.

Bednaršek, N., et al., 'Pteropods on the edge: cumulative effects of ocean acidification, warming, and deoxygenation' (2016) 145 *Progress in Oceanography*, 1–24.

Bergh, Ø., Ingvaldsen, R., Mork, K. A., 'Fiskeoppdrett i varmere hav'/'Aquaculture in warmer oceans' (2012) 1 2°/C, 36–38.

Berkes, F., et al. (eds.), *Navigating Social–Ecological Systems: Building Resilience for Complexity and Change* (New York: Cambridge University Press, 2003).

Bertram, C., 'Ocean iron fertilization in the context of the Kyoto Protocol and the post-Kyoto process' (2010) 38 *Energy Policy*, 1130–1139.

Berwyn, B., 'Ice loss and the polar vortex: how a warming Arctic fuels cold snaps', Inside climate NEWS, 28 September 2017, available at insideclimatenews.org/news/27092017/polar-vortex-cold-snap-arctic-ice-loss-global-warming-climate-change.

Biermann, F., et al., 'Navigating the Anthropocene: improving earth system governance' (2012) 335(6074) *Science*, 1306–1307.

Billé, R., et al., *Regional Oceans Governance: Making Regional Seas Programmes, Regional Fishery Bodies and Large Marine Ecosystem Mechanisms Work Better Together*, UNEP Regional Seas Report and Studies No. 196 (2016). https://wedocs.unep.org/bitstream/handle/20.500.11822/7701/-Regional_oceans_governance_Making_Regional_Seas_programmes,_regional_fishery_bodies_and_large_marine_ecosystem_mechanisms_work_better_together-2016R.pdf?sequence=3&amp%3BisAllowed=

Birchenough, S., Williamson, P., Turley, C., 'Future of the sea: ocean acidification', Government Office for Science, 2017, available at www.gov.uk/go-science.

Bird, E., Prescott, V., 'Rising global sea levels and national maritime claims' (1989) 1 *Marine Policy Reports*, 189.

Birnie, P., 'The status of environmental "soft-law": trends and examples with special focus on IMO norms' in H. Ringbom (ed.), *Competing Norms in the Law of Marine Environmental Protection* (The Hague: Kluwer, 1997).

Birnie, P., Boyle, A., Redgwell, C., *International Law and the Environment*, 3rd ed. (Oxford: Oxford University Press, 2009).

BLOOM, 'Electric "pulse" fishing: why it should be banned', November 2018, available at www.bloomassociation.org/en/our-actions/our-themes/electric-pulse-fishing/.

Bodansky, D., 'Protecting the marine environment from vessel-source pollution: UNCLOS III and Beyond' (1991) 18 *Ecology Law Quarterly*, 719–777.

Bodansky, D., 'May we engineer the climate?' (1996) 33 *Climactic Change*, 309–321.

Bodansky, D., 'The legal character of the Paris agreement' (2016) 25 *Review of European Comparative & International Environmental Law*, 142–150.

Bodansky, D., 'The Paris climate change agreement: a new hope?' (2016) 110 *American Journal of International Law*, 288–319.

Bodansky, D., Brunnée, J., Rajamani, L., *International Climate Change Law* (New York: Oxford University Press, 2017).
Bodansky, D., O'Connor, S. D., 'The legal character of the Paris agreement' (2016) 25(2) *Review of European, Comparative & International Environmental Law*, 142–150.
Bogojevic, S., 'Legalising environmental leadership: a comment on the CJEU's ruling in C-366/10 on the inclusion of aviation in the EU emissions trading scheme' (2012) 24(2) *Journal of Environmental Law*, 345–356.
Bohannon, J., 'Weighing the climate risks of an untapped fossil fuel' (2008) 319 *Science*, 1753.
Born, D. A., et al., 'Structural basis for methylphosphonate biosynthesis' (2017) 358 *Science*, 1336–1339.
Börzel, T. A., 'Theorizing regionalism: operation, integration, and governance', Prepared for T. A. Börzel and T. Risse (eds.), *Oxford Handbook of Comparative Regionalism* (Oxford: Oxford University Press, 2016), 1–26.
Börzel, T. A., van Hüllen, V. (eds.), *Governance Transfer by Regional Organizations Patching Together a Global Script* (Houndmills: Palgrave Macmillan, 2015).
Boyle, A. E., 'The Southern Bluefin Tuna Arbitration' (2001) 50 *International and Comparative Law Quarterly*, 447–452.
Boyle, A. E., 'Transboundary air pollution and international law', in S. Jayakumar et al. (eds.), *Transboundary Pollution: Evolving Issues of International Law and Policy* (Cheltenham: Ashgate, 2015), 233–259.
Boyle, A., 'Further development of the law of the sea convention: mechanisms for change' (2005) 54(3) *International and Comparative Law Quarterly*, 563–584.
Boyle, A., 'Law of the sea perspectives on climate change' (2012) 27 *The International Journal of Marine and Coastal Law*, 831–838.
Boyle, A., 'Climate change, ocean governance and UNCLOS' in J. Barrett and R. Barnes (eds.), *Law of the Sea: UNCLOS as a Living Treaty* (London: British Institute of International and Comparative Law, 2016), 225–231.
Boyle, A., 'Litigating climate change under Part XII of the LOSC' (2019) 34 *International Journal of Marine and Coastal Law*, 458–481.
Boyle, A., Chinkin, C., *The Making of International Law* (Oxford: Oxford University Press, 2007).
Boyle, A., Singh Ghaleigh, N., 'Climate change and international law beyond the UNFCCC' in C. P. Carlarne, K. R. Gray and R. G. Tarasofsky (eds.), *The Oxford Handbook of International Climate Change Law* (Oxford: Oxford University Press, 2016), 26–54.
Branch, T., et al., 'Impacts of ocean acidification on marine seafood' (2013) 28 *Trend in Ecology and Evolution*, 178–186.
Branson, M., 'A green herring: how current ocean fertilization regulation distracts from geoengineering research' (2014) 54 *Santa Clara Law Review*, 163–200.
Breitburg, D., et al., 'Declining oxygen in the global ccean and coastal waters' (2018) 359 *Science*, 46.
Broadway, R., Anwar, S., *Fiscal Federalism: Principles and Practice of Multilevel Governance* (Cambridge: Cambridge University Press, 2009).
Brown Weiss, E., 'The evolution of international environmental law' (2011) 54 *Japanese Yearbook of International Law*, 1–27.

Brown, E. D., *The International Law of the Sea* (Aldershot: Dartmouth Publishing Company, 1994) vo. I.

Burke, K. D., et al., 'Pliocene and Eocene provide best analogs for near-future climates' (2018) 115 (52) *Proceedings of the National Academy of Sciences*, 13288–13293.

Burke, K. P., Rameka, L., 'Kaitiakitanga active guardianship, responsibilities and relationships with the world: towards a bio-cultural future in early childhood education', available at researchcommons.waikato.ac.nz/bitstream/handle/10289/11216/Kaitiakitanga%20-%20FINAL.pdf?sequence=11&isAllowed=y.

Busch, S. V., *Establishing Continental Shelf Limits Beyond 200 Nautical Miles by the Coastal State: A Right of Involvement for Other States* (Leiden: Brill, 2016).

Busch, S. V., 'Sea level rise and shifting maritime limits: stable baselines as a response to unstable coastlines' (2018) 9 *Arctic Review on Law and Politics*, 174–194.

Caddell, R., 'Precautionary management and the development of future fishing opportunities: the international regulation of new and exploratory fisheries' (2018) 33 *International Journal of Marine and Coastal Law*, 199–260.

Cai, W., et al., 'Acidification of subsurface coastal waters enhanced by eutrophication' (2011) 4 *Nature Geoscience*, 766–770.

Cajete, G., *Native Science: Natural Laws of Interdependence* (Santa Fe, NM: Clear Light Publishers, 1999).

Caldeira, K., Wickett, M. E., 'Anthropogenic carbon and ocean pH' (2003) 425 *Nature*, 365.

Camden, W., *Annales Rerum Gestarum Angliae et Hiberniae Regnate Elizabetha* (as published in 1615 and 1625–1627), with the annotations of Sir Francis Bacon, in D. F. Sutton (ed.), University of California, Irvine, web-publication 2000/01, at www.philological.bham.ac.uk/camden, accessed 25 September 2019.

Campbell, L. M., Gray, N. J., 'Area expansion versus effective and equitable management in international marine protected areas goals and targets' (2019) 100 *Marine Policy*, 192–199.

Carbon Sequestration Leadership Forum, Technical Group, *Final Report from Task Force on Technical Barriers and R & D Opportunities for Offshore, Sub-Seabed Geologic Storage of CO_2*, CSLF-T-2015-06, 20 October 2015 (CSLF, *Offshore Geologic Storage*), available at www.cslforum.org/publications/documents/riyadh2015/tg_OffshoreSubSeabedStorageTaskForceFinalReport-Riyadh1115.pdf, 8–9.

Carlarne, C., 'Delinking international environmental law and climate change' (2014) 4 (1)*Michigan Journal of Environmental and Administrative Law*, available at http://repository.law.umich.edu/mjeal/vol4/iss1/1.

Carlarne, C. P., Gray, K. R., Tarasofsky, R. G., 'International climate change law: mapping the field' in C. P. Carlarne, K. R. Gray and R. G. Tarasofsky (eds.), *The Oxford Handbook of International Climate Change Law* (New York: Oxford University Press, 2016).

Caron, D. D., 'When law makes climate change worse: rethinking the law of baselines in light of a rising sea level' (1990) 17 *Ecology Law Quarterly*, 621–653.

Carpenter, K. E., et al., 'One-third of reef building corals face elevated extinction risk from climate change and local impacts' (2008) 321 *Science*, 560–563.

Carr, M. H., et al., 'The central importance of ecological spatial connectivity to effective coastal marine protected areas and to meeting the challenges of climate change in the marine environment' (2017) 27 *Aquatic Conservation Marine Freshwater Ecosystems*, 6–29.

Cartwright, J., 'Salinity changes affect sea level more than scientists thought', Environmental Research News, 9 February 2015.

Castelos, M. A., 'Marine renewable energies: opportunities, law, and management' (2014) 45 *Ocean Development & International Law*, 221–237.

Centre for International Governance Innovation (CIGI), A. Chircop, M. Doelle and R. Gauvin, Special Report, *Shipping and Climate Change: International Law and Policy Considerations* (2018) (hereinafter CIGI Report), 11.

Centre for International Governance Innovation (CIGI), A. N. Craik and W. C. G. Burns, Special Report, *Climate Engineering under the Paris Agreement: A Legal and Policy Primer* (2016) (CIGI Report 2016), available at www.cigionline.org/sites/default/files/documents/GeoEngineering%20Primer%20-%20Special%20Report.pdf.

Centre for International Law (CIL), Conference Report, *Climate Change and the Law of the Sea: Adapting the Law of the Sea to Address the Challenges of Climate Change* (13–14 March 2018) (Singapore Conference Report), available at https://cil.nus.edu.sg/wp-content/uploads/2018/04/Climate-Change-Law-of-the-Sea-Final-report.pdf.

Chan, F., et al., 'Emergence of anoxia in the California current large marine ecosystem' (2008) 319 *Science*, 920.

Chapin III, F. S., Kofinas, G. P., Folke, C. (eds.), *Principles of Ecosystem Stewardship: Resilience-Based Natural Resource Management in a Changing World* (New York: Springer, 2009).

Cheung, W. W. L., et al., 'Modelling future oceans: the present and emerging future of fish stocks and fisheries' in R. Caddell and E. J. Molenaar (eds.), *Strengthening International Fisheries Law in an Era of Changing Oceans* (Oxford/Portland: Hart, 2019), section 2, 13–24.

Chief Executives Board for Coordination, United Nations, *UNFCCC: Cancun Adaptation Framework*, available at www.unsystem.org/content/unfccc-cancun-adaptation-framework, accessed 21 November 2018.

Chrystostomou, A., Vagslid, E., 'Climate change: a challenge for IMO too' in R. Asariotis and H. Benemara (eds.), *Maritime Transport and the Climate Change Challenge* (Earthscan, 2012), 75–111.

Church, J. A., et al. (eds.), *Climate Change 2013: The Physical Science Basis, Contribution of Working Group I to the Fifth Assessment Report of the Intergovernmental Panel on Climate Change* (Cambridge: Cambridge University Press, 2014).

Churchill, R., 'The LOSC regime for protection of the marine environment – fit for the twenty-first century?' in R. Rayfuse (ed.), *Research Handbook on International Marine Environmental law* (Edward Elgar, 2015), 3–30.

Churchill, R. R., Lowe, A. V., *The Law of the Sea*, 3rd ed. (Manchester: Manchester University Press, 1999).

Cicin-Sain, B., et al., *Toward a Strategic Action Roadmap on Oceans and Climate: 2016–2021* (Washington DC: Global Ocean Forum, 2016), available at: https://globaloceanforumdotcom.files.wordpress.com/2013/03/strategic-action-roadmap-on-oceans-and-climate-november-2016.pdf.

Cicin-Sain, B., et al. (eds), October 2016, Policy Recommendations on Oceans and Climate for Consideration at UNFCCC COP 22 and Beyond, 4, available at: https://globaloceanforumdotcom.files.wordpress.com/2013/03/strategic-action-roadmap-on-oceans-and-climate-november-2016.pdf.

Cicin-Sain, B., Knecht, R., *Integrated Coastal and Ocean Management: Concepts and Practices* (Washington, DC: Island Press, 1998).

Cinnamon, P., et al., 'International climate change law: mapping the field' in P. Cinnamon et al. (eds.), *The Oxford Handbook of International Climate Change Law* (Oxford University Press, 2016), 3–25.

Clark, P. U., et al., 'Consequences of twenty-first-century policy for multi-millennial climate and sea-level change' (2016) 6 *Nature Climate Change*, 360–369.

Climate Transparency, *Brown to Green Report – The G20 Transition to a Low-Carbon Economy* 2018, available at www.climate-transparency.org/g20-climate-performance/g20report2018.

Coleman, M. A., et al., 'Anticipating changes to future connectivity within a network of marine protected areas' (2017) 23 *Global Change Biology*, 3533–3542.

Comeau, S., et al., 'Ocean acidification accelerates dissolution of experimental reef communities' (2015) 12 *Biogeosciences*, 365–372.

Cook, J., et al., 'Consensus on consensus: a synthesis of consensus estimates on global warming' (2016) 11(4) *Environmental Research Letters*, 1–7.

Costanza, R., et al., 'The value of the world's ecosystem services and natural capital' (1997) 387 *Nature*, 253–260.

Cox, P. M., et al., 'Acceleration of global warming due to carbon-cycle feedbacks in a coupled climate model' (2000) 408 *Nature*, 184–187.

Craig, R. K., 'Stationarity is dead: long live transformation: five principles for climate change adaptation law' (2010) 34 *Harvard Environmental Law Review*, 9–75.

Craig, R. K., 'Marine biodiversity, climate change, and governance of the oceans' (2012) 4 *Diversity*, 224–238.

Craig, R. K., 'Dealing with ocean acidification: the problem, the Clean Water Act, and state and regional approaches' (2015) 90 *Washington Law Review*, 1627–1654.

Craig. R. K., 'Oceans and coasts' in M. Burger and J. Gundlach (eds.), *Climate Change, Public Health, and the Law* (Cambridge: Cambridge University Press, 2018), 204–240.

Crutzen, P. J., 'Geology of mankind' (2002) 415 *Nature*, 23.

Crutzen, P. J., Stoermer, E. F., 'The "Anthropocene"' (2000) 41 *Global Change Newsletter*, 17–18.

Crutzen, P., 'We aren't doomed' (interview with C. Schwägerl) in N. Möllers, C. Schwägerl and H. Trischler (eds.), *Welcome to the Anthropocene: The Earth in our Hands* (Munich: Deutsches Museum, 2014), 30–36.

CSLF, *Offshore Geologic Storage*, at 14. The only significant offshore CO_2\EOR project is the Lula Project, Brazil, ibid. at 11.

Cullis-Suzuki, S., Pauly, D., 'Failing the high seas: a global evaluation of regional fishery management organizations' (2010) 34 *Marine Policy*, 1036–1042.

Currie, D., Wowk, K., 'Climate change and CO_2 in the oceans and global oceans governance' (2009) 3 *Carbon & Climate Law Review*, 387–404.

Czybulka, D., 'Article 192, mn 3' in A. Proelss (ed.), *United Nations Convention on the Law of the Sea: A Commentary* (München: C H Beck, 2017), 1277.

Damrosch, L., et al., 'Scholars in the construction and critique of international law' (2000) 94 *ASIL Proceedings*, 317–320.

Daw, T., et al., 'Climate change and capture fisheries: potential impacts, adaptation and mitigation' in FAO, 'Climate Change Implications for Fisheries and Aquaculture: Overview of Current Scientific Knowledge', *Fisheries and Aquaculture Technical Paper* No. 530 (FAO, 2009).

de Buffon, C, *The Epochs of Nature*, J. Zalasiewicz, A.-S. Milon and M. Zalasiewicz (trs.) (Chicago and London: University of Chicago Press, 2018).

de La Fayette, L., 'The OSPAR Convention comes into force: continuity and progress' (1999) 14 *The International Journal of Marine and Coastal* Law, 247–297.

De Lucia, V., 'Oceans commons, law of the sea and rights for the sea' (2019) 32(1) *Canadian Journal of Law & Jurisprudence*, 45–57.

De Santo, E. M., 'Implementation challenges of area-based management tools (ABMTs) for biodiversity beyond national jurisdiction (BBNJ)' (2018) 97 *Marine Policy*, 34–43.

DeConto, R. M., Pollard, D., 'Contribution of Antarctica to past and future sea-level rise' (2016) 531 *Nature*, 591–596.

Dhall, A., 'On the philosophy and legal theory of human rights in light of quantum holism' (2010) 66(1) *World Futures*, 1–25.

Di Gregorio, M., et al., 'Multi-level governance and power in climate change policy networks' (2019) 54 *Global Environmental Change*, 64–77.

Diaz, R. J., Rosenberg, R., 'Spreading dead zones and consequences for marine ecosystems' (2008) 321 *Science*, 926–929.

Dixon, T., et al., 'International marine regulation of CO_2 geological storage: developments and implications of London and OSPAR' (2009) 1 *Energy Procedia*, 4503–4510.

Dixon, T., McCoy, S., Havercroft, I., 'Legal and regulatory developments on CCS' (2015) 40 *International Journal of Greenhouse Gas Control* 431–448.

Doelle, M., 'Climate change and the use of the dispute settlement regime of the Law of the Sea Convention' (2006) 37 *Ocean Development & International Law*, 319–337.

Doney, S., et al., 'Ocean acidification: the other CO2 problem' (2009) 1 *Annual Review of Marine Science*, 169–192.

Druel, E., Gjerde, K., 'Sustaining marine life beyond boundaries: options for an implementing agreement for marine biodiversity beyond national jurisdiction under the United Nations Convention on the Law of the Sea' (2014) 49 *Marine Policy*, 90–97.

Dufour, J., 'EU MRV vs. IMO fuel consumption data collection system', Verifavia Shipping, 2 December 2016, available at www.verifavia-shipping.com/shipping-carbon-emissions-verification/press-media-eu-mrv-vs-imo-fuel-consumption-data-collection-system-155.php; COM(2019) 38 final.

Dunn, D. C., et al., 'The onvention on Biological Diversity's ecologically or biologically significant areas: origins, development, and current status' (2014) 49 *Marine Policy* 137–145, available at http://dx.doi.org/10.1016/j.marpol.2013.12.002i.

Dupont, S., Pörner, H., 'A snapshot of ocean acidification research' (2013) 160 *Marine Biology* 1765–1771.

Durden, J. M., et al., 'Environmental impact assessment process for deep-sea mining in "the Area"' (2017) 87 *Marine Policy*, 194–202.

Eberlein, T., et al., 'Effects of ocean acidification on primary production in a coastal North Sea phytoplankton community' (2017) 12(3) *PLoS ONE*, e0172594.

Edmunds, P., Yarid, A., 'The effects of ocean acidification on wound repair in the coral *Porites* spp' (2017) 486 *Journal of Experimental marine Biology and Ecology*, 98–104.

Edwards, M., 'Sea life (Pelagic Ecosystems)', in T. M. Letcher (ed.), *Climate Change: Observed Impacts on Planet Earth*, 2nd ed. (Amsterdam: Elsevier, 2016).

Ehler, C., Douvere, F., *Visions for a Sea Change*, Report of the first international workshop on Marine Spatial Planning, Intergovernmental Oceanographic Commission and Man and the Biosphere Programme, IOC manual and guides no. 48 (Paris: UNESCO, 2007).

Ekstrom, J., Crona, B., 'Institutional misfit and environmental change: a systems approach to address ocean acidification' (2017) 576 *Science of the Total Environment*, 599–608.

Ekstrom, J., et al., 'Vulnerability and adaptation of US shellfisheries to ocean acidification' (2015) 5 *Nature Climatic Change*, 207–214.

Elferink, A., 'Environmental impact assessment in areas beyond national jurisdiction' (2012) 27 *International Journal of Marine and Coastal Law*, 449–480.

Energy Agency, Energy Technology Network, 'Ocean: pilots, projects and potentials' (2015), available at web.archive.org/web/20150522054948/ http://www.iea.org/techinitiatives/renewableenergy/ocean/, accessed 5 January 2019.

Esmaeili, H., *The Legal Regime of Offshore Oil Rigs in International Law* (Dartmouth: Ashgate, 2001).

Espinosa, C., 'Interpretive affinities: the constitutionalization of rights of nature, Pacha Mama, in Ecuador' (2015) 21 *Journal of Environmental Policy & Planning*, 608–622.

Evans, M. D., *International Law* (Oxford: Oxford University Press, 2014).

Fabricius, K. E., et al., 'Losers and winners in coral reefs acclimatized to elevated carbon dioxide concentrations' (2011) 1 *Nature Climate Change*, 165–169.

Falk, R., 'Voluntary international law and the Paris Agreement' (2016) *Commentary on Global Issues*, blog available at https://richardfalk.wordpress.com/2016/01/16/voluntary-international-law-and- the-paris-agreement/.

Falk, R., Elver, H., 'Comparing global perspectives: The 1982 UNCLOS and the 1992 UNCED' in D. Vidas and W. Østreng (eds.), *Order for the Oceans* (The Hague: Kluwer, 1999).

FAO Technical Guidelines for Responsible Fisheries No. 5, Aquaculture Development (1997).

FAO, *Technical Guidelines for Responsible Fisheries. No. 4 'Fisheries Management', Suppl. 2 'The Ecosystem Approach to Management'* (Rome: FAO, 2003).

FAO, 'Report of the FAO Expert Workshop on Climate Change Implications for Fisheries and Aquaculture, Rome, 7–9 April 2008', *FAO Fisheries Report No. 870* (FAO, 2008).

FAO Technical Guidelines for Responsible Fisheries No. 5, Suppl. 3, Aquaculture Development: Genetic Resource Management (Rome, 2008), www.fao.org/3/a-i0283e.html.

FAO, 'Climate Change Implications for Fisheries and Aquaculture: Overview of Current Scientific Knowledge', *Fisheries and Aquaculture Technical Paper No. 530* (Rome: FAO, 2009), www.fao.org/3/i0994e/i0994e00.htm.

FAO Technical Guidelines for Responsible Fisheries No. 5, Suppl. 4, *Aquaculture development: Ecosystem approach to aquaculture* (Rome, 2010), www.fao.org/3/a-i1750e.pdf.

FAO, C. Shelton, Fisheries and Aquaculture Circular No. 1088: *Climate Change Adaptation in Fisheries and Aquaculture: Compilation of Initial Examples* (Rome, 2014), www.fao.org/3/a-i3569e.pdf.

FAO, P. B. Bueno and D. Soto, FAO Fisheries and Aquaculture Circular No. 1142: *Adaptation Strategies of the Aquaculture Sector to the Impacts of Climate Change* (Rome, 2017), www.fao.org/3/a-i6943e.pdf.

FAO, 'Impacts of climate change in fisheries and aquaculture: synthesis of current knowledge, adaptation and mitigation options', *FAO Fisheries and Aquaculture Technical Paper No. 627* (FAO, 2018), www.fao.org/3/i9705en/i9705en.pdf.

FAO, *The State of World Fisheries and Aquaculture 2018: Meeting the Sustainable Development Goals* (FAO, 2018).

Feely, R. A., et al., *Carbon Dioxide and Our Ocean Legacy* (Washington, DC: NOAA, 2006), available at www.pmel.noaa.gov/pubs/PDF/feel2899/feel2899.pdf.

Fenstad, A., 'Satellitter og maskinlæring kan hindre framtidig fiskedød fra giftalger', Teknisk ukeblad, 22 May 2019, available at www.tu.no/artikler/satellitter-og-maskinlaering-kan-hindre-framtidig-fiskedod-fra-giftalger/465881.

Fiskeri- og kystdepartementet, *Klimastrategi for Fiskeri- og kystdepartementet*/Ministry of Fisheries and Coastal Affairs, *Climate strategy for the Ministry of Fisheries and Coastal Affairs* (2013), www.regjeringen.no/globalassets/upload/fkd/brosjyrer200g20 veiledninger/2013/fiskeridep_klimastrategi_korr3.pdf.

Fluckiger, J., et al., 'High resolution Holocene N_2O ice core record and its relationship with CH_4 and CO_2' (2002) 16 *Global Biogeochemical Cycles* 10–1–10–8, see data at ftp://ftp.ncdc.noaa.gov/pub/data/paleo/icecore/antarctica/epica_domec/dc_co2_hol_flo2.txt.

Four Arrows and Narvaez, D., 'A more authentic baseline' in N. McCrary and W. Ross (eds.), *Working for Social Justice Inside and Outside the Classroom: A Community of Teachers, Researchers, and Activists* (New York: Peter Lang, 2015), 93–112.

Freestone, D., 'International governance, responsibility and management of areas beyond national jurisdiction' (2012) 27(2) *The International Journal of Marine and Coastal Law*, 191–204.

Freestone, D. (ed.), *The 1982 Law of the Sea Convention at 30: Successes, Challenges and New Agendas* (Leiden: Martin Nijhoff, 2013).

Freestone, D., Rayfuse, R., 'Ocean iron fertilization in international law' (2008) 364 *Marine Ecology Progress Series*, 227–233.

Frölicher, T. L., Fischer, E. M., Gruber, N., 'Marine heatwaves under global warming' (2018) 560 *Nature*, 360–364.

Frommel, A., et al., 'Ocean acidification has lethal and sub-lethal effects on larval development of yellowfin tuna, *Thunnus albacares*' (2016) 482 *Journal of Experimental Marine Biology and Ecology*, 18–24.

Fuentes-George, K., 'Consensus, certainty, and catastrophe: the debate over ocean iron fertilization' *The New Security Beat*, 3 May 2017, available at www.newsecuritybeat.org/2017/05/consensus-certainty-catastrophe-ocean-iron-fertilization-debate/.

Galea, F., 'A legal regime for the exploration and exploitation of offshore renewable energy' (2011) 25 *Ocean Yearbook*, 101–129.

Gallo, N. D., Victor, D. G. Levin, L.A., 'Ocean commitments under the Paris Agreement' (2017) 7 *Nature Climate Change*, 833–838.

Gander, K., 'Video shows sea "violently boiling" with methane bubbles in Siberia as Arctic permafrost thaws' *Newsweek*, 30 October 2019, available at www.newsweek.com/video-sea-boiling-methane-bubbles-siberia-arctic-permafrost-thaws-1468686.

Ganopolski, A., Winkelmann, R., Schellnhuber, H. J., 'Critical insolation-CO_2 relation for diagnosing past and future glacial inception' (2016) 529 *Nature*, 200–203.

Garrard, S., Beaumont, N., 'The effect of ocean acidification on carbon storage and sequestration in seagrass beds; a global and UK context' (2014) 86 *Marine Pollution Bulletin*, 138–146.

Gattuso, J. P., et al., 'Contrasting futures for ocean and society from different Anthropogenic CO_2 emissions scenarios' (2015) 349 *Science*, 4722.

Gaunce, J., 'On the interpretation of the general duty of "due regard"' (2018) 32 *Ocean Yearbook*, 27–59.

Geoengineering Monitor, *Ocean Fertilization (technology Factsheet)* (2018), available at www.geoengineeringmonitor.org/2018/05/ocean-fertilization/.

GESAMP, P. W. Boyd and C. M. G. Vivian (eds.), GESAMP No. 98, *High level review of a wide range of proposed marine geoengineering techniques* (2019).

Giannopoulos, N., 'Global environmental regulation of offshore energy production: searching for legal standards in ocean governance' (2018) 28 *Review of European, Comparative and International Environmental Law*, 289–303.

Ginzky, H., 'Marine geo-engineering' in M. Salomon and T. Markus (eds.), *Handbook on Marine Environment Protection* (Springer, 2018), 997–1011.

Gjerde, K. M., 'Challenges to protecting the marine environment beyond national jurisdiction' (2012) 27(4) *The International Journal of Marine and Coastal Law* 839–847.

Glasson, J., et al., *Introduction to Environmental Impact Assessment* 4th ed. (London: Routledge, 2013).

Global Ocean Acidification Observing Network, JA Newton Feely et al., *Requirements and Governance Plan*, 2nd ed. (2015), available at www.goa-on.org/documents/general/GOA-ON_2nd_edition_final.pdf.

Godbold, J., Solan, M., 'Long-term effects of warming and ocean acidification are modified by seasonal variation in species responses and environmental conditions' (2013) 368 *Philosophical Transactions B the Royal Society*, 20130186.

Goettsche-Wanli, G., 'Sustainable production of offshore renewable energy: a global perspective' in M. Kotzur et al. (eds.), *Sustainable Ocean Resource Governance: Deep Sea Mining, Marine Energy and Submarine Cables* (Leiden: Brill Nijhoff, 2018).

Goldin, I., *Globalization for Development: Meeting New Challenges* (New York: Oxford University Press, 2012).

Gore, A., *An Inconvenient Truth: The Planetary Emergency of Global Warming and What We Can Do About It* (Emmaus, PA: Rodale, 2006).

Graham, M., 'Some thoughts about the philosophical underpinnings of Aboriginal worldviews' (1999) 3(2) *Worldviews: Global Religions, Culture and Ecology*.

Great Barrier Reef Marine Park Authority, *Great Barrier Reef Climate Change Adaptation Strategy and Action Plan (2012–2017)* (2012), http://elibrary.gbrmpa.gov.au/jspui/bitstream/11017/1140/1/GBR%20Climate%20Change%20Adaptation%20Strategy%20and%20Action%20Plan%202012-2017.pdf.

Greaves, D., Iglesias, G., *Wave and Tidal Energy* (Hoboken, NJ: Wiley, 2018).

Grip, K., 'International marine environmental governance: a review' (2017) 46 *Ambio*, 413–427.

Grote, R., 'Westphalian system' (2008) *Max Planck Encyclopedia of Public International Law* (Oxford: Oxford University Press, 2008).

Grotius, H. *The Freedom of the High Seas: or the Right Which Belongs to the Dutch to Take Part in the Indian Trade*, R. Van Deman Magoffin (tr.), introduction by J. Brown Scott (Washington, DC: Oxford University Press, 1916).

Group of Experts of the Regular Process, *First Global Integrated Marine Assessment: World Ocean Assessment I* (2016), available at www.un.org/Depts/los/woa.

Gümplová, P., 'Restraining permanent sovereignty over natural resources' (2014) 53 *Enrahonar. Quaderns de Filosofia*, 93–114.

Guruswamy, L., *'Climate change: the next dimension'* (2000) 15 *Journal Land Use & Environmental Law*, 341–382.

Guruswamy, L., 'The promise of the United Nations Convention on the Law of the Sea (UNCLOS): justice in trade and environment disputes' (1999) 25 *Ecology Law Quarterly*, 189–228.

Gutjahr, C., et al., 'Very large release of mostly volcanic carbon during the Paleocene-Eocene thermal maximum' (2017) 548 *Nature*, 573–577.

Harmsworth, G. R. (Te Arawa, Ngāti Tūwharetoa, Ngāti Raukawa), Awatere, S. (Ngāti Porou), 'Indigenous māori knowledge and perspectives of ecosystems' in J. R. Dymond (ed.), *Ecosystem services in New Zealand: Conditions and Trends* (Lincoln, New Zealand: Manaaki Whenua Press, 2013), 274–286.

Harrison, J., 'Recent developments and continuing challenges in the regulation of greenhouse gas emissions from international shipping' in A. Chircop, S. Coffen-Smout and M. McConnell (eds.), 27 (2013) *Ocean Yearbook*, 359–384.

Harrison, J., 'The Law of the Sea Convention Institutions' in D. Rothwell et al. (eds.), *The Oxford Handbook of the Law of the Sea* (Oxford: Oxford University Press, 2015).

Harrison, J., *Making the Law of the Sea* (Cambridge: Cambridge University Press, 2011).

Harrison, J., *Saving the Oceans Through Law* (Oxford: Oxford University Press, 2017).

Harvard Magazine, 'The Ocean Carbon Cycle', November–December 2002, available at harvardmagazine.com/2002/11/the-ocean-carbon-cycle.html.

Harvey, B. J., et al., 'Ecosystem-based management of coral reefs under climate change' (2018) 8 *Ecology and* Evolution, 6354–6368.

Haszeldine, R. S., et al., 'Negative emission technologies and carbon capture and storage to achieve the Paris Agreement commitments' (2018) 376 *Philosophical Transactions of the Royal Society* A, 1–23.

Haszeldine, S., Ghaleigh, N. S., 'Geological factors for legislation to enable and regulate storage of carbon dioxide in the deep subsurface' in I. Havercroft, R. Macrory and R. Stewart (eds.), *Carbon Capture and Storage: Emerging Legal and Regulatory Issues*, 2nd ed. (Portland Oregon: Hart Publishing, 2018).

Haver, G., Bugge, H. C., 'Transboundary chains for CCS: allocation of rights and obligations between the state Parties within the climate regime' (2007) 5 *Journal for European Environmental & Planning* Law, 367.

Hayashi, M., 'Sea level rise and the law of the sea: legal and policy options' in *Proceedings of the International Symposium on Islands and Oceans* (Tokyo: Ocean Policy Research Foundation, 22–23 January 2009).

Hayashi, M., 'Sea-level rise and the law of the sea: future options' in D. Vidas and P. J. Schei (eds.), *The World Ocean in Globalization: Climate Change, Sustainable Fisheries, Biodiversity, Shipping, Regional Issues* (Leiden, Boston: Brill Nijhoff, 2011).

Hayashi, M., 'Sea level rise and the law of the sea: how can the affected states be better protected?' in C. H. Schofield, S. Lee and M.-S. Kwon (eds.), *The Limits of Maritime Jurisdiction* (Leiden: Brill, 2014).

He, P., et al., 'Countering climate change: measures and tools to reduce energy use and greenhouse gas emission in fisheries and aquaculture' in FAO, 'Impacts of climate change in fisheries and aquaculture: synthesis of current knowledge, adaptation and mitigation options', *FAO Fisheries and Aquaculture Technical Paper* No. 627 (FAO, 2018), www.fao.org/3/i9705en/i9705en.pdf.

Heclo, H., 'Thinking institutionally' in R. A. W. Rhodes, S. A. Binder and B. A. Rockman (eds.), *The Oxford Handbook of Political Institutions* (Oxford: Oxford University Press, 2006).

Hendriks, I. E., Durart, C. M., Álvarez, M., 'Vulnerability of marine biodiversity to ocean acidification: a meta-analysis' (2010) 86 *Estuarine, Coastal and Shelf Science*, 157–164.

Henriksen, T., 'Conservation and sustainable use of Arctic marine biodiversity' (2010) 1 (2) *Arctic Review on Law and Politics*, 249–278.

Hinkel, J., et al., 'The ability of societies to adapt to twenty-first-century sea-level rise' (2018) 8 *Nature Climate Change*, 570–578.

Hirdaris, S., et al., 'Considerations on the potential use of Nuclear Small Modular Reactor (SMR) technology for merchant marine propulsion' (2014) 79 *Ocean Engineering*, 101–130.

Hiriart, G., et al., 'Submarine geothermics: hydrothermal vents and electricity generation' in *Proceedings World Geothermal Congress* (2010), www.geothermal-energy.org/pdf/IGAstandard/WGC/2010/3704.pdf.

Hodgson, G. M., 'What are institutions?' (2006) 15(1) *Journal of Economic Issues*, 1–25.

Hoegh-Guldberg, O., 'Climate change, coral bleaching and the future of the world's coral reefs' (1999) 50 *Marine Freshwater Research*, 839–866.

Hoegh-Guldberg, O., et al., 'Coral reefs under rapid climate change and ocean acidification' (2007) 318 *Science*, 1737–1742.

Hönisch, B., et al., 'The geological record of ocean acidification' (2012) 335 *Science*, 1058–1063.

Hopkins, C. R., Bailey, D. M., Potts, T., 'Perceptions of practitioners: Managing marine protected areas for climate change resilience' (2016) 128 *Ocean & Coastal Management*, 18–28.

Hoque, M. N., *The Legal and Scientific Assessment of Bangladesh's Baseline in the Context of Article 76 of the United Nations Convention on the Law of the Sea* (2005–2006), available at www.un.org/depts/los/nippon/unnff_programme_home/f

ellows_pages/fellows_papers/hoque_0506_bangladesh.pdf, accessed 26 September 2019.

Hubert, A. M., *Code of Conduct for the Responsible Geoengineering Research* (2017), available at https://ce-conference.org/system/files/documents/revised_code_of_conduct_for_geoengineering_research_2017.pdf.

Hubert, A. M., Craik, N., 'Towards normative coherence in the international law of the sea for the conservation and sustainable use of marine biological diversity of areas beyond national jurisdiction', The blog of the K.G. Jebsen Centre for the Law of the Sea, 1 February 2018, available at http://site.uit.no/jclos/files/2018/02/JCLOS-Coherence-Blog-Hubert-Craik-v-2.pdf.

Hughes, T. P., Anderson, K. D. Connolly, S. R., 'Spatial and temporal patterns of mass bleaching in the Anthropocene' (2018) 359 *Science*, 80–83.

Hughes, T. P., et al., 'Climate change, human impacts, and the resilience of coral reefs' (2003) 301 *Science*, 929–933.

Hughes, T. P., et al., 'Global warming and recurrent mass bleaching of corals' (2017) 543 *Nature*, 373–377.

Hughes, T. P., et al., 'Global warming transforms coral reef assemblages' (2018) 556 *Nature*, 492–496.

Hulme, M., *Why We Disagree about Climate Change: Understanding Controversy, Inaction and Opportunity* (Cambridge: Cambridge University Press, 2009).

Hunter, K., et al., 'Impacts of anthropogenic SOx, NOx and NH3 on acidification of coastal waters and shipping lanes' (2011) 38 *Geophysical Research Letters*, L13602.

Hurrell, A., 'Can the study of global order be de-centred?' (2015) 3 *PRIMO Working Paper*, available at www.primo-itn.eu/PRIMO/wp-content/uploads/2015/07/WorkingPaper-2_Andrew-Hurrell.pdf.

Hurrell, A., Kingsbury, B. (eds.), *The International Politics of the Environment: Actors, Interests, Institutions* (Oxford: Clarendon Press, 1992).

Institut du Développement Durable et des Relations Internationales (IDDRI), E. Druel, *Environmental impact assessments in areas beyond national jurisdiction: identification of gaps and possible ways forward* (IDDRI, 2013).

Interacademy Panel on International Issues (IAP), *IAP Statement on Ocean Acidification* (2009), available at www.interacademies.net/File.aspx?id=9075.

Intergovernmental Oceanographic Commission, D. W. R. Wallace et al., *Ocean Fertilization: A Scientific Summary for Policy Makers* (2010), available at unesdoc.unesco.org/ark:/48223/pf0000190674.

Intergovernmental Panel on Climate Change (IPCC), J. T. Houghton, G. J. Jenkins and J. J. Ephraums (eds.), *Climate Change: the IPCC Scientific Assessment, First Assessment Report of the Intergovernmental Panel on Climate Change* (1990).

Intergovernmental Panel on Climate Change (IPCC), *Climate Change: The IPCC Response Strategies* (Library of Congress Cataloging-in-Publication Data, 1991).

Intergovernmental Panel on Climate Change (IPCC), *Revised 1996 IPCC Guidelines for National Greenhouse Gas Inventories* (1996), www.ipcc.ch/report/revised-1996-ipcc-guidelines-for-national-greenhouse-gas-inventories/.

Intergovernmental Panel on Climate Change (IPCC), *Special Report on Carbon Capture and Storage* (2005), https://archive.ipcc.ch/pdf/special-reports/srccs/srccs_wholereport.pdf.

Intergovernmental Panel on Climate Change (IPCC), *Special Report on Renewable Energy Sources and Climate Change Mitigation* (2011), www.ipcc.ch/report/renewable-energy-sources-and-climate-change-mitigation/.

Intergovernmental Panel on Climate Change (IPCC), *Special Report on Renewable Energy Sources and Climate Change Mitigation* (2012 Edition), https://archive.ipcc.ch/pdf/special-reports/srren/SRREN_FD_SPM_final.pdf.

Intergovernmental Panel on Climate Change (IPCC), T. F. Stocker et al. (eds.), *Climate Change 2013, The Physical Science Basis: Contribution of Working Group I to the Fifth Assessment Report of the Intergovernmental Panel on Climate Change* (Cambridge: Cambridge University Press, 2013).

Intergovernmental Panel on Climate Change (IPCC), Core Writing Team, R. K. Pachauri and L. A. Meyer (eds.), *Climate Change 2014: Synthesis report. Contributions of Working Groups I, II and III to the Fifth Assessment Report of the Intergovernmental Panel on Climate Change* (Geneva: IPCC, 2014).

Intergovernmental Panel on Climate Change (IPCC), V. Masson-Delmotte et al. (eds.), *Global warming of 1.5°C: An IPCC Special Report on the impacts of global warming of 1.5°C above pre-industrial levels and related global greenhouse gas emission pathways, in the context of strengthening the global response to the threat of climate change, sustainable development, and efforts to eradicate poverty* (IPPC: Geneva, 2018).

Intergovernmental Panel on Climate Change (IPCC), H. O. Pörtner et al. (eds.), *IPCC Special Report on The Ocean and Cryosphere in a Changing Climate* (2019, in press), www.ipcc.ch/srocc/.

International Council on Clean Transportation (ICCT), 'Heavy Fuel Oil use in the IMO Polar Code Arctic by Russian-flagged ships, 2015', available at www.hfofreearctic.org/en/category/publications_en/.

International Energy Agency (IEA), International Energy Association's greenhouse gas research and development program (IEAGHG), *Interaction of CO_2 Storage with Subsurface Resources* (2013) (*IEAGHG Interaction Report*), available at http://ieaghg.org/docs/General_Docs/Reports/2013–08.pdf.

International Energy Agency (IEA), *Carbon Capture and Storage and the London Protocol: Options for Enabling Transboundary CO2 Transfer* (2011), www.iea.org/reports/carbon-capture-and-storage-and-the-london-protocol.

International Energy Agency (IEA), *Global Energy CO2 Status Report 2017*, OECD/IEA (2018).

International Energy Agency (IEA), *World Energy Outlook 2018*, OECD/IEA (2018).

International Energy Agency/Energy Technology Network – Ocean Energy Systems (IEA-OES), Annual Report, *An overview of ocean energy activities in 2018* (2018), available at report2018.ocean-energy-systems.org/documents/OES-Annual-Report-2018/, accessed 18 January 2020.

International Energy Agency/Energy Technology Network, *An overview of ocean energy activities in* 2018, www.oceanenergysystems.org/publications/oes-annual-reports/.

International Law Association (ILA), International Law Association's Committee on Coastal State Jurisdiction relating to Marine Pollution over Vessel-Source Pollution, Final Report (2000), available at www.ila-hq.org/en/committees/index.cfm/cid/12.

International Law Association (ILA), Committee on the Outer Continental Shelf, Berlin Conference Paper, *Legal Issues of the Outer Continental Shelf* (2004), 23; International Law Association, Committee on the Outer Continental Shelf, Toronto Conference Paper, *Legal Issues of the Outer Continental Shelf* (2006).

International Law Association (ILA), Report of the Study Group (2006), *Fragmentation of International Law: Difficulties Arising from the Diversification and Expansion of International Law*, finalized by M. Koskenniemi, Doc. A/CN.4/L.682, https://legal.un.org/ilc/documentation/english/a_cn4_l682.pdf.

International Law Association (ILA), *Report of the Seventy-Fifth Conference held in Sofia, August 2012* (London: ILA, 2012), available at www.ila-hq.org/en/committees/index.cfm/cid/1028.

International Law Association (ILA), *Washington Conference Report (2014)*, report by the Committee on Baselines under the International Law (hereinafter ILA Washington 2014), para. 60, https://cil.nus.edu.sg/wp-content/uploads/2015/10/baselines_under_international_law_of_the_sea_report.pdf.

International Law Association (ILA), *Johannesburg Conference 2016, Report of the Committee on International Law and Sea Level Rise.*

International Law Association (ILA), Committee on International Law and Sea Level Rise, *Resolution 5/2018*, Sydney (2018).

International Law Association (ILA), Committee on International Law and Sea Level rise, *Working Session Report*, Sydney (2018).

International Maritime Organization (IMO), *Guidelines and Standards for the Removal of Offshore Installations and Structures in the Continental Shelf and in the Exclusive Economic Zone*, IMO Assembly Res. A.671(16) (19 October 1989), www.imo.org/en/KnowledgeCentre/IndexofIMOResolutions/Assembly/Documents/A.672(16).pdf.

International Maritime Organization (IMO), *Second IMO GHG Study* (2009).

International Maritime Organization (IMO), *Guidelines for Safety Zones and Safety of Navigation around Offshore Installations and Structures*, IMO Doc. SN.1/Circ.295 (7 December 2010), www.imo.org/en/OurWork/Environment/PollutionPrevention/AirPollution/Documents/SecondIMOGHGStudy2009.pdf.

International Maritime Organization (IMO), Press Briefing to 35th Consultative Meeting of Contracting Parties to the Convention on the Prevention of Marine Pollution by Dumping of Wastes and Other Matter, 1972 (London Convention) 8th meeting of Contracting Parties to the 1996 Protocol thereto (London Protocol), *Marine geoengineering including ocean fertilization to be regulated under amendments to international treaty* (18 October 2013), available at www.imo.org/en/MediaCentre/PressBriefings/Pages/45-marine-geoengieneering.aspx#.XQp1r1wzY2x.

International Maritime Organization (IMO), *Third IMO GHG Study* (2014), www.imo.org/en/OurWork/Environment/PollutionPrevention/AirPollution/Documents/Third%20Greenhouse%20Gas%20Study/GHG3%20Executive%20Summary%20and%20Report.pdf.

International Maritime Organization (IMO), 'EC funding gives green light to ambitious IMO energy-efficiency project', Press Release of 12 January 2016, available at www.imo.org/en/MediaCentre/PressBriefings/Pages/01–2016-MTCC-.aspx.

International Maritime Organization (IMO), webpage, *Carbon Capture and Sequestration*, www.imo.org/en/OurWork/Environment/LCLP/EmergingIssues/CCS/Pages/default.aspx.

International Renewable Energy Agency (IRENA), *Global Energy Transformation: A Roadmap to 2050*, IRENA (2018), www.irena.org/publications/2018/Apr/Global-Energy-Transition-A-Roadmap-to-2050.

International Renewable Energy Agency (IRENA), *Global Energy Transformation: A Roadmap to 2050*, IRENA (2019 Edition), www.irena.org/publications/2019/Apr/Global-energy-transformation-A-roadmap-to-2050-2019Edition.

International Union for Conservation of Nature, G. Kelleher (ed.), *Guidelines for Marine Protected Areas* (1999), available at www.iucn.org/sites/dev/files/import/downloads/mpaguid.pdf

International Union for the Conservation of Nature (IUCN), D. Laffoley and J. M. Baxter (eds.), *Explaining Ocean Warming: Causes, Scale, Effects, and Consequences* (2016), available at portals.iucn.org/library/node/46254.

International Workshop on Greenhouse Gas Emissions and Shipping, Singapore, *Workshop Report* (13–14 November 2018), available at https://cil.nus.edu.sg/wp-content/uploads/2019/01/Greenhouse-Gas-Emissions-and-Shipping-Workshop-Report.pdf, paras. 16, 72.

International Renewable Energy Agency (IRENA), *Salinity Gradient Energy: Technology Brief* (2014), www.irena.org/documentdownloads/publications/salinity_energy_v4_web.pdf.

International Renewable Energy Agency (IRENA), *Wave Energy: Technology Brief* (2014), www.irena.org/publications/2014/Jun/Wave-energy.

International Renewable Energy Agency (IRENA), *Offshore innovation widens renewable energy options: opportunities, challenges and the vital role of international co-operation to spur the global energy transformation*, Brief to G7 Policy Makers (2018), www.irena.org/-/media/Files/IRENA/Agency/Publication/2018/Sep/IRENA_offshore_wind_brief_G7_2018.pdf.

Jabour, J., Smith, D., 'The Ross Sea Region Marine Protected Area: can it be successfully managed?' (2018) 32(1) *Ocean Yearbook*, 190–205.

Jakobsen, I. U., *Marine Protected Areas in International Law: An Arctic Perspective* (Leiden: Martinus Nijhoff, 2016).

Jakobsen, I. U., *Marine Protected Areas in International Law: An Arctic Perspective* (Leiden: Brill Nijhoff, 2016).

Jeffries, G., 'Time for a new international legal regime for ocean fertilization in the high seas?' (Master's Thesis LLM in Law of the Sea, UiT The Arctic University of Norway, 2017), 9, available at https://munin.uit.no/bitstream/handle/10037/12501/thesis.pdf?sequence=2&isAllowed=y.

Jesus, J. L., 'Rocks, new-born islands, sea level rise and maritime space' in J. A. Frowein et al. (eds.), *Verhandeln für den Frieden. Negotiating for Peace: Liber Amicorum Tono Eitel* (Berlin: Springer, 2003), 579–603.

Jia, B. B., 'Effect of legal issues, actual or implicit, upon the work of the CLCS: suspensive or without prejudice' (2012) 11 *Chinese Journal of International Law*, 107–126.

Jickells, T. D., et al., 'Global iron connections between desert dust, ocean biochemistry, and climate' (2005) 308 *Science*, 67–71.

Johansen, E., 'Norway's integrated ocean management: A need for stronger protection of the environment?' (2018) 32 *Ocean Yearbook*, 239–263.

Johansen, E, 'The role of the law of the sea in climate change litigation' (2020) *The Yearbook of Polar Law*, 141–169.

Johnston, I., 'Source of world's biggest pool of underwater greenhouse gas discovered by scientists' *The Independent*, 28 February 2017, available at www.independent.co.uk/environment/underwater-greenhouse-gas-pacific-ocean-hawaii-source-bacteria-discovered-methane-qmul-a7598051.html.

Jokiel, P. L., et al., 'Ocean acidification and calcifying reef organisms: a mescocosm investigation' (2008) 27 *Coral Reefs*, 473–483.

Jones, E., et al., 'Ocean acidification and calcium carbonate saturation states in the coastal zone of the West Antarctic Peninsula' (2017) 139 *Deep-Sea Research II*, 181–194.

Kasoulides, G. C., *Port State Control and Jurisdiction: Evolution of the Port State Regime* (Dordrecht: Brill Nijhoff, 1993).

Kavousi, J., et al., 'Colony-specific calcification and mortality under ocean acidification in the branching coral *Montipora digitata*' (2016) 119 *Marine Environmental Research* 161–165.

Kavousi, J., et al., 'Colony-specific investigations reveal highly variable responses among individual corals to ocean acidification and warming' (2015) 109 *Marine Environmental Research*, 161–165.

Keith, D., *A Case for Climate Engineering* (Cambridge: MIT Press, 2013).

Keller, B. D., et al., 'Climate change, coral reef ecosystems, and management options for marine protected areas' (2009) 44 *Environmental Management*, 1069–1088.

Klein, D., et al. (eds.), *The Paris Agreement on Climate Change* (Oxford: Oxford University Press, 2017).

Knowlton, N., 'The future of coral reefs' (2001) 98 *Proceedings of the National Academy of Sciences*, 5419–5425.

Kojima, C., 'Climate change and protection of the marine environment: food security, evolutionary interpretation, and the novel application of dispute settlement mechanisms under the United Nations Convention on the Law of the Sea' in N. Craik et al. (eds.), *Global Environmental Change and Innovation in International Law* (Cambridge: Cambridge University Press, 2018), 138–158.

Kopela, S., 'Climate change, regime interaction, and the principle of common but differentiated responsibility: the experience of the International Maritime Organization' (2014) 24(1) *Yearbook of International Environmental Law*, 70–101.

Kopela, S., 'Port-state jurisdiction, extraterritoriality and the protection of global commons' (2016) 47(2) *Ocean Development and International Law*, 89–130.

Korff, J., *Meaning of Land to Aboriginal People* (2019), available at www.creativespirits.info/aboriginalculture/land/meaning-of-land-to-aboriginal-people.

Koskenniemi, M., Report, UN General Assembly, *Fragmentation of International Law: Difficulties Arising from the Diversification and Expansion of International Law* (2006), available at http://legal.un.org/ilc/documentation/english/a_cn4_l682.pdf.

Kraemer, S., 'Why now is the time for nuclear cargo shipping', Clean Technica, 28 January 2017, available at cleantechnica.com/2017/01/28/now-time-nuclear-cargo-shipping/.

Kraynak, J., Tetrault, K. W., *The Complete Idiot's Guide to the Oceans* (Indianapolis: Alpha Books, 2003).

Krey, J., et al., 'Gas hydrates: entrance to a methane age or climate threat?' (2009) 4 *Environmental Resources Letters*, 034007.

Kristoffersen, K. J., Lysvold, S. S., '13.000 tonn oppdrettslaks er døde', Norwegian Broadcasting Corporation (NRK), 25 May 2019, available at www.nrk.no/nordland/13.000-tonn-oppdrettslaks-er-dode_-_-vi-snakker-om-dyr_-ikke-_biomasse_-1.14561607.

Kuokkanen, T., 'Integrating environmental protection and exploitation of natural resources: reflections on the evolution of the doctrine of sustainable development' (2004) 22(3) *Journal of Energy and Natural Resources Law*, 341–356.

Kvamme, L., 'Fortviler over rømt fisk'/'Despair over escapees', Bergens Tidende, 14 January 2015, available at www.bt.no/nyheter/okonomi/Fortviler-over-romt-fisk-3280539.html.

Lam, V. W. Y., et al., 'Projected change in global fisheries revenues under climate change' 6 *Scientific Reports* No. 32607, 1, www.nature.com/articles/srep32607.

Lambeck, K., et al., 'Sea level and global ice volumes from the last glacial maximum to the Holocene' (2014) 111(43) *Proceedings of the National Academy of Sciences*, 15296–15303.

Langlet D., 'Safe return to the underground? the role of international law in subsurface storage of carbon dioxide' (2009) 18 *Review of European Community and International Environmental Law*, 286–304.

Langlet, D., 'Transboundary dimensions of CCS: EU law problems and prospects' (2014) 8(3) *Carbon & Climate Law Review*, 198–207.

Langlet, D., 'Exporting CO_2 for sub-seabed storage: the non-effective amendment to the London Dumping Protocol and its implications' (2015) 30(3) *International Journal of Marine and Coastal Law* 395–417.

Langlet, D., 'Transboundary transit pipelines: reflections on the balancing of rights and interests in light of the Nord Stream project' (2016) 63 *International and Comparative Law* Quarterly, 977–995.

Larsen, M. H., 'Laksedøden', Norwegian Broadcasting Corporation (NRK), 19 May 2019, available at www.nrk.no/troms/laksedoden_-_-algene-vil-spre-seg-1.14556083.

Leary, D., Esteban, M., 'Climate change and renewable energy from the ocean and tides: calming the sea of regulatory uncertainty' (2009) 24 *The International Journal of Maritime and Coastal Law*, 617–651.

Lesnikowski, A., et al., 'What does the Paris Agreement mean for adaptation?' (2017) 17 *Climate Policy*, 825–831.

Liftin, K. T., 'Sovereignty in world ecopolitics' (1997) 41(2) *Mershon International Studies Review*, 167–204.

Lin, A., 'Geoengineering governance' (2009) 8 *Issues in Legal Scholarship*, 1–24.

LINGO.org, *History of the idea*, http://leave-it-in-the-ground.org/lingo-history/, accessed 3 December 2018.

Lohbeck, K., Riebesell, U., Reusch, T., 'Adaptive evolution of a key phytoplankton species to ocean acidification' (2012) 5 *Nature Geoscience*, 346–351.

Loughlin, M., 'The erosion of sovereignty' (2017) 45(2) *Netherlands Journal of Legal Philosophy*, 57–81.

Lund, N. J., 'Renewable energy as a catalyst for changes to the high seas regime' (2010) 15(1) *Oceans and Coastal Law Journal*, 108–109.

Macnab, R., 'Third-party reactions to continental shelf submissions and their treatment by the Commission on the Limits of the Continental Shelf' in C. R. Symmons (ed.), *Selected Contemporary Issues in the Law of the Sea* (Leiden: Brill, 2011), 285–304.

Maes, F., 'The international legal framework for marine spatial planning' (2008) 32 *Marine Policy*, 797–810.

Marston, P., et al., 'Carbon dioxide infrastructure: pipeline transport issues and regulatory concerns – past, present and future' (2015) 52 *Rocky Mountain Mineral Law Foundation Journal*, 275–313.

Martinez Romera, B., 'The Paris Agreement and the regulation of international bunker fuels' (2016) 25(2) *Review of European Community & International Environmental Law*, 215–227.

Martinez, C., Lefebvre, C., Herr, D., 'Strengthening the relationship between Marine Protected Areas and ocean protection and measures to deliver climate change adaptation and mitigation' in F. Smiard, D. Laffoley and J. M. Baxter (eds), *Marine Protected Areas and Climate Change: Adaptation and Mitigation Synergies, Opportunities and Challenges* (Gland: International Union for Conservation of Nature, 2016), 17–29, https://portals.iucn.org/library/sites/library/files/documents/2016-067.pdf.

Mascarelli, A. L., 'A sleeping giant?' (2009) 3 *Nature Climate Change*, 46–49.

Massachusetts Institute of Technology, 'Researchers establish long-sought source of ocean methane' *Science Daily*, 7 December 2017, www.sciencedaily.com/releases/2017/12/171207141635.htm.

Mathis, L. et al., 'Ocean acidification risk assessment for Alaska's fishery sector' (2015) 136 *Progress in Oceanography*, 71–91.

Matson, P., Martz, T., Hofmann, G., 'High-frequency observations of pH under the Antarctic sea ice in the southern Ross Sea' (2011) 23 *Antarctic Science* 607–613.

McAdam, J., *Climate Change, Forced Migration, and International Law* (Oxford: Oxford University Press, 2012).

McCauley, D. J., et. al., 'Marine defaunation: animal loss in the global ocean' (2015) 347 *Science*, 1255641.

McCoy II, H. D., *American and International Aquaculture Law* (Oxford: Wiley-Blackwell, 2000).

McDonald, S., VanderZwaag, D. L., 'Renewable ocean energy and the international law and policy seascape: global currents, regional surges' (2015) 29 *Ocean Yearbook*, 299–326.

McDorman, T. L., 'The role of the commission on the limits of the continental shelf: a technical body in a political world' (2002) 17(3) *The International Journal of Marine and Coastal Law*, 310–324.

McDorman, T. L., 'Regional port state control agreements: some issues of international law' (2000) 5 *Ocean and Coastal Law Journal*, 207–225.

McKibben, B., 'Remember this: 350 parts per million', *The Washington Post*, 28 December 2007, available at www.washingtonpost.com/wp-dyn/content/article/2007/12/27/AR2007122701942.html; *About 350*, https://350.org/about/, accessed 16 November 2018; *About 350 Pacific*, https://350pacific.org/about/, accessed 16 November 2018.

McKibben, B., 'Why we need to keep 80% of fossil fuels in the ground', 350.org, 16 February 2016, available at 350.org/why-we-need-to-keep-80-percent-of-fossil-fuels-in-the-ground/.

McLeod, E., et al., 'Designing marine protected area networks to address the impacts of climate change' (2009) 7(7) *Frontiers in Ecology and the Environment*, 362–370.

Meeder, J. F., Parkinson, R. W., 'SE Saline Everglades transgressive sedimentation in response to historic acceleration in sea-level rise: a viable marker for the base of the Anthropocene?' (2018) 34 *Journal of Coastal Research*, 490–497.

Meybeck, M., 'Global analysis of river systems: from Earth System controls to Anthropocene syndromes' (2003) 358 *Philosophical Transactions of the Royal Society*, 1935–1955.

Millennium Ecosystem Assessment, *Ecosystems and Human Well-being: Synthesis* (Washington, DC: Island Press, 2005).

Milligan, B., 'Planning for offshore CO_2 storage: law and policy in the United Kingdom' (2014) 48 *Marine Policy*, 162–171.

Moeckli, D., White, N. D., 'Treaties as "Living Instruments"' in M. J. Bowman and D. Kritsiotis (eds.), *Conceptual and Contextual Perspectives on the Modern Law of Treaties* (Cambridge: Cambridge University Press, 2018), 136–171.

Molenaar, E. J., 'The 1996 Protocol to the 1972 Convention' (1997) 12 *The International Journal of Marine and Coastal Law*, 396.

Molenaar, E. J., *Coastal State Jurisdiction over Vessel-Source Pollution* (The Hague: Kluwer, 1998).

Molenaar, E. J., 'Participation in the central arctic ocean fisheries agreement' in A. Shibata et al. (eds.), *Emerging Legal Orders in the Arctic: The Role of Non-Arctic Actors* (Oxon and New York: Routledge, 2019), 132.

Molenaar, E. J., Caddell, R., 'International fisheries law: achievements, limitations and challenges' in R. Caddell and E. J. Molenaar (eds.), *Strengthening International Fisheries Law in an Era of Changing Oceans* (Oxford/Portland: Hart, 2019), 3–10.

Monzón, J., Moyer-Horner, L., Baron Palamar, M., 'Climate change and species range dynamics in protected areas' (2011) 61 *BioScience*, 752–761.

Moore, S. S., Seavy, N. E., Gearhart, M., *Scenario planning for climate change adaptation: A guidance for resource managers* (2013), available at ipclimatechange.trg-learning.com/wp-content/uploads/2013/11/Moore_et_al_2013_Scenario_Planning_for_Climate_Adaptation.pdf.

Mossop, J., *The Continental Shelf Beyond 200 Nautical Miles: Rights and Responsibilities* (Oxford: Oxford University Press, 2016).

Müller, H. K., 'Legal bases for offshore grid development under international and EU law: why national regimes remain the determining factor' (2013) 38(5) *European Law Review*, 618–637.

Munday, P., et al., 'Replenishment of fish populations is threatened by ocean acidification' (July 2010) 107 *Proceedings of the National Academy of Sciences*, 12930–12934.

Munday, P., et al., 'Selected mortality associated with variation in CO2 tolerance in a marine fish' (2013) 1(1) *Ocean Acidification*, 1–5.

Nandan, S. N., Rosenne, S. (eds.), *United Nations Convention on the Law of the Sea, 1982: A Commentary*, vol. 2 (Dordrecht: Martinus Nijhoff, 1993).

Nandan, S. N., Rosenne, S. (eds.), *United Nations Convention on the Law of the Sea 1982: A Commentary* (Dordrecht: Martinus Nijhoff, 1993), Vol. II.

Narita, D., Rehdanz, K., 'Economic impact of ocean acidification on shellfish production in Europe' (2017) 60 *Journal of Environmental Planning and Management*, 500–518.

National Aeronautics and Space Administration (NASA), Earth Observatory, H. Riebeek, *The Carbon Cycle* (2011), available at earthobservatory.nasa.gov/Features/CarbonCycle/.

National Aeronautics and Space Administration (NASA), *What Are Climate and Climate Change?*, www.nasa.gov/audience/forstudents/5–8/features/nasa-knows/what-is-climate-change-58.html, accessed 3 December 2018.

Neil, S. P., Reza Hashemi, M., *Fundamentals of Ocean Renewable Energy: Generating Electricity from the Sea* (Oxford: Elsevier, 2018).

Nerem, R. S., et al., 'Climate-change-driven accelerated sea level rise detected in the altimeter era' (2018) 115(9) *Proceedings of the National Academy of Sciences*, 2022–2025.

Nerus Program, 'Policy brief: Climate change in oceans beyond national jurisdictions', *Neurus Scientific & Technical Briegs on ABNJ series* (Undated), available at nereusprogram.org/reports/policy-brief-climate-change-in-oceans-beyond-national-jurisdictions/.

Newman, D., 'The Lines that Continue to Separate Us: Borders in Our "Borderless" World' (2006) 30/2 *Progress in Human Geography Lecture*, 143–161.

NOAA Fisheries, 'U.S. signs agreement to prevent unregulated commercial fishing on the high seas of the central Arctic Ocean', 3 October 2018, available at www.fisheries.noaa.gov/international/international-affairs/us-signs-agreement-prevent-unregulated-commercial-fishing-high-seas-central-arctic

NOAA Ocean Service, *Salinity*, oceanservice.noaa.gov/education/kits/estuaries/media/supp_estuar10c_salinity.html, 3 January 2020

Nordquist, M. (ed.), *United Nations Convention on the Law of the Sea: A Commentary* (Dordrecht: Nijhoff, 1991), vol. IV.

Norwegian Institute of Marine Research, ES Grefsrud and T Svåsand, 'Status oppdrett'/'Status aquaculture', *Risikorapport norsk fiskeoppdrett* (2018), available at www.imr.no/filarkiv/2018/02/risikorapport_2018.pdf/nb-no

Norwegian Polar Institute, *The Arctic System: The Sea is Getting Warmer*, available at www.arcticsystem.no/en/outsideworld/oceancurrents/warmer-ocean.html.

Nursey-Bray, M., 'Which way? The contribution of indigenous marine governance' (2014) 6 *Australian Journal of Maritime and Ocean Affairs*, 27–40.

O'Leary, A., Brown, J., 'Legal bases for IMO climate change measures', Report by Environmental Defense Fund (Columbia Law School, 2018), available at columbia climatelaw.com/files/2018/06/OLeary-and-Brown-2018–06-IMO-Climate-Measures.pdf.

O'Brien, K., 'The courage to change: adaptation from the inside-out' in S. Moser and M. Boykoff (eds.), *Successful Adaptation: Linking Science and Practice in Managing Climate Change Impacts* (London: Routledge, 2013), 306–319.

O'Brien, K., Sygna, L., 'Responding to climate change: the three spheres of transformation' Proceedings of Transformation in a Changing Climate 19–21 June 2013 (Oslo, Norway. University of Oslo, 2013), 16–23. ISBN 978-82-570-2000-2.

Oberthür, S., 'Institutional interaction to address greenhouse gas emissions from international transport: ICAO, IMO and the Kyoto Protocol' (2003) 3(3) *Climate Policy*, 191–205.

Oberthür, S., 'Interactions of the climate change regime with ICAO, IMO, and the EU burden-sharing agreement' in S. Oberthür and T. Gehring (eds.), *Institutional Interaction in Global Environmental Governance* (Cambridge, MA: MIT Press, 2006), 53–78.

Oberthür, S., 'Regime-Interplay management, lessons from environmental policy and law' in K. Blome et al. (eds.), *Contested Regime Collisions: Norm Fragmentation in World Society* (Cambridge: Cambridge University Press, 2016), 88–108.

Oral, N., 'Integrated coastal zone management and marine spatial planning for hydrocarbon activities in the Black Sea' (2008) 23 *The International Journal of Marine and Coastal Law*, 453–476.

Oral, N., 'Implementing part XII of the 1982 UN law of the sea convention and the role of international courts' in Boschiero, N., Scovazzi, T., Pitea, C., Ragni, C. (eds.), *International Courts and the Development of International Law* (T.M.C. Asser Press, The Hauge, 2013), 403–423.

Oral, N., 'Ocean acidification: falling between the legal cracks of UNCLOS and the UNFCCC' (2018) 45 *Ecology Law Quarterly*, 9–30.

Organisation for Economic Co-operation and Development (OECD), *The Ocean Economy in 2030* (2016), www.oecd.org/environment/the-ocean-economy-in-2030-9789264251724-en.htm.

Orr, J., et al., 'Anthropogenic ocean acidification over the twenty-first century and its impact on calcifying organisms' (2005) 437 *Nature*, 681–686.

Oude Elferink, A. G., Freestone, D., 'Flexibility and innovation in the law of the sea: will the LOS Convention amendment procedures ever be used?' in A. G. Oude Elferink (ed.), *Stability and Change in the Law of the Sea: The Role of the LOS Convention* (Leiden/Boston: Brill, 2005), 169–222.

Oxman, B., 'The duty to respect generally accepted international standards' (1991–1992) 24 *New York University Journal of International Law and Politics*, 109–160.

Oxman, B., 'The territorial temptation: a siren song at sea' (2006) 100 *American Journal of International Law*, 830–851.

Pan-Arctic Network of Marine Protected Areas Arctic Council (PAME), *Framework for a, Arctic Council* (April 2015), available at pame.is/images/03_Projects/MPA/MPA_Report.pdf

Pandolfi, J. M., Connolly, S. R., Marshall, D. J., 'Projecting coral reef rutures under global warming and ocean acidification' (2011) 333 *Science*, 418–422.

Pearce, F., *With Speed and Violence: Why Scientists Fear Tipping Points in Climate Change* (Boston: Beacon Press, 2007).

Pelling, M., *Adaptation to Climate Change: From Resilience to Transformation* (London: Routledge, 2010).

Peters, A., 'The refinement of international law: From fragmentation to regime interaction and politicization' (2017) 15(3) *International Journal of Constitutional Law*, 671–704.

Pinsky, M. L., et al., 'Greater vulnerability to warming of marine versus terrestrial ectotherms' (2019) 569 *Nature*, 108–111.

Pinsky, M. L., et al., 'Preparing ocean governance for species on the move' (2018) 360 *Science*, 1189–1191.

Platzöder, R. (ed.), *Third United Nations Conference on the Law of the Sea: Documents* (Oceana Publications, 1983), vol. IV.

Poto, M. P., Fornabaio, L., 'Participation as the essence of good governance: some general reflections and a case study on the Arctic Council' (2017) 8 *Arctic Review on Law and Politics*, 139–159.

Prescott, V., Schofield, C., *Maritime Political Boundaries of the World* (Leiden/Boston: Brill, 2004).

Proelss, A. (ed.), *United Nations Convention on the Law of the Sea: A Commentary* (Munich: Beck, 2017).

Psaraftis, H. N., 'Market-based measures for greenhouse gas emissions from ships: a review' (2012) 11(2) *World Maritime University Journal of Maritime Affairs*, 211–232.

Punt, A., et al., 'Evaluating the impact of ocean acidification on fishery yields and profits: the example of red king crab in Bristol Bay' (2014) 285 *Ecological Modelling*, 39–53.

Purdy, R., Macrory, R., *Geological Carbon Sequestration: critical legal issues* (Tyndall Centre for Climate Change Research, 2004), Working Paper 45, 18–26.

Queirós, A. M., et al., 'Solutions for ecosystem-level protection of ocean systems under climate change' (2016) 22 *Global Change Biology*, 3927–3936.

Quemmerais-Amice, F., Baxter, J., 'Executive Summary' in F. Smiard, D. Laffoley and J. M. Baxter (eds.), *Marine Protected Areas and Climate Change: Adaptation and Mitigation Synergies, Opportunities and Challenges* (Gland: International Union for Conservation of Nature, 2016), https://portals.iucn.org/library/sites/library/files/documents/2016-067.pdf.

Rajamani, L., *Differential Treatment in International Environmental Law* (Oxford: Oxford University Press, 2006).

Rajamani, L., 'Ambition and differentiation in the 2015 Paris agreement: interpretative possibilities and underlying politics' (2016) 65 *International and Comparative Law Quarterly*, 493–514.

Rajamani, L., Werksman, J., 'The legal character and operational relevance of the Paris agreement's temperature goal' (2018) 376(2119) *Philosophical Transactions of the Royal Society* A, 1–14.

Raustiala, K., Victor, D. G., 'The regime complex for plant genetic resources' (2004) 58 *International Organisation*, 277–309.

Rayfuse, R. G., *Non-Flag State Enforcement in High Seas Fisheries* (Leiden: Brill Nijhoff, 2004).

Rayfuse, R., 'W(h)ither Tuvalu? International law and disappearing states' (2009) *University of New South Wales Faculty of Law Research Series*, Paper 9, 3, www.austlii.edu.au/au/journals/UNSWLRS/2009/9.html

Rayfuse, R., 'Climate change and the law of the sea' in R. Rayfuse and S. V. Scott (eds.), *International Law in the Era of Climate Change* (Cheltenham: Edward Elgar, 2012), 147–175.

Rayfuse, R., 'Sea level rise and maritime zones: preserving the maritime entitlement of "disappearing" states' in M. B. Gerrard and G. E. Wannier (eds.), *Threatened Island Nations: Legal Implications of Rising Seas and a Changing Climate* (Cambridge: Cambridge University Press, 2013), 167–194.

Rayfuse, R., 'Regional fisheries management organizations' in D. R. Rothwell et al. (eds.), *The Oxford Handbook of the Law of the Sea* (Oxford: Oxford University Press, 2015), 439–462.

Rayfuse, R., 'Addressing climate change impacts in regional fisheries management organizations' in R. Caddell and E. J. Molenaar (eds.), *Strengthening International Fisheries Law in an Era of Changing Oceans* (Oxford: Hart, 2019).

Rayfuse, R., et al., 'Ocean fertilisation and climate change: the need to regulate emerging high seas uses' (2008) 23 *International Journal of Marine and Coastal Law*, 297–326.

Rayfuse, R., Warner, R. M., 'Securing a sustainable future for the oceans beyond national jurisdiction: the legal basis for an integrated cross-sectoral regime for high seas governance for the 21st century' (2008) 23(3) *International Journal of Marine and Coastal Law*, 399–421.

Redgwell, C., 'Mind the gap in the GAIRS: the role of other instruments in LOSC regime implementation in the offshore energy sector', in N. Bankes and S. Trevisanut (eds.), *Energy from the Sea: An International Law Perspective on Ocean Energy* (Brill, 2015).

Redgwell, C., 'Treaty evolution, adaptation and change: is the LOSC "enough" to address climate change impacts on the marine environment?' (2019) 34 *International Journal of Marine and Coastal Law*, 440–457.

Rees, A., et al., 'The inhibition of N_2O production by ocean acidification in cold temperature and polar waters' (2016) 127 *Deep-Sea Research II*, 92–101.

Reisman, W. M., Westerman, G. S., *Straight Baselines in International Maritime Boundary Delimitation* (New York: St. Martin's Press, 1992).

Rérolle, V., Floquet, C., Mowlem, M., 'Seawater-pH measurements for ocean-acidification observations' (2012) 40 *Trends in Analytical Chemistry*, 146–157.

Rhein, M., et al., 'Observations: ocean' in T. F. Stocker et al. (eds.), *Climate Change 2013: The Physical Science Basis. Contribution of Working Group I to the Fifth Assessment Report of the Intergovernmental Panel on Climate Change* (Cambridge: Cambridge University Press, 2013), 255–317.

Rignot, E., et al., 'Ice-shelf melting around Antarctica' (2013) 341 *Science*, 266–270.

Rignot, E., et al., 'Four decades of Antarctic ice sheet mass balance from 1979–2017' (2019) 116(4) *Proceedings of the National Academy of Sciences*, 1095–1103.

Rignot, E., Jacobs, S. S., 'Rapid bottom melting widespread near Antarctic ice sheet grounding lines' (2002) 296 *Science*, 2020–2023.

Ringbom, H., 'Global problem – regional solution? International law reflections on an EU CO_2 emissions trading scheme for ships' (2011) 26 *The International Journal for Marine and Coastal Law*, 613–641.

Ringbom, H., Henriksen, T., 'Governance challenges, Gaps and Management Opportunities in Areas Beyond National Jurisdiction' (Washington, DC: Global Environment Facility – Scientific and Technical Advisory Panel, 2017).

Risser, M. D., Wehner, M. F., 'Attributable human-induced changes in the likelihood and magnitude of the observed extreme precipitation during hurricane Harvey' (2017) 44(24)*Geophysical Research Letters*, 12,457–12,464.

Roach, A. J., Smith, R. W., 'Straight baselines: the need for a universally applied norm' (2000) 31(47) *Ocean Development & International Law*, 47–80.

Roach, J. A., Smith, R. W., *Excessive Maritime Claims*, 3rd ed. (Leiden: Brill, 2012).

Roberts, C. M., et al., 'Marine reserves can mitigate and promote adaptation to climate change' (2017) 114 *Proceedings of the National Academy of Sciences of the United States of America*, 6167–6175.

Roberts, J., Cairns, S., 'Cold-water corals in a changing ocean' (2014) 7 *Current Opinion in Environmental Sustainability*, 118–126.

Robertson, H. B., 'Navigation in the exclusive economic zone' (1984) 24(4) *Virginia Journal of International Law*, 866–915.

Robin, L., 'A future beyond numbers' in N. Möllers, C. Schwägerl and H. Trischler (eds.), *Welcome to the Anthropocene: The Earth in our Hands* (Munich: Deutsches Museum, 2014), 19–25.

Roderburg, J., 'Marine aquaculture: impacts and international regulation' (2011) 25 *Australian and New Zealand Maritime Law Journal*, 161–179.

Rodgers, C., 'A new approach to protecting ecosystems: The Te Awa Tupua (Whanganui River Claims Settlement) Act 2017' (2017) 19(4) *Environmental Law Review*, 266–279.

Rodrigues, L., van den Bergh, J., Ghermandi, A., 'Socio-economic impacts of ocean acidification in the Mediterranean Sea' (2013) 38 *Marine Policy*, 447–456.

Rosenne, S., 'The international maritime organization interface with the law of the sea convention' in M. Nordquist and J. Moore (eds.), *Current Maritime Issues and the International Maritime Organization* (The Hague: Martinus Nijhoff, 1999), 251–268.

Rothwell, D. R., Stephens, T., *The International Law of the Sea* (Oxford: Hart Publishing, 2010).

Rothwell, D. R., Stephens, T., *The International Law of the Sea*, 2nd ed. (Oxford: Hart Publishing, 2016).

Rothwell, D., et al. (eds.), *Oxford Handbook on the Law of the Sea* (Oxford: Oxford University Press, 2015).

Royal, T. A. C., *Indigenous Worldviews: A Comparative Study: A Report on Research in Progress* (2002), available at https://static1.squarespace.com/static/5369700de4b045a4e0c24bbc/t/53fe8f49e4b06d5988936162/1409191765620/Indigenous+Worldviews.

Royal, T. A. C. (ed.), *The Woven Universe: Selected Writings of Rev. Maori Marsden* (Otaki: Estate of Rev. Maori Marsden, 2003).

Ruppel, C. D., Kessler, J. D., 'The interaction of climate change and methane hydrates' (2017) 55(1) *Reviews of Geophysics*, 126–168.

Rydberg, N., Langlet, D., Work Package 4 – Legal and Fiscal Aspects (nd), available at www.globalccsinstitute.com/publications/ccs-baltic-sea-region-bastor-2-work-package-4-legal-and-fiscal-aspects.

Sander, G., 'International legal obligations for environmental impact assessment and strategic environmental assessment in the Arctic Ocean' (2016) 31(1) *The International Journal of Marine and Coastal Law*, 88–119.

Sands, P., 'Climate change and the rule of law: adjudicating the future in international law' (2016) 28 *Journal of Environmental Law*, 114–134.

Savaresi, A., 'The Paris agreement: a new beginning?' (2016) 34(1) *Journal of Energy & Natural Resource Law*, 16–26.

Scharf, M., *Customary International Law in Times of Fundamental Change: Recognizing Grotian Moments* (Cambridge: Cambridge University Press, 2013).

Schatz, V., Proelss, A., Liu, N., 'The 2018 Agreement to Prevent Unregulated High Seas Fisheries in the Central Arctic Ocean: a primer', EJIL Talk!, 26 October 2018, available at www.ejiltalk.org/the-2018-agreement-to-prevent-unregulated-high-seas-fisheries-in-the-central-arctic-ocean-a-primer/.

Schmidtko, S., Stramma, L., Visbeck, M., 'Decline in global oceanic oxygen content during the past five decades' (2017) 542 *Nature*, 335–339.

Schofield, C., 'Holding back the waves? Sea level rise and maritime claims' in O. C. Ruppel, C. Roschmann and K. Ruppel-Schlichting (eds.), *Climate change: International Law and Global Governance: Volume I: Legal Responses and Global Responsibility* (Baden-Baden: Nomos, 2013), 593–615.

Schofield, C., 'Rising waters, shrinking states: the potential impacts of sea level rise on claims to maritime jurisdiction' (2019) 53 *German Yearbook of International* Law, 189–231.

Schofield, C., Sas, B., 'Uncovered and unstable coasts, climate change and territorial baselines in the Arctic' in S. Lalond and T. L. McDorman (eds.), *International Law and Politics of the Arctic Ocean: Essays in Honour of Donat Pharand* (Leiden: Brill, 2015), 291–414.

Schofield, C., Freestone, D., 'Options to protect coastlines and secure maritime jurisdictional claims in the face of global sea level rise' in M. B. Gerrard and G. E. Wannier (eds.), *Threatened Island Nations* (Cambridge: Cambridge University Press, 2013), 141–165.

Schreurer, C., 'The waning of the sovereign state: towards a new paradigm for international law?' (1993), 4 *European Journal of International Law*, 447–471.

Scott, J., et al., 'The promise and limits of private standards in reducing greenhouse gas emissions from shipping' (2017) 29 *Journal of Environmental Law*, 231–262.

Scott, K. N., 'The day after tomorrow: ocean CO_2 sequestration and the future of climate change' (2005) 18 *Georgetown International Environmental Law Review*, 57–108.

Scott, K. N., 'International law in the Anthropocene: responding to the geoengineering challenge' (2013) 34 *Michigan Journal of International Law*, 309–358.

Scott, K. N., 'Regulating ocean fertilization under international law: the risks' (2013) 2 *Carbon and Climate Law Review*, 108–116.

Scott, K. N., 'Engineering the "mis-Anthropocene": international law, ethics and geoengineering' (2015) 29 *Ocean Yearbook*, 61–84.

Scott, K. N., 'Geoengineering and the marine environment' in R. Rayfuse (ed.), *Research Handbook on International Marine Environmental Law* (Cheltenham: Edward Elgar, 2015), 451–472.

Scott, K. N., 'Integrated ocean management: a new frontier in marine environmental protection' in D. R. Rothwell et al. (eds), *The Oxford Handbook of The Law of the Sea* (Oxford: Oxford University Press, 2015), 463–490.

Scott, K. N., 'Climate change and the oceans: navigating legal orders' in M. H. Nordquist, J. N. Moore and R. Long (eds.), *Legal Order in the World's Oceans: UN Convention on the Law of the Sea* (Leiden: Brill Leiden, 2017), 124–153.

Scott, K. N., 'Marine geoengineering and the law of the sea' in R. C. Beckman et al. (eds.), *High Seas Governance: Gaps and Challenges* (Leiden: Brill Nijhoff, 2018), 34–57.

Scott, K. N., 'Legal aspects of climate change' in International Ocean Institute, Canada, *The Future of Ocean Governance and Capacity Development: Essays in Honor of Elisabeth Mann Borgese (1918–2002)* (Leiden: Brill Nijhoff, 2019), 169–174.

Scott, K. N., 'Integrated oceans management and climate change' in J. McDonald, J. McGee and R. Barnes, (eds.), *Research Handbook on Climate Change, Oceans and Coasts* (Edward Elgar, *forthcoming* 2020).

Scottish Carbon Capture and Storage, *CO_2 Storage and Enhanced Oil Recovery in the North Sea: Securing a Low Carbon Future for the UK* (2015) at 2, available at www.sccs.org.uk/images/expertise/reports/co2-eor-jip/SCCS-CO2-EOR-JIP-Report-SUMMARY.pdf.

Secretariat of the Convention on Biological Diversity, 'Scientific synthesis of the impacts of ocean fertilization on marine biodiversity' (2009) *CBD Technical Series No. 45*, www.cbd.int/doc/publications/cbd-ts-45-en.pdf.

Secretariat of the Convention on Biological Diversity, S. Hennige, J. M. Roberts and P. Williamson (eds.), *An Updated Synthesis of the Impacts of Ocean Acidification on Marine Biodiversity*, Montreal, Technical Series No. 75 (2014).

Secretariat of the Convention on Biological Diversity, *Scientific Synthesis of the Impacts of Ocean Acidification on Marine Biodiversity*, Montreal, Technical Series No. 46 (2009).

See COP23 website, *The Ocean Pathway*, available at https://cop23.com.fj/the-ocean-pathway.

See UN Environment Programme website, *Adressing Land-Based Pollution*, available at https://www.unep.org/gpa/.

Sefrioui, S., 'Adapting to sea level rise: a law of the sea perspective' in G. Andreone (ed.), *The Future of the Law of the Sea: Bridging Gaps Between National, Individual and Common Interests* (Cham: Springer Open, 2017), 3–22.

Shelton, D., 'Nature as a legal person' (2015) *VertigO: La revue électronique en sciences de l'environnement, special issue*, 22.

Shepherd, J., et al., The Royal Society Report on Geoengineering (2009) *Geoengineering the climate: Science, governance and uncertainty* (Report 10/09) 1, available at https://royalsociety.org/~/media/Royal_Society_Content/policy/publications/2009/8693.pdf.

Shi, Y., 'Are greenhouse gas emissions from international shipping a type of marine pollution?' (2016) 113 *Marine Pollution Bulletin*, 187–192.

Shi, Y., 'Reducing greenhouse gas emissions from international shipping: is it time to consider market-based measures?' (2016) 64 *Marine Policy*, 123–134.

Shi, Y., Gullett, W., 'International regulation of low-carbon shipping for climate change mitigation: development, challenges and prospects' (2018) 49(2) *Ocean Development and International Law*, 134–156.

Shields, M. A., 'An introduction to marine renewable energy', in M. A. Shields and A. I. L. Payne (eds.), *Marine Renewable Energy Technology and Environmental Interactions* (Dordrecht: Springer, 2014), 1–3.

Sicilianos, L. A., 'The European Court of Human Rights facing the Security Council: towards systemic harmonization' (2017) 66(4) *International & Comparative Law Quarterly*, 783–804.

Simma, B., 'From bilateralism to community interest in international law' (1994) 250 *Recueil des Cours*, 293–301.

Sivakumaran, S., 'The influence of teaching of publicists on the development of international law' (2017) 66 *International and Comparative Law Quarterly*, 1–37.

Slaughter, A. M., 'The Paris Approach to global governance' (2015) *Project: Syndicate*, blog available at www.project- syndicate.org/commentary/paris-agreement-model-for-global-governance-by- anne-marie-slaughter-2015–12;

Smiard, F., Laffoley, D., Baxter, J. M. (eds.), *Marine Protected Areas and Climate Change: Adaptation and Mitigation Synergies, Opportunities and Challenges* (Gland: International Union for Conservation of Nature, 2016).

Smith, L. T., *Decolonizing Methodologies: Research and Indigenous Peoples* (Dunedin: University of Otago Press, 2008).

Smith, T., et al., *CO_2 Targets, Trajectories and Trends for International Shipping* (2015), summarized at www.ucl.ac.uk/bartlett/energy/publications/2015/may/co2-targets-trajectories-and-trends-international-shipping.

Smyth, D., Report for the Department of Sustainability, Environment, Water, Population and Communities on behalf of the State of the Environment 2011 Committee, *Indigenous land and sea management: a case study* (2011), available at citeseerx.ist.psu.edu/viewdoc/download?doi=10.1.1.441.6798&rep=rep1&type=pdf.

Sohn, L., 'Managing the law of the sea: Ambassador Pardo's forgotten second idea' (1997) 36 *Columbia Journal of Transnational Law*, 285–305.

Sohn, L. B., et al., *Cases and Materials on the Law of the Sea*, 2nd ed. (Leiden: Martinus Nijhoff, 2014).

Soons, A. H. A., 'The effects of a rising sea level on maritime limits and boundaries' (1990) 37 *Netherlands International Law Review*, 207–232.

Soons, A. H. A., 'An ocean under stress: climate change and the law of the sea', presented at the 2018 Annual Meeting of the Royal Netherlands Society of International Law (KNVIR), available at www.knvir.org/.

Speers, A., et al., 'Impacts of climate change and ocean acidification on coral reef fisheries: an integrated ecological-economic model' (2016) 128 *Ecological Economics*, 33–43.

Spijkers, J., Boonstra, W. J., 'Environmental change and social conflict: the northeast Atlantic mackerel dispute' (2017) 17 *Regional Environmental Change*, 1835–1851.

Spijkers, J., et al., 'Marine fisheries and future ocean conflict' (2018) 19(5) *Fish and Fisheries*, 798–806.

Steffen, W., Crutzen, P. J., McNeill, J., 'The Anthropocene: are humans now overwhelming the great forces of nature?' (2007) 36 *Ambio*, 614–621.

Steffen, W., et al., *Global Change and the Earth System: A Planet under Pressure* (Berlin: Springer, 2004).

Steffen, W., et al., 'The trajectory of the Anthropocene: the great acceleration' (2015) 2 *The Anthropocene Review*, 81–98.

Steffen, W., et al., 'Stratigraphic and Earth system approaches in defining the Anthropocene' (2016) 8 *Earth's Future*, 324–345.

Steffen, W., et al., 'Trajectories of the Earth system in the Anthropocene' (2018) 115(33) *Proceedings of the National Academy of Sciences*, 8252–8259.

Stephens, T., 'Warming waters and souring seas: climate change and ocean acidification' in D. R. Rothwell et al. (eds.), *The Oxford Handbook of Law of the Sea* (Oxford: Oxford University Press, 2015), 777–798.

Stone, C. D., 'Should trees have standing? Towards legal rights for natural objects' (1972) 45 *Southern California Law Review*, 450–501.

Stoppani, A., *Corso di Geologia*, Vol. II, *Geologia stratigrafica* (Milan: G Bernardoni e G Brigola, 1873).

Stoutenburg, J. G., *Disappearing Island States in International Law* (Leiden: Brill Nijhoff, 2015).

Stramma, L., et al., 'Expansion of oxygen minimum zones may reduce available habitat for tropical pelagic fishes' (2011) 2 *Nature Climate Change*, 33–37.

Streck, C., Keenlyside, P., von Unger, M., 'The Paris agreement: a new beginning' (2016) 13 *Journal for European Environmental & Planning Law*, 3–29.

Summerhayes, C. P., 'Climate', in J. Zalasiewicz et al. (eds.), *The Anthropocene as a Geological Time Unit: A Guide to the Scientific Evidence and Current Debate* (Cambridge: Cambridge University Press, 2019), 201–218.

Summerhayes, C. P., 'Ice' in J. Zalasiewicz et al. (eds.), *The Anthropocene as a Geological Time Unit: A Guide to the Scientific Evidence and Current Debate* (Cambridge: Cambridge University Press, 2019), 218–233.

Summerhayes, C. P., *Earth's Climate Evolution* (Wiley-Blackwell, 2015).

Suntrup, J. C., 'The legal person and its other: a comparative view on drawing and effacing boundaries in various cultural contexts' (2017) 3 *The Open Journal for the Study of Culture*, 1–24.

Syvitski, J. P. M., et al., 'Sinking deltas due to human activities' (2009) 2 *Nature Geoscience*, 681–686.

Tams, C., *Enforcing Obligations Erga Omnes in International Law* (Cambridge: Cambridge University Press, 2005).

Tanaka, Y., *A Dual Approach to Ocean Management: The Cases of Zonal and Integrated Management in International Law of the Sea* (London: Routledge, 2009).

Tanaka, Y., *The International Law of the Sea* (Cambridge: Cambridge University Press, 2012).

Tanaka, Y., *The International Law of the Sea*, 2nd ed. (Cambridge: Cambridge University Press, 2015).

Tanaka, Y., 'Principles of international Marine environmental law' in R. Rayfuse (ed.), *Research Handbook on International Marine Environmental Law* (Cheltenham: Edward Elgar, 2015), 31–56.

Tanaka, Y., 'Regulation of greenhouse gas emissions from international shipping and jurisdiction of states' (2016) 25(3) *Review of European Community & International Environmental Law*, 333–346.

Tarling, G. G., et al., 'Effects of acute ocean acidification on spatially-diverse polar pelagic foodwebs: insights from on-deck microcosms' (2016) 127 *Deep-Sea Research Part II: Topical Studies in Oceanography*, 75–92.

Taucher, J., et al., 'Influence of ocean acidification plankton community structure during a winter-to-summer succession: an imaging approach indicates that copepods can benefit from elevated CO_2 via indirect food web effects' (2017) 12(2) *PLoS ONE*, e0169737.

Te Ohu Kaimoana, Report CBD Response, *Te Ohu Kaimoana's response to the Secretariat for the Convention on Biological Diversity on the priorities for negotiations on a new framework for implementing the Convention on Biological Diversity* (2019), available at https://teohu.maori.nz/wp-content/uploads/2019/06/Convention-on-Biological-Diversity-Response.pdf.

Teschke, B., 'Theorizing the Westphalian system of states: international relations from absolutism to capitalism' (2002) 8(1) *European Journal of International Relations*, 5–48.

Teschke, B., *The Myth of 1648: Class, Geopolitics and the Making of Modern International Relations* (London: Verso, 2003).

Teubner, G., 'Rights of non-humans? Electronic agents and animals as new actors in politics and law' (2006) 33(4) *Journal of Law and Society*, 497–521.

The South-east Regional Marine Plan Assessment Reports, *Assessment Report: Sea Country: an Indigenous Perspective* (National Oceans Office, 2002), available at www.environment.gov.au/system/files/resources/271c0bfc-34a2-4c6c-9b02-01204ebc0f43/files/indigenous.pdf.

Thor, P., et al., 'Seawater pH predicted for the year 2100 affects the metabolic response to feeding in Copepodites of the Arctic Copepod *calanus glacialis*' (2016) *POLS ONE*.

Tiller, R., et al., 'The once and future treaty: towards a new regime for biodiversity in areas beyond national jurisdiction' (2019) 99 *Marine Policy*, 239–242.

Tladi, D., *Ocean Governance: A Fragmented Regulatory Framework* (2011), available at http://regardssurlaterre.com/en/ocean-governance-fragmented-regulatory-framework.

Transport & Environment, Position Paper, *Initial IMO GHG strategy* (2018), available at www.transportenvironment.org/sites/te/files/publications/2018_03_TE_position_paper_IMO_Initial_GHG_strategy.pdf, at 4.

Trathan, P. N., Agnew, D., 'Climate change and the Antarctic marine ecosystem: an essay on management implications' (2010) 22 *Antarctic Science*, 387–398.

Treves, T., 'Historical development of the law of the sea' in D. Rothwell et al. (eds.), *The Oxford Handbook of the Law of the Sea* (Oxford University Press, 2015), 1–24.

Trevisanut, S., Giannopoulos, N., 'Investment protection in offshore energy production: bright sides of regime interaction' (2018) 19 *The Journal of World Investment & Trade*, 790–827.

Trouwborst, A., 'International nature conservation law and the adaptation of biodiversity to climate change: a mismatch?' (2009) 21(3) *Journal of Environmental Law*, 419–442.

Tsamenyi, M., Herriman, M., 'Ocean energy and the law of the sea: the need for a protocol?' (1998) 29(1) *Ocean Development & International Law*, 3–19.
Turley, C., Gattuso, J., 'Future biological and ecosystem impacts of ocean acidification and their socioeconomic-policy implications' (2012) 4 *Current Opinion in Environmental Sustainability*, 278–286.
Turner, R. E., Kearney, M. S., Parkinson, R. W., 'Sea-level rise tipping point for delta survival' (2018) 34 *Journal of Coastal Research*, 470–474.
Tyrrell, K. A., 'Humans may be reversing the climate clock by 50 million years', www.Phys.org, 10 December 2018.
UN Division for Ocean Affairs and the Law of the Sea, Office of Legal Affairs (ed.), Other marine based energy industries, *The First Global Integrated Marine Assessment: World Ocean Assessment* (Cambridge University Press, 2017).
UN Environment, *Realizing Integrated Regional Oceans Governance – Summary of case studies on regional cross-sectoral institutional cooperation and policy coherence* (2017), http://cpps.dyndns.info/cpps-docs-web/secgen/2017/taller-proi-oct/docs/6.Realizing%20Integrated%20Regional%20Ocean%20Governance.pdf.
UNFCCC, *Global Climate Action Event: Oceans* (12 November 2016), available at unfccc.int/files/paris_agreement/application/pdf/gcaoceansprogramme.pdf.
Union of Concerned Scientists, *Arctic Climate Impact Assessment* (2008), available at www.ucsusa.org/global_warming/science_and_impacts/impacts/arctic-climate-impact.html, accessed 13 May 2019.
United Nations Climate Change, *Kyoto Protocol: Targets for the first commitment period*, available at https://unfccc.int/process/the-kyoto-protocol, accessed 3 December 2018.
United Nations Climate Change, *What do adaptation to climate change and climate resilience mean?*, available at https://unfccc.int/topics/adaptation-and-resilience/the-big-picture/what-do-adaptation-to-climate-change-and-climate-resilience-mean, accessed 21 November 2018.
United Nations Division for Ocean Affairs and the Law of the (UNDOALOS), *Baselines: An Examination of the Relevant Provisions of the United Nations Convention on the Law of the Sea* (New York: United Nations Publication, 1989).
United Nations, *Transforming Our World: the 2030 Agenda for Sustainable Development* (2015), available at https://sustainabledevelopment.un.org/post2015/transformingourworld.
United States Environmental Protection Agency (US EPA), *Overview of Greenhouse Gases: Methane Emissions*, available at www.epa.gov/ghgemissions/overview-greenhouse-gases#methane, accessed 24 November 2018.
United States Environmental Protection Agency (US EPA), *Overview of Greenhouse Gases: Carbon Dioxide Emissions*, available at www.epa.gov/ghgemissions/overview-greenhouse-gases#carbon-dioxide, accessed 24 November 2018.
van Erp, J. (ed.), *Smart Mixes for Transboundary Environmental Harm* (Cambridge: Cambridge University Press, 2019).
van Hooidonk, R., et al., 'Local-scale projections of coral reef futures and implications of the Paris agreement' (2016) 6(39666) *Scientific Reports* 1–8.
van Ittersum, M. J., *Profit and Principle: Hugo Grotius, Natural Rights Theories and the Rise of Dutch Power in the East Indies (1595–1615)* (Boston/Leiden: Brill, 2006).

VanderZwaag, D. L., 'The international law and policy seascape for aquaculture: navigating tangled currents' in N. Bankes, I. Dahl and D. L. VanderZwaag (eds.), *Aquaculture Law and Policy* (Cheltenham: Edward Elgar, 2016), 11–32.

Vaquer-Sunyer, R., Duarte, C., 'Thresholds of hypoxia for marine biodiversity' (2008) 105 *Proceedings of the National Academy of Sciences*, 15452–15457.

Verkaik, K., Hamel, J., Mercier, A., 'Impact of ocean acidification on reproductive output in the deep-sea annelid *Ophryotrocha sp.* (Polychaeta: Dorvilleidae)' (2017) 137 *Deep-Sea Research Part II: Topical Studies in Oceanography*, 368–376.

Vidas, D., 'Responsibility for the seas', in D. Vidas (ed.), *Law, Technology and Science for Oceans in Globalisation* (Boston/Leiden: Brill/Martinus Nijhoff, 2010), 3–40.

Vidas, D., 'The Anthropocene and the international law of the sea' (2011) 369 *Philosophical Transactions of the Royal Society A*, 909–925.

Vidas, D., 'International law at the convergence of two epochs', in H. N. Scheiber et al. (eds.), *Ocean Law and Policy: 20 Years under UNCLOS* (Brill/Nijhoff, 2017), 101–123.

Vidas, D., Freestone, D., McAdam, J. (eds.), *International Law and Sea Level Rise: Report of the International Law Association Committee on International Law and Sea Level Rise* (Leiden/Boston: Brill, 2019).

Vidas, D., Zalasiewicz, J., Williams, M., 'What is the Anthropocene – and why is it relevant for international law?', 25 *yearbook of International Environmental Law* (Oxford: Oxford University Press, 2016), 3–23.

Vierros. M., Arico, S., 'Governance of Marine Areas Beyond National Jurisdictions', Our World, United Nations University, 14 March 2012, https://ourworld.unu.edu/en/governance-of-marine-areas-beyond-national-jurisdictions.

von Bernstorff, J., 'Non-State Actors in law-making and in the shaping of policy: on the legality and legitimacy of NGO participation in international law' (2007), Conference Draft 2007, available at www.kas.de/c/document_library/get_file?uuid=4e2e1560-2408-8bfd-9f85-5dea3e38c200&groupId=252038.

Wadhams, P., *A Farewell to Ice: A Report from the Arctic* (London: Allen Lane, 2016).

Walker, M. J. C., et al., 'Formal subdivision of the Holocene Series/Epoch' (2012) 27 *Journal of Quaternary Science*, 649–659.

Walker, M. J. C., et al., 'Formal ratification of the Holocene Series/Epoch (Quaternary System/Period): two new global boundary Stratotype sections and points (GSSPs) and three new stages/subseries' (2018) 41(4) *Episodes*, 213.

Walker, M., et al., 'Formal definition and dating of the GSSP (Global Stratotype Section and Point) for the base of the Holocene using the Greenland NGRIP ice core, and selected auxiliary records' (2009) 24 *Journal of Quaternary Science*, 3–17.

Ward, P. C., *Under a Green Sky: Global Warming, the Mass Extinctions of the Past and What They Can Tell Us About Our Future* (New York: Smithsonian Books/Harper Collins, 2007).

Warner, R. M., 'Preserving a balanced ocean: regulating climate change mitigation activities in marine areas beyond national jurisdiction' (2007) 14 *Australian International Law Journal*, 99–120.

Warner, R., 'Oceans in transition: incorporating climate-change impacts into environmental impact assessment for marine areas beyond national jurisdiction' (2018) 45 *Ecology Law Quarterly*, 31–52.

Waters, C. N., et al., *A Stratigraphical Basis for the Anthropocene* (London: Geological Society of London, 2014).

Waters, C. N., et al., 'The Anthropocene is functionally and stratigraphically distinct from the Holocene' (2016) 351 *Science*, 137.

Waters, C. N., et al., 'Palaeoenvironmental archives and their differing suitabilities for candidate global boundary Stratotype sections and points (GSSPs) for the Anthropocene' (2018) 178 *Earth-Science Reviews*, 379–429.

Weibust, I., Meadowcroft, J., Multilevel Environmental Governance: *Managing Water and Climate Change in Europe and North America* (Cheltenham: Edward Elgar, 2014).

Whiteman, G., Hope, C., Wadhams, P., 'Climate science: vast costs of Arctic change' (2013) 499 *Nature*, 401–403.

Whitsitt, E., Bankes, N., 'The evolution of international investment law and its application to the energy sector' (2013) 51(2) *Alberta Law Review*, 207–247.

Widdicombe, S., Spicer, J., 'Predicting the impact of ocean acidification on benthic biodiversity: what can animal physiology tell us?' (2008) 366 *Journal of Experimental Marine Biology*, 187–197.

Wiesmann, A., 'Slow steaming: a viable long-term option?' (2010) 2 *Wärtsilä Technical Journal*, 49–55.

Wikipedia, *Atmosphere of Earth*, en.wikipedia.org/wiki/Atmosphere_of_Earth, accessed 3 December 2018.

Wikipedia, *Prevailing winds*, en.wikipedia.org/wiki/Prevailing_winds, accessed 3 December 2018.

Williams; M., et al. (eds.), 'The Anthropocene: a new epoch of geological time?' (2011) 369 *Philosophical Transactions of the Royal Society* A, 833–1112.

Williamson, P., 'Emissions reduction: scrutinize CO2 removal methods', in *Nature: International Weekly Journal of Science* (10 February 2016), available at www.nature.com/news/emissions-reduction-scrutinize-co2-removal-methods-1.19318.

Williamson, P., Bodle, R., *Update on Climate Geoengineering in Relation to the Convention on Biological Diversity: Potential Impacts and Regulatory Framework* (2016) Technical Series No.84. Secretariat of the Convention on Biological Diversity, Montreal.

Wilson, G., 'Murky waters: ambiguous international law for ocean fertilization and other geoengineering' (2014) 49 *Texas International Law Journal*, 507, 545–546.

Wilson, S., 'Sustainable aquaculture: an organizing solution in international law' (2004) 26(2) *Thomas Jefferson Law Review*, 491–516.

Wolff, E. W., 'Greenhouse gases in the earth system: A palaeoclimate perspective' (2011) 369 *Philosophical Transactions of the Royal Society* A, 2133–2147.

Wolfrum, R., Matz, N., 'The interplay of the United Nations Convention on the law of the sea and the convention on biological diversity' in J. A. Frowein and R. Wolfrum (eds.), *Max Planck Yearbook of United Nations Law* (Zuidpoolsingel, Netherlands: Kluwer Law International, 2000), 445–480.

World Commission on Environment and Development (WCED), 'Our Common Future' ('Brundtland Report'), available at https://sustainabledevelopment.un.org/content/documents/5987our-common-future.pdf.

World Meteorological Organization (WMO), *Greenhouse Gas Bulletin*, No. 12 (24 October 2016), available at library.wmo.int/doc_num.php?explnum_id=3084.

Wright, G., et. al., 'The long and winding road continues: towards a new agreement on high seas governance' (2015) Study N°01/16, L'Institut du développement durable et des relations internationales (IDDRI) Paris, France.

Wright, G., Rochette, J., 'Regional ocean governance of Areas Beyond National Jurisdiction: lessons learnt and ways forward' (2019) *STRONG High Seas Project*.

World Wide Fund for Nature (WWF), Report *Protecting Our Ocean: Europe's Challenges to Meet the 2020 Deadlines* (2019), available at http://d2ouvy59podg6k.cloudfront.net/downloads/protecting_our_ocean.pdf.

Wyatt, T. D., Hardege, J. D., Terschak, J., 'Ocean acidification foils chemical signals' (2014) 346 *Science*, 175–176.

Yamin, F., Depledge, J., *The International Climate Change Regime: A Guide to Rules, Institutions, and Procedures* (Cambridge: Cambridge University Press, 2004).

Yankov, A., 'The law of the sea convention and Agenda 21: Environmental implications' in A. Boyle and D. Freestone (eds.), *International Law and Sustainable development: Past Achievements and Future Challenges* (Oxford: Oxford University Press, 1999), 271–297.

Yong, M. A., 'Introduction: the productive friction between regimes' in M.A. Yong (ed.), *Regime Interaction in International Law: Facing Fragmentation* (Cambridge: Cambridge University Press, 2012), 1–20.

Young, M., 'Building the blue economy: the role of marine spatial planning in facilitating offshore renewable energy development' (2015) 30 *The International Journal of Marine and Coastal Law*, 148–174.

Young, O. R., *On Environmental Governance: Sustainability, Efficiency, and Equity* (London: Routledge, 2016).

Zalasiewicz, J., et al., 'Are we now living in the Anthropocene?' (2008) 18(2) *GSA Today*, 4–8.

Zalasiewicz, J., et al., 'Petrifying earth process: the stratigraphic imprint of key earth system parameters in the Anthropocene' (2017) 34 *Theory, Culture & Society*, 83–104.

Zalasiewicz, J., et al., 'The working group on the anthropocene: summary of evidence and interim recommendations' (2017) 19 *Anthropocene*, 55–60.

Zalasiewicz, J., et al., 'The geological Anthropocene: born in Burlington House' (December 2017/January 2018) 27 *Geoscientist*, 16–19.

Zalasiewicz, J., et al. (eds.), *The Anthropocene as a Geological Time Unit: A Guide to the Scientific Evidence and Current Debate* (Cambridge: Cambridge University Press, 2019).

Zeebe, R. E., et al., 'Carbon emissions and acidification' (2008) 321 *Science*, 51–52.

Zelli, F., van Asselt, H., 'The institutional fragmentation of global environmental governance: causes, consequences, and responses' (2012) 13(3) *Global Environmental Politics*, 1–13.

Zemp, M., et al., 'Historically unprecedented global glacier decline in the early 21st century' (2015) 61 *Journal of Glaciology*, 745–762.

Zou, K. (ed.), *Global Commons and the Law of the Sea* (Leiden: Brill, 2018).

Index

ABMTs. *See* area-based management tools
ABNJ. *See* areas beyond national jurisdiction
acidification, of oceans, 30–31
  area conservation and, 123–125
  carbon dioxide levels and, 104, 106
  climate change adaptation and, 55, 71–72
  control strategies, 121–123
  Convention on Biological Diversity obligations, 111–112
  definition of, 104
  dumping regimes and, 119–121
    under London Convention, 119–121
  fisheries management and, 123–125
    Commission for the Conservation of Antarctic Marine Living Resources, 124
    Regional Fishery Management Organizations, 112
  Global Programme for Action, 118–119
  global regime for, 109–125. *See also* Law of the Sea Convention
    aims and goals of, 110–113
    under soft law norms, 110–113
    Monaco Declaration, 112–113
    Regional Fishery Management Organizations and, 112
    regional level instruments in, 110
    SDGs in, 110–111
  independent obligations for, 121–123
  Law of the Sea Convention obligations, 109–110, 113–125, 126–128. *See also* dumping regimes
    atmospheric pollution prevention, 114–118
    land-based pollution prevention, 118–119
    marine environmental protections, 114
    objectives of, 115
    under Part XII, 105
  marine capture fisheries and, 264–265
  marine ecosystems influenced by, 71–72, 108–109
    positive impacts, 109
  marine protected areas, 125
  mitigation strategies, 121–123
  under Paris Agreement, 116
  pH levels and, historical increases in, 106–109
  in polar regions, 107–108
    Arctic Council guidelines, 112
  UNFCCC guidelines on, 105, 109–110, 115, 122–123, 126–128
    Oceans Pathway Partnership, 116–117
actors, on climate change
  EU as, 156
  International Maritime Organization as, 156
  non-governmental, 159
  in ocean-centered governance models, 358–360
    sectoral and regional actors, 364–366
  regional, 159
  socio-ecological context for, 355–356
adaptation, climate change, 54–58
  aquaculture and, 299
    implementation of measures, 303–307
    monitoring mechanisms, 306–307
    reporting mechanisms, 306–307
    spatial assessment in, 302
  Cancun Adaptation Framework for, 57
  climate change mitigation and, 57–58
  definition of, 54–55
  greenhouse grass emissions and, 54
  jurisdiction of, 56–57
  Law of the Sea Convention and, 78–80
  Law of the Sea Regime and, 376–381

adaptation, climate change (cont.)
  in marine protected areas, 238–240, 241–255
    international legal frameworks for, 247–248
    under Paris Agreement, 245–246
    under UN Climate Treaty Regime, 241–247
    under UNFCCC, 242–244
  ocean's role in, 67–72
    acidification of oceans, 55, 71–72
    changing ocean conditions, 69–72
    marine biodiversity, 69–72
    sea-level rise, 68–69
    weather patterns and, changes in, 67–68
  responses to, 55–56
  scenario planning and, 56
  sea-level rise and, 55, 68–69
  tradeoffs in, 58
  transformational, 56
adaptive aquaculture, 300–303
adaptive ocean-centered governance models, 369–371
  Indigenous governance in, 369–371
Agenda 21, of Rio Conference, 81–82, 87, 356–357
air transport. *See* aviation sector
AMA. *See* Aquaculture Management Area
ambulatory baselines, 325–326, 332, 334–335, 378
ambulatory maritime limits, 312–314
Anthropocene, 23–38, 48
  climate change and. *See* climate change
  definition of, 28
  development of, in natural sciences, 23–25
  Earth System Science approach, 24
  in geology, 25–29
    Geological Time Scale, 26–27, 37–38
    Global Boundary Stratotype Section and Point, 27
    International Commission on Stratigraphy, 26
  Holocene epoch and, 24–25, 28
    dating of, 24
    subdivision of, 28
  international law and. *See* international law
  IPCC and, 22
  Law of the Sea Convention and, 41–48
    climate change and, 41–44
  oceans and, 29–38
  scope of, 29–31
Anthropocene Working Group (AWG), 26, 27
anticipatory approach, 47
aquaculture, climate change impacts on, 291, 377–378
  adaptive, 300–303
  climate change adaptation, 299
    implementation of, 303–307
    monitoring mechanisms, 306–307
    reporting mechanisms, 306–307
    spatial assessment in, 302
  in coastal states, 293
  under Convention on Biological Diversity, 301
  ecosystem approach to, 299–300
  in Exclusive Economic Zones, 293, 294
  food supply principles and, 297–298
  under International Aquaculture Law, 299
  international regulations and guidelines, 293–300
    Food and Agricultural Organization instruments, 289–290, 297–300
    gaps in, 293–294
    for international navigation, 295
    under Law of the Sea Convention, 294–296, 307
    for marine environmental protections, 294–295
    under Paris Agreement, 296–297, 300–302, 304–305, 307
  in maritime zones, 293
  in Norway, 291–293, 302–303, 305–306
Aquaculture Management Area (AMA), 305–306
archipelagic baselines, 312
Arctic Council
  acidification of oceans, 112
  marine protected areas and, regional cooperation over, 260
area conservation, ocean acidification and, 123–125
area-based management tools (ABMTs), 234. *See also* marine protected areas
  marine protected areas compared to, 238
areas beyond national jurisdiction (ABNJ). *See also* biological diversity in areas beyond national jurisdiction
  climate change in, 336–340
    under Convention on Biological Diversity, 339–340
    environmental impact assessment of, 346–350

under International Seabed Authority, 338
Law of the Sea Convention provisions, 338
legal framework for, 337–340
legal instruments on, 340
environmental impact assessment of, 346–352
climate change impacts, 346–350
of climate change mitigation, 350–352
Convention on Biological Diversity and, 347–348
ocean fertilization, 351–352
high seas as distinct from, 336–337
under London Dumping Convention and Protocol, 351–352
in marine protected areas, 234–235, 256–257
strategic environment assessment, 349
atmosphere
composition of, 59
ocean-atmosphere interface, 59–60
atmospheric pollution, acidification of oceans and, 114–118
aviation sector, greenhouse gas emissions by, 149–151
CORSIA and, 150–151
AWG. *See* Anthropocene Working Group

Bangladesh Exception, LOSC, 42, 329
baselines
ambulatory, 325–326, 332, 334–335, 378
archipelagic, 312
delta, 312, 314
BBNJ. *See* biological diversity in areas beyond national jurisdiction
biodiversity. *See also* biological diversity in areas beyond national jurisdiction; marine biodiversity and ecosystems
Convention on Biological Diversity, 85–86
Fish Stock Agreement and, 13
in protected areas, 247–255
biodiversity in areas beyond national jurisdiction, 340–345
bioenergy. *See* marine biomass
biological diversity in areas beyond national jurisdiction (BBNJ), 12, 340–345
climate change and, 342–345
under Convention on Biological Diversity, 345
legally binding instruments for, 340–342
marine protected areas and, 234–235
ocean fertilization and, 202

calcium carbonate levels, 106–108, 264–265
Cancun Adaptation Framework, for climate change adaptation, 57
CAOF Agreement, 285
carbon capture and storage (CCS)
carbon dioxide in, 162–173
under Law of the Sea Convention, 166–173
dumping controls
under Law of the Sea Convention, 171–173
under London Convention and Protocol, 173–175
enhanced oil recovery and, 162–173
under Law of the Sea Convention, 166–173
saline projects compared to, 165
waterflooding operations, 165
function of, 160
implementation of, 162–164
International Energy Agency and, 163, 176
under Law of the Sea Convention
carbon dioxide projects and, 166–173
in coastal states, 169–171
dumping controls, 171–173
enhanced oil recovery and, 166–173
in exclusive economic zones, 166–169
International Seabed Authority and, 170
in marine areas, operational authority in, 166–170
under London Convention and Protocol, 173–178
dumping controls, 173–175
Risk Assessment and Management Framework, 173–175
under regional conventions, 178–181
OSPAR Convention, 179–181
trapping mechanisms, 164
carbon dioxide levels
Anthropocene, 31–32
climate change and, 31–32
geoengineering as influence on, reduction of, 185
ocean acidification and, 104, 106
Carbon Offsetting and Reduction Scheme for International Aviation (CORSIA), 150–151
carbon sequestration, 190, 245, 255, 258, 343
carbon sink
marine protected areas and, 259

carbon sink (cont.)
  oceans as, 60, 64–65
CBD. *See* Convention on Biological Diversity
CBDR approach. *See* 'common but differentiated responsibility' approach
CCAMLR. *See* Commission for the Conservation of Antarctic Marine Living Resources
CCS. *See* carbon capture and storage
CLCS. *See* Commission on the Limits of the Continental Shelf
climate change. *See also* actors; adaptation; Intergovernmental Panel on Climate Change; mitigation
  Anthropocene, 29–38
    carbon dioxide levels, 31–32
    greenhouse gas levels, 31–33
    international law and, 43–44
    Law of the Sea Convention and, 41–44
    methane levels, changes in, 32
    sea-level changes, 33–35
    spectrum of, 29–31
  in areas beyond national jurisdiction, 336–340
    under Convention on Biological Diversity, 339–340
    environmental impact assessment of, 346–350
    under International Seabed Authority, 338
    Law of the Sea Convention provisions, 338
    legal framework for, 337–340
    legal instruments on, 340
  biological diversity in areas beyond national jurisdiction and, 342–345
  biosphere influenced by, 29–30
  greenhouse gas emissions and, 31–33
    adaptation in, 54
    mitigation in, 50–51
  ocean-centered governance models and, 354–358
  oceans and, 58–72. *See also* oceans
    acidification of, 30–31
    sea-level changes, 33–35
climate disputes, under Law of the Sea Convention, 96–102
  compensation and damages, 101–102
  compulsory dispute mechanisms, 96–97
  diplomatic contact in, 100–101
  interpretation of Articles, 97–98
  litigation over, 96–97
  under UNFCCC, 98
climate systems, oceans and
  interdependence between, 1–2, 59–62
  ocean-atmosphere interface, 59–60
coastal states
  aquaculture in, 293
  carbon capture and storage in, 169–171
  international fisheries law in, 271–272
  marine protected areas in, 255–257
  ocean fertilization and, 191
  offshore renewable energy and, 218–222
  sea-level rise near, 335
  vulnerable, 20, 332, 335
Commission for the Conservation of Antarctic Marine Living Resources (CCAMLR), 124, 260–261, 283–285
Commission on the Limits of the Continental Shelf (CLCS), 324–325
'common but differentiated responsibility' (CBDR) approach, 132–133
compensation and damages, in Law of the Sea Convention climate disputes, 101–102
compulsory dispute mechanisms, in Law of the Sea Convention, 96–97
Conference of Parties (COP21), 22
conservation. *See also specific conventions*
  area conservation, ocean acidification and, 123–125
  under Law of the Sea Convention, 77
  in marine protected areas, obligations in, 247–255
    under Convention on Biological Diversity, 252–255
    under Law of the Sea Convention, 248–252
    under Paris Agreement, 251–252
    under UN Climate Treaty Regime, 251–252
    under UNFCCC, 251–252
Continental Shelf Regime, 9–10
Convention for the Protection of the Marine Environment of the North-East Atlantic (OSPAR Convention), 179–181
  offshore renewable energy under, 231
Convention on Biological Diversity (CBD), 85–86, 357
  acidification of oceans and, 111–112
  aquaculture under, 301
  in areas beyond national jurisdiction, 339–340

environmental impact assessments of, 347–348
biological diversity in areas beyond national jurisdiction under, 345
marine protected areas under, 234, 241
environmental protection and conservation obligations, 252–255
ocean fertilization under, 188, 193, 197–198
offshore renewable energy under, 231
COP 21. *See* Conference of Parties
Coriolis effect, 61, 62
CORSIA. *See* Carbon Offsetting and Reduction Scheme for International Aviation

damages. *See* compensation and damages
delta baselines, 312, 314
dissolved oxygen content, in oceans, 70
Doha Amendment, to Kyoto Protocol, 5
due diligence, in Law of the Sea Convention, 102–103
for marine protected areas, 249–250, 254
dumping regimes
acidification of oceans and, 119–121
under London Convention and Protocol, 119–121
with carbon capture and storage
under Law of the Sea Convention, 171–173
under London Convention and Protocol, 173–175

EAF management. *See* ecosystem approach to fisheries management
Earth history, epochs in, 24
Earth System, 36
atmosphere in, composition of, 59
human impacts on, 40
Earth System Science (ESS) community, 24
EBSAs. *See* Ecologically or Biologically Significant Marine Areas
ECJ. *See* European Court of Justice
Ecologically or Biologically Significant Marine Areas (EBSAs), 340
ecosystem approach to fisheries (EAF) management, 272–273, 283. *See also* marine biodiversity and ecosystems
aquaculture and, 299–300
ecosystem services, 69
EEDI. *See* Energy Efficiency Design Index
EEZs. *See* Exclusive Economic Zones
electric pulse trawl fishing, 278–280
emissions reduction units (ERUs), 5
Energy Efficiency Design Index (EEDI), 138–140, 144
enhanced oil recovery (EOR), 160–161, 162–166, 176
carbon capture and storage and, 162–173
under Law of the Sea Convention, 166–173
saline projects compared to, 165
waterflooding operations, 165
entitlements. *See* maritime entitlements and limits
environmental impact assessments (EIAs)
of areas beyond national jurisdiction, 346–352
climate change impacts, 346–350
of climate change mitigation, 350–352
Convention on Biological Diversity and, 347–348
ocean fertilization, 351–352
on offshore renewable energy, 215, 228
EOR. *See* enhanced oil recovery
ERUs. *See* emissions reduction units
ESS Community. *See* Earth System Science community
EU. *See* European Union
European Court of Justice (ECJ), 94
European Union (EU). *See also specific countries*
as actor on climate change, 156
electric pulse trawl fishing in, 279–280
offshore renewable energy and, 217
unilateral regional action, by IMO, 151–154
definitions of greenhouse gas emissions, 152–153
Directives for, 151–152, 153–154
exception rules, in Law of the Sea Convention, 20, 310, 312, 325–335
for baselines surrounding highly unstable coastlines, 326–330
for intent of parties, 326
maritime limits and, 325–326
permanent continental shelf limits, 330–333
Exclusive Economic Zones (EEZs)
aquaculture in, 293, 294
carbon capture and storage in, 166–169
international fisheries law in, 268
Law of the Sea Convention and, 9–10, 73
marine protected areas in, 255–256
maritime limits in, 317–318
offshore renewable energy in, 219–220, 224

FAO. *See* United Nations
fertilization techniques
  under Law of the Sea Regime, 188, 204
  marine geoengineering and, 187–188
Fish Stocks Agreement (1995), 13, 79
  ecosystem approach to fisheries management, 272–273
  in international fisheries law, 272–273, 276, 287–288
fisheries management. *See also* international fisheries law
  acidification of oceans and, 123–125
    Commission for the Conservation of Antarctic Marine Living Resources, 124
    Regional Fishery Management Organizations, 112
  ecosystem approach to, 272–273
Food and Agricultural Organization (FAO). *See* United Nations
food supply principles, 297–298
freedom of the seas doctrine, 8

gas exchange, 59–60
geoengineering. *See also* marine geoengineering
  carbon dioxide reduction through, 185
  definitions of, 185
  ocean fertilization through, 185
    marine geoengineering, 187–188
  techniques, 185
geoengineering, in climate change mitigation, 53
Geological Time Scale
  Anthropocene, 26–27, 37–38
  Holocene epoch, 24–25, 28
    dating of, 24
    Law of the Sea Convention and, 38–41
    subdivision of, 28
  Jurassic Period/System, 27
  Pleistocene epoch, 28
  Pliocene epoch, 37
geology
  Anthropocene, 25–29
    Geological Time Scale, 26–27, 37–38
    Global Boundary Stratotype Section and Point, 27
    International Commission on Stratigraphy, 26
  international law and, 39
geothermal energy, 209, 212
Global Boundary Stratotype Section and Point (GSSP), 27
global climate regimes, IMO and, 147–149
Global Programme for Action (GPA), 118–119
global warming. *See* warming
globalization
  ocean-centered governance models influenced by, 366–369
  public law influenced by, 368
governance. *See specific topics*
GPA. *See* Global Programme for Action
greenhouse gas (GHG) emissions. *See also* International Maritime Organization; shipping
  Anthropocene, 31–33
  by aviation sector, 149–151
    CORSIA and, 150–151
  climate change and, 31–33
    adaptation, 54
    mitigation, 50–51
  under Kyoto Protocol, 5
  ocean fertilization and, 186–188
  in Paris Agreement, 91–93
Grotius, Hugo, 8, 38
GSSP. *See* Global Boundary Stratotype Section and Point

harmonization. *See* systemic harmonization
heat sink, oceans as, 63–64
  anthropogenic heat, 64
  heat storage capacity, 33
  warming of oceans, 63–64
heavy fuel oil (HFO) use, 280
high seas, 336–337
holism, in ocean-centered governance models, 372
Holocene epoch
  Anthropocene and, 24–25, 28
  dating of, 24
  Law of the Sea Convention and, 38–41
    ideological foundations of, 38
  subdivision of, 28
hydrocarbons industry, 217
hypoxia, from ocean warming, 70–71

ice melt, 33, 34, 35–36, 58
ICJ. *See* International Court of Justice
ICS. *See* International Commission on Stratigraphy
IEA. *See* International Energy Agency
ILC. *See* International Law Commission

IMO. *See* International Maritime Organization
impact assessment. *See* environmental impact assessment
Indigenous governance, 357–358, 361, 369–371
inherent rights, 47–48
Intergovernmental Panel on Climate Change (IPCC), 1
  Anthropocene, 22
  on climate change mitigation, 50, 52–54
  Conference of Parties, 22
  on global warming, 49
  ocean fertilization and, 184
  ocean-centered governance models and, 360–361
  Paris Agreement and, 6–7
International Aquaculture Law, 299
International Commission on Stratigraphy (ICS), 26
International Convention on the Prevention of Pollution from Ships (MARPOL Convention), 93, 102, 131
  offshore renewable energy under, 230–231
International Court of Justice (ICJ), 346–347
International Energy Agency (IEA), 163, 176
  offshore renewable energy and, 208
international fisheries law, climate change and
  under CAOF Agreement, 285
  climate change mitigation and
    electric pulse trawl fishing, 278–280
    Food and Agricultural Organization and, 273–274, 281–284
    heavy fuel oil use and, 280
    higher fuel use intensity, 277–278
    for marine capture fisheries, 277–284
    Regional Fishery Management Organizations and, 281–287, 288
  in coastal states, 271–272
  in Exclusive Economic Zones, 268
  global components of, 267–276
    actions by global bodies, 273–276
    Fish Stocks Agreement, 272–273, 276, 287–288
    Law of the Sea Convention, 267–272, 287–288
    UN General Assembly Resolutions, 268, 275–276
  marine capture fisheries under. *See* marine capture fisheries
  in marine protected areas, 271
International Geosphere-Biosphere Programme, 23–24
international institutions. *See specific institutions*
international law
  Anthropocene and, 44–48
    climate change, 43–44
    conceptual change in, necessity for, 46
    methodological approaches to, 46
    objectives of, 46–47
    periodization in, necessity for, 46
    relevance of, 35–38
    responsibility and role of, 46
  geology and, 39
  inherent rights, 47–48
  International Aquaculture Law, 299
  International Maritime Organization under, 158–159
  pacta tertiis principle, 287–288, 380–381
International Law Association (ILA) Committee, 310, 315
  on sea-level rise, 318–321, 326
    baseline maintenance, 319
    Commission on the Limits of the Continental Shelf, 324–325
    maritime zone limits, 319–320
    Resolution 5/2018, 321–325
International Law Commission (ILC), 375
International Maritime Organization (IMO), greenhouse gas emissions guidelines and, 138–156
  as actor on climate change, 156
  assessment of, 144–147, 154–156
  aviation sector and, 149–151
    CORSIA and, 150–151
  cost implications of, 145, 146–147
  Energy Efficiency Design Index, 138–140, 144
  global climate regime and, 147–149
  global pressures on, after Paris Agreement, 147–156
  initial strategies, 143–144
  international law and, 158–159
  Law of the Sea Convention and, 148–149, 158–159
  mandatory data collection system, 142–143
  marine protected areas and, 256–257
  market-based measures, 141–142, 144, 146
  regulatory developments, 138–147
  ship energy efficiency management plan, 140–141, 144

International Maritime Organization (cont.)
standards for, 130
UNFCCC and, 147–148, 149, 155
as influence on IMO, 145
unilateral regional action, in EU, 151–154
definitions in, 152–153
Directives in, 151–152, 153–154
International Renewable Energy Agency (IRENA), 208–209
International Seabed Authority (ISA), 10, 77, 90
in areas beyond national jurisdiction, 338
carbon capture and storage and, 170
offshore renewable energy and, 222
International Tribunal for the Law of the Sea (ITLOS), 82
International Union for Conservation of Nature (IUCN), 237
International Union of Geological Sciences (IUGS), 27
IPCC. *See* Intergovernmental Panel on Climate Change
IRENA. *See* International Renewable Energy Agency
ISA. *See* International Seabed Authority
ITLOS. *See* International Tribunal for the Law of the Sea
IUCN. *See* International Union for Conservation of Nature
IUGS. *See* International Union of Geological Sciences

Jurassic Period/System, 27
jurisdiction. *See also* biological diversity in areas beyond national jurisdiction
climate change adaptation and, 56–57
under Law of the Sea Convention
Exclusive Economic Zones, 9–10, 73
national jurisdiction areas, 73–74
regulatory approach to, 9, 11

Kyoto Protocol
Clean Development Mechanism in, 4–5
Doha Amendment to, 5
emissions trading mechanism in, 4–5
greenhouse gas emissions under, 5
Joint implementation mechanism in, 4–5
mitigation commitments in, 5
ocean fertilization and, 188–190
Paris Agreement and
comparisons between, 6–7
implementation through, 91–93
UNFCCC and, 4–5

land-based pollution, acidification of oceans and, 118–119
Law of the Sea Convention (LOSC), 8–13, 38–48. *See also* Part XII
acidification of oceans under. *See* acidification
Anthropocene and, 41–48
climate change and, 41–44
aquaculture under, 294–296, 307
areas beyond national jurisdiction and, 338
assessment of, 13–15
Bangladesh Exception, 42, 329
carbon capture and storage and. *See* carbon capture and storage
climate change adaptation and, 78–80
climate change mitigation and, 74–77
conservation duties and, 77
International Seabed Authority, 77
marine pollution and, 75–77
climate disputes and, 96–102
compensation and damages, 101–102
compulsory dispute mechanisms, 96–97
diplomatic contact in, 100–101
interpretation of Articles, 97–98
litigation over, 96–97
under UNFCCC, 98
climate in, 2–3
as 'constitution of the oceans', 8–9
Continental Shelf Regime, 9–10
due diligence mechanisms, 102–103
economic profit under, 40
exception rules in. *See* exception rules
Fish Stocks Agreement (1995) and, 79
function and purpose of, 81–82
under Holocene conditions, 38–41
ideological foundations of, 38
international cooperation under, 73–74
international fisheries law and, 267–272, 287–288
International Maritime Organization and, 148–149, 158–159
International Seabed Authority, 10
International Tribunal for the Law of the Sea and, 82
marine protected areas under
biological diversity challenges, 258

due diligence obligations, 249–250, 254
environmental protection and conservation obligations, 248–252
establishment under, legal opportunities for, 255–257
legal constraints and challenges, 257–259
maritime limits under. *See* maritime entitlements and limits
national jurisdiction areas established by, 73–74
ocean fertilization under, 188, 191–195, 200–203
in coastal states, 191
as marine scientific research, 201
pollution and, 192–195
ocean governance under, 11–13
for BBNJ, 12
ocean-centered governance models and implementation of measures, 364–366
Part XII, 361–364
rules systems in, 360–366
offshore renewable energy under, 217–232
balancing of interests under, 222–226
coastal state jurisdictions, 218–222
legal instruments for, 229–232
Part XII, acidification of oceans in, 105
regulation of oceans and
history of, 8–9
Mare Liberum, 8
regulatory approach in, 9–11
Exclusive Economic Zones, 9–10
jurisdictional framework in, 9, 11
maritime zones in, architecture of, 9–11, 42–43
scope of, 3, 39
Sustainable Development Goals and, 82–83
territorial appropriation of seas and, 39–40
UN Climate Treaty Regime, 74–75, 78
UNFCCC and, 88–89
climate disputes under, 98
Law of the Sea Regime, 2–3, 13–15, 126, 374–376. *See also* Law of the Sea Convention
climate change adaptation and, 376–381
climate change mitigation and, 376–381
constraints of, 15
dynamic interpretation of, 378–379
fertilization techniques under, 188, 204
flexibility of, 378–379
framework for, 376–378
future applications of, 382–385
legal research on, 383–385
marine protected areas and, 255–259, 379–380
obstacles in, 379–381
Regional Fishery Management Organization and, 380–381
UN Climate Treaty Regime as complement to, 381
London Dumping Convention and Protocol, 90, 93, 102
acidification of oceans, 119–121
areas beyond national jurisdiction under, 351–352
carbon capture and storage and, 173–178
dumping controls, 173–175
Risk Assessment and Management Framework, 173–175
ocean fertilization under, 194–199, 200–203
jurisdiction of, 202
offshore renewable energy under, 231
LOSC. *See* Law of the Sea Convention

Māori population, governance by, 369–371
Mare Liberum (Grotius), 8, 38
marine biodiversity and ecosystems
in areas beyond national jurisdiction, 266
climate change adaptation and, 69–72
ocean's role in, 69–72
warming of oceans as influence on, 69–70
marine biomass, as bioenergy, 209, 212
marine capture fisheries, international law impacted by, 264–267. *See also* Regional Fishery Management Organizations
Atlanto-Scandian herring, 266–267
calcium carbonate levels, 264–265
climate change mitigation and, 277–284
ocean acidification and, 264–265
species productivity and distribution, 266–267
marine environment protections, under Law of the Sea Convention
acidification of oceans, 114
Part XII, 85–86
marine geoengineering, 120, 185, 196–197, 377–378, 383
ocean fertilization and, 187–188
regulation of, 198
marine pollution
under Law of the Sea Convention, 75–77
Part XII, 87–88

marine pollution (cont.)
- ocean fertilization and, 192–195

marine protected areas (MPAs), 55, 125
- area-based management tools compared to, 238
- in areas beyond national jurisdiction, 231–235, 256–257
- biological diversity in areas beyond national jurisdiction and, 234–235
- biological diversity obligations in, 247–255
- carbon sinks and, 259
- climate change adaptation in, 238–240, 241–255
  - international legal frameworks for, 247–248
  - under Paris Agreement, 245–246
  - under UN Climate Treaty Regime, 241–247
  - under UNFCCC, 242–244
- climate change mitigation in, 238–240, 241–255
  - under Paris Agreement, 245–246
  - under UN Climate Treaty Regime, 241–247
  - under UNFCCC, 242–244
- in coastal states, 255–257
- conceptual development of, 237–240
  - definitions in, 237–238
- under Convention on Biological Diversity, 234, 241
  - environmental protection and conservation obligations, 252–255
- ecosystems in, 235
- environmental protection and conservation obligations in, 247–255
  - under Convention on Biological Diversity, 252–255
  - under Law of the Sea Convention, 248–252
  - under Paris Agreement, 251–252
  - under UN Climate Treaty Regime, 251–252
  - under UNFCCC, 251–252
- in Exclusive Economic Zones, 255–256
- under international fisheries law, 271
- International Maritime Organization and, 256–257
- International Union for Conservation of Nature and, 237
- under Law of the Sea Convention
  - biological diversity challenges, 258
  - due diligence obligations, 249–250, 254
  - environmental protection and conservation obligations, 248–252
  - establishment under, legal opportunities for, 255–257
  - legal constraints and challenges, 257–259
- Law of the Sea Regime and, 255–259, 379–380
- under Paris Agreement
  - climate change adaptation in, 245–246
  - climate change mitigation in, 245–246
  - environmental protection and conservation obligations, 251–252
- regional cooperation for, 260–261
  - through Arctic Council, 260
  - through CCAMLR, 260–261
- Regional Fisheries Management Organizations and, 256–257
- Sustainable Development Goals for, 234–235
- under UN Climate Treaty Regime
  - climate change adaptation in, 241–247
  - climate change mitigation in, 241–247
  - environmental protection and conservation obligations in, 251–252
- under UNFCCC
  - climate change adaptation in, 242–244
  - climate change mitigation in, 242–244
  - environmental protection and conservation obligations in, 251–252

marine spatial planning, 55, 123, 213, 225, 238
- offshore renewable energy and, 226

maritime entitlements and limits, 309, 310–316, 317–318
- ambulatory, 312–314
- baselines law and, 312–314
- in Exclusive Economic Zones, 317–318
- ILA Committee and, 322, 334–335
- under Law of the Sea Convention, 316–335, 378
  - alternative approaches to, 316–318
  - sea-level rise and, 314–316
- sea-level rise and, 311–316. *See also* sea-level rise
  - global frameworks for, 314–316
  - predictions of, 311–312
- unstable, 311–316

maritime zones
- aquaculture in, 293
- ILA Committee on, 319–320

under Law of the Seas Convention, 9–11, 42–43
sea-level rise and, 319–320
market-based measures (MBM), 141–142, 144, 146
MARPOL Convention. *See* International Convention on the Prevention of Pollution from Ships
MBM. *See* market-based measures
methane levels
Anthropocene, 32
climate change and, 32
oceans' influence on, 65–67
in polar regions, 65–67
mitigation, climate change, 50–54
climate change adaptation and, 57–58
geoengineering in, 53
greenhouse gas reductions in, 50–51
international fisheries law and
electric pulse trawl fishing, 278–280
Food and Agricultural Organization and, 273–274, 281–284
heavy fuel oil use and, 280
higher fuel use intensity, 277–278
for marine capture fisheries, 277–284
Regional Fishery Management Organizations and, 281–287, 288
IPCC reports on, 50, 52–54
in Kyoto Protocol, 5
Law of the Sea Convention and, 74–77
conservation duties and, 77
International Seabed Authority, 77
marine pollution and, 75–77
Part XII, 84–91
Law of the Sea Regime and, 376–381
marine capture fisheries and, 277–284
in marine protected areas, 238–240, 241–255
under Paris Agreement, 245–246
under UN Climate Treaty Regime, 241–247
under UNFCCC, 242–244
ocean fertilization and, 186
ocean's role in, 63–67
as carbon sink, 60, 64–65
as heat sink, 63–64
as methane source, 65–67
UNFCCC on, 63
offshore renewable energy and, 207–213
scope of, 50–54
tradeoffs in, 58
UNFCC and
ocean's role in, 63
protocols, 50, 51–52
Monaco Declaration, 112–113
MPAs. *See* marine protected areas

negative emissions technology, 191–192
Norway, aquaculture in, climate change impacts on, 291–293, 302–303, 305–306

ocean fertilization
in areas beyond national jurisdiction, 351–352
biological diversity in areas beyond national jurisdiction and, 202
as climate change mitigation measure, 186
under Convention on Biological Diversity, 188, 193, 197–198
coordination between regimes, 203
definition of, 185–186
through geoengineering, 185
marine geoengineering, 187–188
greenhouse gas emission reductions through, 186–188
IPCC and, 184
Kyoto Protocol and, 188–190
under Law of the Sea Convention, 188, 191–195, 200–203
in coastal states, 191
marine pollution and, 192–195
as marine scientific research, 201
legal perspectives on, 186–187, 199–203
under London Dumping Convention and Protocol, 194–199, 200–203
jurisdiction of, 202
as negative emissions technology, 191–192
under Paris Agreement, 184, 189–191
under UN Climate Change Treaty Regime, 188–191
UNFCCC and, 188–190
ocean governance. *See also* ocean-centered governance models
under Law of the Sea Convention, 11–13
for BBNJ, 12
ocean thermal energy conversion (OTEC), 210
ocean-atmosphere interface, 59–60
ocean-centered governance models, 383
actors in, 358–360
sectoral and regional, 364–366
adaptive, 369–371
Indigenous governance in, 369–371
climate change and, 354–358

- ocean-centered governance models (cont.)
  - conceptual approach in, 354–358
    - expansion of, 367–368
  - convergence of, 371–372
  - globalization as influence on, 366–369
  - integration of, 371–372
    - holism in, 372
  - Intergovernmental Panel on Climate Change, 360–361
  - Law of the Sea Convention
    - implementation of measures, 364–366
    - Part XII, 361–364
    - rules systems in, 360–366
  - law of the seas institutions in, 358–360
  - polycentric, 359
  - rules systems in, 358–360
    - of Law of the Sea Convention, 360–366
  - state-sovereignty-centered, 358–359
  - UNFCCC, 360–361
- oceans. *See also specific topics*
  - acidification of. *See* acidification
  - Anthropocene, 29–38
  - as carbon sink, 60, 64–65
  - climate and
    - interdependence between, 1–2, 59–62
    - ocean-atmosphere interface, 59–60
    - redistribution of heat, 61–62
    - thermohaline conveyer system, 62
  - climate change and, 58–72
    - acidification of oceans from, 30–31
    - adaptation and. *See* adaptation
    - mitigation and. *See* mitigation
    - sea-level changes, 33–35
  - definition of, 1
  - fertilization of. *See* ocean fertilization
  - as heat sink, 63–64
    - for anthropogenic heat, 64
    - heat storage capacity of, 33
    - warming of oceans, 63–64, 69–70
  - offshore renewable energy and, 213–214
  - 'Polar Vortex' and, 58
  - regulation of
    - history of, 8–9
    - *Mare Liberum*, 8
  - stewardship of, by Indigenous peoples, 357–358, 361, 369–371
  - warming of
    - dissolved oxygen content and, 70
    - as heat sink, 63–64, 69–70
    - hypoxia as result of, 70–71
    - marine biodiversity influenced by, 69–70
    - salinity levels influenced by, 70
    - sea-level rise and, 311–312
- Oceans Pathway Partnership, 116–117
- offshore renewable energy
  - climate change mitigation and, 207–213
  - competition over oceans, 213–214
  - under Convention on Biological Diversity, 231
  - development of, challenges in, 213–217
    - environmental impact assessments, 215, 228
    - impacts on marine environments, 214–216, 226–229
    - legal challenges, 216–217
    - regulatory challenges, 216–217
    - strategic environmental assessments, 215
  - under EU law, 217
  - in Exclusive Economic Zones, 219–220, 224
  - geothermal energy, 209, 212
  - hydrocarbons industry, 217
  - International Energy Agency and, 208
  - International Renewable Energy Agency and, 208–209
  - International Seabed Authority and, 222
  - under Law of the Sea Convention, 217–232
    - balancing of interests under, 222–226
    - coastal state jurisdictions, 218–222
    - legal instruments in, 229–232
    - Part XII, 225, 226–228
  - under London Dumping Convention and Protocol, 231
  - marine biomass as bioenergy, 209, 212
  - marine spatial planning and, 226
  - under MARPOL Convention, 230–231
  - ocean thermal energy conversion, 210
  - under OSPAR Convention, 231
  - salinity gradients, 210–211
  - solar energy, 211–212
  - tidal power, 209–210
  - UNFCC and, 209
  - wave power, 210
  - wind power, 211
- OSPAR Convention. *See* Convention for the Protection of the Marine Environment of the North-East Atlantic
- OTEC. *See* ocean thermal energy conversion

- *pacta tertiis* principle, 287–288, 380–381
- Paris Agreement (2015), 2, 6–7, 91–96
  - acidification of oceans and, 116

aquaculture under, 296–297, 300–302, 304–305, 307
greenhouse gas emissions standards in, 91–93
IMO after, 147–156
IPCC and, 6–7
Kyoto Protocol and
comparisons between, 6–7
implementation of, 91–93
lex specialis problem, 93
marine protected areas under
climate change adaptation in, 245–246
climate change mitigation in, 245–246
environmental protection and conservation obligations, 251–252
objectives of, 6
ocean fertilization under, 184, 189–191
operational guidelines, 7
Part XII (Law of the Sea Convention) and, 94–96
ratification of, 6
UNFCC compared to, 6–7
U.S. withdrawal from, 6
Part XII, Law of the Sea Convention
acidification of oceans and, 105
climate change mitigation obligations under, 84–91
marine environment protections under, 85–86
marine pollution under, 87–88
ocean-centered governance models and, 361–364
offshore renewable energy under, 225, 226–228
Paris Agreement and, 94–96
Particularly Sensitive Sea Areas (PSSAs), 238
permanent continental shelf limits, 330–333
pH levels, acidification of oceans and, 106–109
polar regions
acidification of oceans in, 107–108
Arctic Council guidelines, 112
ice melt in, 33, 34, 35–36, 58
pollution. *See also* marine pollution
atmospheric, 114–118
land-based, 118–119
polycentric ocean-centered governance models, 359
power. *See* tidal power; wave power; wind power
PSSAs. *See* Particularly Sensitive Sea Areas
public law, globalization as influence on, 368
RAMF. *See* Risk Assessment and Management Framework
regime complex, 375
regimes. *See* dumping regimes; Law of the Sea Regime; UN Climate Treaty Regime
regional agreements. *See specific agreements*
Regional Fishery Management Organizations (RFMOs), 79, 112
under international fisheries law, 281–287, 288
Law of the Sea Regime and, 380–381
marine protected areas and, 256–257
SPRFMO, 282
renewable energy. *See* offshore renewable energy
RFMOs. *See* Regional Fishery Management Organizations
Rio Conference, Agenda 21, 81–82, 87, 356–357
Risk Assessment and Management Framework (RAMF), 173–175
rules, in ocean-centered governance models, 358–360
Law of the Sea Convention, 360–366

salinity, of oceans
climate change adaptation and, 68–69
ocean's role in, 68–69
warming as influence on, 70
salinity gradients, as offshore renewable energy, 210–211
scenario planning, in climate change adaptation, 56
scientific predictions, 23, 43–44, 46, 383–384
SDGs. *See* Sustainable Development Goals
sea-level rise
Anthropocene, 33–35
climate change adaptation and, 55, 68–69
climate change and, 33–35
ILA Committee and, international law and, 318–321, 326
baseline maintenance, 319
Commission on the Limits of the Continental Shelf, 324–325
maritime zone limits, 319–320
Resolution 5/2018, 321–325
near coastal states, 335
warming of oceans and, 311–312
ship energy efficiency management plan (SEEMP), 140–141, 144
shipping, greenhouse gas emissions from
applicable principles, 131–137

shipping, greenhouse gas (cont.)
  carbon dioxide emissions, 129
  competent global regimes, 132–133
    'common but differentiated responsibility' approach, 132–133
  global setting for, 131–132
  International Maritime Organization and. *See* International Maritime Organization
  Kyoto Protocol guidelines, 133–135, 137
  under Law of the Sea Convention, 131–132
  under MARPOL Convention, 93, 102, 131
  under Paris Agreement, 135–137
  standards for, development of, 129
    by International Maritime Organization, 130
  UNFCCC guidelines, 132–133
    options for, 133
sink. *See* carbon sink; heat sink
socio-ecological context, for climate change actors, 355–356
soft law, acidification of oceans under, 110–113
solar energy, 211–212
South Pacific Regional Fisheries Management Organization (SPRFMO), 282
spatial planning. *See* marine spatial planning
SPRFMO. *See* South Pacific Regional Fisheries Management Organization
storage. *See* carbon capture and storage
storms. *See* coastal storms
strategic environmental assessments
  of areas beyond national jurisdiction, 349
  of offshore renewable energy, 215
Sustainable Development Goals (SDGs)
  for acidification of oceans, 110–111
  Law of the Sea Convention and, 82–83
  for marine protected areas, 234–235
systemic harmonization, 13–14

temperature differences, in ocean currents, 61. *See also* heat sink; warming
thermohaline conveyer system, 62
three-dimensional currents, 61–62
  Coriolis effect, 61, 62
  salinity differences in, 61
  temperature differences in, 61
tidal power, 209–210
tradeoffs, in climate change adaptation/ mitigation, 58
transformational climate change adaptation, 56

UN. *See* United Nations
UN Climate Treaty Regime, 1–7. *See also* Law of the Sea Regime; Paris Agreement; UN Framework Convention on Climate Change
  assessment of, 14–15
  Law of the Sea Convention and, 74–75, 78
  Law of the Sea Regime as complement to, 381
  marine protected areas under
    climate change adaptation in, 241–247
    climate change mitigation in, 241–247
    environmental protection and conservation obligations in, 251–252
  ocean fertilization under, 188–191
  scope of, 3
UN Framework Convention on Climate Change (UNFCCC), 1–2
  acidification of oceans and, 105, 109–110, 115, 122–123, 126–128
    Oceans Pathway Partnership, 116–117
  climate change mitigation
    ocean's role in, 63
    protocols, 50, 51–52
  climate disputes and, 98
  International Maritime Organization and, 147–148, 149, 155
    influences on, 145
  Kyoto Protocol and, 4–5
  Law of the Sea Convention and, 88–89
    climate disputes under, 98
  long-term objectives, 4
  marine protected areas under
    climate change adaptation in, 242–244
    climate change mitigation in, 242–244
    environmental protection and conservation obligations in, 251–252
  Montreal Protocol and, 4–5
  ocean fertilization and, 188–190
  ocean-centered governance models and, 360–361
  offshore renewable energy and, 209
  Paris Agreement compared to, 6–7
UNCLOS III, 42

UNFCCC. *See* UN Framework Convention on Climate Change
unilateral regional action, in EU, through IMO, 151–154
  definitions in, 152–153
  Directives in, 151–152, 153–154
United Nations (UN). *See also* UN Climate Treaty Regime; UN Framework Convention on Climate Change
  Charter of, 46–47
  Food and Agricultural Organization, 273–274, 281–284
    aquaculture and, 289–290, 297–300
  General Assembly Resolutions, on international fisheries law, 268, 275–276
unstable maritime limits, 311–316
U.S. *See* United States

Vienna Convention on the Law of Treaties, 46–47, 95, 177, 326
vulnerable coastal states, 20, 332, 335

warming, global
  IPCC on, 49
  of oceans
    dissolved oxygen content and, 70
    as heat sink, 63–64, 69–70
    hypoxia as result of, 70–71
    marine biodiversity influenced by, 69–70
    salinity levels influenced by, 70
    sea-level rise and, 311–312
waterflooding operations, in carbon capture and storage, 165
wave power, 210
wind power, 211
World Meteorological Organization, 34

For EU product safety concerns, contact us at Calle de José Abascal, 56–1°,
28003 Madrid, Spain or eugpsr@cambridge.org.

www.ingramcontent.com/pod-product-compliance
Ingram Content Group UK Ltd.
Pitfield, Milton Keynes, MK11 3LW, UK
UKHW021934210626
472431UK00010B/350
* 9 7 8 1 1 0 8 8 2 7 4 3 0 *